IN THE PRESENT perplexing times, amid what seems to be the gravest crisis in world affairs, an extraordinarily large discussion goes on, mainly of a pessimistic nature, about our historic Western civilization.... I have scant sympathy with contemporary criers of doom. I unblushingly persist in believing that our Western civilization has long been and still is a great liberal and progressive civilization—the greatest the world has ever produced—and that, having survived other troubled ages, it is likely to survive the present one.

Carlton J. H. Hayes (1882-1964)
Raymond Fred West Memorial Lectures
at Stanford University, 1954

Volume I: To 1650

HISTORY OF WESTERN CIVILIZATION

HISTORY OF

The Parthenon.
Courtesy of the Royal Greek Embassy Information Service, Washington, D.C.

WESTERN CIVILIZATION

Second Edition
Volume I: To 1650

CARLTON J. H. HAYES
MARSHALL WHITHED BALDWIN
CHARLES WOOLSEY COLE

The Macmillan Company
Collier-Macmillan Limited, London

Fourth Printing, 1970

Earlier Editions

History of Europe by Carlton J. H. Hayes, Marshall W. Baldwin, and Charles W. Cole, Copyright 1949 by The Macmillan Company; also published in separate volumes as follows: *History of Europe, Volume I, To 1648,* by Carlton J. H. Hayes and Marshall W. Baldwin; *History of Europe, Volume II, Since 1648,* by Carlton J. H. Hayes and Charles W. Cole; *History of Europe Since 1500* by Carlton J. H. Hayes, Marshall W. Baldwin, and Charles W. Cole.

History of Europe, Revised Edition, by Carlton J. H. Hayes, Marshall W. Baldwin, and Charles W. Cole, © 1956 by The Macmillan Company; also published in separate revised volumes as above.

History of Western Civilization by Carlton J. H. Hayes, Marshall W. Baldwin, and Charles W. Cole, © 1962 by The Macmillan Company; also published in separate volumes as follows: *History of Western Civilization, Volume I, To 1650; History of Western Civilization, Volume II, Since 1650; History of Western Civilization Since 1500.*

Library of Congress catalog card number: 67–13595

THE MACMILLAN COMPANY
866 THIRD AVENUE, NEW YORK, NEW YORK 10022
COLLIER-MACMILLAN CANADA, LTD., TORONTO, ONTARIO

Printed in the United States of America

Prefatory Note

This book is a new edition of the first volume of a work which was published in 1962. That in turn was based on the authors' *History of Europe* which first appeared in 1949 and was revised in 1956. The new version, like its predecessor, tells a story from antiquity, through the middle ages, to 1650 A.D. It embodies amendments of both statement and interpretation necessitated by advancing historical scholarship and broadening knowledge. As befits its title, *History of Western Civilization,* it treats of cultural as well as political and economic developments.

Moreover, the publishers have given the work an attractive and useful format, with double-columned pages, with a profusion of pertinent maps and illustrations, with select lists of supplementary readings for each of the six parts into which this volume is divided, and with an exhaustive index. Of the more than two score maps, about half are adapted from excellent ones provided originally by Mr. Vaughn S. Gray. The other half have been drawn anew by Dr. Francis Barkóczy, to whom the authors gratefully acknowledge their indebtedness. The authors are likewise indebted to Mr. and Mrs. Frederick J. Woodbridge for advice in selection of illustrations.

Altogether, this volume should serve as a survey of medieval history, with an introduction in ancient history. Modern history is surveyed in a second volume, starting in 1650; or, if one prefers, in a special volume starting in 1500.

CONTENTS

Prefatory Note v

List of Maps *xiii*

Introduction: Europe, the Seat of Western Civilization xv

PART I. THE MEDITERRANEAN CRADLE OF WESTERN CIVILIZATION 3

1. Original Heritage of the Ancient Near East 5

A. Origins in the "Near East." B. Ancient Kingdoms and Empires of the Near East. C. Institutions and Cultural Contributions. D. The Empires of Assyria and Persia.

2. Added Intellectual and Artistic Heritage of Greece 17

A. The Greeks in the Aegean and the Mediterranean. B. City-State Politics of the Greeks. C. Hellenic Culture. D. Alexander's Empire, and the Hellenistic Age.

3. Fusing Heritage of Roman Republic and Empire 29

A. Formation of the Roman Republic. B. Expansion and Corruption of the Republic. C. Transition from Republic to Empire. D. Life in the Roman Empire.

4. The Judaeo-Christian Spiritual Heritage 41

A. Origins of Christianity in Judaism. B. Christian Doctrine and Church Organization. C. Christianity and the Roman Empire. D. The Problem of Heresy. E. Summary of Europe's Ancient Inheritance from Mediterranean Lands.

SELECT SUPPLEMENTARY READINGS FOR PART I 49

PART II. CONTRACTION OF THE ROMAN EMPIRE AND EXPANSION OF THE CHRISTIAN CHURCH, FROM MARCUS AURELIUS TO GREGORY THE GREAT 51

5. Decay and Reorganization of the Roman Empire, the Third and Fourth Centuries 53

A. Military and Social Factors in the Collapse of the Augustan Principate. B. Diocletian and the Establishment of Imperial Absolutism. C. Continuing Social and Cultural Decline. D. Development of Christian Literature and Art. E. Orientalizing the Empire and Transfer of its Capital to Constantinople.

6. Barbarian Neighbors and German Settlers on West Roman Soil, the Fifth to the Seventh Century 63

A. German Tribesmen beyond the Roman Frontier. B. First German Migrations into the Empire. C. Collapse of Imperial Government in the West. D. Temporary Imperial Recovery under Justinian, and Renewed Invasions. E. Institutions of the German Kingdoms. F. Gradual Fusion of German and Roman Society: Romanizing the Germans.

7. *Byzantine Continuation of the Roman Empire in the East* **77**

A. Byzantine Institutions. B. Policies and Achievements of the Emperor Justinian. C. Narrowing of the Byzantine Empire in the Seventh Century.

8. *Consolidation and Expansion of the Catholic Christian Church* **87**

A. Conversion of Celts, Germans, and Slavs. B. Consolidation under the Papacy from Leo I to Gregory I. C. The Bishops. D. Development of Monasticism. E. Church and Culture: Education, Literature, and Art after the Barbarian Invasions.

9. *Rise and Conquests of Islam* **99**

A. Role of Arabs Different from that of German and Slavs. B. Mohammed and his Religion of Islam. C. Arab Moslem Conquests. D. The Moslem Empire of the Seventh and Eighth Centuries: the Caliphate. E. Disruptive Effects on Christendom. F. Moslem Culture and its Influence on Europe.

SELECT SUPPLEMENTARY READINGS FOR PART II **110**

PART III. THE EARLY MIDDLE AGE IN THE WEST AND THE NORTHWARD PROCESS OF EUROPEANIZATION, FROM CHARLEMAGNE TO HILDEBRAND **113**

10. *Rise and Disintegration of the Frankish Empire, and New Barbarian Invasions of the Ninth Century* **117**

A. The Frankish State: Transition from Merovingian to Carolingian Rule. B. Charlemagne and his Administration. C. Coronation of Charlemagne as "Roman Emperor." D. Emergence of Feudal Kingdoms. E. Education and Culture under Charlemagne and his Successors. F. Ninth-Century Attacks from South and East: Saracens, Slavs, Bulgars, and Magyars. G. Norse Incursions and Settlements.

11. *The Beginnings of Recovery: Feudalism and Feudal Society* **131**

A. Origins of Feudalism. B. Feudal Procedures. C. Chivalry and Feudal Warfare. D. Feudalism and the Church.

12. *Emerging Feudal States of the Tenth and Eleventh Centuries* **139**

A. Capetian France. B. Germany and the Formation of the Holy Roman Empire. C. Kingdoms in Northern and Southern Europe. D. Eastern Frontier Kingdoms. E. Political and Cultural Revival in the Byzantine Empire.

13. *Economic Conditions Under Feudal Society* **153**

A. Commerce and Industry in the Early Feudal Period. B. Agricultural Revival. C. The Seigneurial Regime. D. Peasant Obligations and Rights.

14. *Religion and Society in the Feudal Age* **161**

A. Cluny and Monastic Reform. B. Gregorian Reform. C. The Church and the Laity. D. The Investiture Controversy. E. The First Crusade.

SELECT SUPPLEMENTARY READINGS FOR PART III **171**

PART IV. THE MIDDLE AGE OF THE TWELFTH AND THIRTEENTH CENTURIES AND THE FLOWERING OF EUROPE, FROM URBAN II TO DANTE *173*

15. New Frontiers *175*

A. The New Frontiers of Western Europe. B. Western Christian States in the Levant. C. Later Crusades. D. Results of the Crusades. E. The Mongols, and European Medieval Contacts with China.

16. Economic Development in the Twelfth and Thirteenth Centuries *189*

A. Expansion of Maritime and Inland Trade. B. Medieval Industry, Money and Credit. D. Development of Urban Communities. D. Town Institutions. E. Agricultural Development.

17. Consolidation of Feudal Monarchy in Western and Southern Europe *201*

A. English Monarchy in the Twelfth and Thirteenth Centuries. B. French Monarchy in the Twelfth and Thirteenth Centuries. C. Developing Christian Kingdoms of the Iberian Peninsula. D. Norman Kingdom of Sicily and Naples.

18. Medieval Empires and Border States of Central and Eastern Europe *213*

A. Emperor Frederick Barbarossa and his Effort to Build a Consolidated Feudal Monarchy in Germany. B. The Hohenstaufen Emperors and Italy. C. Frederick II, German Emperor and King of Sicily. D. Northern and East-Central Europe. E. Russia, the Byzantine Empire, and the Balkans.

19. The Church in the Twelfth and Thirteenth Centuries *227*

A. The Papal Curia. B. The Secular Clergy. C. The Regular Clergy. D. Preservation of the Faith against Heresy. E. Church and Laity.

20. The Medieval Revival of Learning *239*

A. Medieval Intellectual Interests: Liberal Arts and Philosophy. B. Law, Medicine, and Science. C. Schools, and the University of Paris. D. Bologna and Other Medieval Universities. E. Medieval Students.

21. Popular Literature and Art of the Middle Age *251*

A. Epics and Romances. B. Other Vernacular Literature, the Troubadours, and Dante. C. Medieval Music. D. Romanesque Art and Architecture. E. Gothic Architecture.

SELECT SUPPLEMENTARY READINGS FOR PART IV *260*

PART V. LATE MIDDLE AGE: THE FOURTEENTH AND FIFTEENTH CENTURIES, FROM EDWARD III OF ENGLAND TO LEONARDO DA VINCI *263*

22. Social and Economic Developments of Late Middle Age *265*

A. "Closing the Medieval Frontier," and Economic Depression. B. The Land and the Landed Classes. C. Industry and Banking. D. National Economy and Commercial Expansion. E. Improving Technology: Mining and Navigation.

23. *Monarchy in France and England: the Hundred Years' War and Its Aftermath* **277**

A. The Hundred Years' War, 1337–1453: First Stage. B. Second and Final Stages. C. Expansion and Strengthening of the French Monarchy. D. English Political Developments in the Fourteenth and Fifteenth Centuries.

24. *Central and Eastern Europe in the Late Middle Age* **289**

A. Disintegration in the Holy Roman Empire. B. Major Separate States within the Empire. C. Scandinavia, the Baltic Lands, and East Central Europe. D. Byzantine Empire, the Balkans, and Russia.

25. *Mediterranean Europe, Conquest of the Atlantic, and Advent of Ottoman Power* **299**

A. Portugal and Overseas Expansion. B. Spain and Overseas Expansion. C. End of the Byzantine Empire and Rise of the Ottoman. D. Disunited Italy and Its City States. E. The Papal State and the Kingdom of Naples-Sicily.

26. *Learning and Art in the Late Middle Age: the Renaissance* **313**

A. Italian Humanism and the Italian Renaissance. B. Invention of Printing. C. Humanism in Northern and Western Europe. D. Science and Philosophy. E. Progress of Vernacular Literature. F. Painting. G. Sculpture, Architecture, Music.

27. *The Church in the Late Middle Age* **325**

A. The "Babylonian Captivity" of the Papacy. B. The Great Schism. C. Deterioration in Ecclesiastical Morale and Growth of Heresy. D. Age of the Councils. E. Popular Religious Life in the Late Middle Age.

SELECT SUPPLEMENTARY READINGS FOR PART V **334**

PART VI. EARLY MODERN TIMES AND RELIGIOUS UPHEAVAL IN THE WEST, FROM CHARLES V AND LUTHER TO GUSTAVUS ADOLPHUS AND PHILIP IV **337**

28. *Emperor Charles V in Europe, Overseas, and Against the Turks* **339**

A. Charles First of Spain and Fifth of the Holy Roman Empire. B. Wars of Charles V in Europe. C. Wars of Charles V against the Turks. D. Charles and the Spanish and Portuguese Dominions Overseas.

29. *Protestant Revolt Against the Catholic Church: Lutheranism and Calvinism* **351**

A. Catholic Beliefs. B. Luther and Lutheranism. C. Emergence of Radical Sects. D. Calvin and Calvinism. E. The Expansion of Calvinism.

30. *Revolt Against the Catholic Church: Anglicanism* **361**

A. Henry VIII and the Separation of the Church of England from the Papacy. B. Edward VI and Mary, and Religious Fluctuations in England. C. Elizabeth and the Final Establishment of Anglicanism. D. The Elizabethan Age.

31. *Catholic Reformation, and the Cultural Life of the Sixteenth Century* **369**

A. Reforming Popes and the Council of Trent. B. St. Ignatius Loyola and the Jesuits. C. Catholic Revival, Political and Religious. D. Catholic Overseas Missions. E. General Effects of the Religious Upheaval. F. Cultural Trends in the Sixteenth Century.

32. *Successes and Failures of Philip II of Spain* **383**

A. Philip II, the Man and the Monarch. B. Spain's Many Problems Abroad. C. Spain Overseas. D. Successors of Philip II: Philip III and Philip IV, 1598–1665.

33. *The Age of the Thirty Years' War, 1618–1648* **395**

A. Issues at Stake in the War. B. Phases and Course of the War. C. French Intervention and the Peace of Westphalia. D. Results of the Thirty Years' War, and the Continuing Franco-Spanish War to 1659. E. Economics and the Price Revolution of Early Modern Times. F. Culture in the Early Seventeenth Century: Emergence of the Baroque.

SELECT SUPPLEMENTARY READINGS FOR PART VI **410**

Partial List of Sovereigns **413**

Index **425**

Sculpture of peasant from facade of Cathedral at Chartres.

Maps

The Near East in the Second Millenium B.C. 8
Western Half of the Persian Empire about 500 B.C. 14
Principal Settlements of Greeks and Phoenicians about 550 B.C. 18
The Peloponnesian War 23
Hellenistic Empire of Alexander and His Successors to about 200 B.C. 25
Expansion of the Roman Republic to 44 B.C. 31
The Roman Empire about 120 A.D. 36–37
Ancient Palestine 42

Early Christian Centers (before 325 A.D.) 46
The Roman Empire under Diocletian 55
Anglo-Saxon, Pict, and Celtic Britain 67
Germanic Kingdoms in the West and the Roman (Byzantine) Empire in the East, about 525 A.D. 68
The Byzantine Roman Empire under Justinian 70
Europe and the Mediterranean about 620 A.D. 84–85
Expansion of Islam: Arab Conquests 102

Formation of the Carolingian Empire 119
Partition of the Carolingian Empire 122
Norse Raids and Settlements 128
Feudal France 140
Feudal "Roman" Empire of Otto the Great 142
Europe about 1000 A.D. 148–149
Islam and Christendom on the Eve of the First Crusade 168
Crusader States in the Near East 178
The Mongol Empire and Certain Medieval Travel Routes between Europe and the Far East 184–185

Principal European Commercial Centers in the Middle Ages 191
Growth of French Royal Domain in the Twelfth and Thirteenth Centuries 206
The Iberian Peninsula in the Twelfth and Thirteenth Centuries 210
German (Holy Roman) Empire under the Hohenstaufen 215
Germanic Eastward Expansion at Slavic and Magyar Expense 223
Europe Toward the End of the Thirteenth Century 228–229

Major Medieval Universities (prior to 1400) and Pilgrimage Centers 247
The Hanseatic League 272
France at the Start of the Hundred Years' War, 1328 278
France at the Time of the Treaty of Troyes, 1420 281
France at the Close of the Hundred Years' War (1453), and Its Expansion (1453–1500) 285

Germany (The Holy Roman Empire) in the Fifteenth Century	292
Russia and Its Neighbors about 1500	297
Italy and Spain in the Fifteenth Century	301
Rise of Ottoman Empire and Extinction of Byzantine Empire, 1355–1481	304
European Dynastic Dominions of Charles V	340
The Ottoman Empire at its Height (about 1550)	345
Spanish and Portuguese America in the Sixteenth Century	348
Major Christian Divisions in Europe about 1600	374
The Netherlands in 1609	392
The Holy Roman Empire in 1618	396
The Westphalian Peace Settlement of 1648	403

Volume I: To 1650

HISTORY OF WESTERN CIVILIZATION

EUROPE, SEAT OF WESTERN CIVILIZATION

Geographically, Europe is usually designated a continent. As such it is the smallest (except Australia) of the six continents which constitute the bulk of the Earth's surface. Actually, however, Europe is not a continent in the strict sense of the word. It is not a major area completely or almost completely separated by water, like the American continents or Africa or Australia, from other large landed areas. Rather, it is only a western extension of Asia—a minor part of the vast land mass geographers call Eurasia.

But Europe is not simply an arbitrary geographical expression. It signifies something much more important. It denotes a particular kind of historic civilization. And it is this distinctively civilizing Europe which in modern times has spread far beyond the merely geographical Europe, encompassing the American continents and Australia and exerting no little influence on the whole world. It is Europe in this cultural sense whose long historical development will concern us in the following pages.

At the outset we should note that Eurasia, at once the most extensive and the most diverse land mass on our globe, and yet lying largely in the north temperate zone, is the seat of several great and enduring civilizations. Each of these is commonly distinguished by the geographical section of Eurasia where it arose and flourished. Thus, "Far Eastern" civilization is peculiar to China and Japan; "Middle Eastern" and "Near Eastern" civilizations, to India, Persia, and Arabia; "Western" civilization, to Europe. These civilizations have existed longer and been much more fruitful than any native culture of America or Africa or Australia. Though they have touched one another in many ways throughout the countless ages of their formation and development, and though particularly in recent times their interrelationship has been greatly quickened, they are still distinctive. There is as yet no single "world civilization."

To this day, the manners and customs and thoughts of the Chinese are basically determined by their heritage of Far Eastern civilization, just as those of the Persians and Arabs are principally derived from the legacy of Near Eastern civilization, and our own from that of European, or Western civilization. It is this last of which Americans, as well as Italians, Englishmen, Scandinavians, and Germans, are heirs. It has conditioned our past. And whether we are aware of it or not, it conditions our present and future.

In what does this "Europe"—this Western civilization—consist? *First,* in the results of a fusing of ancient peoples and empires of the eastern Mediterranean into a conscious community of settled life, commercial intercourse, expansive effort, and artistic and literary achievement. *Second,* in the

INTRODUCTION

added Graeco-Roman tradition, with its abiding heritage of literature and language, of philosophy, of architecture and art, of law and political concepts—monarchy, aristocracy, democracy, dictatorship. *Third*, in the superimposed Judaeo-Christian tradition, with its fructifying spirituality and ethics, its permeating influence on personal and social behavior, its continuing distinction between the individual and the race, between liberty and authority, between mercy and justice, between what is Caesar's and what is God's. *Fourth*, proceeding from joint effects of the first three, it comprises distinctive traditions of both individualism and socialism, of limitations on the state, of social responsibility, of repeated revolt and revolution. *Finally*, and likewise proceeding from the others, it includes a pretty constant tradition of expansiveness, of missionary and crusading zeal, which has inspired a steady pushing out of European and Western frontiers—from the Mediterranean to the Arctic and across the Atlantic, in turn over lands of Latins, Celts, Germans, and Slavs, over the full width of both American continents, and beyond to at least the Philippines and Australia.

"Europe," in the sense of its distinctive historic civilization, is not a matter of geography or race or nationality. From its origins, it has embraced a variety of peoples, differing from one another in heredity and habitat, in speech and local culture. Predominantly, its inhabitants have been describable as "white" or "Caucasian," and its languages as "Indo-European" or "Aryan." But "white" or "Caucasian" are generic terms covering many racial strains and mixtures, some of which are found outside the area of European civilization, while numerous non-whites (including American Negroes) have been brought within its orbit. In like manner, the words "Indo-European" and "Aryan" merely denote a big family of distantly related languages, not only the Greek, Latin, Celtic, Germanic, and Slavic traditionally associated with Europe, but also the Sanskrit, Hindustani, and Persian of the Middle East; while within Europe have flourished quite alien languages, such as Semitic (Hebrew and Arabic), Turkish, Magyar, and Finnish.

"Europe," that is, the "West," has always had a multiplicity of nationalities, and since ancient times none of the repeated attempts to subject it to political unity has met with any real or lasting success. Yet in the domain of civilization and culture, it has long possessed a unity and distinctiveness marking it off from "Asia," whether of the "Far East," "Middle East," or "Near East." How "Europe" began, and how, during the past three thousand years, it grew and expanded, is the theme of the present book.

The story is long and complicated. It can here be told only in bald outline.

Rome. The Forum and the Arch of Septimius Severus.

Courtesy Italian State Tourist Office, New York

Prehistoric Art. The Lascaux Cave Paintings (see p. 6).

Courtesy French Government Tourist Office, New York

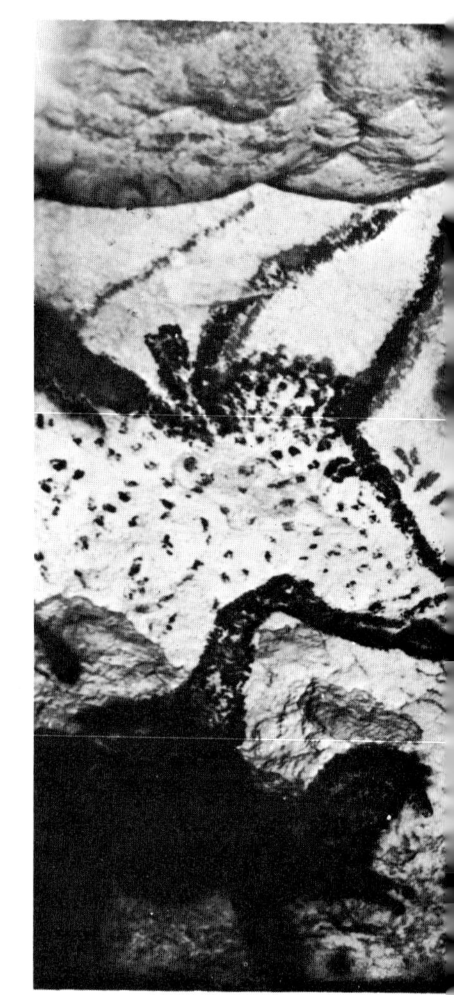

PART I
THE MEDITERRANEAN CRADLE

OF WESTERN CIVILIZATION

THE FIRST part of the story of European, or Western, civilization covers a very long period of time, roughly from 4000 B.C. to A.D. 300. It starts with a gradual rise and fusing of peoples and cultures in lands adjacent to the eastern end of the Mediterranean, in what is known as the ancient "Near East" of Egypt, Mesopotamia, Asia Minor, Syria, Phoenicia, Crete, and the Aegean.

Eventually, the civilization, thus developed in the Near East, is carried westward across the Mediterranean, and modified and added to, first by the Greeks and then by the Romans. Finally, when the entire Mediterranean basin (southern Europe and northern Africa, as well as southwestern Asia) is brought under Greek cultural influence and Roman imperial sway, Christianity, springing from Palestinian Judaism, provides new religious faith and ideals for the Mediterranean world. Without the original, many-sided heritage of the ancient Near East, without the added intellectual and artistic heritage of Greece, without the heritage of law and order of Roman Republic and Empire, and without the Judaeo-Christian spiritual heritage, Europe could not be the Europe of the last nineteen hundred years, nor the home of the Western civilization of today.

Civilized Europe, throughout its early formative period, does not embrace the geographical continent of Europe. It is evolved in, and confined to, the Mediterranean. To the north of a line drawn from Britain up the Rhine and down the Danube to the Black Sea, there still prevails, in the third century A.D., a primitive barbarism analogous to that of most American Indians in the time of Columbus. The expansion of Western civilization over the whole continent of Europe belongs to a later part of our story. And still later is its extension over the American continents.

Queen Hatshepsut of Egypt from the temple at Thebes, c. 1490–1480 B.C. (see p. *11*).

Courtesy Metropolitan Museum of Art, New York

CHAPTER 1

Original Heritage of the Ancient Near East

A. Origins in the "Near East"

The origins of what we understand as European civilization are to be found, not in Europe itself, but in the eastern Mediterranean basin and the adjacent hinterland. Although modern geographical classification includes this area in either northeastern Africa or southwestern Asia, the achievements of its inhabitants in ancient times constitute the first important heritage of Mediterranean and hence of European civilization. Long before Europeans as such had emerged from barbarism, men had reached a relatively high degree of civilization in the lands bordering the eastern Mediterranean.

The geographical explanation of this development becomes clear as one studies a map, for that region includes two vast river basins, the Nile and the Tigris-Euphrates, and the intervening coastal lands of Syria and Palestine. Partly because these lands encircle the "desert bay" of Arabia, the whole area has been called the "fertile crescent." And from earliest times peoples of the neighboring territories—northeast Africa, inner Arabia, and the lands north and west of the Tigris-Euphrates valley—were attracted to the "fertile crescent." Moreover, it is possible that there were also contacts with ancient centers of culture in the Indus valley of northwest India. At any rate, the culture of the Nile and the Tigris-Euphrates and of intervening lands was the achievement of many different peoples.

The peoples throughout the Near East were already, in ancient times, of mixed blood. There was no purity of race among them, except only that most of them could be described in a very general way as "white," rather than "yellow" or "black." They belonged to many different tribes, or nationalities, each with a distinctive language. Some of these diverse languages, by reason of similarity in vocabulary and syntax, can be grouped together in the so-called Indo-European (or Aryan) "family" of languages, which embraces the ancient Hindu (or Sanskrit) of India and also Persian, Armenian, Greek, and Latin, as well as most modern European tongues. Another "family" of languages is the Semitic, which in the ancient Near East characterized the bulk of the peoples in the valley of the Tigris-Euphrates, in Syria, Palestine, Arabia, and in a few isolated areas elsewhere. As the Persians and Armenians were Indo-European (or Aryan), so the ancient Hebrews, Arabs, Phoenicians, Babylonians, and Assyrians were Semitic. A related "family" of languages was the Hamitic, spoken by Egyptians, Ethiopians, and certain other peoples of northern Africa. In addition, there were some languages, such as the Hittite in Asia Minor and the ancient speech on the eastern Mediterranean island of Crete, which do not appear to be related to any of the three language "families" already mentioned.

An important caution should be entered

here against confusing language with race. Language is a badge of common nationality, but not necessarily of blood-relationship. Whites and blacks may speak the same language, and such terms as Aryan, Semitic, and Hamitic refer to languages, not to races. This was true of the ancient Near East, as it is true of modern Europe.

The Near East, with its "fertile crescent," is one of the oldest habitations of man, if not absolutely the oldest. Here man dwelt for many thousands of years before the existence of any written records, before even the most primitive inscriptions were carved in rock or on clay tablet. In that distant "prehistoric" time, man devised tools and weapons of stone, from the character of which we divide time, for convenience sake, into a Palaeolithic (or Old Stone) Age and a Neolithic (or New Stone) Age. The exact beginnings or precise duration of these Ages can, of course, never be determined. The Palaeolithic may tentatively be said to have ended about 8000 B.C., while the Neolithic lasted in the Near East until about 4000 or 3500 B.C., and in the more backward Europe until a later date.

Inscriptions and other written records appeared earlier in the Near East than elsewhere, as did also the use of copper for tools and weapons. The resulting transition from the prehistoric New Stone Age into an historic Bronze or Copper-Bronze Age occurred in the Near East about 4000 B.C. In Europe copper was not generally used until two thousand years later, and writing was correspondingly backward. Finally, iron metallurgy, with its Iron Age, which represented a still more important advance over copper, began in Mesopotamia perhaps as early as 2500 B.C. and was certainly well developed in Asia Minor by 1300 B.C.

The northeastern part of the "fertile crescent" is the land between the rivers, or Mesopotamia, as the Greeks called it. Both the Tigris and the Euphrates flow down from the Armenian highlands in courses which, though varied, are roughly parallel. At modern Bagdad, the two rivers are only about twenty miles apart. Thence the valley broadens into the vast alluvial plain of Babylonia where the annual overflow of the rivers deposits a rich soil, and the gradual silting of the river mouths has added to the length of the plain through the ages at the rate of perhaps three miles a century. But nature, though generous to Babylonia, has occasionally brought disaster. Accordingly, from very early times men had to learn how to build dikes against floods and to construct irrigation works to make agriculture possible during the long dry seasons. Yet so great were the natural advantages of the region that it is easy to understand why it early became a center of civilization.

Equally important to the inhabitants of its basin was the Nile River. The longest of all African rivers, the Nile rises in east central Africa many miles south of Egypt. Somewhere near the modern Khartum it is joined by a great tributary, the Blue Nile. Thence it flows northward through Nubia where a number of rocky rapids, commonly called cataracts, make navigation difficult but not impossible for small boats moving with the current. Near Syene (Aswan) the rapids cease and the valley broadens into a vast depression averaging a dozen miles in width and some five hundred miles long, bounded by the edges of a desert plateau. As this great stream approaches the Mediterranean it divides into the several branches of the delta, so called because it resembles in shape the Greek letter Δ. Adequate rainfall is lacking in this region, but every year the Nile overflows its banks for a period of about two months. And as the waters recede they leave a deposit of exceedingly fertile sediment. Thus from time immemorial Egyptian peasants have seen their soil renewed. And they also discovered various methods of impounding water for local irrigation. Fertile soil and a warm dry climate have combined to make civilized life possible for the Egyptian.

Despite the unique configuration of the river valley, ancient Egypt was not completely isolated from other lands. Caravan routes led from the Nile eastward to the Red Sea, and the river itself, despite the rapids, was a line of communication from the south. Moreover, the delta region was accessible from both sides, and passage eastward to the Sinai peninsula and to Syria was by no means difficult. Notwithstanding, throughout most of its history Egypt was rather less affected by outside influences than any other ancient state.

B. *Ancient Kingdoms and Empires of the Near East*

It would be manifestly impossible here to rehearse in detail the history of the successive kingdoms and empires of the Near East during some four thousand years before Christ. What is important, however, in our study of European civilization, is some understanding of those achievements in government, social and economic organization, and science and art, which were passed on to the West. Accordingly, what will be attempted here is a brief outline of ancient history designed to show how the culture of the Near East was brought into contact with the more primitive Europe and contributed to its civilization.

The earliest evidences of settled political and social life appeared about the same time—during the fourth millennium before Christ—in both the Nile and the Tigris-Euphrates valleys.[1] But since Egypt attained to a political unity somewhat earlier than Mesopotamia, it will be well to commence our story with the origins of political life in the Nile valley. Sometime around 3000 B.C. a number of formerly separate communities were consolidated into the two kingdoms of Upper and Lower Egypt. The former included the valley south of the delta. The latter was the region of the delta itself. Sometime late in the third millennium before Christ the two kingdoms were united, with Memphis, a city near the borders of the upper kingdom, designated as capital. Then began what is called the dynastic period in Egyptian history, the dynasties being distinct lines of rulers, or pharaohs as they were called.

An important aspect of early Egyptian history is the expansion of its authority over neighboring lands. As early as the sixth dynasty (2420–2270 B.C.), for example, the tribes of lower and upper Nubia were subjugated, and Egyptian sovereignty was extended southward as far as the second cataract. The Sinai peninsula with its mineral deposits was also exploited, and commercial expeditions took the Egyptians by sea and land as far as Punt (modern Somaliland) on the lower Red Sea coast. Then, following a protracted period of political trouble, civil war, and even foreign invasion, the pharaohs of the eighteenth dynasty (1580–1356 B.C.) embarked upon a new career of conquest. Security from attack was the initial motive. But, as has so often happened in history, adequate frontier protection seemed to demand expansion over adjacent buffer states. At any rate, during these years, especially under the great Thutmose III (about 1500 B.C.), Egypt advanced to occupy Palestine, Syria, and Phoenicia, which were garrisoned with Egyptian troops and required to pay tribute. Even Crete, Cyprus, and other eastern Mediterranean islands were forced into alliance with Egypt.

The Egyptian Empire, however brilliant, exceeded its own strength as army after army was sent out of the country. A protracted struggle with the Hittites, a people who, as will presently be explained, had moved eastward and southward from Asia Minor, was ended by a treaty (1280 B.C.) which delimited spheres of influence and which, in fact, marks the culmination of the power of both states. Thus by the thirteenth century before Christ, Egypt's days as an expanding world power were over. But contacts with the rest of the Near East had been established and subsequent events there were to affect the course of Egypt's history.

Meanwhile, in Mesopotamia, by the second half of the fourth millennium a people known as the Sumerians had developed a culture superior to any then existing. Around 3200 B.C. the evidence justifies somewhat fuller discussion. Then we hear of a number of separate city-states both in northern Mesopotamia (Akkad) and in the south (Sumer). During the period after 3200, Semitic peoples appeared in increasing numbers, especially in Akkad, and eventually the Sumerian people became submerged. Not, however, until the reign of Sargon (about 2637–2581 B.C.) did a Semitic dynasty rule over Sumer and Akkad.

Toward the end of the third millennium before Christ, a new Semitic people, the Amorites, entered Mesopotamia and settled at Babylon in western Akkad on the Euphrates. Thenceforth, Babylon, which up to that time had not figured prominently in

[1] Also, interestingly enough, at almost as early a time, in the valleys of the Indus (in India) and of the Yellow River (in China).

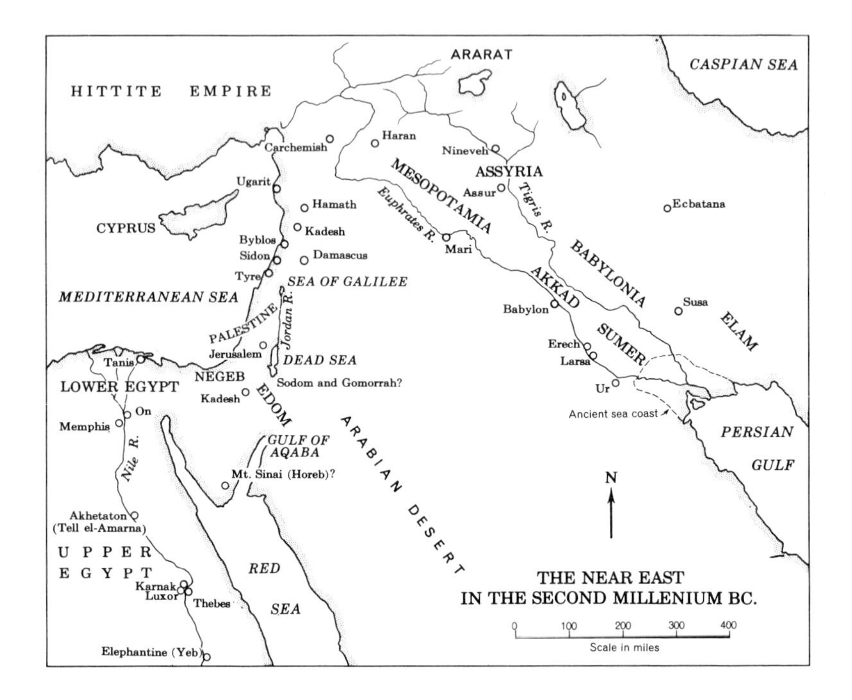

Mesopotamian history, was to take the lead. And the rulers of Babylon, after first merely maintaining their independence, began a career of expansion. Hammurabi (1947–1905 B.C.), the sixth of the Babylonian kings, challenged the rival and threatening power of the Elamites to the north, effectively subdued all Sumer and Akkad, and even extended his sway toward Assyria, the region north of Babylonia. Thus what was to become a remarkable centralized administration commenced to develop throughout Mesopotamia.

The military and political successes of Hammurabi did not long endure, for shortly after his death the unity of the old Babylonian kingdom was broken, partly because of internal dissension, but principally as a consequence of invasion by neighboring peoples. The most important of these invaders, the Hittites, destroyed Babylon in 1750 B.C. and, a little later, established a strong state centering in Asia Minor. The origin of the Hittites is still a matter of dispute, although it seems probable that they migrated from the region north of the Black and Caspian Seas. Presumably the ruling classes were Indo-European, though not, apparently, the main body of the population. The importance of the Hittites lies partly in their introduction of the domesticated horse and their progress in the manufacture of iron implements. But perhaps even more significant were their contacts with neighboring peoples. For it was the Hittites who, as a consequence of their occupation of Asia Minor, formed one of the links between the ancient Near East and the primitive culture of the Aegean and eastern Mediterranean. Further, their pressure southward into Syria threatened Egypt and brought about a long rivalry which, as has been explained, curbed Egyptian expansion. Not until around 1200 B.C. did the Hittite power begin to show signs of decline.

The meeting between the cultures of the Nile and the Tigris-Euphrates, which was a consequence of Egyptian expansion northward and Hittite pressure southward, focuses attention on the intervening coastlands of Palestine and Syria. Moreover, the decline after the thirteenth century B.C. of Egyptian and Hittite prestige provided an opportunity for the independent development of the peoples inhabiting those coastlands, especially the Aramaeans, Hebrews, and Phoenicians. The Aramaeans, a Semitic people, had gradually moved into Syria from the lands bordering on Mesopotamia. As they established themselves in cities like

Damascus and obtained control over the caravan routes, they forsook their earlier nomadic ways for settled agriculture and commerce. Their language was widely adopted and remained, even after their dispersion by the Assyrians, a kind of universal tongue in the Near East. It was presumably the speech of Jesus Christ and was certainly the language of important parts of the Bible.

The Hebrews were also Semitic nomads who entered Palestine probably around the middle of the second millennium B. C., at a time when the western part of the country was under Egyptian control. Many sojourned for a considerable period in Egypt, but eventually the "Exodus" took place, and probably by the middle of the thirteenth century the Hebrews were well established in the region west of the Jordan. The Canaanites, former inhabitants of the land, were defeated, but subjection again followed at the hands of the Philistines. Then, after the first efforts toward liberation under Saul and Samuel in the late eleventh century, there came the final triumph of David of Judah (1020–975 B.C.). During the reign of his son, Solomon (975–935), the old Hebrew kingdom reached its height.

The Semitic Phoenicians are chiefly noted as sailors, traders, and colonizers. Their famous cities on the coast of northern Palestine, especially Tyre, Sidon, and Byblos, flourished first under Egyptian domination. By the end of the second millennium B.C., the Phoenicians had not only outstripped the Egyptians, but were founding colonies throughout the length and breadth of the Mediterranean and even penetrating the Atlantic.[1] Thus, like the Hittites in Asia Minor, the Phoenicians formed a link with the Mediterranean world. But as traders and colonizers their contacts to the west were at once more frequent and spread over a larger area. Greek merchants visited their harbors and, among other things, imitated their method of writing. And at Carthage (near modern Tunis), their most famous colony, the Phoenicians developed a commercial and political power which dominated the central and western Mediterranean until the expansion of Rome.

Another important intermediary between the ancient Near East and the culture which was later to flourish in Greece was the island of Crete, for it seems likely that Cretan culture was first developed by immigrants from Egypt perhaps as early as the fourth millennium before Christ. Later came settlers from Asia Minor and, finally (about 1400 B.C.), invaders, presumably from the Greek mainland, who destroyed the distinctive institutions of the island. Of necessity Cretans were a sea-faring people. Their mariners plied the sea to Egypt and western Asia and extended Cretan influence to the Aegean islands, the Greek mainland, and Asia Minor. Two of the earliest examples of Cretan influence were Mycenae in southern Greece and Troy in northwestern Asia Minor. Indeed, the "sea kings" of Crete exercised authority over a considerable maritime empire.

Clearly, then, with the decline of the old Egyptian and Mesopotamian land states, the westward expansion of Phoenicia, and the emergence of Crete, we pass into a new age in the ancient Near East. But before undertaking an examination of the subsequent centuries, we must attempt an estimate of the contributions made toward the perfecting of government and the advancement of art and science.

C. *Institutions and Cultural Contributions*

Generally speaking, the ancient Near East was organized on a basis of absolute monarchy. Moreover, monarchy was closely associated with religion, and the ruler's authority was commonly regarded as of divine origin. This was especially true in Egypt where the monarch was a theocratic despot—that is to say, he was chief priest as well as supreme law-giver and judge. Indeed, he was regarded as the incarnation of a god and bore various titles emblematic of his divine character. He was the "son of Ra," the sun-god, and later, after the Theban god Amen was introduced, the "son of Amen-Ra."

Over all his people the pharaoh possessed unlimited authority. Not only did he levy taxes, promulgate laws, and administer justice, but, since he was regarded as owner of all the land, he decided for each farmer how many and what fields should be culti-

---

[1] See map, below, p. 18.

vated. The products of artisans and the ex changes of merchants were similarly regulated. In practice, theocratic absolutism was exercised through officials placed over the various provinces and districts. There developed an administrative bureaucracy. And, as a consequence of the identification of religion and government, a priest class acquired considerable authority even outside the purely religious sphere. The vast majority of the population, however, was composed of peasants living as serfs on the estates of the nobles or of the king. Until recent times, history offers few comparable examples of such complete regimentation of life by the state.

Centralized bureaucratic administration fostered a number of necessary public works. Reservoirs and canals, for example, made possible at least a partial control over the life-giving waters of the Nile and facilitated irrigation. Indeed, the absolute dependence of Egyptian agriculture on water control necessitated a large measure of governmental intervention. But the government also encouraged commercial expeditions abroad, which enhanced and varied Egyptian life.

Although in Babylonia, no less than in Egypt, the pressures of corporate life left little opportunity for the individual, the autocracy there seems to have been tempered somewhat by a greater regard for individual rights to both life and property. This is evident in a famous ancient Babylonian code of law which bears the name of Hammurabi, who coördinated and systematized earlier practices. In fact, this famous code, perhaps the first of its kind, presumably mirrors Mesopotamian life of an even earlier date. Class distinctions were recognized. There were wealthy landed magnates, a priest class, petty landowners, tenants bound to the soil, and various categories of persons engaged in agriculture and trade. Slavery also existed. Punishments, often severe, and in many cases based on the primitive "eye for an eye" principle, were graded accordingly. But there is evidence, too, of a more enlightened and humanitarian attitude. Woman's position was generally higher than in other lands. Slaves enjoyed certain very definite rights, even over property. Thus, although in Babylonia religion and government were theoretically inseparable and the king's power was considered to be of divine origin, a regard for individual rights and property moderated an otherwise autocratic governmental system.

It should not be thought that the association of the ruler with divinity exhausted the religious aspirations of the ancients. Babylonians believed in some form of existence after death and lavishly adorned the subterranean tombs of their kings. In the course of time more attention was paid to temples and palaces. Egyptian preoccupation with death and the life hereafter is also evident in their funeral customs. The bodies, at least of the great, were mummified, some existing mummies being of considerable antiquity. The pyramids and the many smaller and later temples were in reality tombs designed and equipped to serve the departed in another world. Although Amenophis IV (*d.* 1358 B.C.) of Egypt changed his name to Ikhnaton ("pleasing to Aton," the god of the sun's disk) and tried to enforce this cult as the sole worship, the ancients were, in general, polytheists—that is, worshippers of many deities. The persistent loyalty of the Hebrews to the one god, Jahveh, is, therefore, highly significant and will merit further discussion in a subsequent chapter.

Both Babylonians and Egyptians made important contributions to the art of writing. The Semitic Babylonians adapted to their own language the earlier Sumerian method of writing. This was a script composed of wedge-shaped or cuneiform (from *cuneus*, wedge) characters which could be made relatively easily on rock or clay tablets. Symbols were provided for some five hundred syllables. Thus, the Babylonians had progressed beyond the more primitive stage of picture writing. The Egyptians were able to designate certain sounds of the human voice by single letters. But in their hieroglyphics, they did not abandon signs for syllables or even for words and ideas. The Egyptians also developed papyrus, a writing material made by pressing together certain reeds which were plentiful in their country. Papyrus rolls served as the books of the ancient world.

It remained for the Phoenicians to produce a set of symbols, adapted from the

Egyptian Sculpture (from about 1400 B.C.). The Temple of Karnak at Luxor.
Courtesy Egyptian State Tourist Administration, New York

writing of other peoples, which represented twenty-two consonants (vowels were not written until later). Named and arranged in order, these symbols constituted an alphabet in the modern sense of the term. And it was this alphabet which was adapted and carried to the west by the Greeks and to the east by the Aramaeans. Thus, even in ancient times, it came to be known from India to the Atlantic. Further, since a great deal of the Egyptian papyrus used by the Greeks was obtained at the Phoenician port of Byblos, completed written works came to be known as *biblia.* Hence, there has come down to us from ancient Phoenician, through Greek and Latin, not only the word paper but the word-root so familiar in such terms as bible and bibliography.

As a consequence of their belief that heavenly bodies influenced the course of human events, the ancient Babylonians made a number of astronomical discoveries. They named the days of the week after the planets, divided the year into twelve months, and the day and night into twelve hours each. This sexagesimal computation was also used in dividing hours into sixty minutes, minutes into sixty seconds, and the circle into three hundred and sixty degrees. In Egypt, scientists also observed the heavenly bodies with simple instruments and distinguished between planets and fixed stars. And probably in the third millennium before Christ, though possibly earlier, the Egyptians reckoned time by a solar year of twelve thirty-day months with an added five extra days. The scientific lore of the ancients was passed on to their successors. And it is significant that it was the Greeks of Ionia in Asia Minor, those whose contacts with the Near East were closest, who were pioneers in the advancement of Greek science.

The most familiar and most striking evidences of ancient culture are to be found in the architectural monuments of Egypt. For the Egyptians achieved a grandeur and massiveness rarely, if ever, surpassed in human history. And stone monuments of astonishing size were possible in a civilization where the king commanded an unlimited supply of forced labor. The oldest and in many ways the most impressive structures were the pyramids which date from the IVth dynasty. In fact, the period from about 3200 to 2500 B.C. is sometimes called the Pyramid Age. Vast funeral monuments, the pyramids reflect the power of this ancient civilization and, taken all together, they form a veritable "city of the dead." In the empire period were completed the great temples at Karnak and Luxor, with their tremendous columns and their brilliantly colored sculptured reliefs. From the same period the huge seventy-foot statues of the pharaohs and the colossal figure of Rameses II (*d.* 1255 B.C.), carved out of the face of a rock, stand in mute testimony to the skill of sculptors thousands of years ago.

Egyptian artistic achievements were not confined to the gigantic, for Egyptians also excelled in portrait sculpture and in the minor arts of the jeweler and the goldsmith. Some of the smaller statues and sculptured busts are exquisite. And the jewels and furnishings of the lately discovered tomb of Tut-ankh-Amen, the successor of Ikhnaton, display a remarkable wealth of artistic talent.

No structures comparable to the Egyptian have survived from Mesopotamia, largely because scarcity of stone forced builders to use unburnt brick, a far more perishable material. Nor was the portrait sculpture of Mesopotamia as remarkable as that of Egypt. But the Babylonians developed to a high degree of perfection the carving of intricate scenes and groups.

To moderns, these ancient masterpieces are important in themselves. But we are also concerned with the cultural influence of the Ancient Near East on Greece and Europe. It is important to observe, for example, that the early Greek sculptors imitated the Egyptians. It is appropriate, therefore, to conclude this section with a word about Cretan art. For Crete was one of the links between the ancient Near East and the Mediterranean civilization which was first to develop in the Aegean area. Although scholars have in part been able to decipher a form of Cretan script, it is not yet possible to present a clear picture of Cretan political life. Other evidence, however, points to a highly developed culture. During the "golden age" (2200–1500 B.C.) Cretan builders raised large palaces, especially at Cnossus, and devised water conduits and drainage systems. Artists adorned walls with handsome frescoes, created beautiful figurines of gold, silver, and bronze, and painted pottery. Curiously enough, although the Greek writer Thucydides alluded to a great maritime empire on the island of Crete, his statement was long discounted and it was not until recent times that archaeologists have disclosed the actual existence of this great ancient culture.

D. The Empires of Assyria and Persia

The scene of our narrative thus far has shifted repeatedly from Egypt to Mesopotamia, with brief glances at the small states in Palestine and Syria and the island of Crete. And, while there has been evidence of cultural relations between these three areas, there has been no sign of any political coördination. The last thousand years before Christ witnessed the formation of new empires, each greater than its predecessor. As a consequence, the predominant characteristic of the first millennium before Christ was the welding together of formerly disparate cultures into unity. Indeed, this is the beginning of a process which reached a climax under the later leadership of Rome.

The first in this succession of empires was the achievement of a Semitic people who around 3000 B.C. had built in northeastern Mesopotamia a city called Assur, whence the name Assyrian. Subjected for many centuries to the Babylonians, the Assyrians developed a civilization influenced by Sumerian culture, but none the less distinctive. Their opportunity for expansion came toward the beginning of the first millennium with the decline of the Egyptian, Babylonian, and Hittite states. A people remarkably efficient in war and employing new weapons and tactics, the Assyrians soon overran Mesopotamia, Syria, and Palestine, and for a time occupied Egypt. Under Sargon II (722–705 B.C.) and his successor, Sennacherib, the Assyrian empire attained the summit of its power. Although often ruthless in their treatment of enemies and conquered peoples—thousands of Jews, Aramaeans, and others were deported to Mesopotamia—the Assyrians were noted for institutions of centralized government and administration which excelled those hitherto developed either in Egypt or in Babylonia. Absolute monarchical power was secured by such measures as an efficient postal service which enabled the king to keep in constant touch with outlying provinces. In spite of this, a large degree of municipal autonomy was permitted within the framework of the central administration.

Assyrian strength was at length challenged by a combination of Indo-European Medes and Persians and Semitic Chaldeans who encompassed the fall of Nineveh, the Assyrian capital, in 612 B.C. The Medes and Persians were destined ultimately to gain the mastery, but for a brief interlude Babylon again achieved an outstanding if temporary brilliance with the rule of the Semitic Chaldeans. Under Nebuchadnezzar, (604–561 B.C.), the capital city reached its maximum size and surpassed in magnificence all other cities. Under Nebuchadnezzar, too, the Jews were again defeated, Jerusalem destroyed, and many Jews endured a half century of captivity, the "Babylonian Captivity" of the Bible.

The passing of the Assyrian and Chaldean

Mesopotamian (Assyrian) sculpture of the ninth century B.C. Alabaster winged lion from the palace gate of Ashur-nasir-apal II, 885–860.

Courtesy Metropolitan Museum of Art, New York; gift of John D. Rockefeller, Jr., 1932

empires brings to a conclusion an era of ancient history marked by the supremacy of Semitic civilization, for the coming of the Medes and Persians heralded the beginning of a long predominance of Indo-European peoples over the Near East. Thus far, Indo-Europeans have not figured prominently in our narrative. In the period we have been considering, they inhabited for the most part the vast grassland, plain, and steppe country to the north, which stretches from central Asia through southern Russia into the Danube basin. When they moved south and west into the Mediterranean region, the lands of eastern and southern Europe began to come into prominence, as our next

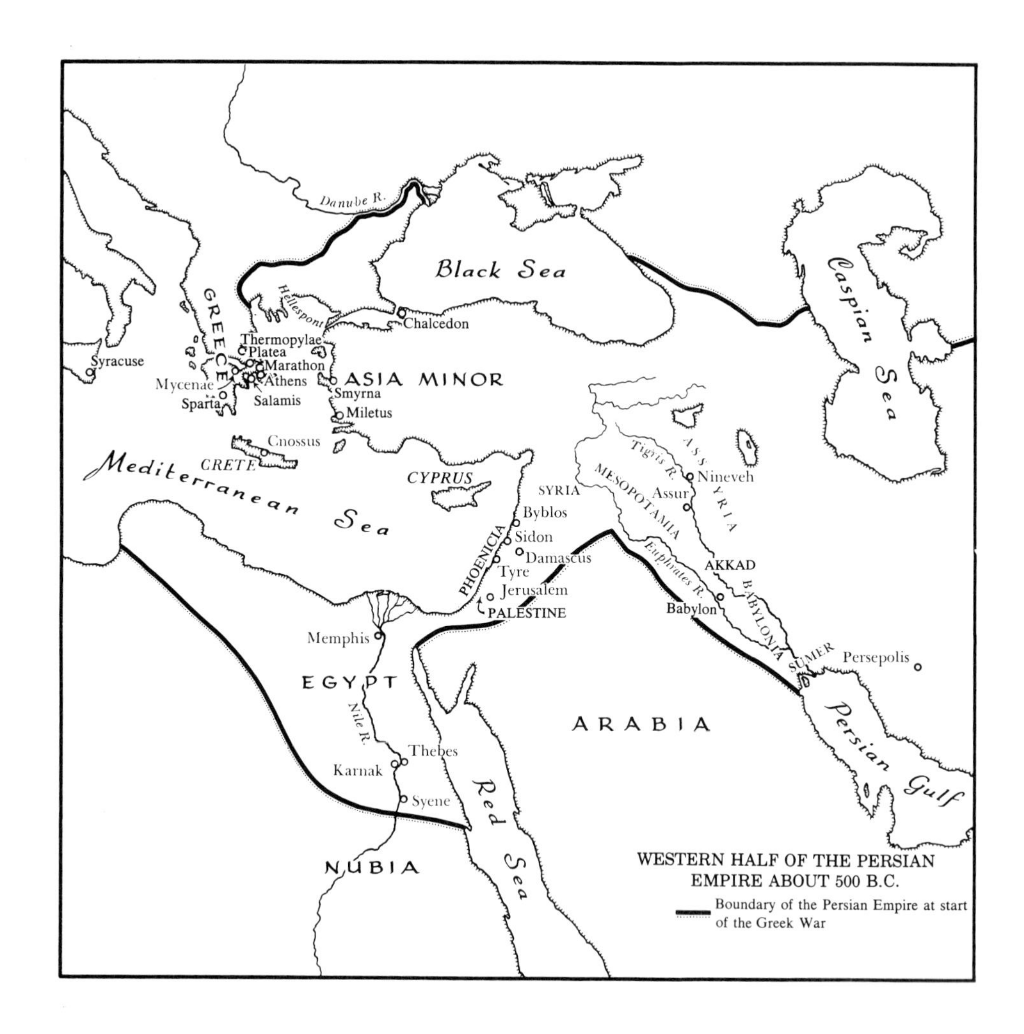

chapters will indicate. But one Indo-European people, the Iranians,[1] of whom the Medes and Persians were the most prominent, pushed southward into the fertile crescent. At the time of the destruction of the Assyrian empire, to which they contributed heavily, the Medes were dominant, the Persians in a state of vassalage. But under their chieftain Cyrus, the Persians turned the tables on their kindred and followed their triumph over the Medes by successful attacks first on the kingdom of Lydia in Asia Minor, then on Babylon which fell in 539 B.C. When Cyrus's successor, Cambyses, conquered Egypt (525 B.C.), the Persian empire embraced the entire ancient Near East from the Nile delta and the eastern Mediterranean to the borders of India.

Persian civilization owed much to its predecessors. Its architecture seems largely derived from the Egyptian, Babylonian, and Assyrian. Throughout the entire western part of the empire Aramaic was an official language. But the Persians also devised a cuneiform alphabet of thirty-nine letters.[2] It seems probable that Hebrew religious influence was not inconsiderable, although in the field of religion the Persian contribution was largely original. Through the *Magi* (or priestly "wise men") of the Medes had been preserved beliefs and rituals of

[1] Iran, which is derived from "Aryan," has become the name of the plateau stretching from the Zagros mountains to the Indus river, and has been adopted as a name for the modern state of Persia.

[2] Among the inscriptions on the famous triumphal monument carved out of a huge rock face at Behistun, near Ecbatana, was a passage in Persian, Babylonian, and Susian, which has provided a key to the language of old Babylonia.

great antiquity, which among other things emphasized the ceaseless struggle of good and evil, of the spiritual powers of darkness and light. It remained for Zoroaster (probably seventh century B.C.) to teach a kind of monotheism which exalted the power of Ahura-Mazda, the supreme god of good. Among Ahura-Mazda's helpers was Mithras. And Mithraism, as an offshoot of Zoroastrian beliefs, developed in a later time into a serious rival of primitive Christianity.

Ancient Persia's most significant contribution lay in the field of government. Never before in the ancient world had so large an area been administered so efficiently. The entire empire was divided into provinces (satrapies), some twenty in all, each under the supervised control of a local governor. The authority of each satrap was checked by the presence of a secretary and a military commander, both responsible directly to the emperor. Moreover, government officials, the famous "eyes and ears of the monarch," constantly traveled over the numerous and excellent roads on the emperor's business. Beneath this superstructure of centralized administration, local life and customs went on much as before. Different religions were tolerated, and Cyrus permitted the Jews to return to their Palestinian homeland and rebuild their temple at Jerusalem.

As we have mentioned, the rise of Persia ushered in an age of great empires. In their expansion the Persians turned north and west in an attempt to subjugate Greece, where a brilliant culture had already developed. Accordingly we shall direct our attention westward from Asia to Greece and the developing civilization of Europe.

Egyptian Sculpture, Queen Nefertiti c. 1375 B.C., Berlin Museum.

Courtesy Marbury Art Reference Bureau

Greek Architecture in Magna Graecia. The Greek Theater at Syracuse, Sicily.

Courtesy Italian State Tourist Office, New York

Fourth or fifth century B.C. Greek-Athenian vase. Combat of Greeks and Amazons.

Courtesy Metropolitan Museum of Art, New York; Fletcher Fund, 1944

CHAPTER 2

Added Intellectual and Artistic Heritage of Greece

A. The Greeks in the Aegean and the Mediterranean

In the previous chapter we were concerned with the achievements of successive cultures in the ancient Near East. With the study of Greece we encounter the very foundations of European and Western civilization. For not only is the Greek peninsula in Europe proper, but Greek habits of life and especially Greek artistic and intellectual accomplishments are recognizable as integral parts of our distinctive Western culture. Greek art has inspired countless artists from the days of Rome to the present. Indeed, there is hardly a city in the western world which does not in some of its buildings reflect Greek influence. The contribution of the Greek mind is less apparent, but no less real and important. Down through the centuries Greek literary forms, Greek scientific achievements, and, perhaps above all, Greek skill in rationalizing the problems of life have repeatedly left their mark.

The Indo-European ancestors of the Greeks moved through the Balkans into the Greek peninsula about the time that the Indo-European Medes and Persians were wandering southward east of the Caspian Sea (about 1300–1100 B.C.). Somewhat later they began to occupy the Aegean islands, Crete, and the coast of Asia Minor. Thus the ancient Greek world included the entire area washed by the Aegean Sea. The irregular and indented coasts of both Asia Minor and Greece are rich in excellent harbors. As the Greek peninsula is broken not only by bays, inlets, and gulfs, but by rugged mountains, communication even in ancient times was often less difficult by sea than by land. It would seem inevitable that the inhabitants of such a region should become a seafaring people.

As the early Greeks came into contact with the ancient Near East, they were particularly influenced by the Cretans. In fact, Crete was a kind of intermediary between the old culture of the west Asiatic mainland and the new world of the Aegean and Mediterranean. The Cretans, it will be recalled, had established settlements of considerable size at Mycenae in southern Greece and at Troy in northwestern Asia Minor. Not only did the Greeks absorb these Cretan outposts, but they invaded Crete itself. The tables were turned. The old Cretan civilization declined and became merged with the new culture of Greece. Thus, about the time of the famous siege of Troy (about 1184 B.C.), immortalized by Homer, the Greeks were beginning to develop customs of their own.

Although the ancient Greek world was one of separate city-states which did not form an administrative national unity, there did develop among them a sense of cultural nationality based upon the many elements of life which all Greeks held in common. Foremost among these was a common language, for, despite differences of dialect, men from various parts of the Greek world could understand one another. Literature

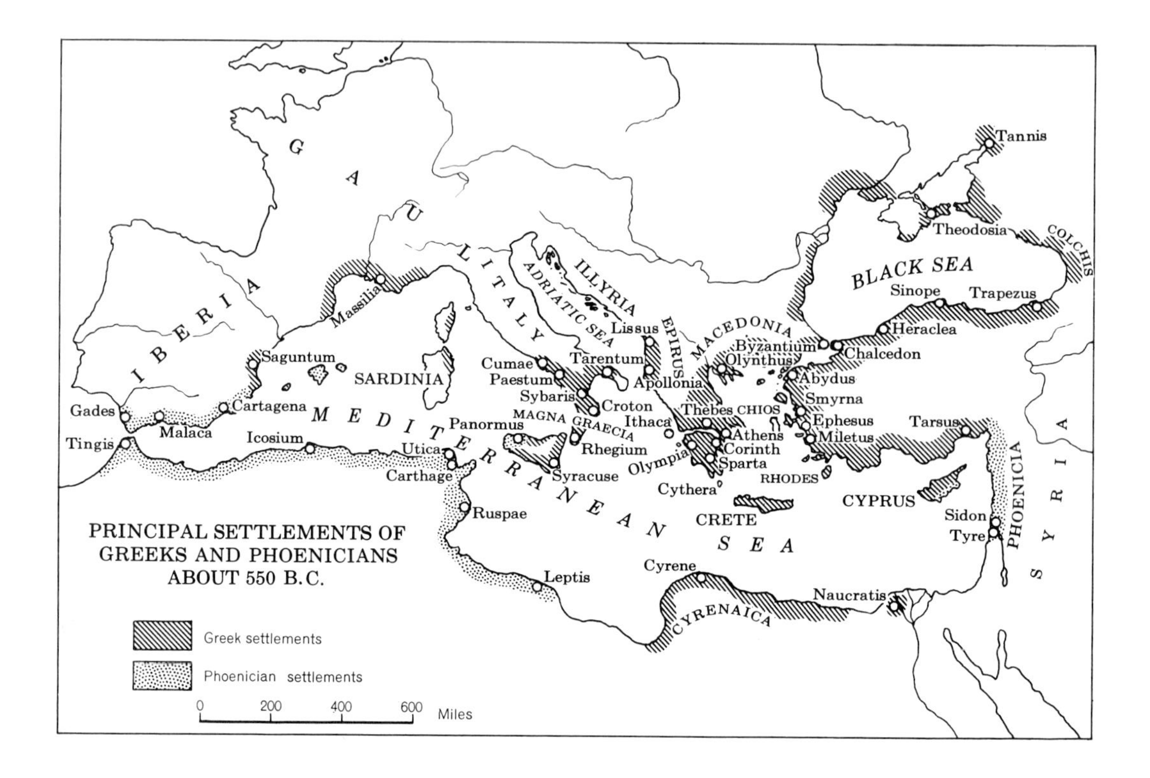

PRINCIPAL SETTLEMENTS OF GREEKS AND PHOENICIANS ABOUT 550 B.C.

and religion also fostered common traditions. Through the Homeric epics all Greeks became familiar with the same gods and with the heroic deeds of their own ancestors. Representatives of Greek communities occasionally met to arrange for such common religious celebrations as the famous festivals of Olympia, which date from the early eighth century. The oracle of Apollo at Delphi was also universal in its attraction. Thus it was that the Greeks became conscious of themselves as culturally distinct from others. They gradually began to think of themselves as Hellenes, one and all descended from a common legendary ancestor, Hellen. Hellas was a culture, if not a nation.

A striking manifestation of a community of culture can be seen in Greek colonization, a feature of Greek life which began in the eighth and extended into the seventh and sixth centuries before Christ. Greek colonization was motivated as much by political as by economic factors. In certain cities such as Corinth and Miletus (Miletus founded more colonies than any other Greek city) the original area was so limited that emigration was almost a necessity. Prestige was not unimportant in colonization; nor, of course, was the desire to increase the opportunities for trade. However motivated, Greek colonial expeditions were thoroughly organized and equipped. Colonists, when they had established themselves, kept on good terms with their mother city while at the same time jealously preserving the sovereign independence of the new community.

Geographically, Greek colonization spread westward throughout the entire Mediterranean area and eastward along the shores of the Black Sea. The Thracian coast, the Straits where the Greek city of Megara founded the colonies of Chalcedon and Byzantium, and the whole length of the Black Sea coast, including the northern shore, attracted Greek settlers. Intrepid pioneers reached the shores of the Iberian peninsula. The modern French city of Marseilles was once a Greek colony. Cyrene (Cyrenaica) and Naucratis, near the later Alexandria, were established in North Africa. The most important Greek colonies were in Southern Italy and Sicily, an area later known as *Magna Graecia*. For there, from centers like Syracuse, founded by Corinth in 735 B.C., Cumae on the bay of Naples, or Croton on the boot of Italy,

Greek ways of life first influenced the Romans.

To a surprising degree the new settlements retained a distinctively Greek character. The architectural and artistic forms of the homeland were employed. Greek speech persisted, and the religious and political institutions of the mother city were set up. As a consequence, colonization proved to be the means of an extraordinary expansion of a truly Greek culture. The modern traveler may visit Greek temples in Sicily, and the modern archaeologist may uncover Greek statues in Africa.

Another evidence of community of feeling among the Greeks is the capacity of at least some of them to coöperate against common danger. This was demonstrated in the fifth century before Christ, when Greeks stood off successive attacks from mighty Persia. In the preceding chapter, we followed the expansion of the Persian empire and its conquest of Asia Minor. This involved the subjugation of Ionian Greek cities. These, however, revolted; and Athens, sensing the ultimate threat to the Greek peninsula, sent twenty ships to assist them. In retaliation, the Persian king Darius launched an attack on Greece and in 490 B.C. successfully landed an army on the shores of Attica in the bay of Marathon. The Athenians mustered a citizens' army and sought aid from Sparta and other Greek cities. Though outnumbered two to one, the Athenians were fortunate in having in Miltiades a capable commander who was familiar with Persian tactics. Instead of awaiting a Persian assault, his army advanced to the hills overlooking the plain of Marathon. The Persians, unable to lure the Greeks from their advantageous position, finally marched towards Athens, thereby exposing their flank to a Greek attack. The result was a resounding Greek victory. The surviving Persians took refuge in their ships and sailed away.

A decade later, Xerxes, Darius's successor, renewed the struggle. Having built a formidable fleet with the assistance of the Phoenician cities, he planned a combined sea and land attack on Greece, together with an advance on Sicily from Carthage. But the Athenians, as a result of the first Persian campaign and the insistent advice of Themistocles, had strengthened their navy; and Sparta helped them with an army under its king, Leonidas. n this occasion (480 B.C.), a big Persian army, supported by the fleet, crossed the straits and moved southward toward the Greek peninsula. It was the Greek plan to fight a delaying action on land until the Athenian navy could overcome the Persian fleet. The plan succeeded only in part. The Persian fleet was halted but not defeated. Meanwhile, the heroic Leonidas, with a force of some four thousand Hellenes, fell at the historic pass of Thermopylae; and the Persians marched into the peninsula, devastating it and burning Athens.

The Greeks were rallied by Themistocles; and presently the Persian fleet was drawn into an attack on the Athenian navy, which had taken up a favorable position in the bay of Salamis. After an engagement which lasted all day, the Persian fleet was disastrously defeated. Themistocles urged that the victory of Salamis be followed up by an attempt to cut off the Persian army, but the Spartans at first hesitated to risk so bold a maneuver. As a consequence, the war dragged on into the following summer, and Attica was again devastated. Then the Spartan King Pausanias, with the combined armies of Athens and Sparta, defeated the Persian host at Plataea (479 B.C.), while the Athenian navy overwhelmed the remnants of the Persian fleet north of Miletus. Already, Syracuse had repulsed the Carthaginians in Sicily. Thus the entire Greek world was saved from conquest. It was a splendid achievement, and the following age was a time of unparalleled brilliance in Greek civilization.

B. City-State Politics of the Greeks

The political development of the Greeks was characterized, not by the formation of a Greek nation, but, doubtless much influenced by geographical conditions, by the growth of separate city-states. Yet even a brief examination of early Greek political life reveals a remarkable political maturity. Many of the governmental terms still in current use, such as monarchy, democracy, tyrant, politics, to mention only a few, are of Greek origin. The conception of a city-state is in itself important, and it lasted into Roman times and far beyond. Indeed, the Greek word for city, *polis,* has been absorbed into words of governmental significance in more than one Western language. The term means a sovereign and independent state whose area is either confined to the environs of a single city or, perhaps, includes several smaller communities dominated by one large city.

Despite the political diversity which is evident in the history of the Greek city-states, there were certain developments which many experienced in common. In early times most cities were petty monarchies. But by the time of the great expansion, that is, around the eighth century before Christ, the predominance of the aristocracy was fairly general, and most kings were overthrown. The mercantile tendencies which characterized that age produced profound social and political changes. In the cities of Ionia, the Greek coastland of Asia Minor, which had been in the van of economic progress, and in the commercially progressive cities of the Greek mainland and Sicily, seizure of power by violence was not uncommon. Dictators made their appearance. Some were beneficent rulers and championed the oppressed lower classes. Indeed, the word "tyrant" did not then have its modern sinister meaning. Nevertheless, benevolent tyranny could and sometimes did degenerate. And there were tyrants who were removed by the same methods which had maintained them in power. By the sixth or fifth century before Christ the principal Greek city-states had developed that form of government which, in general, they were to maintain, and some were beginning to achieve a certain prominence which singled them out over their neighbors. Corinth, for example, owed much to its favorable location at the head of the Gulf of the same name. Sparta was to attain prestige in the south. Miletus, Ephesus, and Phocaea on the mainland of Asia Minor, and certain of the islands such as Naxos or Lesbos remind us that the ancient Greek world embraced both sides of the Aegean Sea.

Since it would be impossible here to trace the development of all the Greek city-states, it must suffice to discuss two famous and strikingly different cities, Sparta and Athens. Spartan social and political organization was not typical. But its peculiar militaristic culture undoubtedly contributed to Spartan predominance in the Peloponnesus, the peninsula of southern Greece. Unlike commercial Athens, Sparta was an agricultural state with an exaggerated emphasis on the military discipline of its citizens. Rigorous training under the aegis of the state began for boys at the age of seven and continued through early manhood. Even girls were required to undergo physical training. Such preoccupation with things physical and military left little time for the finer things of life, and Spartan contribution to the arts was negligible. But Spartan discipline, though not typical of Hellenic civilization, had its importance and in some measure justified itself in the military trials with Persia and later with Athens.

Although the democratic institutions for which Athens became famous were noticeable early in the city's history,[1] the climax of Athenian political development came in the fifth century before Christ. This was a brilliant period in Greek history which followed the long and successful defense of the homeland against Persian attacks, a defense in which Athens played a major part. In accordance with a pronounced tendency toward more popular government, the authority of the old aristocratic council of elders, which formerly met on a hill called the Areopagus, was curtailed. A popular council of five hundred citizens, divided into small groups, now conducted most of the state business. Citizen juries were enlarged to include about six thousand citizens divided ordinarily into smaller units of five hundred and one. To enable poor citizens to serve, jurors were paid, As these juries gained prestige they became, together with the popular assembly, virtual law-making bodies.

The right to hold office was extended to all men who possessed some property, and the choice of office-holders by lot was introduced. This practice, although

[1] It was at Athens that any citizen could write the name of a person deemed dangerous to the state on a broken piece of pottery or *ostracon* (hence our word "ostracize").

democratic, had its obvious disadvantages, and it is noteworthy that the important post of military commander (*strategos*) remained elective. The president of a body of ten generals might, as the principal elected official, wield considerable power. Pericles, for example, champion of the now popular cause of reform and progress, was elected *strategos* (461 B.C.) and, since he was reelected repeatedly, became virtual dictator of Athens for a period of nearly thirty years.

Athenian democracy was also qualified by the restriction of its advantages to citizens. Citizens included only the children of free-born parents. Thus, the foreigners (*metics*) resident in Athens, numbering more than 25,000, and the 115,000 slaves of Attica, not to mention most workingmen, were denied the privileges of citizenship. And no women enjoyed the franchise. Athenian democracy, however full for those who shared its privileges and responsibilities, was severely limited as to the number of those participating.

Of far greater importance than any single political achievement was the impact of the Greek mind on politics. In Greece, perhaps for the first time in history, the greatest thinkers sought to rationalize the theory as well as the practice of government. Above all, they were concerned with ethics as applied to the life of the city-state. As Athens developed a popular government, an increasing number of men sought an education, at least in things political and moral. They acquired, too, a training in persuasive speech. A group of teachers called sophists (Greek *sophia*, "wisdom") helped fill this need. And although their practices degenerated later into an emphasis on mere tricks of speech and reasoning (sophistry), the sophists at their best contributed much to Greek intellectual development.

Indebted to the sophists, and yet standing apart from them, was Socrates (*d.* 399 B.C.). Professing to be an earnest seeker after truth, particularly an inquirer into such things as abstract justice and goodness, Socrates became a notorious questioner. He embarrassed and evidently irritated many of those whom he interrogated by the ease with which he cast doubt on established beliefs. With disarming frankness he pretended to know nothing and sought to lead others toward a more sound rationalization of their own ideas. Posterity has paid his method of teaching the supreme compliment of imitation.

Plato (*d.* 347 B.C.), Socrates' famous pupil, presented a reasoned picture of the ideal state governed by the "philosopher-king" in his book *The Republic*. And finally Aristotle (*d.* 322 B.C.) not only pondered over the nature of ethics but examined the constitutions of some 158 city-states in his treatise on *Politics*. The rational examination of political institutions has ever since been characteristic of Western civilization. The Greeks gave us the foundation and much of the technique for this rationalization.

C. Hellenic Culture

The rationalization of politics is, of course, only one example of Greek intellectual achievement. The interests of Greek thinkers were wide and deep. The word "philosophy" is of Greek origin and means, literally, "love of wisdom." Moreover, Greek philosophers took all knowledge as their province. Philosophy to them included what would today be designated the natural sciences, such as physics, astronomy, and mathematics, as well as the more narrowly "philosophical" subjects of logic, ethics, and metaphysics.

The earliest Greek thinkers of prominence were primarily concerned with the nature of the universe. And because of its closer contacts with the ancient Near East, Ionia (the Greek coast of Asia Minor) witnessed the beginnings of Greek natural science. Thales of Miletus, on the basis of Babylonian calculations, correctly predicted an eclipse of the sun (585 B.C.) and proclaimed, contrary to former beliefs, the dependence of the heavenly bodies on natural laws. Somewhat later came Pythagoras (*d.* about 500 B.C.), who, in addition to enunciating a famous geometrical theorem, was a philosopher and something of an educational theorist. He conducted a sort of "model school" at Croton in southern Italy. Students graduating from our modern medical schools still take a professional oath which is a paraphrase of the words of Hippocrates of the island of Cos (born about 460 B.C.). For centuries physicians followed Hippocrates's teaching.

The sophists were not interested in political matters exclusively. They also laid the foundations for the systematic study of rhetoric and logic. In emphasizing clarity of speech and in giving precise meaning to words they helped to form the tradition of rationalism which became characteristic of Greek intellectual life. Moreover, Socrates and Plato posed the great questions of all philosophy: What is being? What exists? Plato insisted on the reality of abstract ideas—justice, goodness, and the like—which existed in the mind of God and only as pale imperfect reflections in the world of sense. This philosophy of "idealism" has profoundly affected later thinkers, even into modern times.

Aristotle, Plato's illustrious pupil, was a painstaking scholar, who, in addition to his interest in the theory of politics, gathered an enormous amount of information on biology, anatomy, zoölogy, and other sciences, which he systematically classified. In the realm of metaphysics, while conceding that the human mind could "abstract" the general from the particular and, for example, classify into *genus* and *species*, he insisted on the reality of the individual. Aristotle's voluminous writings on almost every conceivable subject constitute a veritable encyclopedia of ancient knowledge. On many matters his authority was unquestioned for centuries. As late as the fourteenth century the Italian poet Dante could hail him as "the master of those who know."

Both Plato and Aristotle strengthened the Greek tradition of rationalism which lies at the foundation of Western thought. Moreover, in their striving to understand the nature of the universe and of man, and, in particular, in attacking the central philosophical problem of being, the Greek philosophers were gradually led away from the primitive polytheism which had characterized Greek popular religion. Although the gods of Olympus continued to figure prominently in literature and art, they began to lose their appeal as objects of real religious worship. More important, Plato and Aristotle presented, at least to intellectuals, the rational conception of a single supreme being, a "first cause" or "prime mover," which was to be of increasing significance.

The Greek literary tradition, which commenced with such works as the Homeric epics, *The Iliad* and *The Odyssey*,[1] includes the lyric verse of Pindar of Thebes, and Sappho, poetess of Lesbos, and, above all, the tragedies of Aeschylus (*d.* 456 B.C.), Sophocles (*d.* 406 B.C.), and Euripides (*d.* 406 B.C.). Their dramas, as also the "comedies" of Aristophanes (*d.* about 385 B.C.), found intelligent and critical audiences in Athens. So skillful was the handling of the timeless themes of life, death, fate, and religion that Greek tragedies have become "classics" for every subsequent age. Athens also produced three renowned historians—Herodotus (*d.* 425 B.C.), chronicler of the Persian wars; Thucydides (*d.* 400 B.C.), who somewhat later described the decline of Athenian hegemony in Greece; and Xenophon (*d.* 355 B.C.), who was an essayist as well as an historian.

Pericles, the great statesman who guided the destinies of Athens in the period after the Persian wars, was also an enthusiastic and discerning patron of the arts. And while it would be incorrect to associate Greek art solely with the "age of Pericles" or even exclusively with Athens, nevertheless it remains true that his régime produced an unrivalled effort of artistic creation. It was distinguished by a revival of building, especially by a rebuilding of the Acropolis, the hill in the heart of the city. Athenians spent little on their private dwellings, but they supported Pericles' appeals for expenditure on the public edifices which adorned the famous hill. Thus they made possible such a masterpiece as the Parthenon, the temple of Athena, designed in the Doric style by Ictinus. The Doric is the most severely simple of Greek architectural styles. The plain columns are surmounted with unadorned "capitals." Yet it seems

[1] These famous epics were composed presumably in the second half of the ninth century before Christ. They reflect, however, Greek life in the period before 1000 B.C.

ideally suited to the Parthenon. Harmoniously proportioned, faultless in every detail, it is one of the most nearly perfect temples ever erected.[1]

The Parthenon and the many other public buildings on the Acropolis and elsewhere bear witness to a combination of architectural skill and artistic taste which has seldom been equaled. In addition to the Doric style which reached its perfection in the Parthenon, there was also the Ionic, employed in the delicately ornamented Erechtheum, and the Corinthian with its more elaborate capitals. Subsequent ages, in paying Greek architecture the compliment of conscious imitation, have made Doric, Ionic, and Corinthian columns and capitals familiar throughout all Europe and America.

Greeks also excelled in sculpture. The Parthenon housed the colossal bronze statue of Athena, while above the stately rows of columns was the carved marble frieze displaying a procession of Athenians. These creations of Phidias (*d.* about 432 B.C.) and his pupils display a capacity to handle a variety of subjects and attitudes and an ability to produce adequate detail without destroying the harmony of the whole composition. Praxiteles and others maintained in the fourth century the high standards set in the era of Pericles.

Greek painting is perhaps less appreciated than Greek sculpture. But the achievements of Phidias were equalled by his contemporary, Polygnotus the painter. Indeed, Phidias probably learned a great deal from Polygnotus' work. Best known for his large frescoes, Polygnotus also influenced the art of vase painting. For the best Greek artists were not unwilling to identify themselves with the efforts of craftsmen. And nowhere is the close association of art and industry more evident than in ceramics.

Hellenic culture reached its full flowering in the period following the Persian wars. Although the defeat of the Persians was a splendid achievement, it brought only temporary unity to the Greek city-states.

[1] The frontispiece of this volume depicts the Parthenon as it is now.

For some thirty years, Athens, through the Delian League, dominated the northern half of the peninsula, together with most of the Aegean islands and Ionian towns, and even threatened the south. But what may be called an Athenian empire was opposed by some cities. Finally, Sparta, leader of the cities of the Peloponnesus, challenged Athenian domination in a series of conflicts known as the Peloponnesian War (431–404 B.C.). There followed a brief period of Spartan and then Theban hegemony.

Evidently, temporary military or naval alliances among Greek city-states did not prove adequate foundations for political unity. Thus it was that the peninsula fell an easy prey to a conqueror less distant than Persia. And this Macedonian conquest which we are about to describe brought to a close the splendid age of the Greek city states. Thenceforth, Hellenic civilization was spread far and wide and merged with the culture of many other peoples.

D. *Alexander's Empire and the Hellenistic Age*

The regions to the north of Greece proper —Thrace and Macedonia—had lagged far behind their southern neighbors. In Macedonia, however, Greek influence had penetrated and, at the court of its king, Philip II, Greek culture was so highly respected that the king engaged the philosopher Aristotle as tutor for his son, Alexander. Further, well aware of the opportunities offered by the chronic political disunity of the city-states, he dreamed of welding the entire peninsula together under one government capable of challenging once and for all the dominion of Persia. Part of this dream was realized when he defeated the Greeks at the battle of Chaeronea (338 B.C.) and assumed the leadership over a league of Greek states.

Philip, however, was not destined to carry his plans to fruition, for his untimely death (336 B.C.) left that tremendous task to his twenty-year-old son, Alexander. Alexander inherited his father's admiration for Greek civilization, an admiration strengthened by the tutelage of Aristotle. Moreover, his romantically ambitious spirit was fired by the Homeric epics, and he not only dreamed of establishing a united Greece as a Mediterranean power but deemed it his mission to spread Greek civilization abroad. A young man of action as well as a dreamer, Alexander possessed the military qualities necessary for so gigantic a task. Assisted by a body of competent and devoted colleagues trained in the service of his father, he embarked upon one of the most amazing careers of conquest the world has known.

The first step in the accomplishment of his great design was a bold invasion of Asia Minor. Then, following two brilliant victories over Persian arms, Alexander declined a peace offer which would have flattered many a greedy conqueror and which olders advisers urged him to accept, for the Persian King Darius III was willing to concede the Euphrates as a boundary between the Greek and Persian empires. Alexander hesitated, but not for long. His mission was not yet accomplished. Advancing southward he occupied Syria and all the Phoenician ports, thus neutralizing the Persian fleet which soon dispersed. Egypt, now exposed, fell easily. Persia was overrun, and the immense treasures of the Persian kings at Susa and Persepolis fell into his hands. Then, to the amazement of everybody, this youthful conqueror pressed still farther eastward. For six years (330–324 B.C.) he led his armies north and east across the Oxus river, even across the Indus into the Ganges valley. And only the complaints of his weary soldiers forced him to turn back.

What was the political result of the stupendous conquest? Alexander had far-reaching political designs which were not merely the result of personal ambition. When he had himself deified at the temple of Amen-Ra in Egypt, he was establishing a kind of religio-political order which he hoped would facilitate a world unity of Greeks and Asiatics. And although the outward manifestations of divine right offended many of his sturdy old companions-at-arms, Alexander doubtless calculated that he might thus win the loyalty of Egyptians and Asiatics, to whom such customs were familiar. His plan for Hellenizing the entire Near East involved the establishment everywhere of cities on the Greek model. Actually some seventy were founded, many of them bearing his name. The most famous, Alexandria in Egypt, remained one of the foremost Mediterranean ports for centuries. Alexander did not live long enough to enjoy the fruits of his conquests. Estranged from his former associates and worn out by exertions and dissipation, he died while still a young man in 323 B.C.

The Empire as a unit did not long survive its creator. It was soon divided into separate kingdoms, some of them ruled by Alexander's generals. But since the various states and kingdoms of the post-Alexandrian period were all monarchies after the original model, a characteristic political order did remain as the legacy of the original single state. Further, there developed in the age following Alexander a civilization which, though diversified, was common to a great part of the area of the Macedonian's conquests. We speak of this age as "Hellenistic," a word which denotes the predominantly Greek basis of its culture yet avoids the connotation of "Hellenic," or the purely Greek. For Alexander's dream of Hellenizing the Orient was realized to a surprising extent, while in its dispersal Greek culture was fused with the oriental.

The significance of Hellenistic culture, therefore, lies partly in the fusion of Greek and oriental culture, but more in the spread of Greek institutions and thought over a wide area. In fact, the heritage of Greece was eventually to be transmitted not only to the Near East but westward by Rome to Europe. It was, therefore, Hellenistic, not Hellenic, culture which directly influenced subsequent civilizations.

It was a prosperous age, a time of commercial and industrial expansion, which affected the entire Mediterranean as well as western Asiatic areas and is evident in the building of cities and in the development of banking. Unlike Athens, where most of the energy went into beautifying the Acropolis, most Hellenistic cities boasted broad and straight streets, sumptuous residences, handsome public buildings. Even the smaller towns had their libraries, assembly halls, baths, theaters, and public squares. It was, therefore, a frankly luxurious and materialistic society, and the cleavage between rich and poor was marked.

Although the subsequent loss of the greater part of Hellenistic literature makes adequate criticism difficult, it is evident that this was preëminently a literate age. Moreover, the Greek political predominance forced all important public servants to learn the tongue of their conquerors. Thus, diplomats, men of commerce, and, most

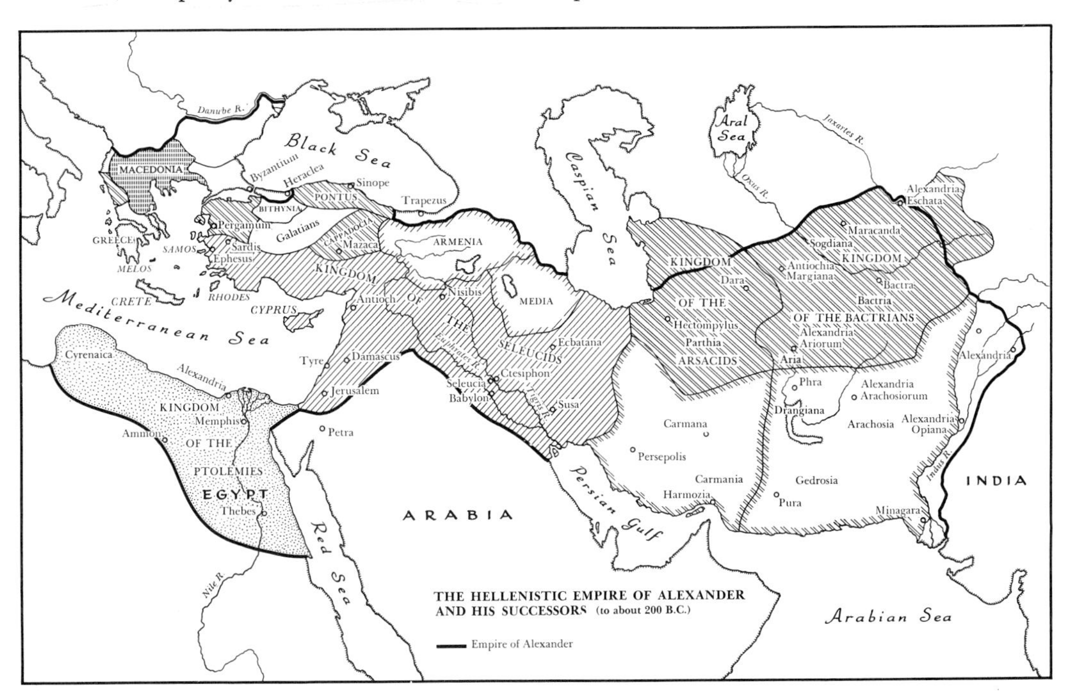

THE HELLENISTIC EMPIRE OF ALEXANDER AND HIS SUCCESSORS (to about 200 B.C.)

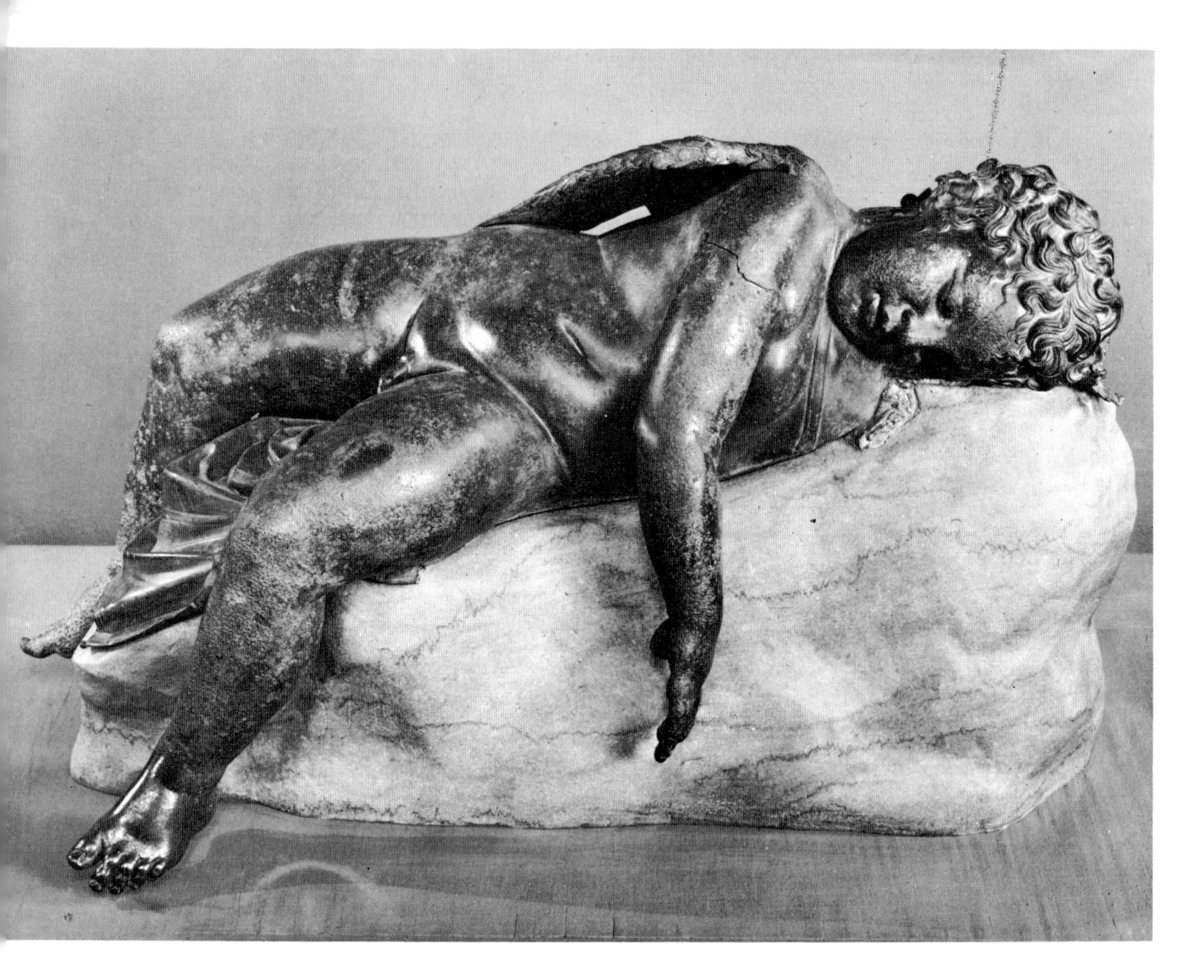

Hellenistic sculpture. Bronze figure of Eros sleeping.

Courtesy Metropolitan Museum of Art, New York; Rogers Fund, 1943

important, men of learning made Greek a virtually universal language throughout the entire area. For this larger audience many books were written, and in certain cities important libraries were collected. The most famous was the library at Alexandria which helped to make that metropolis the foremost center of Hellenistic learning.

Although there are some who hold that Hellenistic art failed to maintain the exacting standards of the Hellenic period, the artists of the later age continued the work of their predecessors. Technical skill and mastery of material were perfected. Painting, especially mural painting, enjoyed a wide popularity. Greek architectural forms persisted, becoming under oriental influence more ornate. Corinthian capitals were especially popular. The large and grandiose had great appeal. The lighthouse at the entrance to the harbor of Alexandria, the Colossus of Rhodes, a huge bronze statue of the sun-god, 105 feet high, and the third temple of Diana at Ephesus were numbered among the traditional seven wonders of the world.

The crowning achievement of the period was in science where the climax of Greek thinking was reached. This was the age of Euclid, who taught at Alexandria and compiled a treatise on geometry wherein he coordinated the work of many predecessors, both known and unknown. Equally famous is the name of Archimedes of Syracuse, who again reminds us that the Greek world extended westward into the Mediterranean. Primarily a mathematician, Archimedes made important inquiries in the fields of mechanics and hydrostatics. Hipparchus of Nicaea was an astronomer of renown whose positive contributions were somewhat dimmed, at least in the eyes of modern critics, by his attack on the heliocentric theory of the universe as proposed by Aristarchus of Samos. The weight of his authority, along with that of Euclid, decided the matter for ancient times. Hipparchus also made a number of important additions to the sum total of astronomical knowledge and its mathematical implications, including a great deal of trigonometry. The *Almagest* (about A.D. 140) of Ptolemy, for centuries the foundation of western astronomical thinking, was based largely on the work of Hipparchus. And lastly we may mention Eratosthenes of Cyrene, who compiled a treatise on geography and whose computation of the earth's circumference was in error by only some two hundred miles.

Hellenistic philosophy failed to live up to the promise of its past. Aristotle, to be sure, lived and worked as the tutor of Alexander, but he was, after all, of the Hellenic tradition. The escapist arguments of Epicurus of Samos, who sought happiness in the intelligent pursuit of pleasure, failed to satisfy many. Stoicism, so named because its first proponent, Zeno, taught at the *Stoa Poecile* (Painted Porch), had a more lasting influence, though its devotees were never numerous. For the Stoic, morality was inseparable from religion, and man must surrender to the will of God who is Nature and the Law of the World. Thus the man who does not question the course of Nature, even though it bring evil or pain to himself, finds peace. Stoicism was a noble philosophy and it reflected a hunger for the spiritual which was increasingly noticeable as the old paganism lost its appeal.

The subject of the preceding pages has been the development of a culture which lies at the foundation of western civilization. Not much has been said of Greek political history, still less of economic progress. For the legacy of Greece to subsequent generations was not economic or political. Rather, it must again be emphasized, it was the rationalization of man, his place in society and, indeed, in the universe of things seen and unseen. Evidences of the pervading influence of Greek thought will multiply as our narrative progresses. And in art, the touch of Greek genius is apparent throughout the west and not a little of the east. Thus what germinated in the relatively restricted area of the Aegean and the central Mediterranean was eventually to flourish throughout the European world.

A Roman wall painting of the first century B.C.

Courtesy Metropolitan Museum of Art, New York; Rogers Fund, 1903

CHAPTER 3

Fusing Heritage of Roman Republic and Empire

A. Formation of the Roman Republic

The geographical center of Alexander's Empire had been in western Asia. Roman civilization developed first in the central Mediterranean region, then expanded westward as well as eastward to include the entire Mediterranean basin. Under Rome, Mediterranean civilization embraced for the first time all the coast lands of southern Europe, north Africa, and, finally, considerable areas to the north in Europe.

Less speculative and philosophical than the Greeks, the Romans were far more practical, and their greatest achievements were in the fields of law and government. Rome was able to remedy the political failures of the Hellenistic world and to preserve and transmit the Hellenistic cultural heritage. The remarkable combination of the Greek and the Roman achievement, which we call Graeco-Roman culture, lies at the base of our western civilization.

The Mediterranean basin which was the scene of this Graeco-Roman civilization is a natural geographic unit. From earliest times it has been an avenue of communication. As we have already seen, the ancient Phoenicians and Greeks founded colonies throughout its length and breadth. Compared with the Atlantic it is a body of water more easily navigated by small vessels. As a consequence, there has been, at least since Roman times, an intimate connection between southern Europe and northern Africa. At the Strait of Gibraltar, Europe and Africa are in close proximity. Many historically significant crossings have been made there. Sicily is not far from the African coast. And in the eastern Mediterranean we have already noticed the contacts between Egypt, Crete, and Greece. The climate of northwestern Africa is roughly comparable to that of southern Europe. The Atlas mountains contribute largely to this condition by breaking the winds which blow over the Mediterranean and the eastern Atlantic, causing precipitation, and impeding the hot airs which blow north out of the Sahara.

Midway in the Mediterranean, and extending southward from Europe toward Africa, is the long peninsula of Italy. This is at least three times as large as Greece and it is the cradle of Roman civilization. Three distinct peoples contributed to the early development of civilization in Italy. A western wing of the Indo-European peoples entered the peninsula from the north sometime after 2000 B.C. To these the Greek colonists of southern Italy later gave the name "Italic." Around 1000 B.C. the Etruscans, a people of unknown origin but more advanced than the early Italic peoples, came, perhaps from Asia Minor, and occupied large sections of western Italy. Then came the Greeks to southern Italy and Sicily. The latter two of these peoples, with their relatively advanced cultures, were to affect the development of the more primitive Italic people. Indeed, it is remarkable that it was these and not one of their more advanced rivals who were des-

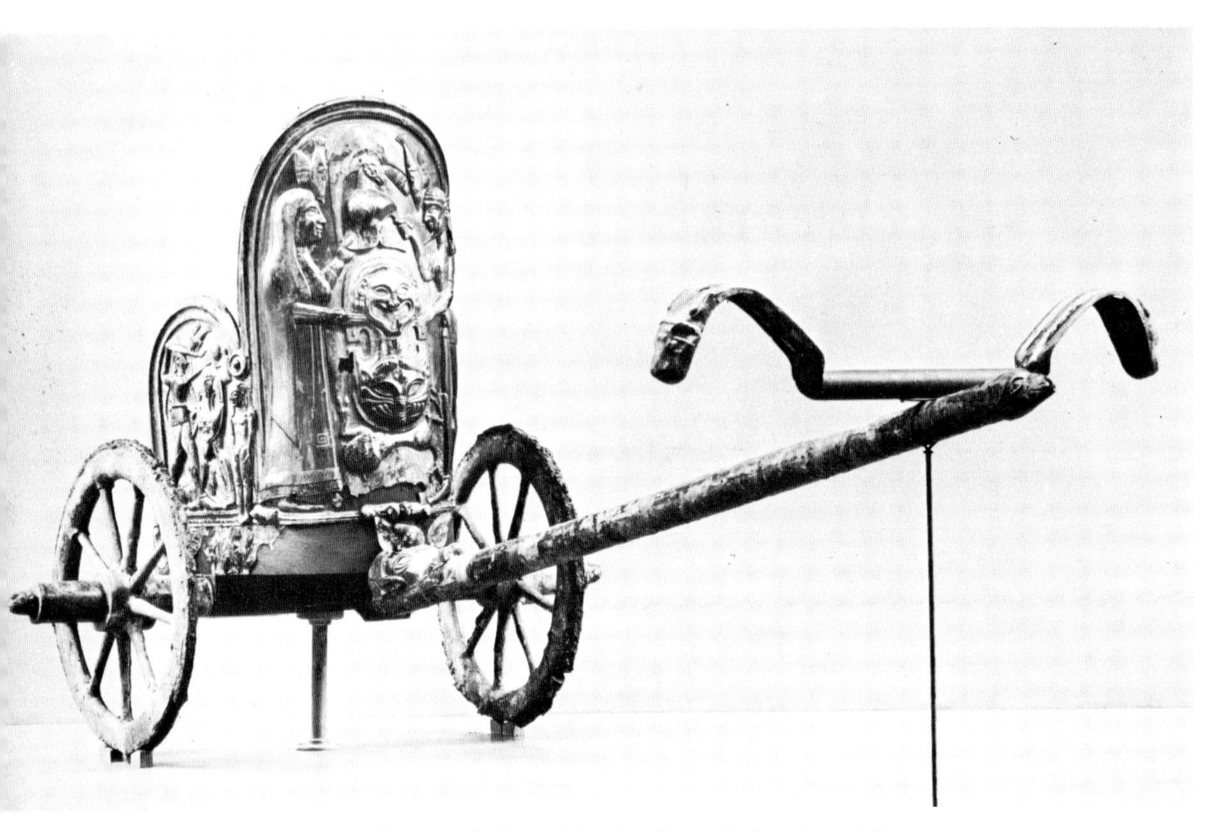

Etruscan chariot of the fourth or third century B.C.

Courtesy Metropolitan Museum of Art, New York

tined finally to dominate the peninsula. Meanwhile, the Carthaginian descendants of the Phoenician colonists, builders of a formidable sea power and commercial state in north Africa, were branching out to include parts of Sicily, Sardinia, and Corsica.

South and east of the Tiber river lies the plain of Latium. There, in various scattered communities, had settled an Italic people known as Latins. One of their settlements was a kind of trading-post, at a point where an island and shoals in the Tiber made possible a crossing and an ancient bridge. Overlooking the shallows was the Palatine hill, and on the lowlands along the bank was the market-place or Forum. Sometime before 800 B.C. the more powerful Etruscans on the north bank overran the Latin settlements and coordinated them into a nucleus which came to be known as Rome. Thus Rome commenced its political history as a monarchy under a line of Etruscan kings.

Under Etruscan domination Rome progressed in many ways, learning both from its conquerors and from the Greeks of southern Italy with whom it continued to trade. Greek coins and oriental measures of length and weight made their appearance as, also, did Greek vase-painting and architectural forms. The Latins had preserved their own language and now they began to adopt, with some modification, the Greek alphabet which thus became part of our general European heritage. Many Greek words also found their way into Latin. And the Romans discovered that some of their own traditional gods had their counterparts among the Greek deities.

Meanwhile, the Roman people had developed certain political ideas and practices which they were able to bring to maturity after the overthrow of the monarchy (about 500 B.C.). A council of older men, the Senate (from *senex,* old), had acquired considerable influence. And this was enhanced by the high esteem the ancient Romans had for the father as head of the family. A family (*familia*) could include an entire household, relatives, and servants, as well as members of the immediate family group. Moreover, the father's authority (*patria potestas*) was supreme. Then, as a natural consequence of the passing of monarchy, the Romans came to think of their government as a "public thing," a notion preserved in the expression *res-publica,* or "republic." Sovereignty, or *imperium* as they called it, rested ultimately in the people, who entrusted it temporarily, or for long periods of time, to their rulers.

Immediately after the overthrow of the kings, the Romans gave form to these ideas by entrusting political power to elected magistrates. Two *consuls,* holding office for a year only, served as an executive. And in the early days of the republic only wealthy patricians served as *consuls* and sat in the Senate. Moreover, they dominated the assembly which elected the magistrates. But since the poorer citizens and peasant farmers, the *plebs,* were indispensable in time of war, the aristocratic element was forced to concede to the *plebs* the right to elect in their own assembly officials known as tribunes who could veto a magistrate's action.

As the volume of state business grew, other magistracies were added. *Quaestors* cared for financial matters. *Censors* kept lists (*census*) of citizens and assessed taxes. *Praetors* were judges who relieved the *consuls* of many judicial matters. And in the event of dire emergency it was decided that supreme power could be entrusted to one person (*dictator*).

Having acquired the protection of the tribunician authority, the people were able to achieve certain additional objectives. About 450 B.C. Roman laws were written

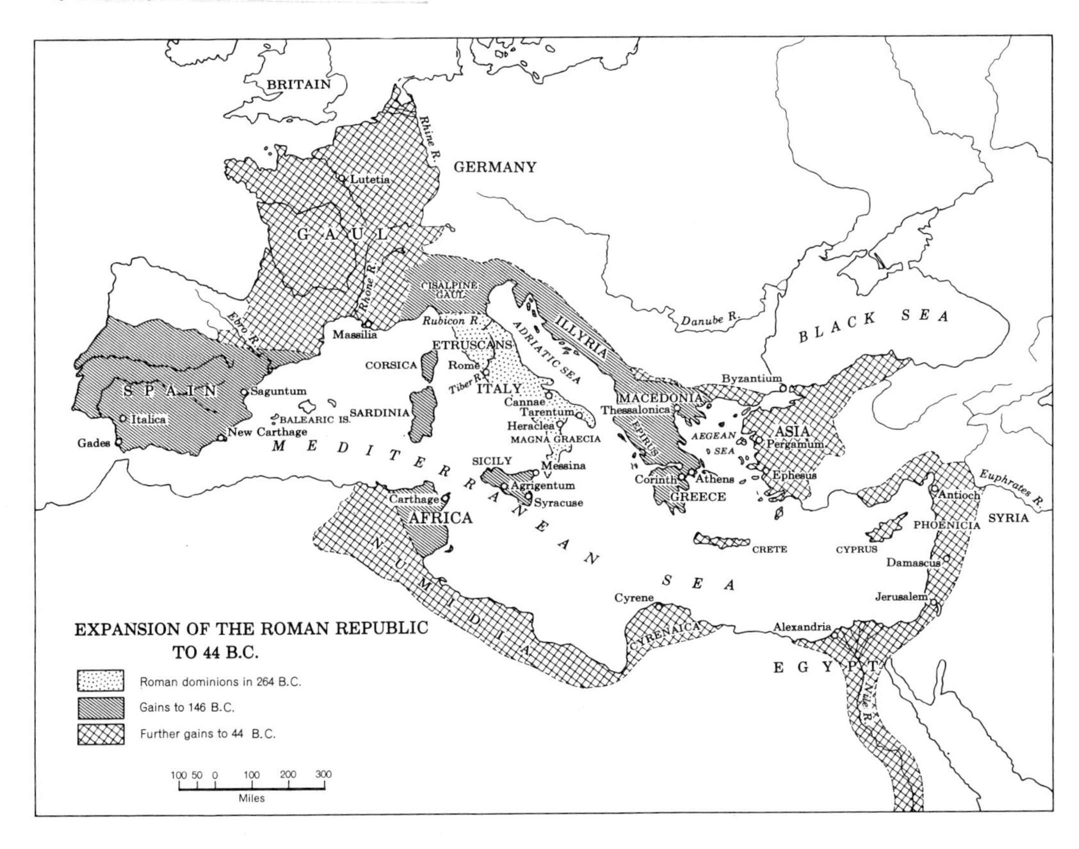

down for the first time, being engraved on the famous twelve bronze tablets. In the making of new laws the plebs also enjoyed some influence in legally constituted assemblies. Gradually the right of any citizen to hold office as *censor, praetor,* and at length even as *consul* was conceded. In addition, the formerly exclusively patrician Senate came to include ex-magistrates. Thus was formed a kind of new nobility of office-holders along with the patrician land-owners.

Despite the increase of popular influence in the Roman government, the republic remained to the end a predominantly aristocratic state. This resulted largely from the unique position held by the Senate. Although no formal additions to its constitutional powers were made, it gained markedly in political influence. First, it was a permanent assembly, its members serving for life. And, with the addition to its membership of ex-magistrates, it included the wisest and most experienced men in Rome.

Moreover, especially in time of war, when many younger men were away from the city on military service, it was frequently difficult to assemble the other bodies, whereas the senate could always be convened with a minimum of delay. Thus it was that, although in theory the senate's functions were advisory only, magistrates often found themselves listening to proposals from the senate instead of initiating measures themselves.

B. Expansion and Corruption of the Republic

In its early days the Roman republic was no more than a small city-state. But since the neighboring Latin tribes realized that for purposes of defense Roman leadership was indispensable, they consented to incorporation into a Latin league of cities, a league which was later replaced by separate treaties negotiated with each city. In this way Etruscan supremacy in the region north of the Tiber was effectively challenged and other unfriendly Italic tribes or cities subdued. Then the Romans turned southward and conquered the various Greek colonies in southern Italy. And in so doing they exposed themselves even more than before to the elevating influence of Greek culture.

Thus by about 275 B.C. Rome had become master of all Italy south of the Po valley.[1] Moreover, to the Latin inhabitants of the territory immediately surrounding Rome, comprising about one-sixth of the peninsula, full citizenship was granted. Elsewhere colonies of Roman citizens were planted or the conquered cities were regarded as allies and given a number of the privileges of citizenship. Voting, impractical anyway because of distance, was not included, but rights under Roman law were universally granted. This policy, so far-sighted in contrast with that of the Greeks, insured the Romans a peasant citizen-army which could expand as need arose, and facilitated Roman domination over Italy.

Roman expansion over Italy had been primarily agricultural in nature. It was accomplished by a small agrarian city-state. But this very expansion, especially as it included the Greek cities of the south, increased the commercial opportunities of Roman and Italian merchants and added to the responsibility of Rome as the protector of its allied communities. This became particularly apparent as Roman merchants looked out over the central and western Mediterranean only to find the commerce of that region monopolized by Carthage. Carthage, originally a Phoenician colony, had developed into a large and prosperous city. All of the north coast of Africa from Cyrenaica to the Atlantic, the southern coast of Spain, the Balearics, Corsica, Sardinia, and lately Sicily had fallen under Carthaginian control. In fact, it was feared that the Carthaginians might, by seizing the Sicilian city of Messina, close the passage to Roman ships. It was inevitable that further commercial expansion on the part of Rome would necessitate challenging the power of Carthage.

The long struggle between the two Mediterranean powers ended in the defeat and destruction of Carthage. In three separate periods of armed conflict, known as

[1] The Celtic Gauls who had invaded the Po valley were later subdued.

the Punic Wars (264–146 B.C.), the Romans, often in dire straits, proved their strength on land and sea against a truly formidable adversary. For if in the illustrious Hannibal, Carthage possessed a commander of outstanding qualities, Scipio, surnamed "Africanus," performed brilliantly for the Romans. At home the Romans displayed remarkabl fortitude in the face of successive emergencies. In the end Carthage was completely destroyed.

Dominion over the central and western Mediterranean made Rome an imperial power which, to protect itself, felt obliged to oppose any other Mediterranean state whose strength rivaled its own. Thus, expansion led to further conquest until the entire Mediterranean world was brought under Roman domination. A pretext for intervention in the eastern Mediterranean arose shortly after the fall of Carthage. Further, this region was ripe for conquest after the disintegration of Alexander's Empire. Accordingly, Macedonia, Greece, Syria, and even Egypt were conquered. Moreover, after a league of Greek cities which had taken up arms had been crushed, as though to teach the Greeks a lesson comparable to that of Carthage, Corinth was burned (146 B.C.) and thousands of Greeks sent to Rome as slaves. The city-state of Rome was henceforth mistress of the entire Mediterranean basin.

This spectacular transformation from humble Italian city-state to mistress of a far-flung empire was not accomplished without tremendous changes in the political, social, and economic life, especially of Rome and Italy, but also of the entire imperial area. So profound were the effects of conquest that they ultimately produced a revolution in the Roman way of life. First, the administration of conquered areas involved a host of new problems. In these areas Roman "provinces" were set up. Regulations were made by the senate and carried out by provincial governors whose authority was, in turn, supported by a sufficient number of troops. Although provincial governors or *proconsuls* often held office for only a year, not all were experienced and not all resisted the temptations for great private gain and personal power.

Another result of conquest was the marked increase in wealth. But since the wealth was not evenly distributed, Rome began to face the problem of a large and impoverished proletariat whose tastes, in this age of increasing luxury, seem to have run to the bloody and brutal gladiatorial contests. Moreover, many a political aspirant sought election by wholesale bribery of the Roman electorate. This added to the debasement of the proletariat. Finally, the state offered food and entertainment, the famous *panem et circenses* (bread and circuses).

Rural conditions were little better. The long campaigns of the Punic Wars had devastated many agricultural districts of Italy beyond repair. A new grain supply was now available from Africa, Egypt, and Sicily. And in Italy and Sicily great estates appeared, bought up by the senators and other wealthy Romans. These large-scale farms, worked by slave labor of which the conquests had unfortunately produced an ample supply, were far beyond the competition of the small farmer. Thus the yeoman citizen-farmer, the backbone of the republic and its army, faced ruin. Many gave up and joined the ranks of the city proletariat.[1]

Extensive and rapid conquest also created new military problems, for the new frontiers required constant vigilance. Critical military situations frequently presented themselves to plague a government already shaken at home. In short, the Roman republic, a government which had arisen to answer the needs of a city-state, was now faced with domestic and external difficulties which proved too formidable for its limited capacities. The last century of the republic, one of intermittent revolution and civil war, demonstrated that a city-state government could not manage an empire.

[1] One important consequence of the wars, representing a change from former ways, was the patronage by rich and educated Romans of Greek literature and art. Such was the vogue of Greek that well-to-do Roman children were commonly educated in schools conducted by emancipated Greek slaves. Greek, therefore, became the language of culture, and Latin literature developed in a large degree as an imitation of the Greek.

C. Transition from Republic to Empire

While it would be impossible to describe the civil war in detail here, it can easily be imagined that it proved disastrous for the institutions of republican Rome. As we have seen, actual power had fallen largely into the hands of the senate. Therefore, as the plight of the small farmer became acute, remedies sought by popular leaders were likely to be blocked. For the senate represented the aristocratic element in Roman society and above all the large landowners. When in 104 B.C., despite a hostile senate, Marius, a farmer's boy who had risen to be a successful general, was elected consul, it seemed as though the popular element had found a worthy champion. Unfortunately, although he was an excellent general and had instituted important reforms in the army, Marius was no statesman. Riots accompanied his election as consul for the sixth time (100 B.C.), and after his retirement the senate also found a military champion in Sulla, one of Marius' officers. Ignoring popular opposition, Sulla marched his troops into Rome and forced the passage of several new laws which destroyed the power of the popular assembly. Thus, for the first time, military power was openly used to secure political action. But this led to open civil war in which, as each side won temporary advantage, it avenged itself ruthlessly on its hapless adversaries. With the death of Marius (86 B.C.) and the retirement of Sulla (79 B.C.), the first period of the revolution ended.

Not only did civil war endanger republican institutions; it provided an opportunity for ambitious opponents of Roman expansion. Mithradates, king of Pontus in Asia Minor, challenged the Roman protectorate over Greece. At the same time his ally, Tigranes of Armenia, occupied Syria and Judaea while Cilician pirates terrorized the seas to the shores of Italy itself. Finally, the presence of foreign danger increased a tendency, already dangerously prevalent, for the military to assume political powers.

The careers of Gnaeus Pompey and Julius Caesar illustrate this emergence of the generals into public life. Pompey, despatched to the east by the senate, effectively crushed both Mithradates and Tigranes, overran Judaea, and captured Jerusalem. A new eastern frontier, comprising newly created provinces and certain areas under indirect Roman influence, carried Roman dominion to the line from the upper reaches of the Euphrates to the Arabian desert. In the many negotiations and treaties involved in the creation of the new border, Pompey acted on his own initiative; and when the senate refused to sanction his decisions, he sought the help of Julius Caesar, the other consul of 59 B.C. Caesar secured the ratification of Pompey's measures and in return was given the military command in Gaul.

Transalpine Gaul, which at that time included only parts of what is today southern France, was then threatened both by the Germanic *Suevi* and the Gallic *Helvetii*. Caesar's successes and his ultimate conquest of the entire area west of the Rhine to the English channel are well known. Equally familiar is the jealousy of the senatorial leaders who refused to abandon the constitution and persuaded Pompey to oppose the successful general. But Caesar was a man of sufficient stature as a statesman to identify himself with the best interest of Rome. Thus not only did he defeat Pompey and his armies in Italy, in Spain, and in Greece, but, as dictator, inaugurated a number of much needed reforms. The assassins who struck him down in 44 B.C. undoubtedly regarded themselves as patriotically removing a tyrant. But Caesar was more than a tyrant. Though a general and an authoritarian, he possessed many statesmanlike attributes.

Caesar's death plunged Rome once again into civil war which lasted until 31 B.C. We need not follow its gloomy details. Mark Antony was the first to gain prominence by seizing Caesar's fortune and securing his own election to the consulship. More important was his acquisition through military power of the eastern half of the empire and his marriage to Cleopatra, queen of Egypt. But the mantle of Caesar's power eventually fell on his nephew Octavian. Too young, at first, to be taken seriously, he gradually strengthened his position, and as some of Antony's legions came over to

A Roman of the first century B.C.

Courtesy Metropolitan Museum of Art, New York

him he prevailed upon the senate to declare war on Egypt. In a combined land and sea engagement at Actium his forces triumphed. The long civil war was over, and to Octavian was given the golden opportunity to reorganize the Roman government and save the empire.

Octavian, whom we may as well now refer to as Augustus,—the title a grateful people bestowed on him,—was eminently fitted for the stupendous task of imperial reorganization. Though not a general, he was a statesman in the best sense of the word and, despite recurring ill health, he kept persistently at the work he had assigned himself. He was capable of bold, resolute action, but never acted impetuously. During his tenure of power (31 B.C.–A.D. 14) the revolution was consummated and a governmental system devised which endured for nearly three hundred years. The beginning of the Roman Empire is customarily reckoned from his reign.

After the battle of Actium, what the entire Mediterranean world most desired was peace and order. Augustus sensed this. He also realized that although the Roman citizens of Italy were still jealous of the ancient city-state constitution, this had to be brought into harmony with the new situation. For henceforth a city-state was to govern the entire Mediterranean world. Augustus, therefore, developed a system of government which was in a sense a combination of monarchy and republic, an empire under republican forms. Sometimes described as a "dyarchy" (double rule), it has usually been designated the "principate," because Augustus himself preferred the title of *princeps*, or first citizen, which the senate conferred upon him.

Augustus preserved the forms of republican government by maintaining the senate and the magistracies in the administration of the city of Rome. But outside the city the senate's powers were limited. Further, Augustus prevailed upon a grateful senate to elect him to all the key offices. Thus, in addition to being *imperator*, or commander-in-chief, with control over the military forces, he possessed the tribunician authority, by which he could veto the acts of the senate. And as *censor* he could in a measure control its membership. He was also *pontifex maximus*, head of the pagan state religion, and the proconsular authority made him supreme in the provinces. Provincial governors were appointed by and directly responsible to him, and their activities were frequently checked. Yet even here he wisely shared power with the senate to whose charge he entrusted the inner provinces. Those on the frontiers where military power was significant he reserved to himself.

Augustus endeavored within the framework of this system to carry out various reforms. Italy was pacified and cleared of bandits. Rome was adequately policed and a rebuilding program commenced. Augustus counseled against any further conquests, a bit of advice prompted by the defeat of his legions east of the Rhine. Britain, however, was added later in the century. He realized, too, that the events of the past century had weakened the old devotion to the state and had created no new loyalty capable of enlisting the support of Romans and provincials alike. As a consequence, he sought to reinvigorate the Roman religion. Nor was it mere personal ambition which led him to accept the senate's enrolling him among the gods. It is possible that he urged Vergil to compose a poem glorifying the deeds of his family. Certainly

Atlantic Ocean
Antoninus' Wall
Hadrians Wall
NORTH SEA
HIBERNIA
Eboracum
Deva
BRITANNIA
Londinium
Strait of Dover
English Channel
Baltic
Elbe R.
Rhine
(19 B.C. - 9 A.D.)
GERMANIA
Colonia Agrippina
GERMANIA Inferior
Limes Germanicus
BELGICA
Aug. Trevor
Superior
Seine R.
Lutetia
LUGDUNENSIS
Loire
Danube R.
Vindelicia
Vindobona
RHAETIA
NORICUM
PANNONIA
GAUL
Lugdunum
AQUITANIA
Tarraconensis
NARBONENSIS
Nemansus
Narbo
Massilia
Pyrenees Mts.
Ebro R.
Po R.
Ravenna
DALMATIA
Adriatic Sea
HISPANIA
Lusitania
Tagus R.
CORSICA
ITALY
Tiber R.
Rome
Ostia
Tarraco
Saguntum
Corduba
Baetica
BALEARES IS.
SARDINIA
Puteoli
Neapolis
Dyrrachium
Brundisium
New Carthage
Strait of Gibraltar
Mediterranean
Tyrrhenian Sea
Messina
SICILY
Strait of Messina
Syracuse
MAURITANIA
Carthage
Cirta
NUMIDIA
Theveste
AFRICA
THE ROMAN EMPIRE ABOUT 120 A.D.
The Empire in 120 A.D.
0
100
200
300
400
500
Scale in miles

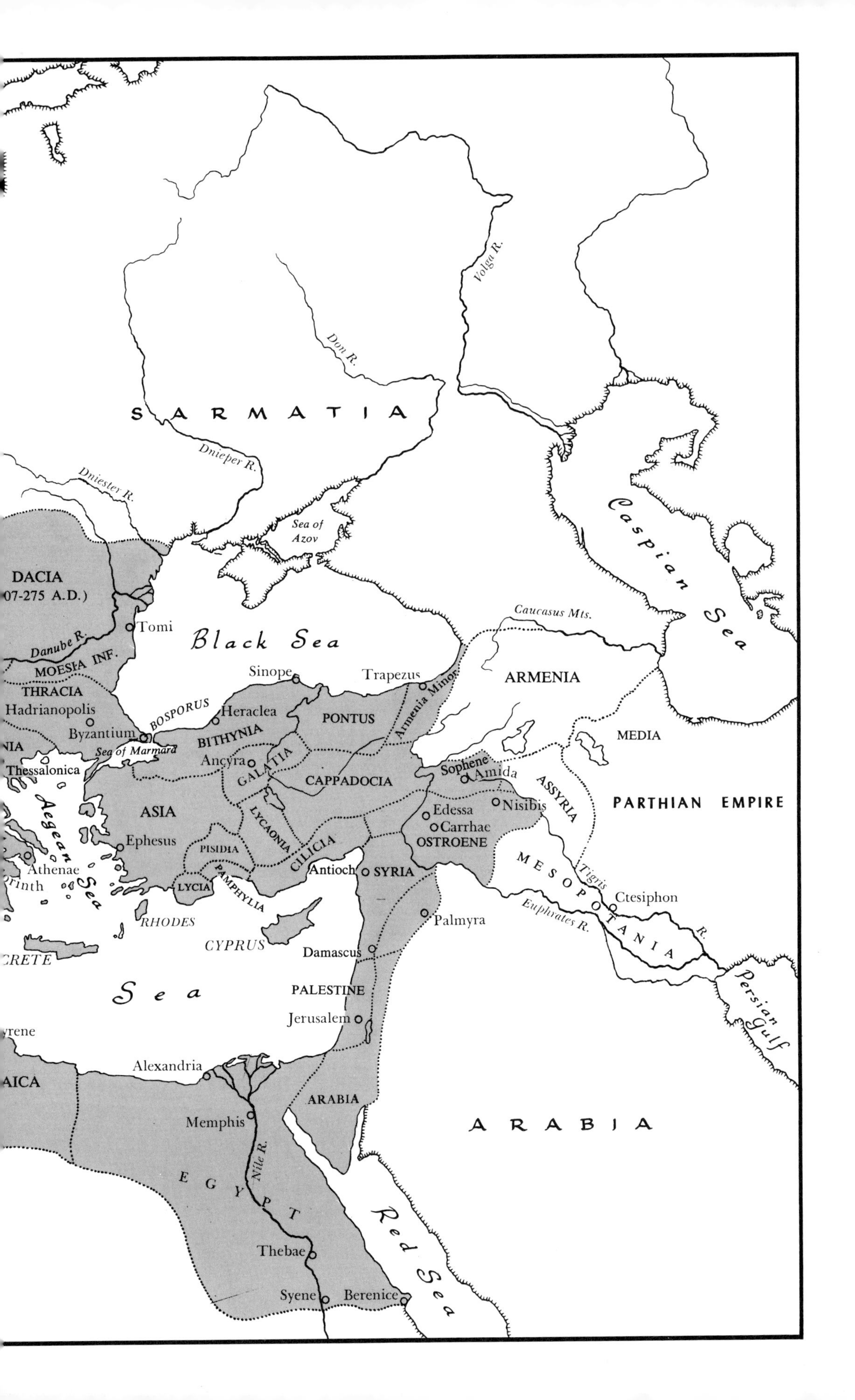

SARMATIA
Volga R.
Don R.
Dnieper R.
Dniester R.
Sea of Azov
Caspian Sea
Caucasus Mts.
DACIA
(107-275 A.D.)
Tomi
Black Sea
Danube R.
MOESIA INF.
THRACIA
Hadrianopolis
Sinope
Trapezus
Armenia Minor
ARMENIA
BOSPORUS
Heraclea
PONTUS
Byzantium
BITHYNIA
Sea of Marmara
MEDIA
Ancyra
GALATIA
Thessalonica
CAPPADOCIA
Sophene
Amida
ASSYRIA
Aegean Sea
ASIA
LYCAONIA
Edessa
Nisibis
PARTHIAN EMPIRE
Carrhae
Ephesus
PISIDIA
CILICIA
OSTROENE
MESOPOTAMIA
Athenae
Antioch
SYRIA
Tigris R.
LYCIA
PAMPHYLIA
Ctesiphon
RHODES
Palmyra
Euphrates R.
CYPRUS
Damascus
Sea
PALESTINE
Persian Gulf
Jerusalem
Alexandria
ARABIA
Memphis
ARABIA
EGYPT
Nile R.
Red Sea
Thebae
Syene
Berenice

The Aeneid is an epic whose hero Aeneas, in whom are found all the old Roman virtues, is held to be the ancestor of the Julian family.

Augustus deserved well of the Roman people, and his reign inaugurated a period of internal peace unparalleled in duration and in the wide area affected. As the years passed the powers granted the Princeps, which were in a sense emergency measures, became permanent. Thus the word *imperium*, which originally signified sovereignty, came through its new association with one man to mean monarchical rule over a vast state. And *imperator* similarly acquired its later connotation of single ruler, or emperor. Moreover, the system Augustus created was even able to survive a number of bad emperors during the first century A.D. Since the republic had never formally been abolished, there could never be adequate provision for the succession. This was the most conspicuous weakness in the system. Augustus associated Tiberius with him and he was accepted after his death. But there were occasions when the rival claims of army and senate caused serious disturbances. Yet the Roman government survived, despite the faults of men like Caligula (37–41) and Nero (54–68), and passed in the second century into the age of the "good emperors."

Under a series of remarkable men Mediterranean civilization prospered as never before. Here we can only name these rulers and then conclude with a brief survey of life during this brilliant period. Trajan (98–117) is perhaps best known for incorporation of the province of Dacia, north of the Danube, and an extension of the eastern frontier to include Armenia, Mesopotamia, and Assyria, and for his correspondence with Pliny the Younger, governor of Bithynia. His remarks concerning the treatment of Christians will be discussed in a later chapter. It is significant that Trajan, who was born in Spain, was the first provincial to hold the imperial title. Hadrian (117–138) built the wall protecting the province of Britain from the north, and commenced the coördination of Roman law. Finally, we must mention the two Antonines, Antoninus Pius (138–161) and Marcus Aurelius (161–180), both men of preeminent ability, the latter a philosopher as well. With his death this happy age passed into more troubled times.

D. Life in the Roman Empire

The unity of the Mediterranean world within the Roman Empire was maintained by a disciplined standing military force and an admirable system of communication. Augustus had attempted to restore the citizen character of the Roman army, but with the passage of years the legions were composed more and more of provincials and mercenaries. Sometimes citizenship was the reward for service, and army pensions often included a plot of land on which veterans could settle. The Romans had organized the army into units called legions, each containing about 4,500 men, the majority of whom were heavily armed infantry. These were variously divided, the smallest unit being the century, originally one hundred men, later usually less, commanded by a centurion. Every mile of the long frontier was policed, and no point was far from a Roman encampment. Great permanent fortifications were erected, for example, to protect Britain, as already mentioned, or to connect the upper Rhine and Danube. Except for Dacia, the two rivers constituted the northern frontier in Europe proper.

The Romans were skillful road-builders. Roadbeds and stone block surfaces were designed for durability as well as speed of travel. Primarily military, they served civilian traffic and a postal system. They greatly aided overland commerce, and made possible the profitable exploitation of the mineral resources of Spain, Gaul, and Britain. Sea traffic showed less progress. Although Roman galleys regularly plied the Mediterranean, the Atlantic was little used.

Not only did the Romans divide the Mediterranean world into provinces, they established cities everywhere—unless these already existed. A Roman *civitas* often resembled the mother-city and boasted a forum, theaters, arenas, and the like. Roman expansion into the provinces was no log-cabin pioneering. Rather, it was a veritable transportation of everything familiar at

Rome. It is possible for a traveler today to gaze on the ruins of an amphitheater at Nîmes in southern France, to visit a Roman theater at Orange, to view mighty aqueducts in southern France and Spain or a forum in north Africa. In the east, most cities were already built, though even there Roman influence was by no means negligible. In the newer western provinces, a tribal center was often chosen as the original nucleus of a *civitas*, a practice reflected in names which have survived to the present. Paris (*Parisii*), Soissons (*Suessiones*), and Trier (*Augusta Treverorum*) are examples.

The *civitates* were of the essence of Roman civilization. To understand the empire it is essential to grasp their significance. Indeed, it has often been said that the principate was a federation of partially self-governing communities.

In the realm of the mind, the Roman contribution is less impressive than the Greek. Indeed, the educated Romans themselves paid tribute to Greek culture by learning Greek, and their writers, by imitating Greek forms. And yet the Latin language as perfected by the Romans became the vehicle for some of the greatest works of our western civilization. Surely literature is the richer for the works of Cicero, the poetry of Vergil and Horace, the histories of Livy and Tacitus, the dramas of Plautus and Terence, to mention only a few. And the Latin tongue lived to become the language of the Catholic church, a language sufficiently flexible to meet the demands of theological precision as well as of religious poetry.

One of the greatest of Rome's legacies was its law. This had grown from the time of the Twelve Tables to the time of Augustus and later into a formidable mass of literature. Judges' (*praetors'*) decisions became precedents. The opinions (*responsa*) of legal experts (*juris prudentes*), at first unofficial, then some officially sanctioned, added to the volume. Moreover, the jurisdiction of Roman law expanded with the extension of citizenship. Thus it came to include first all Italians. Finally, under Caracalla (212), it was extended over the entire imperial area. Just as Greek practices affected the laws of the early republic, so new procedures came in as the entire cosmopolitan citizenry enjoyed rights under Roman law. Such a vast literature finally required codification, a work begun much earlier but not completed until the reign of Justinian in the sixth century. As later chapters will indicate, Roman law has directly or indirectly affected the laws of almost every European country.

Next to law and government, architecture most clearly represents the character of Graeco-Roman civilization. It can be styled Graeco-Roman because Roman builders owed so much to the Greeks whom they sometimes rather slavishly imitated. The Greek orders, especially the Corinthian, were widely used. But, generally speaking, Roman building lacked the exquisite proportions of the Greek. Roman structures were more massive and grandiose. Moreover, many, such as triumphal arches, the Colosseum, and the baths in Rome, were frankly built for pleasure or display. There were, of course, innovations. The round arch, taken probably from the Etruscans, was employed not only by itself but as the structural base of a dome or a vault. Roman engineering also achieved some notable triumphs. The city was supplied with water from fourteen aqueducts, the water being conducted in stone conduits both over and under the ground. Huge dams and drains were constructed and sewage was surprisingly well disposed of. Roman building reflects the Roman emphasis on organization, wealth, and material success in general. It also manifests, even to the modern traveler, the expanse and cultural unity of the Mediterranean world. For from the borders of Scotland to the olive groves of north Africa and from Portugal to the Arabian desert, the all-pervading influence of Rome is still evident in its monuments.

The very existence of the Roman Empire with its uniting of the Mediterranean world left an indelible impression on men's minds. The centuries during which the Empire flourished became the "golden age" for subsequent generations to venerate. So great was the spell cast by Roman civilization that men ever afterwards continued to imitate many of its features. And Rome as the city of the popes, the heart of Christianity, was to live on in a new spiritual empire. Truly, Rome may be called "eternal."

A second century sculptured representation of the Founder of Christianity, now in the Lateran Museum in Rome.

Alinari Photo

CHAPTER 4

The Judaeo-Christian Spiritual Heritage

A. Origins of Christianity in Judaism

Now it came to pass in those days that there went forth a decree from Caesar Augustus that a census of the whole world should be taken. This first census took place while Cyrinus was governor of Syria. And all were going, each to his own town, to register.

And Joseph also went from Galilee out of the town of Nazareth into Judaea to the town of David, which is called Bethlehem—because he was of the house and family of David—to register, together with Mary, his espoused wife. . . . And . . . while they were there . . . she brought forth her firstborn son, and wrapped him in swaddling clothes, and laid him in a manger, because there was no room for them in the inn.[1]

In these words a Palestinian physician, living in the early decades of the Roman Empire, described an event which a substantial proportion of the world's population today regards as the most important in history. It is a simple, straightforward account, but it gives us a glimpse of the Roman administrative system at work in the census ordered by the Emperor, and it reveals much about Christ's birth. The Founder of a great religion was born in humble circumstances, and lived His entire life within the orbit of Roman civilization. The influence of Christianity upon Rome and of Rome upon Christianity is of vital importance to our understanding of both.

It was Judaea, an eastern province of the Empire and one inhabited by a people despised by the Romans, which provided the scene for a history unique in ancient times. Judaea (or Palestine) was the repository of a religious tradition unlike that of any other country of its day. The Roman governmental tradition and the Hebrew religious heritage were two significant formative influences in the development of Christianity.

The Jewish religion was unique, because in a world characterized by various forms of polytheism the Jewish people had persisted in their loyalty to the one God. Moreover, to them, Jahveh was a God of spirit, creator of the world, ruler of the universe, and not a deity fashioned after man's own imperfect imagination. As the ancient psalmist so eloquently put it:

But our God is in heaven: he hath done all things whatsoever he would.
The idols of the Gentiles are silver and gold, the works of the hands of men.
They have mouths and speak not; they have eyes and see not.
They have ears and hear not: they have noses and smell not.
They have hands and feel not, they have feet and walk not; neither shall they cry out through their throat.[2]

Successive Hebrew prophets had striven to convince their people of the gravity of sin. They had preached repentance and emphasized the idea of sacrifice in atonement for sin. And the offering of sacrifices to God became an essential part of Jewish ritual. Finally, the prophets had taught that man-

[1] Luke, II, i–vii.

[2] Psalm CXIII, iii–vii.

kind, in a fallen state since Adam in pride rejected God's command, required a redeemer. Thus they had long foretold the coming of a Messiah or Savior.

The teachings of the prophets, along with the inspired poetry of the psalms and many books dealing with the creation of the world and of man and with Hebrew history, amounted to a literary as well as a religious heritage of extraordinary richness. Moreover, since Christianity embodied a number of Jewish religious ideas, it was only natural that the sacred writings of the Jews should have been incorporated into Christian literature. They formed, in fact, the "Old" Testament, distinct from the specifically Christian "New" Testament books.

The religion preached by Christ was, to his followers, a fulfilment of the Hebraic heritage. They believed Him to be the promised Messiah, both God and man—God who, in the person of Christ, had assumed a human nature from His Virgin Mother, Mary. This doctrine, known as the "Incarnation," is indissolubly linked with man's "Redemption" in the minds of Christians. To them, Christ's crucifixion and death constituted the one perfect sacri-

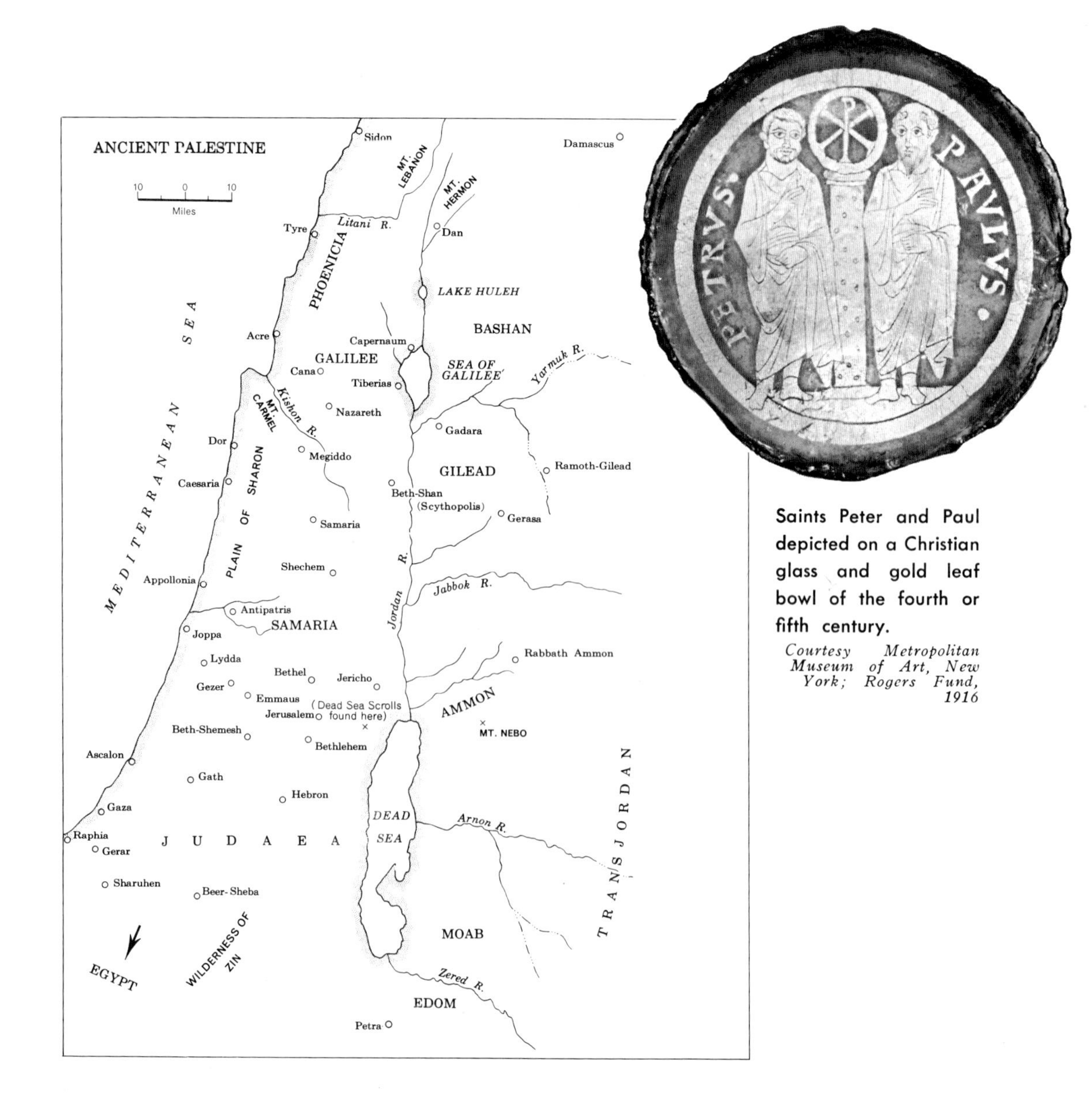

Saints Peter and Paul depicted on a Christian glass and gold leaf bowl of the fourth or fifth century.

Courtesy Metropolitan Museum of Art, New York; Rogers Fund, 1916

fice for men's sins. Humanity was reconciled with divinity, and all men were offered the hope of life after death in a "kingdom not of this world."

Christ startled and dismayed some of His Jewish audiences by His seeming departure from Hebrew tradition. To over-strict observance of the "old" law, as evidenced by the Pharisees, He gave short shrift. Rather, as in His famous *Sermon on the Mount*, He exalted true humility, meekness, even suffering and poverty. His first faithful followers were mostly untutored men. His sympathy for the poor and unfortunate was unbounded, and He commanded His disciples to "love one another."

B. *Christian Doctrine and Church Organization*

Christ's teachings were both moral and theological. The former, embodying the noble concept of the brotherhood of man, are perhaps the more familiar today. However much they have been disregarded, they still form the ethical basis of European, or Western, civilization. The theological teachings, on the other hand, have been the subject of many controversies. As a consequence, it will be well here to mention briefly the principal beliefs of early Christianity. Later chapters will discuss controversial matters as they arise.

The kernel of Christian teaching is the doctrine of the Trinity, that God is triune, three distinct persons in one divine nature, the Father, Son, and Holy Ghost, to use the familiar terms. Christ frequently insisted on His "oneness" with the Father. And before He took leave of His apostles, He promised that His Father would send them the "Paraclete," the "Spirit of Truth." In the person of Christ, therefore, were united, it was taught, a divine and a human nature. This mystery is an important corollary to the doctrine of the Trinity, for from it developed the Christian teaching with regard to the relation of man and God and, indirectly, the idea that the Christian church was divine as well as human.

As a consequence of belief in the Incarnation, or Christ's taking a human nature, there could not be in Christianity any view of flesh and matter as intrinsically evil such as was held by the ancient Zoroastrians of Persia or by the Manichaeans, of whom there were considerable numbers in the Roman Empire. On the contrary, Christ provided the means by which, after His departure from the world, future disciples might continue that union with divinity enjoyed in a different way by those who associated with Him on earth. These means were later called sacraments and, to quote a formal definition, were "outward signs instituted by Christ to give grace." By "grace" was meant a supernatural gift of God freely bestowed on man to prepare him for eternal life. Among the sacraments, baptism was the one which made a person a Christian, while the eucharist, as the sacrificial repetition of Christ's last supper, became the central act of Christian worship.[1]

It has already been pointed out that the early Christians appropriated the sacred scriptures of the Jews and added others of their own, known as the New Testament. The New Testament included the three gospels of St. Matthew, St. Mark, and St. Luke, which tell the story of the life of Christ. Though they evidently existed in oral tradition considerably earlier, they were probably not reduced to writing until thirty or forty years after the crucifixion. The fourth gospel, that of St. John, written towards the end of the first century, is quite different and relates many incidents not found in the others. In addition to the gospels there were the *Acts of the Apostles*, an historical account of the earliest days of the infant church, the *Apocalypse* or book of *Revelation*, and a number of letters, especially those of St. Paul.

The New Testament was only the beginning of Christian literature, for the various struggles against the Roman government, as well as the inner controversies within Christianity itself, occasioned many works of an apologetic nature. These were treatises justifying, explaining, and defending the faith against its adversaries. Although distinct from the Bible ("book"), as the Old and New Testaments came to be called, some of these writings which were regarded as especially inspired or particularly impor-

[1] Other sacraments, as subsequently defined, were confirmation, penance, extreme unction, holy orders, and matrimony.

tant received a kind of official sanction. Their authors were known as the "Fathers" of the church. Among the most famous were St. Ambrose of Milan, St. Jerome, and St. Augustine of Hippo, whose works will be described more fully in a later chapter.

The infant church founded in Jerusalem spread with remarkable rapidity throughout the Roman Empire. Indeed, the Empire by virtue of its very existence immensely aided the progress of the new religion. The *pax Romana* (Roman peace) guaranteed safe travel, and hence made possible the passage of ideas as well as the materials of commerce. As a consequence, the early Christian communities were ordinarily found in the cities. Moreover, it frequently happened that the original nucleus of a Christian community was a group of Jews, many of whom had been dispersed far and wide and had commonly settled in the cities. Any and all Christians were, in those days, "missionaries," for in the course of their travels they brought the faith to others. But there were also some who dedicated their lives to the spread of Christianity and were, therefore, in a more formal sense missionaries. Such, of course, were the immediate apostles of Christ and those closely associated with them.

Foremost among the early missionaries was St. Paul. Paul (originally Saul) of Tarsus was an educated Jew and a Roman citizen who became one of the earliest converts to Christianity. Since he was thoroughly conversant with Hellenistic thought, he was admirably fitted to synthesize the Christian tradition with the Greek and the Hebrew. Although he preached and wrote to his own people, particularly those "Hellenized" Jews who were to be found throughout the Roman world, he firmly believed that the Christian gospel was intended for all races and nations. Hence he traveled the length and breadth of the Empire as an "apostle to the Gentiles." He was especially successful in interpreting Christian theology to educated minds influenced by the Greek philosophical tradition. His epistles which are included in the New Testament are the letters he wrote to the communities where he had preached and founded churches.

Christianity early developed a visible human organization known as the church (*ecclesia*). Those whose function it was to administer the sacraments were known as the clergy, distinct from the body of the faithful or laity. The twelve apostles, the immediate associates of Christ, had been, as it were, the original clergy. And their successors came to be called bishops (*episcopi*). Moreover, since the first Christian communities were in the towns, a bishop's "see" (seat) was invariably a city. The entire area of his jurisdiction, known as a diocese, a word borrowed from Roman usage, was customarily coterminous with a Roman *civitas*. The various smaller parish churches within a *civitas* were administered by priests, who in turn were assisted by deacons.

An episcopal (or bishop's) see founded by an apostle enjoyed a preëminence, and among these Rome came to have a unique position. First, an early tradition held that at Rome, where both St. Peter and St. Paul suffered martyrdom, the former founded his bishopric. And, as was recorded in St. Matthew's gospel,[1] Christ had singled out St. Peter as the leader of his apostles. These things combined with the city's political position to give to the Roman see a supremacy over all others. This was not, of course, so evident in the days of persecution as later. Moreover, records for those early days are scanty. But even as early as 95 A.D., St. Clement, bishop of Rome, exhibited a strikingly authoritative tone in a letter addressed to the Corinthians. During the first century, therefore, the Christian church began to take shape as an hierarchical organization.

C. Christianity and the Roman Empire

The Roman government did not, at first, welcome Christianity. Customarily tolerant of all faiths, the Empire officially banned Christianity and on frequent occasions made determined efforts to suppress it. This was partly because the early Christians usually lived apart and, as a consequence, were often popularly suspected of engaging in various questionable practices in secret meetings. But the principal reason for persecution was the fact that the conscientious Christian

[1] XVI, 17–19.

Rome. The Colosseum, place of Christian martyrdoms, as seen through the Arch of Titus.

Courtesy Italian State Tourist Office, New York

refused the one act of pagan worship still required of everyone. This was a formal outward obeisance to the shrine of the god-emperor. To the Christian such an act was idolatry and signified repudiation of the eternal God. To the Roman government, on the other hand, the refusal was tantamount to treason and punishable by death. The result was an impasse which drove Christians to worship in secret and at the risk of the martyrdom which many suffered. Yet so bravely did men and women, even the very young, face the lions in the public arena that others were inspired by their heroic example. Persecution did not succeed in its objective. It was not continuous, but burst forth sporadically, on the impulse of an irresponsible ruler like Nero, or as a consequence of the considered judgment of a statesman like Marcus Aurelius. Actually most emperors were more lenient than certain provincial governors who were sensitive to the pressure of popular anti-Christian feeling. But for many intervening years the policy of the Roman government was that outlined by Trajan in a famous letter to Pliny, the governor of Bithynia. So long as Christians did not openly flaunt their faith, they were to be left alone.

By the early fourth century it became evident that despite governmental measures, whether severe or moderate, the number of Christians had so increased that some form of recognition was inevitable. Accordingly, in A.D. 313, the Emperor Constantine issued the famous Edict of Milan, which legally tolerated Christianity and placed it on an equal footing with all other religions. The motives which prompted Constantine to this act are not clear. According to an ancient account, he called on the God of the Christians in a critical battle and be-

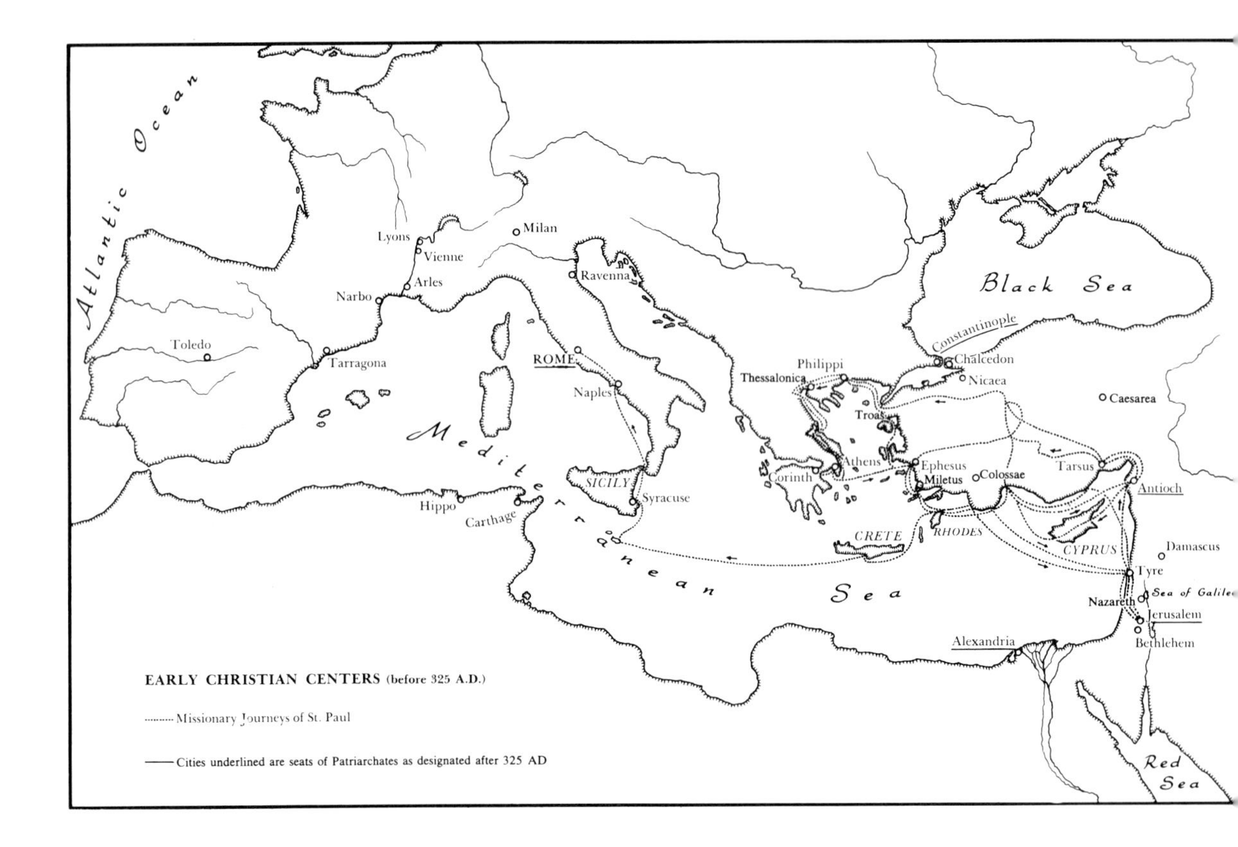

held in the sky the sign of the cross and the words *In hoc signo vinces* (In this sign thou shalt conquer). Constantine did not, however, become a Christian himself until shortly before his death many years later. And he never entirely abandoned, at least in the east, the concept of a god-emperor. But whatever Constantine's own ideas may have been, the future lay with Christianity. A temporary pagan reaction under Julian "the apostate" (A.D. 361–363) merely served to emphasize the power of the new faith. By the reign of the Emperor Theodosius (*d.* 395) public profession of paganism was proscribed and Christianity thus placed in a privileged position. As a consequence, the Roman Empire, before it disintegrated, was a Christian Empire. The persecutor became the ally.

The tremendous mystery of the rise of Christianity, from its humble beginnings among unlettered men in an obscure corner of the Roman Empire to its triumphant recognition as the imperial religion, lies hidden in the hearts of those who became Christians. In a secular history, such as this, we can at best only enumerate contemporary conditions which seem pertinent. Accordingly, we have emphasized material facts, the *pax Romana,* the admirable Roman system of communication. There are also certain developments in the fields of intellectual and religious history which will bear examination. First, it is significant that at the time of the beginnings of Christianity Graeco-Roman paganism had already lost much of its former appeal. Greek intellectual achievements had weakened the belief in the Homeric deities and, with Plato and Aristotle, had pointed toward a rational monotheism. Much the same thing occurred in Rome. Augustus tried in vain to restore the veneration of the ancient Roman gods. But virtually all that remained was an emperor-worship which actually was a religion of the state. Educated, high-minded Romans like Cicero and Seneca turned to Stoicism.[1]

Philosophical rationalization of religious questions could not satisfy the common man. He craved a more tangible, a more

[1] See above, p. 27.

emotionally satisfying faith. And this explains the popularity of various so-called mystery religions which made their way, usually from the Near East, into the Graeco-Roman world. All of these cults seem to have had in common an appeal to the emotions through elaborate ritual. Some embodied the important idea of purification, even of sacrifice. The most popular oriental cult, especially in the Roman army, was that of Mithras. This was of Persian origin, Mithras being the helper of Ahura Mazda and thus elevated into a sort of sun-god.[1] Elaborate and arduous initiations served to give the devotees a sense of fellowship. The military virtues were stressed and a future life was promised. The cult of Mithras was for a time a serious competitor with Christianity.

During the time of Christianity's early growth, educated people were inclined to seek the answer to the riddle of life in some sort of philosophical speculation, while common folk looked to the sensuous rituals of the East. And although the philosophy called Neo-Platonism, as expounded by Plotinus, did in some measure bridge the gap, it is significant that Christianity appeared in a world strikingly barren of real religion. Moreover, it appealed to rich and poor, to educated and illiterate. Christ's teachings gave comfort and hope to those on whom the burdens of life pressed heavily. His promise of beatitude in Heaven was simple and clear. And yet, as explained by a St. Paul or elaborated by the early apologists, Christianity could and did satisfy the intellectual aspirations of the learned. And in contrast to the vague myths of the mystery religions, the Christ of the New Testament appeared as a distinct, historic personality, born into a recognized Jewish family, a man who had lived under Roman governors recorded by name and who had walked and talked with real people.

D. The Problem of Heresy

Even before the days of toleration, the infant Christian Church faced the problem of heresy. Heresy meant deliberate departure from the accepted doctrines of the church. It was intellectual and spiritual dissent and concerned the beliefs of Christianity, not the morals of its adherents. It was distinct, therefore, from the ordinary human moral failings or sins, however great. When heretics were numerous, the church was forced to act as an organization. In fact, the inner organization of the church was materially strengthened as a result of combating heresy. Two types of action were called forth by the prevalence of a particular heresy: first, formal and precise definition of the dogma questioned; and, second, disciplinary measures to suppress heresy.

Most of the heresies of the early centuries of Christianity concerned the doctrine of the Trinity. This mystery, admittedly difficult to understand, puzzled many especially in the Hellenistic East where subtle philosophical speculations were extraordinarily popular. Questions were raised with regard to the person and nature of Christ and his relation to the Godhead. Most important was the heresy known as Arianism, from its founder Arius. Arius held that Christ had not co-existed eternally with the Father. This implied a denial of Christ's equality with God the Father and undermined the entire theology of the Incarnation and Redemption. Arianism acquired a considerable vogue despite the efforts of such stalwart champions of the Trinitarian doctrine as Athanasius of Alexandria. Finally, under the auspices of the Emperor Constantine, there assembled at Nicaea (A.D. 325) a council of bishops and prelates from all over the Christian world. This, the first great ecumenical council, affirmed the orthodox doctrine of the Trinity and in a formal statement of faith, the Nicene Creed, carefully defined Christ's co-eternity and consubstantiality with the Father.

Arianism persisted for some years. But ultimately, and partly with the assistance of the imperial government, orthodoxy triumphed throughout the Empire. Arian missionaries had, however, taught their faith to various German tribes beyond the frontiers, thus creating serious problems, both religious and political, during the later period of the Germanic invasions.

Arianism tested the ability of the early church to coördinate its authority against its enemies. Moreover, the practice of hold-

[1] See above, p. 15.

ing universal councils was continued. The church recognizes seven ecumenical councils within the first seven centuries of its existence, as well as many local councils. The Council of Ephesus (431) again upheld the Trinity against the teachings of Nestorius who held that the two natures in Christ, the divine and the human, amounted to two personalities and that the Virgin Mary was the mother of his human personality alone. In condemning Nestorianism the Council of Ephesus affirmed Mary's title of "Mother of God" and thus officially sanctioned the popular veneration of the Virgin Mary, as the greatest of the saints, which has become so characteristic of Catholic Christianity.

Going to another extreme the Monophysites held that Christ possessed only a single combined nature. This doctrine was condemned by the Council of Chalcedon in 451, a council which was further distinguished by the active leadership demonstrated by Pope Leo I. It was his letter to the Patriarch of Constantinople which was accepted by the assembled prelates as the authoritative expression of orthodoxy on this matter. It is worth noting that the Monophysite heresy persisted in Eastern parts of the Roman Empire, especially Syria, Palestine, and Egypt, and considerably embarrassed later emperors.

By the fifth century Christianity had not only emerged from the "catacombs" and triumphed over external enemies, it had overcome inner schism. It had also commenced a work destined to be in a sense perennial, that of perfecting its organization and adapting it to the conditions of the world about. This important task was retarded, as we shall presently see, by the chaos into which the Roman Empire was plunged in the fifth and sixth centuries.

E. Summary of Europe's Ancient Inheritance from Mediterranean Lands

In looking back upon ancient civilization, philosophers of later days sometimes conceived of the legacy of the past as symbolized by three cities—Athens, Rome, and Jerusalem. For Athens signified the supremacy of the intellect, Rome the benevolent authority of law, and Jerusalem the spiritual heritage of religion. It would be difficult to find a more appropriate summary of the material of the preceding chapters. All that was best in the science and art of the ancient Near East was fulfilled and surpassed in Greece. The Romans were a race of conquerors with a genius for law and government. But as their own poet, Horace, remarked, they were "conquered" culturally by their Greek captives. And as we have just seen, Rome, before its fall, was a Christian empire. Therefore, perhaps the greatest achievement of the Romans was the fusion of the ancient heritage into one organic whole.

With Rome, civilization moved westward to embrace the entire Mediterranean basin. Thus was formed what might appropriately be called a Mediterranean community. Moreover, for several centuries to come the center of gravity of civilization remained within the limits of that community. But Julius Caesar and his successors advanced the Roman standards well into Western Europe. And before many years had passed, new peoples in eastern as well as western Europe were to come under the influence of Graeco-Roman-Christian civilization. What we have been describing is not merely the development of a series of ancient cultures, but the very foundations of European civilization, its inheritance from the past.

Christian marble sarcophagus, fourth century, Allegory of the Last Judgment, the separation of the sheep from the goats.

Courtesy Metropolitan Museum of Art, New York

Greek Coin from Syracuse, c. 400 B.C.
Courtesy Frederick J. Woodbridge

SELECT SUPPLEMENTARY READINGS FOR PART I

Note. The books listed here and at the end of the other Parts of the volume are exclusively in English, and are only a very few of the many important historical works relating to the present text. For additional titles, students should consult the bibliographies in the more recent general books cited below, and also the *Guide to Historical Literature* (new ed., 1961). Two useful surveys of Western civilization, copiously illustrated with artistic material from successive periods, are: *Life Picture History of Western Man* (1951), and F. van der Meer, *Atlas of Western Civilization* (tr. 1954). Useful surveys of art are: H. W. and P. J. Janson, *History of Art* (1963); H. Gardner, *Art Through the Ages* (new ed., 1959); N. Pevsner. *An Outline of European Architecture* (1957); W. H. McNeill, *The Rise of the West* (1963) is a suggestive synthesis.

General for Part I. The standard work of reference for the ancient world is the *Cambridge Ancient History*, 12 vols. (1923–1939). Other comprehensive treatments are: E. Barker, G. N. Clark, and P. Vaucher, *The European Inheritance*, vol. I (1952); J. H. Breasted, *Ancient Times* (1935); W. G. De Burgh, *The Legacy of the Ancient World* (3rd ed., 1960); T. R. Glover, *The Ancient World* (1935); M. I. Rostovtsev, *A History of the Ancient World*, 2 vols. (1923–1939).

Chapter 1. J. H. Breasted, *A History of Egypt* (1942); V. G. Childe, *What Happened in History* (1946), and *The Dawn of European Civilization* (1958); C. H. Dawson, *The Age of the Gods* (1933); H. M. Orlinsky, *Ancient Israel* (2nd ed., 1960).

Chapter 2. W. R. Agard, *What Democracy Meant to the Greeks* (1942), and *The Greek Mind* (1957); G. W. Botsford and C. A. Robinson, *Hellenic History* (4th ed., 1956); C. M. Bowra, *The Greek Experience* (1957); G. L. Dickinson, *The Greek View of Life* (1958); E. Hamilton, *The Greek Way* (1930); H. D. F. Kitto, *The Greeks* (1951); S. Barr, *The Will of Zeus, a History of Greece* (1961); M. I. Rostovtsev, *The Social and Economic History of the Hellenistic World*, 3 vols. (1941); M. Hadas, *Hellenistic Culture* (1959); A. Zimmern, *The Greek Commonwealth* (1931).
For Greek (and Roman) art, see the works of Gardner and Pevsner, cited above.

Chapter 3. M. Hadas, *Imperial Rome* (1965); R. H. Barrow, *The Romans* (1949); J. Carcopino, *Daily Life in Ancient Rome* (tr. 1940); S. Dill, *Roman Society from Nero to Marcus Aurelius* (1920); D. Dudley, *The Civilization of Rome* (1960); H. Mattingly, *Roman Imperial Civilzation* (1959); F. G. Moore, *The Roman's World* (1946); M. I. Rostovtsev, *Rome* (new ed. by E. J. Bickerman of vol. II of *History of the Ancient World;* 1960); H. Scullard, *From the Gracchi to Nero* (1959); C. Starr, *The Emergence of Rome as the Ruler of the Ancient World* (1953).

Chapter 4. R. Bainton, *Early Christianity* (1960); P. Carrington, *The Early Christian Church*, 2 vols. (1957); P. Hughes, *A History of the Church*, vol. I (1934); A. H. M. Jones, *Constantine and the Conversion of Europe* (1949); K. S. Latourette, *A History of the Expansion of Christianity*, vol. I (1937).

Roman building in the provinces. The Arena at Arles.

Courtesy French Government Tourist Office, New York

PART II

CONTRACTION OF THE ROMAN

OF THE

From Marcus Aurelius to Gregory the Great

St. Paul. Late sixth or early seventh century ivory plaque from Roman-Frankish Gaul.
Courtesy Metropolitan Museum of Art, New York

EMPIRE AND EXPANSION CHRISTIAN CHURCH

A Roman aqueduct in southern Gaul. The Pont du Gard.

Courtesy French Government Tourist Office, New York

THE second part of the story of Western civilization extends from the close of the third century to the beginning of the seventh. It is marked by social decay and political reorganization of the Roman Empire, by the practical loss of the western provinces of the Empire (Spain, Gaul, Britain, and most of Italy) to Germanic invaders and settlers, and by the consequent shift of the center of gravity of the Empire from old Rome to newly founded Constantinople. The Empire continues, but henceforth it is described more properly as Byzantine (or Greek) than as Roman; and it confronts, on one hand, a quite different civilization to the east in Asia, and, on the other hand, a relative barbarism among Slavs and Germans to the north and west in Europe.

This part of the story is also marked by consolidation and expansion of the Catholic Christian Church. Indeed, the Church now succeeds the Empire as the chief agency in preserving and extending the Western civilization of the Mediterranean. It gradually converts and helps to civilize the Germanic and Slavic invaders and settlers in southern Europe, and begins to push its missionary and civilizing work northward beyond the former confines of the Roman Empire.

At the same time, Christianity loses the eastern and southern shores of the Mediterranean to the new and rival religion of Mohammed—the religion of Islam. Henceforth, the old traditional unity of the Mediterranean world is broken. Half of it (Syria and northern Africa) becomes identified with the Near and Middle East in an essentially Islamic civilization, while Western and Christian civilization becomes more strictly European.

Test

CHAPTER 5

THE THIRD AND FOURTH CENTURIES:

Decay and Reorganization of the Roman Empire

A. Military and Social Factors in the Collapse of the Augustan Principate

A preceding chapter has described the Roman Empire at the height of its prosperity in the second century. Although a succession of powerful emperors had gradually implanted a habit of autocratic rule, the principate (or dyarchy) founded by Augustus had, in the main, been preserved. Unfortunately, peace and prosperity did not last into the third century; and in the hundred years from the death of Marcus Aurelius (A.D. 180) to the accession of Diocletian (A.D. 284) the Augustan system collapsed. Political disturbances were accompanied by economic and social disintegration, while military anarchy was followed by military despotism until, under Diocletian and his successors, the whole constitutional order was openly changed into an absolutism of the Oriental type.

Thus, at the threshold of European history—at the very time in the third century when Christianity was spreading throughout the Roman Empire and becoming a mark of the advanced civilization of the whole Mediterranean basin—we meet the great problem of the decay of that Empire and the decline of its civilization. It is a problem because our modern attitude of mind, conditioned as it still is by the notion that human history represents continuous progress, rebels at the thought of a great civilization in decay.

Probably no question has engaged the attention of more scholars or produced more varied explanations than the so-called "fall of Rome." According to predilections of various writers, different phases of Rome's decline have been emphasized—the political, the economic, the military, the religious, the agricultural, even the biological. Moreover, to the old question of "why" has been added in recent years the question "when." Obviously, no definitive statements as to the causes or even the chronology of Rome's decay can be given, least of all within the brief compass of this chapter. We must be content with a short description of the transformation of ancient society during the third and fourth centuries, and we must pay particular attention to the new forms which that society assumed. Further, it will become increasingly evident that the drama of the "decline of Rome" was enacted principally in the western and central portions of the Mediterranean basin. The continuing political and economic stability of the eastern provinces is a noteworthy feature of this period.

A primary cause of the troubled conditions which afflicted the Empire was the renewal of the struggles over the imperial throne. This was not new; and the absence of any system of succession has already been noticed. But in the third century the disorder spread beyond Rome to the provinces. As the army discovered its power to make and unmake "barrack emperors," civil war with its destruction of property, including the plunder of cities, ended the long Augustan peace. Since each new emperor owed his power to the army, the soldiers were privileged at the expense of others. Constitutional forms and civilian rights were increasingly disregarded.

Meanwhile the composition of the army changed. Partly because of peace and prosperity, partly because military service became almost exclusively frontier guard duty, the city bourgeoisie were no longer willing to assume the burdens of defense. More and more, therefore, in the third century the army was recruited from the peasants of the less Romanized provinces. Military leaders and even some of the emperors were drawn from non-Italian peasant stock. Ultimately, as numbers of barbarians were settled within the frontiers, the army ceased to be Roman in the old sense. A soldier's loyalty was to his commander rather than to the state, with whose cultural traditions he was apt to be unfamiliar.

The influence of the military was further enhanced by foreign war, for the internal anarchy of the third century invited attacks on the formerly quiet frontiers. In the east, for example, the new Sassanid dynasty of Persia (A.D. 226) was able to capture and temporarily hold the city of Antioch. The province of Dacia north of the Danube was abandoned. Goths and other Germans raided and even penetrated the frontiers from the Black Sea and the Aegean to Gaul. So serious was the crisis that it was deemed necessary to fortify many cities of the interior and finally Rome itself.

The social and economic deterioration which accompanied the military crisis is less easily explained. Certain developments, however, seem clear. To the ravages of civil war was added pestilence. The population markedly declined. Large tracts of land were left uncultivated. With government disorganized, bandits infested the roads, and pirates again roamed the Mediterranean. It is also probable, although exact statistics are not available, that the balance of trade between the western provinces and the eastern Mediterranean favored the latter. At any rate, it seems that a drainage of cash eastward was accompanied by a decrease in the productivity of the European mines. Besides, when the government, in the second half of the third century, resorted to the expedient of debasing the coinage, inflation and speculation followed and trade between east and west was further curtailed. Also, although Rome had formerly exploited the growing trade of the area beyond the northern frontier through its contacts north and east of the Danube and the Rhine, these contacts now diminished.

Whatever the cause of the commercial decline, economic disintegration went hand in hand with a distintegration of local political life, especially in the western provinces. Moreover, it must be remembered that the cities of the Romanized west were newer than those of the east. In many instances their growth reflected that artificial political and military aspect which characterized a great deal of Roman expansion. It is significant, as a later chapter will indicate, that, throughout the disturbances of the third century, the older urban centers of the east successfully maintained themselves. Whether economic deterioration was accentuated by the increasing intervention of the central government, or whether the failure of local initiative left a void which had to be filled, is a debatable question. Certainly city self-government was demoralized and municipal officials and bourgeoisie were ruined by the arbitrary exactions of the military despotism. Public office-holding, which in better times was considered an honor, was now only a burden. The more fortunate left the towns to become farmers, often in a dependent status. Many remained to swell the ranks of the proletariat enjoying the "bread and circuses" which a paternalistic central government dared not curtail. The moral and material decline of the *civitates* is of the highest significance, for upon them and upon the political vitality of the bourgeoisie rested the whole fabric of the Augustan system.

As a result of these depressing economic conditions, the enervation of the municipalities, and the inroads of military despotism, Roman citizenship, once a privilege, became a burden. It was also cheapened by the edict of Caracalla (212) which granted citizenship to all freemen in the Empire. No longer were Italians the privileged ruling class. But if Gauls, Spaniards, Africans, Syrians, and Greeks were thenceforth equal before the law, that law now reflected absolutist tendencies. Further, since the depression had curtailed the taxing facilities of the government, it is permissible to interpret Caracalla's edict as an extension of obligations rather than of rights.

In marked contrast to the poverty of the city bourgeoisie and proletariat and the small farmers was the wealth of the large landowners. Those who were fortunate enough to inherit or to acquire great estates were able to weather the political and economic storms of the later empire. Their extensive villas were sufficiently large to include small local industries as well as large fields. Members for the most part of the so-called senatorial class, the landowners were also politically privileged. They were now powerful enough to defy government agents and tax-gatherers. In competition with them the small farmers were helpless. To escape the tax-collector large numbers of these gave up their independent status and became tenants on great estates. Usually these *coloni,* as they were called, retained the use of their land in return for service. A villa, therefore, was normally composed of a large tract of land cultivated for the owner and an indefinite number of smaller plots, often widely separated, of the *coloni.* These, legally free at least in theory, were economically dependent, while the great landowner was further enriched in both land and service. Large-scale cultivation on an efficient basis was now possible. Thus the best and most carefully managed of these villas became virtually independent principalities over which the central government's power was tenuous in the extreme. The western provinces of the Empire—Gaul, Spain, and parts of North Africa and Italy—ceased to be the home of thriving urban centers with a politically active bourgeoisie. Instead, a new social order based on the country was emerging.

It is evident that the federation of free self-governing municipalities under the enlightened guidance of philosopher-statesmen had been destroyed. The Augustan principate had collapsed. The only hope for the preservation of the state lay in stabilizing the military despotism. This is the meaning of the reorganization inaugurated by Diocletian (284–305) and carried forward by

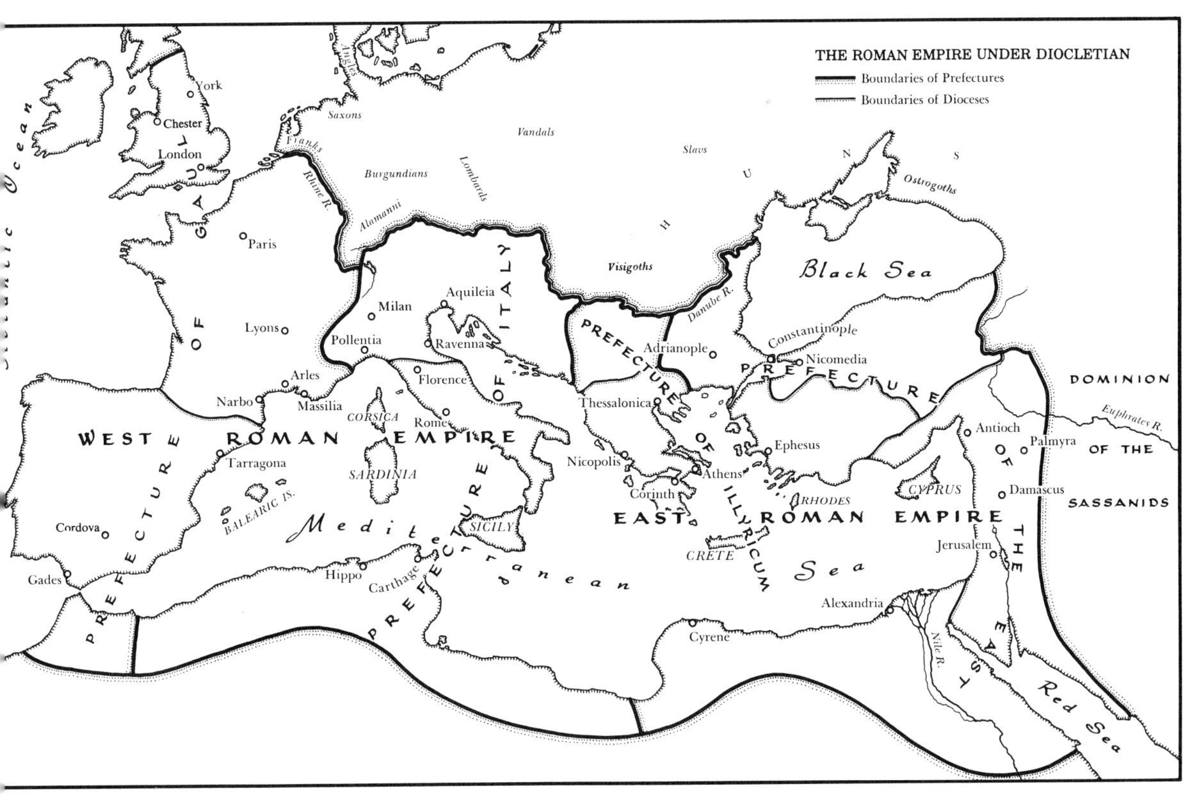

Constantine (306–337) and his immediate successors.

B. Diocletian and the Establishment of Imperial Absolutism

Diocletian was born of Dalmatian peasant stock. Service in the army brought him prominence and eventually acclamation by the troops as Emperor. Thus his career illustrates both the political power of the army and its non-Italian composition. He was distinctly a man of his age. But he had never known and therefore would never understand the cultural and political traditions of the early Empire. A soldier, he viewed the crisis as military. The Empire must be protected against its external enemies at whatever cost.

Diocletian's first move was to exalt the person and power of the emperor. The senate was deprived of all its functions in the central government and became merely a Roman municipal council. A new, elaborately graded and titled hierarchy of officials, dependent solely on the emperor, controlled every phase of life from the central government down to the smallest municipality. Thus the old dyarchy of senate and emperor with its maintenance of republican forms was replaced by a frankly absolute monarchy resting on a huge centralized bureaucracy. Mindful, perhaps, of the discredit into which the imperial dignity had fallen during the days of the "barrack emperors," and realizing that an army could confer power but not the prestige of constitutionally established authority, Diocletian set up an elaborate court with all the paraphernalia of oriental despotism. The "divine" character of the imperial office was given a new emphasis.

Diocletian also decided that the Empire was too big to be governed efficiently by one man. Accordingly he divided it into two parts, each part being further subdivided into two sections (prefectures). Two *Augusti* (himself and Maximinian,), assisted by two Caesars, governed the sections. Since the latter were to succeed the former, it is possible that he intended in this way to settle the thorny question of the imperial succession. This plan, however, did not succeed, although during the fourth and fifth centuries there were commonly two coemperors, one for the eastern half and one for the western. The four prefectures were further divided into dioceses and provinces. The latter, designed to be roughly uniform in size, were much smaller than the former provinces and numbered over one hundred. All administrative heads were appointed and shifted about by the emperor and subjected to constant supervision by special agents. Moreover, practically all civil servants were stripped of military authority.

Although local political power was in this way curbed, various personal privileges continued to exist. Officials of the government service formed a hierarchy of nobility with high-sounding titles of rank: *illustres, spectabiles, clarissimi, perfectissimi, nobilissimi.* Members of the senatorial order, whose actual duties were, for the most part, now only theoretical, were *clarissimi.* All these noblemen—and their number increased as the emperor rewarded old servants or created new ones—were granted various immunities from taxation and other governmental obligations. Many of them rarely left their great estates in the provinces. Moreover, although offices were not hereditary, they tended to become so, since men in other walks of life were prevented from changing their occupations.

The army was similarly reorganized and its own hierarchy of officers rigidly subjected to imperial control. The policy of fortifying the interior cities was continued. Since the frontier legionaries had become resident and privileged landowners, a new and mobile force was created in which infantry and cavalry were separate units. To fill the desired quota of some half million men, "barbarian" Germans, Arabs, Moors, and others, were admitted not only as auxiliaries, but even into the "citizen" legions. Whole tribes were allowed to cross the frontier as allies (*foederati*).

Diocletian's efforts to reëstablish the Empire's economic life were no less far-reaching. They involved control of the currency and prices, a new system of taxation and rigid restrictions on all mercantile and agricultural enterprise. Only the outlines of this policy can be given here. The greatest problem was financial and was made more difficult by the inevitable expense of the bureaucracy. Diocletian did succeed in restoring the coinage,[1] but specie remained scarce and many taxes as well as wages had to be paid in kind. Soldiers, for example, were paid in land, and since they were permitted to marry, they thus became an agrarian peasant class. Food prices had soared during the chaos of the third century and Diocletian sought without appreciable success to achieve stability by price-fixing.

Trades essential to the state, which virtually meant those required by the military, were rigidly restricted. Most of these were already organized into guilds (*collegia*) which proved to be convenient units for taxation. Since many artisans hesitated to undertake contracts because of the depressed condition of business, the government now made a minimum production compulsory and required sons to succeed their fathers in their positions. Merchants and artisans, therefore, became a hereditary caste. The military needs of the state were met, but private enterprise was gravely hampered if not ruined.

Although real local self-government had disappeared from the provincial *civitates*, some of the burdens of local administration remained. Tax collecting was among the most onerous. As commercial decline increased the difficulty of obtaining taxes, the government made members of the local senates (*curiae*)—the *curiales*—personally responsible for certain amounts. Their task was difficult. Any deficit had to be made up out of their own pockets. For a time the system worked and, under the immediate successors of Diocletian, provided the state with revenue. But as their burdens became intolerable, many *curiales* sought to avoid their responsibilities. Here again the government intervened and in no less than one hundred and ninety-two edicts throughout the fourth century closed the army, the church, and the civil service to the *curiales* and forbade their travel abroad. Finally, as in the guilds, membership in the curial class was made hereditary. Nevertheless, despite all these measures, many did escape. Some managed to enter the less important guilds, others placed themselves under the protection of the powerful landowners, even giving up their own property and becoming *coloni*. Some even escaped to the desert of Egypt to become hermits. The "flight of the curiales," indicative of the ruin of the middle class throughout the Empire, is a significant feature of late Roman society.

The long arm of the government also reached out to the countryside, although there the influence of the great landowners limited its effectiveness. Notwithstanding, the peasant was the basis of the state, and land taxes were an important source of revenue. Therefore, the *coloni*, who composed the bulk of the tenants on the villas, were forbidden to leave and became a hereditary caste of laborers. The responsibility for the collection of the tenants' taxes was placed upon the landlord. But, unlike the curial, he was wealthy and powerful and able to defy the government's collector and sometimes to retain the revenues for himself. In the course of time, other governmental duties, including even local police power, devolved upon the landlords, thus completing the formation of another hereditary caste, the great landed magnates. It should be remembered, nevertheless, that, although landowners were in some measure able to defy centralized control, the production of their villas remained an integral part of the organization of defense.

In evaluating the reforms of Diocletian and his successors it must first be emphasized that they resulted from a realistic appraisal of a desperate situation. The heritage of the third century left little opportunity for innovation. The principate with its theoretical division of power between senate and "citizen" emperor had long since ceased to function in the original manner. Diocletian did not set out to destroy Augustan institutions; he found them nearly defunct. Neither did he attempt to revive them. He proceeded along lines familiar to himself, a former peasant and soldier, to establish a regime of discipline and force. What were the results? In certain respects they were noteworthy. Order was restored. The frontiers were held for another century. Diocletian's successor, Constantine, ended one source of unrest by tolerating Christianity, and built a new and magnificent capital on the shores of the Bosphorus. Economic life was restored at least enough to support the army and the bureaucracy.

[1] Constantine introduced a gold *solidus* which remained a standard coin for centuries.

C. Continuing Social and Cultural Decline

Despite these successes, Diocletian's system in the long run only perpetuated the evils which had appeared during the third century. Moreover, the cost in human freedom and individual enterprise was so terrific that the cure proved worse than the disease. The leveling process by which peasants and proletariat were favored at the expense of the bourgeoisie really resulted in a kind of enslavement of all classes to the state. With all freedom of movement between occupations prohibited, society was divided into fixed castes. For the less fortunate—the *curiales*, the artisans, the small landowners, the *coloni*, even the soldiers—there was no escape. The result was a widespread feeling of resignation. If it is permissible to speak of a Roman spirit which had enlivened the institutions of the Augustan age, the prevailing mood of the late fourth century was a sort of discouraged apathy. Barbarian invaders found little resistance left in the fifth century.

The internal disintegration of Roman society is reflected in the realms of culture and the old pagan religion. Classical culture was the product of the city and its religion. This was true of ancient Greece as well as of Rome. The best efforts in the arts and in literature belonged to the periods when civic consciousness was alive and bourgeois prosperity unimpaired. The decline of classical culture, therefore, followed the decay of the city community and the disappearance of the city's gods. It is a phenomenon both spiritual and material. As the central government crushed the community politically, community spirit, manifested in loyalty to the city's gods, disappeared. The incentive to build and dedicate handsome buildings was no longer present either in Rome or in the provinces. The establishment of paternalistic despotism destroyed the old Roman religion, because that religion had been so closely identified with the earlier and freer state. Therefore, until Christianity provided a new source of inspiration, art remained a feeble imitation of the past. Finally, poverty destroyed the material basis upon which the patronage of art rested.

So also it was with secular Latin literature, a faint reflection of the golden age. Ausonius (*d.* about 400) was a poet of some distinction, and Symmachus (*d.* 405) wrote eloquently in defense of a dying paganism. Ammianus Marcellinus (*d.* 400) produced a useful and occasionally vivid continuation of Tacitus's *Histories*. Certain works of compilation were likewise valuable. Dona-

Roman building in the provinces. A Roman amphitheatre at Palmyra, Syria.

Courtesy Syrian Government Tourist Office, New York

tus' (fourth century) treatise on grammar was regarded as the standard work for centuries, and the *Marriage of Philology and Mercury* by Martianus Capella (late fourth century) introduced the classification of learning by the "seven liberal arts" so familiar in the middle ages. Furthermore, some responsibility for preserving the heritage of old Graeco-Roman culture was assumed by the best of the aristocracy on the great estates. From the letters of men like Sidonius Apollinaris, Gallo-Roman country gentleman of the fifth century, later a Christian bishop, and from fragments of mosaics and the extant ruins of villas, comes a picture of a life of genteel ease with a lively appreciation of Rome's cultural tradition. Thus the cultivation of grammar and rhetoric, while not productive of an original literature, kept alive some of the achievements of the past and handed them down to a later age.

D. Development of Christian Literature and Art

In this generally dismal picture of Roman society in the fourth and fifth centuries there are, however, two bright spots. First, what the decadent state now failed to offer, an opportunity for loyal and capable service and an inspiration to intellectual and artistic energy, was being supplied by the rapidly expanding Christian church. Second, the eastern half of the Empire not only remained stable, but in some respects experienced a revival.

Among the representatives of Christian learning in the later Empire were certain men who have been designated the "fathers" of the church. This term was applied to those religious writers whose works were of sufficient importance to warrant a special recognition as authoritative sources of the church's doctrine. All were educated men, steeped in the classical learning of their age and versed in its literature and philosophy. Owing to the general cultural decline of the west, the work of the "Latin" fathers, so-called to distinguish them from their colleagues, the "Greek" fathers of the east, is of particular significance in the intellectual history of that area. In a real sense the Latin fathers were the interpreters of an age that was passing to a new age that was beginning.

The life of St. Ambrose of Milan (*d.* 397) demonstrates how an educated and energetic young man could find a stimulating career in the church. The son of a Roman official, Ambrose advanced in the imperial service to the governorship of Milan. Then, on the death of the bishop of the city, he was chosen by popular acclaim as successor. Accepting this new responsibility, Ambrose became as successful in ecclesiastical administration as he had formerly been in the service of the state. Moreover, though never an accomplished scholar, his writings were of sufficient importance to warrant his inclusion among the Latin Fathers.

The writings of two other Latin Fathers further illustrate how the church enlisted the best intellectual energies of the late Roman period. St. Jerome (*d.* 420), like Ambrose formally educated according to contemporary standards, was an enthusiastic devotee of secular Latin literature, especially the writings of Cicero. But he too entered the church and during a sojourn in Syria learned Hebrew. This enabled him to accomplish his most important work, a complete Latin translation of the Bible. Known as the Vulgate, Jerome's version is still recognized by the Catholic Church as authoritative.

St. Augustine of Hippo (*d.* 430) was one of those rare figures whose destiny it was to influence subsequent generations in an outstanding manner. Born in Numidia, the son of a pagan father and a Christian mother, he too was educated in grammar, rhetoric, and law. Throughout a wayward youth, he was given to intellectual pursuits and especially the study of philosophy, and he was constantly searching for a religion which would satisfy the mind. For a time he embraced Manichaeism, a cult then moderately popular in the Empire, stemming from the Zoroastrian dualism of Persia. But eventually, and apparently owing in no small measure to the preaching of St. Ambrose, he returned to the Christian faith of his youth. Thus, as he relates in his remarkably frank memoirs, the *Confessions*, the prayers of his saintly mother, Monica, were answered. Augustine was finally made Bishop of Hippo in North Africa where he completed a distinguished career and died as the German Vandals besieged the city.

No author was more widely read during the middle ages than Augustine and there is hardly a theological or philosophical question that he did not consider. Since he had been influenced by contemporary Neo-Platonism, the philosophical trend of the early middle ages was Platonic. Perhaps he is best known for his monumental and discursive *City of God*, a work occasioned by the Gothic sack of Rome in 410. Written in part as an answer to the pagan accusation that the abandonment of Rome's gods had caused her fall, the *City of God* presents, for the first time, a Christian philosophy of history. Divine providence is seen in all earthly events, and men's minds are directed from the transitory vicissitudes of human affairs to things eternal.

Another result of the new inspiration which Christianity offered was the beginning of a Christian religious poetry. Ambrose, for example, had composed a number of Latin hymns. More important in the development of hymnody was Prudentius (*d.* 405), who is regarded as one of the founders of the great tradition of Latin religious verse. Indeed, a number of Prudentius' hymns have become familiar in English versions.

Early Christian art had developed in the catacombs where modern archaeology has discovered some remarkable frescoes and sculpture, in particular carved stone tombs or *sarcophagi*. But except for the building of small underground chapels (*cubicula*), the development of architecture had perforce to await the days of toleration. Since the catacombs contained the tombs of martyrs, a number of the earliest churches, not only in Rome but in the provinces, were built over such burial places. Frequently, private dwellings served as places of worship. Portions of these early edifices have been found beneath later structures. The first formal buildings devoted exclusively to worship were, as a rule, adaptations of the Roman basilica. In fact the depression in Roman society had put a number of these typical public buildings out of use. Many early Christian basilicas were actually secular structures made over.

The basilica was a rectangular building with a flat roof supported commonly by two and sometimes four rows of columns which separated the main body of the church from the aisles. At one end, to house the altar, an apse was added, usually semi-circular in shape with a quarter-sphere dome. At the other end of the basilica was often a sort of lobby (narthex) and an outer court. For in primitive Christianity, the catechumens—those not yet baptised—were not permitted to view the sacred ceremonies in their entirety. Apse and walls above the columns were decorated with mosaic, a form of pictorial art which flourished widely both in the west and in the east. Finally, it is important to note that comparatively recent studies of mosaic, sculpture and pictorial decoration justify the contention that early Christian art even in the west was not exclusively Latin. Rather does it show definite traces of oriental influence. But most important of all is the fact that Christian church-building so vividly symbolizes late Roman society. For here in the realm of architecture is an absorption by the Christian religion of a venerable secular tradition. And as it was in art, so it was in literature and in virtually every human activity.

E. Orientalizing the Empire and Transfer of Its Capital to Constantinople

In the eastern provinces of the Empire, the economic depression had been less disastrous. Here, the older and more stable cities retained their commercial contacts with the Asiatic hinterland—with Persia and India and even the Far East. Moreover, bureaucratic despotism was not a novelty to the eastern Mediterranean. The vast state socialism which the new system implied closely resembled the political and economic organization of ancient Egypt. The idea of a god-emperor which Diocletian and Constantine, despite the latter's recognition of Christianity, deliberately inculcated was indigenous to the ancient Near Eastern empires. Indeed from the time of Augustus the Egyptians had regarded him and his successors as heirs of the pharaohs rather than chiefs of a republic. It is not

Fifth century Roman mosaic at Ravenna. The Tomb of Galla Placidia, half-sister of the Emperor Honorius, wife of the Visigothic King Athaulf, later of the Roman general, Constantius, and mother of the Emperor Valentinian III.

Courtesy Italian State Tourist Office, New York

surprising to find that the later emperors recognized the importance of the eastern part of the Empire and even preferred it to Rome as a place of residence. Further, during the third and fourth centuries the most dangerous frontiers were in the east. For this reason, Diocletian moved the imperial residence to Nicomedia in Asia Minor, and Constantine finally decided to build a new capital on the shores of the Bosphorus. We conclude this chapter with discussion of the new city and its influence in the later Empire.

The decision to move the capital, already foreshadowed by Diocletian's abandoning of Rome, probably resulted from a combination of the developments described in this chapter. Rome and the western provinces no longer seemed to be the natural center of imperial life. Moreover, as the home of once thriving republican institutions, it no longer attracted men who completed their destruction. Byzantium, an old Greek colony and the site of the new city, was ideally situated at one of the great gateways to the east where trade continued to flourish. Its location, surrounded on three sides by water, possessed marked natural advantages for defense. Great walls across the fourth side rendered it impregnable to ancient methods of attack. Finally, it was near the important Danube frontier where constant vigilance would alone preserve the Empire intact. In 325 the construction of the new capital began, and in 330, although a great deal of building remained to be done, the city was officially dedicated.

This city which Constantine founded and named after himself was destined to become the seat of a flourishing culture which historians have called Byzantine from the name of the original Greek colony. The story of its development belongs to a later chapter. We are concerned here only with the fact that its foundation by no means signified a surrender of the western provinces or any sudden change in the traditions of the Roman state. Constantinople was the "new Rome," the new seat of the old Empire, not the capital of a new state. When, as was often the case after Diocletian's reorganization, two coemperors were named, one for the east and one for the west, this signified the desire to preserve the Empire intact. It is a mistake to speak of the "eastern empire" and the "western empire" as though they were two separate units. And although the two parts developed along diverging lines, the sense of imperial unity was too strongly implanted to disappear. It was to survive the shock of the barbarian invasions which shook the Empire to its foundations in the fifth century.

Theodoric's tomb at Ravenna. The top is a single piece of stone.

Courtesy Italian State Tourist Office, New York

CHAPTER 6

THE FIFTH TO THE SEVENTH CENTURIES:

Barbarian Neighbors and German Settlers on West Roman Soil

A. German Tribesmen Beyond the Roman Frontier

Beyond the long frontier of the Roman Empire lived peoples of many different nationalities. Some of these, like the Persians, who had held the upper Euphrates against Roman advance for centuries, represented civilizations more ancient than the Roman. Most of the frontier peoples, however, were still in a relatively primitive stage of culture and were regarded by the Romans as barbarians.[1] By the third century the regions beyond the northern and northeastern boundary were being occupied by Germans. First appearing centuries earlier in northern Europe, they had gradually moved, sometimes by devious routes, in a generally southward direction. Occasionally their progress toward, and ultimately across, the border of the Empire was hastened or disrupted by periodic pressure from Asiatic nomads in back of them.[2]

Little is known of the primitive Germans. Julius Caesar mentioned them briefly. A hundred and fifty years later, the Roman historian Tacitus gave a more detailed picture, colored somewhat by his attempt to shame his "decadent" fellow Romans with a description of the "simple, virtuous, and rugged Germans." What struck the Romans particularly was the reddish or blond hair, blue eyes, great stature, and generally powerful physique—in short, what popular imagination still denotes as "Nordic."

In general, German society was tribal, that is, it emphasized the relations and loyalties of kinship rather than of citizenship. An injury to an individual, for example, was an injury to his kin and must be avenged by them unless they were compensated by a graded system of penalties known as *wergeld*. Some tribes, however, had coalesced into groups which, for lack of a better term, might be called "nations." Over such nations ruled kings, at first hardly more than war leaders, elected by the freemen and subject to their wishes. But by the time they entered the Empire there was already a tendency to choose rulers from the same family, thus paving the way for hereditary succession.

Since certain fairly distinct "nations" were later to migrate into the Empire, it will be well to mention the most important. On the lower Rhine were the Franks. Ultimately the strongest of all the German nations, they were originally divided into two groups, the Ripuarian (from *ripa*, riverbank) and the Salian (from *sal*, salt, signifying sea). The Alamans (*Alamanni*, whence the French word "allemand" for German) had occupied the lands between the upper Rhine and the Danube and had

[1] The Latin word, *barbarus*, was used by the Romans in the sense of "foreigner," and had no such depreciatory connotation as is conveyed by the modern English word, "barbarian."

[2] Along the African frontier, Berbers and Moors frequently caused minor problems as did the Arabs in Syria and Palestine. Behind the Germans in eastern Europe were Slavic peoples who later invaded the eastern part of the Empire.

been pushed aside by the Burgundians who came toward the Rhine from central Germany. Behind were the Vandals and Suevi in the interior, the Saxons and Angles along the North Sea in what is now Holland and Western Germany, and last of all, the Lombards who in their southward migration, did not reach the limits of northern Italy until the middle of the sixth century. On the Danube and north of the Black Sea were the Goths, divided into the West Goths (Visigoths) and East Goths (Ostrogoths). By the end of the fourth century A.D., therefore, Germanic peoples had settled along the entire northern frontier from the Black Sea to the North Sea.

It is difficult to estimate how numerous were these Germans. Larger nations, like the Goths, numbered perhaps 80 to 120 thousand. Only about one-fifth of these were freemen or warriors. At any rate, all the German peoples together constituted but a fraction of the total population of the Roman Empire.

On the eve of the fifth-century invasions, the Germanic world was still far from stable. Tribal jealousies and wars enabled the imperial authorities to play one German nation against another. It is a great mistake to think of the Empire as menaced by united German hosts. And as a result of close contact with Roman civilization over a period of centuries, most Germans had become acquainted with Roman ways and some had acquired a veneer of Roman culture. Some of the Germans had also been subjected to influences emanating from the Middle East. In the area north of the Black Sea the Goths, for example, had been preceded by the Sarmatians, an Indo-Iranian people with contacts reaching into Persia. Accomplished horsemen and archers, they used a coat of chain mail and a conical helmet and introduced into Europe stirrups and spurs. Moreover, from them the Goths learned the art of making jewelry of cloisonné enamel, an art form which they carried westward.

It must also be remembered that those Germans who had taken up a position along the boundary, had been preceded across the line by thousands of their compatriots. Individual Germans had crossed to become peasants or *coloni* or to serve in the Roman

Visigothic gold and silver work of the seventh century. Facsimile of the crown of King Swinthila.

Courtesy Hispanic Society of America

army. Occasionally a whole tribe was settled as allies (*foederati*) and given the congenial duty of guarding the border against other Germans. Indeed, the Romans felt no particular racial animosity to those Germans whom many had come to regard as neighbors.

It should be borne in mind, too, that the Roman legions of the late fourth and early fifth centuries were composed largely of German and other "barbarian" troops. The attitude of these Romanized Germans has been admirably summed up in the often quoted phrase: "The Empire was not an enemy but a career." They were not, to use a modern phrase, a "fifth column" seeking to destroy the Roman state. To a considerable degree their attitude of respect for the Empire was shared by the Germans beyond the frontier. The Roman Empire was part of the world they knew. Its institutions and fertile fields were superior to anything they had encountered. They wanted nothing more than to become a part of it, to settle peacefully within its frontiers. For their chieftains, as some of them frankly stated, there was no greater honor than high position in the imperial service. This feeling persisted even after the Empire in the west had crumbled.

B. First Germanic Migrations into the Empire

By the end of the fourth century, thousands of Germans had peacefully entered the Empire and in varying degrees had become Romanized. Beyond the frontier many more had settled and turned their eyes toward the broad cultivated acres and the more secure life to the south. There were times when the pressure on the boundaries was very great, presumably during those periods when the perennial German desire for fertile fields as well as for freedom from attack was more impelling. It is possible that the process of peaceful penetration could have gone on indefinitely and that the entire German world, which was not overwhelmingly numerous, could ultimately have been absorbed without the violent upheaval which came in the fifth and sixth centuries. That this was not the case was largely owing to the coincidence of two factors: first, the weakness of the imperial government which the previous chapter has explained; and, second, the pressure on the Germans from Asiatic nomads, in particular the Huns.

Across the steppes and deserts of central Asia and Russia there have come into central and southeastern Europe at periodic intervals roving nomadic peoples who have terrorized wide areas. Because they inhabited the region between the Ural and Altai mountains, their similar languages have been designated Ural-Altaic. Such a people were the Huns whose round heads, flat noses, slanting eyes, swarthy complexion, and dark hair distinguished them from their Indo-European adversaries whether German or Roman. Dependent on their flocks and herds, they followed the pasturage south in winter and north in summer, often ranging a thousand miles. They became excellent horsemen, and what pastoral life failed to provide they took in raids which terrorized or enslaved more settled agricultural peoples. Their endurance and their ability to withstand hunger and thirst for incredibly long periods were phenomenal.

By the end of the fourth century A.D., after many struggles along the way, the Huns had reached eastern Europe. Shortly thereafter they attacked the Goths north of the Black Sea and the Danube and precipitated a major crisis in both German and imperial affairs. In A.D. 375 the Ostrogoths were overwhelmed and remained for several decades in subjection to the Huns, except for a few who fled westward into Dacia. But when the Huns advanced on the Visigoths, the latter sought permission from the imperial authorities to cross the Danube frontier.

This request of the Visigoths was a turning point in the relations between the Romans and the Germans. As we have seen, many groups of Germans had entered the Empire, but never before had a whole nation sought admission. Though embarrassed by the request, the Emperor, Valens (364–378), could hardly refuse, and the Visigoths were settled as *foederati* south of the Danube. Thus the first German nation to cross the frontier *en masse* came as suppliants, not as invaders. Unfortunately, the incompetent and high-handed officials in charge of the crossing and the subsequent settlement so angered the Goths that they commenced to loot the neighboring provinces. Valens led an inadequate force against them which was badly defeated, and he was killed at Adrianople (378). Though significant as the first victory of Germans over Romans within the Empire and a demonstration of the superiority of Gothic cavalry over Roman infantry legions, the battle of Adrianople can be overestimated and it must be understood in relation to contemporary events. Actually it was a mutiny of Gothic troops who were technically a part of the Roman army. Moreover, under Theodosius (379–395), one of Rome's great emperors and a worthy successor of Diocletian and Constantine, the Goths were again settled peacefully as *foederati,* bound to furnish contingents for the imperial army in return for an annual tribute. Although a considerable territory was in Gothic hands and the Romans' capacity to absorb the Germans was put to a new test, the Empire was still intact under a strong ruler.

It was Rome's misfortune that Theodosius was the last emperor to rule both the eastern and the western parts of the Empire. He was succeeded by his two incompetent sons, Arcadius and Honorius, who divided the Empire, Honorius taking the west and Arcadius the east. Since neither was qualified to assume the responsibility of government, actual power fell to subordinates. In the west, Stilicho, a Romanized German of exceptional ability who had risen in the imperial service, now virtually ruled as *magister militum* or commander-in-chief. Indeed, he was called upon to meet one of the gravest crises in Rome's history. For, under their new king, Alaric, the Visigoths, sensing the weakness of the imperial government, had become dissatisfied with their position and marched through the Greek peninsula, looting as they went. After a temporary occupation of the Illyrian provinces, they appeared in north Italy, entered the Po valley and attempted an assault on Milan. Stilicho temporarily stopped them by a resounding victory at Pollentia (402). But, at this fateful moment in Rome's history, a court clique persuaded the weak and jealous Honorius to have Stilicho, the last hope of the western provinces of the Empire, executed for treason (408).

Meanwhile, the removal of troops from Gaul and Britain, in order to strengthen Italy, left those frontiers vulnerable to attack. In 406 the Alans, Suevi, and Vandals crossed Gaul and the Pyrenees and established themselves in Spain, though still nominally as *foederati.* Alaric, seizing the moment to reverse the defeat at Pollentia, led his Visigoths into Italy again. In 410 he marched on Rome and his troops pillaged the city for three days.

Although the famous sack of Rome by Alaric was not particularly devastating, it was a terrible blow to Roman morale. As has been mentioned, St. Augustine of Hippo felt called upon to write his famous book, *The City of God,* to refute the charge that the abandonment of the old pagan gods had caused Rome's fall. Even hermits of the desert came to St. Jerome in Palestine seeking counsel. The Empire's weakness was now apparent to everybody.

Seventh century Visigothic pottery tablet.

Courtesy Hispanic Society of America

The Visigoths did not remain in Italy. Since they were still facing a serious food shortage, Alaric led them south with the intention of crossing to Sicily. But a storm ended this plan by destroying his ships. Discouraged, he turned north again only to meet a premature death in Calabria. Somewhat later, the imperial government, still attempting to save itself by playing one German nation against another, commissioned one of Alaric's successors to drive the Vandals out of Spain. This the Goths did, virtually destroying the Alans in the process, and leaving only the Suevi in the northwest. Thus was established a Visigothic kingdom, which included southern Gaul and (somewhat later) Spain.

The importance of sea power was further demonstrated by those Vandals who survived the Visigothic attacks on Spain. Temporary control of the Spanish ports and mastery over the Roman fleet of Spain enabled them, under a new and vigorous king, Gaiseric, to cross the strait of Gibraltar to Africa. Thence Gaiseric pushed eastward and overpowered the resistance of the Roman governor. Accordingly, the imperial government, following its now customary procedure of accepting what it could not prevent, established the Vandals as *foederati* in Numidia. But the famous city of Carthage was too tempting a prize for Gaiseric to resist. Its fall in 439 completed the Vandal conquest of North Africa from the Atlantic eastward to modern Tunisia. Meanwhile the Vandal fleet took heavy toll of Mediterranean shipping. Finally, in 455 the Vandals raided Italy and delivered Rome over to a second pillage lasting two weeks.

Along the northern frontiers of Gaul and Britain, Rome had to concede territory. Britain had been denuded of troops in the crisis and left prey to raids from Picts on the north, Scots from Ireland, and Saxon pirates along the east coast. The latter, accompanied by Angles and Jutes, eventually occupied most of what is now England, driving many of the Celtic and Romanized Britons into the remote regions of Wales and Cornwall. No trace of Roman government remained in Britain, and the Anglo-Saxon victors were not regarded as *foederati.*

Meanwhile, the Franks and Burgundians had been installed as *foederati* within the Rhine frontier. The Franks settled along the lower Rhine and westward along the North Sea in what is now Belgium. The Burgundians, after unsuccessful conflicts with Aetius, the harassed Roman commander in Gaul, occupied the territory around Geneva, from which they later spread southward into the Rhone valley. The territory left vacant along the upper Rhine and in Switzerland was taken over by the Alamans. It was precisely at this juncture that the Huns appeared in western Europe.

It will be recalled that the Huns had subjugated the Ostrogoths and driven the Visigoths to seek shelter across the Danube. Continuing their conquests, the Huns gained control over the vast area between the Don and the Danube and captured many German peoples. In 444 Attila, a frightening man, cruel and treacherous, but a capable leader of his people, became their king. Under this "scourge of God," who was to become a sort of legendary figure, the Huns invaded the Balkan peninsula and exacted from the imperial government at Constantinople a yearly tribute, thinly disguised as pay for military service. In 451, with an army composed of Huns and thousands of captured Germans, Attila moved westward and commenced the invasion of Gaul. Sensing the danger, the Visigoths and other Germans made common cause with the Romans under Aetius. The result was a defeat for Attila at Châlons, which stemmed the Asiatic invasion and proved that Roman-German co-

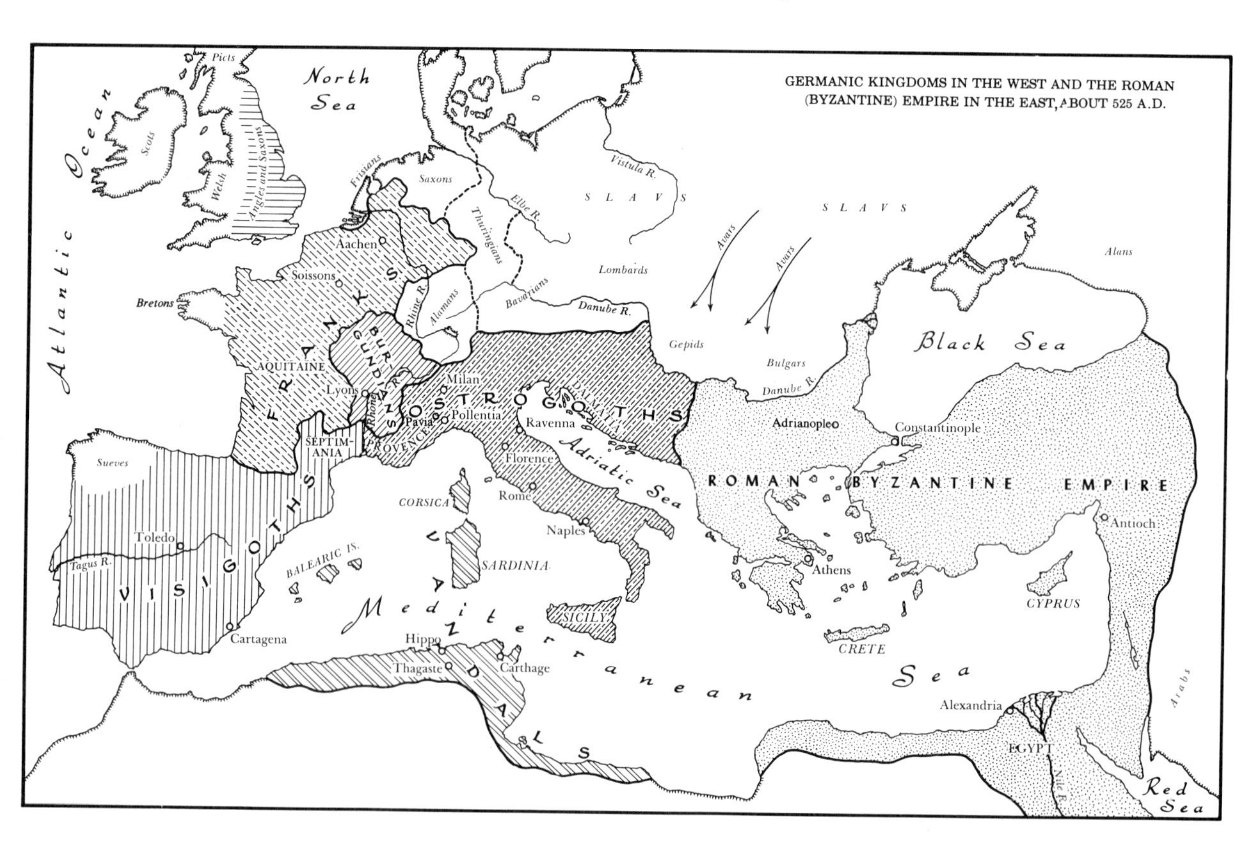

operation was not impossible. Attila's army had not been destroyed, however, and he moved south into Italy. There, he was persuaded to turn back by Pope Leo the Great. When the Hunnic chieftain died in 453 his great empire disappeared completely and his people found their way back to Asia.

C. Collapse of Imperial Government in the West

The fact that it was the Pope, not the Emperor, who went out to meet Attila is eloquent testimony of the low state to which the imperial government in Italy had fallen. The details of the pitiful story of the last co-emperors in the west need not detain us here. When the Theodosian dynasty came to an end (455), there followed a series of puppet co-emperors controlled by German military leaders with no consistent opposition from the Emperor at Constantinople. The last of these puppets was Romulus "Augustulus," the son of Orestes, an ex-secretary of Attila, who had temporarily gained control of the Roman army. When Romulus was deposed (476) by Odovakar, another German chieftain, no successor was chosen and the imperial insignia were sent to Constantinople.

For a few years Odovakar ruled Italy in the name of the Emperor at Constantinople, but without his express approval. Meanwhile, the Ostrogoths, now liberated by the defeat of the Huns, had become dangerously powerful. Settled as *foederati* in the Danubian province, they had developed remarkable political cohesion under their king, Theodoric. Theodoric had spent many years at Constantinople. He was familiar with Roman administration and a great admirer of Roman ways. At one time he had been named one of the consuls of the city. But he was anxious to further the interests of his people. Accordingly, the Emperor Zeno decided to placate Theodoric by commissioning him to remove the usurper, Odovakar. In a few years (489–493), Theodoric mastered the Italian peninsula. Odovakar was invited to a banquet and murdered. Italy itself, the heart of the old Empire, was now a German kingdom, nominally dependent on the emperor at Constantinople, actually governed independently by Theodoric, the Ostrogothic King.

Fortunately for the Italians who had endured many decades of chaos, the wise rule of Theodoric (493–526) brought a generation of peace and prosperity. Genuinely devoted to Roman ideals and scrupulously correct in all his relations with Constantinople, Theodoric attempted to devise a system whereby Roman ways of life could be preserved under German military control. The Roman civil administration was continued. Consuls and magistrates were maintained and Theodoric surrounded himself with officials bearing the familiar Roman titles. Although his capital was at Ravenna where some of the later co-emperors had resided, the city of Rome was not neglected. Its aqueducts were repaired and its people fed and amused. Ravenna was adorned with buildings, some of which still stand; and Theodoric brought to his court the greatest scholars of the day, including Boethius and Cassiodorus. Both of these served as important government officials. Although an Arian, Theodoric protected the Roman church and was even asked on one occasion to settle a disputed election to the papacy.

As a permanent development, however, Theodoric's work must be reckoned a failure. Toward the end of his reign, the jealousy of the Romans and their active hostility to Gothic Arianism finally embittered the Ostrogothic King and led to such unfortunate acts as the imprisonment and execution of Boethius. Not long after Theodoric's death, the Ostrogothic kingdom fell before a new conquest.

Meanwhile, the Franks, who had not figured prominently during the first wave of invasion, were coming into prominence. In fact, they were destined to play a far more important role than any other Germanic nation. Under Clovis (481–511), a Salian Frank, one of the earliest and certainly one of the most important kings of the Merovingian dynasty, the Franks began a remarkable career of expansion.[1] In successive campaigns on the part of

---

[1] The name Merovingian presumably comes from Merovech, Clovis's grandfather.

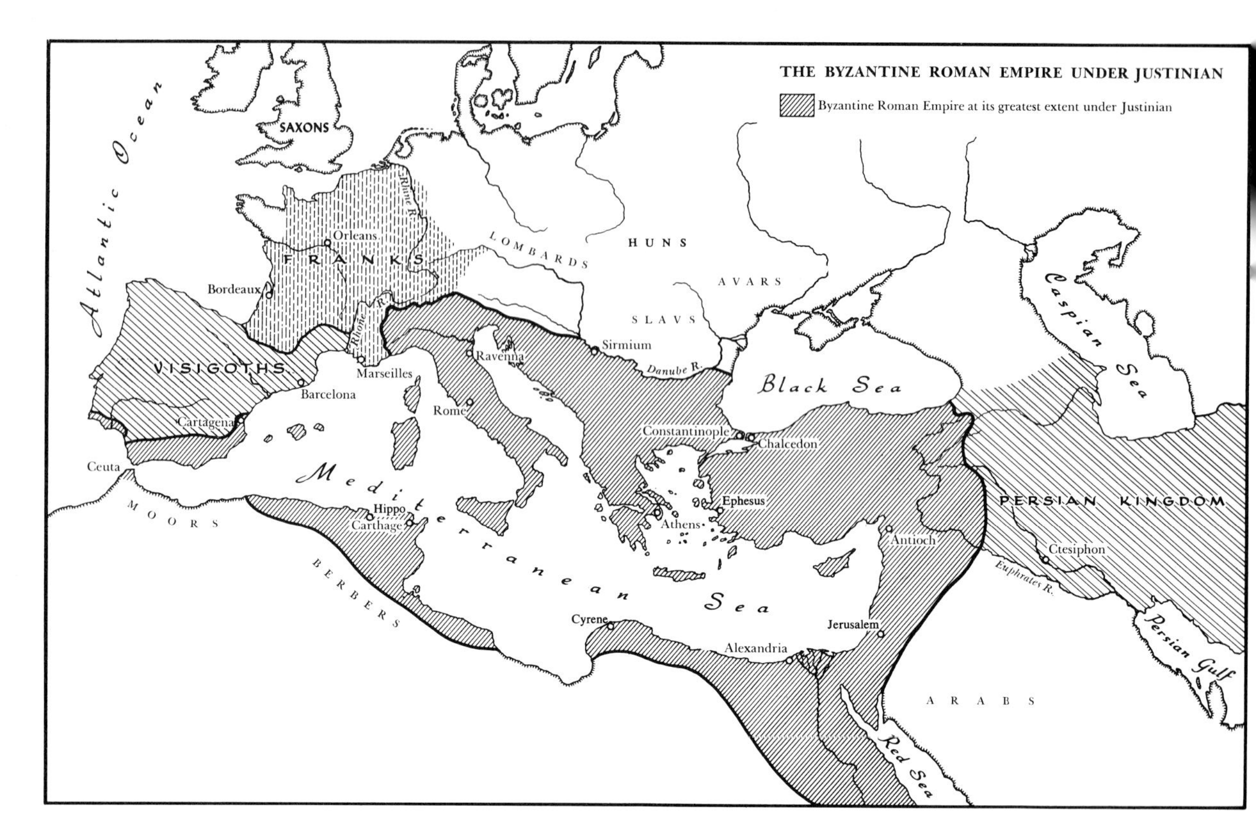

Clovis and his successors against Romans, Alamans, Visigoths, and eventually Burgundians, most of Gaul was taken. As Clovis became convinced that the Christian God had given him victory over the Alamans, he accepted Catholic Christianity. Clovis's Catholic baptism, which led to the acceptance of Catholicism rather than Arianism by the Franks, was an event of capital significance. It assured Clovis a welcome by the Gallo-Roman clergy as the champion of orthodoxy against heresy. Thus the Franks had an advantage in their relations with the native Roman population which other German kingdoms did not at first possess.

The expansion initiated by Clovis differed from other German invasions. Goths, Vandals, Burgundians, and others had left their Germanic homeland and migrated into Roman territory where their Teutonic institutions lost much of their vitality. The Franks, on the other hand, remained on both sides of the lower Rhine and expanded southward into Roman territory. No less respectful of Roman institutions, they never lost touch with their Germanic homeland. Eventually their remarkable expansion carried them eastward as well. In the Frankish kingdom there took place a real fusion of the two cultures, the German and the Roman, not merely an absorption of German population by Rome.

D. Temporary Imperial Recovery and Renewed Invasions

Little has been said thus far of the attitude of the emperors at Constantinople toward the new situation in the western half of the Empire. Indeed, little can be said because for many years they were powerless to change the course of events. Therefore, they temporarily accepted what they could not prevent and saved a vestige of their authority by installing the Germans as *foederati*. Most of the German kings admitted the formal suzerainty of Constantinople. It is important to notice that at Constantinople there was no thought of abandoning the west or of accepting the new situation permanently.

Toward the middle of the sixth century a great Emperor, Justinian (527–565), thought the moment propitious for recovering actual control over the western provinces. Theodoric's kingdom had collapsed, the Franks were divided, and neither Visigoths nor Vandals were any longer formidable. Justinian's career will merit further attention in the next chapter. We are concerned here only with his keen interest in Latin culture and his desire to reunite the entire Empire. Although his capital was Constantinople, a city now more Greek and oriental than Roman, it was he who codified Roman law and recovered, at least partially, the west.

Justinian's first efforts were directed toward Africa where his famous general, Belisarius, destroyed the remnants of Vandal rule in six months (533). Roman provincial administration was restored, although the turbulent Moors, who took this opportunity to revolt, were never entirely pacified. Meanwhile, Belisarius had moved northward and occupied Sicily, Naples, and Rome as another force reconquered Dalmatia.

But Justinian and Belisarius under-estimated the power of Gothic resistance. Not for another twenty years (553) did Narses, who replaced Belisarius, bring the war to an end. Ostrogothic rule was completely erased, and no significant vestiges of it remained except the buildings erected by Theodoric.

The long campaign had sadly devastated Italy. Five sieges and the destruction of the aqueducts ruined Rome and reduced the population to a miserable few thousand in the lower city along the Tiber. Justinian made no attempt to restore the ancient capital, and its administration passed into the hands of papal officials. Ravenna, rebuilt and refortified, became the seat of the exarch, as the imperial representative in Italy was now called. The recovered territory was divided for purposes of administration into units called duchies.

Justinian extended his conquests to Sardinia, Corsica, the Balearics, and a portion of southern Spain. But the major part of Spain and all of Gaul escaped him. Important as his success was, he failed to restore the Empire to its former greatness. The long campaigns so weakened his military system that his successors were unable to maintain what he had regained. North Africa continued another century under Roman rule, but Italy succumbed to the attacks of the Lombards a few years after Justinian's death (565).

Unlike former Germanic invaders, the Lombards possessed no particular reverence for Roman institutions. They had moved from the German forest after the Empire had lost its western provinces. Once in Italy they occupied the valley of the Po (572) with Pavia as the seat of their monarchy. Powerless to thwart them, the exarch concentrated his energies on retaining Ravenna and parts of southern Italy and Sicily. The Lombards overran all the rest of the peninsula except Rome and its environs. But the Lombard monarchy was not strong; and from the first, various dukes, whom the kings set up in imitation of the system established by Justinian, rivaled each other in establishing principalities. No longer could imperial authority be maintained even under a fiction of "alliance"—and indeed there was none in the case of the Lombards. The future of Italy and the west lay with others.

The transformation of the western part of the Empire was now complete. In the space of some two centuries this entire area had succumbed to barbarian attacks and had been forced to permit their entry *en masse*. Everywhere, Germanic kingdoms had replaced the Roman provincial administration. The conquest was not, however, a cataclysmic, sudden development. The fact that it has been described here in a few pages should not mislead the reader. In human history two centuries are a long time. Throughout this gradual process, for it was gradual, Roman civilization—its law, its language, and its institutions—retained sufficient strength to influence the conquerors to a marked degree. Military power, it is true, rested with the Germans. But they were relatively few compared with the Roman population, and the traditions of centuries lay behind Rome even in defeat. The extent to which the Germans preserved Roman institutions and the importance of their own customs will be discussed in the following sections.

E. Institutions of the German Kingdoms

The German kingdoms on Roman soil represent a gradual mixture of Roman institutions and Germanic customs. This was not, however, a meeting between the Romans of the Augustan age and the Germans of the primitive forests. It is evident from the preceding pages that both had changed. The Germans were but a small minority of the total population and totally lacking in any sense of German "unity." Moreover, as some Roman provinces had been less deeply affected by Roman ways than others, so some German peoples preserved their own customs less well than others. The Franks, it will be remembered, did not migrate as did Goths and Vandals, and, as a consequence, kept closer touch with their Germanic background. And the Lombards, who entered Italy late in the sixth century when Roman ways had been altered by time and long years of war, were lacking any sense of respect for things Roman. We must expect to encounter considerable variation in the degree of Romanization. And the following pages must, in emphasizing the characteristics common to all the German kingdoms, note many exceptions.

It should likewise be observed that, for at least the first century of the German occupation, there was a disposition on the part of both natives and invaders to live side by side, as it were, rather than to achieve a fusion into one society. Germans were proud of being Goths, Burgundians, Franks, or Vandals. They wore German costumes and followed German customs. Romans continued to regard them as aliens temporarily quartered in their midst. Only later did a real fusion take place.

Most of the German nations had developed into monarchies, mainly elective in principle, but with tendencies toward dynastic succession. Superficially, the German kings maintained a "court" consistent with their dignity as lieutenants of the emperor. They surrounded themselves with officials bearing high-sounding Latin titles and wore purple vestments on state occasions. Theodoric most nearly approached the Roman system in this respect. But appearances may be deceiving. Although to his own people a German ruler was king, to the Roman natives he remained merely the *magister militum* (master of the troops). Moreover, the Roman conception of the state as a public thing (*res publica*) was hardly understood by the Germans. They viewed territory and governmental authority which went with it as a kind of patrimony, the estate or personal possession of the king. The king's court, therefore, was the center of attraction for the powerful magnates, Roman and German, rather than the seat of a highly developed administrative system. And, of course, military authority was everywhere German. Germans were the conquerors and, although they were willing to preserve Roman institutions, they had no intention of letting military control slip from their hands.

Local government preserved its Roman aspect longer. Since the German peoples had not, as a rule, developed any permanent administrative organization, Roman administrative machinery was retained under German supervision. Latin remained the language of government, and natives continued to occupy civil positions. In Italy, for example, Theodoric, the Ostrogoth, preserved the senate and the magistrates—indeed, all the Roman civil administration—and dated his edicts (as did the Burgundian monarchs) after the year of the consuls whom he named in collaboration with the emperor at Constantinople. Roman provincial divisions and financial organization were commonly retained. The latter proved indispensable to most German kings; and the lot of the remaining *curiales* was not bettered.

Some German kingdoms followed the Roman practice of systematizing their law. Visigothic, Frankish, Burgundian, and Lombard legal codes were drawn up in Latin. These codes, especially the *Lex Salica* of the Salian Franks, present an excellent picture of German society in its new environment. German law was still fundamentally the product of ancient custom and generally reflected an earlier pastoral existence and a strong individualism. More settled conditions never entirely removed these earlier characteristics, but they did produce an increased emphasis on public responsibility for preserving order and dispensing justice. Accordingly, while the relatives of the victim of a crime were still free to take vengeance on the criminal or his kin, or to receive the stipulated money payment (*wergeld*), it was more emphatically insisted that all disputes be settled before the regularly constituted tribunals.

Germanic courts were groups of tribesmen. When an accused appeared he might clear himself, if the court so ruled, by summoning a specified number of men who would swear either to his innocence or to the validity of his oath. This process, called compurgation, required no evidence and was more often accepted in the case of noblemen. Trials by ordeal continued for several centuries. An ordeal consisted in the successful endurance of some physical test such as carrying a hot iron for some specified distance. The ordeal by battle was especially popular. It was believed that in an ordeal God would directly reveal the guilt or innocence of the accused.

Class distinctions were recognized in Germanic law. According to the tariff of *wergeld,* it was more expensive to injure a nobleman than a person of modest means. Great importance was attached to injuries done to or committed by cattle. Burgundian law fixed the death penalty for stealing a cow. On the other hand, since Roman agricultural customs were widely imitated, Germanic codes gave ample protection to enclosed lands, vineyards, and gardens.

The distinction between German and Roman is clearly evident in the attitude of the two peoples toward law and social practices. Both the Visigoths and the Ostrogoths, for example, followed the Roman usage and forbade intermarriages between Goths and Romans. The *wergeld* was invariably higher for an injured German than for a Roman. Romans generally had to pay larger fines and even to suffer capital punishment for lesser offenses against Germans. And although the Germans governed themselves according to their own legal customs, they usually preserved Roman law for Roman provincials.

The distinction between Roman and German, evident in law, was accentuated by difference in religion. With the exception of the Franks, practically all the Germanic peoples who settled on Roman soil were Arians. On the other hand, the bulk of the Roman population was Catholic. There is no doubt that the mutual hostility felt by Catholics and Arians aggravated the natural antipathies of nationality. This situation did not remain permanent. The Franks were converted directly to Catholicism, as has been described. By the end of the sixth century the Visigoths had adopted Catholicism. Gundebaud, king of the Burgundians, was converted to Catholicism as early as 517, and he proscribed Arianism. The conquest of Justinian restored orthodox Catholicism to Italy and North Africa. Even the Lombards who ruined Justinian's work in Italy were converted soon after the middle of the seventh century.

Economic life was not profoundly modified by the Germans. Late Roman provincial society had already become predominantly agricultural owing to the prolonged depression since the third century. Germans easily fitted into this society. The German magnates who settled on Roman soil became landowners and lived on great estates or villas just as their Roman contemporaries. Since the Germans were established in an official capacity, an orderly method of dividing the land had to be devised. Usually the former public domain went to the king. In Gaul the Visigothic magnates took two thirds of the private land. In Italy Theodoric's troops took only one third. But the method was the same and the results roughly comparable. It was not a geographical division of territory, with certain areas Gothic and others Roman. Each domain, that is, the sum total of the cultivated estates belonging to an individual, including the dependent population of *coloni* and slaves, was partitioned. An Ostrogothic magnate probably received one third of a larger domain. Provincial Roman proprietors, therefore, were deprived of at least a portion of their patrimony. While German and Roman magnates lived as neighbors, the latter in somewhat reduced circumstances, the dependent slaves and *coloni,* perhaps both Roman and German, continued their former life uninterrupted except for a change of masters.

The commercial system of the later Empire was less drastically affected by the

German invasions than was once believed. Contacts between the eastern and western provinces were not cut off. Syrian and Jewish merchants peddled their wares in Gaul. The western Mediterranean ports of Marseilles and Narbonne continued to preserve their relations with the eastern Mediterranean. As the Germans sought, at least in theory, to preserve the political unity of the Mediterranean world, so they did not deliberately interfere with its economic life. True, they added nothing to it, and economic life continued to stagnate. Industry languished as before, and the transition from urban to agricultural economy continued. But the economic unity of the Mediterranean world, which the Roman Empire had made possible, they did not destroy. This was endangered only by a new and hostile invasion, that of the Arabs, which will be discussed in a later chapter. Its effects began to be felt in the later seventh century.

F. Gradual Fusion of German and Roman Society: Romanizing the Germans

Thus far we have emphasized the factors which tended to keep Germans and Romans apart. It must not be supposed, however, that the separation was permanent. In the

Sixth century basilica. Sant'Apollinare in Classe, Ravenna.

Photograph by M. W. Baldwin

course of the late sixth and seventh centuries many of those elements which separated German from Roman disappeared, and it is possible to speak of a gradual fusion of the two peoples. First, religious disagreement was removed with the decline of Arianism and the conversion of the Germans to Catholicism. Second, the inability of the imperial government at Constantinople to maintain any semblance of authority, outside of certain parts of Italy, destroyed even the fiction of imperial power throughout the western provinces. Therefore, with confessional differences removed, Hispano- and Gallo-Romans and Italians were no longer unwilling to admit the sovereignty of a German king, now *de facto* ruler of their native province. In short, they came to accept the new situation as permanent and legal. Roman magnates served with the troops of German kings. Nobles—German, Roman, and ecclesiastical—often combined to curb the power of an over-ambitious monarch.

As administrative institutions and popular customs changed, the separation of the two legal systems became less marked. In 654, for example, a Visigothic king promulgated a code of law applicable to both Roman and German subjects. Intermarriages became frequent, and it is significant that late in the sixth century a Visigothic king officially removed the ban on them. As a consequence, racial antagonism between Goths and Romans declined and eventually disappeared. The descendants of the Hispano-Roman aristocracy gloried in Gothic ancestry. Romans in Gaul began to adopt Frankish names, and during the seventh century Gallo-Roman and Frankish magnates fused into a single aristocracy.

Not only did Latin remain the official language of government and church, but Germanic speech apparently disappeared in an area only slightly smaller than the former western half of the Empire. Throughout this territory, which is sometimes referred to as *Romania*, a speech derived from the spoken Latin of the natives survived. Many Germans words were added, more in Frankish Gaul and Lombard Italy than elsewhere. But basically this *lingua Romana*, as it was called, was a Latin speech, and out of its various dialects came the Romance languages of later times. The boundary between *Romania* and the peoples of Germanic speech has hardly changed through the centuries, and has proved far more stable than political frontiers. The border provinces along the Rhine and Danube frontiers were Germanized. Therefore, the dividing line must be drawn west of the Rhine and south of the Danube. The inhabitants of most of what is today eastern Belgium, Alsace, eastern Switzerland, Bavaria, and Austria—speak a Germanic tongue. The only exception is modern Rumania where a Romance language has survived.

It is evident that during the course of the seventh century, if not before, a process of fusion had begun and it is no longer correct to speak of two separate societies. Broadly speaking, the Roman element predominated in this fusion. After all, the Germans were not numerous, and Rome represented an older and much more highly developed civilization. Its language triumphed over German as a written medium of official and intellectual intercourse. Spoken tongues derived from the Latin displaced the speech of the invaders. Arianism disappeared and Catholicism spread. Roman law, although in a greatly modified form and unsupported by any Roman political institutions, survived in some towns. Centuries later it could be deliberately revived with considerable success. Roman economic life, its agricultural system, and what was left of its commerce, the Germans adopted.

Thus by the year 700 a new society was being formed in the western provinces of the old Emipre. Profoundly changed as it was by the German migrations, it had not entirely lost its fundamentally Roman character. Nor had its contacts with the ancient seat of civilization in the eastern Mediterranean been completely severed. Meanwhile, beyond the frontier those Germans who did not move southward, together with other peoples, were also contributing to the formation of a new society, a European as distinct from a Mediterranean civilization. But before proceeding further, it will be well to cast a glance at the fate of the eastern half of the Empire during the same sixth and seventh centuries.

Interior of the church of Santa Sophia showing the pendentives.[1]

Courtesy Turkish Information Office, New York

[1] For an exterior view see below, pp. 346–347.

CHAPTER 7

Byzantine Continuation of the Roman Empire in the East

A. Byzantine Institutions

The barbarian invasions, which disturbed the Roman Empire in the fifth century and resulted in the formation of Germanic kingdoms in its western part, did not permanently disrupt life in the eastern part. Gothic and other tribesmen attacked and even passed through the eastern provinces, but they did not remain to form kingdoms. Nor was the prolonged economic depression which we described in an earlier chapter so disastrous in the eastern provinces. Therefore, while the whole Empire suffered, the collapse which we have been considering was primarily a western phenomenon.

As time went on, the east became separated politically from the former western provinces, and a culture developed there which was a somewhat different composite of Roman, Greek, and Oriental elements from what obtained in the west. This East European culture is generally referred to as Byzantine, a term derived from the old Greek town of Byzantium upon whose site Constantinope had been founded. Although derived mainly from earlier cultures, especially from ancient Near Eastern, the Byzantine possessed a vitality and originality of its own which was particularly manifest in the realm of art. Moreover, as the traditions of "old Rome" proved to be the civilizing influence on the western barbarians, so the institutions of "new Rome," or Constantinople, profoundly affected the development of the eastern European peoples. Basically, the culture of the Balkan peninsula and Russia is still Byzantine. Even Sicily and parts of Italy show traces of the temporary Byzantine occupation of those areas. Some knowledge of Byzantine institutions is, therefore, essential to an understanding of European history, particularly in the east.

Byzantine government was mainly a continuation of the institutions devised by the later Roman emperors. The conception of imperial authority as absolute and divinely instituted, which Diocletian and Constantine had emphasized, was perpetuated. It will be recalled that the "god-emperor" idea was native to the east, and deeply implanted in it; and this conception was now given a Christian form in the Byzantine Empire. The patriarch of Constantinople, theoretically representing the electors and expressing, as it was held, the will of God, anointed the new ruler. The emperor thus became the anointed of God and was expected to fulfill the will of Heaven. While the method of choosing the emperor remained uncertain, senate and army usually concurring in the choice, there developed a marked tendency toward dynastic succession. Such ruling families as the Justinianean, the Heraclian, the Comnenian, the Paleologian, and others are famous in Byzantine history.

Since all pretense of free republican or popular forms had long disappeared, administrative routine was carried out by an elaborate bureaucracy. Well paid and on the whole educated and efficient, the civil service was something on which the Byzantines could justly pride themselves. The reorganization of the Empire into prefectures, dioceses, and provinces, undertaken by Diocletian, was maintained, as was his practice of separating the civil and military jurisdictions. One was a check on the other. The vicars who were in charge of the dioceses were appointed by and responsible to the emperor and exercised a restraining influence on the prefect. The separation of the two jurisdictions also made for greater efficiency, although there developed in the civil jurisdiction a strong administrative conservatism. While this traditionalism sometimes prevented reforms, it did serve to stabilize Byzantine government and to curb the vagaries of a willful emperor.

Inevitably, special circumstances dictated modifications. The exarchs of Italy and Africa, created by Justinian, were military commanders to whom the civil administration was subordinate. In the seventh century the Empire, then greatly reduced in size, was redivided into "themes" for military reasons. In a theme, the military governor had precedence. The Isaurian dynasty in the eighth century took a further step and combined the civil and military jurisdictions.

While Roman imperial ideas and practices formed a basic substratum in all matters of government, native influences, Greek and Oriental, became increasingly evident. This was particularly true after the final loss of Italy and the west. We have already noticed the appropriation of the oriental idea of the god-emperor. And while Latin remained the official language through most of the sixth century, it afterwards gave place to Greek. Roman law was codified for the last time in Latin by the Emperor Justinian (527–565), but even he was forced to publish later imperial laws in Greek and could not prevent the appearance of Greek paraphrases of the original code.

Generally speaking, the Byzantine army, though small, was excellently trained and equipped. While many earlier Roman practices were continued, others were abandoned. The old Praetorian guard, with its baneful influence on government, was abolished. New frontier forces were created (the *limitanei*) and the soldiers were rewarded with inalienable grants of land. Cavalry troops, medical services, and engineers' corps were parts of an effective organization, and several contemporary books on tactics have survived which give evidence that the Roman scientific military tradition was faithfully and intelligently carried forward.

Naval power was developed by the Byzantines far more than it had been by republican or imperial Rome. Constantinople was defended (673–678; 717–718) against the Arabs with the aid of ships, and the highly inflammable and explosive Greek fire was used with telling effect.

The secret of Byzantine political and military strength lay largely in its continued economic prosperity. The development of the eastern Roman provinces presents a marked contrast to the fate of the west. The same regimentation of life, the same oppressive taxation, necessary to support the civil service and the military establishment, which ruined the western half of the Empire, fell on the east. Here also, broadly speaking, agricultural society became stratified, with large estates worked by *coloni* or dependent peasants, bound to the soil. Yet the eastern provinces survived and actually flourished because they possessed old cities whose commercial life was based on well established trade contacts and a thriving native industry. Constantinople, the newest great city, became the depot for merchandise from all over the known world and its fabulous wealth and exotic eastern wares astonished travelers from western and northern Europe.

While products reached Byzantium from southwestern Europe, her great commercial wealth resulted from trade with the east. And although a few Syrian and Alexandrian merchants visited the Far East and returned with wondrous tales of Ceylon and India, or even ventured down the African coast to the marts of Ethiopia, most of the eastern trade, especially that in silk, was monopolized by Persia. Since the shortest route to the Far East by Samarkand and Bokhara lay through Persian territory, the Persian monopoly could only be avoided by occasional use of the old northern route by the Black and Caspian Seas or through contact with the merchants of Ethiopia. Ethiopian ships regularly plied the Indian Ocean and Ethiopian traders penetrated the interior of Africa. To Adule on the Red Sea they brought their wares and met the ships and merchants of Byzantium.

Since silk was increasingly in demand for ecclesiastical vestments and altar draperies, and for private luxury use by the wealthy, measures were taken to bargain with Persia. Most important, however, was the smuggling of silk worm eggs from China by Byzantines. This eventually made possible a thriving native silk industry.

To all this evidence of Byzantine economic prosperity there should be added, finally, the stability of its coinage. The gold besant (Byzant) was the standard coin of the Mediterranean region for centuries.

The heart and center of the Byzantine imperial system was Constantinople. To make this city, the "new Rome," worthy of its dignity as the capital and successor of the "old Rome," Constantine and his successors spared no expense. Not only was it admirably fortified, but great churches, palaces, public buildings, with gilded domes, marble steps, and magnificent mosaic decorations, made the city a show place of the east. In the center of the city was a great marble paved square, the *Augusteum*, its very name reminiscent of Roman grandeur. On the north side of the *Augusteum* was the famous church of Santa Sophia. Opposite was the imperial palace which also overlooked the blue waters of the Bosphorus and the Sea of Marmora.

Near the *Augusteum* was the Hippodrome which, despite its dedication to circus games, public shows, triumphs, and even executions, played a not inconsiderable part in the political life of the Empire. Gathered in its sixty thousand seats the populace cheered their favorite charioteers and, on occasion, denounced the policies of the government. By the sixth century there had appeared two rival circus factions, the Blues and the Greens. Not only did each of these factions support a particular set of charioteers, but, urged on by a turbulent crowd, they intervened in politics. Ministers, judges, even emperors, for they were often present in the lofty royal box, favored or belonged to one faction or the other. Outrages and assassinations occasionally followed victory or defeat in the Hippodrome. As a result, a dangerous popular influence over policy, based on an emotional factional loyalty, threatened to undermine orderly administration. When Justinian attempted to discipline both factions, he was faced with an insurrection, the famous *Nika* ("conquer") riots, which nearly cost him his throne. Only the slaughter of some thirty thousand people and the destruction of a section of the city ended the menace. Thereafter, the political influence of the Hippodrome crowds diminished.

But the ill controlled and somewhat degraded populace of Constantinople did not represent Byzantine society in its entirety. The citizens of the Empire were profoundly interested in matters of religion, and nowhere did religion play a greater role in political and social life than in the Byzantine Empire. Not only did emperors take an active part in ecclesiastical affairs, but the average citizen was absorbed in the great theological controversies of the day and habitually discussed them with his friends in the market place. It will be recalled that it was in the east that the early heresies like Arianism and the Monophysite doctrine of the single nature of Christ developed. Religious ascetism, both in its individual or hermit form and in its communal or monastic aspect, flourished in the eastern provinces. Christian monasticism originated in the east. Monks or hermits from the desert ranked with the charioteer as popular heroes, and pilgrims journeyed far to visit them. On occasion mobs of desert monks from the Thebaid region south of Alexandria even entered that great city to applaud or denounce the policies of the bishop.

B. Policies and Achievements of the Emperor Justinian

The most famous of the Byzantine Roman Emperors of the sixth century was Justinian the Great (527–565). Although of humble, Latin-speaking, Illyrian peasant stock, he possessed, as a man, that dignity which becomes a ruler. He was intelligent, industrious, and concerned with every detail of government. He expected all his subordinates to be equally diligent, and he insisted on, and to a large degree secured, an honest, efficient administration. An enthusiastic patron of the arts, he was also a great builder and many churches in Constantinople were started during his reign, the most celebrated being the great Santa Sophia. Justinian was also a religious poet and composer of hymns. His weaknesses were a want of that capacity for decisive action which a ruler so often needs, and a tendency to overemphasize details.

Justinian's wife, Theodora, was the daughter of a bear-trainer at the Hippodrome and a former circus performer herself. Of somewhat dubious reputation, she was a strange consort for the rather strait-laced Justinian. Yet she made an excellent Empress and her resolute will often strengthened her wavering spouse. It was her refusal to flee at the time of the Nika riots that galvanized the more timid Emperor into the action which suppressed the rebellion and saved his throne. Throughout the reign her influence over her husband and over imperial policy remained considerable, and after her death Justinian was pathetically irresolute. Not without reason did the artists who created the beautiful mosaics of the church of San Vitale in Ravenna portray both Emperor and Empress.

Two great aims guided all of Justinian's policies: the restoration of the Roman Empire to its former greatness, and the championship of Catholicism. If there was a strong tendency for Byzantine culture to become increasingly Hellenized, it was Justinian's distinctly Latin and Roman policy which limited that tendency and preserved in Byzantine civilization an important substratum of Roman influence. The codification of Roman law stands as one of his greatest achievements; the recovery of the western provinces was the task to which he bent most of his energies.

By the sixth century Roman law was in a confused state. The old law (*ius vetus*), composed of statutes of the republic and empire, decrees of the senate, comments of jurists, judicial decisions and the *responsa* of the *jurisprudentes*, had become a mass of ill ordered and often conflicting material. The so-called new law (*ius novum*), or the provisions of later emperors, being more recent, was in somewhat better shape. Hence Justinian first appointed a commission headed by a distinguished jurist, Tribonian, to purge the new law of repetitions and inconsistencies. The result, known as the Code (*Codex Justinianus*), was a greatly reduced amount of material contained in some ten volumes.

The success of this first attempt emboldened the Emperor to appoint another commission to reorganize the *ius vetus*. An enormous amount of material was reduced and compiled into the fifty books comprising the *Digest* or *Pandects*. There were added the *Institutes*, a statement of legal principles, and the Novels (*Novellae*) or new imperial laws which came into existence as the work was being carried forward. The four parts, Code, Digest, Institutes, and Novels, came to be known as the *Corpus Juris Civilis* (Body of Civil Law).

It is impossible to overestimate the significance of the Justinian code. It was compiled at a time when Greek and oriental influences threatened to overpower the Roman. These influences are noticeable in the work of Justinian's jurists. Nevertheless, the *Corpus Juris Civilis* is basically Roman. In feudal western Europe, Roman law soon ceased to be practised as a scientific system. Yet the *Corpus Juris Civilis* was never lost. And when in the eleventh and twelfth centuries a more settled society in the west again demanded a scientific law, the Justinian code proved to be the instrument of a remarkable legal renaissance. Subsequent generations in almost every corner of the earth have been greatly influenced by Roman law.

The partial recovery of the western provinces was perhaps Justinian's most spectacular achievement. It was natural that his Roman policy should lead to an attempt to restore the Empire to its former glory. A Roman Empire permanently separated from Old Rome was to him unthinkable. The suppression of Arianism was in accord with Justinian's Catholic policy. But despite their theoretical subjection to the Emperor's rule, which had never been abandoned, the western barbarian kingdoms, by the middle of the sixth century, were fast losing touch with Constantinople. Justinian's task in this respect was not an easy one. Nor did he ever bring it to completion.

We have already related the story of Justinian's western campaigns and demonstrated how, after a comparatively easy conquest of North Africa, it took his generals, Belisarius and Narses, twenty years to subdue the Ostrogoths in Italy. A few years later imperial armies entered Spain, but could only wrest the southern coast and the Balearics from the Visigoths.[1] Justinian's reconquest was, therefore, not complete. In a sense the Mediterranean was again a "Roman lake," but Britain and Frankish Gaul and most of Spain remained untaken. Nor was Roman administration everywhere reinstated. True, the African provinces were restored to something like their former prosperity. The old systematic irrigation was revived and olive culture again flourished. The Arianism of the Vandals was effectively suppressed in line with Justinian's policy of championing Catholic orthodoxy. But the Berbers and Moors took advantage of the Vandal war to revolt and were never entirely pacified. It will be remembered that in Italy twenty years of warfare had left widespread devastation.

The cost of Justinian's wars was terrific and increased the tax load on his already overburdened subjects. Further, war in the west necessitated a neglect of the eastern frontiers and spread dangerously thin the empire's military forces. Therefore, in spite of the numerous frontier fortresses which Justinian built, and the organization of border patrols (*limitanei*), his conquests scarcely survived his death. In the next generation Italy was again invaded by the Lombards and the Danube frontier broken, and a serious crisis with Persia emerged. The latter had arisen before Justinian's death. The Emperor's western conquests merely added temporary glory. In the long run they weakened the Byzantine state.

[1] See map, p. 70, above.

The Empress Theodora and her court. Sixth century mosaic in the church of San Vitale, Ravenna.

Photograph by John M. Woodbridge

It is a mistake to regard Justinian's western policy as entirely fruitless. It must be considered as part of his plan to recover the entire Roman heritage, to preserve its religion and its law. Moreover in parts of Italy where Byzantine rule lasted for upwards of two centuries, Byzantine culture left an ineradicable impression. This was especially true in the south, in the region around Ravenna, seat of the imperial exarch, and later in Venice. Thus by a strange paradox one result of Justinian's Latin policy was the Byzantinizing of sections of Italy. Byzantine art, for example, was employed in Italy and influenced other areas of western Europe. The Greek language was maintained in monasteries in southern Italy where Greek monks chanted the Byzantine liturgy.

The second great aim of Justinian was the championship of Catholicism and the maintenance of the unity of Christianity. He was deeply interested in religious affairs, and regarded the church as legitimately subject to him as absolute ruler. He appointed bishops and even interfered in theological controversies. And since he regarded religious uniformity as essential to political unity and internal peace, all pagans and heretics felt the heavy hand of official intolerance.

Paganism still existed, although it was fast dying out. A number of pagan philosophers still frequented the schools at Athens, and Justinian considered these vestiges of a once great tradition important enough to suppress. The schools were closed and the scholars scattered. But since the Athenian "Academy" then represented only a faint reflection of earlier glory, the consequent loss to scholarship was slight.

Heretics constituted a more formidable problem, especially the Monophysites who were numerous and powerful in Syria, Palestine, and Egypt. Justinian's early policy of close relations with Rome and the papacy, particularly his enforcement of the decrees of the Council of Chalcedon which condemned the Monophysite doctrine, aroused considerable discontent in the eastern provinces. Here was a religious problem with serious political implications. To appease the west meant to alienate important areas in the east. For a time the Emperor attempted to bring about a theological compromise, a course which resulted in satisfying neither party. One pope was summoned to Constantinople and virtually held prisoner for several years. Toward the end of his life, under the influence of Theodora, Justinian favored the Monophysites. Thus he did not establish religious uniformity and the Monophysite provinces remained a religio-political problem until their conquest by the Arabs in the seventh century.

C. *Narrowing of the Byzantine Empire in the Seventh Century*

Justinian's reign marked the culmination of Latin influence in Byzantine civilization. Thereafter, while certain Roman ideas continued to determine the course of Byzantine history—the emperors never ceasing to regard themselves as the legitimate successors of Augustus—Greek and Oriental influences prevailed. Greek became the official language of the administration and of the law as it had been of the church in the east.

Besides, the loss of the western provinces rendered contact of the east with Rome and Italy more difficult. It is true that southern Italy, Rome, and Ravenna were not taken by the Lombards, but continued as nominal possessions of the Emperor. Yet imperial power in Italy was tenuous in the extreme. More and more, people there turned for guidance, even in temporal matters, to the pope rather than to the exarch. The unity of eastern and western Christianity was also endangered by this loss of contact between the Latin—and, in the Byzantine view, barbarian—west and the Greek east. Finally, Justinian's successors were forced to deal with pressing eastern problems which he had neglected. Foremost among these was the defense of the frontiers.

During Justinian's reign communities of southern Slavs had been established along the northern Byzantine frontier. The Slavs were an Indo-European people who migrated in various directions from the region of the Pripet marshes. In later chapters we shall notice the western Slavs of Bohemia and Poland and the eastern Slavs of Russia. Here we are concerned with the south Slavs

Interior of the basilica of San Vitale at Ravenna built by the Emperor Justinian, sixth century.

Alinari photograph

EUROPE AND THE MEDITERRANEAN ABOUT 620 A.D.

Baltic Sea
SLAVS
SLAVS
Vistula R.
Khazars
AVAR KINGDOM
Danube R.
Bulgarians
SLAVS
Black Sea
Caspian Sea
Odessus
Sinope
Trapezus
Sardica
MOESIA
Adrianople
THRACE
Constantinople
Heraclea
Amasea
Thessalonica
Nicomedia
Nicaea
Ancyra
CAPPADOCIA
Nineveh
Edessa
Mosul
PERSIANS
Smyrna
CILICIA
Tarsus
Aleppo
Ephesus
Corinth
Athens
PAMPHYLIA
ISAURIA
Antioch
Tigris R.
Bagdad
RHODES
CYPRUS
CRETE
Damascus
SYRIA
Euphrates R.
EMPIRE
Sea
Caesarea
Jerusalem
Gaza
Cyrene
Alexandria
ARABS
EGYPT
Nile R.
Medina

(or Yugoslavs) who by the fifth and sixth centuries had settled in some numbers north of the Black Sea. Although they had frequently suffered at the hands of Germans and also of Asiatic nomads, they were tenacious and prolific and maintained their identity. Unlike the nomads, they had reached an agricultural stage of civilization.

In the sixth century, much as the Goths had previously been driven on by the savage nomadic Huns, large numbers of south Slavs were pushed by the Avars, another Hunnic people, into the Balkan peninsula. Sometimes in conjunction with the Avars, but finally on their own initiative, they advanced into imperial territory. By the end of the century a great many had settled in Thrace and Greece. And in 620 the Emperor Heraclius officially recognized a number of them as allies against the Avars. Somewhat later, as Avar raids continued, these Yugoslavs, ancestors of the modern Serbs and Croats, moved into the Illyrian provinces.

Thus it was that the Roman Empire of the east was forced in its turn to permit barbarian immigration. And although it was many years before the Yugoslavs were able to form stable kingdoms, the ethnic character of the Balkan peninsula was permanently changed.

Meanwhile, the Avars remained a formidable military menace. In 591, in 619, and again in 626, together with Slavs, they appeared before Constantinople. But the redoubtable fortifications of the city frustrated all their attacks. Thereafter, the Avars ceased to trouble the Byzantine Empire seriously, and the Slavs settled down within its frontiers.

Defense of Constantinople was complicated by an even more serious menace to the eastern frontier. This resulted from a remarkable resurgence of Persian power. Under their King Chosroes, the Persians passed through Armenia and Syria and advanced into Palestine. Capturing Jerusalem, they carried away part of the relic of the Holy Cross, the Cross upon which Christ had been crucified. That the Emperor Heraclius (610–641) was able to cope with this situation is a tribute to his skill and courage as well as to the inherent strength of the Empire. The Avars were temporarily appeased, and between 622 and 627 a series of brilliant campaigns not only drove the Persians from Syria and Palestine, but carried the Emperor to a signal victory near the ruins of Nineveh on the Tigris. In the following year Chosroes's successor sued for peace. Meanwhile Constantinople had successfully withstood Avar assaults by sea and land. In 629 Heraclius returned in triumph to Constantinople bearing with him the relic of the True Cross. He was a savior of the Empire.

But except in name it was no longer a Roman Empire. The Balkans were henceforth predominantly Slavic, for the Yugoslavs, profiting from the exploits of the destructive Avars, were now firmly settled in the Balkan peninsula. And though they were presently converted to Christianity and nominally incorporated in the Empire, they retained their own Slavic speech and ignored both Latin and Greek. Moreover, the long Byzantine war with Persia exhausted both countries and left them a prey to the Arabs, who, even before Heraclius' death, had invaded Egypt, Syria, Palestine, and Mesopotamia.

Thus the Empire of the early eighth century consisted only of Constantinople, a portion of the Balkan peninsula, Asia Minor, and a few areas in Italy and Sicily. But even in its reduced state—and more losses were to follow—the Byzantine Empire was to remain for centuries a rampart of Graeco-Roman and Christian civilization in the eastern Mediterranean.

CHAPTER 8

Consolidation and Expansion of the Catholic Christian Church

A. Conversion of Celts, Germans, and Slavs

In an earlier chapter we described how the Christian church became in the fourth century the official religion of the Roman Empire. The hundred years of comparative peace between 325 and the German invasions of the fifth century permitted the church to spread throughout the Empire and to develop as a stable institution. As the history of many subsequent centuries testifies, much remained to be accomplished in church organization and in making its operation more effective. But the fundamental principles upon which the organization was based—hierarchy, pope, and bishops—were clear. When the Roman political structure disintegrated in the fifth century, the organized church already possessed sufficient stability to survive and to exert a growing influence over society. In a sense, it replaced the Roman Empire as the principal civilizing agent of Europe.

Not alone did the church develop as an organization; it spread geographically beyond the bounds of the Roman state. With the Saxon conquest of Britain, Christianity had been almost destroyed there and completely isolated. In the fifth century St. Patrick (*d.* 461), who as a youth had spent six years in captivity in Ireland, and then become a monk in Gaul, returned to evangelize the land of his former captors. Before his death he had the satisfaction of seeing the bulk of the Irish people Christian and imbued with missionary zeal. Irish missionaries followed St. Columba (*d.* 597) across the water to the northern coast of England where they found inhabitants of a similar Celtic speech. Since the Latin name for these Irishmen was *Scoti,* the northern part of Britain came to be known as Scotland. Other Irish crossed to Celtic Brittany whence they penetrated the Frankish kingdom which was then still largely pagan. St. Columbanus (*d.* 615) was a famous Celtic missionary to the continent.

Late in the sixth century (597), Pope Gregory sent a monk, St. Augustine, to convert the Saxons of southern England. Thus was started a movement which later converged with the Celtic Christianity of the north. And it was not long before Anglo-Saxon missionaries were carrying the gospel to those parts of the Frankish kingdom where paganism still flourished. The Northumbrian, Willibrord, after an education in Ireland, so successfully labored among the Frisians of the Rhine estuary that he was called to Rome and made bishop of Utrecht. Another Saxon missionary, Winfrid, later known as Boniface (*d.* 754), was a man of exceptional ability. He established the church in the East Frankish dominions and organized its hierarchy under direct papal authority. Even today most Germans regard St. Boniface as their patron saint.

In the east, a century later, the Greek Saints Cyril and Methodius, who were brothers, labored with considerable success in Moravia. The Germans, who aspired to dominance in this Slavic region, were hostile, but Rome upheld the efforts of Cyril and Methodius and sanctioned the Slavonic liturgy they introduced and for which they had devised an alphabet (Cyrillic, Glagolithic). Although Slavonic did not remain the liturgical language of Bohemia and Moravia, it did persist, along with the Cyrillic alphabet, among many Slavic peoples.

Wherever the church spread, its religious ideas permeated all life—political, economic, and social. The church's mode of operation, however, necessarily differed according to the manifold and changing conditions of post-Roman society. In the east, for example, under the stable political institutions of the Byzantine Empire, the development of the church took on a different aspect from its progress in the west where political instability was the rule. Such things must be considered in any discussion of the church in the fifth, sixth, and seventh centuries. And yet the essential unity of Christendom, though jeopardized by the cultural estrangement of east and west, persisted despite political divisions. This is an historical fact of no little significance. It is appropriate, therefore, to treat the church in the period after the Germanic invasions in its entirety, making whatever distinctions geographical variation may require.

B. Consolidation under the Papacy from Leo I to Gregory I

One of the most significant developments during the decline of the Roman Empire was the increasing prestige of the bishops of Rome in both spiritual and temporal matters. We have seen that the supremacy of these bishops as successors of St. Peter was of primitive origin and had been asserted in the days of persecution. In the period of Roman decline, despite the transference of the seat of Empire to the east, the Roman see and papal supremacy became more effective.

This is particularly noticeable in the case of the church's action against heresy. Most of the early heresies—Arianism, Monophysitism, and the like—had developed in the east and were in the beginning, at least, problems for the eastern bishops. The first seven ecumenical councils which were called primarily to deal with such matters were all held in the east. But Rome's decisive leadership in the resulting definition of orthodox dogma was impressive. At the Council of Nicaea (325), the Roman formula on the "consubstantiality" of the Father and the Son was adopted. Two Roman priests were present as representatives of Rome and it is probable that Bishop Hosius of Cordova, who presided at most of the sessions, was actually a papal legate. Similarly, when the bishops in the Council of Chalcedon (451) failed to reach an agreement, Pope Leo I issued his famous *Tome,* or letter, which ended the controversy and upheld the doctrine that Christ possessed two natures, human and divine, in one divine person. Thus the Monophysite belief in a single combined nature was condemned largely as a result of papal initiative.

In the sphere of jurisdiction, that is, the actual power of the pope as supreme governor in administering the church's daily affairs, various political developments of the post-Roman world gravely impeded the pope's freedom of action. In the former western provinces, unstable conditions hampered communications. In place of a single political jurisdiction there were now four or five German kingdoms. For some time, all but one of these, the Frankish, had Arian rulers. Moreover, bishops who had originally been selected by the clergy and people of a city were, by the sixth and seventh centuries, often appointees of the German kings. Under such conditions effective papal jurisdiction was extremely difficult.

Notwithstanding these and other difficulties, there were certain distinct gains, especially in the northwest. Celtic Christianity long retained many local peculiarities which resulted partly from the tribal organization of the Irish. Most of these, such as the calculation of the date for Easter, were in themselves of minor significance, but they represented to their adherents aspects of a whole ecclesiastical system. Scottish and north English Christians clung tenaciously to the practices taught them by the Celtic monks in the face of the determined opposition of the disciples of St. Augustine in the south. Accordingly, when the synod of Whitby (664) accepted the Roman method

Ruins of the St. Simon monastery in Syria.

Courtesy Syrian Government Tourist Office, New York

of determining the date of Easter, something far more important than a date was decided. For the acceptance of the Roman formula signified that the English church—and eventually the Irish—was thenceforth an integral part of Roman Christianity. And it will be recalled that it was with a strong sense of the importance of papal supremacy that the Saxons, Willibrord and Boniface, carried the faith to the continental dominions of the East Franks.

In eastern Europe, the persistence of imperial power meant the continuance of the ecclesiastical organization which had already been developed and which was based largely on the imperial administrative system. As long as the Byzantine Empire remained a unit, so too within its boundaries did the church in the east.

Byzantine Christianity was centered in Constantinople. This had not always been the case, because an old tradition which the west emphasized placed the foundation by an apostle as the criterion of the precedence of a bishopric. But in the east, after Diocletian's reorganization of the Empire, political and ecclesiastical administrative units were identical. Thus "it was a city's position in the civil hierarchy which decided its precedence in the ecclesiastical sphere." [1] Moreover, the Council of Constantinople (381) officially sanctioned this position, at least as far as the east was concerned, by giving Constantinople first place after Rome, "because Constantinople is new Rome." Thenceforth the patriarch of Constantinople, while recognizing the apostolic supremacy of the Roman see of Peter, claimed jurisdiction over all the eastern churches. Only Alexandria seriously contested Constantinople's supremacy. And this was partly because Egypt had always occupied a unique position within the Roman Empire, amounting almost to a kind of autonomy, and partly because Alexandria under Athanasius had so valiantly championed orthodoxy against the Arians. But in the fifth century Constantinople successfully asserted its primacy over the bishops of Alexandria.

Thus it can be seen that the jurisdiction of the pope over the eastern bishops was not direct, as in the west, but was exercised through the patriarch of Constantinople. Moreover, the latter's position was not an independent one, for the continuation of stable imperial government in the east meant the persistence of imperial interference in matters of religion. Even in purely ecclesiastical affairs, the relation of pope and emperor was of paramount importance. Almost from the very moment of imperial toleration of Christianity, the problem of the emperor's position with regard to the church existed.

And it was soon discovered that imperial protection was not an unmixed blessing. The Council of Nicaea met under imperial auspices and Constantine presided over its initial sessions. Later, Justinian regarded himself as head of the church, appointed the bishops in the east, and occasionally interfered in religious concerns. Fortunately, Justinian's strong Roman propensities and his anxiety to promote orthodoxy led him to give full recognition and support to the pope's position. But even with Justinian there were difficult moments, especially during that period when the Emperor attempted to effect a compromise with the Monophysites. Pope Vigilius was virtually prisoner at Constantinople for several years.

When imperial authority was temporarily reëstablished in the west by Justinian, the interference of the Byzantine emperors became a factor even in Italy. The archbishop of Ravenna and other bishops in Byzantine territory were often encouraged by the imperial exarch to resist such expressions of papal authority as the confirmation of an episcopal election or the attendance at a papal synod. Finally, it should be remembered that Justinian's Roman policy scarcely outlived him and that many of his successors wavered in their orthodoxy. And in so far as they gave support to the Monophysites or other heretical groups they tended to turn away from Rome and to encourage the patriarch of Constantinople to do likewise.

An acute issue between Rome and the east was raised early in the eighth century. Partly as a result of the rise and spread of Mohammedanism, whose followers accused the Christians of making gods of their saints and idols of their images, there arose a sort of puritanical faction in the church in Asia Minor which attempted to do away with all statues and images and to repudiate the traditional veneration of saints. Since some of the adherents of this view carried their beliefs into action, they became known as the Iconoclasts (image-breakers). And when their cause was supported by certain emperors, notably Leo III (717–741), a real ecclesiastical crisis developed. The church in the east was nearly rent asunder in the struggle between the imperially supported Iconoclasts and the defenders of the proper use of images led by the patriarch strongly backed by the monks. Fortunately, the church in the east was not permanently divided. The defenders of the traditional veneration of saints held their ground and Iconoclasm eventually disappeared. Although Iconoclasm did not greatly affect the church in the west, the pope as head of

[1] N. H. Baynes, *The Byzantine Empire*, p. 77.

the entire church was seriously concerned. He upheld the patriarch and defended the veneration of saints. As a result of the policy of Leo, relations between the pope and the emperor were badly strained.

It should be emphasized that as the eastern and western provinces of the old Roman Empire drew apart politically, a similar tendency toward division developed in the ecclesiastical sphere. There had long been minor doctrinal and liturgical divergencies. The Christians in the east followed in their public services the Byzantine rite in the Greek tongue, while those in the west used Latin in their liturgy. The more sophisticated, cultured, and economically prosperous east inclined to regard the west as barbarian. There was a noticeable reluctance on the part of some patriarchs to admit that the bishop of the populous and flourishing "new Rome" should be subordinate to the bishop of what had become a comparatively small Italian town. In spite of papal protests, the title "ecumenical patriarch" was adopted and occasionally used by the bishops of Constantinople. During the seventh and eighth centuries the rift widened and there were actually one or two temporary schisms or separations between the two churches.

But none was permanent and it is important to note that, despite political and cultural divergencies and occasional disputes, the religious unity of Christendom was not formally broken for centuries thereafter. Indeed between 650 and 750 there were no less than six popes of Greek or Syrian origin. Nevertheless, papal jurisdiction over Byzantine Christianity was hampered by imperial interference, by the growing cultural differences between east and west, and by the ambitions of several patriarchs.

An important aspect of church history during the period of the invasions was the growth of papal authority outside the purely ecclesiastical sphere. This was the time when the foundations of papal temporal power—a power of great importance in subsequent centuries—were laid. In the first place, the failure of imperial authority in the west left a void which had to be filled. Except for Theodoric's reign, Italy was in constant turmoil. Owing to the prestige of the papal office, the pope was often regarded as the only real symbol of authority and stability. It was Pope Leo I, not the emperor, who went out to meet Attila, the Hun. The popes, like all bishops in the late Roman period, were magistrates. And since a decree of Constantine had empowered the church to own property, the papacy had received many donations of land. Most of these were in the environs of Rome and eventually formed a sizeable strip of territory along the coast north and south of the city, known as the Patrimony of St. Peter. But some estates were as far away as Sicily. Both magisterial authority and the fact that they were large landowners forced the popes in an unstable age to assume the duties and responsibilities of civil government. This was especially true after the Lombard invasions had separated the various sections of Italy which were still claimed by the Byzantine sovereigns. From the sixth century it was the popes who governed the city of Rome and the Patrimony, fed the populace with the grain shipped from the papal estates in Sicily, and, since the imperial exarch rarely fulfilled his proper functions, negotiated with the Lombard kings.

All the tendencies in papal history which we have described were exemplified in a most brilliant manner by Pope Gregory the Great (590–604). Gregory was a Roman of noble family, educated in the Roman tradition. He knew no Greek, little church history, and generally held style and classical scholarship to be of secondary importance. But he was an intelligent student of the Bible and the Church Fathers.

After beginning a political career which carried him to the office of prefect of the city, he gave up his possessions to charity and converted his house into a monastery. Later he was called from monastic seclusion to the position of archdeacon of Rome, a post of high importance in the papal administration. Twice he visited Constantinople, once as a papal representative. Throughout his career as pope, he consistently upheld the legitimate authority of emperors. But with equal insistence he resisted those imperial policies which either aimed at subjecting the church in

Italy or bowed to Monophysite or other heretical opinion. Moreover, since imperial help against the Lombard invaders of Italy was entirely lacking, he was forced to political measures of the type we have described and which to all intents and purposes transferred political authority over Rome and parts of central Italy to the papacy.

Gregory was also zealous in his concern for the church's welfare beyond the Alps. The Frankish kingdom was Catholic, and even in Visigothic Spain Catholicism was making progress. Gregory's letters to bishops and rulers indicate his constant solicitude. Saxon England, of course, was a more decisive conquest. And after St. Augustine's mission was established, it was Gregory's intelligent direction which laid the foundations for the English church's full communion with Rome in the seventh century. As a former monk, he was naturally deeply interested in the progress of monasticism, and the weight of his authority contributed largely to its development.

Gregory was not merely a competent administrator. His deep interest in the church's liturgy induced him to instigate an arrangement of church music then in use at Rome. As a result, the official chant of the church has borne his name ever since (Gregorian chant). Among his many published sermons and writings were the *Pastoral Care*, written for the guidance of bishops and priests, and the *Moralia*, a commentary on the book of Job, and the *Dialogues*. His works earned him the designation of a "Father" of the church. All in all, St. Gregory was one of the great figures in the history of the papacy. And while papal supremacy was by no means perfectly realized in practice, the way was paved for the triumphs of his successors.

C. The Bishops

Emphasis on the prestige of the papcy should not obscure the significant activities of bishops, priests, and monks, for it was through them that the ecclesiastical organization touched the life of every community. Since the ecclesiastical organization had been based on the Roman administrative system, each *civitas* possessed an episcopal church presided over by a bishop. As a consequence, most of the later *dioceses* took their names from the Roman *civitates*. In the eastern provinces the heart of a *civitas* usually remained a metropolis, a city in the actual sense of the word. In the west, where city life declined, the *civitas* was often no longer a flourishing town, but simply a community inhabited by the bishop, his clergy and a population dependent on them. These would consist of the bishop's principal assistants, of whom the most important was the archdeacon, and the clergy of the cathedral who, especially in the west, were usually organized into a community and known as canons. Then in addition to the clerical population, there were the servants in the episcopal household, shopkeepers, and tenants or laborers on the episcopal estates. Finally, since bishops were also magistrates and since the bishop's court was frequented by suitors in a variety of cases, civil and ecclesiastical, there would probably be a considerable transient population. The entourage of a bishop might constitute a fairly sizeable community.

Parish organization tended to become identified with the *latifundia* and great estates. For throughout Christendom the powerful landed magnates maintained small churches or chapels for themselves and their dependents, the *coloni*. Often, despite the decrees (or canons) of church councils, the proprietors exercised a right of patronage over these village churches which thus became the forerunners of the rural manor parishes of the middle ages.

While the bishops of the east had to combat the various heresies which have been mentioned, western bishops, after the decline of Arianism, had to contend with survivals of paganism and with the low moral tone of a semi-barbaric society. Numerous local church councils held in Gaul in the sixth century attest to their activity in this regard. And the decrees of these councils indicate the church's interest in the sanctity of marriage and its concern for the poor and for slaves. As the Roman civil administration passed out of existence, people looked to the local bishop, the representative of a great and stable institution, as a guide and protector in temporal as well as spiritual affairs. Many bishops like St. Caesarius of Arles, St. Remigius of Reims, St. Germanus of Auxerre, St. Avitus of Vienne, and Gregory of Tours, historian of the Franks, gained considerable prestige which they used to further their spiritual missions.

Unfortunately, not all bishops were so active or themselves such shining examples of godly living. All too many sank nearer to the level of the rude society in which they lived. Although bishops were supposed to be elected by the clergy and people of a city and the choice approved by the other bishops of the province, there was actually considerable interference on the part of kings and magnates. And as Frankish and other German kings began to influence episcopal elections or even to appoint bishops, too many selections were made for political or personal reasons. The result was a deterioration of the clergy, and a number of prelates behaved like secular princes and warriors. Notwithstanding, most of the bishops of Spain, Gaul, Africa, and Italy strove valiantly and with no little success to uphold the principles of personal and social morality. Their civilizing role in a barbarian world was of paramount significance.

D. Development of Monasticism

Monasticism is a way of life. It means a complete or partial withdrawal from the world and voluntary abstinence from certain of the ordinary lawful activities of life for the sake of undisturbed prayer and worship of God. True monasticism, as distinct from the solitary life of the hermit, also signifies life in a community according to a fixed rule or daily routine. Monasticism is not exclusively a Christian institution. In various forms it has flourished in other world religions. In fact, asceticism or self-denial, combined with the urge to remove oneself from the world for the sake of religious contemplation, has appealed to people of many races and faiths.

In the days when Christianity was repressed and persecuted by the imperial Roman government, most Christians were called upon to lead a life of self-sacrifice, even of danger, as a matter of course. But after official toleration and support had removed the threat of persecution, an increasing number of heroic souls felt that ordinary life no longer provided the constant challenge to self-denial which a good Christian should face. In the eastern provinces, many such persons betook themselves to remote places to live as solitary hermits. The desert of the Thebaid south of Alexandria, where the climate made such an existence possible, was especially popular. Some, like St. Anthony (*d.* 355), achieved a real sanctity through fasting and prayer. But too many, mistaking the means for the end, fell into excessive self-mortification, vying with their fellows in a strange sort of ascetic competition. The hermit was a popular figure with the average Byzantine citizen who regarded him, despite his excesses, as a sort of spiritual hero. In the west the solitary hermit life was not unknown, but it had less appeal and was less prevalent.

In the main, the asceticism of the solitary hermit did not commend itself to the ecclesiastical authorities. All forms of religious expression, they felt, must be brought within the scope of the church's jurisdiction. The solitary, for his own good as well as for that of the church, must be restored to contact with the community. There arose the demand for a regulated asceticism and there were not lacking men who combined the ascetic spirit with an organizing ability. Three of these deserve mention here, St. Basil in the east, St. Columbanus and St. Benedict in the west.

St. Basil (329–379) elaborated a rule of life to be practiced, not by individual hermits each following his own inclinations, but by a community of monks wherein the individual will was subjugated to the will of the group. Basil felt that solitary asceticism was unfruitful and that prayer was more likely to be spiritually satisfying when varied with labor in the field. He insisted that prayer according to the official liturgy of the church was the foundation of spiritual life. A daily routine of public prayer and worship was added to individual meditation. This was true monasticism, a life of prayer and fasting, but a life lived with others and regulated in every detail. The Basilian rule was soon adopted by many communities throughout the eastern provinces. The Council of Chalcedon (451) ordered that monasteries be subject to the local bishop, and the Emperor Justinian authorized the rule and urged its spread. Its success is indicated by the fact that it is still followed by monasteries in the eastern church and by some in the west.

A number of separate monastic communities had arisen in the west during the later Empire. St. Martin of Tours (*d.* 397) founded a community at Marmoutier. St. John Cassian, who had visited eastern monks, formulated a rule for his community at Marseilles. In Ireland, which was evangelized during the fifth century by St. Patrick, monasticism dominated the Christianity of that land. Early Ireland was predominantly tribal and rural in its organization. Ecclesiastical and social life centered around the great abbeys, and in many cases the abbot, the head of a monastery, was a far more important personage in the community than the bishop.

Irish monks were also missionaries. Many of them went across to Scotland and northern England, whence, as has been explained, they traveled through Saxon England and ultimately to the continent. One of the greatest of these "Scoti" was St. Columbanus (*d.* 615). A native of Ireland, he traveled widely on the continent and founded a number of monasteries in Gaul and northern Italy, of which Luxeuil and Bobbio were the most famous. For all these foundations he also drew up a rule which was markedly ascetic and was later modified under the influence of the rule of St. Benedict.

Most famous of all the monastic founders and the author of the rule which eventually superseded most others in western Europe and influenced all later rules, was St. Benedict of Nursia (about 480–543). St. Benedict was originally a hermit. Subsequently, in association with other hermits who had sought his guidance, he founded a community of monks at Montecassino in southern Italy. There in 529 he published the rule of life which bears his name. It has been said that the Benedictine rule admirably combines the Greek ascetic spirit with the Roman love of law. Every detail of the daily life of the monks was provided for, thereby forestalling laxity or excess. Before taking the irrevocable threefold vow of poverty, chastity, and obedience, each candidate was required to spend a year of trial as a novice (the novitiate). The head of each monastery was the abbot whose rule was supreme. Food and clothing were simple but adequate. Like St. Basil, St. Benedict believed that "idleness is the enemy of the soul," and work and religious study were provided for. Above all, the Benedictine rule carefully outlined the daily life of public prayer, the *opus dei,* as it was called, for this after all was the purpose of the monastic life. In addition to daily Mass, the religious observances of the monastic day consisted of eight "offices" or services. Prime, Terce, Sext, None and Vespers, named after the Roman hours, divided the day into three hour intervals. Compline came at nightfall. Matins and Lauds were the night "vigils." And while the times varied according to latitude and season, matins was invariably sometime not long after midnight. Three or four of the Psalms formed the nucleus of each office, and the entire Psalter was recited in the course of each week.

The Benedictine Rule did not, however, win immediate acceptance in western Europe. In fact, Montecasino was destroyed before the end of the century. Early in the ninth century, through another St. Benedict (of Aniane), and the later Frankish rulers, Benedictine monasticism gradually predominated. Meanwhile other systems continued to flourish. With St. Augustine, Benedictine monasticism penetrated Saxon England, and the later Saxon missionaries introduced it into the newer parts of the Frankish kingdom and ultimately into Scandinavia as well.

By the strictness of their life, the regular clergy, as the monks came to be called (from *regula,* rule), set an example to those members of the secular clergy (from *saeculum,* time) living in the world who strayed from the path of duty. Without doubt they raised the standards of all religious life. As time went on, some monasteries emphasized learning more than others. Thus in monastic libraries were preserved and copied the writings of the ancients, both religious and secular. Diaries, or rather annals, of local happenings were kept, many of which later expanded into important sectional chronicles. Knowledge gained from Roman books on agriculture, combined with experimentation and above all with an orderly and steady regimen of work, made of many a monastery, perhaps originally built in a secluded wilderness, a kind of model farm for the neighborhood. Cattle-breeding, sheep raising, viticulture, the brewing of wine and beer were all activities in which the monks excelled and others learned from them. The tradition of hospitality which developed from St. Benedict's admonition that every traveler should be "received as though he were Christ" made each monastery a kind of inn. For centuries the monasteries were virtually the only establishments for travelers. In short, in a world where agriculture, not commerce, was the prevailing basis of existence, Benedictine monasticism was of paramount importance religiously, culturally, and economically.

E. Church and Culture: Education, Literature, and Art after the Barbarian Invasions

The great Roman tradition of secular learning and education passed with the decay of Roman society. Even in the east, where an educated civil service was still required and where the systematic practice of law long persisted, learning and literature were profoundly affected by the religious spirit of the age. Alike in east and west most scholars and men of letters in the sixth and seventh centuries were churchmen. Although the Latin literary traditions were preserved in the west and the Greek classics cultivated in Byzantium, learning and education became increasingly the monopoly of the clergy.

In the east, a great flowering of Byzantine culture, especially in art and architecture, came during the sixth century and owed much to the patronage of the Christian and Catholic Emperor Justinian. His reign might be said to have marked a period of Greek literary revival in both poetry, especially religious poetry, and prose. Justinian himself composed some hymns. In prose, perhaps the greatest achievements were in the field of historical writing. Procopius, secretary and adviser to Belisarius, and therefore in a positiion to obtain valuable information, produced three significant works: the *History in Eight Books;* the *Buildings,* which lauds the Emperor by describing all his manifold building operations, and is therefore important from an artistic, military, and economic standpoint; and the *Secret History.* In the last, the author, by a strange shift of opinion, relates all the scandal of Justinian's court and villifies the Emperor, his wife Theodora, and others.

Two other historians who deserve mention were Agathias and John of Ephesus, whose *Ecclesiastical History* in Syriac contains interesting and important material on the Monophysites. And although Cosmas Indicopleustes in his *Christian Topography* set out to prove that the earth was shaped like an oblong box similar to Moses's tabernacle, and was not round as Ptolemy had claimed, he contributed, nevertheless, a vast amount of information on geography and commerce.

Generally speaking, the sixth-century Byzantines produced very little original literature. Their foremost contribution was the preservation of the knowledge of Greek and of the Greek classics. After Justinian, the knowledge of Latin disappeared rapidly in the east.

Perhaps the most striking Byzantine cultural achievement was its art. A number of manuscript miniatures and beautiful religious ivory carvings have come down to us from the sixth and seventh centuries. More widely known are the Byzantine mosaics, a form of art which had already been developed to a notable degree in the west. The most famous are those in the interior of Santa Sophia which, although whitewashed by the Turks in the fifteenth century, have recently been partially restored.[1] There are also Byzantine mosaics in the churches built by Justinian and his predecessors at Ravenna.

In the realm of architecture, the Byzantines carried on the Roman tradition and added something of their own. Justinian was a prodigious builder, and the influence of the style of Constantinople was felt throughout the Empire, west as well as east. The churches of San Vitale and Sant'Appolinare in Ravenna and the monastery of St. Catherine on Mount Sinai [2] are examples. Justinian's most famous creation was Santa

[1] See p. 76.
[2] See pp. 74, 83, 89.

Sophia in Constantinople. For this work he chose two gifted architects, natives of Asia Minor, Anthemius and Isidore. The building was completed in five years, and it accomplished what hitherto had not been deemed possible, the raising of a huge circular dome over a rectangular substructure. This was done by means of pendentives (spherical triangles of masonry) and half domes. Santa Sophia was the glory of Justinian's reign. Indeed, there are those who consider two things as justifying his title "the Great": the Law Code and Santa Sophia.

In the former western provinces, civil education and learning gradually died out. And while a number of lay folk, mostly of the upper classes, could read and write (the number is greater than was once supposed), practically all the schools of the sixth and seventh centuries were maintained by the church, either by the bishops or by monasteries. Since most of those who attended such schools did so with the intention of entering the clergy, secular or regular, the content of the education was largely religious. Pope Gregory the Great held the pursuit of profane learning to be merely time taken from more important things. Nevertheless, the ability to study the church fathers and other religious works presupposed a knowledge of Latin, and helped to preserve the classics. The study of the great Latin writers, even for the sake of mastering the language, kept alive a literary spark which others in a later and more peaceful time could fan into a flame.

Among the chief literary figures in the period of the German kingdoms, Boethius (*d.* 524) stands out. He was one of the last of the Romans to be educated in the secular tradition. He entered the service of Theodoric, the Ostrogothic king, firmly believing that in doing so he was serving the best interests of Roman society. It will also be recalled that as a result of a tragic misunderstanding he spent his last days in prison awaiting execution. But there, out of adversity, he produced one of the literary masterpieces of the west, the *Consolation of*

Twelfth century cloister at Moissac, France.

Photograph by Frederick J. Woodbridge

Early medieval manuscript illumination. An initial page from the *Book of Kells,* a manuscript of the Gospels executed in Ireland about the year 800.

Courtesy Library, Trinity College, Dublin

Philosophy. This is not a treatise on philosophy. Rather, it is the voice of a philosopher rationalizing suffering and sorrow with calm resignation. While not specifically Christian, it breathes a truly religious spirit and is by no means incompatible with Catholic Christianity which, it seems clear from his other works, Boethius professed.

More important in the long history of learning was Boethius' attempt to translate the works of Aristotle and Plato. Appreciating that the knowledge of Greek was fast disappearing, he hoped to preserve the thought of the ancient philosophers by translating them into Latin. Unfortunately, he only finished part of Aristotle's logical treatises and some of the comments of Plotinus, a neo-Platonist. Yet what he did accomplish had a tremendous importance in the history of western philosophy.

A contemporary of Boethius, Cassiodorus also felt the passing of the old learning. It was he who, by introducing the practice of copying manuscripts in the monastery where he lived, commenced that all important activity which spread to other monasteries. He too may be called one of the "transmitters" of the ancient heritage.

In the Frankish kingdom, Bishop Gregory of Tours (*d.* 594) represents what was left of the literary tradition in Gaul. His *History of the Franks,* despite its ungrammatical and badly spelled Latin, faults which Gregory himself recognized and lamented, has great vigor and originality and is a priceless record of the times. Bad Latin, however, is not necessarily characteristic of the period. Fortunatus, a sixth-century poet, composed two beautiful hymns which still form part of the church's official liturgy, the *Vexilla regis prodeunt* and the *Pange lingua.* Meanwhile in Visigothic Spain, Isidore, bishop of Seville (*d.* 636), wrote his *Etymologies,* a curious compound of fact and fancy which preserved some of the scientific and literary learning of the past.

Perhaps the most striking example of the preservation of ancient culture during the centuries after the disappearance of the Roman Empire in the west is found in Ireland. For Irish monasticism produced in the sixth and seventh centuries a remarkable flowering of classical learning. Scholars who fled Gaul to escape the turmoil of the continent found a haven in Ireland. And there both Greek and Latin literature were not only studied as steps toward the mastery of sacred learning, but enjoyed with true literary enthusiasm. And this is the more remarkable because with the Irish scholars theology formed the goal of all other learning. A tangible evidence of the Irish achievement consists in the handsomely lettered and decorated manuscripts which have come down to us from that remote period. The *Book of Kells* (after 800) is perhaps the most famous.

Irish missionaries, the *Scoti,* carried their enthusiasm and their knowledge to the continent, but especially to Scotland and England. A veritable "renaissance" of learning flowered in Saxon England in the seventh and eighth centuries. This Anglo-Irish culture was strengthened by the renewed contacts with Rome which followed St. Augustine's mission and the synod of Whitby. Especially important was the appointment of Theodore of Tarsus (*d.* 690) as archbishop of Canterbury. For Theodore was formerly a Greek monk and was consecrated by Pope Vitalian himself at a time when Greek influence in Italy and Rome was more than usually prominent.

Under Theodore's direction the school of Canterbury became renowned and the ties between England and Rome were strengthened. Meanwhile, other schools were founded. Malmsbury was made illustrious by Aldhelm who taught from 675 to 705. Benedict Biscop, a convinced adherent of Rome's authority, founded a monastery and school at Jarrow which was destined to become famous as the home of Bede.

Bede (*d.* 735), surnamed the Venerable, was the most famous of all the Saxon scholars. As priest and monk he was, of course, devoted to sacred learning and theology. But his interests were extraordinarily wide. He knew Greek, which he probably learned from some Irish-trained teacher. He was interested in and wrote treatises on scientific questions. Above all a teacher with an absorbing interest in the problem of religious education, he composed works on grammar and spelling for the monastery school pupils.

Most of Bede's works, and those most frequently referred to by his contemporaries, were his commentaries on the Bible. But the production which has earned the acclaim and gratitude of later generations was his *Ecclesiastical History of the English People,* a history of the English to the year 731. And while the first chapters were compiled from older writers, the author took great pains to secure information from every available source. Fortunately, he was constantly encouraged as well as aided by a number of contemporary clerics. One even consulted the papal archives in Bede's behalf. The *Ecclesiastical History* is an indispensable source for English history, both ecclesiastical and secular, before the early eighth century.

Thus in the distant British isles, where Roman influence had been slight or nonexistent, there began a revival of learning which was later to prove of great assistance to continental scholarship in recovering its ancient heritage and in building upon it. In fact, largely because it was uncontaminated with a similar popular speech, the Latinity of the Celts and Saxons was often more correct than that of Gaul. Unfortunately, as the Greek east lost contact with Latin, so the Latin west gradually lost the knowledge of Greek. The Irish monks were familiar with Greek, and Greek literature was studied in Saxon England as late as Bede (*d.* 735). Charlemagne is said to have understood Greek slightly. But apparently after the eighth century Greek survived in the west only in a few places in Byzantine Italy. As a consequence a cultural rift between east and west was accentuated.

first

CHAPTER 9

Rise and Conquests of Islam

A. Role of Arabs Different from that of Germans and Slavs

For centuries all lands surrounding the Mediterranean, and embraced in the Roman Empire, had shared in a common Graeco-Roman civilization, and latterly Christianity had become a central characteristic of this civilization. The Germans who invaded the western regions of the Empire in the fifth century were gradually assimilated and converted, and became a part of the Graeco-Roman world. Ensuing Slavic invaders of the Balkans were similarly affected. This was not true, however, of the seventh-century Arab invasions into eastern and southern regions of the Empire. For the Arabs were fanatical Moslems, devotees of a new religion—Islam, or Mohammedanism. They spurned conversion to Christianity or other assimilation into the Roman world.

The rise and spread of Islam brought an alien and disruptive force which finally broke the unity of the Mediterranean world. The previous Graeco-Roman-Christian civilization of the entire southern shore of that sea—and most of its eastern shore—was transformed by conquest into an essentially Arab-Moslem civilization. And the conquest proved decisive and complete. Henceforth the Mediterranean was no longer the center of a common civilization but a dividing line between two quite different civilizations, which for centuries were to be largely hostile. The one is "Western," or "European," civilization; the other is "Near Eastern" and "Middle Eastern" civilization. Although each has borrowed heavily from the other, Christendom and Islam have remained two separate worlds.

In the early years of the seventh century no one could have predicted the extent of the assault that was to split the Mediterranean world. Least of all would anyone have suspected that it was to originate in Arabia. Relatively little was then known of the Arabian peninsula, and to the outside world it seemed unimportant. On its fringes were a number of petty quarrelsome states, and a few towns of some commercial significance, including Palmyra and Petra (Arabia Petraea of the Romans) in the north, and Mecca and Medina near the Red Sea coast. The first two of these towns were in contact with the Roman Empire, and the last two with the African kingdom of Ethiopia. Most of the interior of Arabia was arid, and was inhabited by nomadic Bedouin tribes, typical desert Arabs of popular imagination. These were warlike people whose unsettled life was largely given over to predatory raids on neighboring tribes or passing caravans. Yet hitherto they had always been held in check by the more settled border states which in turn were supported by Rome or Persia. Both of these powers considered the Arabs merely a perennial frontier problem.

Why the seventh century brought revolutionary change to Arabia is not entirely clear. It is possible that economic conditions in the period just before Mohammed created a special wave of unrest among the tribesmen, and certainly the economic needs of the Arabs, town dwellers as well as nomads, played a part in the Islamic movement. But material circumstances alone can hardly explain the great Arabian upheaval which had such far-reaching effects. Mohammedanism was first and foremost a religion, and it was the fanatical devotion of the Arabs to that religion which proved to be the driving force in their expansion.

Prior to the advent of Mohammed, Arabia had been subjected to a number of outside religious influences which varied with the geographical environment. Jewish and Christian influences had entered the northwest by way of Syria and Palestine, and the southwest from Ethiopia, while the northeastern Arabs had been affected by the Zoroastrian religion of the Persians. Such external influences had mingled with a native and rather degraded heathenism which manifested itself in the worship of idols or sacred objects of nature, and especially in the veneration of a black stone lodged in the Ka'aba, a temple at Mecca. But there had been no indication that these varied religious trends could be welded into a religious unity, any more than that the perennial conflicts among the tribesmen could be submerged in a national thrust outward, for Mohammed was born (570) at a time when Arabia was a land materially and spiritually divided.

B. *Mohammed and His Religion of Islam*

Mohammed came of a fairly well regarded, though not wealthy, Arab family of Mecca. After some years in the service of a rich widow, Kadijah, he married her and became financially independent. He was familiar with the merchant people and, generally speaking, possessed their outlook on life and their contempt for the lawless desert Arab. But he also had some of the daring of the latter and, no doubt owing to his travels in the service of Kadijah, he was familiar with the desert way of life. He also had some partial familiarity with Judaism and Christianity.

Mohammed's character is difficult to appraise. For his followers there was hardly a fault, while to his enemies he was everything

The Mosque of Ibn Tulun, Cairo, 876–79.
Courtesy Egyptian State Tourist Administration, New York

that was evil. He was highly sensitive, and in some manner came to believe himself the repository of divine revelation. His utterances, therefore, often communicated to his followers in a remarkable rhythmic prose, were regarded as the word of God given directly to Mohammed by the Angel Gabriel. These sayings, many of which were taken down or remembered later by his disciples, constitute the Koran, the "bible" of the Mohammedan religion. Mohammed finally became convinced of his mission to regenerate his people. Two ideas especially seem to have animated him: submission to the one God, Allah (hence *Islam*, submission, and *Moslem*, one who has submitted); and elevation of the moral tone. As time went on his own position as God's last and greatest prophet received more emphasis.

So long as he confined his teaching to his family and immediate friends, Mohammed was tolerated as a harmless eccentric, but when he tried to convert the Meccans he met considerable resistance. The merchants were alarmed at what seemed to them a subversive doctrine and the ordinary town folk were scandalized by his attacks against their idols. So great was the opposition that he was forced to leave Mecca. This was the friendly Yathrib, which was subsequently renamed Medina. The year of the *Hejira* (622) is year one of the Moslem calendar.

At Medina, Mohammed won a large following, and his religion and with it the life he preached were put on a more established basis. Laws and regulations began to form a sort of penal code. The first mosque, or place of worship, was erected. At Medina, too, Mohammed was forced to satisfy the economic needs of the many nomads who espoused his cause. Attack on the Meccan caravans was regarded as religiously justifiable. Thus began in a small way the holy war (*Jihad*), which later turned the warlike energies of the desert Arab from blood feud to national conquest.

Mohammed was able to avenge his early defeat at the hands of the Meccans, for the pillaging of caravans soon led to a war in which Mohammed and his followers were victorious. In 630 he returned to Mecca in triumph. Dramatically he destroyed the idols of the temple, but discreetly kept the black stone of the Ka'aba, already sacred to many Arabs, as the symbol of his one God. Mecca, the town of his birth, thus became the religious center of Islam. When Mohammed died two years after his return, his religion was well established in western Arabia and his military successes had won him prestige throughout the peninsula. Within a few years of his death, his religion overspread all Arabia and served to unify the country.

The religious precepts of Islam, or Mohammedanism, are very simple. The Moslem God is the God of Judaism and of Christianity, and strict emphasis on monotheism is paramount. Mohammed did not reject the Old Testament prophets. Christ he regarded not as divine, but as the next to the last in the line of prophets which culminated in himself, the last and the greatest, the messenger (*rasul*) of Allah. Paradise, pictured in vivid imagery, awaited the faithful believers after death, especially those who died in battle against the infidel. A frightful hell punished the damned.

Mohammed's moral teachings were equally simple. Polygamy was permitted, each man being allowed four wives, a number less than had been customary. (By a special dispensation Mohammed himself had thirteen.[1]) Slavery was also condoned. Otherwise the moral code was almost puritanically strict. A rule that compensations, when offered, must be accepted was designed to limit the blood feud. Pork and wine were prohibited. Alms were to be given to the poor. All believers were to constitute a single fellowship.

Islam has neither priesthood nor sacraments. There are, however, a number of ritualistic observances. Prayer in common at the mosque is recited after a leader, and usually consists of passages from the Koran. Prayer five times a day facing Mecca is a strict requirement and has to be preceded by elaborate ablutions and prostrations. Mohammed was very particular about cleanliness. Every Moslem is required to fast from sunrise to sunset each year during the Arab month of Ramadan, and, provided he can afford it, to make a pilgrimage to Mecca at least once during his lifetime.

Such is the faith and practice of Islam. The simplicity of it appealed to the desert folk and yet it is not exclusively the religion of the nomad, for it has flourished in great cities. Moreover, its later exponents and teachers, in seeking to reconcile it with philosophical and scientific knowledge, rationalized it into a complicated moral and theological system. In the early decades after Mohammed's death, however, it was a fighting faith; and the desire to conquer and subdue the infidel, to subject all people to Allah, was in a large measure the secret of the amazing success of Arab Moslem arms.

C. Arab Moslem Conquests

The rapidity and extent of the early conquests of the Arabs, fired by their new religion and national unity, are astonishing. A century after Mohammed's death, the territory over which the crescent banners of Islam waved stretched from the Pyrenees

[1] Mohammed's marriages were dictated in large part by political considerations and helped to consolidate the tribes of Arabia.

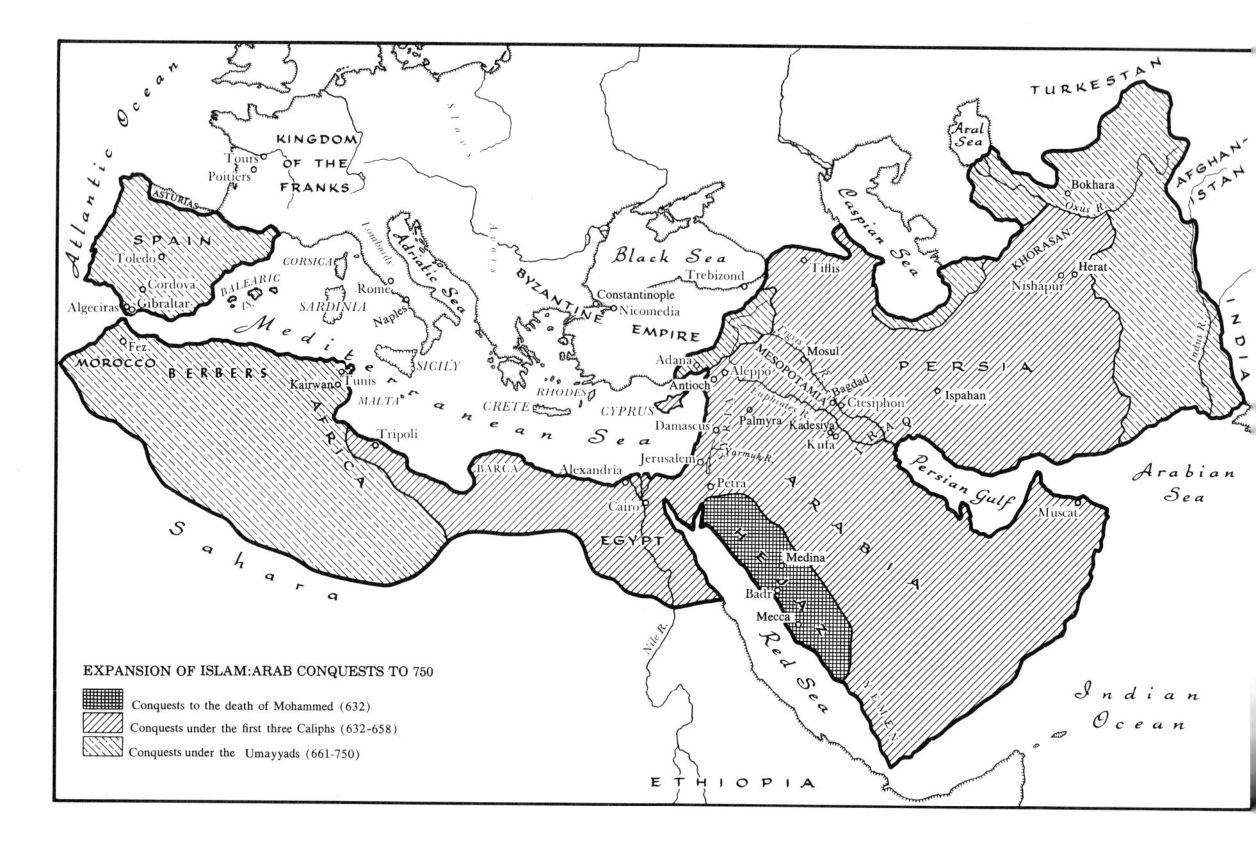

and southern France to the Indus river. But the reasons for such prodigious success are not far to seek.

First, the conquerors were militant Arabs, whose new-found Moslem faith inspired them with a kind of fanaticism. It was not simply that they expected the rewards of Paradise. They gloried in the subjection to Allah of other peoples, often of more advanced culture. It was a sign of their own superiority. Then too, the desert Arab has always been a fighter, and now his bellicose propensities were channeled, so to speak, into one great undertaking. He was serving a cause at once national and religious.

Equally important as explanations of Moslem military success were the weakness of the opponents, and the disaffection of many of the subject peoples in the conquered countries. Both the Byzantine and Persian Empires had been exhausted by long war between them. The triumphs of the Byzantine Emperor Heraclius over the Persian King Chosroes left the former's forces so weakened that he was unable to cope with the advancing Arabs. Persia was an even easier prey. Moreover, there were thousands of Roman Byzantine subjects in Egypt, Syria, and Palestine—Jews and heretical Christians especially—who were only too glad to exchange Byzantine masters for Mohammedan. For the latter promised them religious toleration and imposed upon them a smaller tribute than the Byzantine tax. Egyptian Coptic monks, for example, sang chants of rejoicing at the downfall of the Byzantine "heretics."

The conquest was not an elaborately planned affair. After the unity of Arabia had been won, border raids, long familiar to Arab warriors, betrayed unexpected weaknesses in Byzantine and Persian defenses and tempted the Arab Moslems to more extensive efforts. The Byzantine Emperor Heraclius, after losing Damascus and other Syrian cities, made a determined effort to throw the invader back. But early successes were nullified in the decisive battle of Yarmuk (636). By 640 the fate of Palestine and Syria was sealed. These provinces of the old Roman Empire, with their Christian and Jewish population, passed under Arab rule. Meanwhile, Arab raids into Mesopotamia developed into an extensive campaign, and at the battle of Kadesiya (637) a Persian force was so badly defeated that by 650 the Persian Empire had ceased to exist as an independent state and had been incorporated in the Arab Empire. Thence the impetus of conquest carried the followers of the Prophet through western Turkestan into India and to the shores of the Indus river.

More significant to the ultimate fate of the Graeco-Roman and Christian Mediterranean was the conquest of Egypt. Alexandria fell in 642 and the Moslem conquerors moved the Egyptian capital to Cairo. With Egypt in Arab hands, any danger of a flanking movement by the Byzantines was removed. Alexandria had been a great Byzantine naval base, and in the hands of Moslems it gave them power in the Mediterranean.

The conquest of north Africa followed that of Egypt, though compared to the earlier successes it proved to be slow going. Berber resistance was formidable. But the foundation of a city at Kairwan in Tunisia and the winning of the Berber chieftains over to Islam eventually weighted the scale heavily in Moslem favor. Nevertheless the Berber and Moorish tribesmen remained a problem for the Arabs, and the necessity of offering them booty was partly responsible for the continuation of the Moslem march across north Africa and into Spain.

The Moslem attack on Spain (711) began as a glorified raid. But Visigothic resistance proved so pitifully weak that with the assistance of the Spanish Jews, anxious to avenge their own persecution, the Moslem Arabs and Berbers overran Spain, drove past the Pyrenees, and occupied Narbonne. Later they captured the Balearic Islands. In Frankish Gaul their drive spent itself. And although the great defeat at Tours (732), accomplished by Charles Martel, Frankish *major domus* (mayor of the palace), must still be considered one of the world's decisive battles, it is hardly probable that Moslem armies could have continued their uninterrupted series of successes. Meanwhile in north-western Spain the tiny kingdom of the Asturias harbored what was left of the Gothic armies, which were being reinforced steadily. Not long afterwards Asturias provided the base for a gradual Christian reconquest of Spain.

Meanwhile, in the eastern Mediterranean, Moslem marauders, now joined by sea raiders, were menacing Constantinople itself. Therefore, Emperor Leo III's stout defense of Constantinople in 717–718 deserves recognition as a very important military engagement. Thereafter the defeated Moslem armies retired behind the Taurus mountains and for three centuries Asia Minor remained a Byzantine province. Byzantine Africa, Syria, and Palestine were lost, but eastern Europe was saved.

In only one other area was Christendom to fall back during the early middle ages. In the ninth century the Moslems of north Africa, based at Kairwan, pushed across the Mediterranean, occupied Sicily, Sardinia, and Corsica, and repeatedly harried the coasts of Italy and southern France. They sacked Rome in 846.

D. *The Moslem Empire of the Seventh and Eighth Centuries: the Caliphate*

The conquest we have just described was tremendous in its geographical extent. And although much of the occupied territory was of desert character and therefore sparsely populated, the countries of Egypt, Syria, Palestine, and Persia were the seats of old cultures vastly superior to that of the relatively primitive Arabs. The early Moslem rulers realized this, and it is to their credit that for the most part they did not destroy what they found.

Moreover, they were now faced with the serious problems of government which could not be solved by religious fervor alone. Although their conquering zeal was maintained for the better part of a century, the Moslems were forced to become statesmen as well as warriors. Two problems called for immediate solution: the treatment of subject peoples; and the choosing of a ruler who would succeed to the mantle of Mohammed and preserve the political as well as religious unity of Islam. On the whole the first problem offered less difficulty than the second.

In general, the Moslem Arabs did not

seek to convert their newly won subjects. "Tribute or the sword" sums up their attitude, at least to all those who possessed a "Book," that is, a collection of sacred writings which they themselves understood and respected, like the Old and New Testaments. Tribute from the unbeliever was a tax, usually not greater than that formerly paid to the Byzantine or Persian empires. To the Moslem overlord it was a symbol of subjection to Allah, and it was an important source of revenue which the infant government needed. The conversion of large numbers in the conquered areas was not a feature of early Islam. That came later when Islam was more firmly established as a government, when its brilliant material successes gave it added prestige, and when the civil rights and privileges enjoyed by all the faithful tempted many unbelievers into conversion to Islam. As a consequence, except for occasional sporadic persecution, the denial of certain legal privileges, and the requirement of special dress, Christian and Jewish communities continued to exist within the Moslem world. Churches were maintained, even monasticism continued. The principal difficulties for the Christians were, first, the maintenance of contact with their co-religionists in non-Moslem lands, and, second, the social pressure upon them to turn Moslem.

In the early days, the plunder of caravans and the division of the spoils constituted the Moslem financial system. The Arabs were then a kind of army of occupation living from the tribute of the unbeliever. But such a simple system could not meet the demands of stable government. As far as the routine of administration was concerned, the Arabs appropriated or copied Byzantine and Persian systems. And in the course of time many Greeks, Syrians, and Persians held office under Moslem supervision. Thus the daily life of large areas continued with little change except for new masters.

The method of choosing a successor to Mohammed, as political and religious head (or Caliph) of the Moslem world, proved a bone of contention. On this problem of what might be called central government of a farflung empire, the primitive politico-religious unity of Islam was destroyed. Since Mohammed left no son, the idea of hereditary succession was not at first accepted, and "orthodox" Moslems always held that the caliphate was elective. Since they also respected traditions (*sunna*) which were not included in the Koran, they were known as Sunnites. The first caliphs or "successors" of Mohammed were respected personal associates of the Prophet—Abu Bakr, Omar, and Othman. After the brief reign of Ali (655–661), Mohammed's cousin and son-in-law, which ended in his assassination, the Umayyad family got possession of the caliphate and held it until 750. In this way, hereditary succession finally found a place in the Mohammedan system. But with its acceptance came the confused and bitter rivalries—personal, geographical, tribal, and national—which mark the history of the Islamic "dynasties." Only the bare outlines can be indicated here.

The principal opponents of the Umayyads were the *Shi'a* (Shiites), or partisans of Ali, Mohammed's son-in-law, who held that the succession must be in the family of the Prophet. Except for the reign of Ali, the Shiites were only temporarily and locally successful. They may be described as a powerful minority which existed in many parts of the Moslem world; and in encompassing the murder of Othman they commenced the bloody rivalry between Shiite and Sunnite which created a permanent schism in Islam. Meanwhile other claimants appeared and strange "heresies" developed. Almost from the beginning, Islam was divided religiously and politically.

The Umayyad family ruled from Damascus and under their auspices Syria was the center of the Moslem world, with Damascus and Jerusalem enjoying remarkable prosperity. But Syrian predominance was not acceptable to Persia, where a large number of non-Arab inhabitants had embraced the new faith and found themselves, notwithstanding, in a position of political and social inferiority. A great reaction swept the Umayyads from power, and in 750 Abu'l-Abbas became the first of the Abbasid dynasty which was to rule for several centuries from Bagdad.

One member of the Umayyad family escaped, found his way to Spain, and there proclaimed a virtually independent state

Arabic decorative art. The ceiling of the Manial palace, Cairo.

Courtesy Egyptian State Tourist Administration, New York

(756), which in 929 became a second caliphate. A generation later (972) a third caliphate was set up in Cairo by the Fatimites, a Shiite dynasty of north Africa. Meanwhile throughout the Moslem world, and especially in north Africa, various administrative divisions became virtually independent. It was one of these, Tunisia, which spread Moslem power throughout the islands of the western Mediterranean in the ninth century.

These political and religious schisms did not destroy certain aspects of Moslem unity. Every Moslem learned the same Koran, recited similar prayers, and made the pilgrimage to Mecca. Since the only authorized version of the Koran was in Arabic, every Moslem, whatever his nationality, had to know at least enough Arabic to recite it. Thus the Arabic tongue became a medium of communication over a large section of the world. As an instrument in spreading Islamic culture this was of incalculable importance.

A further evidence of Moslem unity is seen in the extent of its commercial prosperity. Men of similar faith and speech now controlled the Mediterranean from end to end, and likewise the western terminals of the great trade routes to the Far East. Appropriation of Byzantine sea bases in the eastern Mediterranean, together with occupation of the islands in the western and central Mediterranean, guaranteed a common Moslem sea control which was virtually unchallenged before the eleventh and twelfth centuries. Rarely has history witnessed a more extensive commercial monopoly.

The fall of the Umayyads in 750 and the removal of the caliphate to Bagdad marks the end of the first era of Moslem history. At Bagdad a new spirit entered. The faith spread with Islamic material success. With increasing social pressure, conversions from Christianity and other religions became more frequent, until Islam no longer signified a privileged minority of Arabs ruling subject peoples. Thus the way was paved for a continuous expansion in the following centuries, southward into Africa and eastward into Asia and eventually to Indonesia and part of the Philippines. Moreover, as the Moslem empire lost its predominantly Arab character, there commenced that remarkable assimilation of Persian, Byzantine, and Hellenistic culture for which it became so noted during the later middle ages, and which was to prove so important in the cultural progress of medieval Europe.

E. Disruptive Effects on Christendom

The immediate effects on Christian Europe of the early Moslem expansion were serious. In the first place, in so far as the Arabs removed from the control of Christian Europe all the eastern and southern coastal lands of the Mediterranean, including Spain and Sicily, which had formerly belonged to the Roman Empire, their conquest constituted a major military setback for Europe. And since Europe was not willing to admit the losses as permanent, warfare between the two continued. The Spanish reconquest commenced almost immediately with the formation of a little Asturian kingdom. Byzantine resistance strengthened in the ninth and tenth centuries. Later, Italian sailors and Norman adventurers cleared southern Italy and the mid-Mediterranean. These advances were followed in time by the organized crusades of the eleventh and twelfth centuries. Christian Europe's first response to the Arab conquest was military, and military hostility remained a feature of Christian-Moslem relations for centuries. War was not constant and did not prevent, in later times, highly significant commercial and cultural interrelationships which affected the civilization of both. But until modern times, Europe lived under the shadow of a Moslem menace.

A second consequence of the rise of Islam was a major numerical and territorial loss to Chrisianity. It is true that, for the most part, the Moslems were fairly tolerant. Yet the Christians in Moslem lands were isolated, and many, especially in Syria, Palestine, and Egypt, were already disaffected toward the churches of Rome and Constantinople and hence more inclined to accept the Moslem faith as well as Arab rule. Then, too, the material successes of Islam and the legal and social privileges offered to the believers induced many conversions from Christianity to Islam. While Christian communities with surprising vitality survived in Spain and Sicily and, to a much lesser extent, in Syria, Palestine, and Egypt, north Africa (and later Asia Minor) became almost entirely Moslem. The Moslem control of the Mediterranean weakened the contacts between Rome and Constantinople and accentuated the already marked tendency toward political and religious separation. Religiously and culturally, the old Mediterranean world was disrupted. So also were economic ties broken or imperiled.

A third important result of Moslem expansion which can appropriately be considered here is economic. By occupying the Mediterranean coasts from southern Gaul to Asia Minor, together with Sicily and the other principal islands, the Moslems for a time virtually monopolized Mediterranean trade. Western European commerce was gravely impeded and an already weakened economic system was further damaged. Certainly an accelerated trend toward agrarianism and the accompanying deterioration in trade are features of eighth and ninth century western economy. But before many decades trade with the Moslem area began to grow. Accordingly, although the initial rise of Islam must clearly be considered a disruptive force in European history, there were also to be positive contributions.

F. Moslem Culture and Its Influence on Europe

Although Moslems might disagree over the succession to the caliphate and might form innumerable petty states, in all essential matters religious unity remained. In the intellectual sphere, unity of language was also significant, for every good Moslem, whatever his native vernacular, was expected to know the Koran, or at least something of it, in the original Arabic. It is, therefore, possible to speak of an Islamic culture, and what scholars of Bagdad did soon became the common property of their confrères at Cordova.

The classic age of Islamic culture, the age of its foundation and formation, was the first hundred and fifty years of the Abbasid caliphate (750–900). During the preceding period of the Umayyads the Moslems had been content to adapt to their own uses the institutions of the conquered peoples. And this was true not only of the political and economic institutions. Mosques were frequently converted churches, or else buildings newly erected in Graeco-Roman style with columns, capitals, and marbles taken from older Christian edifices.

The accession of the Abbasids (750) did not at once usher in a period of originality. Islamic culture was and is an essentially borrowed and adapted culture. But when the capital of the Moslem world was moved to Bagdad, it was exposed to the influence of an ancient and richly variegated civilization.

Moslem cities came to resemble those of the old Roman Empire and were in striking contrast to the small urban communities in contemporary western Europe. Bagdad, as early as the reign of the Caliph Harun al-Rashid (785–809), was a fabulously prosperous city with many public buildings, markets, residences, baths, and hospitals. So also was distant Cordova in Spain. Under the Abbasids, therefore, Moslem savants found themselves in an intellectual atmosphere which was many-sided and already thousands of years old. And, just as the Mohammedan world was composed of diverse nationalities, so Islamic culture was produced by the amalgamation of various component elements. The particular genius of the Mohammedan scholars was their ability to organize the achievements of others into a harmonious system of their own.

This composite Moslem culture was derived principally from three sources: the Greek, or rather the Hellenistic; the Hindu; and the Persian. The Hellenistic heritage was philosophical and scientific rather than literary or artistic. Classical Greek literature and art were too closely bound up with the polytheism of the old pagan Greek religion to appeal to the severely monotheistic Mohammedans. On the other hand, the writings of the great Greek philosophers, especially Aristotle, had been preserved and studied by the Monophysite Christians of Syria and the Nestorians in Persia, both of whom were in close touch with their Mohammedan conquerors. Of primary importance was the work of translation, and this, too, was often accomplished by Christian or Jewish scholars, or recent converts, who knew Greek and Syriac as well as Arabic, and who passed it on to the Islamic world. The patronage of the caliphs in the diffusion of knowledge was also extremely important. Mamun the Great (813–833) went so far as to found at Bagdad a "House of Wisdom" with a library and observatory—in short a university which proved to be the model for similar schools of higher learning elsewhere.

Greek mathematics and medicine especially interested the Moslems who devoted their attention to Euclid, Galen and Hippocrates, Ptolemy and Archimedes, in addition to Aristotle. But an especially significant mathematical contribution of the Moslems came from India. Thence, sometime before the end of the eighth century, was brought the principle of decimal numeration and of computation with the cipher (0). This the Europeans later named Algorismus after al-Khwarizmi, the Persian mathematician in whose works the system was developed. The same author also composed an important treatise on algebra.

From Persia, which was the home of a series of ancient civilizations, the Arabs gained medical lore that added considerably to the Greek systems of Galen and Hippocrates. Moreover, Persian literary forms influenced contemporary Moslem literature, especially such famous tales as those included in the *Arabian Nights.* In Persia, too, was produced such famous poetry as that of the *Rubaiyat* of Omar Khayyam (*d.* 1123).

Moslem art was also an ingenious amalgam of earlier and varied forms found or developed in different parts of the Mohammedan world. Byzantine, Persian, Egyptian, even Visigothic elements can be discerned in Moslem building and decoration. In time all these diverse features became common Moslem property and Moslem art became a distinctive creation in its own right. Multicolored decoration, geometric design later known as arabesque, "horseshoe" arch, ample cupola, and colonnaded halls can be found throughout the length and breadth of the Islamic world. Two famous structures in Europe might be mentioned here as examples: the mosque of Cordova, and the palace of the Alhambra at Granada.

Moslem civilization which developed in the ninth and tenth centuries as an appropriation or fusion of the higher and more ancient cultures of Greece, Mesopotamia, and India began in the eleventh century to display considerable originality of its own. This took the form at first of a notable clarification of the diverse material which had been assimilated. Then, especially in mathematics, medicine, and astronomy, Moslem scholars surpassed their ancient masters. Avicenna (Ibn-Sina, 980–1037) was not only the greatest of the Moslem philosophers, but an accomplished medical scholar as well. Omar Khayyam (*d.* 1123) was an astronomer as well as a poet. Al-Farabi (*d.* 950) discussed the theory of measured music. Others, whom even a brief treatment should mention, were al-Razi (865–925), composer of a famous treatise on small-pox, and al-Biruni (973–1048), a general scientist. The fact that most of these men came from the region of the Oxus, where the Mohammedanism of Persia touched the civilization of India, illustrates the cosmopolitan character of Mohammedan culture.

In medicine, Islam contributed most to pharmaceutical knowledge. Although in surgery there was some slight advance, it was hampered by a slavish devotion to the authority of Galen and by religious opposition to dissection. The persistence of ancient superstitions with regard to the transmutation of metal, made "alchemists," rather than real scientists, of most Moslem students of chemistry and medicine. But superstition did not prevent treatises on animals, trees, dyes, glass, and miscellaneous subjects.

In the field of astronomy, the names of many stars and such terms as zenith and nadir illustrate the remarkable observations and discoveries of Moslems. These were all based on Ptolemy's conception of a geocentric universe. As in chemistry, so in astronomy, the ancient lore of Mesopotamia survived in the belief that heavenly bodies exercise a determining influence over earthly events. As a consequence Moslem astronomers were also astrologers.

The wide extent of Moslem commerce naturally fostered a special interest in geography and navigation. And in these fields Mohammedans made significant practical contributions. One of the most famous medieval geographers, the Moslem Idrisi, resided at the court of King Roger II of Sicily in the twelfth century. And Moslem trade with the Middle and Far East brought to Europe useful new knowledge from China, and such things as fireworks, paper, and block printing.

Inspired partly by the breadth and diversity of the knowledge opened to them, and partly by the Greek, especially the Aristotelian, philosophical tradition, certain Moslem scholars attempted with considerable ingenuity to embrace and coördinate all human knowledge in one great synthesis. Philosophy to men like Avicenna was not merely metaphysics. Physics, astronomy, cosmology, theology, indeed all knowledge, must be reconciled to and combined with metaphysics. Such was the all embracing encyclopedic ideal of men like al-Kindi, al-Farabi, and especially Avicenna. The reception of Aristotelian philosophy by the Mohammedans raised those same problems of science and faith which were later to trouble the Christian world. Aristotle was hardly compatible with orthodox Moham-

Moslem architecture in Spain. Interior of the Mosque at Cordova. Eighth and ninth centuries.

Courtesy Anderson Art Reference Bureau

medanism. In the main, the philosophy of the Moslem scholar remained apart from the faith of the orthodox religious teacher. Yet Moslem rationalism persisted and exercised no small influence, as we shall later see, on the European scholasticism of the twelfth and thirteenth centuries.

By the eleventh century Moslem culture was formed. Although its debt to past civilization was enormous, it possessed a brilliance and a synthetic originality which insured it an important place in the history of man's material and intellectual progress. That Mohammedan civilization of the ninth, tenth, and early eleventh centuries, in its material aspect at least, was in advance of feudal Europe's is obvious. Early in the twelfth century Christian scholars of western Europe, making contact with Moslem centers of learning, especially in Spain and Sicily, began through translations to acquaint their fellows at home with Arabic learning, and to stimulate a veritable intellectual renaissance. But before we can understand this notable development, we must consider what western Europe had accomplished by the middle of the eleventh century with its own resources.

Byzantine cloisonné enamel on gold of the twelfth century or later. St. John the Evangelist

Courtesy Metropolitan Museum of Art, New York; gift of the estate of Mrs. Otto H. Kahn, 1952

SELECT SUPPLEMENTARY READINGS FOR PART II

General. Two standard works of reference for the entire period from the fall of Rome to 1500 are the *Cambridge Medieval History*, 8 vols. (1911–1936), and the *Cambridge Economic History of Europe*, 3 vols. (1941, 1952, 1961). See also C. W. Previté-Orton, *The Shorter Cambridge Medieval History*, 2 vols. (1952); S. Baron, *A Social and Religious History of the Jews*. vols. III–V (1957–1958). An important guide for further study is L. J. Paetow, *Guide to the Study of Medieval History* (2nd ed., 1931); J. B. Morall, *Political Thought in Medieval Times* (1958); W. Ullmann, *Principles of Government and Politics in the Middle Ages* (1961). L. Bernard and T. B. Hodges, *Readings in European History* (1958) is designed to accompany this volume.

Particularly relevant to the period covered in Part II are: W. C. Bark, *Origins of the Medieval World* (1958); C. D. Burns, *The First Europe* (1947); C. Dawson, *The Making of Europe* (1932); M. Deanesly, *A History of Early Medieval Europe, 476–911* (1956); E. S. Duckett, *The Gateway to the Middle Ages* (1938). H. St. L. B. Moss, *The Birth of the Middle Ages, 395–814* (1935); A. Jones, *The Later Roman Empire, 284–682*, 3 vols. (1964); R. E. Sullivan, *Heirs of the Roman Empire* (1960). J. M. Wallace-Hadrill, *The Barbarian West, 400–1000* (1952). A discussion of some of the problems of the interpretation of this period can be found in A. F. Havighurst, *The Pirenne Thesis* (1958).

Chapter 5. R. M. Haywood, *The Myth of Rome's Fall* (1958); J. B. Bury, *History of the Later Roman Empire*, 2 vols (1923); S. Dill, *Roman Society in the Last Century of the Empire* (1910); S. Katz, *The Decline of Rome and the Rise of Medieval Europe* (1955); F. Lot, *The End of the Ancient World* (new ed., 1961). For the cultural life of the later Empire, see W. L. MacDonald, *Early Christian and Byzantine Architecture* (1962); C. R. Morey, *Christian Art* (1958) and *Medieval Art* (1932); E. K. Rand, *The Founders of the Middle Ages* (1928); H. O. Taylor, *The Classical Heritage of the Middle Ages* (1911), also newly edited by K. M. Setton, *The Emergence of Christian Culture in the West* (1961).

Chapter 6. J. B. Bury, *The Invasion of Europe by the Barbarians* (1928); S. Dill *Roman Society in Gaul in the Merovingian Age* (1926); A. Dopsch, *The Economic and Social Foundations of European Civilization* (1937); C. Gordon, *The Age of Attila* (1960).

***Chapter* 7.** In addition to J. B. Bury, *Later Roman Empire*, already mentioned, N. H. Baynes, *The Byzantine Empire* (1926); N. H. Baynes and H. St. L. B. Moss, *Byzantium* (1948); C. Diehl, *Byzantium: Greatness and Decline* (1956); G. Ostrogorsky, *History of the Byzantine State* (1957); G. Downey, *Constantinople* (1960); J. Hussey, *The Byzantine World* (1957); S. Runciman, *Byzantine Civilization* (1933); A. A. Vasiliev, *History of the Byzantine Empire*, 2 vols. (1928).

***Chapter* 8.** For ecclesiastical history in general: A. F. Flick, *The Rise of the Medieval Church* (1909); P. Hughes, *A History of the Church*, vol. II (1935); H. Daniel-Rops, *The Church in the Dark Ages* (1959); K. S. Latourette, *A History of the Expansion of Christianity, vol. II* (1938); H. K. Mann, *The Lives of the Popes in the Middle Ages*, 18 vols. (1906–1932).

On the rise of monasticism: Dom J. Chapman, *St. Benedict and the Sixth Century* (1929); Dom David Knowles, *The Monastic Order in England* (1940); J. McCann, *St. Benedict* (1958); L. J. Daly, S.J., *Benedictine Monasticism* (1965). For intellectual developments, in addition to the citations for chapters 5 and 7: H. M. Barrett, *Boethius* (1940); E. S. Duckett, *Anglo-Saxon Saints and Scholars* (1947); M. Laistner, *Thought and Letters in Western Europe, 500–900* (1957). On the relation of religion to medieval civilization: C. Dawson, *Religion and the Rise of Western Culture* (1958).

***Chapter* 9.** Tor Andrae, *Muhammad, the Man and His Faith* (1956); T. W. Arnold and A. Guillaume, *The Legacy of Islam* (1931); R. V. C. Bodley, *The Messenger: the Life of Mohammed* (1946); E. Dermenghem, *Muhammad and the Islamic Tradition* (1957); H. A. R. Gibb, *Mohammedanism* (1949); G. E. von Grunebaum, *Medieval Islam* (1946); P. K. Hitti, *History of the Arabs* (1946), and *The Arabs: a Short History* (1956); A. Jeffery, *Islam: Muhammad and His Religion* (1958); B. Lewis, *The Arabs in History* (1950); A. Guillaume, *Islam* (1954).

Hispano-Moorish ivory box, tenth century.

Courtesy Hispanic Society of America, New York

Carolingian art. The figure of St. Mark from an illuminated manuscript of the Gospels produced at Reims at the time of Archbishop Hincmar, 845–882.

Courtesy Pierpont Morgan Library, New York

PART III

THE EARLY MIDDLE AGE IN THE NORTHWARD PROCESS OF

Norman architecture in England. Peterborough Cathedral. Nave with Norman arches. Flat, pointed wooden ceiling of the twelfth century.

Courtesy British Information Services, New York

From Charlemagne to Hildebrand

WEST AND THE EUROPEANIZATION

Medieval warfare. A thirteenth century French manuscript presented by the pope to the shah of Persia in the seventeenth century and annotated at his direction.
Courtesy Pierpont Morgan Library, New York

"MIDDLE AGES" is a term invented in modern times to describe the thousand years of European history from the break-up of the Roman Empire in the fifth century to the so-called renaissance of classical Roman culture in the fifteenth century. Nobody who lived in those thousand years imagined he was living in any "middle age." And certainly those ten centuries witnessed more of continuity than of change in the development and expansion of European and Western civilization.

True, the thousand years had certain peculiar features which may justify us in applying to them a special label, and for this purpose the conventional label of "Middle Ages" will do as well as any. Moreover, in order to distinguish various stages of development during the period, we may conveniently divide it into three parts: (1) an "Early Middle Age," from the seventh to the eleventh century; (2) a "Middle Age proper," from the eleventh to the thirteenth century; and (3) a "Late Middle Age," of the fourteenth and fifteenth centuries.

The immediately ensuing chapters treat of the Early Middle Age, which is often called the "Dark Age." Though doubtless the sun shone as brightly then as in any other age, it was a time when European civilization suffered a series of grave set-backs and something of an eclipse.

While Germanic tribes are gradually emerging from their earlier barbarism, they fall far short of attaining the settled life and rich culture of the old Roman Empire. For a time in the eighth and early ninth centuries, a line of Frankish rulers—the Carolingian—makes valiant efforts, in coöperation with the papacy, to restore order in the West; and under Charlemagne, the greatest of the line, a new empire is constructed, embracing not only Gaul and northern Italy but also the Netherlands and Germany, and fostering throughout its territories a revival of learning and a spread of Christianity. But this promising advance is halted by fresh incursions of fierce Saracens from the south, of barbarous Slavs, Bulgars, and Magyars from the east, and of piratical Scandinavians from the north. Again commerce declines, disorder increases, and ordinary government collapses.

To meet the most pressing needs of the hour—especially the assurance of local security and the production of a minimum food supply—feudalism appears and becomes characteristic of medieval society. To this feudalism and its agricultural support we shall devote special attention.

In the late tenth century, and during the eleventh, matters slowly mend, thanks in no small degree to ecclesiastical activity. Originally inspired by a new monastic movement, centering at Cluny, and eventually headed by one of the greatest medieval popes (Hildebrand, or Gregory VII), the Church manfully opposes the disintegrating and demoralizing tendencies of the age. Simultaneously, ardent missionaries spread Christianity and church influence northward over Scandinavia and eastward among the Slavic peoples. The European continent as a whole is becoming Christian.

Then, too, wherever the Church is established, it contributes to the building up of European states, as yet basically feudal, but already embryonically national. In this connection we shall note the development of France under Capetians, of Germany under a newly founded western "Roman Empire," of England and southern Italy under Norman kings, and of other emerging Christian kingdoms for Scandinavians, Czechs, Poles, Magyars, and Russians. We shall likewise refer to the beginnings of Christian reconquest of Spain from its Moslem invaders.

Finally, we must stress that the Early Middle Age—the so-called "Dark Age" of intellectual and cultural eclipse—is temporary and limited. It is peculiar to western and central Europe. There is no comparable slump in the continuing Byzantine Empire of southeastern Europe, and there is an extraordinary brilliance of Moslem culture from Syria and Persia around northern Africa into Spain. From the Moslems and from Byzantium, as well as from increasing internal stability and education, Europe will presently derive impetus for a real flowering of its own Western civilization in the succeeding Middle Age of the twelfth and thirteenth centuries.

St. Michael's Church, Fulda, one of the oldest in Germany, c. 800.

Courtesy German Tourist Information Office, New York

Test

CHAPTER 10

Rise and Disintegration of the Frankish Empire

AND NEW BARBARIAN INVASIONS OF THE NINTH CENTURY

A. *The Frankish State: Transition from Merovingian to Carolingian Rule*

The consolidation and expansion of the Frankish kingdom under the Merovingian chieftain, Clovis (*d.* 511),[1] was followed by a period of confusion. The kingdom was soon divided into two large units: Austrasia, comprising the Rhine country and lands west of it; and Neustria, the "newest" territory, lying along the Seine. Further subdivisions resulted from the chronic weakness of the monarchy and the Frankish practice of dividing the kingdom, as though it were a private estate, at the death of a ruler. The Merovingian family degenerated, and the seventh-century descendants of a great house have been styled the do-nothing kings (*rois fainéants*). As a consequence, political authority was exercised by the king's principal subordinate, the mayor of the palace (*major domus*). In 687, Pepin, the second of the name and mayor of the palace in Austrasia, defeated the Neustrian mayor in a battle which again brought together the two halves of the Frankish kingdom. Thereafter, the descendants of Pepin continued to occupy the position of mayor and, although they did not as yet possess the royal title, were actually a ruling dynasty.

Two of the most famous of the mayors were Charles Martel (714–741), whose defeat of the Moslems at Tours (732) we have already noted, and Pepin III "the Short" (741–768). Pepin was a ruler whose capabilities were second only to those of his illustrious son and successor, Charlemagne. Lingering separatist tendencies were suppressed. Frisia and all Septimania on the Mediterranean were added to the kingdom, the latter removing from Moslem control the commercially important coastal region west of the Rhone and bringing Frankish power to the Pyrenees. Following in the footsteps of Charles Martel, Pepin supported the organizing activities of the church and the efforts of St. Boniface, a monk who was a product of the religious and cultural revival in Saxon England, together with other missionaries, to convert the Germans beyond the Rhine. Equally significant were his relations with the papacy.

The success of the Franks in reëstablishing political order, in defeating the Mohammedans, and in spreading the Christian faith had attracted the attention of the papacy. The Lombards, who had caused trouble for the popes ever since the time of Gregory the Great, had acquired renewed vigor in Italy. At times even Rome was threatened. Normally such a situation would have induced the pope to seek the assistance of the Byzantine Emperor. But the support given the iconoclasts by Emperor Leo III had accentuated the estrangement between Rome and Constantinople.[2] In 739 the pope had sent messengers to Charles Martel; and although Charles had been

[1] See above, pp. 69–70.

[2] See above, p. 90, and below, p. 150.

unable to render any assistance, a new development in papal relations with the Franks was imminent.

It was doubtless this friendly atmosphere which prompted certain Frankish prelates to consult Pope Zacharias on the state of the monarchy. The pope handed down a judgment that he who possessed actual authority deserved the title of king. Accordingly, in 751 an assembly of Frankish chieftains acclaimed the Mayor of the Palace, Pepin III, as King, whereupon he was solemnly anointed by St. Boniface and other bishops as King Pepin I. Thus, with papal sanction, the now decadent Merovingian dynasty was set aside, and succeeded by the Carolingian.

Three years later Pope Stephen II moved one step farther in the orientation of papal policy toward the Franks. The Lombard King Aistulf occupied the exarchate and the duchy of Spoleto and, in recognition of his sovereignty, demanded tribute from Rome. The Pope, to make sure of Frankish assistance, actually journeyed across the Alps to Aachen, where he personally anointed King Pepin and threatened with excommunication all who resisted his lawful authority. His reward came when in two expeditions (754, 756) Pepin decisively defeated the Lombards and restored the territory of the exarchate, not to the emperor at Constantinople but to the pope. Although the papal lands along the west coast of Italy (the Patrimony of St. Peter) were already considerable, Pepin's "donation" is sometimes regarded as the foundation of the papal states.

This whole episode of Franco-Papal cooperation is highly significant and amounted almost to an alliance, and Italy became an area of Frankish activity.[1]

B. Charlemagne and His Administration

Pepin's son and successor, known to history as Charlemagne or Charles the Great, was well endowed physically and mentally with qualities which make a successful ruler. His secretary, Einhard, has left a vivid picture of this extraordinary man. According to Einhard, Charlemagne was over six feet tall with limbs in proportion. Like most men of his day he was fond of exercise and especially of hunting. Though not abstemious in food and drink, he abhorred drunkenness. Under the influence of the churchmen at the royal court Charlemagne, despite a flexible attitude toward his own matrimonial affairs, developed a deep piety and a sense of the religious purpose of government. Indeed, there was a marked Old Testament flavor about the King's administration. He delighted in being called "David," modeled his regime after the ancient Hebrew kings', and regarded himself as a latter-day moral and religious leader of a chosen people. He felt an obligation not only to protect the church, but to promote a healthy moral and religious life within his realm and to spread the faith to those outside.

Charlemagne was not a genius, nor given to the elaboration of far-sighted plans. But he was persistent in the face of obstacles and setbacks. Above all, he was a man of abundant energy, who allowed no detail of administration to escape him. His capitularies, as the royal decrees are designated, reveal a comprehensive grasp of the realities of the world in which he moved.

Like his predecessors, Martel and Pepin, Charlemagne was a warrior whose conquests further expanded the Frankish dominions. The Lombard power he ended once and for all by decisively defeating King Desiderius and then assuming the Lombard crown himself. He extended his dominion southward, occasionally intervened in Spoleto and Benevento and, as a matter of course, regarded himself as overlord of Rome and the papal states. The longest of his campaigns was with the pagan Saxons who inhabited the territory lying roughly between the lower Rhine and the Weser. Although all of Charlemagne's campaigns were in a sense "holy" wars, and priests always accompanied the armies, the Saxon War was especially so because it signified the conversion—albeit forcible—of an entire people. Saxon opposition to both conquest and conversion was so stubborn that it required 33 years to overcome. But eventually, young

[1] At about this time there appeared a charter known as the *Donation of Constantine*, later shown to be a forgery. By it the Emperor Constantine had supposedly bestowed Rome and Italy on Pope Sylvester I.

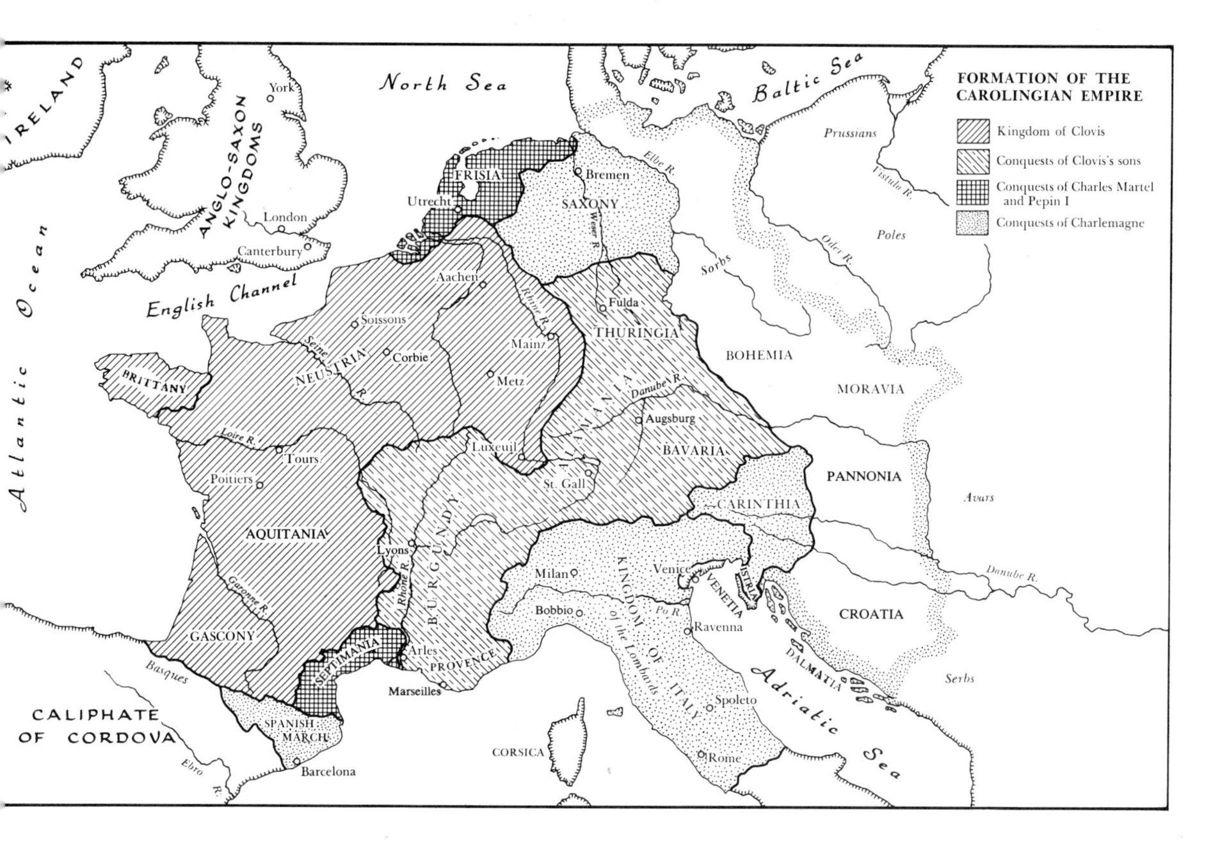

Saxon men were educated for the priesthood, a bishopric was created at Bremen, and monasteries soon flourished in the land. Moreover, the inclusion of Saxony in the Frankish empire prevented the emergence of a non-Frankish Germany and assured to the future German nation the influence of Carolingian culture.

Charlemagne likewise subdued Slavic tribes in the region of the Elbe river and commenced the *drang nach osten,* or pressure eastward, which was to become a characteristic feature of later German policy. He was equally successful in south-central Germany. Bavaria, hitherto dubiously loyal, was forced again into obedience. The Avars, who from their settlements had menaced both Frankish and Byzantine lands, were crushingly defeated. The Carolingian frontier, therefore, reached from Saxony to the upper Adriatic and included Carinthia along with Bavaria and Thuringia. Beyond lay a series of loosely organized Slavic states—Croatia, Pannonia, Moravia, Bohemia, and the northern Slavic and Baltic peoples. These paid tribute and for the most part were to become Marches (border provinces) in later times. In the west the effective work of his predecessors enabled Charlemagne to push southward and to form a march south of the Pyrenees in Spain.

In governing this greatly enlarged domain, Charlemagne followed the pattern set by previous rulers and added certain important innovations made necessary by contemporary conditions. The principal agents of administration were dukes and counts appointed to govern various divisions of the domain, and margraves (*Markgrafen,* counts of the march) who were given special powers over frontier provinces. Charlemagne also elaborated a system whereby the activities of each count could be supervised. Every district of the realm was periodically visited by two men, usually a bishop and a layman, who investigated each county, heard the grievances of any persons, and generally checked upon all the affairs of the district. Since these agents were sent from the King's entourage, they were called *missi dominici.* All matters religious and secular came under their supervision and their own actions were governed by detailed instructions from the King.

Charlemagne's capacity for practical organization and his desire to promote a healthy moral and religious tone can also be noticed in his efforts to regulate economic life. Certain capitularies (or decrees), following papal or conciliar precepts, dealt with money-lending and usury. Others were concerned with weights and measures and food prices. Slavery still existed, but the slave trade was restricted. Metal currency was scarce and the standard coin of the day, the *denarius*, was silver. But Charlemagne insisted on the exclusive right of the palace mint to issue coins or to authorize their issue.

Since the decline of trade and city life which had commenced in the later Roman period continued unabated, the organization of the great landed estates was of first importance, for these provided in last analysis the stable income and economic basis of political power whether of king or of magnates. To the stewards of his own private estates, which he expected to be always ready for his personal use, Charlemagne issued detailed instructions, and he expected his magnates to exercise comparable care and to keep accurate accounts. Moreover, a glance at the King's directive on his farms, the capitulary "On Villas," with its minute regulations on such matters as tenants, cattle, fowl, agricultural produce, cloth-making, forests, mines, and forges, reveals not only a concern for the details of farm administration, but also the fact that a Carolingian *villa* was something more than an agricultural institution. It was, in fact, a center of local industry.

Important as were the great domains of the Carolingian kingdom, two factors must be emphasized further. First, every large domain or *villa* included, in addition to the reserve land cultivated for the landlord, a considerable and often widely scattered collection of tenant farms. Second, it seems clear that there existed throughout the Carolingian period a large number of small privately owned farms. Thus continued the trend toward smaller individualized exploitation which was to become a feature of medieval agriculture.

The administrative procedures devised by Charlemagne seem impressive, and he was doubtless a more capable administrator than most rulers of his time. But directives are not necessarily accomplishments. The decentralizing tendencies of the day were slowed, but not halted. In the gradual transformation of Europe from the cosmopolitan, urban, and unified society of the Roman Empire to the congeries of feudal monarchies of the Middle Ages, the Carolingian kingdom represents a brief pause, a significant but temporary recovery.

That the church should play a major role in Carolingian administration was characteristic of the age. According to current practice bishops were invested with considerable governmental authority and many bishoprics and abbeys were conceded grants of immunity from the jurisdiction of the local count. Thus bishops and abbots were in a position analogous to that of secular magnates.

It was equally natural that the King should make little distinction between the secular and ecclesiastical administrations and should regard religious affairs as his responsibility. Episcopal elections often followed the King's wishes. The papal states in Italy were governed by the pope, but under the King's suzerainty. Indeed, somewhat more than half of the Carolingian capitularies dealt with ecclesiastical matters. To all intents and purposes, therefore, Charlemagne was as much the head of the western church as the emperor at Constantinople was of the eastern. And since, in contemporary theory, church and government were regarded as but supplementary branches of a single society, the position of Charlemagne took on a quasi-religious aspect. He was "God's vicar," the "leader and guide of all Christians."

C. Coronation of Charlemagne as "Roman Emperor"

The politico-religious form of society headed by Charlemagne, despite his generally beneficent attitude and his many excellent reforms, could not be entirely acceptable to the papacy. The situation was not without serious dangers for the future freedom of the church.[1] Unfortunately, the

[1] Even under Charlemagne there were serious problems. In 787 the second Council of Nicaea had condemned the iconoclasts in the Byzantine

pope was between two fires. The Byzantine emperor had removed certain Italian bishops from papal jurisdiction. Now the Franks, on whom the papacy had come to rely, were in a too commanding position. To break with both would have meant complete isolation. The church in the eighth century relied on the support of the secular power, and, so great was the force of the Roman imperial tradition, that it still conceived of secular power as normally and properly the Roman Empire. Prayers for the Roman emperor had long been included in the Roman liturgy. These things must be considered if we are to understand what was perhaps the most spectacular event of Charlemagne's life, his coronation as Roman Emperor by the pope.

In the year 800 Charlemagne celebrated Christmas at Rome. At the solemn Mass, Pope Leo III stepped down from the altar, placed a crown on the Frankish King's head, and proclaimed him Emperor. The interpretation of this event has occasioned innumerable controversies among historians from that day to this. Particularly in the thirteenth century the adherents of pope and emperor discovered all sorts of implications of papal or imperial supremacy, of which Charlemagne and Leo probably never dreamed. The coronation acquired a religious and symbolic value in the later history of what came to be known as the Holy Roman Empire.

As far as Charlemagne's reign is concerned, the coronation altered nothing. He continued to govern the church and to claim suzerainty over Rome as before. As a matter of fact, the interminable arguments over the bearing of the coronation of the year 800 on the relations between emperor and pope have tended to obscure what was really of central importance about it. Actually it consummated a revolution whereby the political suzerainty of the Byzantine "Roman" Empire of the east over the pope or over western Europe was irrevocably repudiated. To Byzantium the coronation was sheer usurpation, and it was only after Charlemagne intervened in Venice that a Byzantine government, hard pressed by eastern invaders, reluctantly admitted the existence of a rival "empire" in the west. Thus Charlemagne's coronation marked the last step in the political separation of Rome and Constantinople.

D. Emergence of Feudal Kingdoms

It cannot be overemphasized that calling Charlemagne's state a "Roman Empire" obscured its real character. The imperial title and other Roman designations gave only an appearance of the sovereignty that had been exercised by the ancient Roman government. In reality, Charlemagne's Empire was a semi-feudal kingdom held together by the genius and energy of one man. The forces of decentralization which he had temporarily stayed proved too powerful for his successors. In addition, the natural tendency of the Frankish kingdom to break up into smaller units was hastened by a wave of invasions far more devastating than those of the fifth century.

An immediate cause of disintegration was the Frankish practice of dividing the royal domains among the sons of the ruler, a practice which had never been abandoned, even by Charlemagne. Since magnates ordinarily followed suit, each major division of the realm was further subdivided.

Royal power was also weakened by the lapse of those checks which Charlemagne had instituted, such as the *missi* and the practice of regular supervision. As a consequence, within each section of the original Empire, the counts, bishops, and other local magnates were practically unhampered in their natural propensity to pursue independent policies. Other developments helped to crystallize this tendency toward local autonomy into a sort of system. Counts came to be succeeded in office by their sons. Thus the great administrative offices became hereditary, and, as the restraints were lessened, innumerable petty dynasties emerged. As the power of the magnates became greater, each Carolingian king or

church and upheld traditional veneration of saints and proper use of images. In 794 Charlemagne summoned a council of bishops at Frankfurt, which questioned the decision of Nicaea. Frankish churchmen added to the Nicene Creed: "The Holy Ghost proceeds from the Father [and the Son]." The pope was embarrassed, and the alteration in the creed was seriously opposed in the east.

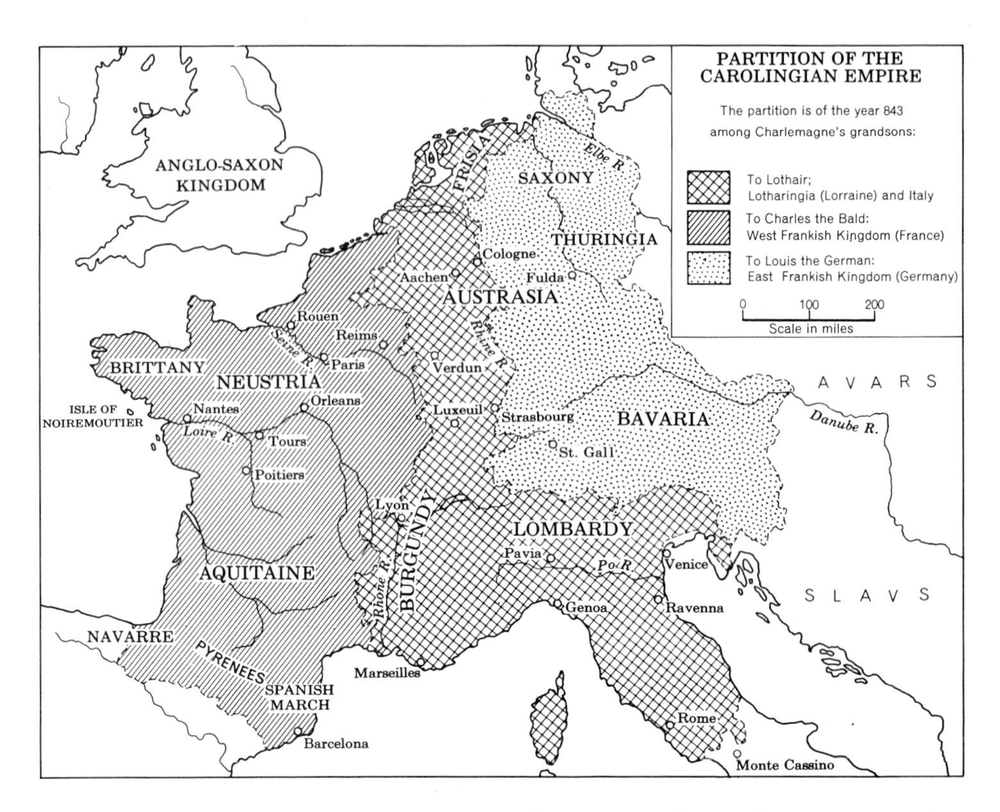

"emperor," in order to win support, was constrained to purchase it, in the only way possible, by grants of land. But this process diminished the royal estates and revenues which had already been curtailed by the divisions. The diminution of the Carolingian estates in relation to the lands of the magnates is a major factor in the decline of the Empire.

Although Charlemagne, following the Frankish custom, had provided for the division of his Empire, only one son, Louis, survived. Known as Louis the Pious (814–840), he failed to maintain his father's system. Norse raids, frontier wars, and local rebellions punctuated his troubled reign. Strongly influenced by clerical opinion regarding the indivisibility of the Empire, Louis arranged a division which conceded the imperial title and a position of superiority to his eldest son; but after his death his already rebellious sons transferred their quarrels to each other. Louis, known as the German, because he had been given Bavaria and other regions east of the Rhine, joined with Charles the Bald against Lothair. To Lothair, the oldest of the three, had been entrusted Italy and the imperial crown and, by implication, a superior authority. In 842 Louis and Charles solemnized their pact by oaths which each had written in the language prevalent in the territories of the other. Historically these "Strasbourg Oaths" are important as early written examples of the *lingua romana* and the *lingua teudesca*—Romance and Germanic languages. In the following year (843), after Charles and Louis had defeated Lothair, an important political settlement was reached in the treaty of Verdun, which became the foundation of all later divisions. Three kingdoms were formed. Charles the Bald governed the land west of an irregular line running from the Scheldt to the Rhone and the Mediterranean. Louis the German reigned over the territory east of the Rhine, exclusive of Frisia. Lothair was left the imperial title and a middle kingdom stretching from the North Sea to the southern boundary of the papal states.

The eastern and western kingdoms of Louis and Charles were relatively homogeneous and proved comparatively stable. As the kingdoms of the East and West Franks, respectively, they became the nuclei of the later feudal kingdoms of Germany and France. Although the middle kingdom included the main lines of communication between Italy and northern Europe, its boundaries were vulnerable and it lasted only a short time in its original form. Lothair died in 855 and, according to Frankish tradition, his middle kingdom was divided among his three sons whose individual fortunes we cannot follow here. One of them, however—Lothair II—had a northern section which thereafter was called *Lotharii regnum* and hence Lotharingia or Lorraine. On Lothair II's death, the weakness of his kingdom proved an irresistible source of temptation to Charles the Bald and Louis the German, who appropriated and partitioned it by the Treaty of Mersen (870). Henceforth a territory of varying boundaries, known as Lorraine, was to be disputed between the eastern and western kingdoms, that is, between Germany and France. The treaty of Mersen also provided a boundary which made these two countries contiguous. So they have remained until now.

Meanwhile, the southern portion of the original middle kingdom was divided into a kingdom of Italy, whose history was indescribably turbulent, and the kingdoms of Upper and Lower Burgundy (Provence) in the Rhône valley.[1] The imperial title passed from one branch of the Carolingian family to another, but the office had little meaning. Charles the Bald held it for two years, 875–877. In 884 the magnates chose Charles the Fat, son of Louis the German, and then in 887 deposed him. He died in 888.

To all intents and purposes the year 888 marks the end of the Carolingian Empire. The political future lay with the more stable of the states then existing, particularly with the eastern and western kingdoms—Germany and France. For many years the strongest of the local counts and dukes within these kingdoms provided such protection and stability as remained. It was Count Odo of Paris who saved his city from one of the worst Norse raids (885–886). For this exploit Charles the Fat made him duke of the Franks, and the grateful magnates later elected him King of the West Franks (888). Thereafter for a century his successors alternated with the later Carolingians as kings of the West Franks, or of "France." Finally, in 987, following the death of the last Carolingian, a descendant of Odo—Hugh Capet—was elected and started the new French dynasty which bears his name.

In the East Frankish kingdom of Germany, the Carolingian line died out earlier, and in 918 the election of Henry the Fowler commenced the Saxon dynasty there. The confused history of Italy and the Burgundian kingdoms during the ninth and tenth centuries need not trouble us. Their ultimate inclusion in the kingdom of Germany will be noted in a later chapter.

E. Education and Culture under Charlemagne and His Successors

Among the concerns of Charlemagne was an anxiety to improve the schooling and general cultural conditions in his dominions, especially among the clergy. There was great need of improvement, for the cultural and educational level of West Christian Europe in the eighth century was far below that of the Byzantine Empire or of the Moslem world. In Gaul, the real center of the Carolingian Empire, the old Roman schools had completely disappeared, and surviving institutions for training the clergy were few and of inferior grade. To help him in his educational task, Charlemagne assembled at his court at Aachen such scholars as he could obtain from other Christian regions of the West, notably Italy, Spain, and England, where something of the old Graeco-Roman tradition of scholarship had survived.

The most distinguished of these scholars, and the Emperor's trusted confidant on many matters, was Alcuin of York (730–804). Alcuin was a product of that flowering of culture in Saxon England which had profited from both Irish and Roman traditions. As a boy he had known the reputation of Bede, and had received his education

[1] A small kingdom of Navarre in southwestern France, reaching across the Pyrenees into northern Spain, was a sixth section of the original Carolingian Empire.

and then had taught at a cathedral school at York founded by one of Bede's pupils. In 781, on his return from a journey to Rome, Alcuin met Charlemagne, who prevailed upon him to take up his residence at the Frankish court. There, and later as Abbot of Tours, he carried on his invaluable work as supervisor and as teacher. Thus the Carolingian intellectual revival was, to a large extent, an outgrowth of previous Anglo-Saxon scholarship.

Charlemagne appreciated that a solid intellectual foundation was necessary if his church reforms were to succeed. He strove to provide enlarged facilities for education. Under the immediate auspices of leading prelates of the Empire—bishops and abbots—many of whom were trained by Alcuin or associated with him, two types of schools were fostered. These were the cathedral schools and the monastic schools. Both were concerned with the religious education of the clergy, but their aims were not identical. The cathedral schools were more practically motivated because they were principally engaged in the training of young men for the clergy. In them, too, under Alcuin's direction, there was a certain amount of specialization. Some, for example, specialized in music, and uniformity of ritual and chant throughout the realm was expected.

Monastic schools were likewise concerned with the religious training of young men, but by reason of their more detached position they were often centers of higher learning. In writing rooms attached to them were copied and preserved the texts of both secular and ecclesiastical authors which any advanced scholar would find indispensable. The importance of the work of the Carolingian monastic copyists is illustrated by the fact that the great majority of the classical texts which have come down to our day date from the Carolingian era. And to the same copyists we owe a beautifully executed form of lettering known as the Carolingian minuscule (lower case letter).[1]

As a kind of crown to his educational reforms, Charlemagne instituted, or rather reorganized, a royal palace school at Aachen for the training of his own children and those of his relatives and chief magnates. Under his predecessors such a school had existed simply to give the royal children the rudiments of military education. Charlemagne injected into it the intellectual element. Although he himself never learned to write, he could read and understand Latin and knew some Greek, and he was an enthusiastic patron of learning. Accordingly the palace school was a favorite creation of the Emperor, who frequently attended its conferences and enjoyed familiar discourse with the scholars he had assembled. Indeed, aside from the education of a few young persons closely associated with the royal family, the principal function of the palace school was to provide a place for the congregating of learned men.

The Carolingian revival was not productive of many original literary works. Rather it produced a significant, if limited, educational curriculum and preserved the contributions of the past. The principal emphasis in the schools was on grammar and rhetoric. But grammar and rhetoric implied the mastery not only of the classical Latin grammarians, but also of the most prominent of the Latin authors of antiquity. There emerged, especially later in the ninth century, a love of literature and a real humanist spirit, out of which grew a desire not only to learn but to create. And while the first step in composition proved to be conscious imitation of the style and form of ancient writers, this training enabled some to produce works of considerable importance and not a little originality. This was especially true of history and poetry.

A few writers merit attention. We have already mentioned Einhard, author of the *Life of Charlemagne*. Paul the Deacon, after sojourning at Aachen, returned to his native Italy and there wrote a *History of the Lombards*. Abbot Lupus of Ferrières possessed an unusually fine library and became a polished letter writer. Mention should also be made of John Scotus Erigena, a philosopher markedly influenced by Neoplatonic ideas, but withal an original thinker. His *On the Division of Nature* appeared around 865.

[1] Later renaissance humanists admired the Carolingian minuscule and imitated it. Thus it came to be adopted by fifteenth-century printers in Italy and has survived to our own day as "Roman" type.

Carolingian art. A ninth century silver-gilt and jewelled binding for the Gospels.

Courtesy Pierpont Morgan Library, New York

There were several poets of some distinction. Not only did they add to the treasury of medieval religious poetry and hymnology, but they sang of nature and human emotions. Paul the Deacon left two gems, one a description of Lake Como, another a plea to the Emperor to liberate his brother. Alcuin also wrote poetry, although it was in the manner of a classical teacher and more imitative than inspired. Theodulf of Orléans, on the other hand, showed real poetic feeling and skill.

Carolingian art also showed a modest but significant revival and exhibited the same diverse influences that are observable in learning. The Emperor's chapel at Aachen was octagonal and evidently inspired by Justinian's church of San Vitale at Ravenna. Indeed, Pope Hadrian permitted Charlemagne to use marbles taken from Ravenna. Such "round" churches were popular as stone gradually replaced wood in building. Some architects also modified the rectangular form of the Roman basilica by enlarging the apse and sometimes adding chapels. Theodulf of Orleans, who came from formerly Visigothic Spain, built a church at St. Germigny-des-Près which is strikingly reminiscent of the Romano-Visigothic style of his native country. Carolingian illuminated manuscripts show not only strong Byzantine characteristics but also barbarian, and especially Celtic, influences in design. Some bibles or gospelbooks were handsomely bound with ivory-carved, or gold-and-jewel, covers.

Although the Carolingian intellectual revival had its limitations, arising from the ideals of the age and the purposes of the Emperor, it was a big step forward. Because it was one of those occasions in western European history when there was a deliberate reaching back for inspiration to the Graeco-Roman past, it has been called the "Carolingian renaissance." Moreover, it was not as ephemeral as the Carolingian Empire. It is true that Charlemagne's educational system suffered considerable damage from renewed barbarian invasions of the ninth and tenth centuries. But not all was lost. The greater cathedral and monastic foundations at Fulda, Tours, Corbie, St. Gall, Reichenau, Lorsch, Orléans, Reims, Pavia, *etc.*, remained centers from which came later cultural revivals. And it is a tribute to Charlemagne's energy and foresight that such was the case.

As the Carolingian Empire disintegrated, there survived no single center of cultural activity comparable to the palace school of Charlemagne. It was left to local cathedral and monastic schools and to an occasional enterprising local ruler to carry on the tradition. Alfred the Great in England (871–901) proved to be a devoted patron of learning, although his efforts bore fruit in the vernacular Saxon language rather than in Latin. He fostered the development of the *Anglo-Saxon Chronicle* and had certain of the works of Gregory the Great translated. With respect to the vernacular, Saxon England was ahead of the continent. The great heroic epic, *Beowulf*, dates from about the eighth century.

F. Ninth-Century Attacks from South and East: Saracens, Slavs, Bulgars, and Magyars

The principal invaders of the ninth century were Norsemen, Slavs, Bulgars, Magyars, and Saracens. All except the Norsemen attacked from the south or the east, and none of them felt the respect for the institutions of Roman Christendom which had animated the German invaders of the fifth century. Nor was the supremacy of European culture as apparent in the two centuries following Charlemagne's death as it had been in the fifth century. For ninth- and tenth-century Christendom, beleaguered from north and east, was encircled on its southern side by Islamic civilization which, in its material aspects at least, was far superior.

Yet the situation was not hopeless. In the west, as we have seen, strong centers of local resistance often succeeded where central government failed. And in the Byzantine Empire, as a later chapter will explain, there was a significant recovery. More important, Europe, thanks especially to the vitality of the church and the surprisingly durable quality of Roman-German institutions, retained remarkable powers of assimilation. In the end most of the barbarians were civilized.

Western Europe's capacity to assimilate its enemies did not, however, extend to Moslems. For in the Moslems, Europe faced not barbarians but the possessors of a rival civilization which had encircled the southern fringes of Christendom. Their ninth-century depredations were an aftermath of the great conquests of preceding centuries. From Tunisia, Moslems—or "Saracens," as these were now called—expanded across the sea to envelop Sicily and menace southern Italy. In 846 Rome was sacked and the tombs of the apostles profaned, with the result that Pope Leo IV encircled the Vatican palace and St. Peter's with a wall.[1] Montecassino was also ravaged and various Italian and Provençal ports were taken and held for some time. Saracen raids on land reached as far as the Alpine passes. Since Corsica, Sardinia, and the Balearics also fell under Moslem control, European commerce was virtually swept from the western and central Mediterranean for many years.

Slavic raids along the northeastern frontier of the East Frankish kingdom were often a source of considerable danger. But even during the period of decline the Germans occasionally renewed their eastward pressure with some success against primitive Slavic states in Poland, Bohemia, and Moravia. Both Slavs and Germans were greatly affected by the advance of two other peoples, the Bulgars and the Magyars. The former, originally Asiatic kindred of the Huns, had expanded into the Balkan peninsula. At one time they almost captured Constantinople. But the Bulgars were anxious to emulate the civilized ways of their neighbors. The kahn or king assumed the Roman title of tsar (Caesar). Their native speech was gradually transformed into

[1] The area thus enclosed, the "Leonine city," roughly corresponds to the present-day Vatican City.

a predominantly Slavic tongue. Finally, in 871, the Bulgar King Boris I accepted Christianity under Byzantine jurisdiction.

The Magyars, also of Asiatic origin, invaded the Carpathian basin once occupied by the Avars, and conquered Moravia. They destroyed a promising Slavic state centering in Moravia, and separated the Balkan Slavs, the South- or Yugo-Slavs, from their cousins, the western Slavs, in Bohemia, Moravia, and Poland. This proved to be a major disaster for the Slavic peoples, for the division accentuated other cultural differences and undoubtedly contributed to the lack of unity later evident in Slavic history. Meanwhile, the Magyars, who came to be known as Hungarians because of a supposed resemblance to the ancient Huns, terrorized the borders of the East Frankish kingdom and Italy. In their most devastating raids they penetrated as far as Lorraine and Burgundy. Not until their defeat by the German King Otto I in 955 did they settle down to form a stable kingdom. In 1000, under their King Stephen, they accepted Christianity and the spiritual authority of Rome, and opened the way for the entrance of Western civilization into Hungary.

The carved prow of a Viking ship. The Oseberg Ship.

Courtesy Norwegian Information Service, New York

G. Norse Incursions and Settlements

The far northern Scandinavian lands were practically unknown to Carolingian Europe. Their inhabitants, loosely called Danes or Vikings, had only occasionally appeared as raiders. Like the Franks, they were a Teutonic people, but of a distinct speech and culture. The heavily forested Danish peninsula and the rocky soil of Norway and Sweden offered limited facilities for agriculture and turned their naturally rugged and warlike inhabitants to the sea. The deep coves and fiords of Norway formed ideal harbors. In their long double-ended boats manned by warriors who set up their shields along the gunwales as they took the oars or managed the small sails, or in the broader and deeper craft not uncommon in the Northern seas, Norsemen fearlessly ventured across unknown waters. Their skill in navigation, their uncanny knowledge of winds and currents surpassed anything Europe was to see until the compass was developed.

The extent of Norse expansion is amazing. Late in the eighth century Viking attacks were felt on the east coast of England, a land then divided into separate Saxon kingdoms. The raids continued through the ninth century, increasing in size as news got back home of easy successes. Finally, the English King Alfred the Great (871–901), after years of stubborn defense, reached a compromise with Guntrum, the Dane, whereby the entire northeastern half of England was given over to the latter, while the rest of England was spared. The territory given the Danes was known as the *Danelaw*, and although the Danes became Christian and professed an allegiance to Alfred, the *Danelaw* was actually independent. In the course of the next century, however, despite a constant influx of Danes, the *Danelaw* was reconquered, and gradually the Danes adopted Saxon ways.

Ireland, though suffering some Danish raids, became one of the principal areas of

Norwegian activity. Norwegians also explored the islands north of Scotland and established colonies in the Faroë, Shetland, and Orkney islands, in the Hebrides, and as far south as the Isle of Man. Thence, guided by the Irish, they pushed on to Iceland where, in the later ninth century, colonization began and a thoroughly Norse state was formed. Even Iceland did not prove to be the limit of Norse expansion westward. Greenland was discovered and a small colony established, which by the twelfth century was considered important enough for the institution of a Catholic diocese. Thence Leif Ericson, accompanied or perhaps preceded by Bjarni Herjolfson, went on to the northern coasts of the North American mainland, where, perhaps journeying southward by land, they reached a place which they called Vinland.[1] While the exact location of Vinland remains a matter of dispute, and so far as we know no permanent settlement resulted, the Norse voyages to America may confidently be regarded as fact.

Of more immediate influence on Europe was the Viking penetration of the continent. Swedish traders and adventurers had crossed the Baltic at an early date, perhaps in the sixth century, and had begun to ascend the northern Russian rivers into the interior. Thence some descended the Volga to the Caspian and thus made contact with Persia and the Moslem world. Others followed the Dnieper to the Black Sea and established contact with Constantinople and the Byzantine Empire. These early Norse rovers were called *Rus* or *Varangians*. The trade route across Russia to Constantinople was known as the "Varangian route." Russia in those day were merely a collection of small Slavic principalities, some of which employed bands of Vikings or gradually fell under their domination. The leader of one such band was Rurik who in 862 became the prince of Novgorod, a thriving northern metropolis, and whose kinsmen, led by Oleg, later appropriated Kiev on the Dnieper. The principality of Kiev was destined to be the chief Russian state during the early middle age. Although intercourse be-

[1] Recent investigations by Norwegian archeologists have uncovered convincing evidence of Norse settlements in Newfoundland. A recently published map dating from the fifteenth century indicates Vinland as an island with rather vague western outlines. R. A. Skelton, T. E. Marston, G. D. Painter, *The Vinland Map and the Tartar Relation* (New Haven, 1965).

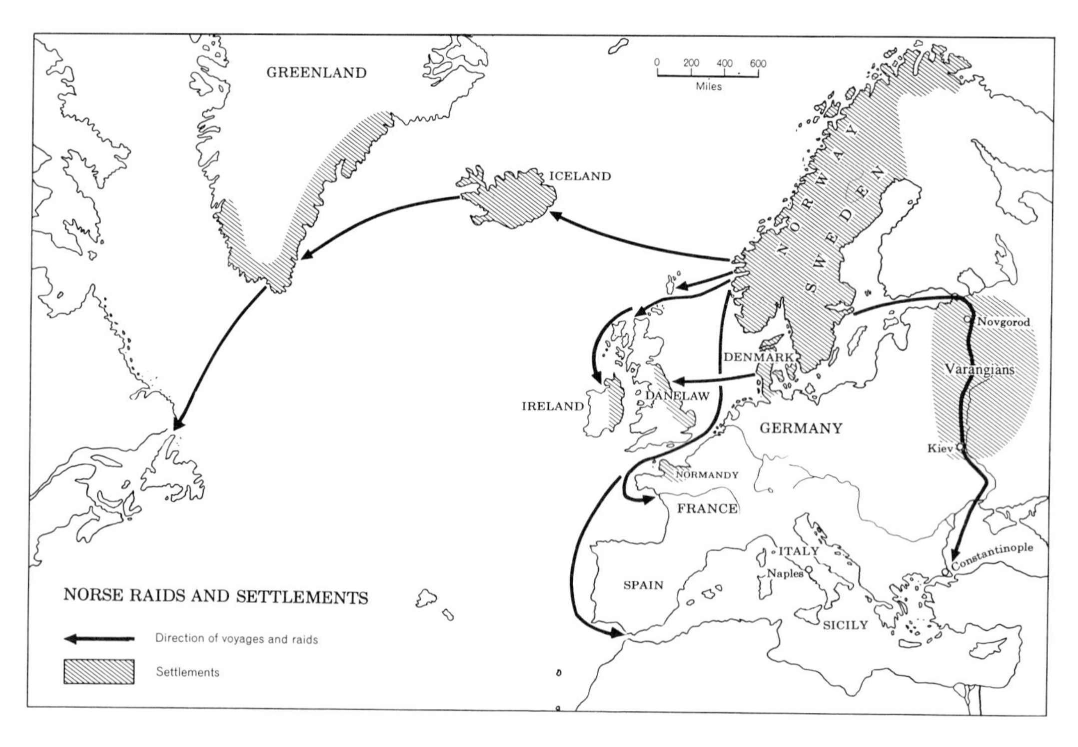

tween the Varangian principalities and the Scandinavian homeland was maintained, the Norse, as was their habit, adapted themselves to their new surroundings and were gradually lost in the development of these early Slavic principalities of Russia.

The western European mainland was also the scene of extensive Norse raids. The French coast, Spain, Mediterranean ports, and Italy were visited by their long boats. The many rivers of the Low Countries and France provided excellent avenues of inland penetration, and toward the end of the ninth century Norse raids in France were noticeably intensified.

One of the greatest attacks on an inland city was the siege of Paris in 885–886 where the heroic defense of Count Odo held several thousand Vikings with a large number of vessels at bay for ten months and saved the city. Even then the French King, Charles the Fat, was forced to pay a tribute. It was evident that the Norse were too firmly entrenched on the lower Seine to be dislodged, and so King Charles the Simple came to terms with the Norse chieftain, Rollo. In the treaty of St. Claire-sur-Epte (911) a statesmanlike compromise was arranged. The Norsemen were permitted to retain that part of the northern Frankish coast which lay between Brittany and the Low Countries, with a hinterland including Rouen, which became their capital. In return, Rollo embraced Christianity and became a vassal to King Charles for what came to be known as the duchy of Normandy.

Although Rollo probably understood but imperfectly the implications of vassalage, the creation of the duchy of Normandy brought the sturdy Vikings of northern France into the orbit of European civilization. Within a surprisingly short time these former marauders were building monasteries instead of pillaging them. And instead of destroying churches they were developing a noteworthy style of ecclesiastical architecture. Yet despite a thorough assimilation of the Latin civilization of western Europe, the Normans, as the inhabitants of Normandy were later called, did not lose the vigor and adventurous spirit of their ancestors. In the eleventh century, Normans carried their fused Norman-French culture to England and to southern Italy and Sicily.

It is difficult to overemphasize the results of the Norse expansion. Its geographical extent was tremendous. Everywhere the Norsemen went they stimulated trade. Skilled sailors, they advanced all the arts of the sea and gave to sea-borne commerce a new impetus. Equally significant was the effect of European civilization on the Norsemen. Everywhere they adopted Christianity, and the church experienced a notable growth. Moreover, while the adventurous Vikings roamed abroad, those who remained at home were forming the three kingdoms of Sweden, Norway, and Denmark. Soon missionaries from the continent and from England were carrying the gospel to heathen Norse in their homeland. By the year 1000, or shortly thereafter, an entirely new and hitherto unknown area had become a part of European Christendom.

That the two centuries following Charlemagne's death were a dark period in European history is undeniable. Political decay was followed by disorder, pillage, and widespread devastation. The losses, both material and spiritual, were terrific. However, it is not inappropriate to conclude this chapter on a happier note. Slavs, Bulgars, Magyars, and Norsemen, were, in the last analysis, absorbed and brought within the orbit of European civilization. Meanwhile, the inhabitants of western Europe were devising a new way of life made necessary by the breakdown of the Roman and Carolingian systems. The result was a slow but steady recovery which will occupy our attention in the following chapters.

Spanish thirteenth century sculpture. Marble relief of a mounted knight in helmet and mail shirt.

Courtesy of the Metropolitan Museum of Art, New York; Dodge Fund, 1913

CHAPTER 11

The Beginnings of Recovery: Feudalism and Feudal Society

A. Origins of Feudalism

The organization of society characteristic of the Early Middle Age is known as feudalism. Although feudalism arose out of the disturbed conditions preceding and following the reign of Charlemagne and may be associated, therefore, with the disintegration of the Roman and Carolingian states, it contained elements of stability and strength. Most important, it made possible a recovery of western European society on a local basis which in turn was to contribute to integration on the wider plane of feudal kingdoms. The latter process, which is first notable during the tenth century, is part of the larger phenomenon of western European recovery—economic, religious, and cultural, as well as political.

Feudalism developed as a kind of amalgam of earlier Roman, German, and perhaps even Celtic practices, modified to suit current needs. Practices varied from place to place and from time to time. There is no typical or "ideal" feudalism. Yet while allowing for very many local exceptions, some sort of general description is possible.

Two kinds of relationships run through the whole development: the personal bond between man and man; and the holding or tenure of land. The former is illustrated by the institution known as "vassalage," an honorable relationship between men based on military service. Though the origin of vassalage is a controversial matter, it appears that in Carolingian times a vassal was a professional fighting man serving someone of higher rank. Meanwhile various magnates—bishops and counts—many of whom held large tracts of land, became associated with the king as his *fideles* or *homines*, that is, as his "faithful men." Further, after the early Carolingians discovered that the great need in combating the Moslems was a well equipped cavalry, the vassal was given a special grant of land in return for service. Such a grant was called a "benefice" and enabled the vassal to meet the added expense of mounted service. Eventually, all landlords, including magnates, were expected to contribute to the military establishment. As customary procedures gradually became fixed as law, they were further emphasized by ceremonial. In becoming the "man" (*homo*) of his lord, the vassal performed some act of "homage." Since his loyalty was all important, he also took an oath of fealty.

Hence landlords, both lay and ecclesiastical, in order to provide military service in proportion to the size of their domains, gave out sections of these as benefices. Carolingian policies also added other elements to the benefice. The holder of a benefice usually retained complete jurisdiction over the dependent peasants. This was an obvious necessity since the land was to provide the economic support for military service. Moreover, a general political jurisdiction over a benefice by its holder was acquired either by a grant of "immunity," which conferred official release from the jurisdiction of the central government, or,

The fortunes and misfortunes of war at the Battle of Hastings.

From the Bayeux Tapestry

as was often the case, simply by appropriation.

The benefice system, which had developed out of late Roman procedures, had not originally or always been associated with military service. Hence a new term, "fief," came into use to designate this novel military benefice developed by the Carolingians. From its Latinized form, *feodum*, is derived the word feudal. A fief was land held in return for military service, but, because governmental jurisdiction was included, it was also an office. In the areas of the former west Frankish kingdom where the Carolingian county system was well developed, inheritance of fiefs came to be, as a rule, by primogeniture (that is, by descent to the eldest male heir). In the east division of the Frankish kingdom, divided inheritance tended to prevail for a longer time.

Then, too, by a process known as "subinfeudation," a vassal holding a fief could subdivide it into smaller fiefs. As a consequence there were sub-vassals (rear vassals) as well as vassals, and fiefs within fiefs. Such fiefs originated out of feudalism itself. They were not former administrative divisions of the Carolingian Empire.

B. Feudal Procedures

The essence of the feudal relation, whether it was between a king and one of the magnates who held directly from him, sometimes called a tenant-in-chief, or between a lesser lord and his vassal, was its contractual nature. Lord and vassal each had reciprocal duties and privileges. Since all lords were also vassals and all but the humblest vassals were also lords, there existed a definite social equality among all the nobility from the king to the poorest knight. Each had similar responsibilities and rights. When we describe the ordinary duties of a vassal toward his lord, we must remember that he expected the same from his own vassals. Vassalage was an entirely honorable estate and implied none of that humiliating subjection which the modern connotation of the word has acquired.

The mutual obligations of vassal and lord were not the same everywhere in Europe and they changed from century to century; but they were sufficiently similar in nature to warrant a general summary. They followed logically from the character of the fief as both a piece of land and an office. First, every vassal was expected to perform the act of homage, that is, to kneel and place his hands between the palms of his lord and take the oath of fealty. Broadly speaking, a vassal's duties can be summarized as governmental or judicial, financial, and military. He had to attend the lord's court at certain intervals or whenever summoned. There he advised his lord on policy or sat in judgment with other vassals, his own peers (*pares*), to decide a case involving one of them. Whatever decision was reached he was required to help carry out. The feudal court attended by those who held directly of the king was usually called the *curia regis* and was the nucleus of such central government as existed. In fact, all the services owed directly to the king were significant in the development of feudal monarchy.

Financial assistance amounted to financial contributions, varying with the size of the fief, on certain specified occasions, such as the marriage of the lord's daughter, the knighting of the lord's eldest son, or the provision of ransom in case the lord was captured. These were the three famous feudal "aids," and like all feudal payments were regulated by custom. One other normal payment, the "relief," recalled the days before the fief was hereditary. It was usually a fairly heavy tax and was expected of every vassal who inherited a fief from his father. A lord might also occasionally profit handsomely from the *droit de gîte,* or compulsory lodging, if he traveled through his vassal's land.

Military service was one of the principal reasons for the feudal system. Each vassal was expected to serve his lord personally (if he had more than one, presumably his liege lord) as a mounted knight. If his fief were large he would have to provide a number of mounted men. These he would secure from his own sub-vassals through sub-infeudation. But military service, however exacting, was limited. A common custom, at least in northern France, stipulated that it should not exceed forty days, although garrison duty at the lord's castle might also be required.

It is obvious that every lord would seek to protect himself from rebellious or otherwise undesirable vassals. If a vassal seriously defaulted in his obligations, the lord had the right, after due trial by peers, to declare the fief forfeit—that is, to expel the recalcitrant vassal and take over the property. Such a procedure required that the lord have adequate force at his disposal and this usually meant the full support of his other vassals. If a vassal died, leaving an unmarried daughter as heiress, it was the lord's privilege to choose a husband for the young lady. Meanwhile, the right of wardship permitted him to administer the fief and collect its revenues. He exercised similar rights over the fief of a young boy whose father died before the son reached his majority.

The obligations of a vassal were counterbalanced by certain definite rights. We have already alluded to the much prized privilege of trial by one's peers. The lord also engaged to protect his vassal in his fief and to support him in righting wrongs done him. Contemporary writers, emphasizing the loyalty due a lord, insisted that the lord ought to act in like manner toward the vassal in all things. It was entirely possible for the lord to violate the feudal contract. And although in theory a vassal might repudiate the agreement because of his lord's default, his chances of redress were, in the nature of things, not great. Nevertheless, since a lord depended on faithful vassals, he dared not press them too far. Feudalism implied limited, not absolute, sovereignty on the part of the king as well as of other lords. This is its greatest contribution to the theory and practice of free government in western Europe.

Feudalism had many complications. There was nothing to prevent a noble, naturally anxious to enlarge his holdings, from becoming the vassal of more than one lord. The counts of Champagne, for example, had nine lords. As a consequence, any baron attending the court of his lord might find there, doing homage to the same man, one of his own vassals. It was possible to be both the lord (or vassal) and the equal (peer) of the same person.

Such situations necessarily complicated the matter of allegiance. Hence arose the practice of *liege* homage, whereby a vassal designated one of his lords as his liege lord to whom he admitted superior allegiance and whom he served personally. In the case of a dispute between two of their lords, most barons followed the course which conscience or apparent self-interest (whichever was stronger) dictated. Feudalism was not without its confusion, its conflicting loyalties and jurisdictions. Feudal warfare, one of its greatest evils, was chronic. But to a marked degree feudal wars, at least in the minds of those involved, were to redress wrongs or to protect rights. Turbulent as were the nobles of the ninth and tenth centuries, they were not entirely lacking in a sense of moral responsibility.

C. Chivalry and Feudal Warfare

The emphasis on fidelity to contract, to plighted word and agreement, is particularly evident in the development of chivalry. Chivalry is not easily defined, for it was never a clearly developed institution. Our principal sources are the great medieval epic poems written in the vernacular.[1] It was natural that the noble audiences for whose entertainment these romances were composed would appreciate most easily

[1] See below, pp. 251–252.

those things which were familiar to them. Derived from the French word for horse (*cheval*), chivalry represents at once a code of conduct and a sort of loose indeterminate fellowship of the warrior class, where king and humble knight were equal. Probably of German origin, and at first purely military and secular, it emphasized courage, loyalty to one's superior, and devotion to military duty. Later, especially in the twelfth and thirteenth centuries, when society was somewhat more sophisticated and more Christianized, the ideas of protection for the weak and defenseless and of courtesy toward women entered. The church also influenced the development of chivalry by inculcating the ideal of the Christian knight sworn to defend the faith against its enemies, in particular Mohammedans. But despite the addition of all these new elements, chivalry retained the predominantly military and secular character of its early days.

Since fighting was the principal occupation of the nobility, a few words about medieval warfare are in order. Private warfare was the great scourge of early medieval society. Yet, in comparison to modern war, it was not especially sanguinary or devastating. For the most part it involved only the noble class and was a privilege which they jealously guarded. Only the necessities of new strategy, required in combating the Moslems, led to the introduction of infantry, bowmen in particular, from the nonfeudal classes. And as late as the fourteenth century, the mercenary infantry troops were despised by the proud French knights. The masses of the population—the peasants—experienced war only when it passed over their crops or when perhaps their lord and his knights were victims of a siege.

Clothed in a long cloak of chain mail, the hauberk, and a conical steel helmet, and carrying shield, sword, and spear, the mounted knight could be knocked down, bruised, and wounded, but less often killed. His ransom was usually more desirable than his life.

The earliest type of castle, and one long considered adequate, was the *motte-and-bailey*. This was a wooden block-house or square tower known as the keep (*donjon*), usually situated on a mound and surrounded by stockades and possibly by a moat and drawbridge. The first stone keeps were also square. Round towers were then developed and, during the period of the crusades more elaborate integrated construction appeared with inner and outer circles of walls forming a concentric design. Towers placed at intervals commanded every section of the walls. The advantage in a siege usually lay with the besieged unless inadequate provisioning made starvation possible. But since only kings or a few virtually independent magnates were likely to afford such edifices, complicated stone castles were never numerous.

The more thoughtful elements in society realized the evils inherent in excessive private war, and various steps were taken, particularly by the church, to curb it. In the late tenth and early eleventh centuries the bishops of France instituted the Peace of God and the Truce of God. The former was designed to protect ecclesiastical persons and property, the poor, and even merchants. Some lords responded by forming societies and taking vows to respect its provisions, but the results were on the whole disappointing. The Truce of God, which prohibited war on weekends and during certain seasons, was somewhat better observed.

The crusades of the twelfth and thirteenth centuries and the earlier wars of reconquest in Spain also diverted much warlike energy. But the most effective deterrent was the growth in authority, either of the central government, as in France, England, and Sicily, or of certain powerful magnates. The duke of Normandy was able to police his duchy and to prevent castle building without his special permission. Other instances could be cited. But such developments marked the decline of feudalism and the recovery, at least locally, of governmental authority. In the high feudal age the problem of private warfare was never really solved.

If fighting was a knight's chief occupation, mock fighting and hunting were his favorite amusements. Tournaments held on festive occasions were little dress-rehearsal wars consisting of a series of jousts, wherein individual knights were paired and rode at each other with lances set, and of an ensuing mêlée or "free for all' which usually resolved itself into individual combats. The fact that tournaments were forbidden, albeit ineffectively, by the church (1179) indicates that they were no mere child's play. Another favorite sport was hunting the deer or wild boar, which provided men of active life with both exercise and food. Falconry, also, became a highly developed art and was enjoyed by women as well as by men.

The position of women under feudalism was considerably improved by the later, more sophisticated chivalry; and their importance as gracious mistresses of considerable households was enhanced by the larger manor houses and castles of the subsequent middle ages. The poetry of romantic love, which had a certain vogue in the twelfth and thirteenth centuries, may also have changed some men's attitudes toward women.[1]

Under feudalism women were regarded primarily as necessary housekeepers and mothers of children, and marriages among the nobility were for the most part arranged for dowries and fiefs, not for love. Nevertheless women could, and often did, administer fiefs by reason of the absence or death of their husbands. And feudal custom jealously guarded woman's rights of inheritance and control over property.

As we have already intimated, feudalism developed spontaneously to meet critical conditions. It must be judged in this light and not by unfair comparison with previous or following ages. It was not perfect, but it enabled western Europe to resist and assimilate barbarians; it provided a rough and ready law and order. Many of its customs have become embodied in the laws of modern states. Trial by peers is still a prized privilege. The concepts of limited sovereignty and individual rights were fundamental to feudal government.

D. *Feudalism and the Church*

The position of individual churchmen under feudalism, like that of all other members of society, was determined by the conditions of land tenure. Bishops and abbots, as custodians of property, were lords or vassals (or both) under the feudal regime, and at the same time proprietors of peasants on ecclesiastical estates. Many served as government officials. Members of the clergy acquired a dual function. They were members of the ecclesiastical order with appropriate duties and, at the same time, they were forced to assume many of the responsibilities normally expected of laymen.

The evils inherent in such a situation were many. Preoccupation with worldly problems necessarily detracted from spiritual concerns. Many a bishop and abbot in the feudal age seemed more statesman than churchman. Moreover, in a very natural way a number of practices developed which were damaging to the church's welfare. Successful kings and great nobles endeavored in every way to control their vassals. As a consequence, the normal process of electing bishops was seriously disturbed. The canons of a cathedral church might formally elect, but the king or neighboring duke or count frequently nominated, the candidate. Younger sons who would not inherit a fief could often be nominated to an ecclesiastical benefice. Such baronial prelates, hurried through Holy Orders without adequate preparation, were seldom fit for their sacred office. A goodly number declined to let their churchly duties interfere with their customary mode of life. Although churchmen were forbidden to bear arms and were not as a rule expected personally to perform military service, too many in the early, rough feudal age were indistinguishable from any other knights. Eventually, there developed the practice known as lay investiture. A king or great lord "invested" the nominee to a bishopric or abbacy, not only with the customary symbols of authority over his fief, but also with the ring and crozier, symbols of his spiritual authority. This implied lay control over matters of ecclesiastical jurisdiction.

All these practices, unfortunate though they were, were a normal consequence of feudalism. More serious was the resultant breakdown of ecclesiastical discipline. Simony, the traffic in church offices, became fairly widespread; and the earlier injunction that clerics must not marry was rather

[1] See below, pp. 253–254.

widely disregarded. Even monasteries were not exempt from the general moral decline.

Not only did feudalism create problems for churchmen as individuals; it seriously endangered the church as an institution. As lay control over ecclesiastical offices increased, the church was in grave danger of becoming decentralized and brought everywhere under the domination of local political authority. For the universal decentralization of western European society accentuated a tendency on the part of certain prelates to assume a quasi-independent ecclesiastical jurisdiction.

It is also true that the machinery of centralization, the means whereby the pope could maintain close contact with bishops and abbots throughout the Christian world, was not yet adequately developed. To build an effective monarchical constitution on the basis of the primacy of the Roman See was one of the great tasks facing the church as it emerged from the Roman Empire. But the fulfilment of this objective was impeded, first, by the disorder of the invasions, and, second, by the development of feudalism.

This dangerous condition was aggravated by an especially acute feudal anarchy which persisted in central Italy. After the collapse of the Carolingian Empire the papal territories fell under the control of nobles of the Roman district. These men were a particularly unruly lot who regarded the bishop of Rome primarily as their temporal ruler—which he was—and paid scant attention to his prerogatives as head of the entire church. Like feudal lords elsewhere in Europe, they attempted, unfortunately with considerable success, to thwart the control of their suzerain. Members of their own families were elected at their behest until the choice of the highest official in Christendom was determined by the factional struggles of a petty local nobility. Needless to say, many of the candidates were unworthy characters and grossly negligent in their duties. There were periods in the late ninth and early tenth centuries when the papacy seemed to have reached the depths of degradation. In such a state, it could offer little leadership to a church caught in the meshes of feudalism.

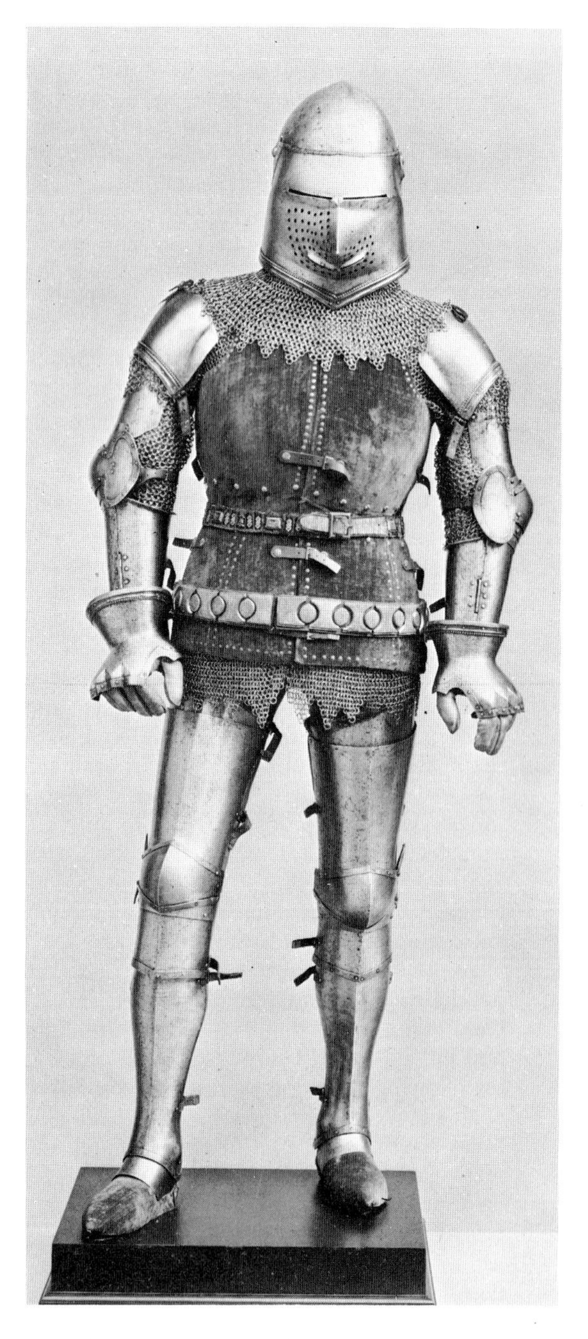

Medieval armor. Italian about 1400.

Courtesy Metropolitan Museum of Art, New York; The Bashford Dean Memorial Collection, gift of Helen Fahnestock Hubbard, 1929, in memory of her father, Harris C. Fahnestock

It would be incorrect to overemphasize the worst aspects of a very bad period in the church's history. There were a number of local efforts to bring about reform. Individual bishops and isolated abbeys struggled to maintain the proper standards, sometimes with notable success. And it must be remembered that, then as now, notorious evil-doers always attract more attention than the rank and file of conscientious people. A number of princes, although jealously guarding their self-assumed prerogatives of appointing bishops and abbots, were, as Charlemagne had been, sufficiently religious, as well as statesmanlike, to be genuinely interested in improving the condition of the church.

Indeed, there was often a real *rapport* between the ecclesiastical authorities and the secular rulers. We have mentioned that many nobles coöperated in maintaining the Peace and Truce of God. Endowment of religious foundations was general. Moreover, the practice of investing clerics aroused no serious objections on the part of the church until toward the mid-eleventh century. And it should be remembered, too, that in contemporary thinking the king was regarded, as Charlemagne had been, as a quasi-religious figure. He was *rex et sacerdos*, king and priest, entitled on solemn occasions to appear in the sanctuary of the church. Accordingly, the church upheld royal authority and expected the king to assist in enforcing ecclesiastical discipline. The ideal of the tenth and eleventh centuries was a coöperation of the two powers, the religious and the secular, to promote a Christian society.

The Romanesque Cathedral of Bamberg. The See of Bamberg was founded in 1007 by the German Emperor Henry II as a missionary diocese and outpost of defense against the Slavs. It became famous for its school and as a resort of the emperors.

Courtesy German Tourist Information Office, New York

Test

CHAPTER 12

Emerging Feudal States of the Tenth and Eleventh Centuries

During the tenth century, after the worst storms of invasion had passed and many of the new peoples had been absorbed, political consolidation was once again possible. The Europe which emerged resembled neither the Roman nor the Carolingian Empire. Rather it was a collection of separate feudal kingdoms. Yet even in the face of political separatism, most of Europe managed to maintain and develop a common culture based upon common religious and political traditions. And it is this unity of culture which justifies, by the eleventh century, the interchangeable use of the words Europe and Christendom.

Political practices in those centuries were generally based on feudalism. This, as we have already seen, had originated in the former Carolingian domains. Elsewhere it developed sometimes in imitation, and sometimes through new settlers to whom feudal institutions were familiar. Invariably it was modified by local conditions. In general, we may say that a feudal kingdom was a collection of fiefs in which the size and management of the fief belonging to the reigning family, the "royal domain," were of first importance as the ruler's primary resource. Beyond this domain the authority of a feudal king was circumscribed by the customary law which evolved from the practical operation of the feudal contract. The idea that a ruler is bound by law and not superior to it is an outgrowth of feudalism. A feudal monarch was "suzerain," not sovereign.

Tenth- and eleventh-century Europe included: (1) those states which had formerly been divisions of the Carolingian Empire; (2) territories consolidated following feudal expansion; (3) kingdoms formed by erstwhile invaders who had settled down and adopted the institutions of the civilization they had previously attacked.

There was also, on an older and different basis, the Byzantine Empire which, though reduced in size, recovered notably in the ninth and tenth centuries and maintained important contacts with central and western Europe. All these will be considered in turn.

A. Capetian France

The former Carolingian kingdom of the West Franks was in the tenth and eleventh centuries considerably smaller than the later French state. Although it extended northward to include Flanders and southward to embrace Barcelona below the Pyrenees, the entire Rhone valley and all of upper Lorraine belonged to neighboring kingdoms. At the accession of Hugh Capet (987),[1] the kingdom was a collection of fiefs loosely bound together. Most of these were larger than the royal domain, the *Ile-de-France*, and many had developed distinctive customs. In Brittany, parts of Flanders, and the southern provinces, different speech prevailed. It would, therefore, be more appropriate to speak of Normans, Angevins,

---

[1] See above, p. 123.

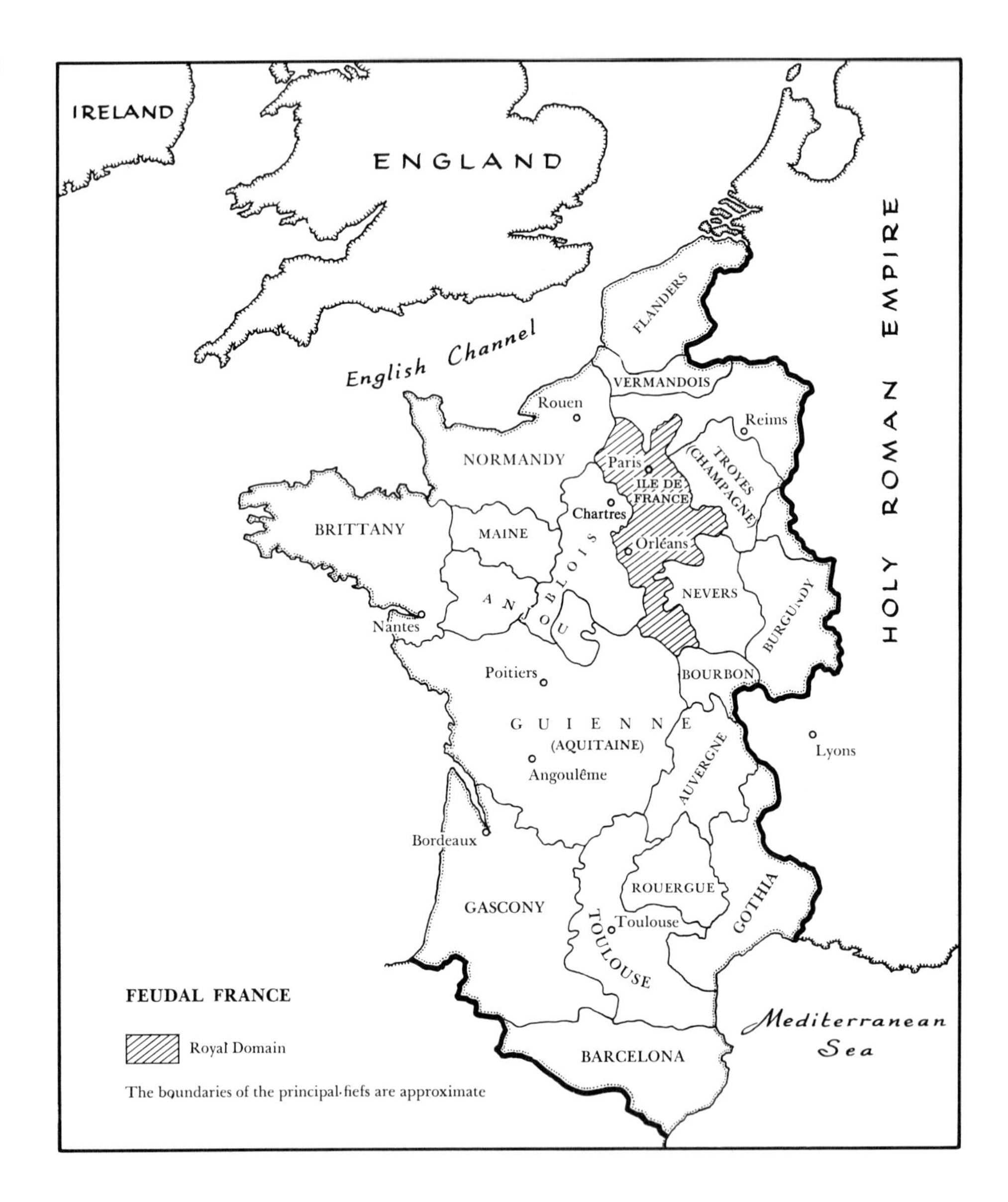

Burgundians, or Flemish, than of Frenchmen. Certainly the history of early medieval France is the history of its fiefs.

Of the first four Capetians who ruled from 987 to 1108 there is little to be said. Hugh set an important precedent for the future by having his eldest son crowned during his own lifetime, thus insuring an orderly succession. The undisputed succession of the early Capetians did much to secure the throne in the family, and hereditary succession by primogeniture became a feature of the French monarchy. Although the early Capetian kings exercised little if any influence outside the *Ile de France,* it must be remembered that there was no unity among the great fiefs which surrounded the royal domain. The perpetual quarrels which marked the relations of the great vassals with each other did much to save the monarchy. A significant event in early Capetian history was the conquest of England (1066) by the Duke of Normandy, for thenceforth France and England were in an unusually close relationship.

B. *Germany and the Formation of the Holy Roman Empire* [1]

The history of the former East Frankish kingdom (Germany) during the tenth and eleventh centuries differs markedly from the development of feudal France which we have just noted. First, the Carolingian dynasty came to an end in Germany in 911, seventy-five years before the accession of Hugh Capet in France, and Germany's consolidation under a new line of Saxon kings commenced earlier. Second, feudalism developed rather later and differently in the eastern Frankish realm. Inheritance of fiefs, for example, was slow to be established. Carolingian traditions of sovereignty lingered longer in Germany than in France. Thirdly, the early German monarchy differed from the French in the location of the crown lands, for the East Frankish monarchs had not lost control of all the Carolingian domains and they retained property scattered throughout the realm. For a time, these were a valuable asset in the early growth of the German monarchy.

The failure of any single dynasty to establish itself for more than a century meant that the elective principle in German kingship was never entirely lost. On a number of occasions the power of the magnates as electors was of special significance. As a result of the crown's passing from one dynasty to another, it was difficult to establish a compact royal domain. And while this was not important during the period under consideration in this chapter, it was a factor in Germany's later development. Finally, the German kings steadily pushed forward their eastern frontiers against the Slavs.

Like its neighbors to the west, the East Frankish kingdom during the period of Car-

[1] Although the designation "holy" was not applied until later, it has become customary to antedate it to the time of Otto I in 962.

An eleventh century amphibious military operation. The invasion of England by William the Conqueror, 1066. Transporting horses.

From the Bayeux Tapestry

FEUDAL "ROMAN" EMPIRE OF OTTO THE GREAT

olingian decline had become divided into a number of semi-independent principalities. At the time of the accession of Henry I "the Fowler" (918–936), the first of the Saxon dynasty, there were four major duchies—Saxony, Franconia, Swabia, and Bavaria. Later other areas, counties, duchies, and marches were added.[1] But Henry the Fowler, so named because the messenger sent to announce his election found him engaged in that traditional feudal amusement, was primarily interested in his own domain of Saxony. For the most part he left the other dukes alone, requiring only a recognition of his royal authority. To secure the frontiers of Saxony and Thuringia against Slavic and Magyar inroads, Henry established numerous fortified communities (*Bürgwärde*). His successors continued this practice and encouraged Germans to settle in the vicinity, thus laying the foundations not only of military security but of German colonization eastward. It was Henry's military reorganization which made possible on the Unstrutt River in 933 the first real victory over the invading Magyars.

Otto the Great (936–973) was even more successful both in protecting and in expanding the kingdom's frontiers. More forts were built by his subordinates in eastern Saxony and in the Slavic marches between the Elbe and the Oder. The northern frontier was pushed forward at the expense of the Danes and a new march of Schleswig created. The Slavic Czechs in Bohemia and Moravia proved sufficiently formidable to warrant a campaign led by the King, with the result that in 950 the Czechs recognized his suzerainty and promised him an annual tribute. Wherefore, the duchy of Bohemia, including the march of Moravia, became a feudal principality within the German kingdom. One of Otto's most signal triumphs was the decisive defeat of the Magyars near Augsburg in the battle of Lechfeld (955).

Otto the Great, not content with a theoretical suzerainty over the East Frankish kingdom, made an important contribution to governmental policy in Germany through his alliance with the church. Bishops and archbishops were given lands and immunities. Some even acquired the jurisdiction of counts. Obviously this policy could succeed only so long as the crown actually controlled the episcopate. Under Otto and his immediate successors this was the case. Bishops were formally elected, but royal nominees were commonly chosen. As a result, tenth-century German bishops were usually loyal feudal servants of the king. They attended court, administered royal lands, gave the king lodging on his travels, and acted as diplomats and regents. They supplied the bulk of the king's troops, and some defied the canon law of the church and appeared in person with their levies.

The successes of Otto in consolidating the German realm must be viewed in the light of his imperial designs. He regarded himself as successor to the Carolingians and, after the manner of his illustrious predecessors, he interested himself in the affairs of Italy. In north and central Italy, originally part of the middle kingdom created by the sons of Louis the Pious,[1] no stable regime had emerged and feudalism degenerated into anarchy. South of Rome the political power was divided among the semi-independent duchies of Spoleto and Benevento and the Byzantine Empire. The peninsula was ripe for foreign intervention.

The occasion for Otto's first transalpine venture was a combination of personal rivalries. Adelaide, widow of one of two candidates for the Italian throne, was imprisoned by the rival. Her brother Conrad, king of Arles (the combined kingdom of Provence and Burgundy), had already fallen under the protection of Otto. On his first expedition across the Alps (951), Otto secured from the Italian king the recognition of his own overlordship and the hand of Adelaide as well.

Some years later Pope John XII was the victim of the now chronic anarchy in Rome. Otto responded to his appeal, and on this occasion, supported by a formidable army, he assumed the Italian crown and in 962

[1] Aside from the eastward expansion and the incorporation of northern Italy which will be described below, the principal additions were Lorraine, taken from the West Frankish kingdom in the reign of Henry I, and (1033) the former kingdom of Burgundy (Arles) which was willed to Conrad II by a king who died childless.

[1] See above, p. 122.

received an imperial coronation at the hands of the Pope. Thus Otto, as Charlemagne before him, assumed the title of emperor, a title which gave greater sanction to his extensive annexations. The danger that a hostile prince might reign in Italy was obviated and a tradition set for his successors. Somewhat later Otto suppressed an insurrection of the Romans, had John deposed by a subservient synod, and secured the election of his own secretary as pope. This success in controlling the papacy and central Italy was not duplicated in the south. But Otto, like Charlemagne, entered into negotiations with Constantinople, and it was agreed that his eldest son, the future Otto II, should marry a Byzantine princess, Theophano.

In the main, Otto's successors were guided by the policies which he had inaugurated. The church remained an important element in government, and imperial domination over the popes was strengthened. Otto III (983–1002), an exceptionally imperially-minded ruler, actually appointed a pope. This was the famous scholar and teacher, Gerbert of Aurillac, who took the title of Sylvester II.

Conrad II (1024–1039), first of the Salian (Franconian) line of German kings and Roman emperors, introduced an important innovation in domestic policy by supporting lesser nobles against the great dukes and by recognizing their fiefs as hereditary. Careful not to deplete the crown lands and rights any more than was absolutely necessary, he made most of his grants to *ministeriales*. These were servants of the monarchy—officials and men-at-arms drawn from the non-noble classes—who, it was hoped, might prove especially loyal and devoted to the King's interests. Finally, Henry III (1039–1056) successfully controlled the magnates in Germany, exercised wide authority in ecclesiastical matters, and in 1046 had three rival claimants to the papal throne deposed and his own candidate, a German bishop, nominated. A second imperial nominee was the reforming Pope Leo IX.

Both the political and the ecclesiastical authority exercised by the German Roman Emperors down to the time of Henry III was destined to pass. Henry III was succeeded by a son, Henry IV (1056–1106), then only six years old, and the period of his minority afforded an opportunity for rapacious nobles to seize whatever royal property and rights they could. Even more significant was the revived prestige and authority of the papacy, for by the middle of the eleventh century, as subsequent pages will explain, the papacy had become strong enough openly to condemn imperial control over the German and Italian episcopate. Obviously such a challenge to royal domination over the church was an attack upon the very foundations of imperial policy. The resultant struggle between empire and papacy halted, at least temporarily, the consolidation of the medieval German kingdom. The details of this controversy will be explained presently.

Meanwhile Otto the Great attempted to imitate Charlemagne's cultural work, as he did his political. He showed zeal in monastic reorganization and in reconstituting libraries. His son and especially his brother, Archbishop Bruno, were both men of letters. And one of his subjects was the remarkable Saxon nun, Hroswita, who wrote Latin poetry and a series of prose dialogues in the style of Terence. Gerbert (*d.* 1003), archishop of Reims and director of its cathedral school, was a friend and confidant of Otto and later became Pope Sylvester II. Gerbert was an accomplished classicist who apparently acquired, from a visit to Barcelona, some acquaintance with Arabic scientific lore. He did special work in mathematics and knew the Hindu numerals one to nine. But the fact that he wrote a treatise on the old Roman system of calculating with an abacus, two hundred years after the Arabs had begun to employ the decimal system and the zero for calculation, indicates the backwardness of scientific knowledge in the western Europe of his time.

By the eleventh century, political and social conditions were again sufficiently settled in western Europe to render possible a greater and broader intellectual revival. Modern scholars have long been accustomed to the term "twelfth century renaissance." The foundations for that achievement were laid in the eleventh century and were particularly marked in the liberal arts, and in law, medicine, and architecture.

At Salerno, in southern Italy, was a center of medical studies which had already won considerable renown as the foremost institution of its kind in Europe. In northern Italy, there developed at Bologna, toward the end of the eleventh century, a center of legal studies, inspired by renewed interest in Justinian's *Digest,* while at the same time Guido of Arezzo produced some remarkable writings on musical theory. In Italy, too, there was considerable secular education.

In France, the liberal arts newly flourished, along with philosophy, theology, and poetry. Here, the intellectual primacy, once held by monastic establishments, was now passing to the cathedral schools. Of the latter, those of Orleans, Chartres, Reims, and Liege were especially prominent, while that of Paris was soon to become the seat of a great university. Fulbert, bishop of Chartres (1007–1029), was an accomplished and versatile scholar, poet, and man of letters, as well as a noted teacher. In Normandy were educated two scholarly archbishops of Canterbury—Lanfranc (*d.* 1089) and St. Anselm (*d.* 1109)—the latter becoming one of the great medieval philosophers.

C. Kingdoms in Northern and Southern Europe

The expansive capacities inherent in feudalism contributed to the formation of new frontier states. Feudal expansion exhibited certain general characteristics. Among the noble classes, love of adventure and the perennial desire for new fiefs sent many young men to distant lands. This often resulted in the adoption by adventurous knights of news ways and a new nationality. Spain and Sicily provided careers for many a French and Norman knight. The gradual expansion of the eastern German frontier, on the other hand, was the joint achievement of knight, peasant, and missionary. Here was a real colonization, the movement of a whole people into a new area. Medieval expansion was often associated with war against the infidel, especially against the Moslem. Pilgrimage to distant shrines was also an inspiration.

One of the best illustrations of feudal expansion is the formation of medieval Spain. There, not only did the church encourage the war against the Moslem conquerors of the peninsula, but the land re-won offered great opportunities for new fiefs. Moreover, at Compostela was the immensely popular shrine of St. James (*Santiago de Compostela*). From every part of France came a horde of knights eager for combat. Medieval Spain was almost as much the achievement of French knights as of the Spanish themselves.

Unfortunately, the Christian armies lacked cohesion; and despite the prodigies of individual valor on the part of men like Rodrigo Diaz whose exploits won him everlasting, if legendary, fame as *El Cid Campeador,*[1] progress was slow. Toledo, the heart of "new" Castile, was taken in 1085. But not until the third and fourth decades of the twelfth century were the boundaries of Castile and Portugal pushed farther south.

The Spanish territory thus re-won was not united. In some respects it resembled feudal France, except that there were four or five separate kingdoms instead of the great fiefs. By 1100 Aragon, Navarre, Leon, and Castile were distinct, and the county of Portugal was soon to become independent. Moreover, French feudal influences which were so important a factor in the reconquest of Spain remained significant in its later political and cultural development.

Southern Italy, also an ideal spot for the activities of restless knights-errant, became the special preserve of Normans. Nominally, southern Italy comprised a few small principalities formerly under Lombard suzerainty: Apulia and Calabria, loosely held by the Byzantine emperors; and the city-republics of Gaeta, Naples, and Amalfi. The entire area was subject to the forays of Saracens who controlled Sicily, Sardinia, and Corsica. Moreover, the presence at Monte Gargano of a shrine to St. Michael, whom the Normans as Christians had adopted as a patron saint, was an added attraction. For pilgrimage demands travel, and travel leads to adventure.

By 1030 one Norman knight had already won a fief near Naples. The news spread, and more Normans arrived, of whom the

[1] On the medieval Spanish epic *El Cid,* see below, p. 252.

The fourteenth century gateway of Battle Abbey. The abbey was established originally by William the Conqueror on the site of the battle of Hastings, 1066.

Courtesy British Information Services, New York

most prominent were the many sons of Tancred of Hauteville. Soon Robert Guiscard (*d.* 1085) and his brother Roger (*d.* 1101), the most famous of twelve brothers, were well on the way toward the conquest of the entire southern part of the peninsula and were even planning an invasion of Saracen Sicily.

Robert's successes eventually brought him into conflict with the papacy. Pope Leo IX led a military expedition against the Normans, who badly defeated him and took him prisoner. A later pope, Nicholas II, in 1059 officially recognized the Norman conquests by formally investing Robert with southern Italy as a papal fief. In addition, the projected conquest of Sicily received the papal blessing as a sort of holy war. It was completed by Roger in 1091. Thus both parties gained—the papacy, an ally; and the Normans, official sanction for their depredations. In the course of time the two states of southern Italy, Naples and Sicily, were united as a kingdom destined to be one of the more important in medieval Europe.

Another famous accomplishment of the Normans was the conquest of England by Duke William (1066). Pre-Norman or Saxon England had never achieved a real stability and had only rarely been blest with a ruler of the stature of Alfred the Great (871–901) who dealt with the Danish invaders. As late as the eleventh century, English weakness was a source of temptation for strong neighbors in Scandinavia and Normandy. For a generation England was part of a Danish empire which also included Sweden and Norway and which was capably governed by King Knut (1016–1035). Knut was a civilized, Christian ruler, not a semi-barbarian Viking. When Harold, the "last of the Saxons," came to the throne in 1066, he was faced with two invading armies, one from Norway led by Harold Hardrada and one from the continent under Duke William of Normandy. Although Harold worsted Hardrada, he went down at Hastings before William.

The Norman conquest is an event of capital importance in English history, for William's occupation of England profoundly affected every aspect of English life. Especially did it bring England more closely within the orbit of western Christendom. These things will become clearer in subsequent chapters.

The temporary incorporation of England into a Danish empire is evidence of important political progress in Scandinavia. During the great period of Norse expansion a considerable degree of stabilization had been achieved under the growing influence of European civilization. As we have seen, Christianity had been introduced and the church organized. During the tenth century and after, three Christian kingdoms begin to. appear as distinct. Harold Bluetooth (*d.* 985) boasted of the reduction of all

Denmark. And by the early eleventh century, Denmark under King Knut was strong enough temporarily to subdue Norway and even England.

Harold Fairhair's trumph over rival nobles (about 872) began the development of a Norwegian monarchy which gained strength under the saintly King Olaf (1016–1029). Moreover, Norway managed to maintain a kind of overseas empire. Olaf received the submission of the colonies in the Faroes, Shetlands, and other islands off the Scottish coast. Contacts with Greenland were kept up, and the Icelanders, though enjoying political independence, were originally of Norwegian stock and were given equal rights with natives when in Norway. Sweden also seems to have emerged as a separate kingdom by the year 1000. Thus the homeland of the Viking marauders became an integral part of Europe.

D. Eastern Frontier Kingdoms

In the period after Charlemagne's death, Slavs and Magyars had pressed against the frontiers of the East Frankish kingdom. By the middle of the tenth century the tables were turned and the historic German *drang nach osten*, or eastward pressure, was acquiring a real impetus. As a consequence, the states which were forming in east-central Europe often developed cohesion as they resisted the German advance.

Slavic resistance was not uniformly successful. The early development of the Czechs had been associated with the ancient principality of Moravia. It was there that the missionaries, Cyril and Methodius, had introduced the Slavonic liturgy.[1] But after the Magyar invasions and the fall of old Moravia, Bohemia replaced Moravia as the Czech political center of gravity. German and western ecclesiastical influences increased and Latin replaced Slavonic in the church's liturgy. Eventually, as we have already remarked, it was the destiny of this young West Slavic principality to become an hereditary fief of the Holy Roman Empire.[2] Yet Czech culture proved stubbornly resistant to German pressure. The political authority of the duke within his own domain was, for that age, extensive and the imperial administrative system was never introduced into Bohemia.

The West Slavs who inhabited the basin of the Warthe and Vistula rivers were more successful in maintaining their independence. Under the Piast dynasty (960–1370) a loose confederation of tribes was organized into a duchy of Poland, which eventually became the most powerful state in east-central Europe. The shrewd Miesko I married a Czech princess and accepted western Christianity (966) at the hands of Czech rather than German clergy. A native Polish bishopric was established at Poznan and, somewhat later, Poland was taken under the special protection of the Holy See. Boleslav the Brave (992–1025), in wars against Germans, Czechs, and Russians, extended the frontiers of Poland to include eastern Galicia, Silesia, and some territory beyond the Carpathians. His religious policy also tended to confirm the independence of the young state. Gniezno, shrine of the distinguished Adalbert of Prague who won a martyr's crown as a missionary to the Prussians (997), was made an archepiscopal see. Shortly before his death, Boleslav was crowned king, thus signalizing the establishment of a new and promising Slavic kingdom.

Meanwhile, the Magyars were also laying the foundations of an independent state. Under their early rulers, of whom St. Stephen (997–1038) was the most famous, the Hungarians had adopted Catholic Christianity and a settled mode of life. The ecclesiastical organization was kept carefully free of German domination. And the crown with which Stephen assumed the title of king was blessed by the pope, Sylvester II.

Farther east, the Russian Slavs were making remarkable progress, particularly in the principality of Kiev, which was established by the Norsemen. A development of the first importance was the marriage of Prince Vladimir to a Byzantine princess and his conversion to Christianity (988). Thereafter, with the growing influence of the church, Byzantine cultural influences permeated Russia. Under Yaroslav (1016–

[1] On Cyril and Methodius, see pp. 87–88, 151.

[2] The suzerainty of Otto the Great was recognized in 950. See above, p. 143.

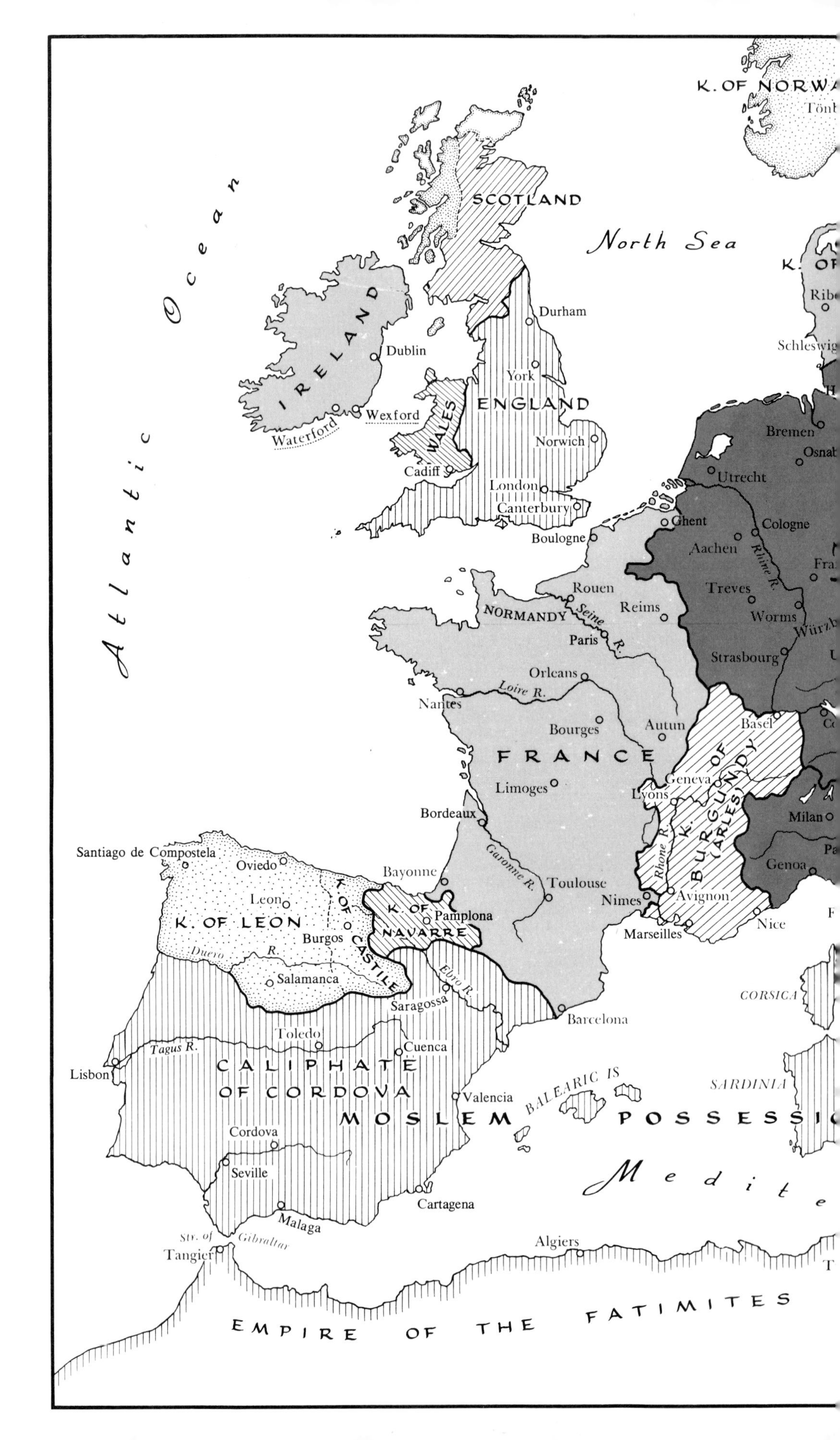

K. OF NORW
Tönb
SCOTLAND
North Sea
K. OF
Ribe
Atlantic Ocean
IRELAND
Durham
Schleswig
Dublin
York
ENGLAND
Wexford
Waterford
WALES
Norwich
Bremen
Osnab
Cadiff
Utrecht
London
Canterbury
Ghent
Cologne
Boulogne
Aachen
Rhine R.
Fra
Rouen
Treves
NORMANDY
Seine R.
Reims
Worms
Würzb
Paris
Strasbourg
Orleans
Loire R.
Nantes
Bourges
Autun
Basel
FRANCE
K. OF BURGUNDY (ARLES)
Geneva
Limoges
Lyons
Bordeaux
Milan
Santiago de Compostela
Oviedo
Garonne R.
Rhone R.
Genoa
Bayonne
Leon
K. OF CASTILE
K. OF NAVARRE
Pamplona
Toulouse
Nimes
Avignon
K. OF LEON
Burgos
Nice
Duero R.
Marseilles
Salamanca
Ebro R.
CORSICA
Saragossa
Barcelona
Toledo
Cuenca
Tagus R.
Lisbon
CALIPHATE OF CORDOVA
Valencia
BALEARIC IS
SARDINIA
MOSLEM POSSESSI
Cordova
Seville
Mediter
Cartagena
Malaga
Str. of Gibraltar
Tangier
Algiers
EMPIRE OF THE FATIMITES

EUROPE ABOUT 1000 A.D.
Scale in miles
0
100
200
300
Estonians
Livonians
Lithuanians
Düna R.
Baltic Sea
Lund
Bornholm
Rügen
Danzig
Prussians
Stettin
Brandenburg
Posen
Plock
POLAND
Oder R.
Breslau
Cracow
Prague
BOHEMIA
Brünn
Danube R.
Pressburg
K. OF HUNGARY
Stuhlweissenburg
Salzburg
Villach
Drava R.
Sava R.
Theiss R.
Minsk
Pinsk
Tchernigov
Pripet R.
RUSSIA
Kiev
Dnieper R.
Halicz
Dniester R.
Pruth R.
Patzinaks
Cherson
Black Sea
Danube R.
Varna
Venice
Ravenna
K. OF CROATIA
Ventian Possessions
Zara
Spalato
Ragusa
SERBIA
Belgrade
Nissa
Triaditza (Sofia)
Philippopolis
BULGARIA
Skopia
Adrianople
Constantinople
Nicaea
Adriatic Sea
Spoleto
Benevento
Gaeta
Naples
Dyrrhachium
Brindisi
Salonica
Castoria
Larissa
Adramytium
Smyrna
Aegean Sea
BYZANTINE EMPIRE
Cephalonia
Corinth
Athens
Attalea
Palermo
Reggio
SICILY
CRETE
Sea

1054) the state of Kiev attained the zenith of its power. A thriving commercial metropolis, second only to Constantinople in eastern Europe, it was noted especially for its churches. St. Sophia and the many other edifices, richly adorned with frescoes and mosaics, rank among the finest examples of medieval Byzantine art. Unfortunately, the brilliant promise of eleventh-century Kiev was not to be fulfilled, for in the period following Yaroslav's death the state was divided among the various branches of the old Kievan dynasty. Medieval Russia suffered from chronic political division.

The Byzantine orientation, so noticeable in old Russian culture, was also characteristic of the Serbs and other southern Slavs who were separated from their northern brethren by the intrusion of the Magyars. There were exceptions, however. The inhabitants of Croatia-Dalmatia, close to the old dividing line between the east and west parts of the Roman Empire, remained within the orbit of Western Christendom. First conquered by the Franks, Croatia became a kingdom when in 924 Tomislav accepted a crown from the pope. In 1102 Croatia joined with Hungary, thus firmly establishing its western cultural orientation.

E. Political and Cultural Revival in the Byzantine Empire

The Byzantine Empire never entirely recovered from the disasters of the seventh century. Some territories—Egypt and North Africa—were permanently lost. Others—Syria, Macedonia, and Thrace—were regained only temporarily. The political recovery of the ninth and tenth centuries did not restore the Empire's former boundaries. It was, however, of great importance, and since it was accompanied by a revival of the Greek classical tradition and a marked advance in art and architecture, it had vital significance for the cultural history of Europe at large.

Military stabilization began to be reestablished under the soldier emperors of the eighth century. It was the Emperor Leo III (717–741) who completed the reorganization of the Empire into the *themes*, in which the civil and military jurisdictions were combined. The army was recruited from the peasants of the eastern provinces.

It was also Leo III who launched the campaign of Iconoclasm against church images.[1] We have hitherto treated of Iconoclasm as a factor in the political separation of east and west, but it should be emphasized here that it caused a severe upheaval in Byzantine society. Temporarily, Emperor, army, and eastern provinces were pitted against the patriarch of Constantinople and the monks. Iconoclasm was really a form of puritanism not uncommon in oriental culture, which disparaged the material element in life and denied its capacity, as in the case of images, to represent the divine and supernatural. As a consequence, and this is more pertinent to the present discussion, when the Byzantine church outlawed Iconoclasm at the second council of Nicaea (787), a notable artistic revival was made possible.

Emperors of the Macedonian dynasty (867–1054) carried the military recovery further. The advance of the Bulgars was first halted, and finally the Bulgar "empire" was conquered and annexed (1018). Thus a portion of the Danube frontier was for a time restored. During the tenth century the Russians of Kiev under their Norse rulers were becoming formidable north of the Black Sea. It was significant that in 988 Emperor Basil II made a treaty with Prince Vladimir of Kiev whereby the latter agreed to become Christian and to furnish the Emperor with 6,000 troops—the famous "Varangian guard." Also during the tenth and eleventh centuries, Byzantine armies re-won ground from the Moslems in Syria, along the upper Tigris-Euphrates valley, in Crete and Cyprus, and in southern Italy. Antioch was a particularly important reconquest (909).

As is so often the case, political success was accompanied by cultural revival. After the defeat of iconoclasm, literature and art were predominantly religious, but they were less exclusively monastic than they had previously been. There was also a rebirth of secular learning marked by a renewed interest in the ancient Greek masters. The university of Constantinople was reëstablished in 863. Men like Michael Psellus, who revived

[1] See above, pp. 90–91, 117.

Platonic philosophy, and Constantine Porphyrogenitus, author of the *Book of Ceremonies,* a manual of court ceremonial, forecast, in their literary tastes and their conscious imitation of classical style, the humanists of the later Italian renaissance. This relatively early revival at Constantinople was not one of great creative genius, but it represented an achievement far in advance of anything then extant in western Europe.

Art, released from the restriction of iconoclasm, exhibited a trend toward naturalism. Painting, ivory carving, illuminated manuscripts, even ecclesiastical mosaics, all showed Hellenic tendencies. Tenth- and eleventh-century Byzantine architecture was less clearly classical, except in the practice of decorating exteriors, porticos, and facades.

Unfortunately, the Byzantine revival was short lived, for the later eleventh century brought, especially at the hands of the Seljuk Turks, new defeats from which the Empire never fully recovered. Yet the "Byzantine Renaissance" of the ninth and tenth and early eleventh centuries profoundly affected the cultural development of many other peoples who came within the sphere of its influence. A few illustrations will make this clear.

Even before the reduction of the Bulgarian "empire" and its incorporation into the Byzantine system, the Bulgarians, though constantly menacing Byzantine frontiers, had developed an admiration for the higher culture of the Byzantines. This was especially true after the Bulgarian Tsar Boris, by becoming Christian in 866, had opened the way for Byzantine influence. Moreover, most of the southern as well as western Slavic peoples (and the Bulgarians were already noticeably Slavic in their speech and customs) were indebted to the civilizing and Christianizing work of Saints Cyril and Methodius. These two famous missionaries had labored in the second half of the ninth century (862–885), especially in Bohemia and Moravia.[1] But the fact that most of the Slavic Christians adopted the "Cyrillic" alphabet, an adaptation of Greek letters to the Slavonic tongue, is proof of the much wider influence of Cyril and Methodius. The late ninth and early tenth centuries witnessed in Bulgaria the formation, through translations from the Greek, of a Christian Slavonic literature which was passed on to other Balkan Slavs and to the Russians.

Byzantine influence greatly increased in Russia during the eleventh century, following the conversion of Vladimir. Greek bishops and missionaries taught the Russians the Slavonic script and brought with them the architectural and artistic traditions of Constantinople. And although the churches and monasteries of Kiev with their Byzantine mosaics are particularly famous, the more northern centers of Novgorod and Moscow, later to become the heart of Russian life, felt the influence of this higher culture.

Direct Byzantine influence in western Europe was significant, though less pronounced than in the east. This was the result partly of the Frankish conquest of the exarchate of Ravenna and the Norman conquest of southern Italy, and partly of a growing cultural and religious rift between eastern and western Christendom.[2] Nevertheless, the Byzantine renaissance was influential throughout Dalmatia and northeastern Italy, and in southern Italy through the Greek-speaking monasteries of Calabria. Byzantine art, as exemplified by St. Mark's at Venice, became in time an inspiration for artists and architects throughout the west.

Such was the Europe of the eleventh century. Though divided politically, it was beginning to manifest signs of governmental consolidation. And this was accompanied by recovery in both economic and religious spheres. To these we shall now turn.

[1] See above, pp. 87–88.
[2] This will be explained later. See below, p. 167.

A tenth century bell tower. A thirteenth century copy of a tenth century Spanish manuscript which substituted, at the right, figures of laymen with drawing instruments for the original monks.

Courtesy Pierpont Morgan Library, New York

test

CHAPTER 13

Economic Conditions Under Feudal Society

A. Commerce and Industry in the Early Feudal Period

In the preceding pages we have noted the predominantly rural character of western European life in the Carolingian age. Such trade as survived was mostly, though by no means exclusively, local; and the many markets for agricultural goods or the products of domain industry were patronized by farm folk. But some necessities and a few luxuries came to the manors from the outside. Salt, iron, grindstones, salt fish, to mention only a few items, were seldom procurable locally. Hence, these and the few oriental luxury products—like spices, pepper, silks, incense, enamels, and ivories which the age sought and could afford—had to be provided by professional traveling merchants.

For some time transportation difficulties were well nigh insuperable. Roads were incredibly bad because no public authority existed with sufficient sense of responsibility to repair them. It was often necessary for monasteries, local benevolent associations, or groups of merchants to repair such roads and bridges as remained. Brigandage was common. And almost equally vexatious were the innumerable local tolls levied by rapacious lords at every crossroad or bridge. Not without reason did the church include merchants in the protection it sought to extend by the Peace of God.[1]

Such a picture of Europe's commercial life is not complete, for the recovery in political life which has been described was paralleled by a corresponding economic growth. Slower in some areas than in others, but everywhere marked by a steady rise in population, this economic expansion which commenced in the tenth century gradually created a new Europe, a Europe different both geographically and economically from the ancient Roman world. Although remaining predominantly agrarian, the New Europe was characterized by a notable increase in the volume of commerce and industry and in the number and size of towns. It is the beginning of this process in the tenth and eleventh centuries which will be described in the present chapter.

The Byzantine Empire never suffered the economic fate of the west either in the fifth or the ninth century. Despite the loss of Syria and Egypt, its naval and military power had preserved Constantinople and (until the eleventh century) Asia Minor. Further, although the Moslems took Sicily, the towns of southern Italy—such as Naples, Amalfi, and Bari—continued for a while under Byzantine sovereignty. And when the southern Italian towns were eventually taken by the Normans in the eleventh century, Byzantine commercial contacts with the west were maintained in Venice. For that city, founded on the islands and lagoons at the head of the Adriatic by refugees from the Germanic invaders, was destined by nature to live from commerce. It would be hard to find a more striking contrast

[1] See above, pp. 134, 137.

than that between commercial Venice and agrarian Europe of that day. Venice was never incorporated into the Carolingian state or into the Holy Roman Empire. Instead, it continued to develop under Byzantine auspices. And when Byzantine sovereignty gradually disappeared, Venice was left an independent republic.

The Venetians did not confine their commercial operations to Constantinople. Undeterred by religious scruples, they made contacts with the Moslems of Africa and Syria, drove a lucrative traffic in slaves, and even sold to Moslems the timber and iron which were undoubtedly used against their fellow Christians. By 1100 Venice, already a great sea power, had mastered the Adriatic and established trading posts all along the coasts of Dalmatia and Greece. In fact, in 1082 the Byzantine Emperor Alexius granted the Venetians privileges and exemptions for trade in his territory which made them a group more favored than his own subjects nearer home.

Ultimately, Venetian enterprise was imitated by cities on the west coast of Italy. Perhaps less exclusively inspired by the love of gain, the Pisans and Genoese required the additional inspiration of religious faith. Their expansion was also an attack on the infidels of Sardinia and north Africa. The Pisan conquest of Mahdia in Tunis (1087) was a crusade in which the Bishop of Modena took part. The cathedral of Pisa was built to commemorate this success. Meanwhile, with Genoese help, the Pisans also established themselves early in the eleventh century in Corsica and Sardinia. Other Mediterranean seaboard towns, including Marseille, were likewise active in this early period.

The commercial and maritime civilization which was emerging during the eleventh century in the Mediterranean had its counterpart in the north. The Norse, it will be recalled, had made contact with the Black Sea and Byzantium and with the Caspian where they met Jewish and Moslem merchants from Bagdad. Honey, furs, and slaves from the north were exchanged for spices, wines, silks, and other luxuries from the orient. Quantities of Arabic and Byzantine coins have been found in Russia. The island of Gothland in the Baltic off the coast of Sweden became a great depot for Scandinavian-Oriental trade, and even greater quantities of Greek and oriental coins have been unearthed there. Moreover, as the three Scandinavian kingdoms developed politically, and as England, particularly in the tenth century, increased its stability, the entire northern area, extending from the British Isles to Russia, moved commercially forward.

It should also be noted that northwestern Europe, especially Flanders, was an early center not only for trade but of a native textile industry. Flemish woolen cloth was everywhere in demand, even in the east. As an article of export, it helped in some measure to restore the balance of east-west trade which was generally unfavorable to the west. As early as the tenth century it proved necessary for the Flemings to import wool from England, their own supply being insufficient. There resulted an economic bond between the Low Countries and England which was subsequently to have important political repercussions.

Also, the quantity of mineral output commenced to increase. Certain areas of north, central, and eastern Europe beyond the old Roman frontiers began to produce not only gold and silver, but iron. The discovery of the Rammelsberg silver mine (960) near Goslar in Saxony might be cited as an example.

Along with the increasing volume of trade and industry, and in part the cause of it, was the increase in the number and size of town communities, that is, those containing a population living by trade and industry, even in inland areas. In Germany which, as we have seen, early enjoyed a measure of political stability, this phenomenon is noticeable even in the tenth century. Owing doubtless to a slower political development this primitive urbanism, outside of such Roman municipalities as had survived, was not common in France or elsewhere before the eleventh century.

B. Agricultural Revival

Urban growth, even of a limited extent, demanded expanded agricultural production. So also, of course, did an expanding population whether in country or town. As

The close association of town and country. Sheep under the walls of Avila, Spain. Sheep-raising has been an important part of Spanish economy since early times.

Courtesy Spanish National Tourist Department, New York

a consequence there followed systematic efforts to effect a more rational use of the land. These took two forms.

First, certain technical improvements were devised. In part these antedated the population rise, and resulted from an initial decline in agricultural man-power caused by the destructive invasions. Slavery, which had persisted into Carolingian times, largely disappeared and with it the human motor-force it supplied. It is noteworthy, for example, that the water-mill for grinding grain, known but not exploited by the Romans, now came into greater use.

Horse-shoes, horse-collar, and tandem harness increased the availability of animals for farm work. As agrarian exploitation moved northward into damper climates and heavier soils, it became necessary to invent a heavier wheeled plow with mould board. It was also discovered that in large areas of northern Europe certain grains could be planted in the fall and harvested early in summer. Romans had commonly employed a two-field rotation, one field being left fallow each year to recover its fertility. In the damper northern areas a three-field rotation (including a fall planting) was possible and therefore correspondingly greater annual yield. Experiments were tried with three, four, and five fields, and, in places where soil was plentiful but poor, a continuous shift of the arable land was made as soon as the soil became unusable.

The second important change in western Europe's agrarian economy was the increase in the total area under cultivation. Begun toward the end of the tenth century and gathering momentum in the eleventh, this phenomenon revolutionized what might be described as the agricultural map of Europe. Though not discernible on ordinary political maps, except those of sufficient scale to show the multiplication of villages, the changes were as important to the history of Europe as the shift of national boundaries.

How were these changes accomplished? A considerable extension of eventually usable land was obtained by diking along the lowlands of the northwest coasts of the Low Countries. Monasteries often pioneered in this enterprise. Comparable techniques were employed in draining swamp areas along the eastern frontiers of Germany. Indeed, skilled Flemings were sometimes employed to further the work. By far the greatest amount of new land was brought under cultivation by systematic deforestation. Abbeys, enterprising landlords, individual peasants, all joined in this pioneer work. Into a new area first came the loggers, charcoal-burners, and the like, who moved on when their work was done. Then came the peasant settlers, often known as *hospites*, and usually given privileged or free status. Although much deforestation took place along actual frontiers which were continually expanding, a great deal was done within the already existing kingdoms. Accordingly, much of what was once forest became a land of alternate woodland and clearing. There persisted, for some two or three centuries, what might be described as frontier conditions which constantly reacted on the older or less recently settled areas.

Finally, it should be noted that in addition to the divergencies between the older southern regions and the more recently exploited north and west, innumerable variations of local custom and differences of soil and climate dictated widely varying farming methods. What is suitable to fertile plains will not suffice in mountain regions. Viticulture, sheep and cattle raising, require techniques different from those for the cultivation of cereal crops. It is in the light of all these possible and actual differences that we must now consider the predominant agricultural institution of western Europe in the feudal age, the seigneurial regime.

Page from a twelfth century English bestiary (book of animals, etc.) Showing a "saw fish" and a contemporary single-masted ship.

Courtesy Pierpont Morgan Library, New York

C. The Seigneurial Regime

The seigneurial regime [1] may be loosely defined as the exploitation of land by a landlord (*seigneur*) or by a single institution such as an abbey, with the aid of a dependent peasantry over whom he (or it) exercised certain governmental and legal functions. For like the feudal relation between lord and vassal, the relation between seigneur and peasant was political and legal as well as economic. It was, in short, a unit of government as well as an economic institution. The seigneurial regime emerged in the post-Carolingian age, when, as a consequence of invasion and general turbulence, the large Carolingian domains were mostly destroyed. Parts of these older domains were delegated to or appropriated by individual landlords and the few remaining free villages or small free farms were absorbed. The system, therefore, marks a further stage in the development of individualized, smaller-scale farming which, it will be recalled, had existed even in the Carolingian period.

Students of medieval economy have found so many different types of peasant community that they have been unwilling to admit that there is such a thing as a "typical" settlement. Speaking from a territorial standpoint, and allowing for many variations, it is possible, however, to distinguish two main types of settlement, the village and the hamlet. The former was a nucleus of houses with fields, often divided up into long narrow individual holdings, occupying a common area outside. It prevailed throughout most of northern and western Europe, the area of predominantly three-field cultivation. The hamlet, on the other hand, was commonly composed of houses with small plots nearby, and other, usually rectangular, fields outside; it was common in the south and in certain extremities of the northwest, for example in Wales, Scotland, and Brittany.

[1] The words manor or manorial regime are usually employed in describing English agrarian organization. A manor, however, signified a complex of relationships between peasants and landlord, and not necessarily a single farm community.

The property under the jurisdiction of seigneur or monastery might all be contiguous and form a single agrarian complex. But it was equally common for parts of villages or hamlets to be held by different lords. The seigneur, or the lord of the manor, to use the expression common in England, was the holder of a collection of rights and obligations owed him by the peasants possibly of one, but often of more than one, community, each separate from the others. Manifestly, it was also possible for a peasant to be obligated to more than one landlord.

Most of the peasants on whose labor the seigneurial exploitation depended were neither slaves nor entirely free. As slavery declined, so also the turbulence of the ninth century tended to reduce the status of the remaining free men. The latter did not disappear, but the typical peasant of the eleventh century was dependent legally and economically on his landlord, owed him services and taxes, and was usually called a serf.[1]

There were, in fact, many gradations of serfdom. Not all peasants, even on the same manor, paid precisely the same taxes or were required to do the same amount of work. Local arrangements of long standing dictated the individual relations of lord and serf. Gradations of manorial peasantry resulted from property. Although the average serf's holding in a manor's separate strips amounted to about thirty acres, many held more, some less. Thrift, inheritance, and marriage (as in fiefs) might expand a peasant's tenure over the years. A few peasants —the cotters—held no land and simply possessed a rude dwelling (cottage, cot) and perhaps a small kitchen garden. Their livelihood was almost entirely the result of labor for the lord. We must not neglect to mention the lord's household servants—the skilled craftsmen, millers, bakers, smiths, carpenters, leather-workers, and the like—whose relations to the lord must have differed from those of the peasant who labored in the fields. There were also certain manorial offices held by men of servile status, such as the reeve, who supervised the manorial economy and prepared its annual accounts.

In general, the status of the peasants with regard to their lord, their rights as well as their obligations, and their relations with one another were regulated by long standing custom which had come, with the passing of years, to have the force of law. It is impossible to overestimate the importance of long established custom in medieval agrarian economy.

D. *Peasant Obligations and Rights*

Broadly speaking, every serf was dependent on his lord, and theoretically required to do whatever work and to pay whatever taxes the lord demanded. Actually, old customs set limits both to work and to taxes. Some lords were cruel, but most of them were sensible, hard-headed farm managers, who recognized that a starving serf was a poor farmhand. Although serfs could be sold off the manor, they could not of their own will leave it, and custom guaranteed that a serf's tenures were his to cultivate and hand down to his son, much as a vassal handed down his fief.[2]

A serf was valuable primarily because of the work he could do, secondarily for the taxes he could pay. Although there were many ways of regulating the serf's labor, a fairly widespread practice stipulated that a certain number of days, commonly three each week (week work), be given over to the lord's demesne, together with extra days (boon work) at especially busy times. Food and drink were often supplied by the lord on such occasions. In the village where open field cultivation prevailed, work was of necessity communal. Each peasant might hold his own land and enjoy its fruits, but, especially after the invention of the heavy plow, he had to pool such draft animals as he possessed with those of his fellow-peasants. Similarly, sowing and harvesting were found

[1] In England the term *villein* was more common, whereas in France the term *vilain* or *franc vilain* ordinarily meant freeman. The student should guard against associating modern connotations of "freedom" or "unfreedom" with medieval serfdom. The status of freeman and serf on a medieval estate did not differ greatly in actual practice and one was not necessarily superior to the other. Freedom of movement, legally conceded the freeman, could often not be denied a serf who chose to escape.

[2] Inheritance customs varied in different parts of Europe.

to be more effectively accomplished if all worked together. The up-keep of roads and bridges was also generally required of serfs. From military service, except in cases of siege or dire emergency, the serf was usually free. The feudal knights placed no high value on the military capacity of the peasant.

The payments expected of an average serf were many, but here again ancient custom and the stern school of experience limited the lord's caprice. The subject is too complicated to treat adequately here. We must content ourselves with a few illustrations. Since money was scarce, payments were usually made in produce, but as the volume of money in circulation increased in the later middle ages, it appears that manorial taxes were sometimes paid in coin.

Some dues grew out of the very conditions which governed manorial economy. If a serf's daughter married outside the manor, involving, at least potentially, a loss to the lord, a payment (*formariage*) was demanded. Marriages outside the manor had formerly been prohibited, but the church's insistence that families not be broken up helped to produce this compromise. A serf's son, on succeeding his father, paid an inheritance tax (*heriot*); and as a serf was not regarded as having the right to inherit movable property, his death might mean the loss to the lord of some of his chattels, possibly his best beast. *Chevage* (head tax) was occasionally levied, and *banalités* were payments resulting from the lord's monopoly over certain necessary services such as wine-press, oven, and mill. Fines imposed in the manorial court were also a source of revenue. And, finally, the peasant owed a tithe (tenth) to the local parish church.

Practically every manor had its church. The parish limits usually, though not always, corresponded with it. In some cases, a monastery had control of the local church and appointed a vicar (substitute). The parish priest had his little land, the *glebe*, along with the rest, and often, if he were a good sort and, as was frequently the case, peasant-born, he lent a hand in the village work. Many a faithful village priest, in addition to regular duties, gave advice, settled disputes, solaced the sorrowing, and

A shepherd depicted in a mid-thirteenth century French manuscript.

Courtesy Pierpont Morgan Library, New York

even gave the rudiments of an education to especially promising peasant lads. It is necessary to add, however, that few parish priests in the early middle age were themselves educated beyond the rudiments of their religion. Facilities for clerical education were woefully inadequate. The efforts of the church to improve this situation will be noted in subsequent chapters.

The peasant's life was undeniably hard. He worked from sunrise to sunset and returned to his little one-or-two-room thatched cottage. It may have lacked a wooden floor and been simply furnished with stools, table, and wooden couch with a straw mattress big enough for the whole family. Cattle were housed in adjacent out-buildings or at the end of one of the rooms. Primitive sanitation (in such matters, the nobles were not vastly superior) fostered disease, and pestilence spread rapidly. Fire was an ever present hazard and, once started in one cottage, could easily wipe out a whole village. Though probably adequate in quantity, the peasant's food was coarse in quality.

It would be a mistake to dwell over long on the hardships of the medieval peasant's life or to picture the medieval agricultural community as absolutely static. Not only did the increase of towns and new farming communities offer opportunities to venturesome peasants; their development reacted on the management of the older settlements. Even before 1100 a tendency is noticeable to commute services into fixed payments, and obligations into rents. This tendency was notably to increase in the later middle ages.

The Monastery Church at Cluny as it appeared before it was dismantled following the French Revolution.

Courtesy Bibliothèque Nationale, Paris

CHAPTER 14

Religion and Society in the Feudal Age

An earlier chapter has indicated the grave problems which feudal decentralization presented for the church: lay control, often exercised for personal or family aggrandizement, over bishoprics and abbeys; the prevalence of simony; the widespread disregard of clerical celibacy which had come to be the rule in the west. It has also been remarked that the picture was not entirely bleak. It is now time to analyze the measures taken to remedy this situation, the church's part in the general renewal of society which characterized the tenth and eleventh centuries. Three aspects of this story will engage our attention: a monastic reform; the reorganization of the secular clergy and the elaboration of a machinery of centralization under the pope; the religious life of the laity and its relation to the renewed church.

A. Cluny and Monastic Reform

Owing perhaps to the shrewdness of a monastic notary, the charter of foundation granted in 910 to the abbey of Cluny in Burgundy guaranteed absolute independence in elections and in all internal affairs. The first Cluny monks devoted themselves to the strict observance of the Benedictine rule but with certain important modifications. Farm work was no longer a major part of the monk's day; it was carried on by peasants, some of them often living under a semi-monastic regime. Instead, the monastic community spent a longer time in the solemn chanting of the liturgy which now became the principal emphasis of the daily life. The Cluny idea spread to other daughter houses established by or adopted by monks from the original abbey. Unlike the typical Benedictine communities, these daughter houses maintained their connection with the mother house at Cluny, each being governed by a prior under the jurisdiction of the abbot of Cluny. Even when, in the course of a century or more, some three hundred Cluniac monasteries had been established in France, Burgundy, western Germany, Spain, and England, there still remained only one abbot. Inevitably the abbot of Cluny was an ecclesiastic of major importance and not a few were men of real distinction.

The growth of the Cluny movement was also significant in Europe's cultural development. The emphasis on liturgy stimulated in the succeeding years a notable development of ecclesiastical music, the chant. Since a larger proportion of Cluny monks were priests, an abbey church needed added chapels or side-altars. In the case of the abbey church at Cluny size was also a factor. And there was dedicated in 1130 the largest church in the west, one of the longest, indeed, ever constructed in the Christian world.[1]

[1] 187 meters. St. Peter's, including the vestibule, is about thirty feet longer. Owing to neglect the great church at Cluny collapsed early in the nineteenth century. From the ruins measurements have been taken and scale reconstructions made.

B. The Gregorian Reform

While it is undoubtedly true that the Cluny achievement affected other areas of the church's organization and that in the reform of the secular clergy and the papacy a markedly monastic spirit prevailed, the two developments were not the same. The more general ecclesiastical renewal has been called the Gregorian reform after Pope Gregory VII (1073–1085), its most zealous promoter. In many respects it was a radical, almost revolutionary, movement which stemmed from earlier efforts, some in north Italy, some in Lorraine, and which aimed at a total reorganization of Christian society.

With the appointment by Henry III of Pope Leo IX (1049–1054), a native of Lorraine and formerly bishop of Toul, this movement reached Rome, and it was in the company of Leo that the future Gregory, then known as Hildebrand, first joined the papal administration. Hildebrand was of humble Tuscan peasant stock. Although not particularly prepossessing in manner, ap-appearance, or voice, he was a man of indomitable will and genuine spirituality. Less intransigent, more diplomatic and flexible, and more patient, but no less dedicated, was Urban II, a Frenchman perhaps best known for his launching of the First Crusade. As reform proceeded, France was to become one of its major areas of support.

Under the auspices of such men, there were taken what have sometimes been considered the first steps in building the modern constitution of the church. Certainly for the first time since the invasions it was possible to begin to create an ecclesiastical constitution with the pope actually, not merely theoretically, at the head, and a governmental procedure supported by canon law. Certain of these initial measures may be mentioned here. It was stipulated by a decree of 1059, for example, that only the principal or "cardinal" clergy of the Roman district should elect the Pope. These cardinal clergy were specifically designated. The seven (later six) cardinal bishops of the suburban sees of Rome actually elected the pope. A somewhat larger number of cardinal priests and deacons, attached to the principal Roman churches, confirmed the election. The role of the "people," who according to ancient traditions were expected to participate, was reduced to mere "acclamation." Thus the interference of the Roman nobility was avoided. With regard to the emperor's rights in the matter, only those enjoyed by the existing ruler were admitted; nothing was conceded to his successors.

While Pope Leo personally traveled a great deal, his successors, notably, Gregory, relied increasingly on legates. Papal legates, usually cardinals clothed with full papal power, were sent everywhere to correct abuses, hold synods, enforce the canons against clerical marriage and simony, even to depose recalcitrant prelates.

Though imbued with the monastic spirit, the Gregorian reformers were not unmindful of the interests of the secular clergy. They supported a tendency on the part of many secular priests to associate themselves with others in communities which adopted a quasi-monastic rule, usually one associated with the name of St. Augustine. Clergy living in such a way were called canons, and their community, sometimes connected with a cathedral church, sometimes with a large town parish or "collegiate" church, was called a chapter.[1] This development helped to restore a spiritual prestige to the town clergy whose reputations had been somewhat tarnished partly as a consequence of their own shortcomings, partly by comparison with the monks.

C. The Church and the Laity

The measures just described were but the beginning of a task which was to occupy the church for centuries. Moreover, its purpose was the sanctification not merely of clerics and monks, but of the vast population of laymen. To understand the magnitude of this problem it will be well to consider briefly the state of lay religion in the feudal age. Owing to the scarcity of evidence any generalizations regarding the religious life of the agrarian or town popu-

[1] One organization of canons founded in 1120 at Premontré by St. Norbert became a new religious order, the Premonstratensians, devoted to the service of parishes.

Italian Romanesque architecture. Orvieto.

Alinari photograph

lation which comprised the majority of Christians must be tentative. But there were occasional demonstrations of considerable religious feeling, though often irrational and disorganized. Hermits, particularly in France, were not uncommonly the objects of popular veneration, and a number of popular preachers—not all of them orthodox—made their appearance. The cult of saints and martyrs, particularly those of local fame, and of their relics was a notable feature of popular religious life. Apparently the attempts to thwart feudal war and banditry and to punish the offenders against the peace sometimes enlisted the support of the peasantry. Many, indeed, were killed in the attempt. There was a disposition to criticize a clergy whose lives were deemed unworthy of their sacred calling. In short, there was among the lower orders of medieval society a religious as well as an economic and social restlessness which in some instances was capable of leading to movements or "crusades" of some magnitude. And in some manner many of the humble folk managed to make pilgrimages to distant shrines.

Somewhat more clear are the religious aspirations of the nobility. Here the church had been at some pains to curb and, at least in part, to Christianize the innate warlike vigor of the typical feudal knight. This is the meaning of such institutions as the Peace and Truce of God and the religious element in chivalry. Knighthood, the status of the noble as a warrior, was originally a purely secular thing. The young squire, his training completed, received a simple accolade, or blow on the back of the neck, sometimes with the flat of a sword, from another knight. Thus he was admitted into the fellowship of the warrior class. But as ecclesiastical influence increased, the candidate spent the previous night in vigil before an altar on which his arms reposed. In the morning his arms were blest in an elaborate ritual, and he took a long and detailed oath symbolizing the ideals he hoped to live up to as a true Christian knight.

During the eleventh century bellicose tendencies were often channeled toward what was coming to be considered a "Holy War," the war against Islam. As early as 1063, for example, papal approbation was given to the expedition of French knights into Spain. Thus the already popular pilgrimage to Santiago de Compostela came to be associated with the great military offensive against the Moslems, the *Reconquista,* a movement by no means exclusively or even predominantly religious, but none the less manifesting a somewhat unsophisticated and enormously heroic sort of religious sentiment quite characteristic of the age.

All these emotions and aspirations, the typical melange of religious, political, and social ambitions, are dramatically and unforgettably expressed in the popular poetry of the time, the *chansons de geste,* composed in the language of northern France, the *langue d'oil.*[1] Originating in the eleventh century or before, many of these epics center around the figure of Charlemagne whose campaigns in Spain now appear in the guise of a great struggle with the Moslem world and who in the popular mind becomes a saint. Prodigious blows are given and taken in battles against countless thousands of Saracens. But battle is always preceded by religious ceremony, the blessing by the priest or by the emperor. Thus religious piety and bloody carnage are mingled together without discrimination. There is much emphasis on vassalage and feudal loyalty, but none on women or romantic love. All in all these epics let their readers and listeners see the Carolingian heroes perform as they would like to perform themselves.

The most famous of the *chansons de geste* is the *Song of Roland,* the story of a gallant but eventually unsuccessful rearguard action fought by Charlemagne's nephew, Roland, when he was ambushed in the Pyrenees by overwhelming thousands of Saracens. Although the story may have originated from an actual incident in Charlemagne's career, what little historical truth remains is highly colored to fit the tastes of later listeners. It must be read to be appreciated. One becomes acquainted in it with great characters of fiction: the knightly Roland; the traitor Ganelon; the fighting archbishop Turpin, who at one moment invokes the Deity, the next, "in the thick of the press, deals well more than a thousand buffets."[2]

Another aspect of the religious life of the upper feudal classes has already been mentioned, the widespread control of religious foundations by rulers and feudal magnates. This had involved, it will be recalled, the intrusion into ecclesiastical office of many men unfit for such duties, an alarming increase of simony, and the usage of lay investiture whereby a bishop was invested with the symbols of his jurisdiction by a layman. The continuance of lay participation in ecclesiastical affairs did not, however, always or necessarily lead to corrupt practices. Many nobles and not a few rulers regarded their religious responsibilities as a solemn obligation. So, for example, did the Emperor Henry III consider his interventions in papal affairs. As we have explained, contemporary opinion held the ruler to be a partly religious figure. And until the advent of the Gregorian reform there had been no consistent objection to lay investiture.[3]

Accordingly, when the Gregorian reformers came to regard the evils of lay intervention in church matters as outweighing the good, and concluded that lay investiture must be abolished, they were proposing a revolutionary reversal of current procedures and they were challenging the traditionally accepted religious character of kingship. These things became evident during the pontificate of Gregory VII in what has been called the "Investiture Controversy," for Gregory felt that lay investiture was the

[1] See below, p. 252.

[2] *The Song of Roland,* tr. by Isabel Butler, in the "Riverside Literature Series," No. 157, p. 77.

[3] The Emperor Henry II (1002–1024), who appointed and invested a considerable proportion of German bishops, is an officially canonized saint.

cause of much of the simony and corruption. The principal offender was the Emperor Henry IV who appears to have been more interested in the political aspects of lay control than in the improvement of the church. Thus the issue was squarely joined. Two men, equally resolved to uphold opposing positions on the matter of lay investiture, stood face to face.

D. *The Investiture Controversy*

In a famous synod held at Rome during the Lenten season of 1075, the Pope added to the now usual decrees against simony and clerical marriage the first outright prohibition of lay investiture. Henry disregarded the papal order. Moreover, when he received from the Pope a letter threatening excommunication and deposition,[1] he summoned a synod of German bishops (1076) who showed their loyalty to Henry by voting the deposition of the Pope.

Faced with such defiance, Gregory's only course was to carry out his threat of excommunication and deposition and to absolve all of Henry's subjects from their oath of fealty. All bishops who failed to make their peace with the Holy See were similarly placed under the ban of the church. Some submitted. A few, like Bishop Herman of Metz, braved the Emperor's wrath and supported the Pope throughout the entire bitter controversy. This first excommunication of an emperor not only frightened some of the bishops, but was eagerly seized upon by a large number of Henry's lay vassals as a religious sanction for rebellion against him. After consultation with Gregory's legates, the rebels demanded of Henry that he obtain absolution or forfeit their loyalty. The Pope was invited to cross the Alps and preside over a synod at Augsburg where Henry's position was to be discussed. Overjoyed at this apparent expression of loyalty, Gregory set out, stopping on the way at Canossa, the castle of a devoted friend, the Countess Matilda.

Henry's shrewdness did not fail in the crisis. Realizing that he must become reconciled to the church before he could hope to subdue his insurgent vassals, he decided to force the Pope's hand before the proposed council could meet. With a handful of followers he eluded his enemies, crossed the Alps in mid-winter, and appeared as a penitent before the Pope at Canossa. There, according to contemporary accounts, he appeared barefoot and without royal insignia on three successive days. At length, on the solicitation of those around him and doubtless much moved by this show of penitence, Gregory gave Henry absolution and reinstated him in his office.

This famous scene has been repeatedly cited as a symbol of the subjection of temporal to spiritual power. Henry's spectacular penitence does not tell the whole story. As events were to show, no permanent advantage was obtained by the Pope. Henry had now righted himself and was again the lawful sovereign, and his rebellious vassals were deprived of all justification for resistance. It soon became abundantly clear that Henry was returning to his old ways. Accordingly, nearly four years after Canossa, the Pope again excommunicated and deposed the Emperor.

Gregory's second sentence found Henry in a stronger position and in no mood for another public penance. The fortunes of the struggle began to go against the Pope. The archbishop of Ravenna was elected anti-pope as "Clement III" by the imperial faction. In 1081 the Emperor invaded Italy, and the year 1084 saw him in possession of Rome with the Pope besieged in the castle of St. Angelo. At this critical juncture Gregory called upon his vassal Normans of southern Italy for assistance. Robert Guiscard responded, but the Norman army was as much interested in sacking Rome as in rescuing the Pope. Since he was not safe elsewhere, Gregory went with them when they retired to the south. The imperialists were again masters of the Eternal City, and Gregory died at Salerno in 1085, a virtual prisoner of his rescuers.

Henry IV's victory over Gregory VII was a triumph over one pope, but not over the papacy. Gregory's successors carried on the struggle. And the added strength which the papacy gained as a result of the reforms

[1] Since no good Christian was supposed to associate with an excommunicated person, the deposition of such a ruler was a logical consequence.

The Bury St. Edmunds Cross. Carved walrus-ivory. English twelfth century.

Courtesy the Metropolitan Museum of Art, New York, The Cloisters Collection

gradually began to tell. The last years of Henry's reign were troubled by renewed rebellions in which even his own son participated. And although Henry V continued his father's policies and invaded Italy, he was eventually defeated by his enemies and in 1122 was ready to negotiate.

The Concordat of Worms (1122) between Emperor and Pope permitted the former to invest a new incumbent of a bishopric with the symbols of temporal rule only. Ring and crozier, symbolizing ecclesiastical jurisdiction, he was no longer to bestow. Episcopal elections were to be conducted, in the manner then customary, by the cathedral chapter. The emperor, however, was allowed to be present and to decide in the event of a disagreement.[1] The concordat was a compromise in that neither party gained the full measure of its demands. Lay investiture was a thing of the past, but interference in episcopal elections was not permanently avoided. Nevertheless, the time when emperors could dominate popes was passing.

The spectacular nature of the controversy between Popes and Holy Roman Emperors tends to obscure the more normal relations between the popes and certain of the other European kings. William I of England, for example, appointed bishops and ruled the English church, but he promoted reforms. Therefore, except for a brief period of strain, Anglo-Papal relations were friendly. In France Philip I did not resist the threat of excommunication and papal legates achieved considerable success, although here it was the magnates as much as the king who were guilty of lay investiture.[2]

The Gregorian reform opened a new era in the history of the church and of Europe. A new morale was evident which had considerable popular support and which continued to animate the church in the following decades. Yet the age of reform was not without its losses. Not all ecclesiastics sympathized with what seemed the overly rigid and sometimes markedly monastic character of the movement. The challenge to the ruler's religious position endangered the *rapport* between king and church, and subsequent decades were to witness considerable tension in certain areas. Excommunication and deposition, even for purely religious reasons, had political consequences and amounted to a claim, albeit vague, of the spiritual power to authority over the

[1] There were minor variations for Italy and Burgundy. A settlement reached in England (1107) seems to have provided a model for the arrangements in the Concordat of Worms.

[2] At this time certain rulers entered into a formal feudal relationship with the Holy See. Papal suzerainty might bring prestige and protection to a king whose position was legally insecure. For the pope a contractual relation seemed to offer, in addition to a regular revenue, the assurance that ecclesiastical policy would have the support of the local government. The actual extent of Gregory's feudal policy was not great. Hungary, Croatia-Dalmatia, the principality of Kiev, the Norman kingdom of southern Italy and Sicily, and a few small principalities accepted papal suzerainty, although in certain instances only temporarily. Others were added by later popes.

temporal. In the current confusion caused by the intimate association of religion and politics, Gregory laid the foundation for papal claims to political supremacy. He did not himself bring this idea to realization, and he probably had not such an intention. But his acts, whatever their motive, set important precedents for his successors. Another unfortunate development of the period which was in part related to the reform in the west was the tragic rift with the church in the east. By the middle of the eleventh century deep-seated cultural, linguistic, and political, as well as certain minor religious, divergencies had produced an estrangement and occasionally an outright, if temporary, break between the two ecclesiastical worlds. Certain recent events, for example the Norman occupation of Byzantine Italy, including dioceses formerly under Constantinople's jurisdiction, accentuated the tension. Most important, the Gregorian conception of an effective jurisdictional supremacy of Rome worried a Byzantium long accustomed to a nominal primacy.

In 1054 a papal legate was sent to Constantinople. He was Cardinal Humbert, an exceptionally able person, but one of the more intransigent Gregorian reformers and notably lacking in diplomatic finesse. The patriarch of the time, Michael Cerularius, was a man not without personal ambition. The details of their contretemps need not concern us here. Suffice it to say that each excommunicated the other. Certainly neither man regarded his action as involving anyone beyond those present. Nor for many decades did either side look upon 1054 as constituting a formal schism. A number of popes, and of eastern prelates, continued their efforts at reconciliation. Nevertheless, the Byzantine church which now included the bulk of the south Slavic population of the Balkans and also the Russians, gradually drifted into schism, and this schism has never been healed. To this day most of the east European churches continue to reject the jurisdiction of the pope.

E. The First Crusade

Toward the end of the eleventh century in the midst of the investiture controversy, there occurred an event which in many respects epitomizes all that western feudal society had come to be. This was the First Crusade to the Holy Land. It would therefore seem appropriate to conclude this chapter of our story with a consideration of that unique achievement.

The origins and causes of the First Crusade have long been the subject of controversy, and have been ascribed to a great variety of human motives, spiritual and material. Certainly the desire to acquire new fiefs, the mainspring of feudal expansion, was one. Another was the urge to extend contacts with lucrative oriental trade. But it must be remembered that the great majority of the participants did not remain in the east. They were moved, it would seem, by a spirit of high religious adventure, an attitude thoroughly characteristic of the age and perhaps of no other period in the history of the West. For the First Crusade was the culmination of the "holy war" against the "infidel." Such war, encouraged by the church, had been going on locally in Spain and elsewhere for some time. Its extension to the east followed certain important developments in the Moslem world, in particular the expansion of the Seljuk Turks in the eleventh century. These people, migrating from Turkestan, overran Moslem Persia and pushed south into Syria and Palestine. After becoming Moslems themselves, they decisively defeated a Byzantine army at Manzikert in Asia Minor (1071). Thereafter bands of Turks commenced an occupation of large sections of Asia Minor, thus bringing a resurgent Islam to the very gates of Europe.

Largely because the Seljuks were only a ruling minority in the conquered territories, there was considerable disorder for a time in Syria which interrupted or endangered Christian pilgrim travel to Jerusalem. Contemporary accounts bear witness of serious mistreatment of pilgrims, with a resulting curtailment of pilgrimages. This was not a permanent situation, but reports reached the west and stimulated a desire to take defensive measures against the Seljuk Turks and to ensure the safety of the Holy Sepulchre, the place of the entombment of Christ, at Jerusalem.

By the eleventh century, indeed long before, pilgrimage had become a venerable

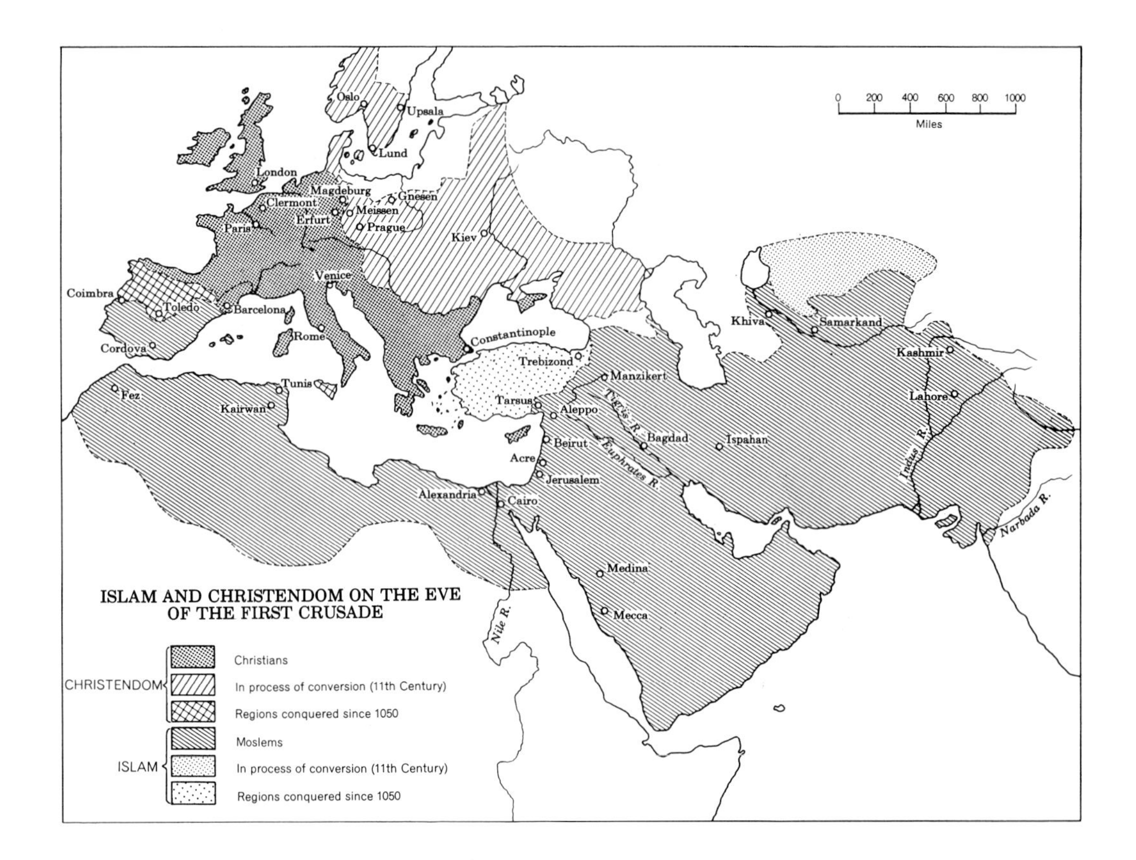

Christian practice. In fact, from the very early days of Christianity, men and women of all walks of life had formed the habit of visiting the places hallowed by the events of Christ's life or by the shrine of a great saint. Sometimes such journeys were prescribed as penances. More often a pilgrimage was a purely voluntary pious act. Rome and Santiago de Compostela were famous pilgrimage centers. But the most famous was Jerusalem, despite its remoteness from western Christendom, for here were the Holy Sepulchre and a portion of the relic of the True Cross of the Crucifixion. Nearby were Nazareth and Bethlehem and many other spots intimately associated with Christ's life. In a sense, the crusades were armed pilgrimages.

The First Crusade was launched as the immediate result of a famous sermon delivered by Pope Urban II at a church council in Clermont, France, in 1095. Urban, a man of broad statesmanship with a remarkable ability to grasp the significance of the current crisis, perceived the danger to all of Europe in the Moslem resurgence. He saw that it existed in Spain as well as in the Orient. Above all, he understood how the safety of eastern Europe depended upon the survival of the Christian Byzantine Empire. Only a few months before his appearance at Clermont, he had received envoys from the Byzantine Emperor Alexius Comnenus I, requesting western assistance against the Seljuk Turks. Evidently, the Pope was thinking in terms of a defensive war. Urban was a Frenchman and a former monk and abbot of the French monastery of Cluny; and it was to Frenchmen, who had already contributed heavily to Christian fighting against the Moslems in Spain, that he made his epochal appeal at Clermont in 1095.

Precisely what Urban said on that famous occasion we do not know. The accounts we have of his sermon were written years after the event. But in calling for an organized effort against the Moslems in the east, he evidently knew how to arouse his audience. He spoke in their native vernacular. His appeal was religious, but not entirely so. He urged his listeners to abandon their fratricidal feudal warfare and to expend their fighting energies in a more worthy cause. He dwelt on the unhappy plight of the eastern Christians, but he also pictured the Levant as a "land of milk and honey." Finally, to all participants who died repentant was offered a plenary indulgence.[1]

The response was immediate; and, according to the chroniclers, a great cry of "God wills it (*Deus lo vult*)" greeted the Pope's words. There is reason to believe that the numbers volunteering for service, and taking the cross, far exceeded Urban's expectations and plans.[2] Large-scale organization had to be provided immediately, and, in order that the expeditionary forces should be properly directed, the Pope appointed Bishop Adhemar of Puy as papal legate in charge. Provision was also made to protect, under threat of ecclesiastical censure, the property and families of those who enlisted. Women had to be specifically prohibited from going without their husbands' consent, and monks and priests without the authorization of their superiors. August, 1096, was set as the departure date for the crusading army.

The first contingent to set out was a miscellaneous, ill-organized band under a fanatical itinerant preacher named Peter "the Hermit." A second was a similar though somewhat better equipped band, led by another fanatic, Walter "the Penniless." Neither of these was of any real military significance, and both were decimated by the Turks in Asia Minor. But the fact that such bands went at all is eloquent testimony of popular enthusiasm for the crusade.

The real military expedition set out in the summer and fall of 1096. As might have been expected, practically all its members were French. Germany, which might otherwise have participated, was then torn by the investiture controversy, and its Holy Roman Emperor, Henry IV, had recently been excommunicated. As a consequence, the term "Frank" became almost synonymous with "Crusader." The expedition as a whole consisted of several separate divisions, each under a distinguished feudal leader. Though they all agreed to meet at Constantinople, there was no effective unified command.

At Constantinople, trouble arose out of conflicting aims of the Crusaders and of the Byzantine Emperor Alexius. The latter had requested assistance in recovering lost territory for his Empire. The Crusaders, on the other hand, were intent on keeping for themselves whatever land they conquered, at least in Syria and Palestine. And the Western divisions of eager and often truculent knights were a source of potential danger to Alexius until he could shepherd them safely over into Asia Minor. Between the Byzantines and the Westerners, differences of language and customs, as well as of war aims, were aggravated by the recent rift between the eastern and western churches.[3] Though some temporary agreements were reached between them, real coöperation, so essential to any permanent success, was never achieved.

In crossing Asia Minor the Crusaders demonstrated an ability to defeat armies of the Seljuk Turks, and, despite hunger and thirst, to triumph over such natural obstacles as the hot Anatolian plateau and the rugged Taurus mountains. At Antioch in north Syria they began the siege of a major city.[4] Lacking siege engines and needful supplies, they were forced to await the arrival of an Italian fleet before pressing the siege in earnest. This intervention of Italian shipping was a development of special significance. For the Crusaders, in their advance southward, were no longer dependent on land communication with the Byzantines, but rather on sea communication with Italy. In this way, commercial contact between the Levant and western Europe was at last revived. The Italians soon learned to exact a high price for their invaluable assistance, and before long traders from Genoa, Pisa, and other Italian city-states were firmly established in Syrian and Palestinian ports.

Meanwhile, the divisions which were to

[1] A *plenary* indulgence signified the remission of all the temporal punishment due to sin. See below, pp. 351–352.

[2] Because those volunteering wore the cross, at first rudely made of cloth, on their armor they were called *crucesignati* or "crusaders."

[3] See above, p. 167. It is probable that Pope Urban hoped that Western aid might create an atmosphere favorable to ending the schism. If so, his hopes were disappointed.

[4] Nicaea had been taken shortly after the Crusaders left Constantinople.

A French twelfth century polychrome oak statue of the Virgin and Child.

Courtesy Metropolitan Museum of Art, New York; Gift of J. Pierpont Morgan, 1916

plague the crusading movement to its very end had already begun to appear. One group had left the main army before the siege of Antioch and had begun operations along the upper Euphrates which eventuated in the capture of the city of Edessa (1098). And it was only a general clamor among the rank-and-file shortly after the fall of Antioch which compelled the leaders to reunite their forces and resume the march to Jerusalem.

Jerusalem, the goal of the expedition, was captured after a six-week siege on July 15, 1099, three years after the crusade had set out and four years after Pope Urban's sermon.[1] The Pope died on July 29, before the news of victory could reach him. When eventually the news did reach western Europe, it was received with the utmost enthusiasm and exultation. The victory crowned a long sustained effort, which cannot be explained by mere ambition for material gain. It betokened a zeal, an idealism, a stubborn persistence against formidable obstacles, and a spirit of high adventure, which have rarely been equalled.

The First Crusade may be taken as marking the climax of the early medieval world. It was unique, both in its character and in being the only one of the crusades which really succeeded. Those Crusaders—and they were the minority—who remained in the east to found principalities, together with the Italian merchants who controlled the trade in the ports, came to be, if they were not already, men of a different stamp. Like their contemporaries in Europe they now set out to build institutions of law and of government, to live and deal with the Moslems as well as to fight them. But such developments were characteristic of a more mature stage in the growth of Western civilization, the stage which may be called the "Middle Age proper" and to which we shall next turn.

---

[1] Jerusalem was taken from the Shiite Egyptian Moslems who had captured the city from the Sunnite Turks in the preceding year.

SELECT SUPPLEMENTARY READINGS FOR PART III

General. Same as for "General" under Part II, p. 110; in addition: R. W. Southern, *The Making of the Middle Ages* (1953); C. Brooke, *Europe in the Central Middle Ages, 962–1154* (1964).

Chapter 10. For the rise and decline of the Carolingian Empire, and the culture of the period: J. A. Wallace-Hadrill, *The Long-haired Kings* (1962); E. S. Duckett, *Alcuin, Friend of Charlemagne* (1951) and *Alfred the Great* (1956); S. C. Easton and H. Wieruszowski, *The Carolingian Empire* (1961); H. Fichtenau, *The Carolingian Empire* (tr. 1957); M. Laistner (cited above, Chapter 8); G. Schnürer, *Church and Culture in the Middle Ages*, vol. I (1956); R. E. Sullivan, *The Coronation of Charlemagne* (1959); R. Winston, *Charlemagne* (1954). On the Norsemen and other invaders: H. Arbman, *The Vikings* (1961); J. Brondsted, *The Vikings* (1940); F. Dvornik, *The Slavs: Their Early History and Civilization* (1956); T. D. Kendrick, *History of the Vikings* (1930); A. R. Lewis, *The Northern Seas* (1958); C. A. Macartney, *The Magyars in the Ninth Century* (1930); F. Mowat, *Westviking* (1965); C. Turville-Petrie, *The Heroic Age of Scandinavia* (1951).

Chapter 11. M. Bloch, *Feudal Society* (new ed., 1961); F. L. Ganshof, *Feudalism* (1952); S. Painter, *Medieval Society* (1951) and *French Chivalry* (1940); E. Prestage, *Chivalry* (1928); C. Stephenson, *Feudalism* (1942).

Chapter 12. G. Barraclough, *The Origins of Modern Germany* (1947); F. Dvornik (cited above, Chapter 10); R. Fawtier, *The Capetian Kings of France* (1960); R. Menendez-Pidal, *The Cid and His Spain* (1934); C. Petit-Dutaillis, *Feudal Monarchy in France and England* (1936); F. M. Stenton, *Anglo-Saxon England* (2nd ed., 1947); J. W. Thompson, *Feudal Germany* (1928); D. Whitelock, *The Beginnings of English Society* (1952); P. Blair, *Introduction to Anglo-Saxon England* (1959).

Chapter 13. H. S. Bennett, *Life on the English Manor* (1937); M. Bloch, *Feudal Society* (1961); G. G. Coulton, *The Medieval Village* (1925), reprinted as *Medieval Village, Manor, and Monastery* (1960); H. L. Adelson, *Medieval Commerce* (1962); R. Latouche, *The Birth of Western Economy* (tr. 1960); A. R. Lewis, *The Northern Seas* (1958); N. Neilson, *Medieval Agrarian Economy* (1936); H. Pirenne, *Economic and Social History of Medieval Europe* (1937); S. Painter, *Medieval Society* (1951); E. Power, *Medieval People* (1924).

Chapter 14. In addition to the general works on church history cited above, p. 49: R. H. Bainton, *The Medieval Church* (1962); G. Tellenbach, *Church, State, and Christian Society at the Time of the Investiture Contest* (1940); W. Ullmann, *The Growth of Papal Government in the Middle Ages* (1955) and *Medieval Papalism* (1949). For the Eastern church and the crusades: S. Runciman, *A History of the Crusades*, 3 vols. (1951–1954), and *The Eastern Schism* (1955); K. M. Setton and M. W. Baldwin, eds., *A History of the Crusades*, vol. I (1955); H. Daniel-Rops, *Cathedral and Crusade* (1957); M. A. Deanesley, *History of the Medieval Church, 590–1500* (1954).

Twelfth century military architecture. The Barbican Gate at Carisbrooke Castle, Isle of Wight.

Courtesy British Information Services, New York

From Urban II to Dante

Gothic architecture in Spain. The elaborate interior of the Cathedral at Burgos.

Courtesy Spanish National Tourist Department, New York

PART IV

THE MIDDLE AGE OF THE CENTURIES AND THE

TWELFTH AND THIRTEENTH FLOWERING OF EUROPE

Late twelfth or early thirteenth century Champlevé enamel work from the famous center of the industry at Limoges, France.

Courtesy Metropolitan Museum of Art, New Yorl

DURING THE MIDDLE AGE of the twelfth and thirteenth centuries, European civilization, with its Graeco-Roman and Judaeo-Christian traditions, is no longer confined to Mediterranean lands, as it had been in antiquity; nor is it diluted with barbarism, as it was in the Early Middle Age—the "Dark Age"—from the sixth to the eleventh century. It is now the civilization of the entire continent of Europe, and it is remarkably lusty and progressive.

True, two major subdivisions of European civilization, long in the making, now become definitive through a rupture of church unity. The "East," including the Byzantine Empire, the Balkans, and Russia, follows a separate Orthodox Church, with strongly Greek and oriental influence, while the "West," embracing western and central Europe, continues to adhere to the Catholic Church under the Roman papacy and with Latin liturgy and usages. Henceforth there is an aloofness, and a more or less open hostility, between "West" and "East."

It is the "West" which flowers in the Middle Age proper, and with which we are here chiefly concerned. The flowering takes many forms. It is evidenced in a great crusading movement against Moslems in the Near East and the Iberian peninsula, in colonial experiments outside Europe in Syria and Palestine, and in pioneer contacts with faraway China. It is shown, too, in the expansion of maritime and inland trade, the increase of commodities, industry, and money, the growth of cities, and the extension of agriculture. It is further exemplified in the consolidation of feudal monarchy, in the development of representative institutions, in the seeming brilliance of the Holy Roman Empire, and in the very real "Drang nach Osten"—the West's "Drive to the East."

Central to this Middle Age in the West is the Catholic Church, which develops a strong papal monarchy, sponsors such new religious orders as the Franciscan and Dominican, successfully combats heresy, and exerts an all-pervasive popular influence. In close connection with the Church, universities arise, scholastic philosophy flourishes, and notable progress is made in science, medicine, and law.

It is an age, moreover, of highly important popular literature and art. Epics and romances and Dante's *Divine Comedy* appear in the ordinary spoken (vernacular) languages, and both romanesque and gothic architecture reach a climax.

CHAPTER 15

New Frontiers

A. The New Frontiers of Western Europe

Earlier chapters have emphasized the expansive character of feudal society. Expansion continued to be characteristic of European civilization during the twelfth and thirteenth centuries—the Middle Age proper—and it was accentuated by such factors as a general rise in population, increasing commerce, and a heightened emphasis on waging a "holy war" against the infidel. Not only was the area of Christendom enlarged by the establishment of new frontier settlements, but venturesome souls journeyed to remote lands prompted by the desire to open new avenues of trade or to carry forward the banners of holy religion. By 1300, Europeans of varied nationality had extended their political boundaries, added to their knowledge of other civilizations, and generally broadened and deepened their own.

From far northern Europe had gone out in all directions the Scandinavian Vikings, or Norsemen. From their settlements in French Normandy, their descendants in the eleventh century went to southern Europe and to England. The *wanderlust* was certainly in their blood, for from all three places young knights pushed on to further adventures. The Norman kingdom of Sicily developed commercial contacts along the north coast of Africa. And Norman-Sicilian barons were active in the crusades in Palestine. Meanwhile, Anglo-Norman warriors and traders helped to extend the territory of the English monarchy, particularly at the expense of the Scottish kingdom, which had included a large section of English-speaking Northumbria. Into this "lowland" area and even into the Celtic "highlands" of Scotland came many knights from the south, especially during the reign of the Scottish King David I (1124–1153), who was receptive to southern and feudal ideas.

A somewhat similar situation developed in Wales. The Anglo-Norman border knights, or "Lords Marchers" as they were called, drove the Celtic Welsh farther into their rugged hills and established new fiefs and towns. Finally King Edward I conquered Wales (1276–1284) and incorporated it into the English monarchy. Since then the heir to the English throne has usually borne the title of "Prince of Wales."

Nor was Ireland immune to Anglo-Norman expansion. Although many Scandinavians had settled there, adopting Christianity and mingling with the native Irish, the Viking raids had left the island a turmoil of warring clans. In 1171 an Anglo-Norman contingent invaded Ireland, ostensibly to aid an exiled chieftain, but actually to establish English barons in new fiefs. Two years later King Henry II placed a royal official in Ireland, organized the east coast under his jurisdiction, and even received the homage of a number of Irish chieftains of the interior. During the thirteenth century the area under English domination increased.

In southern Europe, the Iberian peninsula continued to attract restless French as well as native knights in search of material or spiritual rewards. The formation of Portugal affords an excellent example of what happened. First, a group of northern Crusaders en route to Jerusalem assisted in the conquest of Lisbon (1147) from the Moslems. Then Portugal, already a fief of the Holy See (1143), was recognized as a separate kingdom (1179) through the authorization of Pope Alexander III.

In the expanding Christian kingdoms of Spain, papal influence was especially noticeable under Innocent III (1198–1216). The king of Aragon, for example, submitted his state to the protection of the Holy See in 1204. And during a crisis of temporary Moslem recovery, it was Innocent's organizing activities which procured added assistance from the north and united the several Christian Spanish states into some sort of common front. As a consequence, the Moslems were defeated in a great battle at Las Navas de Tolosa in 1212. Never again was Christian Spain seriously menaced by Moslem advance.

During the thirteenth century the consolidation and expansion of Christian Spain was furthered, first, by the union of the kingdoms of Leon and Castile (1230), and, second, by the growing preëminence of the kingdom of Aragon in the western Mediterranean. Though Aragon lost Languedoc (except Montpellier) to the French monarchy, it conquered Valencia from the Moslems (1245) and won temporary footholds on the north African coast. It regained the Balearic Islands in 1235. Then in 1282, the King of Aragon, Peter III (1276–1285), taking advantage of a popular revolt in Sicily—the so-called "Sicilian Vespers"—intervened in the island and took possession of it.[1] Thus Aragon secured a predominance throughout the Western Mediterranean, and shared the bulk of the Iberian peninsula with three other Christian states—Castile, Navarre, and Portugal. Only Granada, in the extreme south, remained in Moslem hands.

Meanwhile, there had been a notable German expansion eastward in north-central Europe. This had begun, on a wide front from the Danube to the Baltic, under the early Saxon emperors. The internal strengthening of the Slavic states of Poland and Bohemia and the Magyar state of Hungary had at first prevented major extension of the German frontier at their expense, but not the immigration within them of many German settlers. The twelfth and thirteenth centuries did witness, however, an impressive advance of the German frontier along the Baltic. There, in a concerted and often highly systematic movement, thousands of German peasants, merchants, and townsmen followed the leadership of such feudal magnates as Adolf of Holstein, Albert "the Bear" of Brandenburg, and Henry "the Lion" of Saxony.

New towns, bishoprics, and monasteries were founded and German settlers and missionaries introduced. Gradually, the original Slavic inhabitants were submerged by the influx of German peasants in Mecklenburg, Brandenburg, and Pomerania. In this Germanizing process, the church and especially such monastic orders as the Cistercians and the Premonstratensians zealously coöperated. The church's official support of the movement went beyond the organization of missions and the establishment of local hierarchies. In 1147, at the time of the Second Crusade to the Holy Land, the church promised the same spiritual rewards for fighting Slavic "infidels" as for warring against Moslems.

German expansion eastward and northward along the Baltic was speeded in the thirteenth century by religio-military orders, particularly the Knights of the Sword and the Teutonic Knights. The former of these, founded early in the century by Albert, missionary bishop in Livonia, completed the conversion and conquest of that province and extended its sway into Estonia and Kurland. In these regions a kind of ecclesiastical state was founded under a Grand Master of the German Knights of the Sword, and with immigrant German nobles as feudal landlords. Here was a transplanted feudalism, topped by a German aristocracy and supported from below by a conquered and Christianized native peasantry.

The Teutonic Knights, originally established for service in the Holy Land, transferred their activities first to eastern

[1] Later, during the fourteenth and fifteenth centuries, Aragon appropriated Sardinia from the Pisans and Genoese.

Hungary and then (1228), on the invitation of a Polish prince, to Baltic-speaking Prussia, east of the Vistula river. The Grand Master of the Order, Hermann of Salza, then sought and obtained from the Holy Roman Emperor Frederick II confirmation of the "rights" of the Teutonic Knights to all future conquests in Prussia. Many younger sons of German nobles joined the Knights in warfare against the native Prussians. But these Prussians were stubborn fighters, and it took fifty years for the German forces to subdue them. Eventually Teutonic Knights not only reduced the Baltic Prussians along the coast and in a considerable hinterland, but blocked the Polish kingdom from access to the Baltic. This meant a revival of Polish-German rivalry and enmity, with important consequences for the future. Meanwhile, in 1237, the Teutonic Knights absorbed the Knights of the Sword and succeeded them as rulers of Livonia and Kurland. With the conquest of Prussia, and the final acquisition of Estonia from Denmark in 1346, the Teutonic Order and its Germanizing influence were of paramount importance along the whole Baltic coast from the Vistula to the Gulf of Finland.

The expansion which has just been described was one of the major achievements of the German people in the middle ages. A large area which had formerly been Slavic or Baltic was Germanized: Holstein, Mecklenburg, and Brandenburg in what is now the heart of north Germany; Lusatia and Silesia, on the upper Oder; Pomerania and Prussia, on the Baltic. Besides, German rulers and landlords now dominated the northeastern Baltic lands of Livonia, Kurland, and Estonia.

But in considering this achievement, its long-term effect on Germany's neighbors must not be forgotten. The kingdom of Poland was forced to seek expansion southward. Lithuania, threatened with conquest, made common cause with Poland. And the Russians resented and resisted the attempts of the Teutonic Knights to compel their conversion to the Roman church. All these peoples were to provide formidable opposition to the Germans in later years. German eastward expansion reached its climax in the thirteenth and early fourteenth centuries.

B. *Western Christian States in the Levant*

An earlier chapter has described the First Crusade to the Holy Land, a movement which led to a somewhat different form of feudal expansion. The states which the Crusaders founded in Syria were not the result of frontier expansion. Rather, they were settlements of Europeans, predominantly Frenchmen, living in a distant land and in a foreign environment. Four states were established: the county of Edessa; the principality of Antioch; the county of Tripoli; and, farthest south, the kingdom of Jerusalem. The last contained, in addition to the sacred towns of Jerusalem, Bethlehem, and Nazareth, the important ports of Tyre, Beirut, Acre, Sidon, Jaffa, and Ascalon. Its first ruler was Godfrey of Bouillon who was content with the title of Advocate, or Defender, of the Holy Sepulchre, but on his death in 1100 his brother, Baldwin, was given the title of king. Thus was established a feudal monarchy, rather than an ecclesiastical or even a Crusaders' principality. A temporary and largely theoretical suzerainty of the kingdom of Jerusalem over the other states was soon replaced by the actual independence of each.

Each of the states was divided, in typical western feudal fashion, into fiefs and baronies, the vassals forming a feudal *curia*. Thus a superstructure of western feudal administration governed the relations among crusading nobles and knights in the Near East; and these relations were minutely described, so far as the kingdom of Jerusalem was concerned, in the thirteenth-century *Assizes of Jerusalem*, an important compilation of feudal law. Beneath such a superstructure of European feudalism, which represented the usages of the ruling minority, lived the numerous and cosmopolitan native population, Christian and Moslem. Doubtless these people lived in much the same manner as before. The Moslem rulers left the country, and their agricultural estates were parceled out among new Christian masters. But townsmen continued

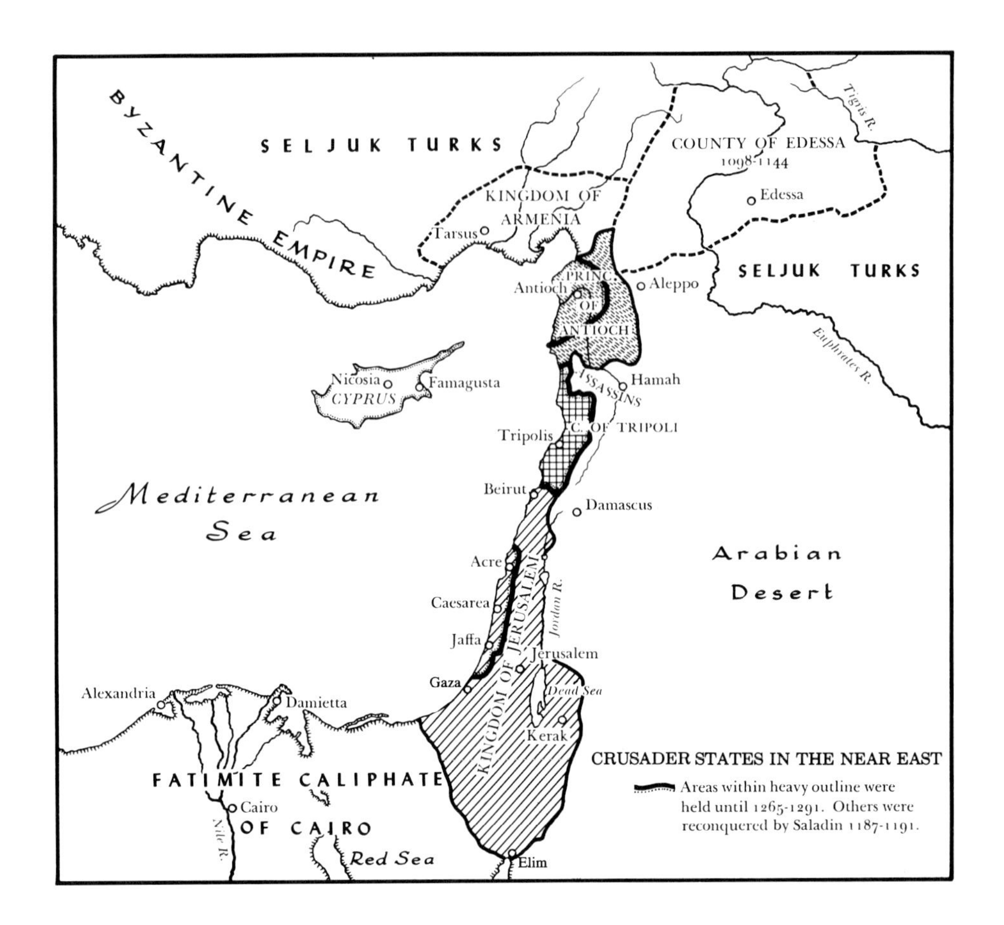

CRUSADER STATES IN THE NEAR EAST

to carry on their business and farmers to till the soil or tend their cattle. Mohammedans were not persecuted, and the various native Christian sects flourished. Some of these, like the Maronites, were reunited with Rome and the papacy. Gradually relations between Crusaders and natives became quite normal and friendly. Crusaders adopted native customs, food, and dress; and they habitually employed native physicians. In short the Franks, as all the Crusaders were called, became acclimated to the orient, and learned by experience the best methods of governing a native population on foreign soil.

A Latin ecclesiastical hierarchy was speedily established in communion with the pope and under the immediate jurisdiction of the patriarchs of Jerusalem and Antioch, two venerable sees of apostolic foundation. Western monasticism also made its appearance, and most of the European religious orders maintained houses in the Levant. The close association of church and government, so characteristic of the west, was equally noticeable in the Latin orient. Ecclesiastics were active in political matters. An occasional prelate, like the famous Archbishop William of Tyre, chancellor of the kingdom of Jerusalem and historian, exhibited superb qualities of statesmanship.

Economic life centered in the coastal towns where the Italian merchants obtained lucrative monopolies. Usually they were given outright control over a section of a port. Since their transport services were indispensable to the furnishing of supplies and reinforcements, privileges were heaped upon them by both ecclesiastical and lay authorities. And in the Western recovery of commercial contact with the eastern Mediterranean, Genoese and Pisans took the lead, breaking thereby the virtual monopoly of eastern trade formerly enjoyed by Venice.

A permanent military establishment was organized to meet the ever present needs of defense against renewed Moslem attacks. Such attacks were frequent if intermittent, and sometimes involved large-scale campaigning. Each barony was expected to provide a stipulated number of men-at-arms, both mounted knights and foot-soldiers, for the common army. The crusaders learned by bitter experience that heavy cavalry unsupported by a disciplined infantry, especially bowmen, were helpless against the Saracen light-armed horsemen and mounted archers. Strong fortresses were erected at vulnerable points along the frontier, and important advances were made in the art of castle building.

Many of the castles were garrisoned by Knights of the Temple or of the Hospital. These were orders of military monks whose lives were dedicated to perpetual "holy war." The Templars were first organized to protect pilgrims on the way to the Holy Sepulchre. Their headquarters were on the site of Solomon's temple, hence their name. The Knights of St. John, or Hospitallers, originally founded to care for sick pilgrims, later assumed military functions. Both Orders required, though not irrevocably, the customary monastic vows in addition to military service. After many privileges and exemptions had been granted them by successive popes, they formed a virtually independent, as well as a permanent, military force.

A great weakness of the Crusaders' states was the lack of numbers, for many of the original Crusaders returned home, and reinforcements from the west were irregular and rarely sufficient. Newcomers were inexperienced in Levantine life and tactics and hence were often as much a nuisance as a help to the "native" Latin Christians. Another difficulty resulted from the rather typical feudal decentralization. Only crises brought effective common action within or among the four states, and even then Antioch, Tripoli, and Jerusalem acted as separate units. There were several attempts to revive the alliance with the Byzantine Empire, for, despite obvious sources of discord, there was great need for coöperation. Unfortunately all attempts proved unsuccessful. Consequently, whenever the surrounding Moslem states achieved a semblance of unity among themselves, they could be a grave menace to the divided and isolated Latin Christian states in Syria and Palestine.

Crusaders' fortifications in Syria.

Courtesy Government of Syria Tourist Office, New York

Such occasions were rare, however, and the Crusaders, though divided themselves, learned to profit by Moslem disunion and to achieve a sort of Near Eastern balance of power. Antioch and Tripoli, and to a lesser extent Jerusalem, were admirably protected by nature. The northern portion of the kingdom of Jerusalem, virtually all of Tripoli, and most of Antioch were guarded by mountainous frontiers. Hence it is not surprising that Edessa, the least protected, was the first to be reconquered by the Moslems, in 1144, and that Tripoli and Antioch survived the Moslem reconquest of Jerusalem in 1187 by at least a century.

Altogether the crusading Christians successfully established and for over a century maintained centers of Western European culture on an alien soil, and though they were influenced by ideas and customs in the new environment, they did not become entirely "orientalized." Some learned Arabic, but all habitually conversed and occasionally wrote in a European, principally French or Italian, vernacular. Chronicles were composed and documents issued in Latin. Churches were erected in contemporary

Moslem fortifications east of the Crusaders' states. The Citadel at Aleppo.

Courtesy Government of Syria Tourist Office, New York

styles of West European architecture. In short, although owing no allegiance to any specific European kingdom, the Latin states in the Levant were western European colonies outside of Europe.

C. Later Crusades

The rise of Saladin, Sultan of Egypt (1171–1193), brought a temporary, though tremendously effective, unity to the Moslems throughout Syria and Egypt; and his success in suppressing the rival Fatimite caliphate of Egypt and in unifying his co-religionists happened to coincide with disastrous political and personal dissensions in the Latin Christian kingdom of Jerusalem. These, rather than any clear-cut military superiority, enabled Saladin to defeat a Christian army at Hattin near the Lake of Tiberias in 1187 and to open the way to the re-conquest, in the same year, of the city of Jerusalem. By 1191 only a few ports in the former state of Jerusalem, together with the little states of Tripoli and Antioch, remained in Christian hands.

The Third Crusade,[1] organized as a result of the fall of Jerusalem, is perhaps the best known after the First, because it was led at the outset by two kings and an emperor, Philip Augustus of France and Richard I of England and the Holy Roman Emperor Frederick Barbarossa. The last was drowned while crossing a stream in Asia Minor on his way to the Holy Land, and Philip soon pleaded an excuse of illness to return to more inviting French concerns. Though Richard conquered the island of Cyprus, successfully besieged the important port of Acre, and buttressed the Latin Christian states of Tripoli and Antioch, he was unable to recover Jerusalem. This remained under control of Saladin and the Moslems. Both Richard and Saladin, despite many passages at arms, were honorable, one might almost say friendly, enemies. Both displayed the best characteristics of medieval chivalry.

[1] After the First Crusade, many other expeditions set out from the West. The most important have been given numerical titles (Second, Third, Fourth, etc.), but these major organized ventures represent only a part of a continuous effort in which many individuals and smaller groups participated.

During the thirteenth century there was a growing apathy in the West toward crusading. The ardor of 1095 was lacking. Only occasionally did a prince, such as St. Louis IX of France (1226–1270), devotedly take the cross. And since his genuine zeal was shared by few of his associates, his two expeditions, one to Egypt (the Seventh Crusade), and the other to Tunis (the Eighth Crusade), in which he met his death, were fruitless. In the meantime, a great deal of crusading energy was diverted by the popes to their European enemies—heretics of southern France and Hohenstaufen rulers of the Holy Roman Empire. Worldly interests, political, diplomatic, and economic, engaged the attention of Europeans in the thirteenth century so that oversea crusading against Moslems seemed to many a distant and unprofitable undertaking.

Perhaps the most conspicuous example of the predominance of diplomatic and economic motives over religious was the so-called Fourth Crusade. Inaugurated at the beginning of the thirteenth century by one of the greatest of medieval popes, Innocent III, and planned originally for the Holy Land, it was diverted first to Zara in Christian Hungary and then, despite papal censures, to Constantinople which was captured in 1204. This diversion resulted partly from diplomatic intrigues involving a pretender to the Byzantine throne, and partly from financial demands of the Venetians. These shrewd traders had been engaged to transport the crusading army, but finding part of the expected payment lacking, they insisted on compensation through an attack on the wealthy capital of the Christian Byzantine Empire. With Constantinople in western hands, the Venetians not only made its commerce a virtual monopoly of their own, but were enabled to gain more of the other oriental trade which the earlier crusades had fostered for the Genoese and Pisans. Pope Innocent III, at first profoundly disturbed, finally accepted the inevitable and seized the opportunity to organize in the conquered Byzantine provinces a Latin hierarchy in communion with Rome.

The Latin Empire of Constantinople and Greece, which the Fourth Crusade erected in 1204, lasted only until 1261, when the Byzantines, who had held out in Asia Minor, reconquered Constantinople and most of Greece. The net result of this warfare between Greek and Latin, between Christian East and Christian West, was a profound and enduring hostility. Coöperation against the common Moslem enemy was henceforth impossible, and the chances of ecclesiastical reunion of the Catholic and Eastern Churches were more remote than ever. And, despite its restoration, the Byzantine Empire was irreparably weakened by the temporary Latin conquest.

Increasingly neglected by the West, the little Christian states in Syria which had survived the fall of Jerusalem in 1187 gradually became the prey of internal quarrels and external Moslem pressure. In the latter part of the thirteenth century, they were gradually reduced by a remarkable Moslem commander, Baybars, at the head of an Egyptian force known as the Mamelukes. Acre, the last Christian stronghold in the Levant, fell in 1291.[1]

A thirteenth century book about animals. The earliest surviving example of Persian art after the Mongol invasions and the fall of Bagdad, 1258.

Courtesy Pierpont Morgan Library, New York

D. Results of the Crusades

It has sometimes been claimed that the Crusades were responsible for all the great developments—commercial, political, and intellectual—which occurred in Western Europe during the twelfth and thirteenth centuries. This is a gross exaggeration. While they doubtless contributed to many of those developments, in the main they merely strengthened some previously existing trends. In commerce, the Crusades simply accelerated a revival already well under way. Italian fleets completed a reconquest of the Mediterranean and reestablished with the Levant a regular sea traffic, which survived the loss of the Christian colonies that the Crusades had planted there. The result was a greater familiarity with, and a greater demand for, eastern products—spices, sugar, textiles, etc. Returning crusaders helped to transform what had once been luxuries into articles of ordinary trade. Moreover, skillful Europeans, notably Italians, managed to appropriate or imitate certain eastern techniques, for example, in glass-making and in the preparation of dyes. A silk industry appeared in Palermo and later in Lucca. An enterprising Italian named Zaccaria "cornered" the alum production of northwestern Asia Minor. In return for assisting the Byzantine emperor to recover Constantinople in 1261, the Genoese obtained trade privileges in the Crimea which subsequently led to further commercial penetration into the Mongol empire. But such achievements, however important, were only incidentally related to the Crusades.

Similarly, the effect of the Crusades on the political and ecclesiastical institutions of twelfth- and thirteenth-century Europe was not great and for the most part it was indirect. While the success of the First Crusade undoubtedly increased the prestige of the reformed papacy at the time of the investiture struggle, subsequent failures and such episodes as the Fourth Crusade served only to discredit the endeavor

[1] A western Christian kingdom continued on the island of Cyprus. It passed under Venetian control in 1489.

and the ecclesiastical authorities who sponsored it.

Another indirect result of the Crusades was the promotion of Christian missions to the Moslems. Franciscan and Dominican friars, whose convents were established in the Crusaders' states, made some attempts to convert Moslems.[1] But in general these remained stubbornly resistant to Christian teaching, and continued (and still continue) to compete with Christians for the conversion of pagans. Nevertheless, the efforts of the friars marked the beginning of organized and active missions to non-European peoples, which were to persist long after the collapse of Crusader states in the Near East.

To the notable renaissance of learning in western Europe in the twelfth and thirteenth centuries, the Crusades made a small, though significant, contribution in the field of historical writing. The Crusades were the most spectacular achievement of the era, and they inspired several participants to write vivid accounts for the edification of interested people at home. One of the best of these was the *History of Deeds Done Beyond The Sea*, which was written by William, archbishop of Tyre and chancellor of the kingdom of Jerusalem, and which traced the crusading history down to 1183. Histories in the vernacular, in poetry as well as prose—for the Crusade was the great *geste* of the age—were added to those in Latin. *L'Estoire de guerre sainte*, written by an Anglo-Norman minstrel, recounts the expedition of King Richard of England. Villehardouin's chronicle of the Fourth Crusade is an early prose work in old French. On the other hand, western Christian contacts with Arabic learning in the Levant were insignificant. Spain and Sicily, not Jerusalem or Antioch, were the centers of that important intellectual exchange.

In the field of military science the crusades contributed to an advance in castle building and to an increased use of infantry in coöperation with cavalry. The ultimate failure of the Crusades should not obscure the fact that, despite the disastrous rift between Constantinople and the West and the weakening of the Byzantine Empire, the Mohammedans were kept back from the gates of eastern Europe for two centuries.

Finally, the Crusades made real, for a brief time, the Christian ideal of unified endeavor, the dedication of all to a holy cause. So powerful was this ideal and so striking the initial success of the holy war, that the word "crusade" became customary in describing subsequent undertakings in other fields. "Crusades" were preached against Slavs of northeastern Europe, against heretics of southern France, against Hohenstaufen enemies of the papacy. Such diversions undoubtedly helped to lessen support for real crusading in the Holy Land, but they bear testimony to the power of an idea. Even in our own day, one of the surest ways to enlist support for a popular cause is to call it a "crusade."

The idea of crusading against Moslems persisted into the fourteenth and fifteenth and even sixteenth centuries, in the form of a number of projects for the recovery of the Holy Land, including even an economic blockade of the Mohammedans; and occasionally an expedition was launched. But little or nothing was actually accomplished. The later middle age was a period of national monarchies, incipient power politics, and diversified commerce. Although in many respects unique, the crusades were primarily a product of the feudal age, of its religious and material interests. They illustrate the exuberant energy of a feudal day. It is significant that they did not survive the passing of feudalism.

E. The Mongols, and European Medieval Contacts with China

Just before the middle of the thirteenth century, when Christian Europeans were still fighting Moslems, there suddenly irrupted in the Near East a mighty Asiatic power which most gravely threatened both Christendom and Islam. It was the Mongol power. The Mongols, or Tatars as they were more often called by Europeans,[2] were Asiatic nomads who in the first part of the thirteenth century swept over and subju-

[1] Some efforts were also made to teach Arabic and other oriental languages in Europe but with scant success. Ramón Lull, a missionary who was a celebrated proponent of such teaching, met his death in North Africa.

[2] Or, more popularly, *Tartars*. The name is derived from that of the Ta-ta Mongols.

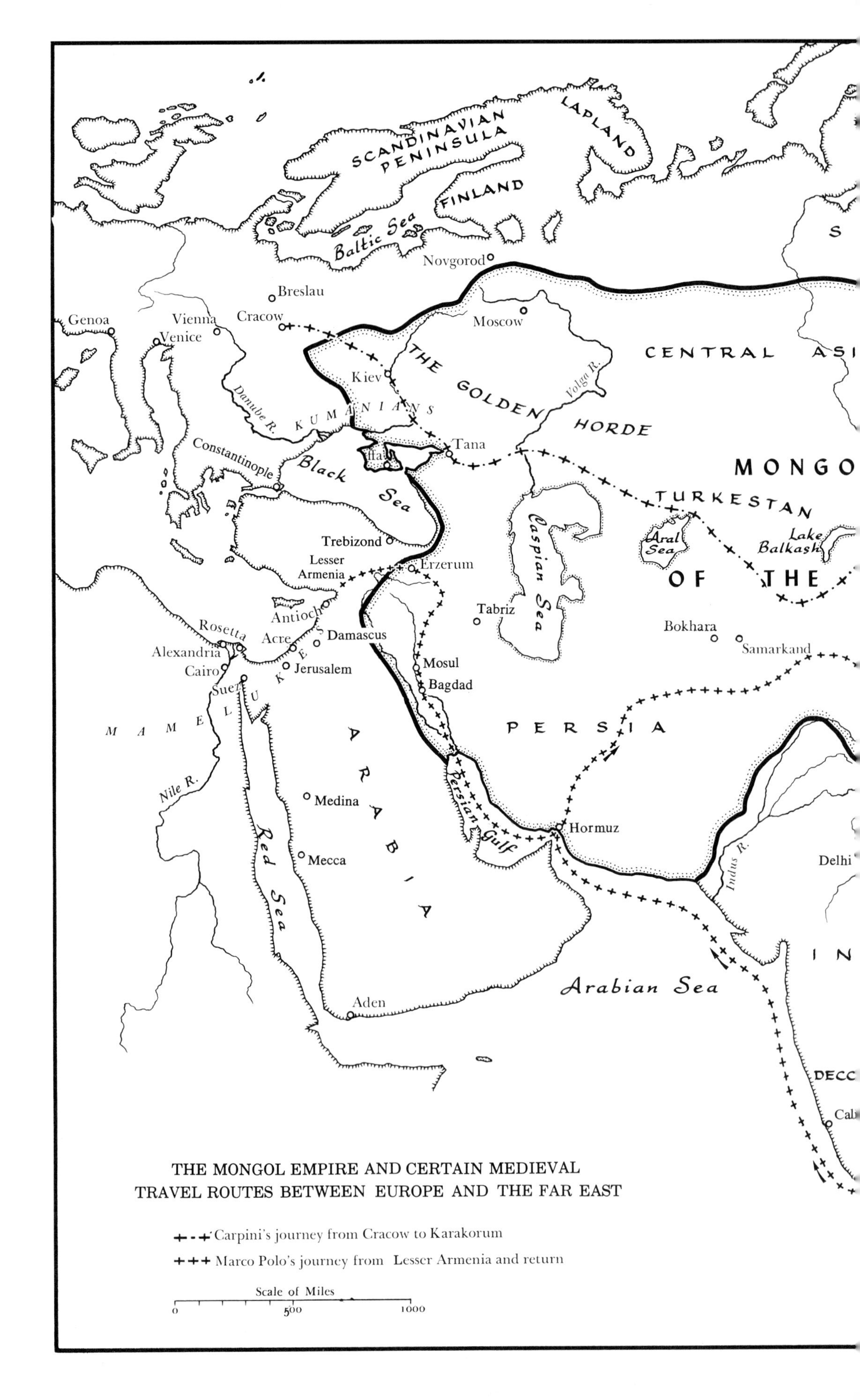

THE MONGOL EMPIRE AND CERTAIN MEDIEVAL TRAVEL ROUTES BETWEEN EUROPE AND THE FAR EAST

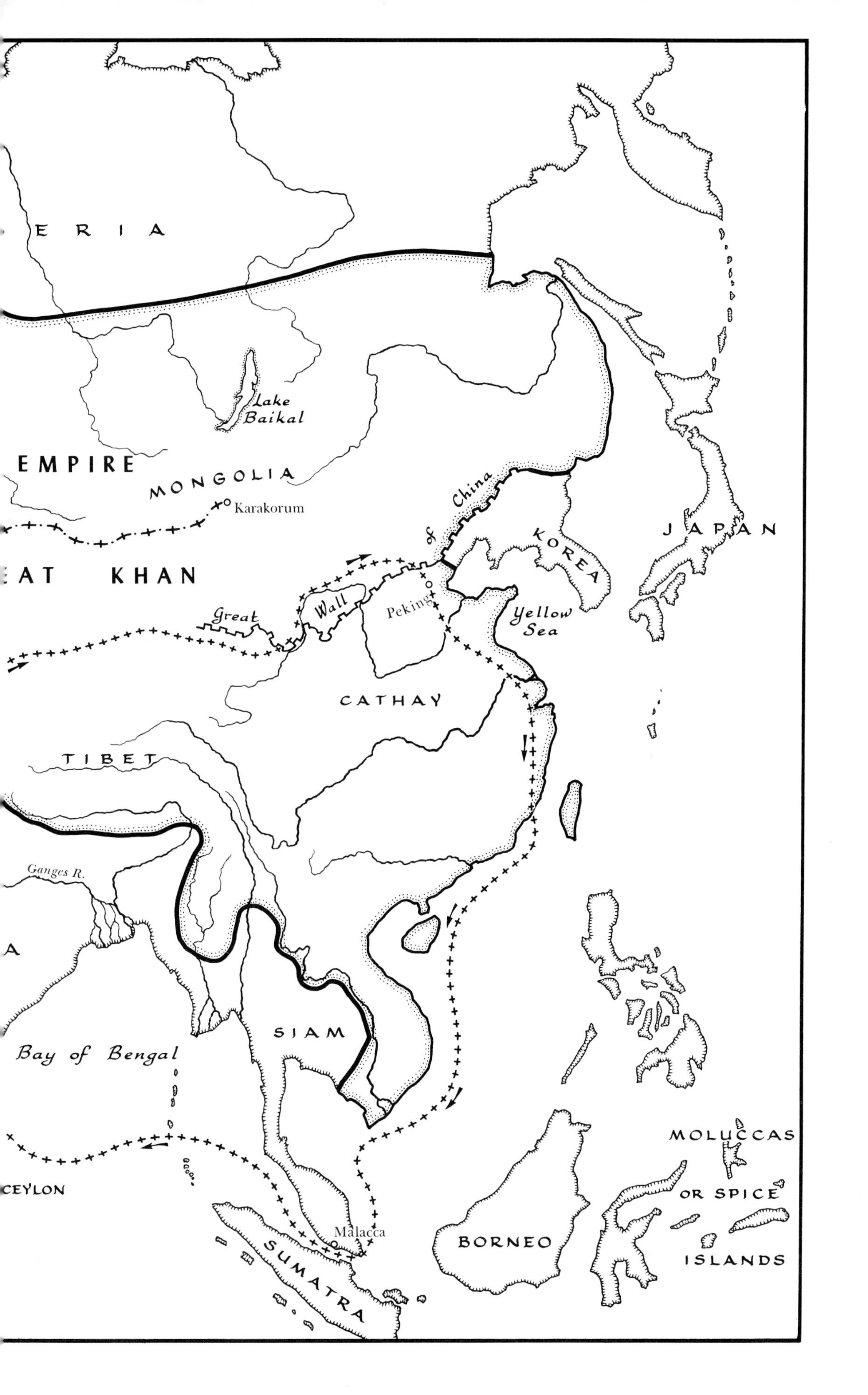

ERIA
Lake Baikal
EMPIRE
MONGOLIA
Karakorum
EAT KHAN
Great Wall of China
Peking
KOREA
JAPAN
Yellow Sea
CATHAY
TIBET
Ganges R.
SIAM
Bay of Bengal
CEYLON
Malacca
SUMATRA
BORNEO
MOLUCCAS OR SPICE ISLANDS

gated an area exceeding all other known empires before or since. Under the redoubtable leadership of Jenghiz Khan (*d.* 1227) and his immediate successors, they conquered the whole Chinese Empire, reduced west-central Asia (including Afghanistan and Persia), and invaded eastern Europe, overrunning southern Russia, Poland, and Hungary. In 1258 they overthrew the Abbasid caliphate of Bagdad and attacked the Moslems in Syria. Wherever they penetrated, whether into Moslem or Christian lands, they displayed a terrifying disregard of life and property.

The Mongol Empire proved too extensive. It soon broke into several "Khanates," which encountered stiffening resistance both in the Near East and in Europe. In 1260, a Moslem force, under the command of Baybars, decisively turned back the Mongols from Syria. And in Christian Europe, while Poland and Silesia suffered further spasmodic raids, only Russia remained under Mongol occupation for any length of time.

Thereafter, the Tatars devoted most of their energies to eastern and central Asia, where they consolidated their territories and gradually abandoned some of the ruthlessness of their conquering days. Before long they became surprisingly tolerant. Under Kublai Khan (*d.* 1294), they made the Chinese Empire their own and frankly adopted Chinese ways. Partly because they felt the Moslems to be their most dangerous enemies and partly because their own religious ideas were ill-developed, the Tatars in China welcomed Christian missionaries and traders. As a consequence, there began a noteworthy period of intercourse between Europe and China, which lasted until the fall of the Mongol dynasty in 1368 and the advance of Mohammedanism into central Asia.

Meanwhile popes and kings in Europe nurtured the hope that the Mongols might prove to be Christendom's allies against Islam. Although this hope proved vain, Western missionaries were able to penetrate the Middle and Far East.[1] A Franciscan friar, John of Plano Carpini, was sent to the court of the Khan, then at Karakorum in Mongolia. So far as is known, he was the first westerner who penetrated inner Asia and returned to describe his travels. His detailed account of the two-year journey is invaluable. In 1253 another Franciscan, William of Rubruquis, also journeyed to the east hoping to found a mission. His account is equally important. Finally, John of Monte Corvino (*d.* about 1330), also a Franciscan, was able to found an archdiocese at Peking, of which he was the first incumbent. The Franciscan Chinese mission lasted only into the second half of the fourteenth century when contacts with the West were lost.[2]

Missionaries were followed by the venturesome Venetian traders, Nicolo and Maffeo Polo, who made two extended visits to China (1255–1266 and 1271–1295). On the second journey, after entering the Chinese emperor's service, they returned part of the way by sea along the coast of southern Asia. Nicolo's son, Marco, who accompanied them, wrote an account of his experiences which was translated into several languages. Among other things he mentioned many ports along the southeastern coast of China and indicated that the China Sea was not separate from adjacent bodies of water. He referred to the island of Zipangu (Japan). And he reported a great many useful things, much of it hearsay, but much too from his own observation, about the East Indies, Ceylon, the coast of India, the Red Sea region, and even the islands off the east African coast. Unfortunately, further pioneering toward the Far East was halted after the middle of the fourteenth century. For then the penetration of Islam into the Middle East and the passing of the Mongol rule in China interrupted communication between Europe and China.

[1] Nestorian Christian missionaries had entered the Middle and Far East as early as the fifth century. In the twelfth century a letter, presumably a hoax and purporting to come from an oriental Christian priest-king, reached the west. For centuries various travelers hoped to find the kingdom of "Prester John."

[2] The ravages of the Black Death in the mid-century, the advances of Islam in Middle Asia, and the supplanting of the Mongol dynasty by the Ming (1368) combined to make the maintenance of the mission impossible.

It is evident from the preceding pages that medieval expansion profoundly altered the map of Europe. The West's economic and institutional progress, which must now be described, affected an area far greater than that occupied by the emerging feudal kingdoms of the year 1100.

The belfry and cloth hall at Bruges. Civic architecture of the thirteenth and fourteenth centuries.

Courtesy Belgian National Tourist Office, New York

CHAPTER 16

Economic Development in the Twelfth and Thirteenth Centuries

A. Expansion of Maritime and Inland Trade

An earlier chapter has described the beginning of Europe's economic recovery in the tenth and eleventh centuries. This expansion continued in the following two centuries along with a steady rise in the population. Three areas were principally concerned in this development: the northern seaboard from the Atlantic to the eastern Baltic, the Mediterranean littoral, and the inland continental region between. One of the achievements of the age was a closer linking of these three areas.

Although trade along the North and Baltic Seas had been stimulated originally by the Scandinavians, these were being rivaled in the twelfth and thirteenth centuries by Germans and Flemings. German expansion eastward, it will be recalled, included not only agricultural settlements, but urban foundations along or near the Baltic coast or on the northern German rivers. Lübeck and Danzig, for example, became important trade centers. But many towns, large and small, made their appearance, and commercial contacts reached as far east as Novgorod in Russia and as far north as Bergen in Norway.

In northwestern Europe, the most important commercial region continued to be the Low Countries. The cloths of Ghent, Bruges, Ypres, Lille, and Arras, woven from English wool, were exported everywhere, even to the Levant. Since the Flemish themselves were more interested in industry than in commerce, foreigners flocked to their country to procure their goods. Flanders attracted English, Scandinavian, and German merchants from the North Sea and Baltic regions, and French, Spanish, and Italian merchants from the Mediterranean. Bruges was the Flemish commercial metropolis, enjoying a reputation in the north comparable to that of Venice in the Mediterranean.

The bulk of the trade of northern and western Europe, except for the important cloth exports of the Low Countries, was in raw materials such as copper, iron, tin, timber, hides, wool, or certain food stuffs, including fish, salt, beer, and grain. The wines from France and from the Rhine and Moselle valleys were in widespread demand. Bordeaux was a major center of wine export. But, as the standard of living rose, there was also exchange of luxury products.

Even before the First Crusade, Genoese, Pisans, Normans, and others had challenged the Moslem and Venetian monopoly of Mediterranean commerce. The Crusades clinched European dominance in the Mediterranean, and since the Crusaders were dependent for the transport of troops and supplies on the maritime towns of Europe, these, and especially the Italian, were enabled to drive hard bargains. Most of the Near Eastern ports, or at least important sections in them, were controlled by merchants of Genoa, Pisa, Amalfi, Venice, Provence, or Aragon. Thus traders from southern Europe were established at the terminals of the chief commercial routes to the east.

Meanwhile, other maritime regions felt the impetus of commercial expansion. Sicilians obtained a temporary foothold in African Tripoli and Tunis (1134–1135). Genoese were active in Ceuta, pushed southward along the Atlantic coast of Morocco, and, following the Fourth Crusade, further accentuated a growing rivalry with Venice by establishing bases in the Crimea. Meanwhile, considerable numbers of Italians, especially Venetians, were taking up permanent residence in the Byzantine Empire and appropriating much of its commerce. Aragon also became a flourishing maritime state with its control over the Balearics and its annexation of Sicily.

Much, though by no means all, of Mediterranean trade was in the luxury products of the east. Oriental spices, which were in general demand throughout Europe for seasoning and preserving foodstuffs, and which had provided a powerful impetus for the expansion of medieval commerce, continued well into modern times to occupy the foremost place. But many other eastern wares were also in demand: certain foodstuffs, such as oranges, apricots, and figs; dyestuffs, textiles like damask (Damascus), muslin (Mosul), gauzes (Gaza), cotton, and raw silk. In exchange, Europe exported some of its primary raw materials, notably timber and iron, and certain manufactured goods, especially Flemish woolens.

The expansion of sea-borne trade was accompanied by, indeed it required, a corresponding progress in shipbuilding and navigation. This was particularly noticeable in the Mediterranean. The galley remained the common type of vessel, but it was enlarged and some Genoese and Venetian craft were upwards of a hundred feet long and with two or three decks. The sailing ships of the North and Baltic Seas were smaller, higher in the water, and of broader beam. Boat construction was generally improved. Better sails, masts, and spars came into use. Perfecting of the stern rudder in the thirteenth century eliminated the earlier and clumsier lateral steering methods. Development of the fore-and-aft rig, known in the Mediterranean as early as the ninth century, came into more general use, though often in combination with square-rigged sails. As sailing became less dependent on wind variation, the number of oarsmen in galleys could be reduced and cargo space correspondingly enlarged. There was also great improvement in ballasting, cargo stowing, and the provision of life-boats. The Venetian government devised a remarkably efficient system of ship inspection which curbed the parsimonious propensities of profit-seeking merchants. Important improvements were also made in harbor facilities, beacons, and lighthouses. Venice and Bruges were noted for their effective management of docks, lighters, and cranes.

Discovery of the properties of the magnetized needle, and its use in the compass, practically revolutionized navigation. Whether Europeans gained this now indispensable knowledge from the Moslems, or *vice versa,* is still a disputed point. At any rate, Europe had knowledge of the magnetized needle in the twelfth century, and put it to practical use in the thirteenth. By the fourteenth century the needle, suspended over a card indicating directions, was coming to be standard equipment for sailing vessels. The astrolabe, an instrument developed by the Arabs for determining latitude, seems to have been more slowly introduced. But taken altogether, these innovations made possible longer voyages out of sight of land. Some of the human obstacles were more formidable than those of nature. And since piracy remained a largely unsolved problem throughout the middle ages, most merchant vessels sailed armed and in fleets.

The inland trade of western Europe progressed less rapidly, because the obstacles to land transportation were removed far more slowly. These obstacles, it will be recalled, were both physical and political: bad roads, bridges, and wagons, and the persistence of man-made impediments in the way of brigandage and innumerable tolls. Some new roads were built and old ones improved. Bridges seemed to have fared somewhat better, and a number of canals were cut. European rivers were as indispensable to medieval trade as they are to-day; and more of them were navigable to the small sea-going ships of the middle ages than to the ocean liners of to-day.

The man-made obstacles to inland trade were both legal and illegal. Tolls, levied by local feudal lords, were numerous. Central government was slow to remedy the abuses of such tolls, and for many years it was powerless to prevent brigandage. Even in France and England, where central government was being strengthened, police jurisdiction long remained local and inefficient or obstructive. Broadly speaking, the "robber-barons," though not extinct, were mainly confined by the thirteenth century to out-of-the-way places. Wherever governmental authority was lacking, merchants took matters into their own hands, formed mutual protective associations, and traveled in large bands whenever possible. German towns, for example, often associated themselves in leagues.

A flourishing commerce requires adequate facilities for the marketing or exchange of goods. In the early middle age, when the volume of trade was small, the individual traveling merchant disposed of his wares as best he could. Markets were usually local and feudal, and concerned chiefly with the exchange of agricultural commodities. But as the quantity and variety of commodities expanded and the number of merchants rose, the older markets proved to be woefully inadequate. Solution of the marketing problem was now found partly in the development of urban communities—a feature of medieval commercial revival which will presently engage our attention—and partly in the institution of fairs.[1]

Fairs sprang up during the middle ages in all parts of Europe, but principally they were established in places through which passed an habitually used trade route, or in some locality sufficiently central to enable merchants from various countries to attend. A fair was not simply a large market; it was a very special kind of institution. Markets were of local and restricted economic importance. Fairs were universal in scope, and customarily privileged by law; they were held under the jurisdiction of a king or high feudatory who offered protection, regulation, and other inducements in order to attract the largest possible number of merchants and prospective buyers. Usually a special court was maintained for the settlement of all law-suits arising out of trade at the fair. In England, this was called the "pie powder" court (*pie poudreus,* dusty feet). Moreover, the convenience of traders was served by

[1] The name "fair" comes from the Latin, *feria,* "feast day." The day on which the fair opened was usually a saint's day or other holy day.

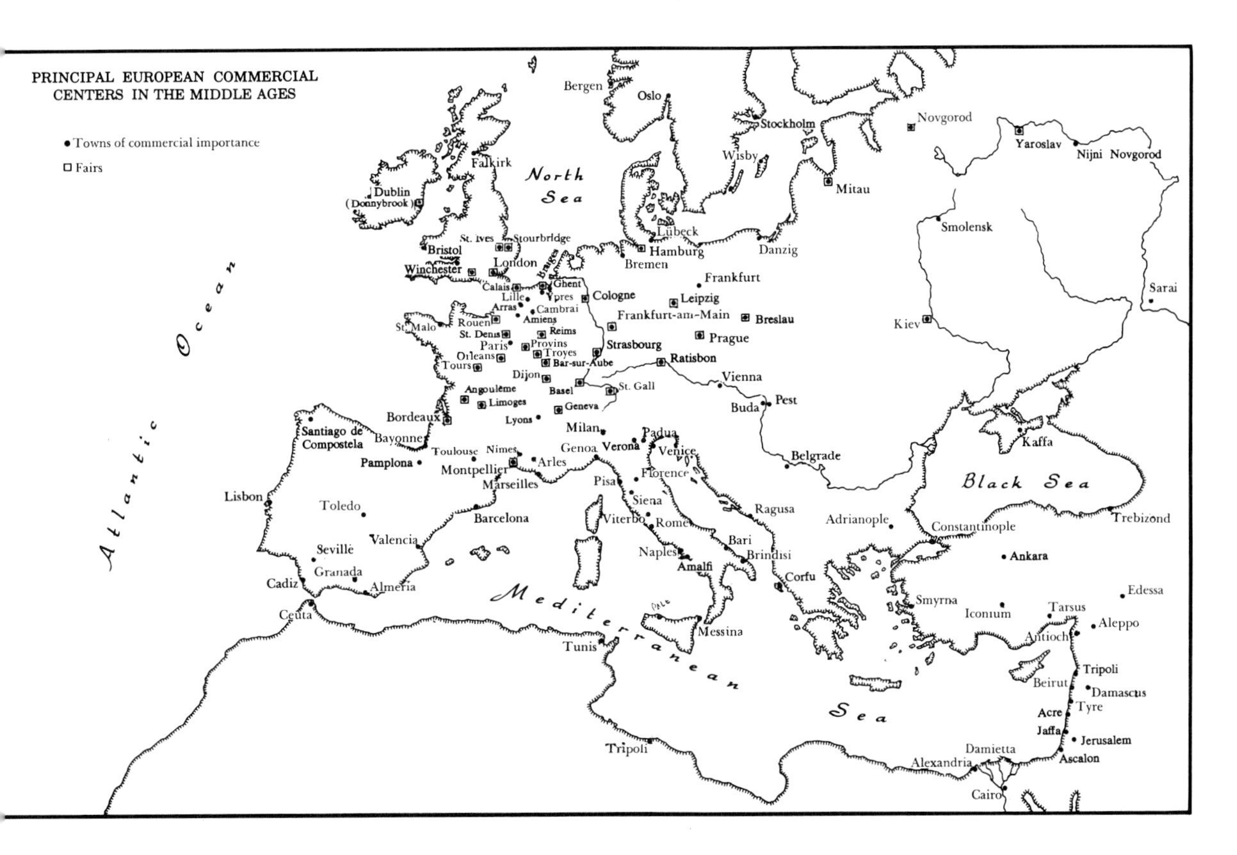

bureaus of exchange for the various moneys in circulation. *Lettres de foire* ("fair letters") were also used. These were promises to pay at some future date, and were sometimes redeemable at a merchant's home establishment. They were early letters of credit.

In addition to the attractions of business, the medieval fair, like its modern counterpart, the county fair, had its social aspects, its amusements and side shows. Strolling jongleurs and acrobats would frequent fairs as they would any large gathering of people. And we may be sure the various prizes and contests which attract people in modern times were equally alluring in the middle ages. The fairs were thoroughly popular institutions.

Although fairs were held all over Europe with similar procedures, those of Champagne were the most famous. These had a peculiarly favorable location at a crossroads of inland commerce. The counts of Champagne were not slow to capitalize on such a location and to afford special encouragement. Moreover, the Champagne fairs performed an especially important function in providing the first large-scale, regular contact between the northern seaboard area and the Mediterranean. Flemish cities built warehouses in the Champagne fair towns and regularly dealt with representatives of Italian business concerns who traveled north. Small wonder that during the thirteenth century there was hardly a time of year when one fair or another was not in progress in the county.

B. Medieval Industry, Money, and Credit

Medieval industrial advance, exclusive of those crafts devoted to local or town consumption, was considerable. There was marked advance in the manufacture of woolen cloth in Flanders. For dyeing it, Florentines and Venetians imported dyes from the Near East, and learned to make new colors. Before long, Florentines were "finishing" Flemish textiles for reëxport, and creating a cloth manufacturing industry of their own. We have mentioned the silk industry at Palermo and Lucca and the glass manufacture which flourished at Venice. Limoges in France was renowned for its enamel ware.

Progress in mining and metallurgy was furthered by certain technical advances in pumping out and draining the pits, in the smelting of the ore, and in the use of waterpower for crushing ore and operating lifts. Iron was in far greater demand for building than had been the case in ancient times. The Tyrol, Bohemia, Carinthia, and Sweden were all important iron producing regions. Some iron ore as well as tin was also obtained in Spain and in England. Copper was procurable in Sweden. Of the precious metals, gold was mined in Bohemia, Hungary, Carinthia, and Spain; silver in Bohemia and Hungary. Coal pits were opened near Liege in the Netherlands.

The expansion of commerce created a need for a more mobile and more stable currency, and before the end of the thirteenth century the monetary situation had greatly improved, although it still left much to be desired. Among the new coins struck were the Venetian silver groat (1192) and the Florentine florin (1252), the latter marking the return of a relatively stable gold coinage to Europe. Unfortunately there remained too many types of coins issued by different feudal principalities. No comprehensive monetary system was attained in the middle ages.

Ordinary demands of economic life require credit, and the borrowing and lending of money. Credit was provided for in the middle ages by the "fair letters" we have previously mentioned. Money lending, on the other hand, was impeded by the stand which the church took against usury, or the charging of interest on loans. In the early middle age, loans had been made, but they were mainly for consumption, and not for productive purposes, and only non-Christians—chiefly Jews—were supposed to charge interest for them. But in the twelfth and thirteenth centuries there is ample evidence that, while the services of Jewish money-lenders were still in demand, traffic in money was becoming widespread among Christians, notably Italians. Successful merchants obtained capital for their expanding enterprises by permitting one or more partners to contribute money in return for a share in the profits. Thus a business partnership was established. Many such associations (and they were increasingly numerous wherever business flourished) also lent money to kings or even to the church. In general, money-lenders were also merchants. Banking as a separate occupation came later.

It seems evident that the church's prohibition of usury was not strictly heeded. What actually happened was, first, the elaboration of various methods of disguising the taking of interest, and, second, a gradual recognition on the part of ecclesiastical authorities of a distinction between legitimate "interest" and prohibited "usury." Nevertheless, the church's formal prohibition remained, and the problem of dealing with it or getting around it continued to plague both clergy and laity.[1]

In another though less obvious way, the teachings of the church ran counter to the spirit of the whole commercial revival. To trade for the sake of gain, for the accumulation of profit rather than simply to provide for the necessities of life, even to charge more than a "just price,"[2] was regarded as falling into the sin of avarice. In the medieval church's outlook on life, there was little room for the kind of capitalistic enterprise which we have described. Yet a genuine and vigorous capitalism did develop and the successful entrepreneurs often attempted to salve their consciences by endowing charitable institutions, churches, and monasteries, and by leaving funds for Masses to be said for the repose of their souls after death. Evidently the conflict between the spirit of gain and the Christian way of life was very real in the middle ages. Medieval capitalism did not entirely deaden the consciences of men who were never allowed to forget the church's teachings.

C. Development of Urban Communities

In our discussion of the commercial revival in the middle age of the twelfth and thirteenth centuries, we have repeatedly referred to towns as economic centers. We have taken them for granted. We must now examine more carefully their development and their relation to the revival of trade. Among the various and conflicting theories as to the origin of medieval towns which still engage the attention of scholars, one thing seems certain. Whatever its former site or the manner in which it came into existence, a medieval town was the creation of enterprising merchants working together. Merchants naturally sought out communities which offered them protection and a market. Those most favorably situated from an economic point of view, on navigable rivers, portages, river junctions, crossroads, or harbors, inevitably attracted the largest number of traders.

In turn, a congregation of traders soon attracted artisans who saw a greater opportunity to dispose of their wares and to procure the raw materials for their craft. Thus a type of settlement appeared whose inhabitants lived a very different kind of life from the ordinary feudal community. Often it was called a "new" *burg* or *faubourg* (*foris burgus*, outside the *burg*), or suburb (*suburbium*).[3] And in countless instances the *faubourg* became larger than, or even engulfed, the original settlement. Since the *faubourg* was usually enclosed by a wall and, as a consequence, became in its own right a *burg*, or fortified community, such terms as "burgher," "bourgeois," or "burgess," came to be applied to its inhabitants. Thus the extension in meaning of a now well-known word illustrates the importance of these new communities.

The communities of merchants and artisans formed an essentially new element in feudal society. The inhabitants of a *faubourg* were not typical feudal personages. Being neither nobles nor peasants, they did not fit into the feudal organization as individuals. Feudal law did not provide for the freedom of movement or for the right to possess movable property which were vital to a mercantile society. Consequently, the members of these new communities strove for some sort of autonomy. Many cities won their freedom dearly against determined

[1] It is worth noting that questions regarding usury were reserved to the ecclesiastical courts.

[2] Theologians held that the "just price" should include the cost of material and labor plus a profit sufficient to enable the craftsman to live according to his station in life.

[3] A *burg* was originally a fortified settlement of peasants, knights, and clergy commonly located in a frontier region.

The Cathedral and Leaning Tower at Pisa.

Courtesy Italian State Tourist Office, New York

opposition and at the price sometimes of years of actual fighting. For many nobles, both ecclesiastical and lay, saw in the rise of towns a threat to their traditional feudal jurisdiction. The association thus forced on the burghers gave rise to a new term, "commune," often used in medieval town history.

Other more fortunate urban communities found their neighboring feudal lord amenable to reason or to regular money tribute. Many lay magnates saw possible advantages to themselves in the development of adjacent commercial towns; and during and after the twelfth century, a number of princes were prompted for reasons of profit to establish towns, often with privileges guaranteed by a written charter. Kings frequently protected cities within the domains of their great vassals. Everywhere, the characteristic feature was the banding together of merchants into corporations in order to deal as legal entities with the nobility and the central government.

However achieved and whatever the degree of freedom attained, self-government of the towns guaranteed personal liberty. And eventually it signified not only a freedom granted to certain individuals, but to the town itself. Town liberty became territorial.[1] Thus the town inhabitants—the bourgeosie—became in reality a privileged class. Moreover, the rights of the merchants and artisans of a *faubourg* were in time extended to include even the inhabitants of the original settlement, the whole forming a single urban community. Not all medieval towns achieved precisely the same degree of independence. The largest measure of autonomy was acquired in those regions, like north Italy or Germany, where monarchical centralization failed. For the flood tide of commercial prosperity coincided with the decline in power of the Holy Roman Empire. As subsequent pages will show, the resistance of the Lombard towns of north Italy contributed largely to the failure of imperial power. By 1250 they were independent in all but name.[2] And during the same period the so-called "imperial cities" of Germany were actually communities which, having thrown off immediate feudal control, were only nominally responsible to the Holy Roman Emperor. In countries like

[1] According to a widespread custom, residence in a town for a year and a day guaranteed freedom.

[2] In the Italian communes there were two factors not usually present elsewhere. First, most of them expanded to include the surrounding countryside, and became city-states. Second, as a result of expansion, the local nobility were drawn into the communal movement. Unlike the French, English, or German landlords who preferred their country castles, the Italian nobility took part in urban life. Only in some towns of southern France and of Spain were there similar developments.

France and England, where royal authority was enhanced, political independence such as the Italian cities enjoyed was rare. Here, even in those instances where autonomy had once been achieved, central government usually gained the upper hand sooner or later.

D. Town Institutions

In matters of internal administration, the burghers were breaking new ground, for there were few earlier institutions to guide them. Town councils, designated by the burghers, took charge of routine matters and displayed remarkable ingenuity in tackling such practical matters as food supply, schools, police, local taxation, and, of course, the regulation of commerce and industry.

The types of government devised by medieval townsmen varied with the degree of autonomy they possessed. And quite commonly single towns passed through extraordinary vicissitudes and many changes in their own institutions. But even in cities with limited rights of self-government, there developed a cohesive civic patriotism. The town became a miniature state, pledged to protect its citizens politically and economically. The outside world (including other towns) was "foreign" soil.

The characteristic institution for the regulation of economic life within the town was the guild. The earliest form of guild, and one that could be found practically everywhere, was the merchant guild, an association of merchants formed to protect and forward their mutual interests. Somewhat later the craft guild appeared. By this, each industry, or craft, devoted to the production of a particular kind of manufacture for local consumption, was organized into a separate guild whose function was to promote and protect the interests of the workers in that craft.

Most craft guilds were organized on a threefold hierarchical basis, embracing masters, journeymen, and apprentices. An apprentice was a young boy bound by his parents, according to a fixed contract and for a stipulated number of years, to some master craftsman. During his apprenticeship, he would live in the master's house, work for him, and be completely under his control. In return the master was required to provide for the moral and physical needs of the apprentice and to educate him, especially in the techniques of the craft.

A journeyman was a young man who worked for some master as a hired day laborer (*journée*, day). So long as the guild system operated for the benefit of all in the craft, there was rarely any unemployment; and the journeyman worked in the master's shop on terms of familiarity if not equality with him.

In order to be accepted by the craft guild as a master and admitted into the full privileges of the association, a former apprentice or journeyman had to demonstrate upon examination his skill as a craftsman. Usually he had to create a "masterpiece," a completed product according to the standards of the guild and often while other masters watched. Then, after paying certain fees and perhaps banqueting his future associates, he became a full-fledged master.

Since the purpose of the guild was to protect its own members, it insisted first of all on a monopoly of its product in the town. Guild wardens periodically inspected their own and other crafts and reported infringements on the monopoly. Thus the guild system exhibited that extreme of protectionism which was characteristic of medieval town life. Since it was felt that the maintenance of a standard quality of output was essential to the good reputation of a craft guild, all guild production was regulated and inspected, and commonly the craftsmen were required to work near a window in full view of passersby. A standard fixed price prevented undue competition and assured the guild's monoply.

Like the merchant guild, the craft guild was also a social and benevolent organization having its banquets and celebrations and caring for its own members or their families in time of trouble. Through the guilds the citizens expressed their civic pride, even much of their religious devotion. Guilds usually had a patron saint whose feast day they honored. And many beautifully stained glass windows in churches and cathedrals were donated by guilds.

At their best, that is in the late twelfth and thirteenth centuries, the guilds provided an organization of local industry without undue profit and with a high standard of work. Masters, apprentices, and journeymen worked together at the same table and in the same shop. And since every apprentice or journeyman presumably had the opportunity one day of becoming a master, the class distinction between employer and employee, so prominent in modern machine industry, hardly existed. Besides, the masters in any craft had perforce to be real craftsmen themselves. There was always, too, a direct exchange from producer to consumer. Competition was at a minimum, and no master was allowed to acquire property or a volume of trade so great as to be injurious to his fellows.

Such conditions could endure only in relatively small communities where the market was known and limited. With commercial expansion and resulting change in circumstances, there was evidence, even before the end of the thirteenth century, that the guild system, as originally conceived and operated, was breaking down. Competition for markets prompted masters to limit the number of apprentices. Requirements for guild membership were deliberately raised, and many apprentices and journeymen were prevented from becoming masters. In some cases, only members of guild families or the sons of wealthy friends were admitted. What was originally a protective monopoly was narrowed, and the relation between master and journeyman tended to become that of employer and employee, while unemployment increased. In short, the guilds evinced embryonic capitalistic tendencies. Further, the guild system inevitably discouraged industrial inventiveness.

It should also be borne in mind that the guilds controlled industrial life only within the town. Over expanding enterprises affecting wider areas, they had no control. In these, the craftsmen usually worked for some wealthy merchant as hired laborers, and, unlike the local guildsmen, they did not themselves sell the product of their own work but rather had to be content with letting their employer dispose of it abroad, perhaps in the Levant or in some other distant market. Although the workers in export industries organized themselves into guilds,

their relation to the merchants for whom they labored was that of employee to employer.

It is obvious from what we have said that the condition of craftsmen in the main middle age was not universally satisfactory. Whether because of growing exclusiveness of the masters of local guilds or because of

A medieval fortified town. Carcassonne.

Courtesy French Government Tourist Office, New York

competition in the export trades, journeymen were frequently exploited. Before the end of the thirteenth century, there were in relatively wealthy and populous Flanders a number of journeymen's strikes, which were drastically curbed by the town authorities representing the merchant class. Unemployment, poor wages, and wretched living conditions are not a monopoly of modern times.

A few words should be added about the appearance of medieval towns. Usually walled, they were apt to be very congested. Houses of five or even six stories were not uncommon, and since the upper stories jutted beyond the first, the streets were dark. Some attempts were made at "zoning."

Reims had a quaint regulation prohibiting houses higher than the level of the eaves of the cathedral. Venice permitted no houses higher than seventy feet. Florence, Paris, and Toledo limited buildings to one hundred, sixty, and seventy-five feet respectively. There was a good deal of overcrowding, and to discomfort was added the hazard of fire, since all houses except those of the very rich were built of wood. An ordinance of King Richard I of England required the separating of houses by at least a two-foot wall. Overcrowding was not evident everywhere within a medieval town, any more than it is in a modern city. There was always a public square or market place, usually in front of the cathedral or other principal church. And we read of gardens and orchards, even of small farms, within town limits. Within a medieval town, there were often distinctive "quarters" for particular or associated trades.

Town authorities, interested in the physical upkeep of the town, were concerned first with its defense. "Watch and ward" on the walls was always necessary, and the maintenance of fortifications was provided by taxation. Despite the popular notion that all medieval towns were extraordinarily dirty, many enterprising urban administrations, at least in the twelfth and thirteenth centuries, made important improvements in sanitation and cleanliness. It is true that in the previous period the narrow streets were unpaved and unlighted, and that refuse was thrown in a common gutter in the middle. But already in the twelfth century London and other cities had latrines and sub-surface sewers. Many communities provided a water supply from without, relieving the inhabitants of the necessity of relying entirely on wells. Cologne and Lübeck paved their market places and adjacent streets, and King Philip Augustus of France paved the street in front of his palace in Paris. By the thirteenth century, many municipal hospitals were established. The population of towns at the time cannot be determined accurately. A community of twenty thousand was considered a rather large town. Probably a majority were under ten thousand. Although a figure of one hundred thousand or over has been attributed to Venice and Paris, only a few others, such as Florence, Milan, and Genoa, exceeded fifty thousand.

Outside the town proper there was usually a belt district, called in France the *banlieu*, which fell under the jurisdiction of the municipal authorities. It was often dotted with villages and farms and was indispensable to the provisioning of the town. Many of the artisans also lived in the *banlieu*.

E. Agricultural Development

The twelfth and thirteenth centuries constituted a period of significant agrarian as well as commercial development. This was in part a continuation of the expansion which had begun in the early middle age, but the growth of trade and urban life also radically affected the economy of the rural manor. Since much of the surplus population was drawn to the towns and since towns depended on food brought from the outside, a heightened agricultural production was necessitated. And the provisioning of towns opened up the possibility of farming for profit, rather than merely for local manorial consumption. Thus the clearing of new agricultural land from the forest, which had commenced in the early middle age, reached its climax in the twelfth and thirteenth centuries. Afterwards, for several centuries, there was not much further addition to cultivated land in central or western Europe. A great deal of the new farming was done in districts opened up along the frontiers, but much also was done within the older regions, where there was forest land to be cleared. Technological improvements furthered agricultural progress. The wheelbarrow, which came into use in the thirteenth century, was helpful; and the appearance of windmills in the same period was of marked utility, especially in areas where natural waterflow was sluggish.

An important role in the agricultural advance was played by the Cistercian monasteries. The Cistercian order was established early in the twelfth century with the idea of observing monastic rules more strictly. Whereas the older Benedictine and Cluniac foundations usually held estates or manors which had long been under cultivation, the Cistercians set themselves to clear new land.

This was accomplished not entirely by the monks themselves, who, according to the Cistercian rule, led extremely strict lives, but often by lay brothers, called *conversi*, who took the monastic vows but did not live the full monastic life. The Cistercians also employed numbers of agricultural laborers knowns as *hospites*. These were free laborers, whatever their original status, who, as a result of overcrowding on the older manors, sought new openings as pioneer farmers.

Not all *hospites* went to Cistercian farms. Many found their way to the fringes of forest borderland not part of any estate under cultivation, where they usually obtained from the nominal proprietor ready permission to settle. Eventually, enterprising landlords sought to attract *hospites* to villages deliberately established in hitherto undeveloped areas. Such settlements were known as *villeneuves* (new towns); and, although agricultural in nature, they often imitated the merchant communities and secured a charter and a measure of self-government. Not quite as independent as the real urban communities, for most lords retained certain rights over the land in the *villeneuves*, they were nevertheless very different from the older manors.

Pioneer free farming was the rule in new frontier regions. But it was also true of the "frontier" of the Low Countries, in the land won from the sea by diking. This work, as we have indicated, began in the early middle age. It continued with the encouragement of the counts of Flanders and often under the direction of monasteries. The Cistercians were particularly active. The abbey of the Dunes, for example, had nearly twice as much diked land as undiked.

The effects of the rise of towns on agriculture were striking. Manors which in the early feudal age produced only for home consumption were now able to produce a surplus for sale outside. Grain became an article of mercantile circulation, brought by the peasant to the town or sold to the merchant who traded in foodstuffs. As a consequence, money circulated more freely in the countryside. Peasants were able to buy freedom or to become tenant farmers paying a fixed rent. Some became laborers for hire. The size of holdings could be increased more readily by hard-working peasants who invested their savings in more land. Even the bourgeoisie speculated in land. The immobility of the manorial relationship was broken.

Since the dues and rents exacted by the landlords were usually fixed by immemorial custom and did not fluctuate, and since the general increase in money caused a rise in prices, many landlords—nobles, abbeys, and bishops—faced serious financial loss if not ruin. These, in order to keep their serfs from running away to the towns and if possible to increase their revenues, were forced to enfranchise serfs and to accept money rent. Since the process of emancipation was primarily the result of economic change, it was more rapid and widespread in the regions where commercial development was most advanced. Accordingly, in western and central Europe, by 1300, a substantial proportion of the peasants were in reality tenant farmers, not serfs in the older sense. In eastern Europe, on the other hand, serfdom was more general and lasted longer.

Another significant effect of the commercial revival was the tendency toward agricultural specialization. Certain regions concentrated on one product. Some landlords devoted all their acres to a crop which could be exported. The Cistercian abbeys of England, for example, were famous for their wool. In certain favorable areas, vineyards spread at the expense of grain growing. All these tendencies quickened in the later middle age.

It should be evident from the preceding pages that the economic life of the twelfth and thirteenth centuries was far from static. Western Europe was now dotted with thriving urban communities whose way of life altered medieval society. Simultaneously there were significant changes in the countryside, many of them induced by the commercial revival. But we must beware of exaggerating the importance of the medieval towns. Europe was still largely agrarian. Only in relatively recent times has European and Western civilization taken on the predominantly urban aspect which it now has.

Château-Gaillard, built by Richard I of England to control the route along the Seine.

Courtesy French Government Tourist Office, New York

CHAPTER 17

Consolidation of Feudal Monarchy in Western and Southern Europe

Political developments of the twelfth and thirteenth centuries followed a similar pattern in France, England, Spain, and Sicily. By 1300 feudal monarchy in these countries was evolving into more centralized royal states.

England and France were bound together by the fact that after 1066 the English rulers, royalty and aristocracy alike, were Norman Frenchmen who spoke French and held large domains in France. Copying and borrowing one from the other was inevitable. And since many French knights sought careers in Spain, French feudal influences persisted there. The Norman occupation of Sicily and southern Italy provided a Norman-French background for political institutions in those regions. In all the countries mentioned, though only temporarily in Sicily, governmental progress was marked.

A. English Monarchy in the Twelfth and Thirteenth Centuries

Among the most important consequences of the Norman conquest of England in 1066 was the introduction of Norman-French feudalism. Although William the Conqueror preserved whatever Saxon practices he found useful, he skillfully utilized such Norman institutions as emphasized the power of the overlord rather than the rights of the vassal. The typical Saxon local divisions—the shires and the hundreds—were maintained, although the shires were now often called counties. The sheriff (shire reeve) became a royal official, commanding the chief castle in the shire. He was appointed by and responsible to the king. Most important of all, the estates of the Anglo-Norman nobles were scattered. Except in the case of the Welsh and Scottish border marches, there were no compact fiefs in England with extensive governmental rights such as prevailed on the continent. A comprehensive and detailed survey of all landed properties as they existed before the conquest was ordered by William in 1086. The results were recorded in a document known as *Domesday Book,* one of the most important sources of information concerning English landholding in the eleventh century.

The foundations laid by William I proved their worth during the twelfth century. Under Henry I (1100–1135) feudal courts declined and many more cases were brought before the king's court (*curia regis*) than had been customary previously. While the *curia* itself accompanied the king wherever he went, agents of it were appointed as itinerant justices (*justices in eyre*) to hear cases on specifically designated circuits in regions not personally visited by the king.

Henry I left no sons, and a generation of feudal anarchy disturbed England until the accession of Henry II (1154–1189), the son of Henry I's daughter, Matilda, and of Count Geoffrey Plantagenet of Anjou. Henry II, the first of the Plantagenet, or Angevin, kings of England, was not merely ruler of England and Normandy, which he inherited from his mother. Maine had been added, and from his father he inherited Anjou and Touraine. In 1152 he married Eleanor, heiress of Aquitaine. As a consequence, although he remained a vassal to the king of France for his French holdings, he personally ruled a domain stretching through England and France, from the Scottish marches to the Pyrenees.

In spite of the manifold responsibilities which obliged him to spend more time on the continent than in England, Henry II was one of England's greatest kings. Perhaps the most famous of his reforms was the employment of juries as a regular part of judicial procedure. The origins of the jury can be traced to much older continental practice, perhaps to practice in the Roman Empire. Its immediate predecessor was the sworn inquest, adopted by the Normans from the Franks. In order to cope with violent crime, a legacy from the turbulent days before his accession, the King ordered (Assize of Clarendon, 1166) that twelve men from each hundred and four from each village should be present when an itinerant justice held a county court. These men who were to tell under oath the names of those suspected of crime formed a jury of presentment or indictment. Usually, the actual trial of a person thus indicted was the early medieval method of ordeal.

In certain kinds of civil cases, particularly those having to do with the land, Henry II directed that the actual trial should be by a smaller (*petit*) jury of twelve men. These twelve were presumed to possess some special knowledge of the case. They were witnesses and jurors combined. Not for many years did a distinction between juror and witness begin to be recognized, and consequently Henry II's use of the jury was only the germ of our modern system of trial by jury. Jury trials in criminal cases, although occasional, were not common much before the end of the thirteenth century.

Two consequences of Henry II's legal reforms should be emphasized. First, they contributed in a large measure to the development of what came to be known as the "common" law, that is, the law common to the entire realm. Second, through the use of the jury the king invaded and curtailed the local jurisdiction of the barons. Accordingly, the twelfth-century jury should be regarded as an extension of royal power, rather than as a curb on arbitrary government.[1]

In one important instance, the extension of royal justice ran into conflict with ecclesiastical jurisdiction. Since the Norman conquest had brought the English church into closer touch with Rome, the procedure in English ecclesiastical courts kept pace with the development of canon (church) law. There were, in twelfth-century England, two parallel and well organized legal systems, one of the king and the other of the church. And in view of the intimate relations of church and state, the possibilities of disputes over jurisdiction were very real. The case of clerics convicted of crime in ecclesiastical courts gave rise to a famous controversy between Henry II and a celebrated archbishop of Canterbury, Thomas Becket. Becket had originally been chancellor of the kingdom and a devoted servant of the king. Henry arranged that he be given the see of Canterbury in the hope that, as archbishop, he might coöperate in the king's plan to subordinate the church to the state. But Becket was a person who threw himself wholeheartedly into whatever task he assumed; and to the king's dismay, Becket resigned his chancellorship and became a stubborn champion of ecclesiastical rights.

The king had insisted that "criminous clerks," after conviction in ecclesiastical courts, should be handed over to the king's courts for punishment. These and other matters, for example the curtailment of the right of appeal from English ecclesiastical courts to Rome, were incorporated into a document called the Constitutions of Clarendon (1164). Becket at first gave his consent, with some reservations. But later he changed his mind and resisted to the last. He was forced to spend many years in exile in France. In the course of the protracted struggle, Henry let drop a chance remark

[1] The privilege of bringing suit before the king's justices was obtained by the purchase of a writ, and such purchase money enriched the royal treasury.

which he doubtless did not really mean, but which a few of his followers interpreted literally. For these sought out Becket in the cathedral of Canterbury and there murdered him.

The assassination shocked all Christian Europe, including England, and Henry, genuinely remorseful, submitted to papal legates, took an oath that he had no part in the murder, and conceded on the matters of criminal clerics and freedom of appeals to Rome. Various other matters were settled by subsequent negotiations between papal legates and the king's lawyers. Becket, the martyr, was canonized, and his shrine speedily became the object of popular pilgrimage.

The ensuing century—the thirteenth—was particularly significant in the development of English government, for two reasons. It opened with a struggle between King John (the son of Henry II) and his barons, leading to Magna Carta; and it closed with the summoning by King Edward I of the so-called Model Parliament (1295). Unfortunately both events have received exaggerated emphasis as a result of later interpretations placed upon them. In a certain sense, the really determining development of the century was the growth of the monarchy as an institution governing the realm.

An important feature of John's reign was the loss of all the French possessions except Aquitaine. The details of this change in the relations of the kings of France and England will be described in the following section. What is important to point out here concerning the loss of French possessions by the English king is, first, that it was a serious blow to the king's prestige, and, second, that it necessitated a relinquishing by his English barons of their feudal holdings abroad. These barons tended to become more exclusively English in their outlook, more jealous of their own rights as against those of the king, and more outraged by John's arbitrary actions and occasional injustice. That the reckoning was delayed until 1215 is a tribute to the basic strength of the Norman-Angevin monarchy.

In addition to the protracted struggle over the French lands, John from 1205 to 1213 was engaged in a bitter controversy with Pope Innocent III. A disputed election to the see of Canterbury had been appealed to Innocent, who took the opportunity of persuading the electors present at Rome to accept his own candidate, Stephen Langton. Stephen was an excellent choice, but the king saw in the Pope's action a denial of his own claim to nominate to English sees. He refused to accept Stephen and confiscated the episcopal estates. For seven years

The murder of Thomas Becket from a thirteenth century English manuscript.

Courtesy Pierpont Morgan Library, New York

John defied papal interdict [1] and excommunication, and attacked those who obeyed the Pope, even seizing as hostages the sons or daughters of recalcitrant barons. Eventually all classes of the population were affected by the king's misrule and his conflict with the church. Finally, Innocent III, hearing of a baronial conspiracy against the king, proclaimed his deposition, absolved his subjects from their allegiance, and summoned the assistance of the king of France. But John was clever enough to appease one opponent in order to face others. Not only did he submit to the Pope (1213) and agree to accept Stephen Langton, but he made over his kingdom to the papacy as a fief and promised an annual payment to Rome of a thousand marks. Thereby he solicited papal support against the now rebellious barons in England. But when he returned from a finally unsuccessful attempt to recover his French possessions, he had to face a formidable combination of discontented and defiant nobles. He submitted to their demands at Runnymede and signed the Great Charter in 1215.

Viewed in relation to the situation in thirteenth-century England, Magna Carta was not a revolutionary document. Rather, it was feudal and conservative, a reëmphasis on that fundamental characteristic of all feudalism, the mutual contract between lord and vassal. John had violated such a contract, and no king was to do so again. Yet the conditions of the granting of the charter, as well as the actual wording of certain of its provisions, were susceptible, especially in later times, of a more revolutionary interpretation.

The very act of calling a ruler to account, even though the motive was feudal, together with the somewhat clumsy provision that his acts were to be supervised by a committee of barons, was of the very essence of *limited* sovereignty. Although the clause, "no freeman shall be arrested and imprisoned, or dispossessed, or outlawed, or banished, or in any way molested, nor will we set forth against him, nor send against him, unless by the lawful judgment of his peers and by the law of the land," did not guarantee trial by jury, it did assure, in cases of arrest, an orderly procedure governed by accepted custom. Further, while in 1215 the word "freeman" had a limited meaning, by the seventeenth century it signified almost everyone.

Magna Carta was confirmed six times during the thirteenth century, and many times more during the later Middle Age. For later generations it became an arsenal of rights. It hardly had such significance in the year 1215.

The reign of Henry III (1216–1272) was important principally because a series of royal difficulties with the nobility confirmed the limitations on monarchical power laid down in Magna Carta. In 1258 the king was forced to submit to various baronial restrictions on his authority set forth in an additional document, the Provisions of Oxford. In 1264 he was defeated and captured by a number of magnates led by Simon de Montfort. Only the death of Simon and the more successful maneuvers of Henry's son, Edward I, saved the royal prestige.

Under Edward I (1272–1307), one of England's ablest kings, the worst controversies of the earlier period were avoided and a more normal progress rendered possible. In many respects his policy was more English and less continental than that of his predecessors. Wales was conquered (1276–1284). Scotland was subjugated, although its people soon rebelled under the leadership of Robert Bruce, who defeated Edward II at the battle of Bannockburn (1314) and reëstablished Scottish independence.

Under Edward I there also appeared more clearly than before a distinction within the *curia regis* between an inner group of councillors who met regularly with the king and the more cumbersome and less frequently summoned great council of all the major barons and prelates. Certain meetings of the latter were called parliaments. And in order to obtain a closer contact with elements of the population hitherto not represented, Edward began to summon representatives, chosen locally, from the shires and the boroughs, the

[1] Interdict is the prohibition of normal religious functions within a specified area.

knights and the burgesses. Because all the elements which were to become associated with English practice in this regard were present at a meeting in 1295, this came to be called the "model parliament." [1] It met in four separate groups, not in two as in later times. And though not regarded as particularly important at the time, this meeting marked the beginning of what was to become a celebrated institution.

Edward I had no such serious trouble with the church as Henry II or John had had. He was personally devout and on good terms with the popes, with whom he often coöperated in taxing the English clergy. On one matter he clashed with Pope Boniface VIII. When the latter declared in the letter, or "bull," *Clericis laicos* (1302), that the clergy should not be taxed by lay rulers without papal consent, Edward replied by refusing the clergy access to the royal courts. Edward's stand against Boniface proved successful, though not as spectacularly so as that of his French contemporary, Philip IV.

The foundations of the English constitution were laid in the medieval feudal period. The significance of the developments we have described did not escape contemporary Englishmen. Ranulf de Glanvill, Henry II's justiciar, wrote a *Treatise on the Laws and Customs of the Kingdom of England*. Henry de Bracton produced a similar work in the thirteenth century. These and other writings, together with the recorded decisions of the king's justices, formed an important body of literature on the government and law of England. It is well for modern English-speaking students to appreciate the extent of our debt to the medieval past.

B. French Monarchy in the Twelfth and Thirteenth Centuries

In the twelfth century the strictly royal domain of France—the Île-de-France—was still surrounded by large fiefs with old traditions of independence. In the thirteenth century, however, large areas were added to the royal holdings, and as in England a century earlier, institutions of centralization were elaborated within the framework of feudalism. It is evident that the key to the understanding of medieval French history is the geographical growth of the royal domain.

Toward the end of his reign, King Louis VI (1108–1137) arranged a marriage between his son and Eleanor, the heiress of the duchy of Aquitaine. As sometimes happened in such marriages, the royal couple proved to be ill matched, and the husband, Louis VII (1137–1180), was able in 1152 to procure from a council of French clergy an annulment of the marriage. Thus the French king lost control of Aquitaine, a large fief including the greater part of southwestern France. Eleanor's marriage two months later to Henry Plantagenet, the future Henry II of England, has already been mentioned. It transferred control of Aquitaine to the English crown, which already controlled Normandy, Maine, Anjou, and Touraine, and presently gained Brittany. Thus roughly two thirds of France owed immediate fealty to the English King Henry II. True, Henry was in turn the vassal of the French King Louis VII for these territories, but Henry was a vastly more powerful sovereign than Louis. In the circumstances it is a tribute to the latter's ability that he held his own against the former.

Philip II (1180–1223), generally known by the surname "Augustus," was a wily sovereign and very successful. He occupied Artois and Vermandois, and, after Henry's death, acquired part of Berry and Auvergne. For personal and political reasons, his English contemporary, King John, had married the fiancée of one of his own vassals in Poitou, Hugh of Lusignan. Hugh complained to Philip as John's overlord, although such appeals from a sub-vassal to the king were then rare. Philip bided his time until he felt strong enough to challenge his royal vassal. Then, in 1202, he summoned John to answer Hugh's charges at his court. And when John refused to appear after the customary three summons, Philip declared John's French fiefs forfeit. Though perfectly legal in feudal law, this

[1] In 1295 two knights from each shire and two burgesses from each town were summoned in addition to the principal ecclesiastics and barons.

was a bold maneuver. It succeeded. In the ensuing war Philip was able to drive John from northern France, including all of Normandy, Brittany, Anjou, Maine, and Touraine, and subsequently he conquered Poitou. When John attempted to repair his fortunes and made alliances with the Holy Roman Emperor Otto IV, with the count of Flanders, and with a number of other magnates, Philip, with the support of Otto's imperial rival, Frederick II, decisively defeated John's allies at Bouvines (1214). The French royal domain was trebled in size, and the prestige and power of the Capetian monarchy immensely increased.

It was also during the early thirteenth century that Pope Innocent III proclaimed a Crusade against the Albigensian heretics of southern France.[1] This was espoused by Philip II's successors and utilized to extend their control southward. In 1229, after a devastating struggle, it was arranged that Count Raymond VII of Toulouse, the son of Raymond VI whose refusal to proceed against the heretics had occasioned the conflict, should be allowed to retain only the small part of his lands which had not yet been conquered, but even this reverted to the French crown on the death of Raymond's successor without heirs.[2] Since many northern barons were also rewarded with fiefs in the south, a veritable northern "invasion" added to the devasta-

[1] On Innocent III's policies, see pp. 176, 181, 227, 235.

[2] The French King Louis VIII (1223–1226) had given certain of his younger sons royal fiefs called *apanages*. Two especially deserve mention here: Charles was given Anjou and Maine, to which he later added Provence, east of the Rhone. Alphonse was given Poitou and Auvergne, to which he added Toulouse through his marriage to the daughter of Count Raymond VII.

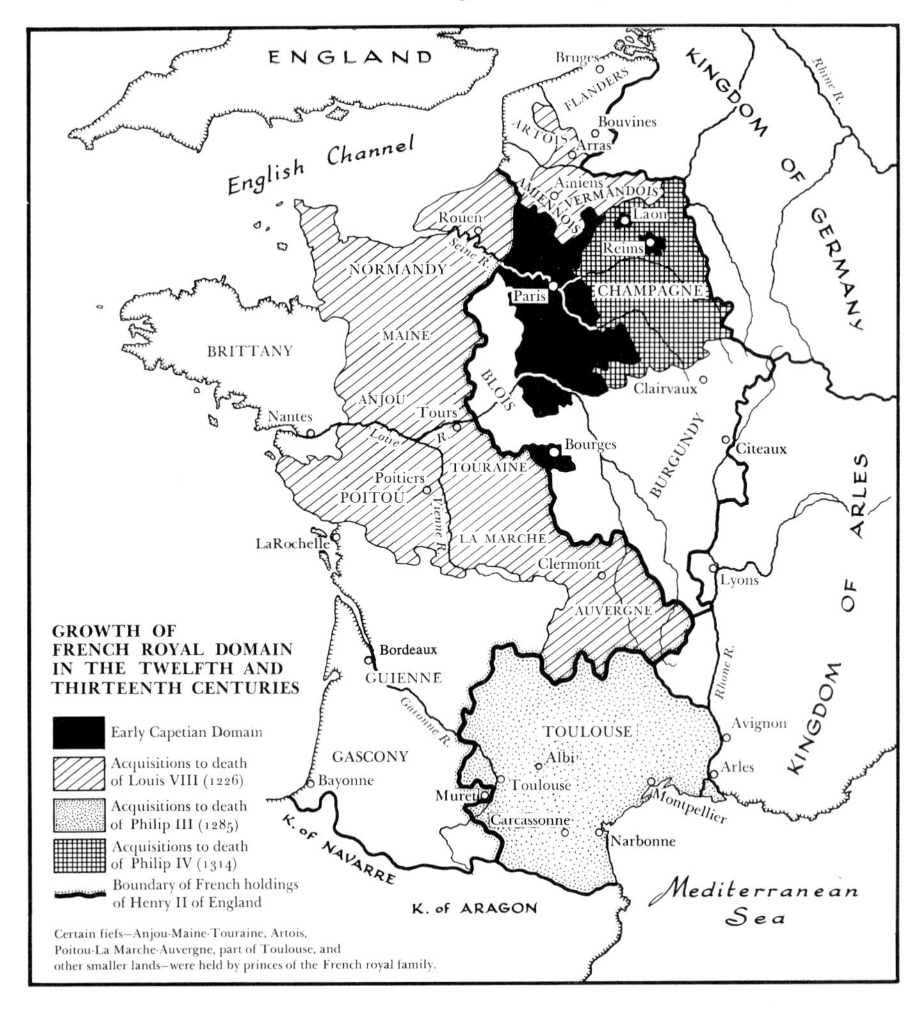

tion wrought by the war and further strengthened the political hegemony of the north over the south. Finally, in the latter part of the century, King Philip IV married the heiress of Champagne and Navarre. Thus, in the space of a hundred years the French royal domain expanded from the Île-de-France to include the greater part of the whole kingdom of France.[1]

French institutional development of the period hardly kept pace with the English. In the first place, it was not until the reign of Philip II (Augustus) that the amount of territory under direct royal control was really significant. Secondly, in many of the lands incorporated during the thirteenth century, as well as in the great fiefs which remained outside of the royal domain, local customs and usages persisted. Nevertheless, as the king's lands increased to the point where he controlled an aggregate of former fiefs far larger than the domain of any existing magnate, the occasions when his authority was exercised outside his domain became rapidly more numerous. Appeals to the king's court, which were exceptional in the days of Louis VI and Louis VII, henceforth became the rule. And, although the kings still traveled frequently, Paris in the thirteenth century was developing into a permanent royal residence and the capital of the French feudal monarchy.

Some of the men who accomplished these things are deserving of special mention. Suger, abbot of St. Denis, a learned man and an ascetic, was also a capable administrator. He was a tower of strength as chief minister for Louis VI and Louis VII. Philip Augustus is naturally best known for his territorial acquisitions, but he also instituted, for his newly expanded domain, a system of local administration modeled on that of the Anglo-Norman-Angevin rulers. Bailiffs (in the north) or seneschals (in the south), drawn usually from the petty nobles or royal knights of the *curia*, supervised alloted districts. As delegates of the king's court, they made royal authority felt in outlying areas. Louis IX strengthened the system by ordering periodic inquests and issuing special ordinances for the conduct of bailiffs and seneschals.

Louis IX (1226–1270), more often known as Saint Louis, was brought up devotedly, but strictly, by his capable mother, Blanche of Castile. It was she who instilled in him an intense loyalty to the Christian religion and a conscientious devotion to the ideal of a true Christian monarch. As regent for eight years during her son's minority, she ably administered the kingdom, and remained a wise adviser to him after he came of age. Louis possessed that rare combination of a deeply religious temperament with a capacity for bold action. No ruler has ever surpassed his zeal for justice. So universal was the confidence in the wisdom of his decisions that he was invited to arbitrate disputes in other lands. And although on occasion his generous impulses got the better of his judgment, his whole reign was one long effort to protect rights and to see that obligations were fulfilled. Thus the "crowned saint" was an exceptionally capable ruler with a remarkable judgment in matters of government.

The character of Philip IV (1285–1314), known to history as Philip the Fair, is less easy to appraise. Certain of his policies and acts, though possibly dictated by influential advisers, have given him a sinister reputation as a ruthless and unscrupulous monarch. Some of these will be described in subsequent pages,[2] but it is appropriate to suggest here that the portrait of Philip as an evil king has perhaps been overdrawn. He regarded himself as following in the steps of his sainted grandfather.

As in England, the chief business of the *curia regis* (or royal court) in France was judicial. As the number and variety of cases increased, the court required the services of professional lawyers who sat in on sessions known as *parlements*. These men were trained, presumably in feudal law, and, as the thirteenth century wore on, many also in Roman law. Thus there came into being a permanent corps of judges resident at Paris which later was

[1] In an agreement with the king of Aragon (1259), the French King Louis IX gave up claims to Catalonia and Roussillon which dated from the formation of the Spanish march in the time of Charlemagne, in return for a relinquishment, on the part of Aragon, of all claims north of the Pyrenees except Montpellier.

[2] See below, pp. 205, 207–209, 227.

to become a separate body known as the *Parlement*, the highest court in feudal France. Since the *curia regis* was occasionally in session for financial matters exclusively, there eventually appeared a specialized personnel, the germ of what in the fourteenth century was called the *chambre des comptes*.

There also appeared in France a general assembly, or Estates General. Philip IV first summoned such an assembly in 1302 during a sharp crisis in his relations with the pope. It comprised representatives of three Estates—clergy, nobility, and third estate—and was the beginning of an institution which at first resembled the English parliament, but whose later history was quite different. The Estates General strengthened rather than limited the French monarchy. It should be remembered that there were also provincial or regional estates.

The summoning of the Estates General indicates the rising importance of the bourgeoisie and the towns. In fact, monarchy and towns were natural allies against the feudal nobility. Louis VII, occasionally, and Philip Augustus, more consistently, granted and confirmed town charters and encouraged the formation of communes. The latter found town militias of considerable assistance. During the reign of Louis IX, however, many towns were under the control of oligarchies of rich guildsmen whose policies often weighed heavily on the poor and whose mismanagement of finances endangered the royal revenues. Accordingly, although Louis IX confirmed some old charters and reëstablished municipal privileges where royal officers had abused them, he founded only one new commune.[1] And wherever possible, he attempted to bring towns, especially their financial administration, under royal supervision.

The young King Louis IX (1226–1270), from a French manuscript of the thirteenth century.

Courtesy Pierpont Morgan Library, New York

The signal advance of the French monarchy had been paralleled by an equally impressive establishment of effective papal supremacy. The papacy of the twelfth and thirteenth centuries, as a later chapter will explain more fully, was in a position to challenge royal encroachments on ecclesiastical liberties. The case of John of England was an illustration. Moreover, Innocent III, one of the great popes of the middle ages, felt it his duty to discipline a monarch for grave immorality. When Philip Augustus repudiated his wife and she appealed to Rome, Innocent ordered the King to reinstate her. Philip refused, but after defying excommunication and interdict for several years, he eventually relented. On the other hand, he would not let the Pope arbitrate his quarrel with the English king, and he maintained his own control over the French clergy by appointing the bishops in his dominions. Even Louis IX, saint that he was, resisted any ecclesiastical interference with what he considered his legitimate authority. For all his intense loyalty to his religion he felt that in political matters pope and bishops might be mistaken.[2]

If Louis IX's relations with the church had been characterized by a pious loyalty

[1] This was Aigues-Mortes, a naval and commercial establishment, founded in connection with crusading.

[2] Note also Louis's attitude toward the controversy between Innocent IV and Frederick II. See below, pp. 220, 237.

mingled with reserve, a famous controversy between his grandson, Philip the Fair, and Pope Boniface VIII was marked by spectacular violence. Boniface was an accomplished canonist, devoted to the extreme temporal claims of the papacy as enunciated by some of his predecessors. Unfortunately, he was deeply involved in the factional and family quarrels of thirteenth-century Italy. Moreover, he was a man singularly lacking in diplomatic finesse. In his bull, *Clericis laicos*, Boniface had forbidden kings to tax the clergy without papal permission. Philip replied by stopping the export of money and precious metals from France to Rome. Later, when the Pope attempted to defend a bishop against the arbitrary decisions of a secular court and issued two other bulls, Philip, by summoning the first Estates General, sought to enlist the support of the country against the Pope. Whereupon Boniface issued still another bull, *Unam sanctam*, which reëmphasized papal supremacy in the strongest language.

Assured of the backing of the Estates General, and following the advice of his minister, Nogaret, Philip intensified the campaign against the Pope. A mission was dispatched to bring the pontiff to trial before a general council. Nogaret, joined by Italian factions, sought out Boniface at Anagni where the Pope met his enemies with great dignity. Nevertheless, he was insulted and seized. And although Nogaret was subsequently forced to release him, the aged pontiff died soon afterwards (1303).

The affair of Philip and Boniface has often been regarded as the first striking victory of the "national state" over the medieval papal theocracy, a sort of "Canossa" in reverse. Such, in a sense, it was. Thirteenth-century France was already becoming a national state. Yet it should be borne in mind that although Philip the Fair was a powerful monarch, he was still only a suzerain over considerable areas. France lacked a common law and even a common language. In 1300 Frenchmen were still Normans, Bretons, Burgundians, Gascons, or Poitevins. French royal power, like that in England, was limited. But it was limited less by constitutional curbs than by considerations of distance and communication, and, above all, by the varied cultural backgrounds of the different parts of the country.

Finally, it should be emphasized that thirteenth-century France, a thriving country with an expanding population, had obtained an eminent position in the cultural life of Europe. It was at once the home of the great university of Paris, of Gothic architecture, and of a vernacular literature of widespread popularity. Such matters will receive more extended consideration in later chapters.

C. *Developing Christian Kingdoms of the Iberian Peninsula*

The rugged mountainous nature of much of the Iberian peninsula and the prolonged wars for its reconquest by Christians from Moslems combined to delay its political unity. Moreover, the constant influx of French knights to participate in the local crusades served to perpetuate in the peninsula the feudalism which was passing in France. As late as 1300, the peninsula was still divided into four Christian kingdoms—Portugal, Navarre, Castile, and Aragon—and a Moslem state of Granada. Political separatism was also accentuated by cultural and linguistic differences. In those years which saw the rise of vernacular languages and literature, the Hispanic peninsula had four different ones—Portuguese, Castilian, Catalan, and Basque, not to mention Arabic.

Communities of *Mozarabs*, Christians who had in large measure adopted Moslem culture, were incorporated in one or another of the expanding Christian kingdoms, or utilized as new settlers on conquered territory. *Mudejares*, free Moslem Arabs, were also numerous in conquered areas and some degree of autonomy was customarily guaranteed them in the treaties of surrender. Jews likewise constituted an important element in the peninsular population. The same Moslem resurgence which threatened Christian Spain toward the end of the twelfth century and in the early years of the thirteenth, led to persecution of Jews in Moslem Spain, and at the time large numbers of them found a cordial reception in Christian areas. Upwards of ten thousand, for example, were welcomed to Toledo, where they were subsequently permitted to hold public office. Only in the later Middle Ages and early modern times did popular and official resentment toward Jews become a factor in Spanish life.

All such elements increased the diversity of Spain's population, while notably enriching its culture. Yet despite political and cultural divergences, there were certain common features of Christian civilization in the Iberian peninsula which it will be well to consider.

The chief difference between the fundamental agricultural life of Spain and that, let us say, of France, was the prevalence of grazing in the former. For while the upland plains and mountainous regions of the peninsula could support many sheep and cattle, they were not suitable for any large-scale cultivation. Thus, while medieval Spain fostered a privileged, land-owning nobility in common with most of western Europe, the type of agrarian community characteristic of western feudalism had scarcely taken root in Spain. But there were a considerable number of towns enjoying special privileges under royal charters (*fueros*). Cities were often founded in reconquered territory, and liberties promised as an inducement to settlers. Leagues or brotherhoods (*hermandades*) of towns, formed usually as a means of protection against the nobles as well as against Moslems, played an important part in Spanish political life and were often highly useful to the kings.

As far as institutions of central government were concerned, considerable progress was made in the larger states. In Castile, Alphonso X "the Wise" (1252–1284) was not only a patron of general learning, but the author of *Las Siete Partidas*, a code of laws based on Roman principles of centralized monarchy. In both Castile and Aragon, *cortes* or parliaments antedated the English Parliament and the French Estates General. The *cortes* of Castile was an assembly summoned by the king and comprising nobles and clergy together with representatives from the towns chosen by lot. Like their counterparts elsewhere, the Castilian *cortes* met only at the king's pleasure, but their powers somewhat ex-

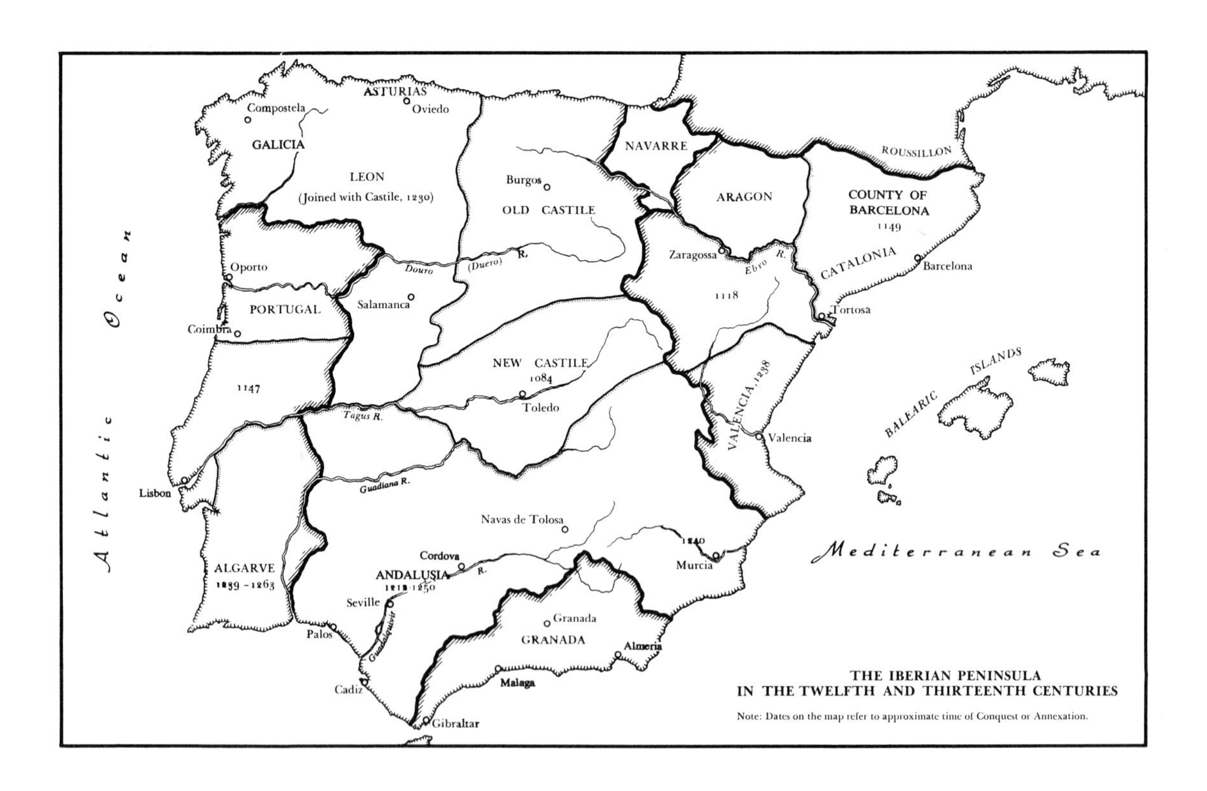

THE IBERIAN PENINSULA
IN THE TWELFTH AND THIRTEENTH CENTURIES

Note: Dates on the map refer to approximate time of Conquest or Annexation.

ceeded those of the French Estates. The *cortes* of Aragon possessed much wider powers, as did also the local *cortes* in each of the provinces composing the realm—Aragon proper, Catalonia, and Valencia. They were all divided into four estates: one of the clergy, another of the chief nobles, a third of the knights, and the fourth of the commoners. England was by no means the only land in which there developed during the middle ages a monarchy constitutionally limited by a parliament.

D. Norman Kingdom of Sicily and Naples

One of the most successfully centralized kingdoms in Europe was the Norman kingdom of Sicily. It will be recalled that Normans from Normandy in the eleventh century had occupied Apulia and Calabria in southern Italy and then conquered Sicily from the Moslems. Under Count Roger, southern Italy and Sicily were united and all attempts at interference by popes, Holy Roman emperors, or Byzantine emperors were frustrated by a skillful combination of force and diplomacy. In 1130 Roger II assumed the title of king, a title the Pope was eventually obliged to recognize. Not content with his existing domains, Roger contemplated a Mediterranean empire and actually secured, at least temporarily, certain holdings in north Africa. His immediate successors continued his policies.

In 1186, with the marriage of the Norman heiress, Constance, to the future Emperor Henry VI, the kingdom was linked with German fortunes and came under the rule of the imperial Hohenstaufen dynasty.[1] Under the brilliant Frederick II (*d.* 1250), the kingdom reached the peak of its development.

In many respects the government of Sicily was unique. Although composed of disparate elements long accustomed to different rulers, it attained a high degree of centralization. The inhabitants were variously Greek, Saracen, Italian, Jewish, Lombard, and Norman French. Roger had shrewdly drawn on all these elements to weld his state into a notably compact unit. Three languages—Latin, Greek, and Arabic—were officially recognized, while royal agents had also to be familiar with Italian and French. Religious toleration for non-Christians was obviously essential, though the Catholic rulers suppressed heresy and strictly controlled the clergy. A heterogeneous army and bureaucracy owed complete loyalty to the king and enabled him successfully to curb the feudal aristocracy. In 1231 Frederick II reconstituted all these institutions and further centralized the state in the *Constitutions of Melfi*, which clearly showed the influence of Roman law. In economic policy Frederick was particularly progressive and leaned heavily on Moslem precedents. Internal tolls were abolished, tariffs being levied only at the frontiers. Fairs were encouraged. The kingdom prospered.

The fall of the Hohenstaufen dynasty, which will be explained in the following chapter, marked also the decline of Naples-Sicily as a strong state. The brother of Louis IX of France, Charles of Anjou, to whom the papacy entrusted the kingdom, lost Sicily to Aragon, and thus retained only Naples and southern Italy. This should not obscure the fact that during the twelfth and thirteenth centuries the Norman kingdom of Sicily-Naples was an important European state, far more important, indeed, than contemporary England. In Mediterranean diplomacy and commerce, it played a highly significant role. Moreover, as the meeting ground of Latin, Greek, and Arabic cultures it contributed in large measure to the medieval revival of learning.

[1] See below, p. 217.

Gothic architecture in Spain. The Cathedral at Toledo.

Courtesy Spanish National Tourist Department, New York

CHAPTER 18

Medieval Empires and Border States of Central and Eastern Europe

A. Emperor Frederick Barbarossa; His Effort to Build a Consolidated Feudal Monarchy in Germany

In the German lands of north-central Europe, various factors combined to prevent the formation of a strong feudal monarchy such as arose in the western countries of France and England. Among these factors were: (1) certain peculiarities of German feudalism, (2) frequent changes of dynasty, (3) prevalence of civil strife, and (4) a pursuit of Italian as well as German policies on the part of German kings. These kings, it must constantly be borne in mind, persisted in regarding themselves as the successors of Charlemagne and Otto the Great: Roman emperors as well as German kings.

The years of the investiture controversy with its attendant civil wars had halted the promising progress of early medieval Germany.[1] Although the kings of that time had fairly successfully curbed the greater dukes, many lesser vassals had seized the opportunity, sometimes with royal encouragement, to establish their own power even to the extent of building castles and surrounding themselves with bands of knights. Nevertheless, in the German kingdom—and in this it was unlike the former western Frankish domains—many royal rights (*regalia*), taxes, mining rights, etc., were still claimed or contested by the king within the various duchies. In other words, feudalism was neither universally nor systematically rooted. Further, despite the setback which the German crown had received as an outcome of the investiture controversy, most German rulers continued to try to use the church in support of the monarchy.

The death of the Emperor Henry V in 1125 without direct heirs confirmed the German practice of election by the chief feudal lords. Two families, in particular, were rivals for the kingship and imperial title—the Hohenstaufen and the Guelf. The former stemmed from the duchy of Swabia, and found supporters in both Germany and Italy, who were usually styled "Ghibellines," presumably from the name of the family's castle of Waiblingen. The Guelf family were dominant in Saxony and Bavaria. After much struggling and disorder, the Hohenstaufen gained the upper hand, and in 1152 the head of the family became Holy Roman Emperor as Frederick I.

Frederick I "Barbarossa" (1152–1190) has become the legendary German hero-king. Handsome, well built, with golden red hair, he could attract by his affable disposition and command with authority. A young man of energy and ability, he was the perfect embodiment of the knightly chivalrous ruler.

Generally speaking, Frederick I strove to do for Germany what his contemporaries in England and France were doing, namely to strengthen the state and to establish monarchical institutions grounded on a constructive feudalism. His relations with Henry "the Lion" of Saxony and Bavaria, the head of the rival house of Guelf, illus-

[1] See above, pp. 164–166.

trates the king's policy with regard to the great duchies and incidentally the lesser nobility. For several years Frederick left Henry unmolested and in practical independence. But though he was deeply engaged with Italian affairs, he apparently did not lose sight of the ideal of making Germany a federation of great duchies bound to him by ties of vassalage. Manifestly such an ideal could not be realized if any duchy was too strong. As time went on, Frederick became alarmed at the success with which Henry was utilizing his independence to build up a formidable domain. Henry was consolidating the duchy of Saxony, patronizing towns, and generally promoting prosperity; he was also extending his sway into Brandenburg and Pomerania. Frederick finally challenged Henry; and his method was typically feudal and not unlike the procedure of Philip Augustus with King John of England.

In 1180 Henry, whose successes had not been won without alienating many of his smaller neighbors, was summoned to the royal court to answer charges. His refusal brought from Frederick a declaration of the forfeiture of his estates. In the ensuing struggle, Henry's forces were crushed, his duchies of Saxony and Bavaria were divided into smaller fiefs dependent on the crown, and only two castles were left to him. Of the previous large duchy of Saxony, only the small eastern part continued to bear the name. The western part was cut off and formed into a new duchy of Westphalia; this was temporarily assigned to the archbishop of Cologne. By thus overcoming and penalizing Henry the Lion, the Emperor redressed in his own favor the balance of power between the duchies and the crown and gave dramatic emphasis to the obligations of vassalage. By dividing Henry's lands and securing the dependence of smaller territories, he put himself in a position to ensure that balance. Like Philip Augustus of France, he was utilizing feudal law and practice to strengthen the monarchy.

There were two other significant aspects of Frederick Barbarossa's German policy: his attempt to build up a royal domain governed by some sort of administrative system; and his continued use of the church. In western and south-central Germany, especially in Franconia, Swabia, and neighboring Alsace, he labored to consolidate his own territories and to exercise an effective control of monastic and other properties. His marriage to Beatrice, heiress to the kingdom of Burgundy, was a significant move. He also won support of numerous cities, particularly in the Rhineland, by granting them liberal privileges. It was not a compact domain in the geographical sense, but Frederick strove to make it so. Moreover, within this expanded royal territory, Frederick hoped to ensure control through the appointment of officials dependent on the crown. As a consequence, *ministeriales* were stationed at appropriate places. The German monarchy was less successful in exercising control over the new frontier districts in the northeast, for there the princes were usually able to establish a relatively unrestricted authority of their own.

With regard to the church, Frederick continued to dominate the German bishops, at least in political matters. He made the most of the right to invest a new incumbent with the temporalities of his see, a right, it will be remembered, conceded by the pope in the Concordat of Worms.[1] Thereby, ecclesiastical princes were associated with the crown. All in all, Frederick Barbarossa made a promising start toward building a consolidated feudal monarchy in Germany.

B. The Hohenstaufen Emperors and Italy

What distinguishes German medieval history from that of other countries is the Italian or "imperial" policy of its monarchs, for, as the years passed, they came to regard themselves as the successors of Charlemagne, the heirs of a Roman Empire. The wisdom of pursuing such a course in the twelfth and thirteenth centuries when Italy, though divided, presented such formidable obstacles as a strong southern kingdom, a revived papacy, and prosperous and powerful northern cities, has been questioned. To some historians it has seemed the principal reason for the failure of a truly constructive

---

[1] See above, p. 166.

GERMAN (HOLY ROMAN) EMPIRE
UNDER THE HOHENSTAUFEN
Boundary of the Empire
Territory added during Hohenstaufen period
Patrimony of St. Peter
Other lands claimed by Papacy
Venetian possessions
K = Kingdom D = Duchy C = County
M = Mark L = Landgraviate
By 1300 the great duchies were broken into smaller feudal divisions.
By 1300 French influence was strong in the Kingdom of Arles
and imperial power in Italy was slight.
DENMARK
PRUSSIA
POLAND
FRANCE
HUNGARY
SILESIA
C. Holstein
Danzig
Pomerelia
POMERANIA
Slavonia
Hamburg
Elbe R.
M. BRANDENBURG
Vistula R.
FRISIA
C. Oldenburg
D. SAXONY
Brunswick Lüneburg
Brunswick
Magdeburg
C. Holland
Guelders
Munster
Weser R.
M. Lausitz
Oder R.
D. BRABANT
C. Loos
Antwerp
Rhine R.
Cologne
Mühlhausen
L. THURINGIA
C. Berg
Hesse
Fulda
M. Meissen
C. Hainaut
Aachen
Luxemburg
Mainz
Worms
Trier
D. FRANCONIA
Prague
K. BOHEMIA
M. Moravia
Ratisbon
D. LORRAINE
ALSACE
Breisgau
Danube R.
D. Austria
Ulm
Augsburg
D. SWABIA
D. BAVARIA
Vienna
Constance
Salzburg
C. Burgundy
D. Styria
D. Carinthia
K. ARLES
Geneva
C. Savoy
Trent
Cortenuovo
Friuli
M. Verona
M. Carniola
Legnano
Milan
Chartreuse
LOMBARDY
Cremona
Venice
Alessandria
Roncaglia
Po R.
Rhone R.
Genoa
Romagna
Zara
C. Provence
(to Anjou, 1266)
Florence
Pisa
TUSCANY
M. Ancona
Ancona
D. Spoleto
Ragusa
CORSICA
To Pisa until 1285
then to Genoa
Patrimony
Rome
of St. Peter
S. Germano
Hohenstaufen, 1194
Anjou, 1266
Apulia
Melfi
Naples
K.
SARDINIA
To Pisa and Genoa
to Aragon 1296-1326
TWO
SICILIES
Calabria
Palermo
SICILY
Hohenstaufen, 1194
Anjou, 1266
Aragon, 1282

German policy.[1] But Frederick, it must be remembered, viewed the world from a twelfth-century, not a nineteenth- or twentieth-century standpoint. To his kingdoms of Germany and Burgundy he must add the kingdom of Italy, traditionally associated with the German monarchy. No doubt the wealth of Italy he needed. Moreover, his rival, Henry the Lion of Bavaria and Saxony, was close to the Alps and had relatives in Tuscany. To have permitted consolidation by the Guelphs would have seriously endangered his work in Germany. It is possible, therefore, to argue that solid realistic reasons prompted Frederick's moves to the South.

All three areas of Italy—the northern cities, the papal lands, and the Norman kingdom of the south—were concerned in one way or another with Frederick's policies. Under Pope Hadrian IV, the only English pope, relations, despite certain tensions,[2] were reasonably friendly. Opinion among the cardinals favored the traditional cooperation of Pope and Emperor. As a consequence, Frederick assisted the Pope in subduing a revolt of the Roman citizenry and captured and executed Arnold of Brescia, an agitator-reformer. In 1155 Frederick was crowned by the Pope.

However, a growing number of cardinals led by Roland Bandinelli, who was soon to become Pope as Alexander III, was becoming uneasy about Frederick's control of ecclesiastical affairs in Germany as well as the possibility of a real instead of a nominal control over northern and perhaps central Italy. Thus in 1156 a Treaty of Benevento was negotiated with the Norman kingdom of the south that was distinctly favorable as regards the ecclesiastical privileges of the monarchy and that Barbarossa regarded as incompatible with a previous Treaty of Constance of 1153 with the Empire.

Meanwhile, Frederick had begun the consolidation of his authority in northern Italy. In a famous imperial Diet held at Roncaglia (1158), after overcoming resistance in Lombardy, the Emperor proclaimed, according to the principles of Roman law then being revived in Italy, his sovereign rights over the cities. Although he had no intention of doing so in all cases, he reserved the right in each to appoint an official, a *podestà*, and to collect certain taxes. But if Frederick's regalian claims were more precisely stated than had been the case previously, so also were the cities better able to resist, for, as we have seen, this was the period of the flowering of town administration throughout Europe and preëminently in Italy.

Such was the situation when Pope Hadrian died and Cardinal Roland was elected to succeed him as Alexander III (1159–1181). A minority of cardinals disputed the election and chose a rival Pope whom the Emperor supported. Most, but not all, of the German bishops—some, no doubt, under pressure—also accepted the anti-Pope and his two successors. And though the Emperor's superior force drove Alexander to refuge in France, the Pope had no intention of surrendering and managed to maintain the papal administration for some years in exile.

Although Frederick was at first successful in Italy and crushed a rebellious Milan his triumph proved only temporary. The Pope soon won the support of other monarchs and of the majority of the clergy everywhere. Moreover, most of the defeated cities formed a Lombard League (1168) to defend their privileges. A few cities and factions remained loyal to the Emperor and were called "Ghibelline." On the other hand, the name of "Guelf" was applied to the Lombard League and others who opposed the Emperor and supported the Pope. The Norman king, and occasionally

---

[1] For a summary of the long controversy over German medieval imperial policy, and a presentation of the traditional adverse criticism, see J. W. Thompson, *Feudal Germany* (Chicago, 1928), Chapter VIII. Since Thompson, himself, figures in the controversy, the student is advised to consult the appropriate pages in G. Barraclough, *The Origins of Modern Germany* (Oxford, 1957), and his "Frederick Barbarossa and the Twelfth Century," *History in a changing world* (1956).

[2] On their first meeting, Frederick refused for two days to perform the usual courtesy of holding the Pope's stirrup. In 1157 a legate, in referring to favors done the Emperor by the Pope, used the word "beneficia." This was translated "fiefs" by the imperial chancellor and was immediately protested. Hadrian later acknowledged that the word meant "benefits," not "fiefs."

even the Byzantine emperor, who was anxious to recover influence in the west, gave assistance. Finally at Legnano in 1176 Frederick suffered a crushing defeat. But in the peace of Venice (1177) he managed, by astute diplomacy, to separate Pope Alexander, whom at long last he recognized, and the Lombard cities with whom final settlement was deferred. In 1183, by the peace of Constance, the emperor conceded the rights of self-government for which the Lombard cities had fought. But in return they acknowledged his suzerainty, including the right to hear appeals from their courts and to receive occasional contributions.

Although partially thwarted in northern Italy, Frederick was more successful in Tuscany and other parts of central Italy. Besides, in the years after the treaty of Constance, he managed to neutralize the formerly hostile south by arranging a marriage between his son, the future Emperor Henry VI, and Constance, daughter of the King of Sicily.

In 1189 this Frederick I, Barbarossa, good Christian knight that he was, embarked for the Holy Land on a Crusade. Did he perhaps hope to lay new foundations of power in the east? It is difficult to say, for the great emperor did not live to complete his project. He died while fording a stream in Asia Minor. Thus ended the distinguished, if not entirely successful, career of one of Germany's most engaging rulers.

It so happened that Constance, the wife of Frederick's son and successor, became sole heiress to the southern kingdom. Hence with the reign of Henry VI (1190–1197) Hohenstaufen policies were more deeply involved than ever in Italian and Mediterranean affairs. But although Henry made the most of his inheritance, subduing his newly acquired kingdom of Sicily, and mastering central and northern Italy, premature death cut short his successes.

Henry VI's death gave the papacy a much needed respite, of which the young and vigorous Pope Innocent III (1198–1216) knew how to take advantage. Henry's heir was his son Frederick, then only three years old. With great energy and skill, but not without considerable difficulty, Innocent recovered the bulk of the papal lands and managed to entrust the remainder to princes loyal to himself. In Germany, the imperial and royal titles were withheld from the boy Frederick, while in Sicily his mother, anxious to obtain papal support for her son,

Gothic architecture in Germany. The Cathedral, formerly abbey, at Altenberg, north Rhineland.

Courtesy German Tourist Information Office, New York

recognized anew the old feudal suzerainty of the Holy See over the kingdom. Consequently, when she died in 1198, the young Frederick II, as King of Sicily, automatically became a ward of the papacy. Thus Innocent was enabled to sever the union between Sicily and Germany.

In Germany itself, the refusal of the princes to accept the young Frederick II precipitated a renewed outbreak of the Guelf-Hohenstaufen feud. Philip of Swabia, Barbarossa's youngest son and candidate of the Hohenstaufen faction, was opposed by Otto of Brunswick, a son of Henry the Lion. Before long, the civil war involved most of Europe, as the English Angevin kings joined the Guelfs and the French Capetian kings threw in their lot with the Hohenstaufen.

Pope Innocent III was at first neutral. He had no desire to question the German custom of electing a king, although he reserved to himself the rights of approving the choice and of reviewing a disputed election —rights implied in his privilege of crowning Holy Roman Emperors. Gradually, because Otto seemed the more conciliatory and Philip refused to agree to any arbitration, the Pope swung his powerful support to the former (1201). But not until Philip was killed (1208) was Otto's position secure.

Unfortunately for all concerned, the Guelf Otto, once he was crowned Emperor, proved to be as tenacious of imperial claims as any Hohenstaufen. As a consequence, Innocent's maneuvers were in vain, and in 1210 he was forced to break with his erstwhile candidate. And when, in 1211, a Diet of rebellious princes finally elected the young Frederick, the Pope gave his backing to his Sicilian ward. Frederick II repeated the protestations of loyalty to the papacy made by Otto and, on Innocent's insistence, made two additional promises. He agreed to undertake a Crusade; and he promised never to unite the Sicilian and German kingdoms under one crown. Then when Frederick, with the aid of Philip Augustus of France, defeated Otto and John of England at Bouvines (1214), Innocent's position seemed secure. Europe was pacified and could, so he hoped, unitedly carry forward the crusade which was so dear to his heart. In 1216 the great Pope died, little realizing how untrustworthy his former ward was to prove.

C. Frederick II, German Emperor and King of Sicily

Frederick II (1211–1250) was one of the most brilliant rulers of his time. Unlike his chivalrous grandfather, who exemplified the Teutonic hero-king, Frederick was the subtle, shrewd, and unscrupulous diplomat. He was far more attached to Sicily with its cosmopolitan culture than to his northern German realm. Although Frederick, like others of his day, had a firm belief in astrology, he was well educated and a good deal of a scholar, with a real intellectual curiosity, especially in matters of science. He arranged for a number of experiments, and transported on his journeys a whole menagerie of birds and animals. He even wrote an important treatise on falconry, displaying considerable scientific knowledge (*De arte venandi cum avibus*). Under his patronage, Moslem, Christian, and Jewish scholars took up residence in Sicily.

Frederick II was known as a skeptic, and contemporary gossip attributed to him the authorship of an anonymous pamphlet entitled, *The Three Imposters: Moses, Christ, and Mohammed.* It was also alleged that he kept a sort of harem in Mohammedan style. Small wonder that his astonished contemporaries spoke of him as the wonder of the world (*stúpor mundi*). Perhaps Frederick's propensity to defy current theological and moral standards has been somewhat exaggerated owing to his long struggle with the papacy. It is noteworthy, at any rate, that in Sicily he treated heresy as a civil crime.

Frederick II was thoroughly devoted to the Hohenstaufen conception of empire which he regarded as divinely ordained to bring about a reign of justice. Only, in his case, the center of the empire would not be Germany, but rather Sicily. In this southern kingdom, with its admirable governmental traditions, Frederick was more at home.

Fortunately for the young Emperor, Innocent III was succeeded by Honorius III (1216–1227), an elderly man not disposed to insist too strictly that Frederick fulfill

Castel del Monte, built by the Emperor Frederick II in southern Italy.

Courtesy Italian State Tourist Office

his promises. The latter readily found reasons for postponing the Crusade, and easily persuaded Honorius to agree to the election of Frederick's infant son as "King of the Romans," or heir-presumptive to the headship of the Holy Roman Empire. Meanwhile Frederick conceded important privileges to German princes, ecclesiastical and lay, as he energetically extended his sway throughout Italy. For a time, it seemed as though the ambition of Frederick Barbarossa was to be realized by Frederick II, and all Italy and Germany joined under the strong rule of a Holy Roman Emperor.

But Honorius's successor, Pope Gregory IX (1227–1241), despite his eighty-odd years, was as stout a champion of papal prerogatives as Innocent III had been. He insisted that Frederick set out for the Holy Land in fulfillment of his promise, and the Emperor, who had recently married the heiress to the Latin Kingdom of Jerusalem, actually made a pretense of going. He conveniently fell ill, however; and his failure to depart brought an excommunication from Gregory. Though still under the ban of the church, Frederick left in the following year for the Holy Land. There he managed, by skillfully playing on the jealousies of the Moslem chieftains, to win a temporary control of Jerusalem. Meanwhile, the doughty Gregory refused to lift the ban and attempted to rouse Frederick's subjects against him. Eventually, in 1230, the Emperor submitted, pledging himself to respect church privileges in Sicily and to protect the papal territories, and was then absolved by the Pope.

Peace with the papacy afforded Frederick II the opportunity to resume pursuit of his imperial plans. After suppressing an insurrection in Germany, he turned his attention to Italy. Claiming that he was not bound by the promises which his grandfather had made at Constance in 1183, he demanded the submission of the Lombard cities. But for these cities, Constance had been a kind of charter of independence, and they now formed a second Lombard League. Their resistance was shattered, however, by a victory of Frederick's forces at Cortenuova (1237). The Emperor followed up his triumph by conquering all north Italy and imposing upon it a Sicilian type of administration under trusted officials of his own. Each city was placed under an imperial *podestà*, the forerunner of the Italian "despot" of the next century. Moreover, since the Pope had sided with the Lombard League, Frederick invaded the papal states. At this point Gregory IX died (1241).

When it was learned that Gregory's successor had been a personal friend of Frederick, the latter, despite his pleasure at the choice, is said to have remarked "no pope can be a Ghibelline." And, indeed, Innocent IV (1243–1254) continued with vigor the struggle against the Emperor. Compelled to flee from Rome, the Pope took refuge at Lyons in France, and there summoned a general church council, in which he solemnly excommunicated and deposed Frederick and proclaimed a Crusade against him. Never before had the ideal of papal predominance over the kings of Christendom been so clearly expressed. But Innocent could not organize forces sufficient to overcome the Emperor and once again it was death which thwarted the imperial plans. Frederick was within sight of the mastery of all Italy when he died in 1250.

The death of Frederick II virtually brought to an end the Hohenstaufen dream of empire. Frederick's son, Conrad IV (1250–1254), survived him only four years; and the grandson, Conradin, who was next in succession, was only a boy. In vain, an illegitimate son of Frederick, Manfred, attempted to stem the tide that was setting in against the Hohenstaufen. The papacy preached a new Crusade against the last representatives of the imperial family, and invited Charles of Anjou, a brother of St. Louis IX of France, to take possession of the kingdom of Sicily. Manfred died in battle and Conradin was finally captured and executed.

All this did not bring peace to Italy. Towns freed from imperial rule presently resumed quarreling and fighting with one another; while the new French Angevin kings of Sicily and Naples soon proved themselves almost as ambitious and dangerous to the papacy as the former Hohenstaufen had been. In 1282, a rebellion broke out in Sicily against the French Angevin ruler, and although he retained control of Naples and adjacent territory in the southern part of the Italian peninsula, he lost Sicily to the King of Aragon, who utilized the rebellion to occupy the island. In this way, the once great Norman kingdom of Sicily and Naples was broken into two parts and sadly weakened.

In a sense, the outcome was a triumph for the papacy, which had prevented the formation of a consolidated Italian monarchy that might have been dangerous to its own independence. But the triumph was achieved at heavy cost. As will later be explained, the political hegemony of the papacy proved as short-lived as that of the Hohenstaufen Emperors.

A just estimate of Frederick II's career must include passing reference to his achievements in Sicily and also in Germany. Sicilian by birth, more Sicilian than German in temperament, he devoted some of his best energies toward furthering the progress of the former Norman kingdom. The results we have described elsewhere. But he did not neglect entirely his northern German realm. Indeed it is possible that the rights conceded to the princes he regarded as a temporary expedient and that he intended ultimately to impose a "Sicilian" regime in Germany. Frederick did foster eastward expansion by encouraging and confirming the Teutonic Knights in their Prussian conquests.[1] He also defended the eastern frontiers against the Mongols. But this very frontier policy worked in the long run against the Hohenstaufen design for a monarchically unified Germany. For it shifted the balance of power within the country farther away from the west, where Frederick Barbarossa had commenced to consolidate a royal domain, to the pioneering and more independent east.

Germany emerged in the later Middle Ages as an agglomeration of principalities, large and small, ecclesiastical and lay. With the fall of the Hohenstaufen went the last attempt to create a crown domain strong enough to dominate the entire realm in manner comparable with that of the Capetian kings in France. Some historians see in this the key to the medieval and much of the modern history of Germany. As we have indicated, another explanation is that the imperial policy of the Hohenstaufen entailed their neglect of Germany and its consolidation; that they sacrificed national to imperial interests. If this be true, there is a temptation to condemn the German rulers of the twelfth and thirteenth centuries for pursuing a policy which lacked realism. This is unfair. Nationalism is a

[1] See above, pp. 176–177.

modern, not a thirteenth-century, conception. If the Hohenstaufen were imperialists in the Roman sense, they were seeking to realize the highest political ideal their contemporaries knew, that of a single empire for all Christendom. Today, we are accustomed to look ahead for progress. In the thirteenth century, men still looked back to what seemed to them the golden age of the past, the days of Charlemagne.

D. *Northern and East-Central Europe*

As we turn from Germany proper to northern and eastern Europe we pass into areas of varying political development. In the latter region, the Tatar invasion [1] had considerably more than temporary significance. Then, too, in many instances throughout both regions, the institutional influences of the older kingdoms, particularly of Germany, were marked. But perhaps the most striking feature about all the smaller or border states of northern and eastern Europe is their membership in the community of Christendom. We shall begin our survey with a brief glance at the Scandinavian lands in northwest Europe.

During the twelfth and thirteenth centuries the three Scandinavian kingdoms of Denmark, Norway, and Sweden developed, in varying degree, the institutions of feudal monarchy. The struggles between crown and nobility, so characteristic of western Europe, were evident in each; and in Denmark the nobles forced from King Eric V a charter (1282) not unlike the English Magna Carta.[2] In Norway and Sweden regular parliaments of the nobility were assembled. But, in general, royal power remained a reality in Scandinavia, while the peasants retained a large measure of personal freedom. The thirteenth century also witnessed here, as in Europe generally, the growth of towns and commerce, the latter stimulated by German capital and German merchants. The fishing industry flourished, and mining came to play an increasingly important role, especially in Sweden. Ecclesiastical organization was also perfected with the establishment of new dioceses, and the growth of monasticism. The institution of archdioceses in each of the kingdoms freed the Scandinavian churches from their earlier dependence on the archbishop of Bremen.

Meanwhile, the northern descendants of the Vikings were not entirely inactive beyond their own frontiers. Norway retained its contacts with Iceland and Greenland, and its hold over the islands off the north coast of Scotland. King Eric IX (1150–1160) of Sweden led a Crusade into Finland, and the Danes were active all along the Baltic coast until their efforts were frustrated by the Germans.

To the east of Germany proper were two Slavic states of growing importance in the middle ages—Bohemia and Poland. Bohemia, peopled largely by Slavic Czechs, was closely connected with Germany and included within the Holy Roman Empire. Both in its internal affairs and in its relations with the imperial government, however, Bohemia retained a very large measure of autonomy. It is true that Frederick Barbarossa's centralizing policies threatened Bohemian independence. But the danger passed with the failure of his efforts and with the simultaneous cessation of internal conflict within Bohemia. In the closing years of the twelfth century and the early years of the thirteenth, the Bohemians were able to utilize for their profit the contemporary political difficulties of their imperial suzerains. Ottokar I (1197–1230), for example, won confirmation for his title of king from both factions in the German civil war, and likewise from the pope (1207). Still more important, Ottokar obtained from the Emperor Frederick II the Golden Bull of 1212, which specifically limited Bohemia's obligations to the Empire and recognized the right of the Bohemian nobility to elect their own king. This latter concession, together with Ottokar's own provisions for the royal succession, resulted in a customary "election" of the king's eldest son and the practical establishment of a hereditary succession to the crown of Bohemia.

Subsequent decades witnessed not only further diminishing of imperial interference in Bohemia, but increasing participation on the part of the Bohemian kings in

[1] See above, p. 186.
[2] See above, p. 204.

German affairs. Their position as imperial electors came to be officially recognized. And partly as a consequence of the chaotic conditions in the Empire attendant upon the fall of the Hohenstaufen, Ottokar II (1253–1278) was able temporarily to extend Bohemian territorial boundaries. Furthermore, despite the fact that many of the clergy in Bohemia were German rather than Czech, the period witnessed a notable development of Czech culture. Several Bohemian chronicles and tales were written, including Cosmas's *Chronicle of the Bohemians*. Finally, the opening of Bohemian silver mines proved important in the economic development of the kingdom.

Though Poland, the other Slavic state in central Europe, was not included within the Holy Roman Empire, its relations with the Germans assumed special significance during the twelfth and thirteenth centuries. The Polish King Boleslav III (1102–1138) successfully withstood the Emperor Henry V, and, by capturing Pomerania, gained access to the Baltic. Less auspicious was his division of the state into five principalities for his sons. Cracow, the old capital, went to the eldest member of the ruling house, with the title of Grand Duke. Resulting quarrels over the succession materially weakened Poland. Furthermore, the country was restricted by the conquest of the adjacent region of Prussia by the Teutonic Knights who, ironically enough, had first been summoned by one of the Polish dukes. Eventually, German settlers outnumbered the native inhabitants. Poland likewise suffered from Mongol raids and the devastation they wrought. It is true that the settlement of Teutonic Knights and other Germans in northern Poland was of immediate advantage for common defense against the Mongols and for the economic development of the region, but it sowed seeds of future rivalry and conflict between Poles and Germans.

In east-central Europe, like a wedge between the West Slav Poles and Czechs and the South Slavs (Yugoslavs) of the Balkans, lay the Magyar kingdom of Hungary. In the twelfth century its rulers reduced to vassalage the Slavic state of Croatia on the Adriatic, but their efforts to extend the Hungarian realm farther into the Balkans were successfully resisted by the Byzantine Emperor at Constantinople. For a short time, the Byzantine Emperors managed to exercise a suzerainty over Hungary.

In the early thirteenth century Hungary was raided and devastated by Mongols, and to protect the country against renewed raids, the nobility were authorized to build castles which increased their power at the expense of that of the kings. Already King Andrew II (*d.* 1235) had disposed of large tracts of the royal domain in order to finance a crusade. And in the Golden Bull of 1222, another document in some measure comparable to the English Magna Carta, he agreed to periodic meetings of a parliament, or diet, and to other curtailments of royal power by the nobility. Thus, medieval Hungary took on a feudal and agrarian character, with a strongly entrenched aristocracy.

E. Russia, the Byzantine Empire, and the Balkans

In eastern Europe, Russian history of the twelfth and thirteenth centuries was marked by two significant developments: (1) the rise of several new principalities following the decline of Kiev; and (2) the Tatar, or Mongol, occupation. Some inhabitants of the Slavic principality of Kiev migrated northward to the region of the upper Dnieper and Dvina rivers, where they contributed to the formation of a distinctive Byelorussian ("White Russian") nation. Others moved in a more north-easterly direction toward the upper Volga and Oka rivers, where they intermarried with other Slavic and Finnish peoples to form the "Great Russian" stock. Still others went west and south into Volhynia and Galicia, which became the historic homeland of the Ukrainians or "Little Russians." In all these regions new settlements were founded or older communities strengthened.

Russia, alone of all the countries of Europe, was forced to endure a prolonged occupation by the Tatars. Practically all the Russian principalities, except Novgorod in the north, came under the Mongol yoke and suffered varying degrees of devastation. In the course of time, however, Tatar dominance came to involve little more than

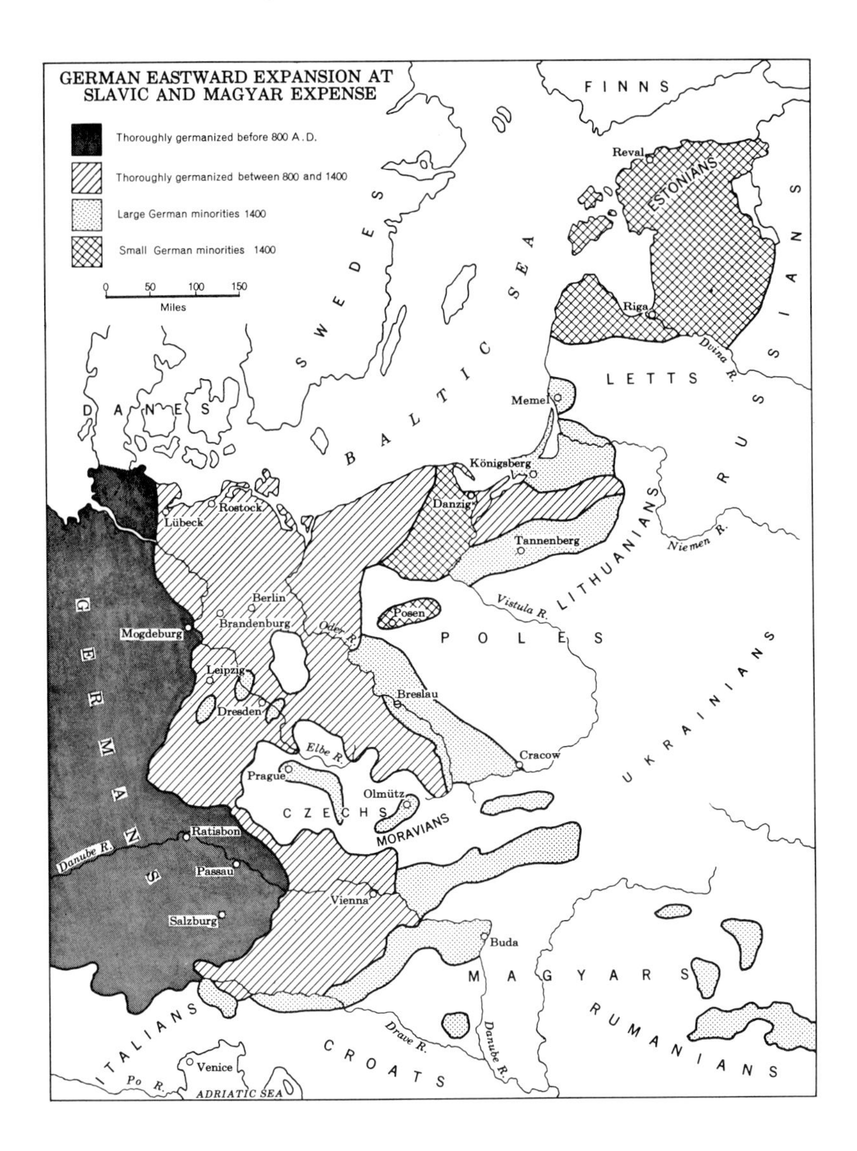

tribute paid by native Russian princes and magnates for lands they actually ruled. And since the Mongols failed to construct any strong central states, their power was wielded by several different, and usually rival, "Khanates."

The Tatar invasions had driven many Russians north and northeast along the rivers and deep into the forests which afforded them escape from assault. One result was the rise of a new principality centering in the town of Moscow—a principality which was destined to be the starting-point for the rise of a great and unified Russian state.

Thus, despite the protracted occupation of a large part of Russia by the Mongols, some independent Russian life and culture precariously survived throughout the middle ages and even gave promise of later resurrection and expansion. This culture had been derived mainly from Constantinople, and it continued to be fundamentally Eastern and Byzantine.

The period immediately following the Mongol conquest was not without occasional moments of native Russian brilliance. For example, one of the grand-dukes of the principalities of Novgorod and Vladimir, Alexander Nevski (1236–1263), defeated the Swedes and the Teutonic Knights, and secured peace with the Mongols and an easing of the tribute they exacted.

In southeastern Europe, the history of

Russian medieval architecture. Cathedral of St. Sophia at Novgorod. Dating from the eleventh century, restored.

Sovfoto, New York

the Byzantine Empire and the Balkan lands during the twelfth and thirteenth centuries is a troubled and confusing story. The Emperor Alexius Comnenus, whose request for assistance from the West against the Seljuk Turks helped to precipitate the First Crusade, was succeeded by John (*d.* 1143) and Manuel (*d.* 1180), both of whom were able statesmen. Manuel continued his efforts to retain influence in the west, as we have seen, by assisting Pope Alexander, and by attempting, although unsuccessfully, to maintain a foothold in southern Italy. The Peace of Venice (1177), which terminated Alexander's long controversy with Barbarossa and brought peace to Italy, marked the end of these efforts. Venetians and Sicilians forced the Byzantine Emperor to confirm their trading privileges; and Venetians, it will be recalled, along with other Italians, were migrating in considerable numbers into the Byzantine dominions.

Meanwhile the Emperor suffered a major defeat at the hands of the Turks at Myriokephalon in Asia Minor in 1176. And a Bulgarian insurrection forced the Byzantine government to cede a large area in the Balkan peninsula to a practically independent Bulgaria. Thus was inaugurated what is called the Second Bulgarian Empire, which reached its apogee under Tsar John Asen II (1218–1241).

The climax of these misfortunes for the Byzantine Empire was the Fourth Crusade (1204) and the establishment of a Western "Latin" Empire at Constantinople. Greece was divided into feudal principalities after the French fashion, and Venice clinched her control of the Adriatic by annexing a number of islands and portions of the Greek mainland. Further, a Roman Catholic hierarchy was established in the Eastern Empire, and papal political influence was temorarily extended to the Balkans. A Serbian and a Bulgarian monarch were crowned by papal legates. The Byzantine government doggedly held out at Nicaea in Asia Minor and established a state at Trebizond which enjoyed brilliant if precarious existence.

Even after the Byzantines, under Michael Paleologus (1261–1282), recaptured Constantinople with the aid of the Genoese, rivals of the Venetians, western influences continued. A Latin duchy of Athens and principality of Achaia and a Venetian principality of the Archipelago remained for some years, while Venetian commercial predominance in the eastern Mediterranean was more firmly entrenched than ever. Other western influences were to be felt in the ensuing years.

Thus the Byzantine recovery was both incomplete and temporary. The Fourth Crusade had irreparably weakened the once great empire. It had also rendered extremely difficult, if not quite impossible, any rapprochement between the eastern and western branches of the Christian Church.

Byzantine architecture in Italy. Interior of the Church of San Marco, Venice. Dating from the eleventh century.

Courtesy Brogi Art Reference Bureau

Gothic architecture in France. The interior of Amiens.

Courtesy French Government Tourist Office, New York

CHAPTER 19

The Church in the Twelfth and Thirteenth Centuries

A. The Papal Curia

It was remarked in an earlier chapter that the Gregorian reformers of the eleventh century took certain significant steps in developing the church's monarchical constitution. The further internal institutional growth of the twelfth and thirteenth centuries should be viewed in connection with the contemporary renaissance of legal studies, canon and civil, and with the progress of secular government. It is significant that after 1150 most of the popes, notably Alexander III (1159–1181), Innocent III (1198–1216), Gregory IX (1227–1241), and Innocent IV (1243–1254), were canon lawyers. As men trained in the law, they left their imprint upon the papal curia and monarchy.

Ecclesiastical government was developed to promote the spiritual welfare of the faithful.[1] Accordingly, it is important not to concentrate too much attention on certain spectacular activities of the papacy, such as crusades and the conflicts with emperors and kings. Even a cursory examination of papal letters will reveal that the vast majority of them deal not with such exceptional matters, but with the many day-to-day concerns of priests, monks, and laymen.

In an age keenly aware of things legal and constitutional, the supremacy of the pope in matters of ecclesiastical jurisdiction was at once more precisely defined and more widely effective. The pope was, as Innocent III said in describing his own position, the "vicar of Christ." As successor of St. Peter, his office was recognized as of divine institution and sanction. His court, the papal *curia,* was a supreme court of appeal from all other ecclesiastical courts, and also a court of first instance.

The principal members of the papal *curia* were the cardinals, who represented the chief clergy of Rome and its vicinity and who elected the pope.[2] As a result of the expansion of papal jurisdiction, what had once been a purely local body became the

[1] That is, of almost everyone throughout the greater part of Europe. Outside of the church were, of course, groups of Jews in various countries and a Moslem minority in Spain. And most Christians in the Byzantine Empire and Russia adhered to the Eastern Orthodox Church which by the thirteenth century was no longer in communion with the church of the west.

[2] In 1179, the right of cardinal priests and deacons as well as of cardinal bishops to participate in papal elections was recognized, and a two-thirds majority was required for such elections. There was an implied jurisdictional equality between cardinal bishops, priests, and deacons. It gradually came to pass that all cardinals outranked other clergy. In modern times, bishops have commonly been appointed cardinal priests and deacons. In 1274, in order to avoid delay (sometimes the result of political pressure), it was ruled that within ten days after the death of a pope, the cardinals were to be placed behind locked doors until they reached a decision. This was the conclave (*clavis,* key), and with minor modifications, the procedure has been continued to the present day. The modern practice whereby a cardinal resides permanently away from Rome was not the rule in the Middle Ages.

EUROPE TOWARD THE END OF THE THIRTEENTH CENTURY
Boundary of the Empire
Scale in miles
0
100
200
300
400
NORWAY
Bergen
Oslo
SCOTLAND
Aberdeen
Glasgow
Edinburgh
North Sea
IRELAND
Armagh
Dublin
Waterford
Cork
Wexford
Carlisle
York
Chester
Lincoln
WALES
ENGLAND
Norwich
Ely
Cambridge
St. Albans
London
Bristol
Oxford
Winchester
Hastings
DENMARK
Viborg
Hamburg
Elbe R.
Bremen
Brandenburg
Brunswick
Magdeburg
Rhine
Amsterdam
Bruges
Liege
Cologne
Frankfort
Treves
Mainz
Metz
Spires
Strasbourg
Augsburg
Basel
Constance
Salzburg
Innsbruck
Trent
Milan
Verona
Pavia
Venice
Alessandria
Po R.
Genoa
Bologna
Lucca
Pisa
Florence
Siena
PAPAL STATES
Rome
Naples
HOLY ROMAN EMPIRE
Rouen
Laon
Paris
Reims
Seine R.
Nantes
Loire R.
Orleans
Tours
Auxerre
FRANCE
Poitiers
Nevers
Angoulême
Limoges
Chalons
Clermont
Lyons
Bordeaux
Vienne
Rhone R.
Avignon
Arles
Bayonne
Toulouse
NAVARRE
Pamplona
Ebro
Atlantic Ocean
Santiago de Compostela
Oviedo
Leon
Oporto
PORTUGAL
Coimbra
LEON AND CASTILE
Lisbon
Tagus R.
Toledo
ARAGON
Lerida
Barcelona
Cape St. Vincent
Palos
Cordova
Granada
GRANADA
CORSICA (To Pisa)
SARDINIA (To Pisa)
Mediterranean
Palermo
SICILIES
ALMOHADS (to 1270)

FINLAND
TERRITORY OF NOVGOROD
Ladoga
Upsala
(to Denmark)
Novgorod
Pskov
KNIGHTS
LIVONIA
Wisby
Baltic Sea
KURLAND
Riga
Samogitia
Memel
Yaroslav
Vladimir
Moscow
Polotski
RUSSIAN STATES (Tributary to Mongols)
MONGOL KHANATE OF THE GOLDEN HORDE
Volga R.
Kovno
LITHUANIA
TEUTONIC
Danzig
Posen
Warsaw
POLAND
Tchernigov
Vladimir
Kiev
Lvov
Olmütz
Cracow
Halicx
Dnieper R.
Don R.
Vienna
Pressburg
Gran
Pruth R.
HUNGARY
Kalocsa
CUMANS
Semlin
WALLACHIA
Black Sea
Spalato
SERBIA
Nissa
Danube R.
BULGARIA
EMPIRE OF TREBIZOND
Sinope
Trebizond
Ragusa
Philippopolis
Adrianople
Constantinople
Nicomedia
Durazzo (to Sicily)
BYZANTINE EMPIRE
Nicaea
Mongol Dominions (Seljuk Turks)
Thessalonica
EPIRUS
THESSALY
Larissa
Corfu (to Sicily)
Euphrates R.
Iconium
ATHENS
Thebes
Athens
ACHAIA
ARMENIA
Antioch
Seleucia
RHODES
Tripoli
CYPRUS
CRETE
Damascus
Acre
Sea
Jerusalem
MAMELUKES
Cairo

governing body of the entire church. Although there could then be fifty-two cardinals (six bishops, eighteen priests, and twenty-eight deacons)—later seventy cardinals and nowadays still more—the number was rarely complete. In 1179 the cardinals were officially constituted as a corporation or *collegium*, whence arose the familiar term "college of cardinals." The cardinals administered the important affairs of the universal church, but they did not legally limit papal authority. Popes could and did consult them and take their advice, but were not bound to do so. And only the pope could create cardinals.

A full meeting of the cardinals with the pope was known as a consistory. And it was through consistories that most of the important affairs of the church were administered even into the thirteenth century. Since added pressure of business required division and specialization, there was a tendency to reserve consistories for particular occasions and to leave routine matters to departments of the *curia*. There were two distinct curial departments by the twelfth and thirteenth centuries, the chancery and the camera. The chancery, one of the oldest of papal bureaus, was responsible for the sending and receiving of letters and bulls.[1] The camera was the papal treasury, headed by a *camerarius* or chamberlain, always a cardinal bishop.[2] Papal curial procedure, especially in regard to finances, has been a subject of criticism from the middle ages to the present. Some of this criticism is certainly justifiable. Delays were frequent, and at times there was considerable financial corruption in the transaction of curial business. Yet the fact remains that, with all its shortcomings, the papal *curia* was better organized and conducted than any secular government of the period and that from it were derived many features of later political organization.

The papal *curia* was organized to care for all the ordinary routine of centralized administration. There were occasions, however, when a pope wished to discuss with prelates from all Christendom important matters of doctrine or policy affecting the entire church. This was done by requiring all the bishops and abbots to attend a general church council. The most famous of these gatherings in the middle ages, the Fourth Lateran Council at Rome (1215), was attended by over four hundred bishops, some eight hundred abbots and priors, and a number of lay delegates. It was this council, together with its predecessor the Third Lateran (1179), which issued a number of canons designed to raise the standards of clerical conduct. And while success in this respect was by no means complete, the general level of clerical efficiency and morality in the mid-thirteenth century was undoubtedly higher than it had been a hundred years earlier.

The Fourth Lateran Council also concerned itself with important matters of faith. The intellectual revival of the twelfth and thirteenth centuries with its marked emphasis on language and logic, particularly where theological or philosophical terminology was involved, raised a demand for more precise definition of certain dogmas. For example, although it had always been believed that in the sacrament of the Eucharist the bread and wine were miraculously transformed into the Body and Blood of Christ, the Fourth Lateran Council solemnly defined the doctrine of "transubstantiation." This meant that while the inner reality, or "substance,"[3] of the bread and wine was changed as the priest pronounced the words of consecration, the appearance, or "accidents," remained the same.

These are only examples of the many matters which engaged the attention of the Fourth Lateran Council. And since Innocent III had committees carefully prepare its agenda beforehand, all the work was

[1] A bull (from the Latin, *bulla*, seal) was a more formal communication than the ordinary letter.

[2] Since the receipts from papal lands in Italy were no longer adequate for its expanding organization, and since such payments as the *census* from papal fiefs and Peter's pence (originally a sort of hearth tax in England and certain northern states) were irregularly paid, the popes were forced to levy income taxes and benefice taxes on the bishops and to charge fees for letters, bulls, and litigation at the *curia*.

[3] There is no adequate English equivalent of the medieval Latin term, *substantia*. The usual material connotation of the modern English word "substance" is very misleading.

Gothic architecture in France. The Cathedral at Chartres.

Courtesy French Government Tourist Office, New York

completed in a surprisingly short time. The Council was at once a testimony of a smoothly functioning organization, and a tribute to the administrative genius of a remarkable pope.

B. The Secular Clergy

The success of any government, however centralized, depends on its subordinate officials. In the case of the church, the most important of these were the bishops. In order more adequately to regulate them, the papacy repeatedly sought to bring their elections under some sort of control. By 1300 it ordinarily confirmed the appointment of all archbishops and many bishops and abbots, and increasingly made "provision" (appointment) even to minor benefices. Papal supervision over prelates once elected, was also made more effective. The system of legates was expanded. Every archbishop was required to receive a *pallium,* the symbol of his office, from the pope, and all bishops were expected to make periodic visits to Rome. More numerous appeals to the papal *curia* were facilitated by the appointment of special judge-delegates to act locally. This diminished the jurisdiction of local episcopal courts, as did also the deliberate "reservation" of certain types of cases, notably those concerning heresy, for papal jurisdiction only.

In spite of the surrender of a good deal

of his formerly independent authority to Rome, the average bishop was burdened with cares both ecclesiastical and secular. First, he presided over a cathedral church, of which the priests, or canons as they were called, were organized into a corporation known as the cathedral chapter. Since it was the bishop's duty to supervise the parish priests of his diocese, he had to travel on regular tours of inspection, and, as a rule, he required his parochial clergy to attend an annual synod. The regular clergy were also a concern, for not all monasteries were exempt from episcopal jurisdiction. To relieve themselves of some of the burden, most bishops either delegated a great deal of their routine to a diocesan official, the archdeacon, or appointed other agents.

The bishop also had obligations to his superiors, the archbishop and the pope. There were frequent provincial synods which the archbishop expected him to attend, and even occasional controversies over judgments rendered in his episcopal court. With more effective papal supremacy there were increasingly numerous dealings with Rome. Bishops were often required to act as judge-delegates in papal cases. Most important of all were the journeys to Rome, either to make the periodic visit, to attend a Lateran council, or simply to participate in a litigation in which he was personally concerned. Moreover, in the Middle Ages, a trip to Rome was long, arduous, and sometimes dangerous. Finally, as previous chapters have indicated, the average bishop's life could not be wholly devoted to the service of the church. He was responsible for the supervision of the episcopal estates with all that entailed in a feudal world, and frequently he was involved in the political life of his country.

What sort of men were the bishops of the twelfth and thirteenth centuries? It is impossible, of course, to generalize. Probably a large majority, though certainly not all, were of noble birth. As a whole they were fond of power and display. A few were wealthy enough to bequeath considerable property to their cathedrals, to monasteries, or to the poor. According to contemporary critics (who were many and outspoken), they were too fond of worldly things.

But we must beware of accepting the testimony of detractors who often exaggerate. Actions speak louder than words. If the worst bishops were little better than robber barons, and the despair of popes and reformers, the best were excellent administrators of their dioceses, faithfully fulfilling the duties of an exacting, even perilous, position. Eudes Rigaud, bishop of Rouen in the thirteenth century, has left in his record of diocesan visitations a priceless source of information, and the evidence of his own conscientious devotion to duty. Maurice of Sully, bishop of Paris in the twelfth century, was the son of a peasant, who, somewhat in the manner of the modern student who works his way through college, begged his food and waited on rich scholars at Paris. Having become Master of Theology, he rose in the church and won renown as a preacher and as a remarkably efficient administrator of his diocese. Like Maurice, a number of bishops were scholars and theologians with a university education. Many were builders, for we must not forget that the great cathedrals, perhaps the most striking contribution of medieval art, were partly the result of episcopal energy and initiative. The bishop's task was essentially an administrative one which left little time for the systematic pursuit of personal sanctity.

It will be remembered that some parish priests of the towns were organized into corporations ("colleges") much as were the cathedral canons, and that their churches were known as collegiate churches. The rural parish priest faced different problems. He was often appointed and to some extent controlled by the local *seigneur*. His duties were manifold and included not only the maintenance of his church and its functions, but often a responsibility for parish discipline. He was always very close to the people of his parish and potentially an important influence for good.

Unhappily, repeated fulminations of popes and councils, together with the reports of episcopal visitations, indicate a continuing need for reform among the parish clergy. Moreover, although better facilities for education became available with the rise of schools and universities, they remained generally inadequate throughout the middle ages.

Doubtless many a parish priest faithfully

fulfilled his duties, and thus attracted no particular attention. But his opportunities to raise the standard of his own life and thus more deeply influence his people were meager.

C. The Regular Clergy

Among the new religious orders founded in the twelfth century, the Cistercians were the most important.[1] The Cistercian order, so named from the original settlement at Cîteaux in Burgundy, was actually established in 1098. But its importance in the ecclesiastical life of Europe dates from the career of its most famous son, St. Bernard of Clairvaux (1090–1153). It was the purpose of the Cistercians to restore the Benedictine observance in all its strictness, for by the twelfth century many Benedictine and Cluniac houses had strayed from the path of primtive discipline. Thus the Cistercian monks were to the twelfth century what the Cluny foundation had been to the era of Hildebrand.

Greatest of all the Cistercians was St. Bernard. In fact so widespread was the influence of this outstanding abbot of Clairvaux, that the designation, "the age of St. Bernard," seems quite appropriate to the mid-twelfth century. For St. Bernard was not only a remarkable ascetic, gifted with an extraordinary capacity to detach himself from worldly affairs in the contemplation of things divine. He was a man of action as well. It was St. Bernard who preached the Second Crusade, aided the pope against his enemies, helped the king of France settle various ecclesiastical problems, and withstood the prominent scholar, Abelard. Many of his sermons and hymns have been published and several of the latter have remained popular to this day.[2] Rarely has a man so towered above his contemporaries.

Until the thirteenth century monasticism had commonly been associated with the countryside. But it was particularly in relation to the growing towns that a new type of regular clergy now appeared under the name of "friars." These, like the monks of earlier times, took vows and lived under a rule. But whereas the monk's life of prayer and contemplation normally centered in a cloister, the friar's life was one of religious activity. He was expected to go out into the world and to serve the laity in particular work associated with his order. There were several different orders of friars, of which two were especially important—the Franciscan and the Dominican.[3] Each of these reflected the character of its founder.

[1] The Cistercians adopted a policy midway between Cluniac centralization and Benedictine separatism. Each monastery was governed autonomously by an abbot, but a system of annual meetings of all Cistercian abbots and periodic visitations by the abbot of Cîteaux ensured uniform practices. In the thirteenth century, the Cistercians obtained exemption from local episcopal control.

[2] *Jesu, dulcis memoria* (Jesus, the very thought of Thee) is the best known of St. Bernard's hymns. He also composed for Eugenius III, the first Cistercian monk to be chosen pope, the *de Consideratione,* a notable treatise on the papal office and its responsibilities.

[3] In addition, there were the Carmelite, the Augustinian, and the Servite.

A monastic complex of buildings. The ruins of the Cistercian abbey of Fountains, Yorkshire, twelfth and thirteenth centuries.

Courtesy British Information Services, New York

St. Francis of Assisi (about 1181–1226) was the son of a wealthy Italian merchant. As a young man, he passed through a deep crisis in his own spiritual life which ended in a resolution to embrace a life of poverty. To live as the apostles, to be poor with Christ and to minister to Christ's poor, enduring the same hardships as they; that was the course ahead of him. This radical decision was accompanied by no morbid melancholy. Rather it seems to have enhanced his naturally buoyant temperament. In a spirit of romantic chivalry which never left him, he devoted himself to his "Lady Poverty."

Although this resolve meant a separation from his family and former associates, Francis with a few faithful followers persisted in the new way of life. He received sympathy and counsel from the bishop of Assisi, and in 1210 he sought papal confirmation for his undertaking. Although Innocent III was opposed to the formation of new orders, he was impressed with the sincerity and persistence of Francis and shrewd enough to see the possible value of his work. As a consequence, he gave a verbal consent to the Franciscan rule of life. This rule, revised later to meet the demands of larger numbers, was confirmed by Pope Honorius III in 1223. It was a simple statement of the Franciscan ideal of apostolic poverty, with needful practical directions for an expanding organization.

It is difficult to overestimate the significance of the Franciscans (or Friars Minor, as they were officially termed) in the Europe of the early thirteenth century. They were simple, sincere men, who, in a world prospering materially, but whence much religious fervor of an earlier day had departed, devotedly ministered to townsfolk who were often inadequately served by the local secular clergy.

The Franciscan order expanded rapidly, becoming numerically the largest in the church. Moreover, before the end of the thirteenth century the activities of the order had expanded far beyond the simple ideal of the founder. Franciscans went as missionaries to distant lands. They maintained schools at the universities and produced famous scholars like Roger Bacon and St. Bonaventure. But never, even when in later times many Franciscans succumbed to the temptations of wealth, did they entirely forget poverty and the poor.

Dominic Guzman (1170–1221)—St. Dominic—differed in temperament and emphasis from Francis of Assisi, and the Dominican order which he founded differed from the Franciscan. Dominic was a Spaniard and primarily a scholar, theologian, and preacher. He was a cathedral canon when, as an associate of a Catalan bishop on a preaching mission, he first came into contact with the Albigensian heretics of southern France.[1] Later, with a small band of followers, officially recognized by the bishop, he began to preach in Toulouse, a hotbed of the heresy. Like St. Francis, Dominic sought papal recognition for a new organization. But since the Fourth Lateran Council (1215) had formally prohibited new orders, the Pope urged him to adopt one of the already existing rules. Dominic then adapted to his own purposes the so-called rule of St. Augustine, which was familiar to him as a cathedral canon. Dominic's rule was formally confirmed by Honorius III in 1216.[2]

Like the Franciscans, the Dominicans lived on the alms of the faithful, and they too were welcomed in the towns where they helped to fill a real need, particularly in preaching. In fact, the official title of their organization is the Order of Friars Preachers. But they were also missionaries, scholars, and teachers. One has only to recall the name of St. Thomas Aquinas, perhaps the greatest of medieval theologians and philosophers, to realize their influence. In 1277 there were three hundred and ninety-four Dominican convents situated in all parts of western and central Europe and in Greece and the Holy Land.

D. Preservation of the Faith Against Heresy

From its beginning, hardly a century passed in which the church did not have to oppose some heresy. But since the disappearance of Arianism and other heresies of

[1] See above, p. 206, and below, p. 235.

[2] The Dominican rule was a constitutional masterpiece, providing for provinces and chapters of the Order, and for representative democracy in its central government.

the fourth and fifth centuries concerning the Trinity and the nature of Christ, heretical movements had been only temporary or of local importance, until the twelfth century. Then, two different heresies arose and attracted a sufficiently numerous following to create a formidable problem for the ecclesiastical authorities. Moreover, heresy was also a concern of governments which, so close was the relation between religion and secular affairs, usually regarded heresy as treason. Not uncommonly, too, heretics were the victims of mob violence.

What at first seemed an innocuous movement was that of the Waldensians, so-called from the name of its founder, Waldo, a rich merchant of Lyons. Waldo was a man of no particular learning, but he possessed generosity and a love of the poor. His followers who preached to the poor were at first not unlike the Franciscans and were known as the Poor Men of Lyons. Pope Alexander III gave official approval to their work on condition that they obtain the sanction of the local clergy. But the Poor Men soon defied clerical discipline, and in censuring publicly and severely the ordinary clergy of the day they adopted a markedly anti-clerical attitude. At length, in 1184, the Waldensian movement was condemned by an ecclesiastical council at Verona, and it passed from simple anti-clericalism to acceptance of the heretical doctrine that personal holiness availed more than the sacrament of Holy Orders. Although Waldensianism spread from southern France into Spain and even into central Europe, it was gradually overcome and eventually survived only in a few places in northern Italy.

The other, and far more formidable, heresy of the time was known as Catharism, from a Greek word, *cathari* (the pure), or as Albigensianism, from the town of Albi in southern France, one of its strongholds. Though it gained an especially large following among the Provencal population, particularly around Toulouse and in Languedoc, its origin seems to have been in the Near East. At any rate, it resembled an ancient Persian religion of "Manichaeism," and in the early middle age it had spread in Bulgaria and thence to Italy and southern France.

The central doctrine of Catharism was a belief in an eternal struggle between a god whose dominion was the realm of the spirit and an evil deity, or the devil, who ruled the material universe. All matter and flesh were considered evil, and their propagation serviceable only to the devil. The Christian belief in the resurrection of the body was also rejected. An important element in Catharism, and one which accounts in some measure for its popular appeal, was the distinction it made between pure or "perfect" believers and ordinary believers. The former, usually numbering only a few members of a community, lived lives of extreme asceticism, and, in some cases, they hastened their release from the flesh by suicide. The ordinary believer was merely required to venerate the "perfect."

Catharism flourished in the lax and sophisticated atmosphere of southern France where clerical wealth and corruption were especially prominent and, as Pope Innocent III himself bluntly remarked, were powerful inducements to loss of faith. The combined efforts of bishops, papal legates, and preaching missions like that of St. Dominic had only limited success in reconverting the heretics. When the local secular ruler, Count Raymond VI of Toulouse, flatly refused to coöperate with the church in suppressing Catharism, he was excommunicated by Pope Innocent III's legate, Peter de Castelnau, and his lands were placed under an interdict. A few months later Peter was murdered by one of the Count's men.

The death of Castelnau was the signal for the abandonment, at least temporarily, of peaceful persuasion and the adoption of more drastic methods in dealing with the Catharist heresy. The Pope now proclaimed a holy war against the Count of Toulouse, and offered the same indulgence to the participants as was promised to those who went to the Holy Land. The ensuing Albigensian Crusade soon developed into a protracted, sanguinary war, in which the conflicting political ambitions of the leading participants overshadowed its original purpose. Northern French barons seized the opportunity to pillage and acquire new lands in the south, and French kings, to extend their power. Count Raymond VI was finally defeated at the battle of Muret (1213), but not until 1229, when his son, Raymond VII, once again submitted and renewed his father's promises to prosecute heretics, was the Albigensian war finally liquidated.

The eradication of Catharism was only obtained by the establishment of a special ecclesiastical tribunal, called the Inquisition. This medieval Papal Inquisition, was a court for judicial inquiry, with a regular procedure based primarily on canon law and secondarily on Roman civil law.[1] From the latter was derived the practice of torturing accused persons in order to obtain confessions from them—a practice which Pope Innocent IV authorized (1252) in "stubborn cases."

The Inquisition recognized various gradations of heretical crime, including mere suspicion of being a heretic, and a harboring of heretics. Lesser offenses, duly confessed, were lightly punished. But even suspects were sometimes required to undertake expensive and difficult pilgrimages, or to wear distinctive markings on their clothes. Fines and confiscation of property were fairly frequent. Only in more severe cases was imprisonment the penalty; and for only two kinds of cases was the death penalty recommended: (1) a final refusal to recant, and (2) a relapse after recantation. In these cases, the recommendation usually meant burning the condemned at the stake, and it was invariably carried out not by the ecclesiastical but by the civil authorities. It is worth noting, too, that such recommendations of the medieval Inquisition were relatively few.[2] After all, though it may seem very strange to us, the medieval Inquisitors were striving to convert the heretic. They did not desire his death, but rather the saving of his immortal soul.

E. Church and Laity

There were two levels on which the church organization dealt with the layman. It had official dealings with rulers, and, more important, it was concerned with the spiritual life of all the faithful. In its dealings with the rulers of Europe, the church of the thirteenth century developed a comprehensive temporal policy. Its purpose was the attainment of peace and justice in Christendom through the universal recognition of papal political predominance. This did not mean direct papal government of Europe. Rather, it implied a kind of administrative unity or federation of European states under papal supervision. Indeed, it was a kind of ecclesiastical counterpart of the Holy Roman Empire, an attempt to revive, under papal rather than imperial suzerainty, the ancient dream of world unity—of a Pax Romana. Thus, although the thirteenth-century popes were still concerned with the protection of the papal states and with the prevention of secular dictation to the clergy, they aspired to something broader and higher. It was their hope that Christendom could achieve an inner harmony necessary to the furtherance of Christian life and to adequate defense against the ever menacing Moslems.

The juridical claims of the papacy to preeminence over the several European realms varied considerably. In the first place, those over the Holy Roman Empire were grounded on a traditional relationship dating from the time of Charlemagne's coronation by the Pope in the year 800. It was strife between Emperors and Popes which occasioned some of the most striking medieval pronouncements regarding papal preëminence.

Second, the papacy utilized contemporary feudal practices to assert and establish its preëminence. Thus, among its fiefs, besides a numbers of towns and petty principalities, were the kingdoms of Portugal, Aragon, Poland, Sicily, Hungary, and, temporarily, England.[3]

Still other opportunities for papal intervention in secular states were afforded by local infringement of clerical privileges, by violation of marriage vows on the part of a ruler, by disputes between kings, etc. The cases of John of England and Philip Augus-

[1] Gregory IX (1227–1241) seems to have definitely established the Papal Inquisition and to have first appointed members of the Dominican Order as its judges, or "Inquisitors."

[2] Over a period of seventeen years, Bernard Gui, generally regarded as a particularly efficient Inquisitor, recommended the death penalty in forty-five cases, while imposing prison sentences in 307 cases, out of a total of 613 adjudged "guilty." Incidentally, the medieval Papal Inquisition should not be confused with the more notorious Spanish Inquisition of the fifteenth and sixteenth centuries.

[3] The first systematic list of pontifical fiefs was included in the *Liber Censum* (1192). Insistence on payment of the *census*, or feudal tax, was often an added occasion for papal intervention.

and Protestant rulers continued to seize church lands when opportunity offered, and there were also a number of cases where Catholic ecclesiastics, bishops or abbots, became Protestant and turned their church holdings into personal estates. The Catholic revival had now gained great strength, spearheaded in many areas by the activities of the Jesuits. Yet Protestantism was still active and seeking to gain new converts. The forces of a rejuvenated Catholicism met the advancing Protestants head on.

The Holy Roman Empire, where the Bohemian revolt had occurred, had failed completely, as previous chapters have indicated, to achieve the kind of consolidation characteristic of France and Spain. Indeed, long before the Peace of Augsburg (1555), the history of the Empire had become the history of its separate states. Certainly in the seventeenth century these states, Protestant and Catholic alike, were determined to thwart any attempt on the part of ambitious emperors to revive a long dormant imperial authority.

Furthermore, the German states which opposed the Habsburg Emperors, particularly in the final stages of the Thirty Years' War, were to be aided by the Bourbon rulers of France who in the seventeenth century, no less than their Valois predecessors of the sixteenth, felt that their country was encircled in a threatening fashion by Habsburg power and that France could gain in strength and prestige only by defeating the Habsburgs. Between Habsburg and Bourbon, therefore, the dynastic stakes were clear; they were nothing less than predominance in Europe.

In addition to the religious and dynastic issues, both of which were continuations of sixteenth-century problems, there had arisen other matters which concerned the Baltic and its trade. Denmark, through its traditional authority in the straits which gave access to the Baltic, was able to collect dues on ships passing by and was also in a good strategic position to extend its commerce and its territory. But so also was Sweden, which, having won its independence from Denmark nearly a hundred years earlier, was growing in military power and in commercial and territorial ambitions. Nor were these the only powers interested in the Baltic. The old Hanseatic cities of Lübeck and Bremen were eager to maintain their commerce and prosperity. Brandenburg, the northern electorate of the Holy Roman Empire, was ambitious to become a Baltic power as a consequence of the war. Even Spain, France, and England were desirous of increasing their commerce with the Baltic countries. And the Netherlands, having already won a major share in the North Sea trade, was anxious to improve its position in the Baltic.

In all these matters, one factor is increasingly evident. The divided condition of Germany, accentuated by religious conflict, dynastic struggles, and economic rivalry, was inviting foreign intervention. By the early seventeenth century, the German problem was an international concern.

B. *Phases and Course of the War*

The Bohemian phase of the Thirty Years' War had been brief (1618–1620), and in it the religious issues had been outstanding, though Czech patriotism was likewise involved. It had ended in the triumph of the Habsburgs and of Catholicism and a ruthless crushing of Bohemian Protestantism. In 1621, Philip IV succeeded Philip III as King of Spain. Since that year marked the end of the Spanish-Dutch truce and since things seemed to be going well for the Habsburgs in Europe, the new King renewed the war with Holland in the hope of reconquering it. Both France and England espoused the cause of Holland. But the French campaign against the Spanish was badly managed, an English attack on Cadiz was repulsed, and a Dutch expedition against Brazil was driven off. In 1625, Spain's success reached a climax, for after a long and painful siege a Spanish army captured the important Dutch town of Breda.

In the meantime, the Protestant princes of Germany had grown increasingly alarmed as they witnessed the triumphs of the Habsburgs of both Austria and Spain and the expansion of Catholic Bavaria. It seemed as if the balance of power in Europe was being upset in favor of the Catholics. At this juncture, Christian IV (1588–1648) of Denmark opened the second, or Danish,

The Club-foot. Painting by José Ribera (*d.* 1652).

Courtesy Louvre Museum, Paris

phase of the war in Germany. An ambitious and impulsive ruler, Christian, as duke of Holstein, was a member of the Holy Roman Empire and like most of the other princes was eager to check any increase in Habsburg power. As King of Denmark and Norway, he was desirous of extending his influence over the northern coasts of Germany and his control over the trade of the Baltic. As a Lutheran, he wished to support his fellow Protestants in their privileges and in their possession of lands seized from the Catholic Church. For these reasons, Christian IV, supported by grants of money from England and aided by many of the German Protestant princes, invaded Germany in 1625.

Against the Danish invasion, Tilly, general of the imperial forces, might have had difficulty in making headway. But fate seemed to have raised up in the nick of time another defender of the Habsburg cause in the person of a remarkable adventurer, Wallenstein. This man had made himself enormously rich out of the confiscated estates of Czech Protestants. He had secured permission from the Emperor Ferdinand II to raise an independent army of his own to restore order in the Empire and expel the Danes. By liberal promises of pay and plunder he had recruited a force of some 50,000 men, soldiers of fortune like himself. Italian, Swiss, Spaniard, German, Pole, Irishman, and Scot, Protestant and Catholic, were welcomed into his army by Wallenstein. Bound together by loyalty to its leader and hope of gain, it was made into an effective military machine by Wallenstein's genius. Supplied from his Czech lands, it became a sort of moving military state. It plundered and ravaged as it went, dragging in its train a motley throng of camp followers, men, women, and children. Where Wallenstein's army had been, it was said that a crow could scarce find sustenance.

The fighting in the Danish phase of the war was in northern Germany. At Lutter (1626), Tilly's forces, combined with those of Wallenstein, crushed the army of Christian IV. The Lutheran states were left at the mercy of the Catholics, and Brandenburg, hastily joining the Habsburg cause, aided Ferdinand's generals in expelling the Danes from German soil. Only lack of naval control in the Baltic and North Seas prevented the victors from seizing Denmark and winning complete mastery of the German Baltic coast. Thus, for example, the city of Stralsund, aided by Danish and Swedish ships which brought in supplies and evacuated non-combatants, successfully withstood an eleven-week siege in 1628 by Wallenstein, who dreamed of carving out a Baltic state for himself and who swore to take the city, "though it were chained to heaven." The desperate straits of Christian IV and the growth of suspicious activity on the part of Sweden resulted in the peace of Lübeck (1629), by which the Danish King was left in possession of Jutland, Schleswig, and Holstein, but deprived of the German bishoprics which various members of his family had taken from the Catholic Church.

As a result of these successes, the Emperor Ferdinand II in the same year (1629) felt strong enough to sign an edict of "Restitution," which restored to the Catholic Church all the lands taken from it in violation of the principle of "ecclesiastical reservation" of the peace of Augsburg of 1555. The edict was executed by imperial commissioners, all Catholics, who worked so effectively that within three years Catholicism in Germany recovered three bishoprics, thirty Hanse towns, and nearly a hundred monasteries, to say nothing of numerous parish churches. Up till then, the weight of the Habsburg power had fallen mainly on Calvinists, but at this point the Lutheran princes became thoroughly alarmed. The enforcement of the edict of Restitution seemed likely to deprive them of many fair lands and to strengthen greatly the position of the Emperor and of the Catholic league which supported him. This dismay of the Lutherans seemed to promise a favorable opportunity for intervention by the foremost Lutheran power—Sweden. In addition, the Emperor weakened his position in 1630, by dismissing, at the behest of the Catholic league, the rapacious but able Wallenstein.

The King of Sweden was Gustavus Adolphus (1611–1632), the grandson of Gustavus Vasa who had established both the independence and the Lutheranism of his country. Gustavus Adolphus was one of the most attractive figures of his age—in the prime of life, tall, fair, blue-eyed, well-educated, and versed in seven languages, fond of music and poetry, skilled and daring in war, impetuous and versatile. A rare combination of idealist, general, and practical man of affairs, Gustavus Adolphus dreamed of making of Protestant Sweden the leading power of northern Europe, and of the Baltic sea a Swedish lake. Setting to work vigorously to achieve his ends, he had occupied Finland and Estonia and had forced Russia in 1617 to recognize these territories as Swedish possessions. Then by a stubborn conflict with Poland (1621–1629) he had secured for Sweden the province of Livonia and the mouth of the Vistula river. In these wars in the eastern Baltic, he had matured his military genius and become a master in handling both artillery and cavalry.

No sooner was his war with Poland ended than Gustavus Adolphus turned his attention to northern Germany. He feared lest the Emperor, gaining control of the coastal cities there, might build up a Baltic sea power threatening Sweden. He viewed with alarm the decline of the Protestant cause, and the edict of Restitution promised him aggrieved allies among the Lutheran princes. It was likewise at this very time that Cardinal Richelieu, chief minister of King Louis XIII of France, was seeking some effective means of prolonging the war in Germany so that France might profit from the defeat and humiliation of the Habsburgs. In Richelieu's mind, cardinal of the Roman church though he was, national and dynastic reasons had more weight than religious ones. He agreed to support Gustavus with money and arms, and asked only that the Protestant leader accord liberty of Catholic worship in conquered districts.

Gustavus Adolphus, landing in Pomerania in 1630, inaugurated the third, or Swedish, phase of the war in Germany. He proceeded to occupy the chief northern fortresses and to seek alliances with the influential but reluctant Protestant electors of Brandenburg and Saxony. While Gustavus tarried at Potsdam in these negotiations, Tilly and the imperialists succeeded after a long siege in capturing the Lutheran stronghold of Magdeburg (May 1631). The fall of the city was attended by a mad massacre of the garrison and of armed and unarmed citizens in the streets, houses, and churches. At least 20,000 perished; wholesale plundering and a general conflagration completed the havoc. Gustavus Adolphus, now joined by the electors of Brandenburg and Saxony and by many other Protestant princes of northern Germany, advanced into Saxony, where, in September 1631, he avenged the destruction of Magdeburg by decisively defeating the smaller army of Tilly on the Breitenfeld, near Leipzig. Tilly was himself thrice wounded and escaped from the field with some difficulty.

Gustavus then turned southwestward, making for the Rhine valley, with the idea of forming a union with the Calvinist princes. Only the prompt protest of his powerful ally, Cardinal Richelieu, prevented the Catholic archbishoprics of Cologne, Trier, and Mainz from passing immediately under Swedish control. Next, Gustavus Adolphus moved east and invaded Bavaria. Tilly, who had reassembled his forces, failed to check the invasion and lost his life in a fierce battle on the Lech (April 1632). The victorious Swedish King, now acclaimed by German Protestants as their liberator, at once made ready to carry the war into the hereditary dominions of the Austrian Habsburgs. As a last resort, Ferdinand II recalled Wallenstein and gave him full control of his free-lance army. About the same time, the Emperor concluded an especially close alliance with Philip IV of Spain.

The memorable contest between the two generals—Gustavus Adolphus and Wallenstein—was brought to a tragic close in November of the same year, 1632, on the fateful field of Lützen. Wallenstein was defeated, but Gustavus was killed. Although the Swedes continued the struggle, their army was not large, and they possessed no general of the calibre of their fallen King. On the other hand, Wallenstein's loyalty to the Emperor was suspect. He had earlier offered to coöperate with Gustavus, and rumors reached Ferdinand II that he was engaged in self-seeking negotiations with the Protestants. In February 1634, Wallenstein was assassinated in his camp by a group of imperialists whose very names (Piccolomini, Gordon, Devereux, Leslie, Butler) indicate the motley nature of the armies of soldier-adventurers warring in Germany at the time.

The removal of both Wallenstein and Gustavus Adolphus, the economic exhaustion of the whole Empire, and the eagerness of the Protestant princes, and the Emperor as well, to rid Germany of foreign soldiers and foreign intervention—all these developments seemed to point to the possibility of concluding the third, or Swedish, period of the war, not as advantageously for the imperial cause as would have been possible earlier, but at any rate by some sort of compromise. In fact, in May 1635, a treaty was signed at Prague between the Emperor and a number of the German princes, whereby the former would gain control of the military forces of the Empire, the leagues of the princes would be dissolved, captured territory would be restored, and church lands would remain in the hands of those who actually held them in 1627, two years before the edict of Restitution was issued. On this basis a fairly satisfactory peace seemed possible. But from such a peace, the Emperor would doubtless have emerged in a considerably strengthened position, and this was contrary to the desires of Richelieu and what he conceived to be the interests of France.

C. *French Intervention and the Peace of Westphalia*

After the death of Gustavus Adolphus it became increasingly evident to Richelieu that France might have to abandon its policy of merely aiding the enemies of the Habsburgs with money. It was the peace of Prague which made it clear that if Richelieu wished to keep the war going to weaken and defeat the Habsburgs he would have to use more direct methods. Richelieu accordingly declared open war on Spain in 1635, and began the final, or French, phase of the war, which was to last thirteen years, almost as long as the other three periods put together. In the earlier phases, religious considerations had been prominent, though German and Baltic questions were also important. In the last period, with Catholic France warring on Catholic Spain and the Emperor, the issues were clearly dynastic, and religious matters played only a secondary role. Furthermore, while Richelieu was eager to humble the Austrian Habsburgs and to add to the French holdings in Alsace, his major designs were against Austria's close ally, Philip IV of Spain. The wily French Cardinal could count upon the Swedes and a number of the German princes to keep up the fight against the Emperor, while French armies attacked the encircling dominions of the Habsburg King of Spain.

From 1635 onward Philip IV had to wage a very different war from that he had previously carried on. Before 1635 he had aided his Austrian kinsmen and sought vainly to crush Holland. After 1635, he was confronted by such violent attacks from the French in the Belgian Netherlands, in Franche Comté, in northern Italy and in Spain itself, that he had frequently to abandon the offensive against Holland and also against the German Protestants. From the start Richelieu's keen strategic eye had discerned the importance of the Valtelline, an Alpine valley which offered the only practicable route by which the Spaniards could bring supplies and men from Italy to the Rhineland and Germany. In that valley, therefore, repeated campaigns were fought and much of the time the French were able to prevent its use by the Spanish.

At first, the Spanish armies, composed mainly of veterans of a dozen campaigns and led by able and tested generals, seemed superior to the French forces, which totaled some 200,000 men but lacked adequate training and competent commanders. In 1636 a large Spanish army invaded northern France and almost captured Paris. The next year, another Spanish force invaded southern France. Gradually, however, the balance shifted. Spanish armies made less and less headway against the French. As the latter gained in experience and acquired more capable generals, they began to press the Spaniards back in the Netherlands, in the Rhineland, in northern Italy, and in southern France.

By 1640, Philip IV was threatened with the disintegration of his dynastic empire. In that year, while the Dutch, with French aid, were successfully maintaining their independence and making inroads into Brazil, an assembly of nobles at Lisbon proclaimed the deposition of Philip IV as King of Portugal. In his place, they put John IV, the head of the native noble family of Braganza and a relative of the king whom Philip II had succeeded in 1580 when he made himself ruler of Portugal. Shortly after 1640, other revolts against Philip IV broke out in Naples and Catalonia (Aragon). Valiantly but hopelessly the Spanish struggled on. The Neapolitans were repressed and so were the Catalans eventually, despite military, naval, and financial aid they received from France. Milan was successfully defended and the Belgian Netherlands were grimly held. But these defensive endeavors quite exhausted the resources of Philip IV. He was unable to recover Portugal or to make headway against the Dutch or the French. In 1643, the long-standing prestige of Spanish arms was shattered when in a fair fight at Rocroi the brilliant young French general, later known as the Grand Condé, crushingly defeated a large body of the far-famed Spanish infantry.

Meanwhile, the fortunes of war had been fluctuating in Germany. For a time the Habsburg Emperor, with the aid of Maximilian of Bavaria and other Catholic princes, more than held his own against the Swedes and the Protestant German princes. But the waning strength of Spain enabled the French to send larger and larger forces into Germany against the Emperor, with increasingly decisive results. Though negotiations for a general peace were undertaken in 1641 by Ferdinand III (who had become Emperor on the death of his father in 1637), they bore no fruit until after the death of Cardinal Richelieu in 1642 and the occupation of Bavaria by the French in 1646. So complicated were the questions involved that after the diplomats had been conferring for many months as to the peace terms, it was decided to hold a general debate to determine what had been the issues over which the war had been fought. At last in 1648, by a series of treaties concluded at Münster and Osnabrück in Westphalia, the Thirty Years' War was ended and peace restored within the Holy Roman Empire. But in signing the peace treaties the Emperor, under pressure from the French, abandoned his Spanish kinsman and ally, Philip IV, and the war between Spain and France dragged on for eleven more years—years that were long and costly for the Spaniards

The peace of Westphalia left the Austrian Hapsburgs in undisputed possession of their dominions in Austria, Hungary, and Bohemia. But its political provisions deprived them of any effective control over the Holy Roman Empire and at the same time wrought numerous changes within the Empire. (1) Practically, each prince was invested with sovereign authority in his own territory; each prince was in effect free to make war, peace, or alliances, without let or hindrance by the Emperor. (2) France obtained Alsace, except the free city of Strasbourg, and was confirmed in the possession of the bishoprics of Metz, Toul, and Verdun. (3) Sweden received the part of Pomerania controlling the mouth of the Oder, and the bishopric of Bremen surrounding the city of that name and dominating the mouths of the Elbe and Weser. (4) France and Sweden, thus securing lands in the Empire and acting as guarantors of the peace, got the right to interfere in German affairs, and Sweden got a voice in the imperial diet. (5) Brandenburg annexed eastern Pomerania and several bishoprics, while Saxony and a number of other smaller states gained or lost certain territories. (6) The Palatinate was divided between Maximilian of Bavaria and the son of Frederick, the "Winter King," and both Bavaria and the Palatinate were henceforth to be electorates. (7) Switzerland and Holland were formally recognized as states free and independent—Holland of the Spanish Habsburgs, and Switzerland of the Austrian Habsburgs.

In addition to the political provisions, the peace of Westphalia included certain stipulations about religion. (1) Calvinists were to share all the privileges of their Lutheran fellow-Protestants. (2) Any piece of church property was guaranteed to such Catholic or Protestant as held it on January 1, 1624 (1618 for Württemberg, Baden, and the Palatinate). (3) An equal number of Catholics and Protestants were to sit in certain imperial courts. (4) The ruler could determine the official religion of each German state, but (except for the hereditary lands of the Habsburgs) he must permit liberty of private worship, freedom of conscience, and the right to emigrate.

D. *Results of the Thirty Years' War, and the Continuing Franco-Spanish War to 1659*

The Thirty Years' War, concluded in 1648, gave a more or less definite solution to the vexing issues which had given rise to it. In the religious sphere the Calvinists won recognition and equality, and the further alienation of Catholic lands was halted. More important, the conflict between an advancing Protestantism and a rejuvenated Catholicism was ended. After 1648 there was little further change in the

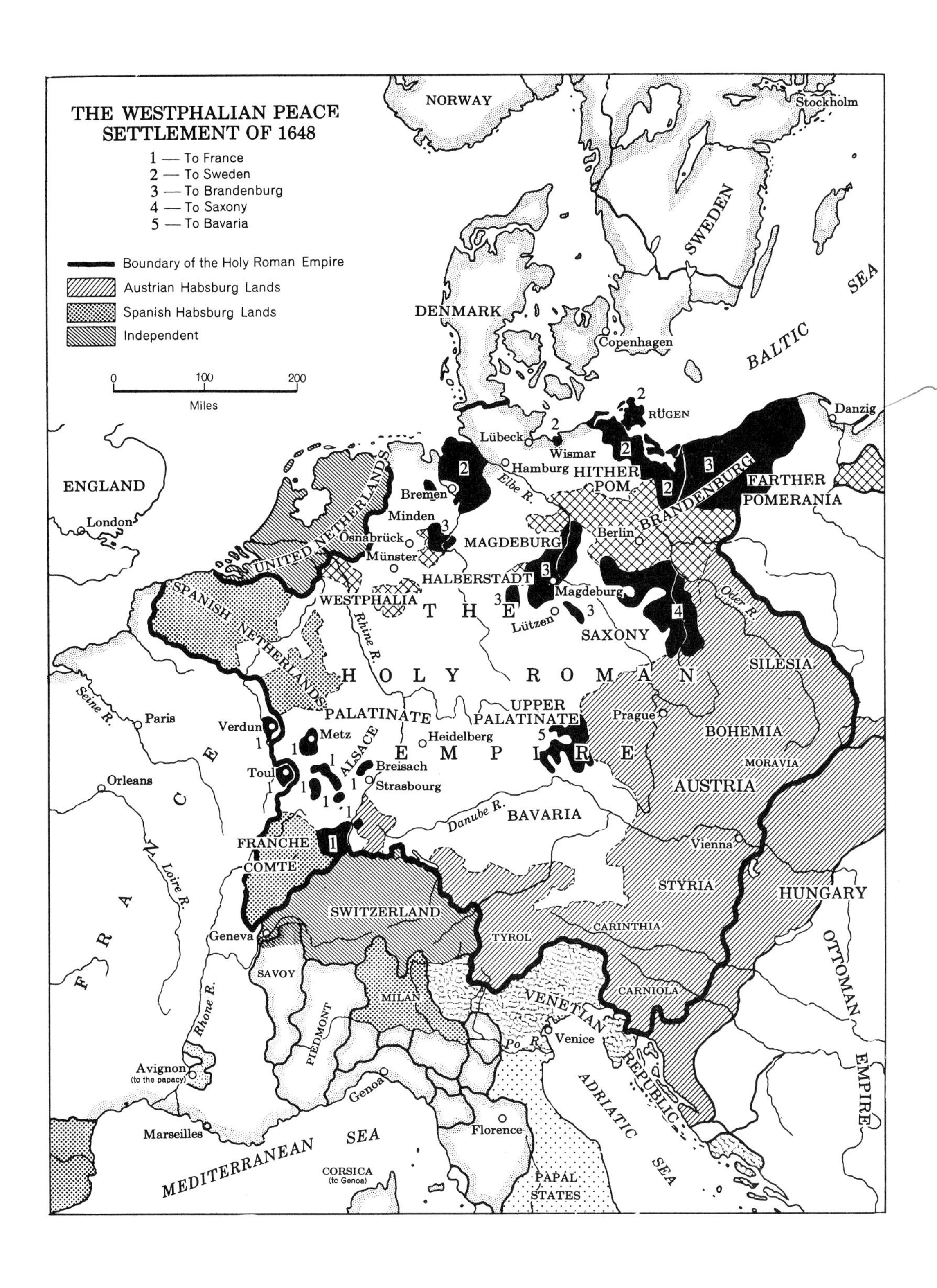

THE WESTPHALIAN PEACE SETTLEMENT OF 1648
1 — To France
2 — To Sweden
3 — To Brandenburg
4 — To Saxony
5 — To Bavaria
Boundary of the Holy Roman Empire
Austrian Habsburg Lands
Spanish Habsburg Lands
Independent
0 100 200
Miles
NORWAY
Stockholm
SWEDEN
BALTIC SEA
DENMARK
Copenhagen
RÜGEN
Danzig
Lübeck
Wismar
Hamburg
HITHER POM
FARTHER POMERANIA
BRANDENBURG
Berlin
Bremen
Minden
Osnabrück
Münster
MAGDEBURG
HALBERSTADT
Magdeburg
Lützen
SAXONY
Elbe R.
Oder R.
ENGLAND
London
UNITED NETHERLANDS
SPANISH NETHERLANDS
WESTPHALIA
Rhine R.
THE HOLY ROMAN EMPIRE
SILESIA
Prague
BOHEMIA
MORAVIA
AUSTRIA
PALATINATE
UPPER PALATINATE
Heidelberg
Metz
Verdun
Toul
ALSACE
Breisach
Strasbourg
Danube R.
BAVARIA
Vienna
STYRIA
HUNGARY
Seine R.
Paris
Orleans
FRANCE
Loire R.
FRANCHE COMTE
SWITZERLAND
Geneva
TYROL
CARINTHIA
CARNIOLA
OTTOMAN EMPIRE
SAVOY
MILAN
VENETIAN REPUBLIC
PIEDMONT
Po R.
Venice
Rhone R.
Avignon
(to the papacy)
Genoa
ADRIATIC SEA
Marseilles
Florence
MEDITERRANEAN SEA
CORSICA
(to Genoa)
PAPAL STATES

religious affiliation of the peoples of the various sections of Germany. In part, the cessation of religious strife in Germany after the peace of Westphalia was due to the exhaustion of the country. In part, it arose from a definite decrease in religious zeal.

Ten years before the end of the war, it had become fairly clear that the religious questions were side issues as compared with political and dynastic matters. Even the pope had been on several occasions accused of favoring the "Protestant" side in the war. Furthermore, as the seventeenth century progressed, it became clear that all over Europe religious bitterness was waning and that, through force of circumstances, tolerance was gradually increasing. In the last half of the century some of the wars had religious aspects, but more and more clearly the main issues were national and dynastic, territorial and economic.

On the whole it can be argued that in Germany the Thirty Years' War represented a victory, partial and qualified, but still a victory, for the forces of Catholicism. Not only had the further advance of Protestantism been checked, but also considerable areas had been won back for the Catholic Church. The triumphs of the Habsburgs in the early years of the war had enabled them to crush Protestantism in Bohemia. At the same time, with the aid of the Jesuits and other religious orders, they had almost wiped out Protestantism in Austria and greatly reduced it in Hungary. The Calvinists in the Palatinate and the upper Rhineland were sharply decreased in number by the course of the war and by Austrian and Bavarian influence. By 1648 the Catholic revival had won back almost all the areas that were to be recovered from Protestantism. Henceforth, its forces were to be expended in strengthening the religious life of Catholic countries in Europe and in winning converts overseas.

The Thirty Years' War helped to prepare the way for the emergence of the modern state-system of Europe, with its formulated principles of international law and diplomacy. Modern diplomatic usages had originated among the Italian states in the fifteenth century [1] and had been adopted by the monarchs of Spain, Portugal, France England, and other countries for the conduct of inter-state business. Yet the modern state-system could not fully emerge as long as one European power—the Holy Roman Empire—claimed even a nominal jurisdiction over states which aspired to, and were capable of, independent existence. The Treaty of Westphalia, by conceding full sovereignty to the member states of the Empire, even in matters of foreign policy, climaxed a development which had been going on since the Golden Bull of 1356 [1] and had made of the Empire merely a nominal federation of self-governing principalities.

Accordingly from the negotiations and treaties of Westphalia emerged the novel principle that all independent sovereign states, regardless of size, were essentially equal. Henceforth, the public law of Europe was to be made by diplomats and by congresses of ambassadors representing theoretically equal sovereign states. The Peace of Westphalia pointed the new path—a path that was made clearer by the fact that with the definite success of the Protestant revolt the pope could no longer speak with spiritual authority to all the rulers. To the Protestant states he was now only a petty Italian prince with somewhat sinister religious connections. Even the Catholic kings, if they still listened to the pope with respect on spiritual matters, were often inclined to ignore his behests when they interfered with political or national ambitions.

Another aspect of international relations was emphasized in the first half of the seventeenth century. It was the Thirty Years' War with its revolting cruelty which turned the attention of a considerable number of scholars to the need of formulating rules for the protection of non-combatants in time of war, the treatment of the sick, wounded, and prisoners, the prohibition of wanton pillage and other horrors which shocked the awakening humanitarianism of the time. The foremost of such scholars was Hugo Grotius (1583–1645), whose famous treatise *On the Laws of War and Peace* (1625) was published in the midst of the struggle.

[1] See above, p. 306 *n*.

[1] See above. pp. 274, 291.

tus of France were thirteenth-century examples.

Although the actions of Gregory VII implied a substitution of papal for royal predominance, the popes of the twelfth century were, despite occasional tension, hesitant about pressing this. Alexander III's patience, for example, in the controversy between Henry II and Thomas Becket, was resented by some of the Archbishop's supporters, and during the long struggle with Barbarossa there was no mention of an anti-Emperor.

It remained for Innocent III, mentioned often in these pages, to be the most brilliant exponent of a papal theocracy. A careful lawyer and a skilled diplomat, he examined the legality of each case before he acted. Later popes asserted more emphatically the papal temporal claims, but no pope before or since has so nearly succeeded in making effective the idea of a Christian commonwealth of nations under the supremacy of the Apostolic See. England, France, the Empire, and many smaller states felt the power of his exalted office. And in most instances, it will be recalled, Innocent III won his point. It is true that several of his successors also won certain triumphs, but their claims to political supremacy went unheeded even by such pious monarchs as Henry III of England and St. Louis IX of France.[1] Philip IV's rejection of Boniface VIII's bull, *Unam Sanctam*, was even more spectacular. In the later ages, the development of monarchies demanding unrestricted control over their territories prevented the realization of the papal dream of a federated Christendom.

The success which the medieval church attained in promoting a genuine spirituality among the laity and in raising the standard of individual and social morality is difficult to estimate. Religion was a real part of every man's life, and modern preconceptions make it easy to forget that religion played a great part in the daily lives of the laity throughout the middle ages and that the average layman was constantly brought into contact with the all-embracing ecclesiastical organization. Indeed, the laity constituted the vast majority of the "body" of the church. Spiritual matters were intermingled with the temporal concerns in a manner baffling to the modern student. Various activities which today are frequently secular, such as education or the care of the poor and sick, were, in the middle ages, ecclesiastical responsibilities. Frequently hospitals for the sick and kindred institutions for lepers, for women and children, or for the aged, were organized under ecclesiastical direction by religious confraternities of laymen. Ecclesiastical courts claimed jurisdiction over all cases involving clergymen and over many matters affecting everybody, such as domestic relations, wills, oaths, and usury. As a consequence, any layman would have recourse to the courts of the church.

[1] During the struggle between Innocent IV and Frederick II, St. Louis promised to protect the Pope if he were attacked at Lyons where he was then staying, but he attempted to mediate in the dispute. Both Louis of France and Henry of England continued to address Frederick as Emperor after the Pope had pronounced his deposition.

Saint Francis preaching to the birds, from a Franco-Flemish manuscript of the thirteenth century.

Courtesy Pierpont Morgan Library, New York

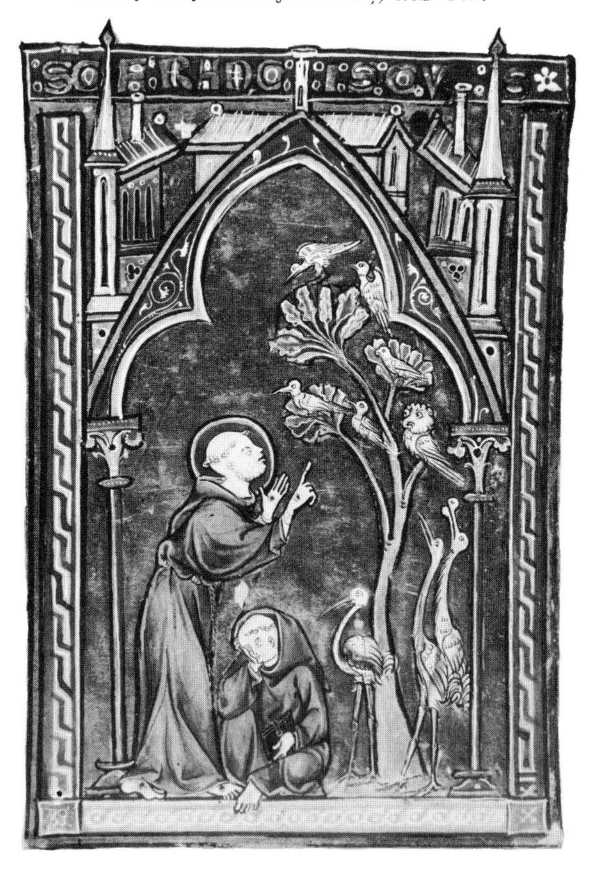

There is also ample evidence of popular devotion. We have seen that while some nobles and kings attacked church property or sought to control the church for their own purposes, others went on crusades and pilgrimages and generously contributed to churches and monasteries. A townsman might laugh at satirical and often ribald stories about clerical shortcomings. But his guild was dedicated to a patron saint and he shared in giving a stained glass window to the cathedral. He was often also a member of a religious confraternity devoted to a charitable or purely devotional purpose.

Medieval popular devotion is evident, too, in the increased veneration of the saints, and especially the Virgin Mary. From early times, and particularly after the Council of Ephesus (431) had solemnly proclaimed her the "Mother of God," Mary had been the chief recourse for pious seekers of spiritual, and even temporal, favors. But it was especially in the main middle age that popular devotion to Mary flourished. Saints, of course, had always been honored in the church and their shrines had been objects of pilgrimage. The saints, in short, were very real to the average medieval man. He constantly sought their intercession. He prayed to them and he swore by them.

Although it seems clear that ecclesiastical and secular authorities working together—and they were part of a single society—did noticeably improve the quality of medieval religion, there remained much that was imperfect. Lay participation in the sacraments, for example, was not always frequent. It is notable that at the Fourth Lateran Council (1215) it was felt necessary to prescribe that every Christian must receive the sacraments of penance and the eucharist at least once a year under pain of excommunication. The medieval church's achievement was principally in perfecting an organization capable of bringing religion into men's daily lives. It was exercising its influence more widely and deeply in the twelfth and thirteenth centuries, but there was much still to be done.

CHAPTER 20

The Medieval Revival of Learning

The intellectual revival of the eleventh century in western and central Europe, rendered possible by increasing political and social stability, was quickened into what modern historians often call the "renaissance of the twelfth century." This was marked by a notable increase in the number of students and teachers and a corresponding demand for better organization of instruction. Two aspects of this revival will concern us here: the content of medieval learning, and the development of schools and universities.

A. Medieval Intellectual Interests: Liberal Arts and Philosophy

The purpose of medieval education was practical, the improvement of the student's position in church, state, or commerce. To some a grounding in the traditional liberal arts sufficed. These numbered seven, it will be remembered, and were divided into the *trivium* and the *quadrivum,* or the "three ways" and the "four ways." [1] The *trivium,* consisting of grammar, rhetoric, and logic, was the basis for all further advanced study. And it is important to notice the use of the terms "art" and "way." Together they designate facility or competence, and also method. They were the instruments of literary expression and thought, what today are sometimes called "skills." Before a scholar could hope to enter the fraternity of higher learning, he must first master the tools. He must be thoroughly competent in the Latin language (grammar), be able to express his ideas clearly (rhetoric), and, perhaps most important, know how to think and reason correctly (logic). Hence the *trivium,* the basis of all education, came to be the core of instruction.

A growing number of students sought further instruction in the three advanced subjects of the day—theology, law, and medicine—which most often led to employment or promotion, and which formed the principal curricula of the medieval universities. It should also be remarked that many scholars, however concerned they might be with professional advancement, acquired at various stages along the way a love of learning for its own sake. Both motives, the practical and the purely intellectual, must be considered in estimating the medieval achievement.

The mastery of grammar and rhetoric involved the study not only of grammatical and rhetorical treatises, but acquaintance with the works of the great classical men of letters. And rhetoric required at least imitation, if not original skill. Hence there appeared during the eleventh and twelfth centuries a genuine literary humanism, a both wider and deeper knowledge of the ancient authors. The quality of Latin composition improved notably. To mention only one example, John of Salisbury, a student and later bishop at Chartres, counsellor of popes and kings, friend of Thomas Becket, was an excellent Latinist. His letters, especially, are masterpieces of style. This was the age, too, of the great Latin hymns, and of poems on nature and love, youthful student songs, satires, all in excellent Latin. And the

[1] See above, p. 59.

twelfth century likewise produced some notable historians whose works reveal considerable acquaintance with the ancients.

Medieval Latin differed from the Latin of Cicero in style and vocabulary. For it continued to be a living language, capable of absorbing ecclesiastical, feudal, and Germanic words and philosophical ideas. Despite a persistent popular notion to the contrary, medieval Latin was not barbarous or ungrammatical.

In the west, medieval literary classicism was exclusively Latin. Greek works were known only in translation, and knowledge of the Greek language was generally confined to parts of southern Italy and Sicily or to those ecclesiastics and diplomats who had dealings with Byzantium. A notable advance in this matter resulted, however, from the establishment of the Latin empire at Constantinople after the Fourth Crusade.

As grammar and rhetoric blossomed into literary appreciation and skill, so logic inspired inquiries into philosophy. And so fascinated were scholars by the problems of logic and philosophy that toward the end of the twelfth century philosophical studies predominated over the humanistic. Thus the thirteenth century, the great "age of the universities," was a period of philosophical and theological, rather than of literary, interest. Men were absorbed by the attempt to understand the nature of the world and of man and to explain the existence of God and the meaning of creation. Above all, they sought answers to the questions which philosophers have always asked and doubtless always will. What is? What exists? What is being? And since these questions were threshed out in the schools, the solutions and reasonings of the medieval "schoolmen" have been called "scholastic philosophy" or "scholasticism."

To the average medieval thinker, philosophy was not an end in itself. It should lead him to truth, and in particular to theological truth, which he deemed the highest of all. The schoolmen did not believe that the truths of revealed religion could be strictly proven, but they did insist that they could be rationally explained, that they could be made to satisfy the human intellect. There emerged a scholastic theology, related to and dependent on, yet intellectually distinct from, scholastic philosophy. A few examples may help to explain the distinction. It was held that the human intellect was capable of understanding the things of nature and of man—his virtues, his vices, his physical and moral attributes. It could also reason from man and nature to God; it could, in fact, demonstrate the existence of a supreme being and in a limited manner understand the divine nature. But there, having reached the limits of what some have called "natural theology," the independent function of philosophy—of the mind unaided by revelation—ended. Beyond that, philosophy was merely the handmaid of theology, the "queen of sciences." As such, it provided the rational basis for an intelligent discussion of what God revealed to man, such as the Incarnation, the Trinity, the sacraments, the theological virtues, divine grace, etc.

Although the basis of logical studies throughout the early Middle Age had largely been those parts of Aristotle's *Organon* which Boethius had translated from Greek into Latin in the sixth century, most of Aristotle's other treatises were then unknown. As a consequence, and also owing to the veneration with which the semi-Platonist works of St. Augustine were held, it was the general philosophy of Plato, rather than of Aristotle, which gave chief direction to European thought well into the twelfth century. On the fundamental question of being, for example, it was held, with Plato, that abstract ideas or "universals," such as justice, goodness, man, etc., were the true realities. Thinkers who entertained such views were called "realists." [1] St. Anselm, scholar and archbishop of Canterbury, was a prominent "realist" in this tradition. His *Cur Deus Homo* was a widely read treatise and contained a famous proof of the existence of God, reflecting the "realist" school of thought.

Medieval Platonic "realism" did not remain uncontested. A veritable revolution in thought resulted from western Christendom's deriving from the Moslems fuller knowledge of the whole philosophical heri-

[1] It should be noted that the modern connotation of the term "realism" is radically different. "Idealism" would more nearly approach the medieval meaning.

Gothic architecture in England. Salisbury Cathedral.

Courtesy British Information Services, New York

tage of ancient Greece. Bit by bit the long forgotten or neglected works of Aristotle reappeared in Latin translations from the Arabic. By the middle of the thirteenth century, practically the complete writings of Aristotle were available. Under this new, or rather ancient, but radically different intellectual influence, the validity of "realism" was challenged. It was urged that universals did not possess true reality, but were only arbitrary collective names. Hence, arose, in the mid-twelfth century, a "nominalist" school of thought.

But we must not overemphasize the controversy over universals. Significant though it was to the understanding of being, it was but one example of the current enthusiasm for the new Aristotelian logic. Meanwhile, men like Peter Abelard (*d.* 1142) were pioneering in methods of reasoning and argumentation. In a treatise called *Sic et Non,* Abelard stated a series of propositions and cited from various authorities opinions for and against each. Since the reader was expected to resolve the contradiction himself, the method aroused considerable criticism. It had, however, many advantages, and later writers adopted it, while usually suggesting solutions to the questions posed. Peter Lombard, who became bishop of Paris in 1159, applied the technique in his *Book of Sentences,* one of the first systematic treatises on theology.

Although Abelard was a remarkable teacher he was as self-assured as he was brilliant. He dared openly to challenge at Paris the most noted realist of the day, William of Champeaux, and soon the latter's students were deserting him and flocking to Abelard's lectures. Abelard's popularity undoubtedly contributed to the reputation of the University of Paris in its early days.

On the matter of universals, too, Abelard made a distinct contribution. To him individual things possessed reality, but universals or abstract ideas, he admitted, had validity as concepts of the mind. This "conceptualism" of Abelard's proved to be a basis for rationalizing the problem of being —a basis which gradually gained wide acceptance. Fortified and modified by further knowledge of Aristotle, it led to the "moderate realism" of St. Thomas Aquinas in the thirteenth century.

Unfortunately Abelard's real gifts were all too often nullified by his egotism.[1] On one occasion his enthusiastic rationalizing brought him into conflict with ecclesiastical authority. Partly at the instigation of St. Bernard, who probably did not fully understand Abelard's purposes, certain of his propositions were publicly condemned. But Abelard was not a heretic and never questioned either the fundamental truths of the faith or the authority of the church. He was simply attempting to make the truths of religion understandable to the human mind through the instrument of logic. Opposition resulted partly from his own somewhat intemperate manner and partly from a mistrust of the new logic which disappeared as soon as it was better understood.

Scholastic philosophy became associated with another intellectual tendency characteristic of the thirteenth century. It was firmly believed that all knowledge, whether it be natural science, metaphysics, or theology, was interrelated and could be fused into an organic whole. As a consequence, there were many efforts to synthesize the sciences and a number of treatises appeared bearing the title "Summa" ("the whole"), or some similar designation. In this endeavor to coordinate all knowledge as well as to rationalize theology, the foremost figure was St. Thomas Aquinas, the greatest philosopher of the middle ages, and one of the greatest of all time.

St. Thomas (*d.* 1274) was a Dominican friar and as such belonged to an order with a tradition of learning, which had already made significant contributions to the coordinating of Aristotelian rationalism with Catholic thought. He was a disciple of Albertus Magnus, also a Dominican, who taught at Paris and stoutly defended the study of the great Greek philosopher at a time when many were questioning its propriety.[2] Firmly convinced that the truths of faith and of natural reason could not conflict, since both were from God, Aquinas set about preparing his synthesis. In the manner of Aberlard's *Sic et Non,* he posed questions and quoted contrary opinions from Greek, Christian, and Arabic sources, and then offered resolutions of the contradictions for each question. Meticulous care was exercised in citing authorities and in distinguishing the conclusions reached by the author. St. Thomas's *Summa theologica,* his greatest work, is, as its title indicates, a complete compendium of theological knowledge. But it is a theological work in the broadest sense and contains a tremendous amount of material on philosophical, psychological, moral, and scientific subjects as well, and all presented in a logical and orderly manner. Not without reason is the *Summa theologica* universally regarded as one of the world's masterpieces.

We must not assume that the thirteenth-century penchant for synthesis resulted in perfectly harmonious systems being universally accepted. For the disputes between rival philosophies and rival schools of thought, always provided they did not question the fundamental truths of revealed religion, were many and acrimonious. We have already mentioned the controversy over universals. Both the Platonic tradition of

---

[1] Abelard is perhaps best known to moderns for his famous love affair with Héloise, his pupil, an affair which not only interrupted his academic career, but brought poignant tragedy into two lives.

Abelard, after a condemnation of certain of his writings, was given asylum at Cluny. Héloise became an abbess. The two corresponded until Abelard's death in 1142.

[2] The original study of Aristotle at Paris occasioned some misgivings. Certain teachings of Aristotle seemed incompatible with Christian thought and much of the work appeared in translation from the Arabic with commentaries by Moslem philosophers. Although Aristotle's scientific writings were temporarily banned in Paris early in the thirteenth century, by 1254 his chief works were required for the degree of master of arts.

realism and an extreme nominalism persisted. The highly gifted Franciscan, St. Bonaventure, following generally the former trend, stoutly championed the importance of the will against the emphasis laid on the intellect by Aquinas.

More damaging to the reputation of Aquinas was the work of certain thinkers at Paris who followed a more uncompromising Aristotelianism and were influenced by the writings of the great Moslem commentator, Averroes. A general condemnation in 1277 by the bishop of Paris included several propositions of Thomas. Although these were later removed, the cause of Thomism was seriously damaged. The teachings of Aquinas were generally not followed in the succeeding two centuries.[1]

B. *Law, Medicine, and Science*

Although the scholastic method of reasoning—the citing of authorities and the balancing of contradictory opinions—is primarily associated with the study of philosophy and theology, it was also generally employed in law and medicine. The renaissance of legal studies is preëminently associated with the city of Bologna and was stimulated by the revival of Justinian's *Digest* of Roman law late in the eleventh century. About 1140 there also appeared the *Decretum*, a codification of canon law by a monk, Gratian.[2] Teachers of both Roman and canon law then appeared, and Irnerius, one of the most famous, established himself at Bologna in the early decades of the twelfth century and attracted many students. In the course of this century, Bologna became the center for an impressive number of other distinguished jurists. But although its law faculty was the most celebrated, Bologna early had a good liberal arts faculty and subsequently established a school of medicine which was the equal of any in Europe.

Medicine had long been studied at Salerno in southern Italy and at Montpellier in southern France. With the revival of learning in the twelfth and thirteenth centuries, other institutions surged ahead, notably Bologna, Padua, and Naples, which eventually absorbed the medical school at Salerno. The fundamentals of medical knowledge continued to be derived from the writings of Galen and Hippocrates, the famous physicians of the Hellenistic age. Indeed, the respect with which the authority of those ancients was held tended to retard progress. But the Arabs had made later and important contributions to the chemistry of medicine, and Moslem textbooks were now widely studied. Little progress was made in surgery in either Christendom or Islam, but toward the end of the thirteenth century, despite adverse popular opinion, occasional dissections of human corpses were performed and the way paved for later advances.

Recent studies have revealed that more progress was made during the middle ages in mathematics and the natural sciences than was once supposed. Mathematics flourished particularly at Oxford where one of the leading lights was Robert Grosseteste (*d.* 1253), one-time chancellor of the university. A pupil, Roger Bacon, a Franciscan friar, won considerable publicity through his eloquent criticisms of contemporary learning. Because of his somewhat stormy temperament, his remarks, many of them justified, often aroused antagonism rather than support. Thus his pleas that mathematics, languages, even oriental languages, and, above all, experimentation be given greater emphasis were not always heeded. In the manner of his day, Bacon conceived of all knowledge, including theology, as one organic whole, but one in which natural science should have a place.

The popularity of scientific and mathematical studies at places like Oxford indicate that European scholars were receiving from the Moslems not only Greek philosophy, but Greek and oriental science. As a result

---

[1] Extreme Aristotelianism and what came to be called Latin Averroism later obtained an important following at the university of Padua in Italy. The principal theological problems involved were Aristotle's teaching on the eternity of matter, and Averroes' questioning of the immortality of the individual soul and his doctrine of the "double truth," that is, one for philosophy or science, another for religion.

[2] The full title of the *Decretum*—*Concordantia discordantium canonum* (Concord or Harmony of Discordant Canons)—indicates that the canonists faced the same kind of problems in reconciling conflicting authorities as did the civilians.

Gothic Exterior. Notre Dame, Paris

Courtesy French Embassy Press and Information Division, New York

of the work of certain pioneer translators, Graeco-Arabic mathematics, astronomy, geography, chemistry—in short, natural science generally—became available to Christian Europeans. In both Western and Moslem traditions the persistence of ancient superstitions retarded progress, though they did not prevent it. For astronomy was confused with astrology, and chemistry was burdened with the alchemist's dream of transmutation. Generally speaking, natural science did not enjoy the popularity of the arts, theology, or law in the thirteenth century. What advances there were in it, and these were not inconsiderable, were made chiefly outside of the universities.

C. *Schools, and the University of Paris*

The first universities were not, of course, "founded." They sprang up naturally and more or less spontaneously in the twelfth century, when increasing material prosperity, especially in the towns, combined with new intellectual interests to multiply the number of students and to tax the facilities of existing monastic and cathedral schools. Monastic schools, which had been the best, if not the most numerous, educational institutions in Europe since the early middle age and which were usually located in rural places, were now being eclipsed in quality and popularity by cathedral schools in urban centers. This was the time, it should be remembered, when cities were growing in size and wealth, developing merchant and craft guilds with much civic pride and vying with one another in building great cathedrals and expanding cathedral schools. Chartres, for example, boasted a school of considerable renown. But at Paris, which was becoming the capital of the French monarchy, the cathedral school became so expanded and famous and so attractive to students from all parts of Christendom that it evolved into what was called a *studium generale* ("general study-place"), or "university."

At Paris, the cathedral school of Notre Dame was located on a little island in the Seine, the *cité*. During the course of the eleventh and twelfth centuries the school drew so many students and teachers that they overflowed the island to the high ground across the river where there were certain other schools associated with the abbey of Ste. Geneviève. In this way, the site of the university of Paris came to be the historic "left bank" of the Seine, "the latin quarter" of later days, so named because of the scholarly language spoken there.

Medieval scholars were not primarily concerned with location or buildings. Actual instruction and its organization first engaged their attention. It was early determined that no one should give instruction without a "teaching license," to be issued by the bishop's chancellor. Still more significant, the scholars early sought an autonomous organization of their own through which they might control their own affairs, determine their own curriculum, and license their own teaching staff. For this they quite naturally borrowed the type of organization then coming into general use in towns—namely, the guild. From the Latin word sometimes used to designate a guild—the word "universitas," meaning corporation—was derived the popular name for the new *studium generale*, or "university."

Thus the unique feature of the university, as distinct from other contemporary schools, was its organization as a corporation after the manner of a guild. Since their "trade" was the liberal arts, it was the "master of arts" who controlled university affairs. Upon the completion of a designated curriculum, an "apprentice" in arts received a certain official recognition as "bachelor" (*baccalaureus*).[1] Later he might be admitted to the guild as a "master" after formal "inception," an elaborate ceremony of investiture with appropriate oaths of obedience. Moreover, since the baccalaureate was a "step" toward becoming a master, it was a *gradus* or "degree." The whole familiar paraphernalia of guild customs now appeared in this academic organization.

The arts guild at Paris became so large that it was found necessary to subdivide it into what were called "nations." The term "nation" in medieval Paris did not signify what it does today. A "nation" was then any convenient grouping of scholars from

[1] The term *baccalaureus* seems to have been borrowed from the contemporary terminology of chivalry, in which it signified the knight bachelor or knight without others serving under him.

particular regions. There were originally four: French, Picards, Normans, and English. And the absence of nationalism in the terms as then used is indicated by the fact that the English "nation" at Paris included Germans, and that all southern Europeans were grouped with the French. Each "nation" was headed by a *proctor*, and, toward the middle of the thirteenth century, a *rector* was chosen to supervise the entire institution.

Since liberal arts remained the fundamental basis of medieval education and were doubtless sufficient for the needs of most people, the great majority of students at Paris pursued their studies under a "faculty of arts." But there soon developed at Paris and elsewhere a demand for instruction in other more advanced and specialized subjects. This was provided by higher "faculties," as they were called, dealing with such fields of learning as theology, civil and canon law, and medicine. Rarely did any one university provide for all "faculties." Paris, for example, specialized in those of theology and canon law. The higher faculties, as well as the faculty of arts, were organized on the guild model with similar terminology, although the term "dean," designating the head of a higher faculty, was borrowed from ecclesiastical usage. There were masters of theology and of law, as well as masters of arts. Meanwhile, the titles "doctor" and "professor" were introduced—titles signifying teacher and used interchangeably with "master." As these academic titles were often sought by men who had no intention of teaching, they came to be, like our modern degrees, certificates indicating the successful completion of specified courses of study.

The University of Paris became a federation of guilds. And perhaps owing to the basic importance of the liberal arts and the greater number of arts students, the original arts guild retained its primacy. After a certain amount of protest on the part of the deans of higher faculties, the rector of the arts faculty was recognized as superior to the others. Moreover, although the term *studium generale* remained in contemporary usage, the word *universitas* gradually replaced it.

In the course of its incorporation as a self-sufficient teaching organization, the university—or federated guilds of masters and scholars—found it necessary to regularize its relations with the civil and ecclesiastical authorities. Toward the end of the twelfth century, comparatively early in the history of the institution, the problem of police jurisdiction over students became serious. Since not all scholars were hardworking, and not all students serious, there were recurrent troubles between "town" and "gown," that is, between officials and citizens of Paris on the one hand, and members of the university on the other. Shortly after one bad riot and a consequent suspension of university activities, King Philip Augustus decreed (1200) that the masters and scholars of Paris should be officially immune from the interference of ordinary civil authority. Masters and scholars were thus confirmed in the privilege of responsibility only to themselves and to the ecclesiastical authorities.

The university rather resented the continued supervision of the bishop and his chancellor, who, in turn, were not altogether pleased at the spectacle of their intellectual child, now grown to man's estate, and demanding an end of paternal control. A series of difficulties between bishop and masters ensued, necessitating papal intervention. The result was that, in the early decades of the thirteenth century, Popes Innocent III and Gregory IX recognized the university as a corporate entity and confirmed its right to determine its own course of study. The *studium generale* at Paris was henceforth a fully independent institution responsible only to itself and to the pope.

In the thirteenth century the new orders of friars sought to establish themselves within the university. At first they were not welcome. The university had been developed by the secular clergy and they were jealous of any encroachment on the part of the "regulars." But the friars eventually won the right to lecture as masters in theology, though not to participate in the faculty of arts.

Teaching and learning are processes which change very little. In the early days of the university of Paris, any available buildings were used for lectures and the students sat on whatever chairs or benches they could find or on the floor. The principal difference between medieval instruction and our own was the scarcity of books, which, of course, were written laboriously by hand and were expensive. More was accomplished orally than is the case today. A medieval lecturer often read aloud the text of some important work and added his own comments as he went along. His auditors might scribble some notes, but we may be sure that memory was normally more depended upon than notebooks. Examinations were oral and the candidate for a degree was commonly required to sustain a "thesis." That is, he was presented with a proposition which he had to defend in the face of vigorous questioning.

Medieval scholars lodged where they could or formed little societies to provide in common the necessities of life. For the poorer among them the pursuit of learning inevitably entailed real hardship. By the thirteenth century, however, conditions improved. The friars provided houses for their own members, and about 1258 Robert de Sorbon endowed for students in theology a hostel or "college," as it was called, which proved to be the first of many similar foundations. Thus the term "college" originally signified merely a place of residence. Presently it included a library and even some instruction. In the later middle ages, many universities came to be dominated by endowed and well-organized colleges which were attached to them and which often boasted teaching staffs of distinguished masters. In the university of Paris, the *Sorbonne* has continued to occupy an important place.

D. Bologna and Other Medieval Universities

While the *studium generale* at Paris was growing into the foremost university of western and northern Europe, a similar institution of higher learning was developing in southern Europe, at Bologna. Here, as we have remarked, the study of law—both civil and canon—prevailed.

The university of Bologna differed in organization from that of Paris. While in both institutions the masters formed guilds to regulate their own affairs and to deal collectively witth the students, at Bologna it was associations of students, rather than of teachers, which exercised real control. For these associations were able to pre-

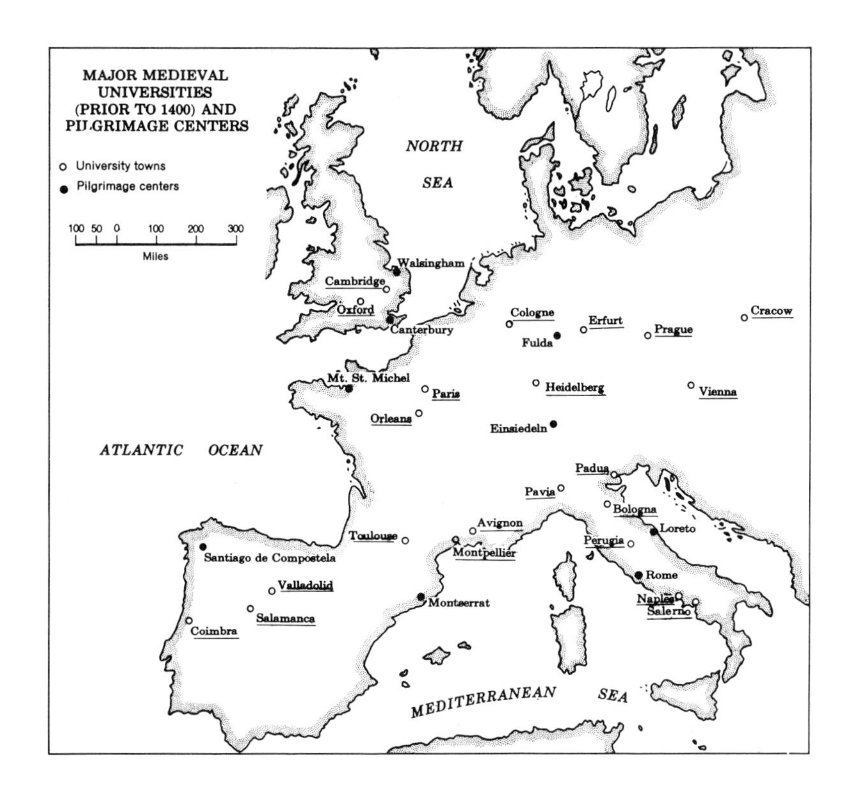

scribe and enforce minute regulations governing the conduct of their professors, including hours of lectures, presentation of subject-matter, absences, fees, etc. Even the powerful civic authorities of Bologna were brought to terms by threats of boycott or migration on the part of the students. The chief explanation of this striking role of the student body at Bologna lies in the fact that they were usually older and more mature than the student body of Paris. Legal study, which was the main pursuit at Bologna, attracted men of business and nobles with estates to manage, as well as younger men anxious to obtain administrative positions.

The examples of Paris and Bologna were soon followed elsewhere. In general, the universities which emerged in northern and western Europe adopted the type of organization at Paris, while those in southern Europe took Bologna as their model. Sometimes new universities started as offshoots from an older one. Padua, for example, was an offshoot of Bologna. Toward the end of the twelfth century a number of masters who had been at Paris took up residence at Oxford, and in the next century a similar migration resulted in the formation of a second English university at Cambridge. It was especially at Oxford that the colleges which, as at Paris, were originally boarding establishments with some equipment for teaching, came to enjoy a dominant position in the university organization.

Salamanca, chartered and privileged by kings of Castile and by the pope toward the middle of the thirteenth century, was the first important Spanish university; and Coimbra, the first in Portugal. The university of Toulouse received a papal charter in 1233, as a sequel to the Albigensian crusade; and in the mid-thirteenth century a university of the papal *curia* was established. Naples, founded by the Emperor Frederick II in 1224, and Montpellier in southern France, dating from about the same time, together with Bologna, soon surpassed older Salerno [1] as famed centers for medical study.

Medieval towers at Bologna.

Courtesy Italian State Tourist Office, New York

[1] Salerno had been famous as a health resort with competent physicians as early as the tenth century, though references to a formal "school" of medicine are later. Its geographical location gave it access to Latin, Greek, Arabic, and Jewish medical lore.

Montpellier was also noted for its instruction in law.

Not until the fourteenth century did universities appear in countries on the Continent north of France and Italy. Then were founded Prague in Bohemia, Cracow in Poland, Vienna in Austria, and Heidelberg in Rhenish Germany. Thenceforth there was a steady spread and multiplication of universities throughout Europe.

E. Medieval Students

Various contemporary sources give the impression that medieval students were an unruly, turbulent lot. Apparently, many were very young, some only fourteen or fifteen. They were likely to be far from home and parental discipline, and in an institution which exempted them from ordinary police jurisdiction. It is not surprising that they got themselves into trouble. But we must beware of exaggerating. The unusual always attracts more attention than the ordinary. The average conscientious student was taken for granted and passed unnoticed.

Some student correspondence has survived. Though commonly composed in the stilted style of professional letter writers, the subject matter—requests for money on the part of students and concern on the part of parents over frivolous behavior and neglect of studies—is perennial.

A unique source of information about medieval students is their verse. Especially in the early days when the universities were in process of formation, there was a great deal of informal changing by students from one place to another. Scholars dissatisfied with a teacher, or merely restless or bored, simply moved elsewhere. Probably they begged en route. In this atmosphere was produced what has been called Goliardic poetry, for the students were the wandering Goliardi, so named perhaps because they pretended to be followers of Goliath the Philistine. The principal themes of these are the time-honored "wine, women, and song." But there is also in many of them a nostalgic melancholy which reflects the uncertainties of life and the rapid passing of youth. Composed in Latin, they demonstrate that the admirable linguistic skill acquired by medieval students could as easily be put by them to the service of a lively full-blooded humanism as to a technical treatise or a hymn.[1]

The remarkable and varied achievements of medieval students, as well as medieval masters, indicate that a very important intellectual class was coming to the fore in Europe of the twelfth and thirteenth centuries—a class which commanded increasing respect. Evidently, the academic or university estate—the calling of the scholar—was coming to be so highly regarded that all the chief authorities in Christendom were only too eager to give it their protection and patronage. Medieval society at large must have believed that the students were pursuing something eminently worth while, and must have acquired a respect for education which our own generation can appreciate.

Thirteenth-century achievements in law, medicine, and theology, and in philosophy in the most inclusive sense of the word, indicate that, at least in university circles, interest in the technical was now surpassing the earlier enthusiasm for the literary and humanistic. But though formal learning in the thirteenth century lacked the humanistic spirit of the twelfth, there emerged a notable literature in the vernacular tongues. This, too, ranks among the major accomplishments of the period, and will be treated in the following chapter.

[1] An important collection of medieval student literature was preserved in the monastery of Benediktbeuren in Germany and hence called *Carmina Burana*.

Fourteenth century French tapestry from the workshop of Nicolas Bataille. Probably King Arthur with cardinals.

Courtesy Metropolitan Museum of Art, New York; The Cloisters Collection, Munsey Fund, 1932, and gift of John D. Rockefeller, Jr., 1947

CHAPTER 21

Popular Literature and Art of the Middle Age

A. Epics and Romances

Throughout the Middle Ages, all over Western Christendom, educated people knew Latin, and scholarly writing was done in it. Professors and students used the same Latin language in university work, whether at Paris, Bologna, Oxford, Salamanca, Prague, or Heidelberg. But alongside the scholarly Latin, and quite distinct from it, were many different spoken languages or dialects, the so-called "vernaculars" of the common people. Some of these had developed, in late Roman and early medieval times, out of a "vulgar" spoken Latin—the *lingua romana*—differing from "classical" written Latin, and had become the parent tongues of the later "romance languages" —French, Italian, Provençal (and Catalan), Castilian, Portuguese, and Rumanian.

Other vernaculars had been developed from early Teutonic speech: Low German, in northwestern Germany and the Netherlands; High German, in southern and eastern Germany; Anglo-Saxon, in England; and distinctive Scandinavian dialects in Denmark, Norway, and Sweden. Besides, different Slavic vernaculars were spoken by Czechs (in Bohemia), Poles, Yugoslavs, and Russians, while Celtic vernaculars survived in Ireland, Scotland, and Wales, and in Brittany (in western France). "Middle English," becoming the common vernacular of England in the thirteenth century, was a combination of Anglo-Saxon with Norman French.

In the early middle age, there was relatively little writing in any of the vernacular languages, beyond some translations of the Bible and of church service books for the religious instruction of newly converted peoples. But gradually the amount of vernacular literature increased and became popular. Having little or no connection, as Latin had, with technical intellectual concerns, it was written primarily to amuse; and, far more than Latin, it reflected the fashions and tastes of secular lay society.

This was especially evidenced by the growing number of medieval "epics," which were long poems recounting deeds of adventure and usually sung by minstrels to the accompaniment of a lute or some similar instrument. Such epics appeared fairly early in Germanic vernaculars. The Anglo-Saxon *Beowulf* dated from the eighth century or even earlier. The *Hildebrandslied,* of which a fragment from the end of the eighth century has survived, was in the old Saxon dialect. The half legendary, half historical Norse sagas, many of which were actually composed in Iceland in the time of the Vikings, are essentially epics in content and form.

Broadly speaking, France produced the most popular and influential vernacular literature of the middle age. France was then, both politically and culturally, the leading kingdom in Europe, and the two vernacular languages which had developed within it were adapted to the production of popular literature. One of these was the *langue d'oil*, or "French," spoken throughout northern France and, after the Norman conquest of England in 1066, by the English court and upper classes. The other was the *langue d'oc*, or "Provençal," spoken in southern France and, with only slight differences of dialect, in northeastern Spain, where it was known as "Catalan.' Each of these vernaculars became the vehicle for a distinctive written literature, which was widely read and imitated abroad.

Some of the literature of the *langue d'oil*, the *chansons de geste*, we have already described as a reflection of early feudal society.[1] The appeal of the *chansons de geste*, especially of the Carolingian cycle, was not merely French; it was broadly European. There were Scandinavian, German, and Italian translations of them.

Meanwhile other heroic epics were appearing in the vernacular languages of Northern Europe and of Spain. Of particular importance was a Germanic cycle which in various forms embodied the tragic stories of *Siegfried* and *Brünhilde*. One version, the *Volsunga-Saga*, was a twelfth-century prose composition, while the more familiar *Niebelungenlied*, originally produced in the late twelfth century, was subsequently remodeled. Then, too, from twelfth-century Spain came the *Poema del Cid*, which celebrated the deeds, largely legendary, of Rodrigo Diaz, a Castilian warrior of the eleventh century. Like the *chansons de geste* of France, the *Cid* reflects the atmosphere of the epic struggle for the liberation of Christian lands from the Moslems.

Side by side with the *chansons de geste*, though not, it would appear, greatly influencing or being influenced by them, there appeared another kind of popular vernacular literature. This was the so-called "courtly romance." One of the most famous examples dealt with the British King Arthur and his court. Original material for this had come from Celtic legends, but it had been added to by Norman Englishmen, in particular by Geoffrey of Monmouth (*d.* 1154), whose *History of the Britons*, while purporting to be a presentation of historical fact, seems to have been largely manufactured out of whole cloth. At any rate, poets and minstrels were thereby provided with numerous suitable themes for the courtly romances which speedily became favorites with aristocratic audiences. Perhaps the most famous poet who so used the Arthurian material was Chrétien de Troyes who wrote in French. But it was also drawn upon by a number of German writers of the thirteenth century, including Wolfram von Eschenbach in his *Parzifal*, and Gottfried von Strassburg in *Tristan*, one of the best renderings of the famous Celtic love story of *Tristan and Iseult*. The courtly romances, unlike the *chansons de geste*, were composed by individual poets, many of whose names are known. Moreover, they evidently catered to a more exclusively aristocratic taste than was the case with the *chansons de geste*. On the whole, the romances reflected that more sophisticated chivalry which idealized woman and romantic love and which emphasized the distinction between the knights and persons of lower estate.[2]

[1] See above, pp. 123–125.

B. Other Vernacular Literature, the Troubadours, and Dante

Epics and courtly romances were only a part of the vernacular literature which appeared and flourished in the twelfth and thirteenth centuries. Examples of several other types and forms may be cited. The *Romance of the Rose* by Guillaume de Lorris was an allegory in French, in which the characters typified vices and virtues. The *Romance of Reynard*, also in French, consisted of a series of parodies on chivalry. *Aucassin and Nicolette* was a delightful novelette, half prose, half poetry. Such German works as *Der Arme Heinrich* of Hartmann von Aue and *Meier Helmbrecht* by Werner der Gartenaere dealt with peasants and their life. Also, there were numerous and very popular *fabliaux*, which were coarsely humorous stories in verse, poking fun at contemporary characters and sparing none, not even the clergy. Equally popular in appeal were the simple scenes,

[2] In addition to the Carolingian cycle of *chansons de geste*, and the Arthurian court romances, mention should be made of contemporary "Roman" epics, in which ancient worthies, such as Alexander, Caesar, Joshua, or David, were celebrated as feudal heroes.

with appropriate dialogue, which were enacted in churches on major feast days, and the more elaborate "mystery plays" which developed from them and constituted a medieval form of drama.

A special literary form, rather different from anything so far mentioned, arose in the sophisticated society of southern France and northeastern Spain. For the land of the *langue d'oc* (that is, of Provençal and Catalan) was peculiarly productive of lyric poetry dedicated primarily, though not exclusively, to various themes of romantic love. The southern composers were called *troubadours*. Most of them were well born, and the names of some four hundred have come down to us from the middle ages. Duke William IX of Aquitaine (1071–1127) was an early and especially famous *troubadour*.

Though the distinctive culture of southern France suffered a good deal from the Albigensian crusade in the early part of the thirteenth century, the influence of its lyric poetry was extensive after, as well as before, that political-religious struggle. *Troubadours* roamed and sang from Provence to Catalonia throughout Spain, France, and Italy, and in all these regions they were welcomed and acclaimed. Moreover, the marriages of Eleanor of Aquitaine, granddaughter of Duke William IX, first to the French King Louis VII and then to the English King Henry II, had literary as well as political importance, since it served to establish southern lyric poetry at the royal courts of both France and England. Before long, this type of literature ceased to be a monopoly of southern *troubadours*. It was successfully practiced in northern France by *trouvères*, and in Germany by a swarm of *minnesingers*. Among the latter, Walther von der Vogelweide was an outstanding lyric poet.

In Italy, the Emperor Frederick II patronized poets using the Sicilian dialect. Meanwhile, a group, greatly influenced by these as well as by the Provençal and Catalan *troubadours*, commenced writing in the thirteenth century in the northern Italian vernacular. The most famous was Dante Alighieri (1265–1321), who utilized for his poetry the idiom of his native Tuscany. He is regarded not only as the greatest of all Italian poets but also as one of the most distinguished literary artists of all time.

Dante came of good Florentine stock and was active in the government of his native city until the vicissitudes of politics drove him into exile. Always a patriot, he retained a deep love for Florence, though he bewailed the petty strife which disturbed it and which divided Italy as a whole; and he dreamed of the restoration of the traditional Holy Roman Empire. Though a layman, he was exceptionally well educated. In fact, the breadth and depth of his learning reveal the advances made in medieval education. Dante had a remarkably wide acquaintance with classical literature and an excellent command of Latin. This language he used for his serious prose works, such as *De Monarchia*, a defense of the idea of empire, and *De vulgari eloquentia*, a reasoned justification of the use of the vernacular. Dante was likewise profoundly versed in theology, and had evidently immersed himself in the writings of the scholastics.

Giotto (d. 1337). Portrait of Dante. National Museum, Florence.

Alinari photograph

Dante's most important work, the *Divine Comedy*,[1] which he wrote in vernacular Italian, is a long allegorical and narrative poem. The symbolic setting of the *Comedy* is the author's imaginary pilgrimage through Hell, Purgatory, and Paradise. After seeing the hopeless torments of the damned and the hideousness of evil, he passes through Purgatory, the abode of those departed spirits whose sufferings are lightened by the hope of Heaven, into the dwelling place of the saints and the presence of God. Thus the poet's own journey is made to represent the general theme of the salvation of the soul. But as he holds converse with many figures famous in Italian and European affairs, Dante boldly criticizes those whom he holds responsible for the evils of church and state. A poem of great vividness and emotional beauty, it is also a work of deep philosophical, theological, and moral significance. Indeed, it has been described as the theology of St. Thomas Aquinas in poetic form. To convey in brief compass the merit of this most famous of poems is manifestly impossible. It must be read and re-read to be understood.

C. *Medieval Music*

To the modern listener, medieval music may seem remote and difficult to understand. This is because our ears have become accustomed to modern harmonies and rhythms which have created for us an entirely different musical atmosphere. The actual changes in the art of music subsequent to the middle ages are more radical than those in the other arts.

The most significant musical advance made during the main middle age was an increasingly successful experimentation with combinations of more than one voice, that is, with polyphony. It will be recalled that the so-called Gregorian chant had enriched the church's liturgy with a variety of melodies designed to be sung in unison. The liturgical tradition of the chant persisted—its subordination to the text, its fitness for performance in church, even the very melodies of earlier days. But now, for the first time, the chant is enriched or

[1] Dante's title was simply *Commedia*. The word "Divine" was added later.

Gothic sculpture. The Cathedral at Bourges.

Courtesy French Government Tourist Office, New York

Stained glass. French thirteenth century.

Courtesy Metropolitan Museum of Art, New York

supplemented by association of two or more melodies simultaneously.

As early as the eleventh century, a practice known as *organum*, the use of voices singing in parallel fourths, fifths, or octaves, appeared. A bit later, contrary motion in a second part was introduced. Thereby different intervals became marked, and a more varied second melody was possible. This was at first called "descant," and later, in the thirteenth century, "counterpoint." Several varying parts began to be incorporated, as contrasting melodies with the central one, not necessarily altogether, but more usually following one another. This provided opportunity and incentive for invention, not so much in the original melody as in the contrasting parts. The central melody, as a rule, continued to be a traditional chant, based on one or another of the earlier medieval modes. It was mainly ecclesiastical, although a few secular melodies were introduced. And this central melody, with which other parts were sung contrapuntally, was called the *cantus firmus*.

Counterpoint, rather than harmony, represents the principal musical achievement of the time. Inevitably, however, the varied intervals which contrapuntal singing produced led toward harmony. And the theory of measured music, necessary in order that notes in different parts should sound together, was familiar to the Arabs and presumably known to Europeans by the thirteenth century. In writing music, a certain Guido of Arezzo (*d.* 1050) seems to have popularized the use of a four (later five) line staff, while square notes, with various symbols to indicate time value, were introduced.

Stringed instruments were, of course, familiar to medieval musicians and especially to the *troubadours*. A bow seems to have appeared in the tenth century and to have provided means for developing many of our modern instruments. Some sort of organ with sliders instead of keys was in use as early as the ninth and tenth centuries. Keys seem to have come into use by the thirteenth century.

D. Romanesque Art and Architecture

Because so much is visible to us in the buildings still standing and in our museums, medieval art is better known than any other feature of medieval civilization. Here we possess tangible evidence of a combination of artistic taste and technical skill rarely equaled in world history. Medieval art was predominantly religious, for in those days the church was the main inspiration and support for the genius of artists and its patronage often best rewarded their efforts. Besides, the flowering of medieval art was a product of that same religious revival which was in back of Cluny and the Cistercians, the medieval papacy, and the friars. Finally, medieval architecture, especially the great cathedral-building of the thirteenth century, represented a popular awakening and movement.

The art of western Europe during the eleventh and twelfth centuries is generally called "romanesque." [1] As the name indicates, romanesque art owed a great deal to the art of classical Rome. But somewhat as the romance languages evolved from ancient popular speech, so romanesque art often developed from provincial rather than strictly Roman models. Moreover, Byzantine influence was highly important. Romanesque building was predominantly monastic, for it flourished especially in the age of Cluny and Cîteaux, and most of it, even in the case of cathedral churches, was supervised by monks. Romanesque churches were also associated with pilgrimages by reason of the fact that so many monasteries in that style were established along the roads to popular shrines.

Among the characteristic features of romanesque church building was a ground plan designed in the form of a cross—the cruciform plan, as it has been called. The basic rectangle, or nave (*navis*, ship), of the ancient basilica was enlarged, and a transept, or crossing, added. Beyond the transept a choir and apse increased the total length. The side aisles of the church were also bigger, sometimes double, and were continued into an ambulatory completely encircling the apse. Finally, a series of chapels or side altars was placed in the semi-circle of the apse.

This more elaborate ground plan was accompanied by corresponding changes in the superstructure. Moreover, frequent losses by fire had created a demand for all-stone structures. Therefore, wooden roofs were replaced by stone vaulting. And the added weight of a stone roof required a substructure of considerable strength. Because the graceful slender columns of the basilica could not bear the weight of a stone roof, they were replaced by rows of massive piers joined by higher and wider semi-circular arches and flanked by correspondingly higher and wider aisles. Above the arcade of the main piers, the wall often extended upward in a second set of smaller round arches (the *triforium*), and these were finally topped by the windows of a clerestory.

The simplest form of stone roof was the so-called barrel vault. This might be described as a plain semi-circular arch extended tunnel-like. Its weight fell equally on all points of the supporting wall, which necessarily had to be massive. Indeed, the outer walls were supported by piers or buttresses built against the side of the building. In some of the later romanesque churches, groined- or cross-vaulting was formed by adding arches which passed diagonally across the piers of the nave and served to distribute some of the weight of the roof.

There were a number of variations in romanesque building which are noticeable in different regions. A distinctive Norman style found its way into England. Southern French types were evident in Spain, thus affording further evidence of the cultural inter-relationship of the two regions. And a north Italian or Lombard school of architecture was also popular in Germany, especially in the Rhineland. Taken all in all, romanesque architecture was by no means mere imitation of the Roman or Byzantine. It was distinctive and original.

Sculpture kept pace with building. Columns were surmounted with carved designs, sometimes reminiscent of the classical orders, but more often departing radically from them. Romanesque sculpture is perhaps seen at its best in the ornamental reliefs and figures adorning the portals of churches. Interior decorative features were surprisingly varied. Mosaics continued to be popular, and polychrome frescoes made their appearance. The romanesque period likewise witnessed advances in the technique of stained glass.

Among the minor arts were metal work and enamels. At Limoges in France, new methods of applying and firing the enamel made possible a greater flexibility, and established a lasting fame for Limoges enamel. Meanwhile, comparable skill and artistry were being displayed by miniaturists who illustrated or "illuminated" manuscripts, and by ivory carvers who produced exquisitely formed articles such as combs, chessmen, or small boxes.

[1] Romanesque art developed in the early Middle Age and reached what might be called the peak of its development in the twelfth century. In many parts of Europe, however, romanesque churches were built long after 1200.

E. Gothic Architecture

Gothic architecture,[1] which many people still revere as the supreme achievement of medieval civilization, reached the summit of its development in a comparatively short space of time, roughly between 1150 and 1350. While the style spread to England, western Germany, northern Italy, and Spain, the most famous gothic cathedrals were erected in north-central France.

The Gothic was intimately bound up with contemporary social and economic developments. If romanesque was a monastic architecture, gothic reflected the new town life. Bishops, of course, took the initiative in cathedral building, but they were earnestly supported by citizens and by the guilds. Guilds usually contributed chapels and stained glass windows. While an initial impetus or "drive" may have enlisted general popular participation, the medieval cathedral was a skilled professional enterprise. Many architects were friars, but an increasing number were laymen and graduates of universities. Masons' guilds contracted with the bishop for their labor. Naturally there was keen competition, as the bishop and townsmen of one city sought to erect a "bigger and better" structure than that being completed by a neighboring community. Gothic building represents, therefore, a unique and fortuitous combination of civic pride, religious zeal, technical skill, and aesthetic understanding.

A number of structural problems were solved by the gothic builders. In particular, they discovered how to achieve greater height and breadth without so enlarging the walls as to shut out light. It was not entirely an accident that grey northern France, rather than the sunnier south, was the locale for the original experimentation. Three distinctive structural features were devised: the groined vault; the pointed arch; and the flying buttress. One of these alone did not necessarily make a building gothic, for, as we have already noticed, a groined vault and even a slightly pointed arch had been employed in earlier romanesque churches. It was rather the combination of all three features just mentioned which constituted the gothic.

The use of a pointed arch enabled the builder to increase the ratio of height to width, for the extra space could be bridged by a number of pointed arches of different heights. This in turn made possible more varied cross-vaulting and the bridging of rectangular as well as square areas. In the simple semi-circular cross-vaulting of the romanesque, only two arches intersected. Gothic vaulting might be quadripartite or sexpartite or even more complicated, while the ridges between the stone panelling were emphasized by ribs which went up fan-like from pier to roof.

There was the problem of the outward, as well as the downward "thrusts," from the weight of a heavy stone roof. This had been met in romanesque churches by increasing the thickness of the supporting walls. In gothic buildings it was solved by a series of "flying buttresses," of stone arcs, which swept out from high points in the main walls, over the roof of the side aisles, to pier buttresses built out alongside the foundations. A gothic church was indeed a miracle of structural engineering, and the skill of its builders is perhaps best proven by the fact that their seemingly delicate creations still stand, resistant to the storms of nature and the bombardments of war.

Since arched vaults and flying buttresses relieved the walls of much of their weight-carrying functions while heightening the whole structure, it was possible to install many glass windows. And this provided far more opportunity than in romanesque churches for the introduction of stained glass. The term "stained glass" is somewhat misleading. Actually the glass was colored in its molten state and part of the design etched and fused. Then innumerable pieces were inserted and held together with strips of lead and masonry. Some of the large "rose windows" commonly placed over the

[1] The term "gothic" is really a misnomer. It has nothing to do with primitive German tribes of Goths. It was invented by an Italian writer of the sixteenth century, Giorgio Vasari, as a contemptuous description of what he deemed a style of architecture very inferior to the classical. Vasari's view, unfortunately, was widely accepted from his time until the romantic revival of "Gothic" in the nineteenth century.

broad front entrance of cathedrals required consummate skill in balancing glass, lead, and supporting masonry. The total effect was singularly imposing and beautiful.

Just as the raising of a cathedral required the coöperation of a whole community, clergy and laity alike, so gothic sculpture and decoration emphasized the union of man and nature in God. Front and side portals were flanked with figures of Christ, the Virgin, and the saints, together with characters from both Old and New Testaments, rulers, scholars pagan as well as Christian, and peasants and artisans at work. And a scene of the Last Judgment invariably completed the cycle of religious life. Innumerable carvings of flowers and leaves, not the formalized acanthus of the classical orders, but real oak leaves and floral garlands, testified to an awareness and love of nature and to a desire that it, too, should glorify God. At the same time, gaiety and humor were evident in accompanying gargoyles and grotesques, some of which adorned inaccessible niches that only the birds could see. And not only did the guilds contribute windows, but in the stained glass which they put into them, they portrayed themselves at work.

Altogether, the Gothic cathedral mirrored the rich life of the age in all its fullness, in its vitality, and, above all, in its movement. Romanesque retained something of classical tranquillity and sense of proportion. With Gothic architecture—and it is equally true of manuscript illumination, of painting, and of vernacular literature—we are in an age of romanticism.

French twelfth century architectural sculpture. A capital from the abbey of St. Michael and St. Germain, Cuxa. Birds and grotesque men.

New York; The Cloisters Collection, Purchase, 1925 Courtesy Metropolitan Museum of Art

SELECT SUPPLEMENTARY READINGS FOR PART IV

General. Same as for "General" under Parts II and III (pp. 110, 171, above); in addition, F. Heer, *The Medieval World* (1962).

Chapter 15. For the expansion of European frontiers, see under the appropriate countries mentioned under Chapter 12 (p. 171) and Chapter 17 (below). For the crusaders' states, in addition to the works mentioned in Chapter 14 (p. 171): J. L. La Monte, *Feudal Monarchy in the Latin Kingdom of Jerusalem* (1932); D. C. Munro, *The Kingdom of the Crusaders* (1935); G. Slaughter, *Saladin* (1955). For the Mongols and European travelers to Asia: C. R. Beazley, *The Dawn of Modern Geography*, 3 vols. (1897–1906); Kim Setton, R. L. Wolff, H. W. Hazard, eds., *A History of the Crusades*, vol. II (1962); L. Olschki, *Marco Polo's Precursors* (1943) and *Marco Polo's Asia* (1960); M. P. Prawdin, *The Mongol Empire, Its Rise and Legacy* (1940); P. M. Sykes, *The Quest for Cathay* (1936); J. K. Wright, *Geographical Lore of the Time of the Crusades* (1925).

Chapter 16. H. Adelson, *Medieval Commerce* (1962); P. Boissonade, *Life and Work in the Middle Ages* (1927); M. V. Clark, *The Medieval City State* (1936); R. S. Lopez and I. W. Raymond, *Medieval Trade in the Mediterranean World* (1955); J. H. Mundy and P. Reisenberg, *The Medieval Town* (1958); S. Painter, *Medieval Society* (1951); H. Pirenne, *Economic and Social History of Medieval Europe* (1937) and *Medieval Cities* (1949); C. Stephenson, *Borough and Town* (1933).

Chapter 17. In addition to the books cited for Chapter 12 (p. 171): W. C. Atkinson, *A History of Spain and Portugal* (1960); F. Barlow, *The Feudal Kingdom of England* (1954); A. Castro, *The Structure of Spanish History* (1954); H. J. Chaytor, *The History of Aragon and Catalonia* (1933); J. T. Appleby, *John, King of England* (1959); S. B. Chrimes, *An Introduction to the Administrative History of England* (1959); D. C. Douglas, *William the Conqueror* (1964); C. L. Haskins, *The Growth of English Representative Government* (1948); A. Kelly, *Eleanor of Aquitaine and the Four Kings* (1950); H. V. Livermore, *History of Portugal* (1948); R. L. Poole, *Domesday Book and Magna Carta* (1955); S. Painter, *The Reign of King John* (1940); M. Powicke, *The Thirteenth Century* (England) (new ed., 1962); F. M. Stenton, *The First Century of English Feudalism* (1932); D. M. Stenton, *English Society in the Early Middle Ages* (1951); W. Warren, *King John* (1961).

Chapter 18. In addition to the works cited for Chapter 12 (p. 171): G. Barraclough, "Frederick Barbarossa and the Twelfth Century" in *History in a Changing World* (1955), pp. 73–96; H. B. Cotterill, *Medieval Italy* (1915); O. Halecki,

Borderlands of Western Civilization (1952); E. Kantorowicz, *Frederick II* (1931); G. Slaughter, *The Amazing Frederick* (1937); G. Vernadsky and M. Karpovich, *A History of Russia*, vols. II and III (1948, 1953).

Chapter 19. The general works on the church cited for Chapter 8 (p. 110) contain material pertinent to this chapter. For more special topics: M. W. Baldwin, *The Mediaeval Church* (1953); R. P. Bennett, *The Early Dominicans* (1937); S. R. Packard, *Europe and the Church Under Innocent III* (1927); A. C. Shannon, *The Popes and Heresy in the Thirteenth Century* (1949); W. Ullmann, *The Growth of Papal Government in the Middle Ages* (1955) and *Medieval Papalism* (1949); E. Vacandard, *The Inquisition* (1924). See also the following biographies: T. S. R. Boase, *St. Francis of Assisi* (1936) and *Boniface VIII* (1933); Fr. Cuthbert, *St. Francis of Assisi* (1913); J. Jorgenson, *St. Francis of Assisi* (1912); B. S. James, *St. Bernard of Clairvaux* (1957); B. Jarrett, O.P., *Life of St. Dominic* (1924); C. E. Smith, *Innocent III, Church Defender* (1951); W. Williams, *St. Bernard* (1944).

Chapter 20. F. B. Artz, *The Mind of the Middle Ages* (1952); F. Coppleston, *Medieval Philosophy* (1961); A. C. Crombie, *Augustine to Galileo* (1952), reprinted as *Medieval and Early Modern Science*, 2 vols. (1959); C. G. Crump and E. F. Jacob, *The Legacy of the Middle Ages* (1926); E. Gilson, *Heloise and Abelard* (1960), *History of Christian Philosophy in the Middle Ages* (1955), and *Reason and Revelation in the Middle Ages* (1938); C. H. Haskins, *The Renaissance of the Twelfth Century* (1927) and *The Rise of the Universities* (1932); P. Kibre, *The Nations in the Medieval Universities* (1948), and *Scholarly Privileges in the Middle Ages* (1962); G. Leff, *Medieval Thought* (1958); H. Rashdall, *The Universities of Europe in the Middle Ages*, 3 vols. revised by F. M. Powicke and A. B. Emden (1936); L. Thorndike, *University Records and Life in the Middle Ages* (1944) and *The History of Magic and Experimental Science*, vols I–IV (1923–1934); D. Knowles, *The Evolution of Medieval Thought* (1962); H. O. Taylor, *The Medieval Mind*, 2 vols. (1930); L. J. Daly, S. J., *The Medieval Universities* (1961).

Chapter 21. There are many available editions and translations of medieval literary works. A convenient selection is given in C. W. Jones, *Medieval Literature in Translation* (1950) and in *Medieval Epics*, Modern Library (1963). See also W. P. Ker, *The Dark Ages* (1904) and *Epic and Romance* (1897). On art, see Gardner, *Art through the Ages*, and Morey, *Medieval Art and Christian Art*, cited above for Chapter 5; J. Gimpel, *The Cathedral Builders* (1960); E. Mâle, *The Gothic Image* (1958); N. Pevsner, *An Outline of European Architecture* (5th ed., 1957); R. Branner, *Gothic Architecture* (1961); W. R. Lethaby, *Medieval Art* (rev. D. Talbot Rice, 1949); H. Saalman, *Medieval Architecture* (1962). For music, P. H. Lang, *Music in Western Civilization* (1941); G. Reese, *Music in the Middle Ages* (1940).

PART V
LATE MIDDLE AGE:

Gloucester Cathedral. An example of English perpendicular style (see p. 322).
Courtesy British Information Service, New York

THE FOURTEENTH AND FIFTEENTH CENTURIES

The Alba Madonna. Raphael (d. 1520), (see p. 320).

National Gallery of Art, Washington, D.C.; Mellon Collection

From Edward III of England to Leonardo da Vinci

A fifteenth century one-masted ship of the Netherlands.

Courtesy Museum of Fine Arts, Boston

THE fourteenth and fifteenth centuries may be designated as the "Late Middle Age." This phrase implies a difference, perhaps a decline, from the particular features of civilization which characterized the preceding two centuries and which may be regarded as strictly "medieval." But the same period includes what has also commonly been called the "renaissance," a term which connotes the revival of a culture long dead or dormant. The period, moreover, was climaxed by certain novel and highly significant developments: the emergence of national monarchy, the invention of printing, the opening of new routes to India, and the discovery of a new world across the Atlantic—developments which have been described as heralding the coming of the "modern age."

It should be remarked that the distinctive cultural movement associated with the term "renaissance" was largely confined, during the fourteenth and fifteenth centuries, to Italy and affected northern Europe only gradually and later. Hence it is possible to speak of a cultural revival in Italy and a lag elsewhere. But this geographical distinction is hardly satisfactory as an explanation of a remarkably complex period. The arc and music of the north, for example, rivaled that of Italy; and in economics, recent studies have indicated that throughout Europe, including Italy, the Late Middle Age, at least until near its close, was one of protracted and occasionally acute depression accompanied by a decline in population.

For years scholars have debated about the "renaissance." Doubtless they will continue to do so. Two observations may be made here. First, while there is general agreement that the concept of a sharp break between middle ages and renaissance must be abandoned, it remains true that if much in the fourteenth century is reminiscent of an earlier day, the civilization of the fifteenth century does differ in certain important respects from that of the preceding middle ages. Second, and most important, the student should realize that in studying this transitional period he is confronting one of the most difficult problems of interpretation in the entire course of European and Western history.

CHAPTER 22

Social and Economic Developments of Late Middle Age

A. *"Closing the Medieval Frontier," and Economic Depression*

Earlier chapters have described the long process of growth which characterized western European civilization: the winning of new land from forest, swamp, and shore; the expansion of commerce and the growth of town life. Before the middle of the fourteenth century this forward movement had apparently reached its peak and a recession had begun. Europe's population, except in east-central areas, leveled off and became relatively stationary. This involved a cessation of the continent's internal colonization, whether through the founding of new towns or the occupation of new agricultural lands. In short, an important "pioneering" aspect of European life was coming to an end. This process has been described as "the closing of the medieval frontier." [1]

In part the recession seems to have been the normal termination of a movement of centuries' duration which had finally run its course. But it was also in large part the result of disturbed political and social conditions in the fourteenth century and the first part of the fifteenth. France suffered grievously from the Hundred Years' War, and England in the fifteenth century was plagued with lawlessness and wars of royal succession. Spain was divided, and the Byzantine Empire which had never recovered from the Fourth Crusade was now beleagured by Turks, Slavs, and Mongols, not to mention French, Italian, and Catalan merchants and adventurers.

Partly, too, the change resulted from natural calamities of famine and pestilence. In the second decade of the fourteenth century a major famine afflicted large areas of Europe. And most terrible of all pestilences was the epidemic of bubonic plague, or "Black Death," which in 1348–1350 ravaged all Europe and carried off an estimated fourth or third of its population. The congested districts of the towns were hardest hit, but the countryside was not spared. All classes of society were affected. There was an especially heavy mortality among the secular clergy, who, with physicians, ministered to the sick and dying; and even isolated monasteries fell prey to this greatest plague in all European history. Economic life, in the circumstances, could not fail to be adversely affected not only by the Black Death itself and by repeated occurrences of pestilence, but by the shortage of labor which followed in its wake.

Gradually, during the second half of the fifteenth century, an economic recovery occurred. This, with the new geographic discoveries, heralded a new era. Hence, as we consider various aspects of European life during the late Middle Age, we must do so with understanding of their setting in a long depression followed by gradual economic restoration and advance.

[1] The phrase is that of A. R. Lewis, "The Closing of the Medieval Frontier," *Speculum*, XXXIII (1958), 475–483.

B. The Land and the Landed Classes

Europe remained throughout the fourteenth and fifteenth centuries predominantly agrarian. But the effects of an expanded commercial and urban life, and of a money economy with consequent rise in commodity prices—effects which were noticeable well before 1300—were now accentuated. It was more common for landlords to pay agricultural laborers with money, and for peasants to lease their holdings for fixed sums of money in lieu of personal services. In short, most peasants in England, the Netherlands, France, and the Rhineland became rent-tenants or farm laborers for hire. And in general the customary law of the land guaranteed to peasants the permanent possession of the holdings for which they paid rent. Thus the French tenant became a *censier* (from *cens*, "rent"), and the English tenant a "copyholder." [1] Since most such leases were on a long-term basis, the landlord was at a disadvantage in an age of rising prices.

Thus what was left of serfdom in western Europe diminished further. Although opportunities to migrate to new farms were lessened, the possibilities for a more flexible rent-relationship with a *seigneur* were enhanced, as were also the opportunities to sell surplus produce to landlords or to town.

The agrarian changes of the period in western Europe were by no means an unmixed blessing for the peasants. The greater flexibility which characterized the western areas was apparently not matched in various parts of Germany and eastern Europe where serfdom persisted. In some places the old coöperative manors were transformed into capitalistic estates practically owned by an individual landlord, and on these the peasants found themselves deprived of the security which manorial organization had afforded them, and transformed into mere hired agricultural laborers, underpaid and possessing nothing they could call their own. Besides, the virtual cessation in the settling-up of new lands removed an important outlet for depressed peasants anxious to improve their lot. There was less opportunity for peasants to leave the manor or estate, and the landlord, knowing this, felt less disposed to ameliorate their living and working conditions. Even for those peasants who enjoyed a relatively low rent, the rise in prices of articles which many now felt they needed could be a real burden.

The change was unsettling, and especially in the fourteenth century it gave rise to widespread peasant disorders and insurrections throughout western Europe. Some of these, like the "Jacquerie" in France, which followed the Black Death and the devastations of the Hundred Years' War, were undoubtedly inspired by dire material distress and active hostility to landlords. But others, such as the Peasants' Revolt in England (1381) and similar uprisings in Flanders in the third decade of the century, seem to have been the work of peasants who were relatively well off and conscious of their strength; and in the case of the revolt in England, there was a well formulated peasant pronouncement of "revolutionary" doctrines concerning the equality of all men. While the peasants' rebellions of the fourteenth century were suppressed by force, the very fact of their occurrence indicated on the part of masses of peasants a class consciousness and ambition unknown in an earlier day.

The landowning classes, nobility and upper clergy, were in general adversely affected by political and economic change. Politically, the rise of monarchical power and the extension of its judicial authority, and in fifteenth-century Germany the integration of some of the larger principalities, deprived the nobility of their functions as governors of fiefs. Long-term rents, as we have seen, proved disadvantageous as prices rose. At the same time, the average noble's normal expenses increased for his now more complex and costly arms and armor, and for luxuries which commerce made more available, which current social convention dictated, and which he, and more particularly his wife and daughters, now desired.

One way to recoup a lost or falling fortune was to enter government service and to become associated with a royal court. Other possibilities were to arrange a mar-

[1] The term "copyholder" signified that the tenant held a "copy" of the manorial court roll which stated the conditions of his tenure.

Early fifteenth century French illuminated manuscript. *The Très Belles Heures* of the Duke of Berry done by the Limbourg brothers, Jean, Pol, and Herman.

Courtesy Metropolitan Museum of Art, New York; The Cloisters Collection, Purchase, 1954

riage with the daughter of a wealthy bourgeois or to encourage younger sons to enter the church. Many nobles sought employment in military service. Royal military forces in this age were largely composed of contingents serving for pay from funds which kings were able to obtain from taxes. While such forces now included archers, pikemen, and other infantry troops drawn from the lower orders, nobles of all ranks continued to serve, not as a feudal obligation, but for pay definitely contracted for. The armies of the Hundred Years' War were in many respects still "feudal," that is, composed of mounted knights in armor. But these were professional soldiers, recruited by and serving under captains. Unhappily, many such companies under English, Irish, French, or Flemish captains remained in arms between formal campaigns, and sold their services to warring factions of France, England, or Italy, or went on distant and often ill-planned expeditions to Spain, Sicily, North Africa, or the Near East, or simply engaged in methodical pillage. In short, the nobles of the late middle age, no longer administrators of fiefs or feudal warriors in the old sense, were extraordinarily restless and generally ill-adjusted to the conditions of life which confronted them.

Perhaps because they felt a challenge to their hitherto dominant position in society, the nobles of the late middle age clung tenaciously to the outward symbols of prestige, to those things which represented the ideals of their class. Hence emphasis was put on an exaggerated and essentially unreal brand of chivalry. When war or distant expeditions failed to provide opportunities for deeds of daring, tournaments abounded. These were at once more formal than in the earlier middle ages and more costly. Full plate armor, though doubtless beyond the means of many petty nobles, came into fashion early in the fifteenth century. Barriers were set up between the contestants, heralds announced the opening of a joust, and ladies in gala attire graced the gallery. And although only the chosen few could join, such elaborate institutions as the *Order of the Golden Fleece*, created by the duke of Burgundy, set a tone for aristocratic society.

It is probable that such institutions also reflected a desire to escape from the crudity, brutality, and suffering which characterized the actual existence of many townsmen and peasants. It savors of paradox, not easily explained, that an age of economic depression should be also an age of fantastic luxury. Certain it is that the royal court of France and the court maintained by the dukes of Burgundy, who were also rulers of the Netherlands, were unparalleled in lavish display and in costly and minutely ordered ceremony of court life. This was not entirely wasteful, for most of the rulers were intelligent and discriminating, as well as generous, patrons of art.[1] But if the modern student can thank these men for making possible some of the most beautiful of tapestries, illuminated manuscripts, and paintings, he should remember the cost. Not without reason was the prodigal and art-loving French duke of Berry hated by his subjects as grasping, dishonest, and totally unconcerned with their welfare.

C. Industry and Banking

It was suggested at the opening of this chapter that the persistence of economic depression did not mean that the capitalistic enterprise which had begun to characterize the economic life of the twelfth and thirteenth centuries now ceased or that large fortunes were not made. Indeed, the contrary is true. Although more evident in the later fifteenth century, progress is notable in the fourteenth. Certain general trends may be mentioned first.

In the preceding age, private capitalistic enterprise had been checked by such essentially coöperative institutions as the craft and merchant guilds, or it had been discouraged by the church's teaching regarding the just price and the taking of usurious interest. Even before 1300 these restraints were weakening. Churchmen were beginning to compromise on the matter of usury and to distinguish between it and "interest," a

[1] Under the auspices of the dukes of Burgundy, Flemish painting reached its apogée, and Flemish influences penetrated Burgundy and other parts of France. The artist Jean Fouquet became court painter to King Louis XI. These are but a few examples of such patronage.

legitimate return on loans. Loaning money at interest was no longer a despised profession of Jews and other non-Christians, but an accepted as well as lucrative occupation of Christian bankers, with whom even popes now had high financial dealings. In this respect, as in so many others, the influence of the church lessened during the late middle age.

Equally significant was the decay of the guilds, with resulting sharpened cleavage between wealthy merchants and poor artisans. Already, prior to 1300, we have had occasion to remark a tendency within the craft guilds toward a rift between master and workman.[1] Apprentices and journeymen were finding it more difficult to become masters. At the same time certain larger industries which depended on distant markets were beginning to break loose from any guild organization or control.

True, guilds persisted through the fourteenth and fifteenth centuries. But after 1300 they underwent a profound alteration. In some parts of Europe, especially in national states, they were seized upon and utilized by monarchs as convenient instruments of governmental control over industry. In regions where the demand for goods outran the supply from local guilds, enterprising merchants established new centers of production, with workmen outside of the guild system and free from its restrictions.

[1] See above, p. 196.

Burgundian cannon of the late fourteenth or early fifteenth century (mounting modern).

Courtesy Metropolitan Museum of Art; The Bashford Dean Memorial Collection, Purchase funds from various donors, 1929

Thus, in Flanders, smaller towns without guild organizations, and sometimes with the encouragement of the ruling dukes of Burgundy, flourished at the expense of older guild cities such as Bruges, Ghent, and Ypres. Large-scale operators would employ workmen widely scattered in various localities, providing them with raw wool and disposing of the finished cloth. Such workmen were often part-time farmers, part-time weavers.

The cloth guilds of Florence, founded much earlier—the *Arte della Lana* and the *Arte di Calimala* [2]—were essentially capitalistic. They monopolized the clothing business of the city, buying out small weavers, and controlling raw materials, dyeworks, transportation facilities, and warehouses. But if Florentine cloth was a rival of Flemish, it, too, was facing serious competition in the latter part of the fifteenth century.

In London, a number of guilds, particularly those engaged in large-scale buying and selling, obtained royal charters of incorporation permitting them to monopolize the trade in designated types of goods. They enriched themselves as monopolists and capitalists, and in the latter role they gained a commanding position in city affairs and in royal councils. And what occurred in London and Florence, became a common occurrence in most other European cities during the late middle age. Even in towns where the market remained fairly static, guilds tended ever more to become closed corporations dominated by wealthy masters and offering little opportunity to aspiring journeymen.

With the decay and alteration of the guilds, the lot of the small artisan in the fourteenth and fifteenth centuries was not a happy one. True, he did not have to experience all the evils of the later factory system. But he was an employee dependent upon various vicissitudes of employment, and with very little likelihood of becoming a master himself. It must not be supposed, however, that artisans submitted quietly to capitalistic exploitation. Journeymen's guilds began to appear, even before 1300, and, though not nearly as powerful as modern trade unions, they participated in strikes and

[2] The *Arte della Lana* manufactured cloth, the *Arte di Calimala* "finished" imported cloth.

urban disorders which increased in frequency during the late middle age and testified to growing unrest of an artisan class.[1]

Broadly speaking, as the feudal order passed, there vanished with it those checks and balances which had made it endurable. Developing capitalism not only rendered possible a great access of wealth; it caused widespread poverty. Political and military complications added to the strains and stresses of economic change. Moreover, the lower classes of society, both urban and rural, had no organs for orderly expression of their political and economic views. Town governments were closed to them. Parliaments and Estates of the national monarchies were representative only of the relatively well-to-do.

Insurrection, therefore, was a crude means of self-expression. But it would be a mistake to interpret the frequency of urban and rural disorder merely as evidence of injustice. Injustice there was in plenty. But violent outbursts reflected the desires of people already conscious of some change for the better and demanding more.

Although there was a tendency, especially in the fifteenth century, for banking to become an independent business of particular families or firms of capitalists, many bankers were, as in earlier days, prosperous merchants who developed money-lending as a side line. Some catered to royal needs or proved themselves useful intermediaries between the papal treasury and its collectors throughout Europe. Several of the chief banking families were Italian. The foremost in the fourteenth century were the Bardi and Peruzzi families, the latter having branch banks in sixteen cities and five different countries, including England. Like some later bankers, the Bardi and Peruzzi families eventually met reverses and failed. The English tariff duties which they administered fell into arrears. The king of Naples repudiated a debt of two hundred thousand florins he owed them, and interest payments from the king of England were suspended. And finally they lost heavily at home in a war between Florence and Pisa. No banking house could stand such a combination of strains, and both families went bankrupt.

What proved to be a bigger and more illustrious banking family, the Medici, profitted by the mistakes of the Bardi and Peruzzi and established financially autonomous branch banks in various key localities. In the middle and second half of the fifteenth century, Cosimo de' Medici and his successor, Lorenzo "the Magnificent," headed this opulent family whose financial ramifications extended throughout the greater part of Europe. Not only did they become "bosses" in their own city of Florence, but they saw their sons elevated to the papacy; and, somewhat later, their daughters married French kings. Meanwhile, there was arising, in the German city of Augsburg, another famous banking family—the Fuggers—who in the early sixteenth century were to outstrip all others.

An example of a great financier and business man who served his country's interest as well as his own was the Frenchman, Jacques Coeur of Bourges (*d.* 1456). Born of a merchant family, he followed a commercial career, dealt in a variety of goods, and owned warehouses in several French cities. He operated mines and owned a fleet of ships which plied the Mediterranean. He even obtained special papal permission to trade with the Moslem Turks. With his enormous fortune and manifold financial connections, he was welcomed as steward of the French king's household and later was appointed master of the royal mints at Bourges and Paris. Members of his family married into high society or were given handsome ecclesiastical benefices; and in return he advanced money to the king, to the pope, and to many of the French nobility. But his conspicuous patriotic service was the raising of sufficient sums to enable French arms to reconquer Normandy from the English. And, as a reward, this merchant's son accompanied his king on the latter's triumphal entry into Rouen in 1449. But if Jacques Coeur's career illustrated the heights to which the wealthy bourgeoisie could rise, it also, by a queer turn of fortune's wheel, demonstrated that those who thus rose might fall. Convicted on a preposterous charge of having poisoned the

[1] Political motives combined with social and economic to produce certain insurrections, such as the Matins of Bruges (1302) and the Sicilian Vespers (1282).

king's mistress, he was banished and his property confiscated. He finally met his death fighting the Turks as a captain of a papal army.

Although the Medici were deep in the politics of their native city and Jacques Coeur served his king, the capitalists of the time rarely sought to influence policy other than to seek privileges, monopolies, mining rights, etc., for themselves. They generally did not aspire to become statesmen, but were content as men of wealth to promote their own and their relatives' private fortunes, or to see their sons and daughters rise in noble or ecclesiastical society.

D. National Economy and Commercial Expansion

To a limited degree, the successful national monarchies of the fourteenth and fifteenth centuries began to foster a national as distinct from an urban economy. As early as 1381 the English government attempted to restrict English trade to English ships. About the same time the English Parliament tried to regulate agricultural wages, which led, in this case, to a peasants' revolt. In the same century, an English company, known as the Merchants of the Staple, was given a virtual monopoly of the export of wool, hides, and tin, and for a time was subjected to close governmental supervision. Partly as a consequence of the dislocation caused by the Hundred Years' War, an English wool industry appeared which began to rival the Flemish. After the middle of the fifteenth century English economic policy was further promoted by a series of measures prohibiting the importation of continental cloth and restricting the activities of foreign merchants within the country. King Henry VII (1485–1509) sponsored the organization of a company of "Merchant Adventurers" to operate, under close governmental supervision, in foreign trade. It should be remembered, however, that until the accession of Henry VII the English government was far from stable, and that until 1453 it was occupied in the French war. Although this had some economic implications regarding trade between England and southwestern France, it seems that many Englishmen who were regularly committing acts of piracy against Flemish, Dutch, and Germans would have preferred a hostile policy aimed at the Netherlands rather than an alliance with them.

France, by reason of the protracted Hundred Years' War fought on its own soil, did not adopt a corresponding national trade policy before the reign of Louis XI (1461–1483). Louis surrounded himself with bankers and men of business, attempted with some success to promote a silk industry, and in other ways sought to protect French merchants. Similar developments occurred in Spain and Portugal.

National economic policy was limited and did not preclude the continued economic development fostered by the relatively autonomous cities or city-states of the Netherlands, Germany, or Italy. It only foreshadowed the more consistent national mercantilism of the following century.

Despite economic depression, Europe's commerce continued to be geographically extensive. Italians, for example, remained active in the Near and Middle East. It was a Genoese base at Caffa in the Crimea whence, it is believed, the Black Death was carried to western Europe. Italian commercial depots (*fondachi*) were to be found in the Mongol hinterland. The discovery, early in the present century, of the Datini archives (1360–1410) has revealed a vast commercial enterprise organized with great sophistication, including double-entry accounting. The Venetians, perennial rivals of the Genoese, maintained a number of areas of exploitation in Greek islands and mainland, which they detached from the Byzantine Empire, at least until conquests of the Ottoman Turks in the fifteenth century menaced the entire area. Nor were Italians the only ones to exploit Byzantine weakness. A Catalan company appeared in the fourteenth century and was followed by Navarrese.

The connection between the commerce of the Mediterranean region and that of northern Europe had been made overland in the twelfth and thirteenth centuries, particularly through the instrumentality of the Champagne fairs. Early in the fourteenth century Venice, employing larger and more seaworthy ships, was able to establish and maintain a regular sea contact with Flanders. A Venetian "Flanders galley" was 120 to 150 feet long, and was manned by a crew of from one hundred to two hundred. The oarsmen were signed on—the use of galley "slaves" was a later development—and the entire ship was under the command of a captain who was usually a representative of the Venetian aristocracy. Though his authority on shipboard was absolute, he was governed by specific instructions from the owners.

During the fourteenth and early fifteenth centuries Bruges remained, as it had been, the principal commercial depot of the north. It was at once the "staple," that is the terminal, for English wool export and a factory of the Hanseatic League. This league, or *Hanse* as it was called from a German word for mercantile association, eventually included some two hundred towns, villages, and districts in an area stretching from England and Flanders on the west, through Scandinavia in the far north, to Russian Novgorod in the east. Moreover, the league came to include not only cities of the Baltic and North Sea coasts, but inland river towns like Magdeburg and Breslau. Though predominantly German, the Hanseatic League was an international affair. In addition to Bruges, it possessed foreign trading centers, or factories, at London, at Bergen in Norway, and at Novgorod in Russia. Documents recording agreements made with the city of Bruges in the mid-fourteenth century appear to be the first official use of the phrase German *Hanse*.

An objective of the League was the securing of trading privileges in foreign ports for merchants of the member cities and eventually the acquisition of a monopoly of northern Europe's export trade. It also devoted itself to the imports of northern Europe and to the protection of the inland trade routes of northern and central Europe. Of necessity, the protection of members required strict rules of trading at home and abroad, and this in turn led to a form of organization. Never rigid, this amounted to little more than occasional meetings and assemblies. There were no league officials and no common treasury or army. Lübeck, Hamburg, and certain other towns came to be recognized as leaders of groups within the whole League. Nevertheless, the League could and did bring recalcitrant members into line by withholding privileges, or forcing the hand of a foreign power by boycott. Moreover, on occasions the League actually went to war to defend its rights, levying contributions of men, money, and ships. The most notable occasion was the struggle with and defeat of Denmark in the four-

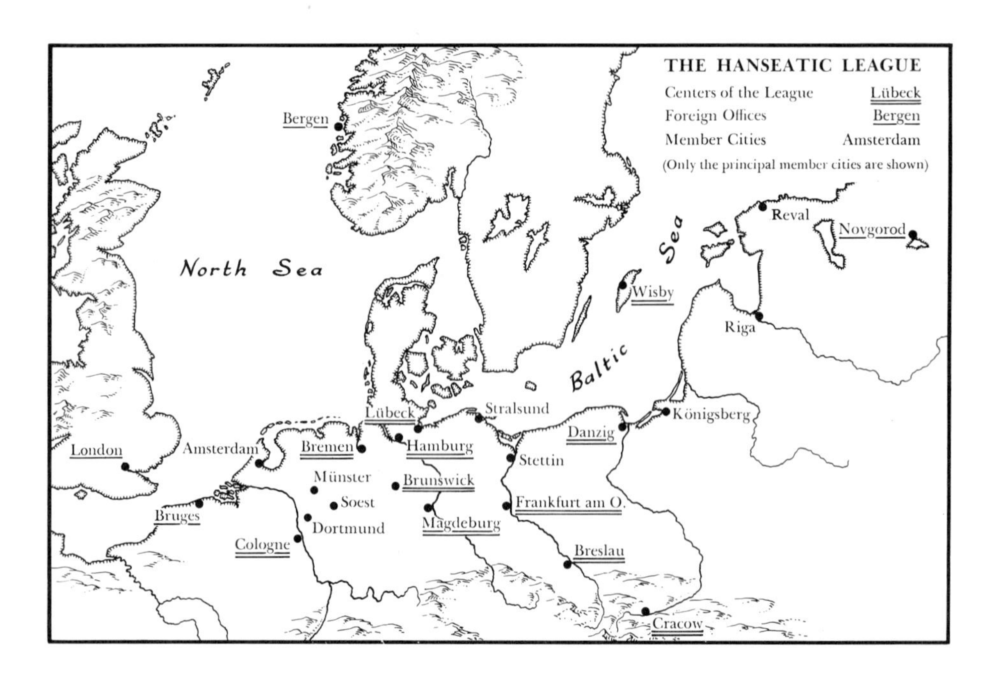

The thirteenth century Wall of Wisby, Isle of Gotland. Wisby was one of the outposts of the Hanseatic League.

Courtesy Swedish National Travel Office, New York

teenth century and the subsequent restoration there of the League's privileges (treaty of Stralsund, 1370).

By the fifteenth century the Hanseatic League was troubled by domestic dissensions. It also suffered from the defeat of the Teutonic Knights, an important ally, by the united kingdom of Poland-Lithuania.[1] Besides, it began to encounter more determined opposition from England, and likewise from the Netherlands under the dukes of Burgundy. Even nature contributed to the woes of the League, as the herring, among the most important items of its trade, became less plentiful in the Baltic and more so in the North Sea.[2]

Important changes also developed within the Netherlands in the second half of the fifteenth century. Bruges now suffered loss of its commercial primacy, partly as a result of serious silting of its harbor with consequent inability to accommodate larger and more numerous ships, partly owing to the persistence of old and now outdated restrictions, and partly because of the promising development, with the encouragement of the dukes of Burgundy, of such other ports as Amsterdam and Antwerp. As the middle ages came to a close, Antwerp with its magnificent harbor, some distance from the

[1] See below, p. 296.

[2] The movement of the herring, presumably following a change in the ocean *flora,* may have resulted from what is now held to have been a progressive deterioration of the climate of the northern areas during the late middle age. A southward movement of the polar ice cap, which lowered northern mean temperatures, may also have accounted for the decline and disappearance of the Norse colony in Greenland.

sea on the river Scheldt, became the leading commercial depot of the north. By 1500 it had surpassed Bruges and other cities and was the seat of a flourishing *bourse* or stock exchange.[1]

E. Improving Technology: Mining and Navigation

Mining of both precious and baser metals had declined during the depression of the fourteenth and early fifteenth centuries. Then, too, many mines, formerly successfully exploited, were abandoned because a point had been reached where water seepage was too great for contemporary drainage techniques to handle. In the later fifteenth century when general economic conditions improved, there were important improvements in mining techniques. Some of these dated from an earlier time, but could now be more fully developed and exploited. They included such things as longer mine passages for gravity drainage, horse-driven pumps, larger and more effective blast furnaces, and bellows driven by water-power which could produce cast iron "pigs" in greater quantity. In the middle of the century an improved method for separating silver from copper ore was devised by Johannes Funcken.

Although fifteenth-century mining was still hardly more than extensive quarrying, the new techniques indicate a combination of technology and industry which had important implications for the future. Moreover, since these techniques were expensive, exploitation tended inevitably to become more capitalistic. Miners' associations which in an earlier day had managed their own affairs under contract with a landlord, were now often forced to borrow money to continue operation. As a consequence, many fell under control of their creditors.

Control over mining, particularly where the precious metals were concerned, was also a political concern. In the Holy Roman Empire, a constitutional document of 1356, the Golden Bull, conceded to the several princes what had previously been jealously guarded regalian mining rights. The princes, in turn, generally conceded the actual management of mining to merchants whose wealth made possible a successful large-scale exploitation. Mining, for example, played an important role in the rise of the fortunes of the Fugger banking family. Independent capital was also important in England and Scotland, but in France the regalian claims of the crown were generally maintained. It should be added here, that, although the cleavage between capital and labor became more marked during the fifteenth century, the miner was still regarded as a substantial member of society.

The commercial and technical achievements of the late middle age made possible, toward the end of the period, a venturing beyond Europe's historic coastal seas. The arts of shipbuilding and navigation were well developed. In the fourteenth century a large number of carefully drawn portable maps (*portolani*) were available, indicating shore lines, harbor channels, and the like; and at least for the well-traveled routes, they were quite accurate. Simultaneously, improvements were made in the compass, and the astrolabe was already known if not universally used. In the fifteenth century, the sailing vessel known as the caravel was developed, usually having three masts.

There had been some venturing into the Atlantic before the fifteenth century. Even in ancient times, both Greek and Phoenician sailors had sailed out beyond the straits of Gibraltar and discovered what they called the "Fortunate Isles" or what we know as the Canaries. Though these Atlantic islands had afterwards been neglected and forgotten, they seem to have been rediscovered in the year 1270 by a Genoese navigator, Malocello by name. Thenceforth, other Genoese penetrated the Atlantic fairly frequently, and certainly visited Madeira and the Azores as well as the Canaries. Moreover, they learned something of the northwest coast of Africa and may well have considered the possibility of reaching India by encircling that continent. Apparently, however, the first European to explore the Atlantic coast of Africa was not a Genoese but a Frenchman, Anselm Desalquier of Toulouse, who

[1] Maritime law codes associated with Lübeck, with Barcelona, and with Oléron, a town on the western coast of France, and generally similar in nature, facilitated the settlement of disputes between merchants, ship-owners, sailors, and governmental authorities in widely separated parts of the continent.

visited Guinea, lived in the Niger region for several years, and returned in 1417 with the story of his exploits. We have already mentioned the regular trips of the Venetian galleys to Flanders.

There was also some penetration into the interior of Africa. Venetians went up the Gambia River in 1455, and a Florentine expedition reached Timbuktu in 1469. In the long run, however, Italians did not profit from these ventures. Rather, it remained for national states along the Atlantic seaboard—Portugal, Spain, England, and France—to be the pioneers in this endeavor. Hence before considering the great voyages of discovery, it will be well to trace the development of the states of Europe in the late middle age.

Fifteenth century air-conditioning by Leonardo da Vinci (*d. 1519*). A full story-high wheel, partly driven by water-power, forced cool air into the apartment of Beatrice d'Este, the wife of Leonardo's patron, Ludovico Sforza (see p. 320).

Courtesy the IBM Collections

The Pietà of Avignon by an unknown French painter of the mid-fifteenth century.

Courtesy Louvre Museum, Paris

CHAPTER 23

MONARCHY IN FRANCE AND ENGLAND

The Hundred Years' War and its Aftermath

Previous chapters have traced the development of the French and English monarchies up to the early decades of the fourteenth century. It will be recalled that, despite considerable progress toward governmental integration, neither country—and this is particularly true of France—had achieved real national unity. This was further retarded in succeeding decades not only by the economic depression described in the previous chapter, but also by protracted war between the two countries and bitter internal strife. Not until late in the fifteenth century was either monarchy able to promote national consolidation in any systematic fashion.

A. The Hundred Years' War, 1337–1453: First Stage

The Hundred Years' War was so named, not because actual fighting was continuous for a whole century, but because certain issues which precipitated the struggle were settled only after that long period of time. Foremost among these was the continued possession by the kings of England of lands in southwestern France. These were Guienne and Gascony, the residue of the great fief of Aquitaine which had first been acquired by Henry II.[1] The French government, which aspired to take over these provinces, continually harassed the English administration with various claims to jurisdiction, especially the hearing of appeals. A further source of conflict was the French insistence, according to treaties made between Louis IX and Henry III (1259), that the English king must do liege homage for these lands.

A more serious bone of contention was Flanders, a fief of the French crown, but closely associated economically with England. The Flemish burghers had been irked by efforts of Philip IV to curtail their traditional liberties and to strengthen French authority over them. Following a victory at Cassel (1328) by Philip VI and further curtailment of privileges, many Flemish emigrated to England.[2] Somewhat later, the Count of Flanders, doubtless acting on the suggestion of King Philip, arrested English merchants. Whereupon Edward III of England, perhaps hoping to stimulate a revolt in Flanders, retaliated by placing an embargo on the export of English wool to Flanders and by arresting Flemish merchants in England.

Minor irritations also contributed to the outbreak of war. English and French sailors frequently came to blows over fishing rights in the English channel, and bloody reprisals occurred. Then, too, just as the English supported the Flemish, so the French maintained an alliance with the Scots, who successfully resisted efforts of English kings to incorporate them into the English monarchy.

[1] See above, p. 205.

[2] The town where most of them settled, Worsted, is appropriately memorialized as the name of a type of cloth.

All these sources of disagreement were critically complicated by a disputed succession to the French throne. With the death in 1328 of the last of the sons of King Philip IV,[1] the direct male line of the Capetian sovereigns of France came to an end. Actually, the nearest surviving male relative was King Edward III of England, who, through his mother Isabelle, was Philip IV's grandson. But the French, maintaining that the royal succession could not pass through a woman,[2] chose Philip of Valois, son of Philip IV's brother. He became King of France as Philip VI (1328–1350).

In the critical years 1337 and 1338 Edward made formal claim to the French crown,[3] and the Flemish under the expert leadership of Jaques van Artevelde, a weaver of Ghent, launched a revolt against the French. After a brief period of neutrality, the Flemish formally allied themselves with the English, and an Anglo-Flemish fleet won a victory off the Flemish coast at Sluys (1340). Meanwhile, highly destructive raiding expeditions were conducted in northeastern France and in Flanders.

The death of the Flemish leader, Artevelde, in 1345, temporarily deprived the English King of military support on the continent. Notwithstanding, he fitted out in England an expeditionary force of some 10,000 men, which he landed in Normandy, moved eastward, put across the lower Seine at low tide, and advanced to a hill at Crécy near the Flemish border. Philip VI, with a larger army, followed the English, but failed to trap them at the Seine; in 1346 he joined battle with them at Crécy, the first important land engagement of the war.

The battle of Crécy was important, not only as a signal triumph for the English, but as an example of the newer methods of warfare which they had learned in recent fighting with the Welsh and Scots. For the traditional feudal cavalry, upon which the French chiefly relied, was mowed down by a veritable hail of arrows from English

[1] See above, p. 207.

[2] The authority for this was the so-called "Salic law," presumably derived from the law of the Salian Franks.

[3] Edward quartered the French lilies on his coat of arms and adopted the French motto, "Dieu et mon droit."

infantrymen, armed with the highly effective long bow. This weapon, a simple though powerful arched bow held upright, was capable of a greater rapidity of discharge than the more cumbersome cross-bow of the French.[1] Crécy was a step in the decline of feudal methods of warfare.

We must not exaggerate the speed or intensity of warfare resulting from the new military tactics employed at Crécy. Compared with modern warfare, the fighting in the Hundred Years' War moved at snail's pace. Except for the capture of the important channel port of Calais by the English, and a certain amount of desultory skirmishing, there were no immediate results of the battle of Crécy. It was ten years before another significant engagement was fought. Then the "Black Prince," Edward III's eldest son, who had moved north from Guienne with a small force, inflicted another defeat on the French at Poitiers (1356). The French King John II "the Good," who meanwhile had succeeded Philip VI, was taken prisoner.

Fortunately for France, John's eldest son, Charles "the Dauphin,"[2] took over the reins of government with such admirable courage and efficiency that in 1360 Edward III agreed to peace with him and signed the treaty of Calais (or Brétigny). Thereby the English King formally renounced his claims to the French crown, and in return was ceded in full sovereignty the territories of Aquitaine (including Poitou), Calais, and Ponthieu. John II was to be ransomed, but as the full amount could not be collected, this old French King, honorable knight that he was, and perhaps hopeful of negotiating further, returned voluntarily to England and died there in 1364.

The reigns of Philip VI and John II were marred not only by military defeat, but by spells of political and social disorder. In addition to strife between factions of nobles. there were insurrections known as Jaqueries —so designated from the common name for peasant (Jaques)—and pillagings by the so-called "free companies." These were bands of soldiers who between formal campaigns were organized, often with considerable skill, by various English, French, Flemish, and Irish captains, and who conducted a terrorizing but methodical pillage. Added to all these woes were the ravages of the Black Death (1348–1350) which, as has been explained, carried off perhaps a quarter of the population.

Meanwhile, the Estates General (or embryo parliament) at Paris took advantage of King John's captivity in England and the accompanying disorders within France to assert extensive authority over revenues and expenditures and even over the royal ministers. For a short period in the middle of the fourteenth century it seemed as though the French Estates General might securely establish itself as a paramount factor in French political life. One of its leaders, Étienne Marcel, member of the third estate and champion of a sort of bourgeois revolutionary movement in Paris, discredited the Estates General by his activities. He and his followers murdered a number of the king's unpopular ministers, and he intrigued with Charles of Navarre, properly nicknamed "the Bad," who was a would-be claimant for the French throne. Eventually, Marcel was repudiated by his native Paris and killed. Another obstacle to the Estates General at Paris was the jealousy of local provincial estates throughout the country. Paris was not France; and the efforts of Marcel and the Estates General had little support outside of the capital.

The Dauphin eventually succeeded to the French throne as Charles V, and throughout his reign (1364–1380) French fortunes fared well. Charles "the Wise," as he was popularly called, combined political insight with a cautious though statesmanlike conservatism. These qualities enabled him to stabilize the disturbed political condition of the country and to restore to the crown much of the prestige it had previously lost. Finances were reorganized, and a number of military reforms accomplished. Particularly important was the liquidation of the "free companies." With the help of Bertrand du Guesclin, a Breton noble who was

[1] The "long bow" was apparently first developed by the Welsh, many of whom were now serving in the English forces.

[2] The title of Dauphin, subsequently held by the French king's eldest son, was derived from the province of Dauphiné, east of the Rhône, which had been secured by Philip VI when its Count died childless.

his Constable and who was a competent commander and tough fighter, Charles managed to disperse some of the companies and to incorporate the others into the French army. As a result of the king's efforts a more effective French fighting force was available for continuing the war with the English.

Despite the peace treaty of 1360, the war did continue. The French king would not recognize as permanent a settlement which deprived him of a large and rich part of of France. Avoiding such full-scale battles as Crécy and Poitiers, Du Guesclin allowed the English forces to penetrate and scatter far in hostile country before he attacked them. Thereby he could overcome them piecemeal. He was aided, too, by a weakening of the English command. The "Black Prince," the ablest of the English generals, became involved in the politics of Castile and presently fell ill and died; and his aging father, King Edward III, encountered rising disaffection within England. By 1380, the French under Charles V and Du Guesclin had been so successful that the English retained in France only the coastal towns of Bordeaux, Bayonne, and Calais.

B. The Hundred Years' War: Second and Final Stages

In that year (1380), both Charles V and Du Guesclin died, and with them ended a period of great promise for a unified France. The succeeding period was marked by renewed disasters, the result not so much of any immediate resurgence of English power as of an outbreak of civil war in France. Since the new king, Charles VI (1380–1422), on his accession was too young to rule alone, the administration was shared by various uncles, including the dukes of Burgundy, Anjou, Berry, and Bourbon. Inevitably there was jealousy, and each sought to promote his own interests at the expense of the country at large. Wherefore, if, as the previous chapter suggested, the world was the richer for the art patronage of the dukes of Berry and Anjou, the French people were the poorer. And the misfortune was tragically prolonged when in 1392 the king was afflicted with recurring insanity.

The most prominent of the royal uncles was Duke Philip "the Bold" of Burgundy (1363–1404). He had been entrusted with the duchy of Burgundy by his brother, Charles V, and encouraged to marry the heiress of Flanders, Margaret, in order to break the traditional alliance between England and Flanders and to bring the latter into alliance with France. Shortly afterwards, Philip was further invested with that part of eastern Burgundy, known as Franche-Comté, which was a fief of the Holy Roman Empire rather than of the French monarchy. Gradually, by various means, he acquired most of the territory between Burgundy and Flanders. Thus it transpired that the wealthy Flemish domain in the Netherlands was combined with a territorial state of considerable size and importance on the northeastern borders of France.

For a time Duke Philip exercised a commanding influence over his royal nephew. But gradually a rival influence was exerted by the king's younger brother, Duke Louis of Orléans,[1] until finally the competition for influence at the royal court developed into active hostility between a Burgundian and an Orleanist faction. After the death of Philip "the Bold" of Burgundy in 1404 and the succession of his son, John "the Fearless," the latter instigated the assassination of the Duke of Orléans. This was the signal for the outbreak of civil war between "Armagnacs" (as the former Orleanists were now called [2]) and "Burgundians." And to make matters worse, Paris fell prey to serious industrial riots led by Simon Caboche, a butcher.

Meanwhile the unrest and internal troubles which had disturbed England during the later years of Edward III and throughout the reign of Richard II (1377–1399), the gifted but erratic son of the "Black Prince," were allayed by an enterprising prince of the Lancastrian branch of the royal family who obtained the throne with the title of Henry IV (1399–1413). This monarch's vigorous son, Henry V (1413–

---

[1] Orléans married Valentina Visconti, daughter of the ruler of Milan. This combined with the Angevin claims to Naples to involve France increasingly in Italian affairs.

[2] Their leader, succeeding the Duke of Orléans, was the Count of Armagnac.

1422), perceived in the French civil strife an excellent opportunity to fulfill his ambition to renew claim to the French crown. Hence during several decades of the fifteenth century English energies were diverted from more constructive pursuits at home to the maintenance of costly military operations in France.[1]

In a well-planned invasion, Henry V led his army across the Channel, took Le Havre, and won a signal victory at Agincourt (1415), a victory comparable with the earlier ones at Crécy and Poitiers. And while Armagnacs and Burgundians contested the mastery of Paris and control of the French government, Henry V proceeded to capture Rouen (1419) and to master all Normandy. In vain, a reconciliation was sought between the two French factions in order to present a united front against the English. It failed by reason of a second murder. John of Burgundy, then in control of Paris, met the Armagnac leaders and the heir to the French throne—the Dauphin—at Montereau. As they conferred on a bridge, angry words led to a scuffle in which the Duke of Burgundy was killed. In revenge, the Burgundians allied themselves again with the English.

Faced with the combined English and Burgundian military strength, the French were forced to make peace. The resulting Treaty of Troyes (1420) was most humiliating. By its terms the unfortunate French King Charles VI was to be succeeded at his death, not by his son, the Dauphin, but by Henry V of England, who was married to Charles's daughter. Two years later both Charles VI and Henry V died, and the rights of the latter to the throne of France passed to his infant son, Henry VI, now formally King of both England and France.

The Duke of Bedford, regent for France during Henry VI's minority, consolidated English control of northern France, gave Normandy an excellent administration, and prepared, with Burgundian support, to overcome French resistance in other parts of the country. Nevertheless, the English position was insecure in many ways. Bedford's regime, however efficient, was not popular with the majority of native French-

[1] On the economic implications of Henry V's policies, see above p. 271.

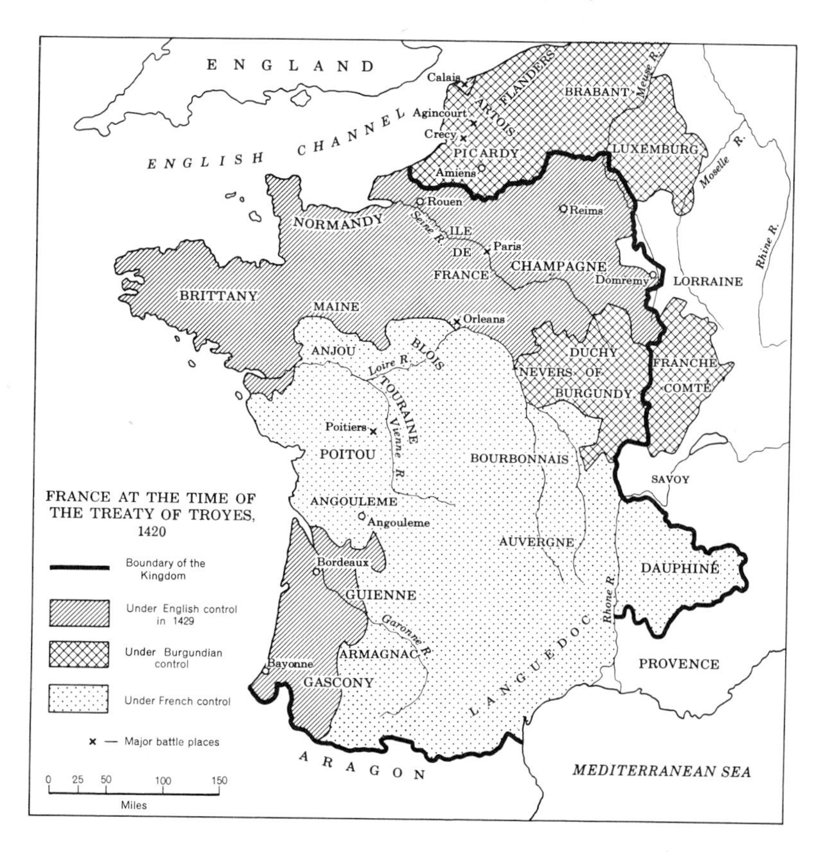

men, who recognized the English as being of different speech and nationality and derisively called them "goddams." Then, too, the Dauphin, the son of Charles VI, refused to recognize the Treaty of Troyes which had disinherited him. He assumed the title of Charles VII, established a temporary capital at Bourges, and maintained some forces in the field. The Armagnacs adhered to his cause, as did most other Frenchmen who disliked the Burgundians. Even the Burgundians were not thoroughly loyal to their English alliance. They regarded it merely as a temporary means of overcoming their Armagnac rivals in France.

The Dauphin, Charles VII, was not exactly a prepossessing figure. He was slight and bandy-legged, and he was nicknamed by his adversaries the "king of Bourges." But he also acquired the appellation of "the Well Served." The first who served him well was a remarkable peasant girl named Joan of Arc.

The story of Joan of Arc has had such universal human appeal as to have become almost a legend. Indeed, much has been claimed for her which never happened. She did not single-handedly drive the English from France. Her military exploits were extraordinary, but not in themselves decisive. But she did help to crystallize an incipient French patriotism. This was her real achievement.

Joan was a humble peasant girl of Domrémy,[1] near the Lorraine frontier, a region which had witnessed a great deal of fighting between Burgundians and Armagnacs. She disliked the Burgundians and was well aware of the distraught condition of France. Though uneducated, she possessed an unusual native intelligence and quick wit. She was deeply religious, much given to meditation, and especially devoted to Saints Michael, Catherine, and Margaret. To their "voices" she listened. They told her to go to the King and bring him to Reims to be crowned. She approached a local lieutenant of the Dauphin, and he was sufficiently convinced by her to give her some sort of escort. That she finally reached Charles VII at Chinon, after traveling some three hundred miles through hostile territory, is a tribute to her inner conviction and her persistence. The King's advisers were naturally very skeptical of this peasant girl dressed in man's clothing, but she convinced the King himself of her sincerity by picking him out of a crowd of courtiers. As a consequence, Charles provided her with armor, a horse, and command over a small contingent.

Joan was not commander-in-chief of the French army, but her presence in it aroused a strange new enthusiasm among a hitherto apathetic and discouraged soldiery. She set a new tone, and, by urging action and more action, raised the morale of the French troops who were convinced that they now had the aid of a saint. Her first military exploit was the driving of English besiegers from the city of Orléans (1428), and so miraculous did it seem that not only were her French soldiers confirmed in their belief that she was "la Pucelle" (the Maid) sent from heaven, but the English became convinced that she was a witch, actuated by the devil.

After the relief of Orléans, the irresolute Charles VII would have preferred to revert to his accustomed lethargy, but Joan, faithful to continuing "voices" of her saints, prevailed upon him to make the journey to Reims, where he was solemnly crowned and anointed in her presence. From a purely military viewpoint, an attack on Paris might have been better, but the coronation at Reims, in the traditional place and manner, was a symbol to the whole country that the "king of Bourges" was now truly King of France. For a moment, Charles could be persuaded to no further activity, and Joan had at first deemed her mission fulfilled when the King was properly crowned. Yet it seems she was persuaded to continue, and presently she was captured by the Burgundians who turned her over to the English. After an imprisonment of nine months, she was tried at Rouen in Normandy, by a local court of the Inquisition, for witchcraft and heresy (1431).

The trial was one of the most famous in history. The judges, presided over by Bishop Cauchon of Beauvais, were French sympathizers with the English and doubtless

[1] Her father's name was Jaques Darc. The name was later changed to d'Arc.

Charles VII of France about 1444. Jean Fouquet.

Courtesy Louvre Museum, Paris

believed, like them, that Joan was bewitched by the devil. They asked her if she was willing to permit the church to decide whether her voices were really of heavenly inspiration or merely the promptings of the devil. Refusal would render her guilty of heresy. For ten weeks the simple peasant girl insisted before the hostile tribunal on her supernatural inspiration and skillfully parried the subtly worded leading questions. Only when worn out in body and mind, and threatened with torture and death, did she admit that the "voices" had been an hallucination. But returning to her cell, she rallied and retracted this admission. Whereupon the inquisitors found her guilty of being not only a heretic and witch, but a relapsed heretic, and as such subject to the extreme penalty. She was turned over to the civil authority, which was English, and by it was burned at the stake in Rouen.

Twenty-five years later, the papacy ordered a posthumous re-trial of Joan's case. This time the earlier verdict was quashed and she was pronounced innocent. Much later, in our own century, the church solemnly canonized the "maid of Orléans" as a saint, not, of course, because of her military exploits, but rather in recognition of the undoubted reality of her personal sanctity and of her intimate converse with things divine. It was the inspiration of her valor and enthusiasm, rather than any military achievement, which counted in the national cause of France.

Following Joan's death, King Charles VII displayed more energy and statesmanship. He opened negotiations with the Burgundians, and at the Congress of Arras (1435), by ceding certain territories to them, he got them to break their alliance with the English. Thereafter, although hostilities with the latter dragged on for another twenty years, the French had the upper hand. Charles obtained appropriations from the Estates General and additional loans, as we have seen, from the banker Jacques Coeur.[1] With such financial backing, he reorganized and enlarged his army. Gunpowder, already in use in the fourteenth century, made possible a primitive sort of artillery. The

[1] See above, p. 270.

English were driven out of Normandy, and in 1453 they lost Bordeaux, their last stronghold in southern France. Only Calais, on the Channel coast, remained to them for another century as a remnant of the former vast possessions and claims of English kings in France.

C. Expansion and Strengthening of the French Monarchy

After the final defeat and expulsion of the English, the French monarchy had still to cope with a number of princes and nobles who in the preceding years had managed to build up a considerable local authority. Most menacing was Burgundy, which had steadily grown in size and strength under the leadership of a line of able and ambitious dukes. Already, Duke John "the Fearless" (1404–1419) possessed not only Burgundy proper, with Franche Comté, part of Lorraine, and Flanders, but also nearly all of the Low Countries, or "Netherlands" (Holland and Belgium). His successor, Duke Philip "the Good" (1419–1467), added Namur and Luxembourg and exercised chief control over the neighboring bishoprics of Utrecht, Liége, and Cambrai. It was possible, therefore, for Philip and his successor, Duke Charles "the Bold" (1467–1477), to build up a strong domain, and even, perhaps, an independent "middle kingdom" between France and the Holy Roman Empire. To this end Charles rounded out the Burgundian-Netherlands possessions by acquiring further territories in Lorraine and upper Alsace. And, as though to prove to the rest of Christendom that Burgundy was actually a great power, the dukes magnified their court and spent money lavishly. Philip founded the celebrated order of chivalry, the Order of the Golden Fleece. The dukes liberally patronized the arts and letters and especially fostered a golden age of Flemish painting. They aspired to be at least the equals of the kings of France, and they succeeded in being a most serious threat to them.

Yet eventually the ambitions of the dukes of Burgundy, and particularly of Charles the Bold, were thwarted by the subtler maneuverings of a French king who had little use for the external trappings of royalty. This was the son of Charles VII, the remarkable Louis XI (1461–1483). Louis was small, unprepossessing in appearance, and frequently afflicted by illness. But he possessed an abundant nervous energy, traveled incessantly, and was passionately fond of the chase. He surrounded himself with able associates, few of whom were of the noble estate, and one or two of whom were of very dubious origin. Often preferring devious to direct methods, Louis earned the reputation of being an intriguing, sinister monarch. This reputation was enhanced in his later years, when, made miserable by his illnesses, he more and more withdrew from society. A hostile Burgundian writer spoke of him as "the Spider King," a sobriquet which has come down through the years and which obscures the more positive side of Louis' character. Although, as we have remarked, he was not fond of court ceremonial, he was by no means uninterested in things cultural. He fostered the establishment of printing in France and invited the celebrated artist,

Portrait of Maria Baroncelli. Hans Memling (*d.* 1494).

Courtesy Metropolitan Museum of Art; Bequest of Benjamin Altman, 1913

Jean Fouquet, to be court painter. We have mentioned his concern for the economic development of the country. All in all, Louis was a capable ruler, an accomplished diplomat, and more than a match for the impetuous Charles the Bold of Burgundy.

Charles managed to form against Louis a league of discontented French nobles anxious to frustrate progress in the royal centralization which was proceeding apace since the close of the Hundred Years' War. This "League of the Common Weal" represented a feudal reaction and proved, with Burgundy, to be a powerful combination. Against it, however, Louis XI succeeded, by diplomacy and bribery, in arraying Alsatian subjects of the Duke of Burgundy and also the Swiss, who were fearful of further Burgundian expansion; and when Charles the Bold attempted an invasion of Switzerland, he was defeated and killed (1477). With his death, the League of the Common Weal collapsed.

Louis utilized the occasion not only to overawe rebellious nobles in his own territories, but also to break up and annex a large part of the Burgundian possessions. Duke Charles' only heir was his daughter, Mary, who was unable to prevent Louis from appropriating, in 1482, the original duchy and county of Burgundy, together with Picardy and Artois (in southern Flanders). The remainder of her inheritance—the Low Countries, or Netherlands (including the former French fief of Flanders)—she managed to retain only by marrying Maximilian of Habsburg, Archduke of Austria and heir to the Holy Roman Empire, whose power and threats gave pause to Louis. Although Louis' successor on the French throne, Charles VIII, was obliged subsequently to re-cede Artois and the county of Burgundy (Franche Comté) to Mary and Maximilian, Burgundy proper (the duchy) and also Picardy remained permanently with France.

Meanwhile, Louis XI, on the extinction of the direct line of noble rulers of the old feudal fiefs of Anjou and Maine (to which Provence had recently been added) extended direct monarchical control over them. Then, when Charles VIII, the son

of Louis XI, married Anne, Duchess of Brittany, this large fief in western France and the only remaining feudal estate of first-rate importance in the country, passed to the crown and was incorporated in the royal domain.

Although the early decades of the fifteenth century had brought to France military disaster and civil war, governmental progress was again possible during the later years of Charles VII's reign. In order to effect the military reorganization which brought the Hundred Years' War to a conclusion favorable to France, the Estates General empowered the King to levy a direct land tax, the *taille*. This tax, voted as a permanent right to a monarch then successful in war, went a long way toward making the crown financially independent. As a consequence, the French Estates General had no effective means of controlling royal policy, and it became a rather useless body. Louis XI seldom convoked it. And since Louis not only repressed the nobles but also consistently sponsored the interests of the bourgeoisie, the latter came to regard the old urban liberties, and the Estates General on which these depended, as less desirable than the security which a strong monarchy could now ensure.

Important military reforms were also begun by Charles VII. Since no formal treaty concluded hostilities in 1453, royal ordinances regarding the organization of companies, including companies of artillery, provided for a standing army. The church in France had also been largely brought under royal control, as a contemporary crisis in the papacy permitted an arrangement, called the Pragmatic Sanction of Bourges (1438), whereby the French king would appoint the bishops.[1]

By 1500, the French crown had subdued most of the older feudal lords, had become mainly dominant over the towns, and had furthered the development of governmental institutions. France was not yet an absolute monarchy, however, and the government was still far from centralized. There remained many local differences of custom, of law, and even of language. Moreover, French kings beginning with Charles VIII, the successor of Louis XI, were tempted by the divisions in the Italian peninsula to expend valuable energy and resources in asserting dynastic claims there. But royal authority, though far from uncontested, was now paramount, and the direction of future political progress clearly indicated.

D. English Political Developments in the Fourteenth and Fifteenth Centuries

Like other European countries, England passed through a period, from 1300 to 1500, characterized by the decline of medieval institutions. Unlike France, where the long Hundred Years' War was actually fought, England escaped its devastation and the depredations of unemployed soldiery. But the Black Death visited England as well as France and occasioned equally profound social disturbance. Nor was the protracted warfare in France without important effect on the development of English government. In the fourteenth century England witnessed a growing constitutional limitation of monarchy by Parliament. The exigencies of foreign war and its consequent drain on the finances had early forced Edward III (1327–1377) to summon frequently the English Parliament; and during his reign it began to assume a bicameral (or two-chamber) form unlike the contemporary Estates on the Continent, which met in three or even four bodies.

In the English Parliament, the upper house, or House of Lords (Peers) to use its later designation, included such tenants-in-chief as had customarily constituted the king's Great Council, together with the bishops and abbots many of whom were bound by ties of kinship to the nobility.[2] At the same time, the lesser gentry, consisting of baronets and knights of the shires

[1] On the contemporary papal crisis of the Great Schism, see below, pp. 325–327.

[2] The representatives of the lower clergy dropped out and never became a part of Parliament.

It is important to distinguish between the king's Council in parliament and the king's Council out of parliament. The latter was the group of officials and regular consultants of the king who assisted him in the daily routine of government.

(or counties) associated themselves with the town representatives and sought a "common" place of meeting. This House of Commons, as it came to be called, was not at the outset the powerful legislative body it is today. For in the fourteenth and fifteenth centuries the nobles in the House of Lords usually took the initiative in political matters. But the Commons, and the burgesses in particular, having more money than anyone else, were not slow to make their influence felt. In the long run, they would prevail.

The functions and powers of the English Parliament, though still relatively undeveloped, were extended and clarified in the fourteenth century. As the king's council, Parliament was primarily a judicial body, a high court where complaints could be heard and decisions rendered on formal petition. But from the king's point of view, Parliament was also a means of obtaining revenue. As a consequence, it was discovered, especially by the Commons, that when the king was in financial straits subsidies could be withheld unless grievances were redressed. And the king's demands for money increased during the Hundred Years' War. Unlike the French Estates General which gladly voted subsidies to a king who would rid the country of an invader, the English Parliament only grudgingly supported a foreign war. Thus there grew in England a tendency toward financial dependence of the king on Parliament. Edward III, for example, was forced in 1340 to agree that no tax should be levied without the consent of Parliament, and in 1343 he promised to make no change in customs duties without parliamentary approval.

Progress toward a general legislative function of Parliament was also evident, though less marked. Some, but by no means all, statutes were promulgated by the king in answer to parliamentary petitions, but even in these cases, they were apt to be issued after an adjournment of Parliament and to undergo royal alteration. Similarly, parliamentary attempts to control the king's ministers and the appointment of royal officials met with only limited success. In the latter part of the fourteenth century Parliament did succeed in establishing a procedure for "impeachment" of officials, whereby they could be indicted by the Commons and tried by the Lords. Broadly speaking, the English Parliament was acquiring a considerable authority and prestige. The lower house was exercising wide powers in financial matters, while the upper house was continuing and developing the restraints over monarchy which had been set forth in Magna Carta.

During the reign of Richard II (1377–1399), the King's high-handed methods and defiance of Parliament aroused a formidable baronial opposition in Parliament, which ultimately brought about his deposition. The role of Parliament in bringing about the succession of Henry IV (1399–1413) of the house of Lancaster added considerably to its prestige.

Following a general tendency of the time throughout Europe, the English government attempted to limit papal jurisdiction within the country. In 1351, a Statute of Provisors prohibited papal appointments to English benefices, and in 1353 the Statute of Praemunire limited appeals to the papal *curia*. These measures indicated an incipient national consciousness, doubtless accentuated by the fact that, during most of the fourteenth century, the popes were resident at Avignon in France and on particularly friendly terms with French kings, with whom the English were at war. Simultaneously, heresy appeared in England, and, as a later chapter will explain more fully, the teachings of John Wyclif attracted a considerable following known as "Lollards." [1] The Lollards were suppressed by government action. In general, English religious opinion continued to be staunchly Catholic. Such measures as were taken against the pope's jurisdiction did not indicate any widespread departure from the faith.

Although England was not devastated by war, the ravages of the plague had important social and economic consequences. For a time after the Black Death, which affected England as disastrously as it affected the continent, the relative scarcity of labor caused a rise in wages. Then in 1351 a Statute of Laborers fixed the wage rate as it had been before the plague. In the resulting atmosphere of discontent, radical political

---

[1] See below, p. 328.

and social ideas found a hearing. In 1381, after the government decreed a poll tax, there was a formidable peasant revolt, which was put down by the cool hard effort of the young King Richard II. As the preceding chapter has indicated, such revolts were characteristic of the transition from an old order to a new. The English peasant was attempting to get a hearing. And it may further be remarked that he had a spokesman in William Langland whose *Vision of Piers Plowman* reflects much of the social unrest of the age.

Henry V (1413–1422) who led England again to continental invasion was followed by Henry VI (1422–1461). Since the claim of the Lancastrians to the throne was not unassailable and in fact was challenged by their cousins, the Yorkists, and since Henry VI was a weak ruler, factional strife developed over the control of, and ultimately the succession to, the throne. Thus it was that after the conclusion of the Hundred Years' War in 1453, with English defeat, the country was torn by a series of civil wars known as the Wars of the Roses. These were wars over the royal succession between rival houses of Lancaster and York, the former with a red rose as its emblem, and the latter with a white rose. The struggle involved much disorder and violence, and in the course of it a large part of the old nobility was killed, while Parliament, split into factions, was temporarily weakened. For a time the Yorkists had the upper hand under Edward IV (1461–1483). But the strife was not ended until Henry Tudor, indirectly connected with the Lancastrian house, gained a decisive victory over the Yorkist King Richard III in 1485 and assumed the crown as Henry VII and married a surviving Yorkist princess.

During the Wars of the Roses, there had been shocking disregard or manipulation of the usual judicial processes. Nevertheless, although common law procedures were endangered by violence and intimidation, they did not collapse. Then, too, in the realm of local administration, officials known as justices of the peace, and appointed by the crown from among the lesser landowners, acquired in the fourteenth and fifteenth centuries considerable administrative, police, and judicial authority.

When Henry VII (1485–1509), the first Tudor, came to the throne, the country was generally sick of war, disorder, and anarchy, and ready to welcome a strong monarchical rule which would put an end to the internal troubles that had so long disturbed the kingdom. And Henry did, in fact, repress disorder with a heavy hand. He established the Court of Star Chamber and other royal or "prerogative" courts which were not bound by the ordinary rules of common law procedure. They could, for example, make the accused testify against himself by means of torture. These courts were used to try political cases and to convict great nobles or important people who might have overawed a regular court.

Realizing that financial difficulties could weaken his position, Henry VII practised careful economy. By a foreign policy of peace, he reduced expenditures. At the same time, he increased his revenues by prudent management of the crown lands, by regular collection of feudal dues and taxes (such as import and export duties), and by imposing fines and "benevolences" (forced gifts) on the wealthy. Thus the king was less dependent on Parliament. And since he promoted foreign trade he won the support of many merchants. With Henry VII began the Tudor policy of controlling, manipulating, bribing, but not abolishing, Parliament.

In international politics, Henry VII sought to increase his prestige by arranging marriages for his children. His son Arthur was married to Catherine, daughter of Ferdinand and Isabella of Spain and aunt of the future Holy Roman Emperor Charles V. When Arthur died a few months after the wedding, Catherine was married to his brother Henry, the King's second son. The King's daughter Margaret was married to King James IV of Scotland, thereby paving the way for the union of the crowns of England and Scotland just a hundred years later (1603). When Henry VII died in 1509, he left to his son Henry VIII a kingdom strengthened internally by peace and good management, used to strong rule, and bolstered by marriage alliances abroad.

CHAPTER 24

Central and Eastern Europe in the Late Middle Age

A. *Disintegration in the Holy Roman Empire*

In the fourteenth and fifteenth centuries, while France and England were overcoming separatist tendencies of feudalism and were emerging as strong national monarchies, the course of events in Germany was in the opposite direction. Here, instead of more centralization, there was less. Instead of a unifying monarchy, there were multiplying local sovereignties.

One explanation of this peculiar development is that the Holy Roman Emperors had never regarded themselves simply as kings of Germany. As previous chapters have indicated, their domains included Slavic Bohemia, part of the Netherlands, much of French-speaking Burgundy and Provence, northern and central Italy. And until at least the middle of the thirteenth century the imperial title still seemed a valuable prize.

With the death of the Hohenstaufen Emperor Frederick II in 1250 and the extinction of his line shortly afterwards, any prospect of bringing both Germany and Italy into a single solid Empire was dispelled. Subsequent emperors made a few desultory attempts to assert claims south of the Alps, but in the main they abandoned the pretense of controlling Italy and retained only a nominal suzerainty over a few city-states in the north of the peninsula.

Although the relinquishment of Italy enabled the emperors of the fourteenth and fifteenth centuries to concentrate their attention upon the affairs of Germany, they were not able to develop a strong German monarchy. The time had passed when such an eventuality was practicable. For the preceding emperors had so privileged their German vassals and so depleted the royal domain that a policy of centralization was out of the question. What their contemporaries were accomplishing in France and England could not now be commenced in Germany.

There were now in Germany hundreds of fiefs, large and small, ruled by princes, who, under various titles such as dukes, counts, margraves, knights, etc., aspired to ever greater independence of central authority and to ever widening territories for themselves. Most of the larger and more prosperous towns had gained charters as free imperial cities. The policy which earlier emperors had pursued of favoring ecclesiastical vassals as a counterpoise to undependable lay vassals, had served to build up several large, and practically independent, ecclesiastical states, such as the "prince-bishoprics" of Cologne, Mainz, Trier, Liége, Magdeburg, Passau, and Salzburg. The history of Germany was already becoming the history of its many different states—ecclesiastical, lay, and "free cities"—rather than the history of Germany as a whole or of the Holy Roman Empire.

But ancient tradition, and particularly the ancient tradition of some sort of an Empire for Christian Europe, died hard. Despite ample evidence of its actual disintegration the Holy Roman Empire continued with a formal semblance of authority. After an interregnum (1256–1273)

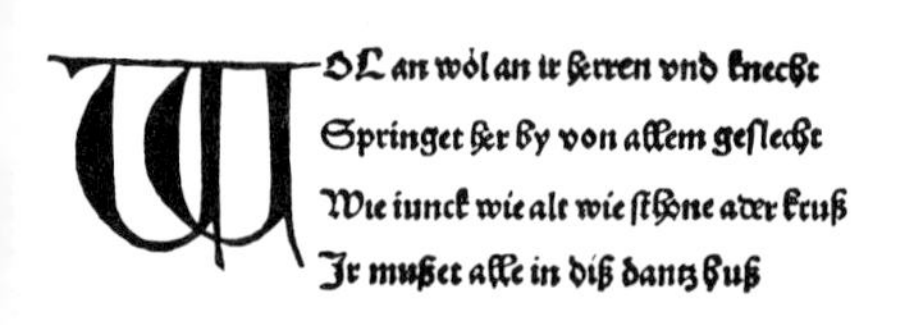

A fifteenth century German woodcut of the "Dance of Death." Heidelberg, 1488.

Courtesy Pierpont Morgan Library, New York

which followed the fall of the Hohenstaufen, a new emperor was elected by the German princes. He was Rudolf of Habsburg (1273–1291), a Swabian prince whose ancestral lands centered in Alsace and Switzerland. Rudolf concerned himself less with trying to rule Germany or the Empire than with utilizing what prestige and influence he had as Emperor to establish an important state for his family within Germany. It so happened that during the preceding interregnum, a particularly ambitious prince of the Empire, Ottokar II of Bohemia, had extended his sway far into the Danube valley.[1] Now, on Ottokar's refusal to recognize Rudolf or to attend his court, the Emperor resorted to force and, after winning a decisive victory at Marchfeld (1278), appropriated for himself the territories of Austria, Styria, Carinthia, and Carniola. These provided the historic center of subsequent Habsburg power and the nucleus for many other possessions acquired by the Habsburg family.[2] However, the very fact that Rudolf was so successful in improving his family fortunes militated against his securing an hereditary Habsburg succession to the Empire. The other princes insisted upon the right of electing the Emperor, and they were averse to electing one who, through too large possessions of his own, might dominate them.

Hence, while Habsburg descendants of Rudolf strove for the imperial title, they were repeatedly thwarted in the fourteenth and fifteenth centuries by rival princely families, especially by the Wittelsbach family of Bavaria and the family of the Dukes of Luxembourg. From the latter was elected in 1308 the Emperor Henry VII, who was haunted by the imperial dream of the Hohenstaufen and attempted to realize it by once more invading Italy. In this he failed dismally. Far more significant was his effort, in imitation of Rudolf of Habsburg, to construct a big family inheritance within Germany. By arranging a marriage of his son with the heiress of Bohemia, he temporarily joined this important state with his original duchy of Luxembourg.

But the other German princes had the same reaction toward Luxembourg power as they had previously had toward Habsburg power. They would have no emperor too strong for them. Consequently, on Henry's death, they chose Louis of Bavaria, a member of the Wittelsbach family, who assumed the imperial crown without papal sanction. His reign (1314–1347) was marked by a controversy with Pope John XXII over the relation of the imperial power to the papacy and the control of Rome and central Italy. Various proponents of anti-papal political theories found refuge at Louis' court. Although the Emperor's attempts to exercise a real power in Italy failed, he did succeed in aggrandizing the Bavarian possessions of the Wittelsbach family and establishing it as one of the major dynasties in Germany.

On Louis' death, the electors transferred

[1] See above, p. 222.

[2] Franche Comté and the Netherlands were added by the marriage of Maximilian of Habsburg (1493–1519) to Mary of Burgundy. See above, p. 285.

the imperial title back to the Luxembourg-Bohemian family in the person of Charles IV (1347–1378). Charles did make an effort, albeit ineffectual, to maintain some authority in Italy. More important was his contribution to the constitution of the Empire in Germany by recognizing its essentially federative character and by regularizing the procedure of electing its emperors. The latter he provided for in a document called the "Golden Bull" (1356). Henceforth there were to be seven electors: three ecclesiastical (the prince-bishops of Cologne, Mainz, and Trier), and four lay (the count palatine of the Rhine, the duke of Saxony, the margrave of Brandenburg, and the king of Bohemia). Within a month of an emperor's death, the seven would meet at Frankfurt-am-Main, and within another month they must choose his successor. If they took more than a month, they would be put on a diet of bread and water. Although papal confirmation was not specifically repudiated, the Golden Bull made no reference to any need of an election's being confirmed by the pope.

The Golden Bull further provided that none of the states of the seven electors should be divided and that, with the exception of Bohemia which was privileged to elect its king, the lay states were to pass from father to son by the rule of primogeniture. Conspiracy against the life of an elector was designated as high treason, and no appeal was allowed from electoral courts. Mining and coinage rights, formerly regarded as imperial *regalia,* were relinquished. Many of these measures, though stipulated for the electoral states, were imitated elsewhere. They operated to preserve the major states of the Empire and to contribute to the acceptance of a divided or federalized Germany.

The seven electors also constituted a kind of upper house to an imperial parliament, or Diet as it was called. This assembly had developed, in the century before Charles IV, from a council, or court, of the suzerain's feudal vassals in much the same way as simultaneously the English Parliament and the French Estates General had developed. The German Diet consisted at first of the chief nobles and clergy who met as two separate estates. Gradually, the "free" imperial cities were invited to submit recommendations, although it was not until the century after Charles IV that burghers constituted a regular "third estate" of the Diet. Altogether, the Diet was unwieldly in size, and its members were so jealous of their respective rights and privileges that it could seldom take any effective action. Its powers remained extremely vague, and as time went on it was called together only in the face of some extraordinary emergency.

Charles IV was succeeded by his son Sigismund (1410–1437), the last of the Luxembourg-Bohemian line.[1] Sigismund was greatly concerned over the contemporary schism in the papacy, as well as over the spread of heresy in Bohemia which resulted from the teachings of John Hus. As will presently be explained, the Council of Constance, which Sigismund was instrumental in assembling, ended the schism and disposed of John Hus.[2] But the heresy persisted and provoked a series of conflicts—

[1] Charles' first son, Wenceslas (1378–1400), was deposed because of drunkenness and general incapacity.

[2] See below, p. 330.

Page from the Constance Missal. Gutenberg. Possibly the first printed book.

Courtesy Pierpont Morgan Library, New York

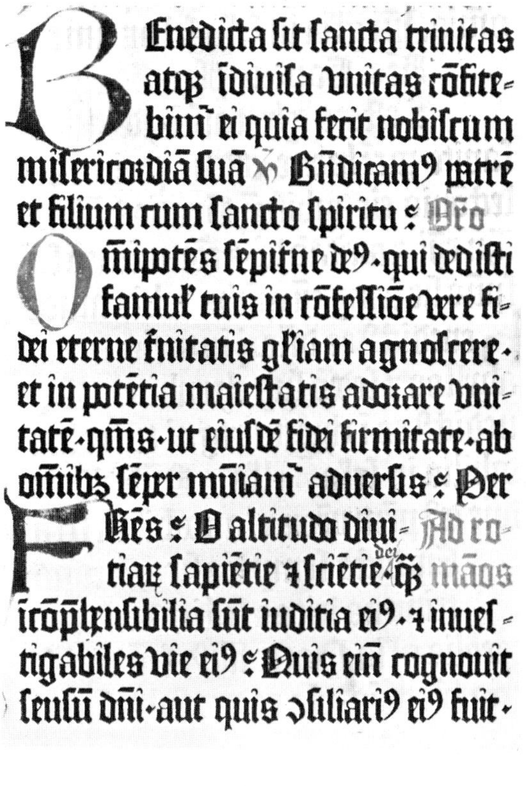
Benedicta sit sancta trinitas
atq; īdiuisa vnitas cōfite-
bim̄ ei quia fecit nobiscum
misericordiā suā. Bn̄dicam9 patrē
et filium cum sancto spiritu. Oro
Omnipotēs sempitne de9. qui dedisti
famul' tuis in cōfessiōe vere fidei eterne trinitatis gl'iam agnoscere.
et in potētia maiestatis adorare vni-
tatē. q̄s. ut eiusdē fidei firmitate. ab
omnib; sēper muniam̄ aduersis. Per
Rēs. O altitudo diui- Ad ro-
tiar; sapiētie et sciētie dei q̄; mānos
icōp̄hensibilia sūt iudicia ei9. et inuesti-
tigabiles vie ei9. Quis eīn cognouit
sensū dn̄i. aut quis consiliari9 ei9 fuit.

the Hussite wars which disturbed the following decades. Sigismund had married the heiress of Hungary, and as so frequently happened in the later history of the Empire, he found his energies absorbed outside of Germany.

After Sigismund's death in 1437, the imperial electors, again fearing a too powerful ruler, turned to a member of the Habsburg family, Albert II (1438–1439). His short reign proved to be the beginning of a long tenure of the imperial throne by members of this family. His successor, Frederick III (1440–1493), the last Emperor to be crowned at Rome, was chiefly noted for his skill in avoiding serious problems throughout a long and rather dull reign. But his son, Maximilian (1493–1519), attempted to improve matters by strengthening the imperial judiciary and by creating, at the Diet of Cologne in 1512, ten imperial "circles" for better enforcement of law and order.

Such measures were taken too late in the history of the Empire to prove efficacious or to halt its development into a collection of states rather than a unity. Moreover, its weakness had tempted more fortunate neighbors. In the course of the fourteenth and fifteenth centuries, France had appropriated Lyons (1307), Dauphiné (1349), and Provence (1481), and had exercised considerable influence in such areas as Lorraine and imperial Burgundy (Franche Comté).

B. *Major Separate States within the Empire*

Really to understand Germany and the Holy Roman Empire in the late middle age, attention must be directed to the separate states. Particularly in the second half of the fifteenth century, certain of the German principalities managed to overcome local particularism, to control or coördinate local estates or diets, and to effect a reasonably successful administrative consolidation. In certain cases, such as the Habsburg lands,

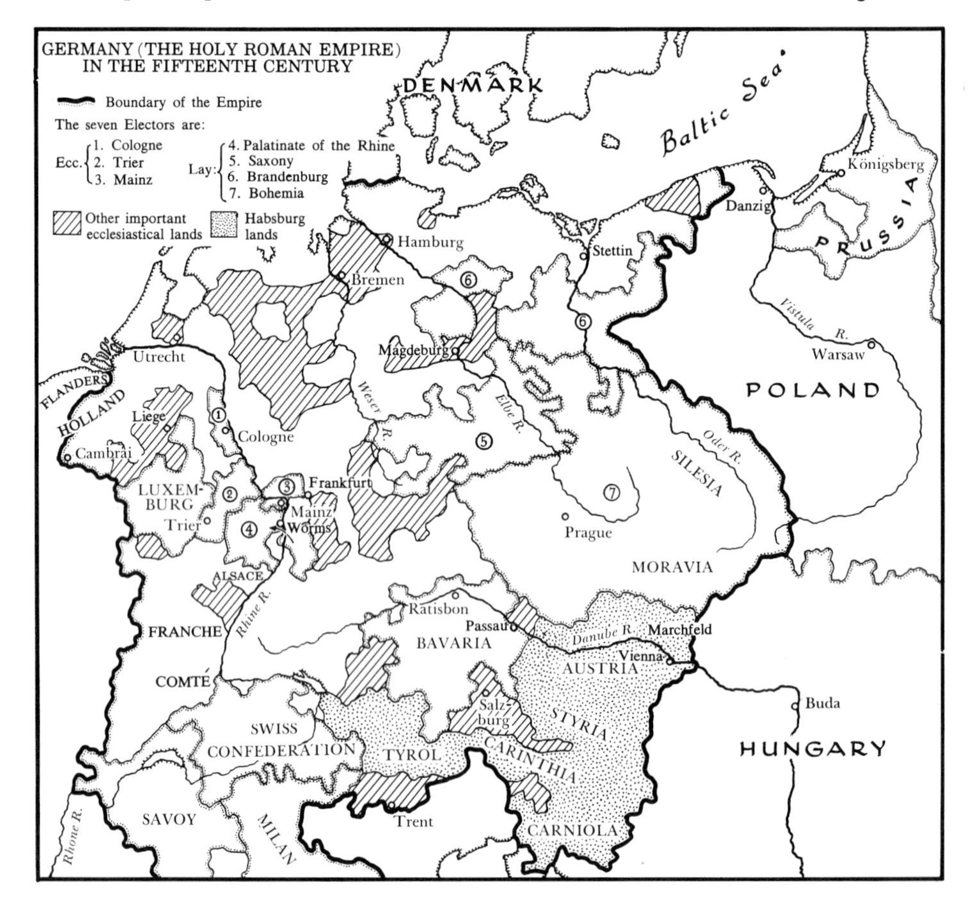

geographical expansion thwarted centralization. For to the already widely scattered territories in the south and southeast of Germany, Maximilian, it will be remembered, added imperial Burgundy and the Netherlands. But other states fared better with consolidation. In 1423 when the previous ruling line of the electorate of Saxony died out, the Emperor Sigismund conferred it upon the Wettin family which already possessed the principalities of Meissen and Thuringia.[1] Both the family and the consolidated Saxony were to play important roles far into modern times.

It was similar with the electorate of Brandenburg in northern Germany. As an original frontier state (*mark*) against the Slavs, it early had considerable military significance. It acquired a new line of rulers (*margraves*) when the Emperor Sigismund in 1415 conferred it upon Frederick of Hohenzollern. Thereby, a previously inconspicuous Swabian family, whose name was derived from a castle on the heights of Zollern, came into possession of territory that would eventually raise the Hohenzollerns to a leading position in Germany, in Europe, and in the world.

German Switzerland differed greatly from Brandenburg or Saxony. It was not a compact state or a rich country. Originally a part of Swabia and the old kingdom of Burgundy, it had developed into a number of mountain and forest communities, or cantons, owing principal feudal allegiance to the Habsburg family of Austria. Three of the forest cantons—Uri, Schwyz, and Unterwalden—had importance because they controlled the main passes through the Alps from Germany to Italy; and transalpine traffic promoted the growth of several Swiss towns. Both townsmen and mountaineers resented outside interference with their local liberties; and in behalf of these they were disposed to seek guarantees or to fight.

The canton of Uri obtained its freedom in 1231 through negotiation with the Habsburg overlord. But when, a few years later, Rudolf of Habsburg became Holy Roman

The Emperor Maximilian (*d.* 1519). Etching and engraving by Lucas van Leyden.

Courtesy Museum of Fine Arts, Boston

Emperor and attempted to enforce his authority over the cantons, the hardy Swiss resisted him.

By a "Perpetual Pact" of 1291 the three forest cantons agreed to united action, and thus laid the foundations for the Swiss Confederation. They administered a stinging defeat to Austria and the Habsburgs in 1315, and in the same year they solemnly renewed their Pact. Fighting continued intermittently for a long time. Occasionally the Swiss suffered reverses in their struggle for independence, but they stubbornly kept on opposing each fresh attack upon them. Gradually the three forest cantons were joined by others, including the towns of Lucerne, Zürich, Berne, Fribourg, and Basel, until by the early sixteenth century there were thirteen cantons in the Swiss Confederation. With increasing strength, they won several victories in the fourteenth and fifteenth centuries over the Habsburgs, sometimes with the assistance of rival Emperors. At length, Maximilian, after still another unsuccessful attempt to subdue the

[1] This Electorate of Saxony consisted of a mark (or outpost) of the much older Saxony, which had been divided by Frederick Barbarossa in the twelfth century after his defeat of Henry "the Lion." See above, p. 214.

Swiss, confirmed their liberties by the Treaty of Basel in 1499.[1]

Their long war of independence, lasting more than two centuries, gave the Swiss the reputation of being the best fighters in Europe. Consequently they were widely employed as mercenaries by foreign rulers. There was long a Swiss Guard in the French army, and there is still a Swiss Guard for the pope.

Bohemia occupied a unique position in the Empire. Its population was predominantly Slavic, and its history continued to be associated, as it had been in the past, not only with Germany but with the kingdoms beyond the eastern frontiers of the Empire. Bohemia quite naturally attained an especial prominence under the Emperor Charles IV of the Luxembourg-Bohemia dynasty. He understood the people of his own kingdom, the native Czechs, and spoke their language. In 1344 he obtained the separation of the bishopric of Prague from the German ecclesiastical province of Magdeburg and its erection into an independent archdiocese. In 1348 he founded the university of Prague. Charles was also a patron of the arts and letters and a friend of the humanist Petrarch who at one time visited Prague.

Although many Germans had penetrated into various regions of Bohemia and neighboring Moravia and were playing a prominent part in the life of the country, a Czech national feeling was growing in the late middle age and was manifested in the multiplicity of Czech literary works and by the warm reception accorded to such popular preaching in the vernacular as that of John Hus.[2] Under Wenceslas, the successor of Charles, the former German domination of the university was ended.

When Sigismund, the last of the dynasty, began to occupy himself with the affairs of Hungary, the fate of the Bohemian kingdom became increasingly linked with developments in eastern Europe. It retained, however, its identity as an important Slavic kingdom within the central European complex of individual states which the Holy Roman Empire was fast becoming.

C. *Scandinavia, the Baltic Lands, and East Central Europe*

The development of the Scandinavian kingdoms was affected by the expansion into that region, and the appropriation of much of its commerce, by the Hanseatic League. As a consequence, the kings of Denmark, Norway, and Sweden were not able, as were the kings of France and England, to utilize an active native middle class against the dominance of landed magnates. Until late in the middle ages the nobility of all three kingdoms played a leading role in military, political, and social life.

Toward the end of the fourteenth century, an extraordinary woman gave promise of improving the political situation. This was Queen Margaret, daughter of a Danish king and wife of a Norwegian king. Following the deaths of father and husband, she joined Norway (and Iceland and Greenland) with Denmark. Then, after protracted negotiations, and no little fighting, she managed to overcome opposition of both nobility and Hanseatic League in Sweden and to secure this country's adherence to the so-called Union of Kalmar (1397), whereby all three Scandinavian kingdoms agreed to form a single monarchy and to accept a common sovereign named by Margaret. Unfortunately, the sovereign so named lacked Margaret's diplomatic and military ability, as did also his successors during the fifteenth century. One of them, Christian I, ceded the Orkney and Shetland Islands to Scotland in 1468 as dowry for his daughter on her marriage into the Scottish royal family. Within the Scandinavian kingdom there was much political disorder and backwardness.

Culturally there was progress. A university was founded at Copenhagen, in Denmark, in 1476, and another at Upsala, in Sweden, in 1477. Both speedily became important centers of intellectual life, and Upsala gave special impetus to nationalist sentiment in Sweden.

The Swedes never took kindly to the Union of Kalmar. They repeatedly challenged it and demonstrated a constant

---

[1] This was internationally guaranteed by the chief European powers in the Peace of Westphalia of 1648. See below, p. 402.

[2] The Hussite movement drew upon the Czech element and Czech national feeling. See below, p. 330.

The Prodigal Son. Albrecht Dürer (*d.* 1528).

Courtesy Museum of Fine Arts, Boston

disposition to break away from it and to set up a separate national monarchy of their own. Moreover, many of them migrated northward and eastward into Finland, and brought this area into subjection to Sweden. Viborg, which would have great modern importance in the northern Baltic, was already, in the fifteenth century, a strongly fortified Swedish outpost.

It had seemed in the thirteenth and early fourteenth centuries as if the greater part of east central Europe, from the northern Baltic to the southern Danube basin, might be dominated by the German expansion eastward which was being promoted militarily and politically by the crusading Order of Teutonic Knights, and commercially by the Hanseatic League. The Teutonic Knights in

1346 added Estonia, just south of the Gulf of Finland, to their earlier conquests of Prussia and other lands along the southern and eastern coasts of the Baltic. Towns on these coasts, such as Riga and Danzig, were being monopolized by Hanseatic merchants, while German colonists, overrunning Prussia, were seeping into Poland and Lithuania. Still farther south, Germans were settling in Slavic Bohemia.[1]

Against the influx and threatened dominance of Germans, not only the Czechs of Bohemia, but also the Slavic Poles and the Baltic Lithuanians developed, in the fourteenth century, a protective national spirit which eventually set limits to German expansion and helped to establish large and powerful Slavic kingdoms in east-central Europe. In 1386 was arranged a union between the kingdom of Poland and the principality of Lithuania which had recently been greatly expanded at the expense of Russians, Tatars, and South Slavs. Jadwiga, heiress of Poland, married Prince Jagiello of Lithuania, who, as part of the agreement, accepted Catholic Christianity with all his people and became joint King of the two countries. Thereby the Teutonic Knights were deprived of the religious basis for their "crusade" against the pagan Lithuanians, and were confronted with combined forces superior to their own. In 1410 a Polish-Lithuanian army invaded Prussia and decisively defeated the Teutonic Knights near Tannenberg. This historic battle not only regained for the victors the province of Samogitia (on the Baltic, between Prussia and Estonia) but it marked the decline of the Teutonic Knights as a military power. Their internal discipline decayed, and a second attack upon them ended in 1466 in the ceding by them to Poland of West Prussia[2] (Pomerelia), including Danzig and its hinterland in the Vistula basin. East Prussia, henceforth separate from Germany, was retained by the Knights, but as a fief of the Polish king. Early in the sixteenth century the territories of the Teutonic Order were secularized, East Prussia being henceforth designated a duchy.

German eastward expansion, a movement of several centuries' duration and one of the major achievements of the German people during the middle ages, was thus finally halted. It had permanently altered the linguistic and national complexion of the coastal area stretching from the Elbe to the Gulf of Finland. The region of Prussia had been thoroughly Germanized, and the Baltic regions to the northeast had acquired, above the native peasantry, a German landholding class. Moreover, Bohemia and Poland, although retaining their essentially Slavic character, had received a considerable number of German settlers. Though Germany failed to become a national state in the middle ages, the eastern areas which it then colonized were to be objectives for the German national state of our modern twentieth century.

As a result of its victories over the Teutonic Knights, the Polish-Lithuanian state achieved great prominence in the affairs of eastern Europe. Already in the fourteenth century, especially during the reign of Casimir III the Great (1333–1370), Poland was making notable advances both politically and culturally. Though forced to admit the absorption of Silesia by Bohemia and of Polish Pomerania (Pomerelia) by the Teutonic Knights, he added to the kingdom's southeastern territories by occupying the Lithuanian (and formerly Russian) province of Galicia, thus increasing the Ukrainian element in an already heterogeneous population. There were many immigrants, not only Germans, but also Jews and Armenians, who swelled the population of Poland, especially of its towns. Something of the development common to the states of western Europe took place in Poland, as the number of cities and the volume of trade increased. Besides, in establishing in 1364 at the capital city of Cracow a school which in 1400 was raised to the rank of a first-rate university, King Casimir enabled Poland to assume a position of leadership in the intellectual and cultural life of east-central Europe.

South of the Polish-Lithuanian state was the Magyar kingdom of Hungary, which for a century after the extinction of its native dynasty (the Arpad) in 1308, was contended for by rival foreign princes of Angevin, Luxembourg, and Habsburg families,

[1] See map above, p. 223.

[2] This territory of "West Prussia" was roughly the same as the Polish "corridor" of 1919–1939.

and also by Polish kings. Sigismund of Luxembourg-Bohemia and the Holy Roman Emperor, for example, was also King of Hungary, and Ladislas I, who died fighting the Turks at Varna (1444), was King of Poland as well as of Hungary. But in no case did rule by a foreign king mean the political incorporation of Hungary into any other state.

The Magyars were intensely jealous of their national independence, and their patriotism was heightened by chronic warfare with the Ottoman Turks who were overrunning southeastern Europe. In this struggle, a leading figure on the Hungarian side was a frontier nobleman, John Hunyadi by name, whose son became one of the country's most famous kings—Matthias Corvinus "the Just" (1458–1490). Matthias built up an efficient administration and patronized scholarship. He collected a celebrated library, the *Bibliotheca Corvina*, containing a large number of valuable books and manuscripts. His successor, Ladislas II, also King of Bohemia, arranged marriages for members of his family with the Habsburgs, thus paving the way for the ultimate succession of both kingdoms in 1526 to the Habsburg family.

D. Byzantine Empire, the Balkans, and Russia

As explained in an earlier chapter, the Byzantine Empire suffered territorial losses in the twelfth and thirteenth centuries to Moslem Turks in Asia Minor, to Christian states of Serbia and Bulgaria in the Balkans, and to the Venetians in Greece.[1] For a time, as the result of the Fourth Crusade, Latin Emperors supplanted Byzantine (or Greek) at Constantinople. Though the latter were restored in 1261, the Empire was never able to recover its former power or prestige.

The rising Yugoslav kingdom of Serbia in the Balkans experienced a notable expansion under King Stephen Dushan (1331–1355). He dominated the whole area from the Danube to the Isthmus of Corinth, subjugated Bulgaria, and even aspired to the imperial throne at Constantinople.

But eventually all three states—Serbia, Bulgaria, and the now diminished Byzantine Empire—proved powerless to withstand the steady advance of the Ottoman Turks in the fourteenth and fifteenth centuries, some details of which we shall narrate in the next chapter. Suffice it here to state that the Turkish conquest of southeastern Europe not only gravely menaced all

[1] See above, p. 224.

Christendom but finally extinguished the Byzantine Empire in 1453 and subjected Greece and the Balkans to several centuries of alien and stagnating rule.

One consequence of the Moslem Ottoman conquest of Constantinople and the Greek Orthodox East was an added significance of Russia as the only remaining independent country whose cultural heritage, however modified by later events, stemmed originally from the Byzantine Empire. For, it was during the fourteenth and fifteenth centuries, while the Byzantines were losing their independence to the Turks, that Russia was winning its independence from the Tatars. This new Russia was not centered as in earlier days around Kiev, which had fallen under Lithuanian jurisdiction, but in the north-central principality of Moscow, which gradually emancipated itself from the Tatar yoke.

The most noted fifteenth-century Duke of Moscow was Ivan III "the Great" (1462–1505), who annexed Novgorod and other rival principalities, conquered certain border territories in White Russia (Byelorussia) and Little Russia (Ukraine) at the expense of Lithuania, and then, after repulsing a final push of Tatars toward Moscow, made his whole dominion entirely independent. After his marriage to Sophia Paleologus, niece of the last Byzantine Emperor, Ivan III emulated contemporary monarchs in pursuit of glory and prestige. He rebuilt the ducal palace at Moscow (the Kremlin), adopted an elaborate court ceremonial, and styled himself "Autocrat of All the Russias."

The church also played an important part in the development of Russia in the later middle age. There had been a notable growth of monastic life. A metropolitan see had been established, first at Vladimir, then in Moscow. And there was growing sentiment that Russia should be, as the Byzantine Empire had latterly been, the exponent and defender of the Orthodox Eastern Church against the Pope and the Catholic Church of the West. Shortly before the fall of Constantinople in 1453, the Byzantine Emperor and a number of prelates of the Eastern Church had agreed at the Council of Florence (1439) to unite with the Western Church.[1] Ivan III's predecessor imprisoned the Russian Archbishop, Isidore of Kiev, who had supported the union, and appointed another. The union lasted, therefore, only temporarily in some southwestern areas, and Russian religious sentiment came to be more and more associated with an incipient national feeling. It was suggested, for example, that as Constantinople had been called the "second Rome," so Moscow was to be the "third Rome." Later, in 1589, the Russian Church was placed under a Patriarch of Moscow whose subordinate relation to the Tsar was analogous to that of the Patriarch of Constantinople to the Byzantine Emperor.

Thus by 1500, though still blocked in the south by Tatars and Turks, and in the west by Poland, Lithuania, the Teutonic Knights, and Sweden, what came to be known as the Grand Duchy of Moscow was emerging as an important state in eastern Europe.

---

[1] See below, p. 331.

CHAPTER 25

Mediterranean Europe, Conquest of the Atlantic

AND ADVENT OF OTTOMAN POWER

Our distinctively Western civilization had originally developed around the Mediterranean. This area remained, throughout the period of the Roman Empire, and on down through the middle ages, the central avenue of cultural as well as commercial progress for the rest of Europe. And although during the late middle age the center of gravity, so to speak, had begun to move northward, events in the lands bordering the Mediterranean continued to be of great significance to the whole of Europe. In the west, much of the ancient Mediterranean unity was still apparent in the close interrelationship of Italy, southern France, and the Iberian peninsula. Such was not the case, however, in the east, where the Moslem Ottoman Turks overran what was left of the old Byzantine Empire and extended their conquests through the Balkans to the Adriatic and across north Africa to Morocco. At the close of the middle ages, a resurgent Islam again menaced European civilization as it had done at the time of the First Crusade in the early middle age.

With the foregoing reflections in mind, we shall now proceed to consider specific happenings in each of the Mediterranean countries during the fourteenth and fifteenth centuries.

A. Portugal and Overseas Expansion

Political life in the Iberian peninsula followed a pattern not unlike that of France and England. True, there was no Hundred Years' War. But there were numerous disputes about royal succession and rebellions on the part of feudal lords or would-be independent towns and provinces; and, until late in the fifteenth century, the peninsula remained divided into the four states of Portugal, Castile, Aragon, and Moslem Granada.

The great achievement of Portugal during the fifteenth century was the exploration of the African coast and the discovery of an all-water route to India. The first step was King John's capture of Ceuta, across the strait of Gibraltar, in 1415. The Portuguese, like the Spaniards, had fought so long to overcome Moslems that crusading was a vital part of their life and thought. Thus they bestirred themselves, at the very time when England and France were locked in mortal combat at Agincourt, to carry the Christian cross into Africa. The conquest of Ceuta was at once a crusading achievement and an incentive to further national expansion.

King John of Portugal had a brilliant son, who, through the greater part of the fifteenth century, was the central figure in Atlantic exploration. This was Prince Henry, commonly styled "the Navigator" (1394–1460). Although he did little navigating himself, he inspired and patronized a vast deal. He was essentially a scientist, intensely desirous of enlarging man's knowledge. Being also a patriot, he aspired to win land and gold and glory for Portugal. And being likewise a devout Christian, he was anxious to gain converts from Islam and to link up European Christendom with the fabled Christian kingdom of "Prester John," formerly thought to have been in Asia, but in the fourteenth century more usually associated with the African Christian Kingdom of Ethiopia. On Cape St. Vincent, whence he could look out upon the broad expanse of the Atlantic, Prince Henry established his headquarters. There he collected and studied all available maps and charts, prepared and equipped expeditions, collated and interpreted reports of returning captains, and constantly encouraged his men and urged them to ever greater endeavor. Incidentally, he employed a number of Genoese as well as Portuguese.

The success of the Portuguese expeditions under Prince Henry's direction was remarkable. Madeira and the Azores were occupied and their colonization begun (1418, 1427). At first, the sailors showed great reluctance to venture southward along the African coast beyond Cape Bojador, but Henry was insistent and the Cape was rounded in 1434. Thereafter progress was more rapid, and Henry's fame mounted. The year 1445 witnessed the passing of Cape Verde, and shortly afterwards Portuguese trading fleets were plying the southern Atlantic. Commercial companies were chartered, and some of them inaugurated a traffic in Negro slaves from the Guinea coast. In 1445 Portugal obtained from the pope an award of all non-Christian territory which its explorers might discover south and east as far as the Indies.

The death of Prince Henry in 1460 did not halt Portuguese advance down the Atlantic coast of Africa. In 1486, Bartolomeo Diaz reached the southernmost tip of the continent, the Cape of Good Hope. Eleven years later, another Portuguese captain, Vasco da Gama, made the first voyage around the Cape into the Indian Ocean, whence he sailed on to Calicut on the western coast of India. This exploit, despite the loss of two of da Gama's three original ships, brought an enormous profit and proved to be the start in the formation of a great Portuguese commercial empire in the sixteenth century.

B. Spain and Overseas Expansion

In both Castile and Aragon, but more particularly in Aragon, the cortes, or parliament, continued during the fourteenth century to play an important part in government. The Castilian cortes obtained the right to propose laws in the form of petitions to the king, who usually accepted them. It also insisted upon its assent to any extraordinary taxation which the king might wish to levy, and upon freedom of speech of its members and their immunity from arrest by the king. The Aragonese cortes possessed even greater powers. It held the king to strict accountability for practically all his actions; and within the kingdom of Aragon, local affairs were regulated by subsidiary provincial cortes for Catalonia and Valencia, as well as for Aragon proper. The English parliament was no unique example of medieval representative government. But just as in France and England, so in Castile and to a large extent in Aragon, monarchy was strengthened in the late fifteenth century through its alliance with the rising middle class; and parliamentary institutions, which had developed out of feudal society, suffered eclipse.

While royal power was being strengthened in Castile and Aragon, an important step was taken toward joining the two kingdoms under a common crown. This was the marriage in 1469 of Queen Isabella of Castile with King Ferdinand of Aragon. They were both highly competent, and quite determined to round out and centralize the common kingdom, henceforth known as Spain. In pursuit of this policy, they resumed warfare with the Moslems in the southern part of the peninsula, and after a long siege they finally, in 1492, captured Granada and incorporated that last Moorish stronghold in their dominions. At Granada still fittingly repose the mortal remains of Ferdinand and Isabella, the "Catholic sovereigns," who brought to successful conclusion the centuries-long crusading of Christians against Moslems in Spain.

In internal policy, Ferdinand and Isabella were confronted with such deep-rooted local patriotism in Aragon and Castile that they retained separate administrations and parliaments for each. Gradually they introduced common practices in both, built up an efficient super-administration, and reduced the meetings and powers of the several cortes. In place of an unreliable feudal force, they established a semi-popular constabulary, called the Holy Brotherhood and subject entirely to the crown. Many feudal castles were destroyed, and privileges of the feudal nobility and knights were notably curtailed. Likewise the charters, or *fueros*, of the towns were revised so that local officials were no longer chosen by the citizens or guilds but appointed by the sovereigns.

The "Catholic sovereigns" were as intent upon cultural and religious as upon political uniformity. Although the long wars of reconquest had bred surprisingly little religious intolerance, measures were now adopted, despite the reluctance of Isabella to accede to her husband's designs, which resulted in the expulsion from Spain of both Moslems and Jews.[1] By means of the ecclesiastical court of the Inquisition, which in Spain passed from papal to royal control, thousands of converted Jews (the *Maraños*) and of converted Moslems (the *Moriscos*) were convicted of heresy and put to death. Though doubtless many of these had professed conversion to Christianity while secretly adhering to their former faith, the wholesale executions were severely criticized abroad. The Pope protested bitterly in 1483, accusing the Spanish sovereigns and their Inquisitors of motives other than religious. But the sovereigns did not desist from their efforts to secure uniformity. They decreed in 1492 that all Jews must accept Christianity or leave Spain. And shortly after the conquest of Granada, despite previous promises of toleration, a similar decree was issued against all Moslems throughout Castile. Thus religious uniformity was forcibly achieved, at the expense of peoples who had contributed largely to Spain's economic and cultural life.

In treating of Spain, we should note that the union of Castile and Aragon combined a vigorous inland state which had dominated the central portion of the peninsula,

[1] It should be observed that much of the anti-Jewish feeling was popular in origin and occasionally the result of inflammatory preaching.

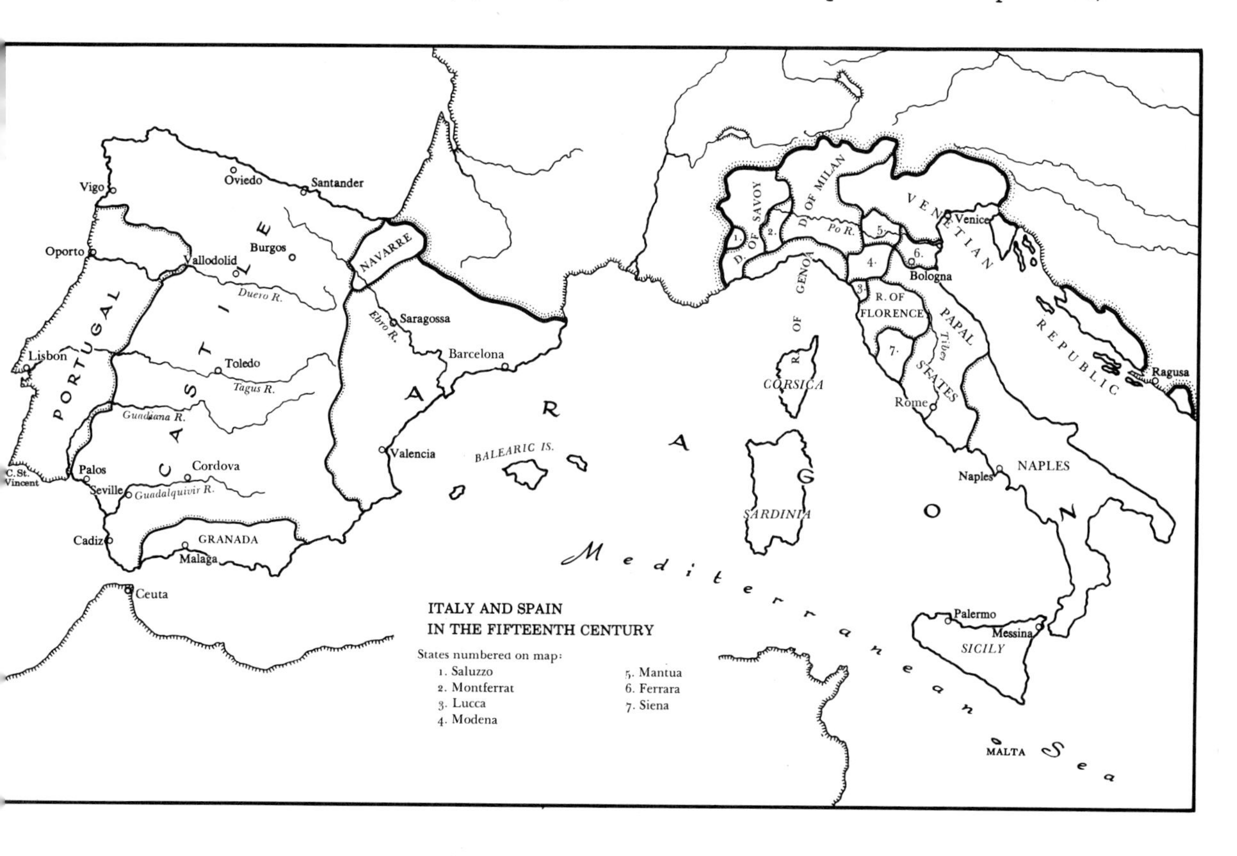

ITALY AND SPAIN IN THE FIFTEENTH CENTURY

States numbered on map: 1. Saluzzo 2. Montferrat 3. Lucca 4. Modena 5. Mantua 6. Ferrara 7. Siena

and which looked westward, with a wealthy maritime state with extensive Mediterranean interests. Aragon had acquired Sicily in 1282. Naples and southern Italy—the other half of the former Norman-Hohenstaufen kingdom of the "Two Sicilies"—remained under Angevin control until 1442 when, as will presently be explained, it too passed into the possession of Alphonso of Aragon. On his death in 1458, the kingdom of Naples was again separated from Aragon, though ruled by kings of the same family until its final incorporation into the united Spanish kingdom of Castile and Aragon in 1504. Meanwhile, before the end of the fourteenth century, Sardinia was also acquired. These acquisitions, together with Malta and a number of ports along the north African coast, constituted a Mediterranean empire of considerable size and strength.

In addition to these possessions, the Spanish, at the very end of the fifteenth century, laid the foundations of what was to become a celebrated and extensive empire overseas. Indeed, in 1492, the very year of the conquest of Granada, Queen Isabella authorized Christopher Columbus to make an attempt to reach eastern Asia and the Indies by sailing due west across the Atlantic.

Columbus' decision to sail west resulted, much as did the Portuguese ventures southward, from a combination of practical experience and theoretical knowledge. The idea of a spherical earth was by no means new; it had been believed by educated men since the days of the ancient Greeks. And although the commonly accepted Ptolemaic geography postulated an earth smaller in size than that of modern calculation, some professors with whom Columbus discussed the matter had made fairly accurate estimates of the Earth's circumference. But Columbus stubbornly clung to his own estimates which were smaller even than those of Ptolemy. As it turned out it was fortunate that he did. With the equipment and supplies at his disposal, he could not possibly have covered the actual distance to the East Indies.

It must not be supposed, however, that Columbus' preparation was inadequate for Atlantic voyaging. A native of Genoa, a city with long-standing maritime traditions, he was a sea captain of much experience which included sailing in the Atlantic. He had studied pertinent geographical writings and he knew Marco Polo's descriptions of the island of Japan and the ports of the China coast. Even so, he had no little difficulty and delay in obtaining needful support for his undertaking. He did receive encouragement from the Franciscan friars at La Rábida, and eventually, in 1492, he secured the invaluable patronage of Queen Isabella. Moreover, he enlisted the practical aid of two Spanish captains, the Pinzon brothers, who supplied him with ships and crews. Incidentally, we may remark that the three ships thus provided (the *Santa Maria*, the *Pinta*, and the *Nina*), though diminutive in comparison with present-day ocean liners, were entirely seaworthy and admirably adapted to the purpose of Atlantic exploration.

After hearing Mass with his men in the little monastery of La Rábida near Huelva on the morning of August 3, 1492, Columbus set sail, and on October 12 made land just about where he had calculated the East Indies should be. It proved to be an island (San Salvador or Watling Island) in the Bahamas off the coast of North America. In the following days, still thinking that he was near the Asiatic coast, he discovered other islands, including Cuba and Hispaniola (Santo Domingo). On the latter island he left a few men to found the first Spanish colony overseas and to locate the gold which he heard about from native "Indians." He then returned to Spain, bringing along some of the natives, and at Barcelona he was received by the Spanish monarchs and their court as a conquering hero. He was fêted and entrusted with a continuing mission of exploring and colonizing lands across the Atlantic.

Columbus made three subsequent voyages to the "Indies," cruising through the Caribbean and finally touching the mainland of South America. The settlers he originally left he could not find again, and in other respects he suffered frustration and disillusionment. True, he eventually founded a permanent settlement at Santo Domingo (1496)—the oldest European town in the New World—but he showed little ability in colonial administration. And, as he failed to disclose any considerable amount of gold or any connection of lands he visited with Asia or the East Indies, his reputation waned in Spain and among his fellow mariners. He died in 1506, ill, worn-out, discouraged, and still imagining that he had reached Asia. He had discovered America without knowing it.

Presently, the truth dawned in Europe that the lands across the Atlantic were not Asia or the East Indies, but a "new world." In 1503 an Italian explorer named Amerigo Vespucci, a native of Florence, claimed to have discovered the "new world." Four years later a German professor suggested that the newly discovered lands should be called "America." The suggestion stuck, and people ever since have described the lands on the western side of the Atlantic as "America" or the "West Indies." just as they have continued to refer to the original inhabitants there as "Indians."

Meanwhile, in 1493, after Columbus's first voyage across the Atlantic, Pope Alexander VI was called upon to arbitrate rival claims of Spain and Portugal to newly discovered lands and seas. He did so by drawing a "line of demarcation" from the north to the south pole, a hundred leagues west of the Azores, and awarding a monopoly east of the line to Portugal and a similar one west of the line to Spain. Portugal protested the award, and the next year, by mutual agreement between the two countries, the line of demarcation was shifted 270 leagues farther west.

Thus it was that at the opening of the new century the states of the Iberian peninsula were not only furthering monarchical consolidation, but were leading the way to new commercial exploitation and the establishment of a new world. At the other end of the Mediterranean, however, an old empire which had stood for centuries as a bulwark against invasion from the east was facing a new and ultimately overpowering attack.

C. *End of the Byzantine Empire and Rise of the Ottoman*

While England and France were engaged in the Hundred Years' War, and while the Holy Roman Empire was disintegrating into separate German states, the historic Byzantine Empire was nearing its end. Weakened by the effects of the Fourth Crusade and the subsequent appropriation of much of its territory and commerce by French, Venetians, and others, it was no longer capable of playing its traditional role as defender of eastern Europe against invasion. As a consequence, when a new and formidable Moslem power, the Ottoman Turks, appeared in the late middle age, it menaced Christendom as gravely as had the Arab conquests in the early middle age.

The Ottomans originated as a small group of Turkish tribesmen who had settled in northwestern Asia Minor following the Mongol conquests in the thirteenth century. They became converts to the religion of Islam, and from the name of their chieftain, Osman, were known as "Osmanli," or, in English, Ottomans. And under Osman and members of his family who succeeded him, they displayed a fighting valor and a fanaticism which rapidly expanded their small territory and population. By 1349 they had breached the Byzantine defenses in northern Asia Minor and captured Brusa, Nicomedia, and Nicaea.

The Ottomans were soon enabled to take advantage of a dispute between rival claimants to the throne of the Byzantine Empire in order to gain for themselves a foothold on the European continent. One of the claimants invited assistance from the Sultan, and in 1356 an Ottoman army crossed the Dardanelles to Gallipoli. Within a few years it subjugated most of Thrace, and the Sultan Murad I (1359–1389) moved his capital from Asia Minor to Adrianople. The conquest of Bulgaria followed, and in 1389 the Serbs were overwhelmed in the battle of Kossovo and their country incorporated in the Ottoman Empire.

With a resurgent and expanding Moslem Empire on the shores of the Danube, western Europe began to take serious notice. The Hungarians were most directly menaced, and their King Sigismund, who was also Holy Roman Emperor, at once joined the pope in urging and sponsoring a new crusade. A temporary lull in the Hundred Years' War made possible the raising of an expeditionary force in the West; and Christian chivalry, mainly French, once more

rode against the "infidel." But the Ottoman armies, under the Sultan Bajazet, were more than a match for the new crusaders. At Nicopolis on the Danube, the latter were badly beaten in 1396.

What saved Europe temporarily was a sudden new irruption of Mongols into Asia Minor under an extraordinary military genius, the Emperor Tamerlane. Tamerlane had already overrun and subjugated northern India, Afghanistan, Persia, and Syria, and he was now invading Asia Minor. Against him the Ottoman Sultan Bajazet, abandoning a contemplated siege of Constantinople, hurried with a Turkish army, only to meet defeat and be captured at Ankara in 1402.

This proved but a temporary set-back to the Ottoman Turks. Tamerlane failed to take advantage of his victory; and his empire was too loose and too far-flung, too much the product of marauding successes, to have any permanence. It began to disintegrate almost as soon as it was formed. Only in northern India did it survive as a compact state. From Asia Minor, the Mongols soon disappeared, leaving the Turks in control and stronger than ever. The fate of Constantinople was delayed but not prevented.

Byzantine Emperors repeatedly pleaded for aid from the west, and these efforts were associated with moves to reunite the eastern and western churches.[1] Successive popes endeavored to enlist crusaders, but they were unable to overcome the divisive forces within Christendom which prevented effective united action. We have already mentioned the attempted crusade of 1396 and its defeat at Nicopolis on the Danube. A half century later, Ladislas, joint King of Poland and Hungary, defeated the Ottoman Turks under the Sultan Murad II at Nish in Serbia, but as he advanced toward the Black Sea he met decisive defeat at Varna in 1444. The Sultan was now master of the entire Balkan area, and ready not only to extend his Moslem Turkish Empire northward into Hungary but also to extinguish, southward, what was left of the Byzantine Empire.

Shortly after the death of Murad II, his successor, the Sultan Mohammed II, laid siege to the venerable Christian Byzantine capital. Only a handful of Venetians were available for help to the hard-pressed Greek

[1] See below, p. 330.

defenders. They fought gallantly, but against overwhelming odds. Constantinople, cut off by land and sea, its walls battered for seven weeks by bronze cannon of the Turks, its last Christian emperor slain, finally capitulated in 1453. Thus fell the "second Rome," the capital of an empire which had continued in unbroken succession the Roman Empire of antiquity.

The Ottoman Empire henceforth centered in Constantinople, or Istanbul as the Turks called it. In a way, it was itself a continuation of the Byzantine, and hence of the old Roman, Empire. But it was Moslem, not Christian; and it represented not a bulwark, but a threat to European Christendom.

Discussion of the government of the Ottoman Empire, of its growing maritime as well as military power, and of its further expansion to include Egypt and nominally, at least, the entire north African coast, must await a subsequent chapter. We would here merely note that Christianity was not extinguished in Greece and the Balkans. Following the usual Moslem practice, Christians in the Ottoman Empire were permitted freedom of belief and worship, subject to the payment of a special tribute. The Orthodox Patriarch of Constantinople was accorded jurisdiction over, as well as responsibility for, all Byzantine Christians. Byzantine administrative procedures were adopted, and many Christian Greeks were retained in civil administrative posts. Under the Ottomans, trade continued and revived throughout the entire eastern Mediterranean region. But it must not be supposed that the lot of the Empire's Christian subjects was entirely happy. They were the *rayahs*, the "cattle" of the Sultan. The great cathedral of Santa Sophia at Constantinople and other famous churches were transformed into mosques. Moslem custom and law favored those who adopted the faith of Islam. Moreover, part of the Sultan's army was obtained by imposing a tax on every Christian family of one boy in five. These were then separated from their families, brought up as Moslems, and indoctrinated with a fanatical loyalty to the Sultan. Reminiscent of the ancient Roman Pretorian guard, they were known as the *Yeni Cheri* (new troops), or Janissaries.

Although persecution of a physical nature was not officially condoned by the Sultans, it was occasionally practiced by subordinates. Nevertheless, the Greek and Balkan Christians not only stubbornly persisted in the practice of their religion; they kept alive the memory of the Byzantine Empire and of the once independent states of Serbia and Bulgaria. Thereby were sowed the seeds of the later intense nationalism in the Balkans.

The impact of the Ottoman power was felt not alone in Christian Europe. Its extension through Syria and Palestine and across north Africa entailed the downfall of other and older Moslem states and the subordination of the Arabs. In the early sixteenth century the Ottoman Empire was the dominant political force in the whole Moslem world. Moreover, the Sultans were champions of the Sunnite, or orthodox, Moslem faith, and, as such, the Sultan Selim I (1512–1520) assumed the title of Caliph, or supreme religious head of Islam. His successors followed his example until the end of the Empire in our own century, so that they were at once Sultans of a political and military state and Caliphs of the religion of Islam.

D. Disunited Italy and Its City States

Italian history in the fourteenth and fifteenth centuries was much affected by the developments in the eastern and western Mediterranean areas which have just been described, but it presents certain features peculiar to itself. It is really the story of separate Italian states, of their internal development, and of their relations with one another and with the outside world. The failure of the Holy Roman Empire of the Hohenstaufen had left the peninsula destitute of any semblance of political unity. Even Germany, divided as it was, still had at least a nominal emperor and a confederation of native princes. In Italy, no prince emerged as a symbol of national loyalty or political federation; no national dynasty claimed the allegiance of all Italians or secured their coöperation.

The defeat of the Hohenstaufen liberated Italy from German domination, but other foreign influences and pressures continued. As has been indicated, French Angevin and Spanish Aragonese dynasties contested control of the south. French interest in Piedmont, Genoa, and Milan added to the problems of those areas. All these external pressures complicated the already chronic rivalries among the separated states of the peninsula.

A further divisive element in Italian history was the absence of the papacy. From 1309 to 1377 the popes resided at Avignon on the frontier of the French kingdom. And for some thirty years after their return to Rome in 1378, a papal schism divided the western Christian world. A subsequent chapter will discuss the religious consequences of these events.[1] Here we are concerned with the political effect on Italy. Not only was a potentially unifying factor temporarily removed, but the absence or weakness of authority in the papal state of central Italy provoked encroachment by neighboring states and usurpation of power by various petty rulers.

While it might appear that all these factors combined to produce a state of hopeless confusion, there is a kind of pattern, not only in internal administration, but also in inter-state relations, which Italian history generally followed in the late middle age. In the fourteenth century, certain of the northern city-states succeeded in expanding at the expense of their smaller neighbors and becoming principalities of some size and strength. Milan and Florence are examples. To some extent, this process continued in the fifteenth century.[2] Venice, hitherto primarily interested in expansion along the Adriatic, pushed westward and southward to become an important land power, and the Papal State acquired a greater stability. But what particularly characterized the developments of the fifteenth century was the creation of an equilibrium, albeit precarious, among the major principalities—Naples, the Papal State, Florence, Milan, and Venice. The equilibrium was precarious, it must be emphasized, because almost without exception these states retained expansive ambitions. Alliances and leagues, therefore, proved temporary.[3] And most dangerous for the future of the peninsula was the tendency, in time of supposed or actual crisis, to seek foreign aid. But it must also be remembered that the danger of foreign intervention which seems so clear to the modern student was evidently not apparent to, certainly not understood by, the Italians of the fifteenth century.

The petty imperialisms of the Italian cities and kingdoms required the maintenance of standing armies more effective than the former communal militias. The common practice was to hire mercenaries who served under, and were organized by, competent captains. From the contract (*condotta*, literally, "leadership"), which was drawn up outlining the terms of service, the armies or "companies" were called *condottieri*. Some of the captains acquired considerable fame. Some changed sides and served more than one city. A few came from outside the peninsula. Manifestly such a system demanded strong government, one able to dominate the troops it employed. In many instances, the *condottieri* system contributed to the decline or abandonment of communal republican institutions.

In internal administration, there is evident a general tendency toward some form of absolutism. Centralization, it is true, was hampered in Naples by survivals of feudalism, the lingering animosity toward a foreign dynasty, and the rivalries of the houses of Anjou and Aragon. And papal government, exceptionally difficult to manage during the Avignon period and the schism, was further endangered by the appearance of local petty despots. Nevertheless, in both these states, an effective monarchy was the goal which their respective rulers sought.

While some of the northern cities boasted old established dynasties, many, as a previous chapter has explained, had adopted some form of republican constitution. But under the pressure of late medieval political and economic conditions, and owing, as we have seen, to the necessity of maintaining companies of *condottieri*, republican

[1] See below, p. 327.

[2] For major states in fifteenth-century Italy, see map above, p. 301.

[3] It is important to note that modern inter-state diplomacy and formal diplomatic usages developed first among the Italian states of the late middle age.

government tended to break down. Power was conceded to or seized by a single person, the lord of the city (*signore*) as the Italians called him. Some—the "despots," as they have often been styled—were descendants of old families. Some were locally prominent citizens who, in one way or another, managed to acquire political power, a few were upstarts, captains of *condottieri*. Often such a ruler was able to secure the support of the less fortunate classes, the *popolo minuto*, against the republican oligarchy, *popolo grasso*. Not uncommonly, too, the *signore* sought from pope or emperor some sort of official sanction as papal or imperial vicar.

A notable example of the development of one-man rule was Milan. Toward the end of the thirteenth century, out of the confusion which had resulted from persistent conflicts of nobles, burghers, and craft guilds, had emerged a rivalry between two great families, the della Torre and the Visconti, in which the latter finally won out. Otto Visconti became archbishop of Milan (1262) and actual ruler of the city. His nephew, Matteo, was appointed imperial vicar, and thus began a succession which was to last until the middle of the fifteenth century.

The Visconti ruled Milan successfully and expanded its domain to the point where it menaced the security of its neighbors. This expansion began, while the popes were at Avignon, with Archbishop Giovanni (1349–1354) and reached a climax under Gian Galeazzo Visconti (1378–1402), who at the time of his death seemed on the point of taking over a large part of northern Italy. This was one of the major crises in fifteenth-century diplomatic history. From the Emperor Wenzel, Gian Galeazzo purchased the title of Duke, and he entered into relations with France by marrying a French princess and by securing for his daughter, Valentina, a marriage with Louis of Orléans, brother of Charles VI. Thus began a diplomatic connection which was ultimately to prove more dangerous than helpful.

Filippo Maria, Gian Galeazzo's successor, was unable to maintain the enlarged Milanese state in the face of Florentine opposition and of Venetian expansion westward. On his death in 1447 there was a brief revival of the republic which, in turn, was followed by the rule of Francesco Sforza (1450–1479), an able captain of *condottieri*. Successful achievement, not dynastic legitimacy, enabled the Sforza family to rule in Milan. Ludovico Sforza (*il Moro*) was something of an economist and promoted agricultural betterment in the surrounding countryside. He was also a patron of arts and letters and brought the celebrated Leonardo da Vinci to Milan.

Ludovico, however, in order to thwart the hostile plans of Naples and Venice, felt it necessary to seek French aid. No doubt he believed that, as had happened often in the past, the threat would suffice. But this time the French were in earnest. The resulting French invasion (1494) will presently be discussed more fully. It was to open a new and unhappy chapter not only in Milanese, but in Italian, history. Ludovico himself miserably ended his days in prison (1508).

The city of Florence rose to eminence in Italy as an industrial and banking center. Commercial success led to imperialism and Florence soon mastered the neighboring towns of Tuscany. Pisa, which controlled the mouth of the Arno on whose banks Florence is situated, resisted for a considerable time, but finally submitted in 1406. Meanwhile, Florence had had its share of class warfare and domestic disturbance. In 1378, a kind of proletarian rebellion, the insurrection of the Ciompi,[1] threatened temporarily the political domination of the aristocratic guilds. Eventually, the Medici, then the leading banking family of the city, gained control of the republican organization. Cosimo, who returned to Florence in 1434 after a brief exile, ruled as a kind of political "boss." His son, Piero, and grandson, Lorenzo "the Magnificent" (1469–1492), built up a strong following and, despite occasional opposition, maintained control over the government. Thus, although Florence remained formally a republic, the Medici were no less *signori*, or "despots," than the Visconti or Sforza.

No less than the Visconti, the Medici sought to promote family interests. Lorenzo,

[1] The leader of the revolt was a certain Michele Lando. The *ciompi* were wool carders.

Lorenzo de' Medici. Verrocchio (d. 1488).

Nation Gallery of Art, Washington, D.C.; Samuel H. Kress Collection

for example, was able to obtain for his son, Giovanni, whom he had destined for the church, important ecclesiastical benefices at an early age. These culminated in his nomination as cardinal at the age of fourteen. We shall hear more of him in the early years of the sixteenth century as Pope Leo X.

The Medici, it should be added, were among the most generous and discriminating of patrons. With the exception of Rome, no city contributed more to the development of art and learning than did Florence. This will be discussed later at some length. But it should be noted here that Lorenzo, as a boy, was brought up to regard some of the greatest artists and men of learning as his companions. Rarely has it been given a head of state to live in such distinguished company.

Toward the end of Lorenzo's career, a Dominican friar, Savonarola, preached a series of sermons which not only won him renown as a popular orator, but carried him to heights of dubious fame in Florentine politics. His eloquent denunciations of current morals and politics gained him a large following among the discontented workmen; and for a few months after Lorenzo's death, Savonarola virtually ruled a city which, in the enthusiasm of the moment, dedicated itself to God. But Savonarola was far from being a prudent or moderate statesman. Moreover, he saw in the invasion of the French King, Charles VIII, God's instrument to purge Italy of its sins.

Savonarola had many enemies, and Medici influence was powerful at Rome. As a result of his defiance of Pope Alexander VI who ordered him to stop preaching, he incurred ecclesiastical censure. In the end, he was tried and burned at the stake in Florence amid the jeers of people who had formerly acclaimed him.

When the Medici returned, they lacked prestige of earlier times. Florence, as all of Italy, now had to adjust itself to foreign invasion.

In many respects Venice stood apart from the main currents of Italian life. Never included in the Holy Roman Empire, it had long maintained close relations with Constantinople. Besides, it was primarily a commercial, not an industrial, metropolis. Its governmental development was conditioned by none of the Guelf-Ghibelline feuds of the Lombard cities and by far less internecine class warfare. Most important, Venice was governed, not by a despot, but by a commercial oligarchy. True, there was a *doge* (duke) who nominally headed the state, but his office was elective and his power originally limited by a popular assembly. Gradually, however, the popular element in the Venetian constitution disappeared. A great council of magnates replaced the popular assembly in 1171, and this in turn was subordinated to a Council of Forty and then to a Council of Ten. Finally, membership in the Great Council was restricted (1297) to those whose paternal ancestors had formerly sat in that body.

Venetian imperialism was of relatively early origin and continued well into modern times. Venice's chief rival, Genoa, was finally worsted and its sea power badly impaired in a war of 1378–1381. During the fifteenth century the Venetian republic possessed the major portion of the Istrian and Dalmatian coasts, various parts of southern Greece, Corfu, Euboea, Crete, Cyprus, and a number of islands in the Aegean. Before the end of the century, however, the Venetians were forced to surrender some of these possessions to the Ottoman Turks. Meanwhile, as we have remarked, Venice, by pushing westward, had become one of the major land powers of northern Italy and a rival of Milan, Florence, and the Papal State.

E. The Papal State and the Kingdom of Naples-Sicily

Milan, Florence, and Venice have been singled out for special mention because in different ways they represented the brilliant, prosperous, secular culture of the city-states of late medieval Italy. Two other states remain to be considered: the Papal State in the middle of the peninsula, and the kingdom of Naples-Sicily in the south.

This latter kingdom, founded by the Normans, had passed to the Hohenstaufen and had then been conceded to Charles of Anjou, brother of Louis IX of France. Following the rebellion of the Sicilian Vespers (1282), Sicily fell under the control of the Spanish house of Aragon, but Naples remained under Angevin kings until 1443 when Alphonso of Aragon temporarily reunited the two parts of the dual kingdom. Again separated on his death (1458), though Naples was still ruled by a member of the family, the two parts were finally brought together in 1504 by Ferdinand, husband of Isabella of Castile. Thus the kingdom of the "Two Sicilies," as it came to be called, formed part of a formidable sixteenth-century Spanish empire.

The Venetian Doge, Andrea Vendramin. Gentile Bellini (d. 1507).

Copyright, the Frick Collection, New York

Although the previous brilliance and power of the southern kingdom did not last into the late middle age, and although it was constantly disturbed by discontented nobles and by the claims of Angevin-French pretenders, it continued to play a major role in Italian politics. Under Alphonso "the Magnanimous," the Neapolitan court enjoyed a certain eminence as a resort of scholars and artists.

The Papal State stood apart from the other Italian principalities as the temporal domain of the Holy See. Yet as a territorial state in the very center of the peninsula, it could not escape the vicissitudes of Italian power politics. During the fourteenth century when the popes were resident in Avignon, the papal lands were menaced by encroachments on its frontiers as well as by considerable internal usurpation of power. For a few years a remarkable individual, Cola di Rienzi (*d.* 1354), gained control over the government of Rome. Playing upon the veneration for past institutions which Romans never lost, Rienzi styled himself "tribune." Temporarily losing his influence, he was driven from the city only to return two years later with the support of the pope. Once again he failed to maintain his power and was killed.

The actual defense and rehabilitation of the Papal State was chiefly the work of Cardinal Albornoz (*d.* 1367) whose combination of military and administrative skill brought a real improvement. But much remained to be done. Ladislas of Naples was in occupation of a large part of the Papal State at the time of his death (1414).

The popes of the second half of the fifteenth century felt compelled to enter the arena of local power politics by raising armies, waging war, and arranging alliances. Moreover, they concluded that, since prestige was then measured by the external display of a court, Rome should be second to none. And Sixtus IV (1471–1484), noting that secular rulers usually had sons and daughters who could profit their countries by holding important offices, contracting useful marriages, and furthering diplomatic policies, decided to make like use of his own numerous nephews and nieces. Systematic "nepotism" had certain advantages, but it was highly dangerous, since the character of nephews greatly varied. A climax may be said to have been reached when Pope Alexander VI (1492–1503), of the Catalan family of Borgia, provided handsomely not only for nephews but for children.

But if the student of religious history is repelled by the career of the notorious Alexander VI, the student of politics can see in the same pope an extremely capable politician and prince. For when Charles VIII of France entered Italy, to the great dismay of all except those who saw him as an ally, Alexander, with consummate skill, made necessary concessions, won over the impressionable King by his affability, ushered him out of Rome into the kingdom of Naples, and then proceeded to build up an alliance behind his back. Once in Naples, disease as well as military inefficiency brought the venture of Charles VIII to an end.

A few years later, Alexander reversed his policy toward the French and secured an alliance with King Louis XII who was making claims to Milan. It happened that Caesar Borgia, Alexander's son, was married to a French princess; and the Pope hoped, with French aid, to break the northern Italian power and thereby to strengthen and enlarge the Papal State. That it did not turn out so was owing in large measure to a new diplomatic orientation which brought Ferdinand of Aragon into possession of Naples in 1504, one year after Alexander's death. This was a critical event in the history of Italy. For to the French in the north were now added the Spanish in the south. Moreover, as we have remarked, Ferdinand represented not merely the dynasty of Aragon, but a united Spain, already a great power.

Shortly after these events a brilliant Italian writer, Niccolò Machiavelli, published a book called *The Prince* (1513), in which, citing examples from Italian history of his time, he outlined the policy which a ruler ought to follow in order to succeed—political expediency and "reasons of state," subordinating all considerations of justice and morality to the needs of the commonwealth. Machiavelli's book, in addition to being the classic expression of what has come to be called "Machiavellianism," has come down through the centuries as an image of fifteenth-century Italy, a land of great brilliance and sophistication, but bereft of unity and lacking in moral integrity, a land of the artist, the artist in statecraft as well as the artist with brush or pen. This, however, is a highly romanticized picture of fifteenth-century Italy. Machiavelli, it must be remembered, was writing in that bleak atmosphere after the French and Spanish invasions had begun. *The Prince* is the treatise of a seasoned but disillusioned politician who has lived to see his hopes shattered and who is groping for an explanation and for a formula for future action. To attribute to Italians an exceptionally large share of unscrupulous political behavior is to misread the history of the age. There were political murders in Italy, it is true.[1] But there was coarse brutality and shocking violence in the north, and calculated intolerance in Spain.

Italy was destined to suffer invasion in the sixteenth century as a consequence of its lack of unity. But Italians had not tried to achieve unity. Rather they sought to create, and in considerable measure succeeded in creating on a small scale, a sense of statehood. To do this they drew on the many sources of their varied political heritage. These were tempered by a searching study of what Rome had once meant and might mean to "Romans" of a later generation. This is one of the significant aspects of what is called the Italian Renaissance and to which we shall now turn.

---

[1] Two murders often singled out as "typical" were the Pazzi conspiracy against the Medici (1478) as a result of which Lorenzo was wounded and Giuliano killed, and the assassination of Galeazzo Maria Sforza (1476). Both were carried out in church. To these might be added Caesar Borgia's "liquidation" of a number of conspirators at Sinigaglia, an affair which Machiavelli described as splendidly executed.

A panel from the door of the Baptistery at Florence. Ghiberti (*d.* 1455).

Alinari photograph

Courtyard of the fifteenth century Bevilacqua palace, Bologna.
Alinari photograph

CHAPTER 26

Learning and Art in the Late Middle Age

THE RENAISSANCE

A. *Italian Humanism and the Italian Renaissance*

Preceding chapters have indicated that the political and economic life of the late middle age presented less uniformity than had earlier centuries. Nascent national states were fostering national cultures, and the intellectual and artistic developments of the fourteenth and fifteenth centuries were correspondingly diversified. Yet there was a pervasive cultural trend which, first noticeable in Italy, ultimately affected almost all Europe. This was a vigorous effort to restore certain important elements in Europe's classical heritage. Although by no means entirely novel—Europeans had repeatedly looked back to Greece and Rome for inspiration—the late medieval emphasis on the ancient inheritance was so extensive as to justify the term "renaissance" (rebirth). In course of time the word, renaissance, has come to signify a period of history, a civilization in all its aspects, political as well as cultural, including, in short, the material of the preceding chapters dealing with European life in the late middle age. Here, however, we are concerned with the renaissance as an intellectual and artistic movement. Basic to it was the literary vogue known as humanism.

Humanism has been variously defined. But in the fourteenth and fifteenth centuries it denoted an enthusiastic devotion to the literature of classical or Graeco-Roman antiquity, the *litterae humaniores* or "humane letters." Latin literature had formed the basis of most medieval education, and during the twelfth century there had developed, as we have seen, a classical culture which might be considered a forerunner of fourteenth-century humanism. That a century elapsed before the literary promise of the twelfth century was fulfilled was largely owing to the more technical spirit of thirteenth-century scholasticism and science which took possession of the universities. The pursuit of metaphysics and the purposeful study of law, medicine, and theology did not, of course, cease in the late middle age. But alongside of these, there grew up, mainly outside of the universities, a veritable cult of antiquity and a searching for those things which, it was felt, would give fullest meaning to the spiritual and intellectual development of the individual man. Thus, although humanism signified to its devotees a fuller appreciation of the good things of this world, it by no means excluded the supernatural or was hostile to traditional Christianity.[1] Indeed, many of its most ardent promoters were ecclesiastics.

It was in Italy, seat of a thriving bourgeois culture and a land where the consciousness of the Roman past had never been lost, that renaissance humanism arose.

[1] The student should realize that at the heart of the present-day debate over the interpretation of "renaissance" lies the question whether it was secular, and "this worldly," as opposed to the "other-worldly" middle ages. See above, p. 264.

Many Italian communities contributed to it, though none more brilliantly than Florence and Rome. And the first of the pioneering humanists, often styled "the father of humanism," was Francesco Petrarca, or Petrarch (1304–1374), who was born of a Florentine family that, like Dante, had gone into political exile. With an absorbing fondness for Latin literature, Petrarch set about collecting the works of ancient Latin authors, and in his many travels he discovered in monastic libraries a number of forgotten manuscripts which he rescued and publicized. Like most succeeding humanists, he was devoted to the works, especially the letters, of Cicero; and in an endeavor to emulate the Ciceronian style, he wrote numerous Latin letters and incidentally composed a lengthy epic poem, *Africa*. Although he failed to master Greek, he appreciated its significance to a well-rounded humanism and encouraged others to study it.

Although Petrarch as a scholar enjoyed the solitude of his country estate near Avignon and retired in later life to a retreat near Padua, he did not hold himself aloof from the life of his time. His travels took him to the Avignon of the popes, and to the Prague of the Emperor Charles IV, as well as to many cities of Italy. Among the many honors which he received was the crown of poet laureate bestowed on him at Rome. He lamented the divisions of Italy and pleaded for the return of the popes from Avignon to Rome. Petrarch was by no means an irreligious man, and one of his most interesting works, the *Secret*, consists of an imaginary dialogue between himself and St. Augustine and reveals the struggle in his soul between the claims of the world and those of eternity. In addition to all these activities Petrarch wrote poetry in his native Italian vernacular. This, as will be explained later, won him undying fame as one of the greatest poets in the history of the western world.

Petrarch as a highly regarded scholar was the center and inspiration of a group of devoted admirers. Among these was Giovanni Boccaccio (1313–1375). Since Boccaccio is best known as the author of the *Decameron*, a collection of stories in Italian, it is easy to forget that he was a classical Latin scholar who managed to obtain some proficiency in Greek. He also lectured in Florence on Dante, a subject of abiding interest to Florentines.

Toward the end of the fourteenth century, a fuller knowledge of Greek considerably broadened the field of classical study and opened the way for that complete humanism to which Petrarch aspired. Manuel Chrysoloras (*d.* 1415), a Byzantine Greek who had been sent to Italy on diplomatic missions, became a much sought-after teacher of his native language and held a professorship at the University of Florence. Among the learned Greeks who attended the Council of Florence (1438–1439) and who remained in Italy were Plethon and Bessarion. Plethon suggested to Cosimo de' Medici the idea of establishing an "academy" to further the study of Plato's works. A coterie of scholars rather than an institution, the resulting academy gained distinction under the direction of Marsiglio Ficino and the patronage of Lorenzo.[1] Bessarion, formerly bishop of Nicaea, later became a cardinal of the Roman church, and a highly respected churchman and scholar. One of the finer products of the revival of Greek studies was Angelo Poliziano (*d.* 1494), who, like so many humanists and artists, was a friend of Lorenzo de' Medici and whose public lectures in Florence won much acclaim. Finally, it should be noted that the Greek works which were added in the period to the West's classical heritage were principally though not exclusively literary—writings of dramatists, poets, and historians which had not been acquired from the Moslems during the earlier middle ages.

In addition to Greek, certain scholars, in an effort to absorb the entire ancient heritage, mastered Hebrew. The most noted was Pico della Mirandola (*d.* 1494), a brilliant scholar in many fields, whose breadth of learning, acquired in a brief career, was phenomenal. He attempted to

[1] The marked interest in Plato was in part a reaction against the Aristotelianism of the thirteenth century, but in part resulted from the humanist desire for a complete classical heritage. "Neo-Platonism" deeply influenced renaissance thought, but did not supersede the study of Aristotle.

coordinate all knowledge in a single system; in addition, he was an extremely devout man, much influenced by the Dominican friar Savonarola.

Although humanists were men of letters primarily, they were not unmindful of other aspects of human life and they recognized the obligations of the scholar to society. Indeed, the ideal of the humanist, as is evident in the educational treatises or experiments of such persons as Guarino da Verona and Vittorino da Feltre who conducted model schools for the rulers of Ferrara and Mantua respectively, or of Leon Battista Alberti, writer as well as architect, was the well-rounded individual whose training should include not merely classical literature, but art, music, athletics, dancing, military skill, "proper bearing," and the study and practice of religion. Thus, although much of the inspiration for this ideal came from pagan Greece and Rome, fifteenth-century humanists, with few exceptions, remained practicing Christians and continued to emphasize the freedom of the individual will and the salvation of the individual soul.

It is not surprising, therefore, that a considerable number of Italian humanists were ecclesiastics or that Rome rivaled Florence as a center of renaissance patronage. Nicholas V (1447–1455) has been called a humanist pope: he invited to Rome Lorenzo Valla who, in a previous service with Alfonso the Magnanimous of Naples, another renaissance patron, had demonstrated the falsity of the celebrated "Donation of Constantine."[1] Pope Pius II (1458–1464), the former Aeneas Silvius Piccolomini, was a humanist of wide learning who among other things was concerned with the preservation of Roman remains, thus lending official support to another facet of the Italian renaissance, archaeology.[2] All these activities reached their apogée during the pontificate of Leo X (1513–1521), the son of Lorenzo de' Medici, who brought to Rome as a young cardinal that love and knowledge of classical culture which was his birthright.

The development of humanism from an intellectual fashion to a general and pervasive vogue, and the principal basis of education, was not—indeed, could not have been—the work simply of humanists who represented a relatively small number of highly educated scholars. It resulted partly from the libraries established or expanded during the fourteenth and fifteenth centuries, partly owing to a limited though important penetration of humanism into the universities, and partly as a consequence of the invention of printing.

Many humanists, commencing with Petrarch, were avid collectors and their efforts uncovered a number of classical manuscripts which might otherwise have been lost. Cosimo de' Medici, with the assistance first of Niccolò Niccoli, the humanist, and later of a remarkable book dealer, Vespasiano da Bisticci, assembled many volumes and housed them in the convent of San Marco which he endowed. The collection grew and subsequently was named the Laurentian after his grandson. Cardinal Bessarion gave his fine collection to Venice, and Nicholas V reëstablished and housed what was to become a celebrated collection, the Vatican library. These are but a few examples.

To account fully for the expansion of humanist interests in Italy and their extension to northern Europe, mention must be made of their impact on the existing institutions of formal education—the universities. What seems to have happened is that most universities continued to provide instruction in the arts and in the still indispensable subjects of theology, law, and medicine. But many, usually simply by expanding the offering in the arts, added the humanistic program of Latin and Greek letters. This was true of such new universities as Florence (founded in the fourteenth century and moved to Pisa in the fifteenth), and Pavia, and of such older universities as Padua, Bologna, Rome, and others outside of Italy. In a few instances, such as the *Collège de France*, founded by Guillaume Budé early in the sixteenth century, humanistic studies constituted an exclusive interest. In one way or another,

[1] See above, page 118, footnote 1.

[2] A Roman Academy, not unlike its Florentine counterpart, expressly dedicated itself, among other matters, to archaeology.

humanism was gaining acceptance as an educational principle.

B. Invention of Printing, and Humanism in Northern and Western Europe

Printing was invented in Germany. The materials necessary, paper, types of ink, etc., had long been known in western Europe, and the printing of full pages or illustrations from blocks of wood was common early in the fifteenth century. All that was additionally necessary was the invention of movable type. And the first to capitalize on this invention, perhaps to have made it, was Johann Gutenberg of Mainz in the decade of the 1440's. The few extant Gutenberg bibles are priceless treasures.

Soon Gutenberg's countrymen were setting up presses in other lands. Two of them, Swenheim and Pannartz, speedily introduced the invention in Italy, and others brought it into Spain. The first press in England was installed by Caxton in 1476. In a surprisingly short time, printing establishments were to be found all over Christendom, including Mexico and Peru. The Aldine press at Venice, named after Aldus Manutius, its founder, was particularly famous.

The effects of printing on the general development of Western civilization were tremendous. The availability of extant works was increased immeasurably, since presses could turn out copies by the thousand while a scribe labored over a few pages. Accuracy, or at least uniformity, was now reasonably assured. And most of the early printers were editors as well. That is to say, they found it necessary to ascertain from perhaps several manuscripts of a given work what was the correct text. Printing, of course, gave an impetus to humanism, although individual humanists were no longer so much in demand. But the fifteenth-century presses also turned out copies of the Bible, the Fathers, and theological, scientific, and legal treatises. In short the output reflected the varied interests of the age.

In a sense, too, the printing press forms a link between the humanism of Italy and the humanism of the northern countries. For although the new learning was not unknown north of the Alps in the days before Gutenberg, the first half of the sixteenth century was the golden age of northern humanism. Its more rapid spread and shorter life resulted in no small degree from the fact that so much was already accomplished and readily available. Indeed, although it may have been desirable, it was no longer necessary to travel to Italy.

Among the German humanists was Nicholas of Cusa (*d.* 1464), a prominent ecclesiastic and eventually a cardinal, a man of wide intellectual interests which included science as well as classical literature, and withal something of a mystic. Rudolf Agricola (*d.* 1485) spent ten years studying in Italy; and through his subsequent teaching, he made Heidelberg a humanist center.[1] Conrad Celtes (*d.* 1508) also studied in Italy, was crowned poet-laureate at Nuremberg in 1487, and taught at Ingolstadt in Bavaria and at the University of Vienna. Johann Reuchlin (*d.* 1522) visited Italy in 1482 and 1490 and acquired from Pico della Mirandola an enthusiasm for Hebrew studies which led him to devote his attention to critical examination of the text of the Old Testament.

Many German humanists were associated with the schools of the Brethren of the Common Life, a religious and educational society which will be discussed in the following chapter. When Alexander Hegius (*d.* 1498) became head of their principal school at Deventer in the Netherlands, a humanist program, including the teaching of Greek, was introduced into the schools of the society. There was, therefore, in these schools an intimate association of humanism and religion which tended to characterize the northern movement and to distinguish it from the Italian.

Preoccupation with ecclesiastical reform was especially characteristic of the greatest of all the non-Italian humanists, Desiderius Erasmus (1466–1536). A native of Rotterdam, Erasmus received his early education

---

[1] Erfurt was another German university where humanistic studies flourished. Martin Luther studied there as a young man.

at Deventer and later pursued theological studies at Paris. Thoroughly absorbed in the new learning, he was an excellent Latinist and obtained a good knowledge of Greek. As his scholarly reputation grew he met many people and became a kind of peripatetic scholar and writer and a welcome guest at princely and university establishments everywhere. He corresponded with scholars throughout western Europe and his letters are a mine of information about contemporary conditions. Among his most happy years were those spent in England, where he formed fast friendships with John Colet and Thomas More. To the latter he dedicated his famous *Praise of Folly* (*Encomium Moriae*). This work and the *Familiar Colloquies* show Erasmus as a master of wit and gentle satire directed especially against decadent scholasticism, corrupt and ignorant clergymen, and the foibles of his day generally.

Erasmus' renown does not rest alone on satire. His *Adagia*, a compendium of selections from classical authors with critical commentary intended for young students, went through many editions including one at the Aldine press in Venice. He dedicated to his patron, Charles I of Spain, ruler of the Netherlands and later Holy Roman Emperor, his *Education of a Christian Prince* (1516), an earnest plea for peace and for an application to government of the principles of Christianity. His most ambitious undertaking was a critical edition of the Greek New Testament. Erasmus' later years were saddened by the shattering of his high hopes for a peaceful regeneration of society.

In England, John Colet (1466–1519) and Thomas More (1478–1535), both friends of Erasmus, stand out. Colet, dean of St. Paul's Cathedral in London, won fame for his critical lectures on the Pauline epistles, an excellent example of the religious earnestness in northern humanism. He also founded at his own expense a grammar school at St. Paul's which was devoted to the new learning. With Thomas More, classical humanism was an avocation. He was a busy man of affairs, a competent lawyer, and ultimately Lord Chancellor of England. Moreover, as his *Utopia*, a kind of Platonic vision of the ideal state, indicates, he grasped the pressing problem of social reform.

French humanism, of which there were indications as early as the reign of Charles V (1364–1380), hardly flourished before the end of the fifteenth century when Greek teachers were brought to Paris and Greek works collected.[1] Francis I (1515–1547) was a patron of learning and established the *Collège de France* with special professorships in Latin and Greek literature. Guillaume Budé was his principal agent in this matter, and in founding the Bibliothèque Nationale.

In Spain the new learning took a distinctly religious turn under the direction of Cardinal Ximines de Cisneros (*d.* 1517). Ximines' objective, a thoroughgoing reform of the Spanish church, required an educated clergy. For this purpose he founded the university of Alcalà which among other accomplishments produced the famous *Complutensian Polyglot*, an edition of the Bible with the original languages and the Latin in parallel columns. Although an awareness of social problems is evident in the literary work of Juan Luis Vives (*d.* 1540), Spanish humanism, generally speaking, took second place to religious reform.[2]

C. Science and Philosophy

Humanism, being a primarily literary movement, contributed to science only incidentally by uncovering and, after the mid-fifteenth century, reprinting certain important classical works. To cite but two examples, Ptolemy's *Geography* reappeared in 1410 and Hippocrates began to supersede Galen in medical teaching. Meanwhile, in both practical and theoretical fields notable progress was made, particularly in the fourteenth century. At the

[1] It has been suggested that the expedition of Charles VIII into Italy (1494) was a means of bringing Italian renaissance ideas into France. This is scarcely true of intellectual matters, but it seems likely that Italian villas with their formal gardens influenced the artistic taste of French nobles.

[2] Erasmus' works, at first well received in Spain, were later banned.

universities of Paris and Oxford, as well as continuing at Padua, there was vigorous re-examination of Aristotle's scientific theories and of Ptolemy's cosmography, and a more penetrating use of mathematics. Nicholas Oresme, Jean Buridan, and Albert of Saxony, among others, developed theories of motion which proved to be important steps toward what Galileo was to demonstrate years later.

Perhaps the most significant applications of applied science were in navigation. We have mentioned the undertakings of Prince Henry the Navigator. Nowhere, in fact, was there a closer association of theoretical and practical science than at the Portuguese court. Portuguese navigators were able to determine latitude by observing with astrolabe or quadrant the vertical angle of the Pole Star, or as they voyaged southward, by observing the sun at noon. For the latter procedure Abraham Zacuto produced in 1478 a table of solar declinations. So also about the same time did Johannes Müller (Regiomontanus), who was later invited to Rome by Pope Sixtus IV to discuss calendar reform.

Medical professors of the fourteenth century regularly dissected human bodies as part of their instruction, and in their surgery they no longer uncritically followed the ancients. The *Anatomy* of Mundinus (1316), in use for the next two centuries, was printed at Padua in 1478; as also was a treatise on surgery by Guy de Chauliac (1363), which, though highly important, was hardly fair to its predecessors. Some progress was also made in the prevention of infection and in the diagnosis of certain diseases previously unknown. During the Black Death (1348–1350) many doctors acquired considerable information, and some displayed notable heroism in ministering to the afflicted.

The fifteenth century seems to have been less productive of scientific accomplishment than the fourteenth, but it is important to observe that the works of the late medieval scientists were printed and that they were known and used by the scientists of the sixteenth and seventeenth centuries.

It was noted in a previous chapter that in 1277 an episcopal commission at Paris condemned a number of propositions held by those scholars known as extreme Aristotelians.[1] And it was further noted that one of the consequences was the transference of this school of thought to the Italian university of Padua. Since the adherents continued to profess the Averroistic doctrine of the double truth—one for science, another for religion—they came to be known as Latin Averroists. Meanwhile, an English philosopher, William of Ockham (*d.* 1349), a Franciscan friar and a nominalist, concluded that rational speculation, however useful for the understanding of man and nature, was of dubious and only "probable" validity as a support for religious truth. Thus in different ways, each of these modes of thought diverged from the basic concept of the unity of all knowledge which Thomas Aquinas had proposed for philosophy and theology, and to which such thinkers as Robert Grosseteste and Roger Bacon had wanted to add natural science, and with which the humanists, in their way, were in accord. The implications for theological teaching will be discussed in the following chapter. Here, it may be observed that since these two streams of thought were to persist into the early sixteenth century, precisely through the period of the origins of modern science, there was gradually produced a dichotomy between religious and scientific thought which had not been prominent earlier, but which was to raise many acute problems regarding the relation between religion and science in later times.

E. Progress of Vernacular Literature

If the classicism of the humanists represented a special interest of scholars, the vernacular literature of the late middle age embraced a broader range, both secular and religious. Petrarch and Boccaccio, both humanists, won enduring fame for their works in Italian. Petrarch perfected the poetic form of the sonnet. Boccaccio, in his *Decameron*, a collection of lively and often bawdy tales preceded by a vivid description of the plague in Florence, proved

[1] See above, p. 243.

An unique equestrian portrait of Geoffrey Chaucer from a manuscript of about 1410.

Courtesy Henry E. Huntington Library and Art Gallery, San Marino, California

himself a master of Italian prose. In the fifteenth century the versatile Leon Battista Alberti defended the use of the vernacular on the interesting "classical" grounds that the Romans had used their own native language. Lorenzo de' Medici, the patron, and Poliziano, the humanist, both composed in Italian. Somewhat later, two Italian epics, Boiardo's *Orlando Innamorato* (1486) and Ariosto's *Orlando Furioso* (1515) testified to the enduring popularity of the Roland theme.[1] Although formal treatises were still composed in Latin, historical writing was increasingly done in the vernacular as is evidenced by the *Florentine Chronicle* of Giovanni Villani (*d.* 1348), and by the more skillful histories of Niccolò Machiavelli (*d.* 1527) and Francesco Guicciardini (*d.* 1540).

French literature of the fourteenth and fifteenth centuries was enriched by the satirical works of Jean de Meung (*d.* 1305); by the poetry of Christine de Pisan (*d.* 1430), a celebrated lady of letters, and of Charles, son of the murdered Louis of Orléans (*d.* 1465); and by the lively, vivid, and often pathetic verse of François Villon (*d.* 1463). To these may be added the historical works of Jean Froissart (*d.* 1405) and Philippe de Commines (*d.* 1509).

In England, the days when Norman nobles spoke French and peasants spoke Saxon had passed, and a common national language, compounded of Germanic and Romance elements, had emerged as "middle English" and was being utilized in the fourteenth century for literary purposes. An early example was the *Vision of Piers Plowman*, written by William Langland in the first half of the fourteenth century. But the outstanding figure in this formative period of English literature was a poet, Geoffrey Chaucer (*d.* 1400), with his famous *Canterbury Tales*. In the following century there appeared a notable prose work, Sir Thomas Malory's *Morte d'Arthur*.

There was a considerable amount of German literature in the fourteenth and fifteenth centuries, and it reflected varied interests of contemporary middle-class people in the German cities. It embraced popular satirical works, like Sebastian Brant's *Ship of Fools* (1498), a good deal of poetry, including ballads and the somewhat artificial pieces which meistersingers used in their singing contests, and also many popular books of devotion. Several German versions of parts of the bible appeared before the end of the fourteenth century, and the first printed edition emanated before 1456, presumably from the press of Gutenberg.

Altogether, it was evident that, though Latin continued to be the language of scholarship, most popular and a good deal of serious writing was now being done in the several vernacular languages. The illustrations mentioned in this section are only a few among many that could be cited. Even governments, like the English, French, and Castilian, were now admitting the respective national tongues to official usage. This encroachment of the vernaculars on a former monopoly of Latin was one of the most significant cultural developments of the late middle age. And it is one of the ironies of history that it occurred amid the humanistic renaissance of classical Latin. In the realm of literature, as in so many others, the growing consciousness of nationality was marked.

F. Painting

The late middle age of the fourteenth and fifteenth centuries witnessed achievements

[1] See above, p. 164.

in the fine arts, especially in painting, sculpture, and architecture, which have made that period, artistically, one of the greatest and most amazing in all human history. It will be possible here to mention only a few of the artistic accomplishments and to relate these to the history of the age.

The art of the period, while still largely religious in subject-matter, was no longer so exclusively fostered by the church. It was more often patronized by lay princes or wealthy townsmen, or commissioned by town governments. Moreover, the vicissitudes of contemporary diplomacy often affected the transference of artistic trends. It is important to remember that Italians often resided in the north, that the Holy Roman Empire had a French-Luxembourg dynasty, that the French Angevins were in and out of Naples, that the popes resided during most of the fourteenth century in Avignon, and especially that the dukes of Burgundy controlled the Netherlands.

Fourteenth-century painting, in Italy as well as in northern Europe, is today generally classified as still within the "international Gothic" age. By this is meant that everywhere in Europe painters continued what the medieval miniaturists and designers of stained glass had begun, a departure from the conventionality of Byzantine art. In short, they pushed further in the direction of a freer naturalism. It was the Florentine Giotto (*d.* 1336) who most notably illustrates this trend and who set a fashion for a number of followers during the fourteenth century.[1] Meanwhile, there flourished at Siena, in the first half of the century, Duccio, Simone Martini, and the Lorenzetti brothers. Martini was invited by the pope to come to Avignon. In France, to the already remarkable technique demonstrated in illuminated manuscripts was added Flemish influence. An earlier chapter has indicated the generous patronage of the royal and ducal courts of the late fourteenth and early fifteenth centuries, and the notable development of miniatures and tapestry. French artists were also doing panel-painting and achieving remarkable success with portraits. Meanwhile, Italian and French influences appeared in the Empire and in Prague.

By the fifteenth century art was being notably influenced by contemporary humanism. Along with religious subjects, it became fashionable to depict characters from Greek and Roman literature. Even the essentially Christian representations were not all designed for churches; many were now produced for private residences, and local persons were used as models. Painters grappled harder with the problems of perspective and space, strove for an ever greater naturalism and a more faithful representation of the human form. By the end of the century some, as, for example, Leonardo da Vinci (*d.* 1519), were making careful studies of anatomy. Leonardo was an exceptional genius, versatile in many fields, who served the Sforza in Milan and subsequently the king of France. Moreover, before him had been a series of artists who helped to make possible what he was able to do. Many of these enjoyed the patronage of the Medici and virtually all owed much to Massaccio (1401–1428) who in a short life started the new post-Giotto trend which many followed. A long list of names could be made, and among the outstanding would be Fra Angelico (*d.* 1455)[2] who did the frescoes in Cosino's convent of San Marco, Benozzo Gozzoli who executed those in the Medici palace, Fra Filippo Lippi, Ghirlandaio, and finally the universally popular Sandro Botticelli (*d.* 1510).

Distinguished as was the Florentine school of painting, it was but one, albeit in many ways the chief, of several Italian schools. There was also a Venetian school represented by Gentile da Fabriano, the Bellini brothers, Mantegna, and, in the sixteenth century, Titian (*d.* 1576). From Umbria came Raphael (*d.* 1520), a pupil of Perugino (*d.* 1524). Raphael was one of the celebrated artists who, toward the end of the fifteenth century and early in the next, were brought to Rome. For after the death of Lorenzo the Magnificent (*d.* 1492), the cultural and artistic primacy in Italy passed from Florence to Rome. This

[1] See example of Giotto's work, above, p. 253.

[2] See example of Fra Angelico's work below, p. 324.

is the "high renaissance," the "golden age," and will be considered later in connection with the papacy in the sixteenth century. Here it may be mentioned that Raphael was not only the creator of several famous Madonnas and of the frescoes of the *stanze* in the Vatican palace, but was commissioned to supervise the preservation and restoration of ancient Roman monuments and works of art.

The fifteenth century also brought a flowering of art in northern and western Europe, equally impressive qualitatively, though smaller quantitatively. This included French and Flemish painters, some of whom were also miniaturists who carried that technique into their panel-painting. Jan van Eyck (*d.* 1441), Roger van der Weyden (*d.* 1464), and Hans Memling (*d.* 1494) who came to Bruges from Cologne, are especially to be noted among the Flemish artists. French fifteenth-century art included the remarkable Avignon *Pietà* by an unknown artist, and the portraits by Jean Fouquet (*d.* 1481), court painter of Louis XI. In Germany, the paintings of Albrecht Dürer (*d.* 1528) show Italian influence, and he was equally skilled as an engraver and wood carver. Hans Holbein the Younger (*d.* 1543), whose work shows somewhat greater Italian influence, won renown as a portrait painter. He spent a number of years in England, and to him we owe the likenesses of a number of early sixteenth-century notables of that country.

G. Sculpture, Architecture, Music

As has been explained, medieval Gothic sculpture had made remarkable progress both in free-standing polychrome wood and stone figures and in those designed to adorn the portals of cathedrals. This forward movement continued; and there was added a greater mastery of technique and, especially in Italy, an increased classical influence. Niccolò Pisano (*d.* 1278) who, despite his name, came from Apulia, was probably influenced by work in that area as well as by Roman *sarcophagi* (carved stone coffins) in the Pisan area where he worked. His most famous creations were

The David of the Casa Martelli. Donatello (d. 1466).

National Gallery of Art, Washington, D.C.; Widener Collection

a pulpit at Pisa and another at Siena, and his work was continued by his son, Giovanni (*d.* 1328), and by his pupils. As in other fields, so in sculpture, Florence excelled in the fifteenth century. And the visitor there today will still marvel at the gilded-bronze doors of the baptistery by Ghiberti (*d.* 1455), the statues of Donatello (*d.* 1466), and Verrocchio (*d.* 1488), whose work inspired the young Leonardo; and the glazed terra cottas of Luca (*d.* 1482) and Andrea (*d.* 1525) della Robbia. The versatile Michelangelo (*d.* 1564) began his work in Florence before he joined the company of artists at Rome.

Outside Italy, special attention should be called to the Dutch sculptor, Claus Sluter (*d.* 1405), who was brought to Burgundy by its dukes and whose most notable works are in Dijon. In both France and Germany, medieval skills in both stone and wood-carving continued to flourish, although design and taste was gradually influenced by what was being done in Italy.

In northern and western Europe Gothic building continued into the fifteenth century. In France, it developed into the more intricately articulated and decorated style known as "flamboyant." In England, structural changes in vaulting made possible the elimination of flying buttresses, and the emphasis on vertical and horizontal lines led to a further modification called "perpendicular." In both countries, Gothic features were incorporated into private residences.

Fifteenth-century Italian architecture did not at first or everywhere show classical influence. The *duomo,* or cathedral, of Florence retained much of the Gothic spirit: Giotto designed its campanile, or bell tower, and Brunelleschi (*d.* 1466) its octagonal dome. But classical influences grew

Renaissance architecture. The Rucellai Palace, Florence. Alberti (*d.* 1472).

Alinari photograph

apace during the century. There was a striving for symmetry, a noticeable revival of classical capitals and entablatures, and an effort to conceal structural features. Renaissance palaces, for example the Medici residence in Florence designed by Michelozzo (*d.* 1472), and the Rucellai palace designed by Alberti (*d.* 1472), show skillful use of capitals, entablatures, pilasters, and cornices. Each enclosed an interior court with classical arcade. Certain churches in Florence designed by Brunelleschi, and the church of San Andrea in Mantua, designed by Alberti, are good examples of the application of the classical style to ecclesiastical building. Most striking is the acceptance of the new style in Rome. But since the fulfillment there came in the following century we shall reserve a discussion of Renaissance Roman building to a later chapter. By the end of the fifteenth century the vogue of classicism in architecture had begun to affect every country in Europe.

The development of music during the renaissance was also significant. The art of contrapuntal composition progressed, especially in England, the Netherlands, and northern France. With the work of Dunstable (*d.* 1453), Okeghem (*d.* 1495), and Josquin des Prés (*d.* 1523), skill in counterpoint reached a high degree of technical perfection and tonal beauty. This was an important achievement in the evolution of modern musical forms and techniques.

It should be evident from the preceding pages that the late medieval, or "renaissance," cultural progress was both impressive and varied. Moreover, despite much political disorder, violence, pestilence, and in certain respects a spirit of pessimism, the prevailing humanist mood was one of optimism. Erasmus, in writing early in the sixteenth century to Pope Leo X, expressed his joy that Christendom was led by a man so much in sympathy with the new learning and under whose enlightened guidance church and society might be regenerated. This hope Erasmus lived to see dashed in the confusion of religious strife. And while the sixteenth-century upheaval was associated with many factors other than religious, it was, at least at the outset, essentially a religious matter. It is, therefore, appropriate to conclude our study of the middle ages with an examination of the state of the church in order that we may better understand the events of early modern times.

Miracles of St. Zenobius. Botticelli (d. 1510).

Courtesy Metropolitan Museum of Art, New York

CHAPTER 27

The Church in the Late Middle Age

A. The "Babylonian Captivity" of the Papacy

The story of the church in the fourteenth and fifteenth centuries presents a melancholy contrast to the record of its brilliance in the thirteenth century. Indeed, this period in its long history has often been entitled "the decline of the church." It is true that both in its functioning as an institution and in its influence over European society, the church of the Late Middle Age showed deterioration. The difficulties which now engulfed it were not all the result of internal weakness or personal derelictions, though these were present. The basic trouble lay in the complex circumstances of the age which we have been describing in preceding pages. It was an age of growing secularism which obscured spiritual ideals and weakened ecclesiastical influences over society.

The particular problems which beset the church included (1) a governmental crisis threatening the position of the pope in the ecclesiastical system, (2) the growth and persistence of heresy, and (3) serious malfunctioning of the administrative system calling for drastic reform. All of these were associated with, and in part caused by, what has been called the "Babylonian Captivity," the residence of the popes for some seventy years (1309–1377) at Avignon in southern France. The removal of the papacy from Rome was an indirect consequence of the fateful conflict between Pope Boniface VIII and Philip IV of France.[1] In 1305 a Frenchman was elected Pope as Clement V (*d.* 1314). Although he had little strength of character and in certain matters sought to appease the French King, he did stand out against Philip's constant pressure that he publicly condemn the actions of Boniface VIII. The Pope's most notorious concession was his acquiescence in French demands for the suppression of the Crusading Order of Knights Templar.[2] Apparently in the hope of stopping hostilities between France and England and promoting a crusade, Clement remained in France and eventually established the papal *curia* at Avignon.[3]

Although Clement V doubtless intended to stay only temporarily at Avignon, his appointment of a large number of French cardinals led to the election of a series

[1] See above, p. 209.

[2] The Templars had undoubtedly outlived their usefulness as a crusading order and had acquired considerable wealth and landed property in Europe, largely as a result of their banking operations. Clement permitted an investigation of various charges brought against them by French royal commissioners coöperating with the Inquisition. Torture produced confessions and many suffered the death penalty for heresy. The Pope decreed that their property should be turned over to the Knights Hospitallers, but the King had already appropriated most of it for himself.

[3] Actually, Avignon was an enclave of papal territory, outside, but surrounded by, French territory. It was purchased from the heiress of Provence in 1348.

The Palace of the Popes at Avignon

Courtesy Marbury Art Reference Bureau

of French popes. These showed less and less inclination to leave Avignon, particularly as conditions in the papal lands in Italy became increasingly turbulent. Eventually a large and sumptuous palace was erected at Avignon to house the *curia*. Criticism from outside of France was inevitable, and the Avignon popes were accused by rulers and people of other countries of subordinating their policies to the kings of France. The English, then engaged in the Hundred Years' War, were especially prone to make the accusation. Both Dante and Petrarch lifted their voices to lament the "captivity." But it should be borne in mind that the French monarchy was in a lamentably weak condition during most of the period, and that, with the exception of Clement V, the Avignon popes were not coerced by it or unduly subservient to it.

Actually, after the entire machinery of administration had been moved from Rome to Avignon, the government of the church went on much as before, and several significant policies were energetically pursued. It was Clement V who answered John of Monte Corvino's plea for assistance by establishing missionary dioceses in China. John XXII (1314–1334), an able administrator, was also a proponent of missions to the Far East.

Particularly important at Avignon was the continued centralization of ecclesiastical administration in the papal *curia*. This was especially significant in the financial realm. Papal taxation increased and was more efficiently collected. Income taxes on benefices were regularized, notably the "annates," payments of the first year's income from a benefice. Papal appointments, or "provisions," to benefices throughout Europe were increased. But while these served to counteract the prevalent tendency on the part of secular rulers to dominate the clergy in their respective realms, papal provisions too often involved questionable financial payments and the appointment of aliens who performed a minimum of service and were resented as "foreign" clerics.[1]

While papal finances at Avignon were a major source of criticism, much of it justified, it seems evident that needful expenses of expanding administration were increasing. In addition, considerable expenditure was necessary to reconquer papal lands in Italy from the various local *signori* and *condottieri* who had appropriated them. There was also, it will be recalled, a greater demand for the higher priced consumer goods, and a relative diminution in revenues derived from land. At the same time, venality and luxury, however exaggerated

[1] Two statutes enacted by the English government illustrate contemporary opposition to Avignon policies. The statute of *Provisors* (1351) forbade papal appointment to English benefices; the statute of *Praemunire* (1353) forbade appeals to Rome. Neither statute was consistently enforced in subsequent years.

by contemporary critics, were indubitably present at Avignon. If the popes themselves were able and honest men, and not notably extravagant, the cardinals, mostly French, lived in sumptuous residences and resisted attempts to curtail expenses; and there were too many "hangers on" who were maintained in comfort and comparative idleness.

In spite of the long residence at Avignon, it had never been deemed a permanent change and return to Rome was delayed only because of conditions in central Italy. Cardinal Albornoz was despatched to restore order in the Papal State, and before his death (1367) he had accomplished a great deal. At length, after considerable hesitation, and encouraged by the letters of two saintly women, St. Brigid of Sweden and St. Catherine of Siena, Gregory XI left Avignon in 1377 to take up residence in the Eternal City.

B. The Great Schism

The return of the papacy to Rome proved but the prelude to a new and even graver crisis. On Gregory's death in 1378, as the cardinals assembled to choose his successor, the Roman populace, milling around outside the conclave, demanded a Roman or an Italian pope. As a compromise, the cardinals elected Urban VI, a Neapolitan—not a Roman, but at least an Italian and not a Frenchman. Urban proceeded in summary fashion to cleanse the *curia* of many abuses for which it had been justly criticized. But his high-handed and tactless methods so antagonized the cardinals that several members of the Sacred College fled Rome into the kingdom of Naples, where they met and declared that the votes they had cast for Urban had been extorted by the threats of the Roman mob, and that Urban's election was consequently void. They then elected Cardinal Robert of Geneva, a Frenchman, who subsequently set himself up in Avignon as "Clement VII." Needless to say, Urban stoutly maintained the validity of his own election and anathematized Clement and the French cardinals.

Western Europe was thus treated to the scandalous spectacle of a pope at Rome and a rival claimant at Avignon. But this was not all. For there were now two *curias*, two sets of legates, conflicting bulls of excommunication, and what was most irksome, two organizations for the collection of revenue. And since successors were elected at both Rome and Avignon on the death of the original incumbents, the "Great Schism" bade fair to continue indefinitely. Pious folk were confused and knew not which way to turn for although this was not the first time that western Christendom had been faced with a schism between a pope and an "anti-pope," previous schisms had usually been rather obviously the result of external pressure on the part, say, of an emperor. In the new case, however, the two claimants had nearly equal support and there was genuine doubt in many minds as to which was the true pope.

Broadly speaking, Europe divided its allegiance in a way characteristic of the time, namely along lines of nationality. France, the Spanish kingdoms, Naples (after changing sides), Sicily, and Scotland followed the popes at Avignon, while England and the Scandinavian kingdoms supported the Roman popes. But the division was by no means clear. Germany and northern Italy were divided in their allegiance, and at one time France questioned the status of the Avignon incumbent.

C. Deterioration in Ecclesiastical Morale and Growth of Heresy

The long papal residence at Avignon and the years of the great schism aggravated various conditions in the church which badly needed remedying. The general standard of clerical conduct and competence had deteriorated. In large part, this was the result of the ravages of the Black Death and the consequent necessity of filling vacancies with imperfectly trained nominees. Thereby the policy, inaugurated by the thirteenth-century popes, of promoting university-trained clerics was bady hampered. Sometimes even worse was the number of dispensations given—often after a payment —to hold an ecclesiastical post without proper ordination, or to remain absent for considerable periods of time. Thus in many areas the faithful lacked proper parochial, and sometimes even episcopal, care. To these ills was added a recurrence of simony. And monasticism, badly hit by the Black Death, suffered greatly both materially and morally.

At the same time that the church was faced with the administrative crisis of the schism and a decline in its morale, it was also confronting serious heresy. Heresy had always been a problem for the church, as preceding chapters have shown. In the fourteenth and fifteenth centuries, it flourished as never before, and in certain instances the discipline of the church proved inadequate for its suppression. The explanation of the marked prevalence of heresy lies partly in the weakness of the church of the time. Corruption in it invited criticism and simultaneously so slackened its internal discipline as to unfit it for coping with its critics and opponents. But ecclesiastical failings were not alone sufficient to account for the volume of dissent. The age was a restless one, in which serfs and artisans engaged in spasmodic rebellions, and scholars broke from old traditions. Something of the spirit of change seems to have permeated the religious sphere as well.

In the fourteenth century, a group known as "Spiritual Franciscans" aroused considerable agitation in ecclesiastical circles. Certain members of the Order of Friars Minor, or Franciscans, sought first to restore the practice of strict poverty as it had originally been taught by St. Francis of Assisi. But in their zeal to reject all the compromises by which the Order held or administered property, the Spirituals went on to insist as a matter of doctrine that Christ and the Apostles had possessed no property whatever. Although condemned by Pope John XXII (1323), the Spirituals persisted for some time, and some found refuge at the court of the Emperor Louis of Bavaria (1314–1347), who for a time was at odds with the papacy.

Also at the imperial court was Marsiglio of Padua (*d.* 1343), a prominent advocate of the conciliar theory of church government. His *Defensor Pacis* is one of the most remarkable political treatises of the age. For Marsiglio conceived of the state as an institution devoted to purely earthly ends and not dependent on any church. He advocated a monarchy limited by a species of popular sovereignty which was to operate, not through a democratic legislature in the modern sense, but through an assembly of the wiser and richer citizens. Further, Marsiglio held that the church was subordinate to the state, and that ecclesiastical authority rested not with the pope and the clergy, but with the community of the faithful (*universitas fidelium*).

If Marsiglio was concerned mainly with questioning the organization of the church, John Wyclif (1320–1384) went further to question fundamental religious doctrine. Wyclif, an English scholar and master at Oxford, was an enthusiastic student of the Bible. At first scandalized, no doubt like many other Englishmen, by the residence of the popes at Avignon, he limited his criticisms to the temporal possessions of the church which, he insisted, the civil government might and should control. Up to this point he had the support of several highly placed persons, including King Edward III's younger son, John of Gaunt. But this support he lost when he denied papal supremacy and rejected the miracle of transubstantiation in the Mass. Wyclif's doctrines were condemned by an ecclesiastical convocation at Canterbury, and he was banished from Oxford. He died in retirement in 1384.

Wyclif's followers, the "poor priests" or "Lollards" as they were called, persisted for some time despite sporadic official action against them. In the main, however, the English rejected Wyclif's doctrines, and throughout the early decades of the fifteenth century civil and ecclesiastical authorities combined to suppress Lollardry.

As a consequence of contacts between England and Bohemia—the marriage of the English King Richard II with a Bohemian princess, and the exchanging of visits by students and diplomats—Wyclif's teachings had considerable influence far from the country of their origin. At the same time, a movement directed toward ecclesiastical reform and including popular preaching in the Czech vernacular was developing at Prague.

The most conspicuous native of Bohemia whose beliefs were derived in part from Wyclif was John Hus. He, too, was a uni-

The Crucifixion. Fra Angelico (d. 1455).
Courtesy Metropolitan Museum of Art, New York

versity man, dean of the Faculty of Arts at Prague, canon of the cathedral, and popular preacher. Although Hus rejected some of the English master's teachings, notably that on transubstantiation, he seems to have been markedly influenced by Wyclif's questioning of ecclesiastical authority and by his views on the importance of scripture. Hus won considerable support, as did also his associate, Jerome of Prague, one of those who had introduced Wyclif's writings into Bohemia.

D. Age of the Councils

It is evident that at the beginning of the fifteenth century the western church was faced with major heresy as well as divided by schism. These, together with the matter of reform, were featured on the agenda of an important church council which met in 1414 at Constance. For some time before this gathering, attempts had been made to persuade one or the other of the papal claimants to withdraw. Since all these attempts had proved unavailing, many groups of Christians, both ecclesiastical and lay, bestirred themselves to devise new means for reuniting Christendom. And it was natural that the means they eventually elaborated should reflect contemporary political ideas and practices. Thus it was proposed that when the head of the church and its central governing body were in default, the entire church could and must assert itself through the instrumentality of a general council. To some, notably the experts in canon law, conciliar action in opposition to a pope was envisaged only as a temporary emergency measure. Others, however, claimed for the proposed council a permanent association with the pope as the supreme governing body of the church. To such theorists it seemed particularly fitting that the government of the church should be parliamentary, and papal authority limited, at a time when parliaments and estates were seeking to restrict monarchical power.[1]

It was, therefore, in an atmosphere of considerable controversy that several prelates, under the auspices of cardinals from both Rome and Avignon, assembled at Pisa in 1409. Too hastily convened and too ill prepared for constructive work, the Council of Pisa lacked general support. Neither

[1] The idea of conciliar supremacy had been advocated in the fourteenth century by Marsiglio of Padua. Early in the fifteenth century somewhat more moderate proposals emanated from the university of Paris. Jean Gerson was a leading proponent of moderate conciliarism.

papal claimant would recognize its validity. Consequently its hasty action in electing a new pope, under the name of John XXIII, did not heal the schism. Rather it broadened and deepened it, for there were now three, instead of two, claimants—Roman, Avignon, and Pisan.

This trebly scandalous situation did not long endure. Five years later a more widely attended and better prepared council was assembled at Constance under the patronage of the Emperor Sigismund. Present were not only churchmen, but numerous representatives of cities and kingdoms. In a sense it was a cross-section of the society of the time, and it proceeded to devote itself to three principal problems: the schism, heresy, and reform.

John XXIII, the Pisan claimant, apparently hoping to wreck the council, left Constance after a brief appearance and was then deposed. Somewhat later (July 1415), Gregory XII, the Roman pope, agreed to resign on condition that the Council accord him the right of officially convoking it. By gaining acceptance of this condition, Gregory not only preserved the papal conception of ecclesiastical government wherein a council must be summoned or approved by the pope, but he secured recognition of himself and his Roman predecessors since Urban VI as the legitimate popes. It likewise followed that a decree concerning conciliar supremacy over the pope which had been issued at a date prior to Gregory's convocation had no validity. At length, in 1417, a group of cardinals of the Pisan and Roman obediences met at Constance, and, with certain deputies of the Council, elected a pope for the whole church, Martin V. The Avignon claimant, now a very stubborn old Spaniard, defied the Council and refused to resign. But he soon lost all his following and lapsed into the position of an insignificant anti-pope.

Even before the delicate matter of the schism had been settled, the prelates at Constance had taken up the matter of heresy. In 1414, under a safe conduct of the Emperor, John Hus appeared, seemingly anxious to defend his views. His safe conduct was not honored and he was imprisoned. After some months he was presented with a list of propositions which he was asked to abjure. He replied that he would recant only those which he had actually professed and only if he were convinced that they were contrary to scripture. In short, he chose to stand for private judgment based on scripture as opposed to the authority of the church. The consequence was that he was condemned by his judges, turned over to the civil authorities, and burned at the stake at Constance in 1415. A year later, Jerome of Prague met a similar fate.

The execution of Hus and Jerome did not put an end to the Hussite heresy in Bohemia. It persisted in parts of the country, associated to some degree with a nascent Czech national feeling, and it occasioned a series of "crusades" on the part of the Emperor. All of these failed. Ultimately a moderate wing accepted a temporary compromise with the ecclesiastical authorities in 1432.[1] The extremists, known as "Taborites" from their mountain retreat which they called "Mt. Tabor," and under the remarkable military leadership of two generals, Procop and Ziska, held out against all attacks. Thus, for the first time in its history, the church had failed to stamp out a major heresy.

Perhaps because it was so occupied with the schism and with heresy, the Council of Constance, despite much talk of "reform of the church in head and members," failed to inaugurate a reform movement of significant proportions. After many discussions, a program was drawn up and formally promulgated, but its implementation was left to future councils which, it was decreed, should be held at regular and frequent intervals. But the popes, fearful of a resurgence of the conciliar theory of ecclesiastical government, were markedly unsympathetic.

Pope Martin V grudgingly acted upon the recommendation of the Council and summoned a council at Pavia (1423), which

[1] These "Compacts," as they were called, permitted the reception by the laity, in the sacrament of the eucharist, of both the consecrated bread and wine, instead of the bread alone as was customary. Hence the moderates were known as "Utraquists" (Latin, "both") or "Calixtines" (Latin, "chalice"). The Compacts were never permanently ratified by the pope.

accomplished nothing. Then, under Pope Eugenius IV another council met at Basel (1431), which had a long and turbulent history. Disagreements between some of its members and the Pope prompted the latter to transfer the council to Bologna and thence (1438) to Ferrara. A minority, refusing to follow Eugenius, remained at Basel, reasserted their superiority over the Pope, and even went so far as to elect an anti-pope. But the Basel assemblage lacked popular support, and the papacy was adept in securing the backing of secular governments. In 1449 the council at Basel came to an inglorious end.

Meanwhile in 1439, the council at Ferrara-Florence (it was moved once again to the latter city) carried on negotiations with representatives of the Eastern, or Orthodox, Church of the Byzantines and Russians, which had been separated from Rome since the eleventh century. Contemporary military pressure of the Moslem Ottoman Turks against the Christian East stimulated serious efforts for reunion of the Churches, and eventually an agreement was reached at Florence, by which the Orthodox Church of the East, like the Catholic Church of the West, would recognize the Pope as spiritual head of all Christendom. When, however, the agreement was made known in the East, it was repudiated by the ecclesiastical authorities at Constantinople and at Moscow.[1] Thus, although the last Byzantine emperors remained personally loyal to the arrangements made at Florence, the two churches remained separate.

Only one thing, therefore—the ending of the Great Schism—was accomplished by the church councils of the fifteenth century. Heresy persisted, and so did the crying need for reform. The papacy, it is true, had survived a major crisis. Its very position in the church had been under attack, and naturally it felt obliged to devote much energy to defending and maintaining its position. This required, as the popes viewed the world in the unstable period of the councils and the Italian wars, a firm hold on the Papal State and the support of the powerful secular rulers of the day.

To the former task the popes, as we have seen, dedicated considerable energy and no little expenditure. Scarcely less demanding of time and money was their patronage of art and letters. Such things, entirely justifiable in themselves, were often pursued at the expense of urgent needs of the church as a whole; and worldly considerations of government, even of art and literature, too frequently took precedence over spiritual concerns.

In dealing with secular rulers, the popes, largely as a consequence of the schism and the conciliar movement, found themselves at a disadvantage. It is noteworthy that the concordats, or arrangements made with contemporary monarchs, usually conceded to them the right of patronage. A notable example is the Concordat of 1516 made by Pope Leo X with King Francis I of France.[2] Similar arrangements had been made with certain German emperors and princes. And to the Spanish monarchy the papacy granted exceptional controls over the court of the Inquisition. Thus, to assure the assistance —or avert the hostility—of monarchs, fifteenth- and sixteenth-century popes conceded what their predecessors since the eleventh century had struggled to preserve. But the early modern monarch, unlike his eleventh-century predecessor, was not a quasi-religious figure in a religio-political society, "priest and king." Rather he was ruler of a secular state which, as it perfected its political machinery, was ready to use this to control the ecclesiastical establishment.

The new system of royal control over

[1] Two Eastern prelates who accepted the union, Bessarion of Nicaea and Isidore of Kiev, returned to end their days in the west after brief visits to their respective homelands. The former, it will be remembered, was highly venerated as a Greek scholar.

[2] The Concordat of 1516, it should be added, did follow a great French victory (Marignano, 1515) in Italy. Moreover, the Pope gained two important concessions. He retained the right of investiture, and he obtained the promise that the Pragmatic Sanction of Bourges (1438), which had included a statement of the superiority of Council over Pope and had proclaimed the virtual autonomy of the French church, would be renounced. The Pragmatic Sanction, it may further be added, is an early example of what came to be known as "Gallicanism," the concept of a partially independent French church.

church affairs did not, in general, promote ecclesiastical reform, but rather the opposite. There was an increase in the number of dispensations, often granted to the relatives of important personages, to hold more than one benefice or to hold ecclesiastical office before reaching the minimum canonical age. The number of major sees whose incumbents during the last half of the fifteenth century were absentees was scandalously high.[1] Similar conditions afflicted many parishes. That this had a disastrous effect on the religious life of the time is obvious. Indeed, such conditions were far more significant than the misconduct, however spectacular, of individual members of the clergy.

In one instance, however, royal control over the ecclesiastical establishment did eventually facilitate an important movement of reform. This was Spain where, it will be recalled, Cardinal Ximenes, an archbishop of Toledo, primate of the Spanish church, and grand inquisitor, obtained extensive powers which he used to promote clerical education and generally to restore proper conditions. Ximenes met much opposition, but he persisted. Moreover, the reform which he inaugurated was not at first, like that of the Gregorians in the eleventh century, an ecumenical effort. Rather it was the Spanish national church which he was restoring. But it so happened that from this Spanish reform came much of the spirit and no small part of the energy for the larger reform of the following century.

E. Popular Religious Life in the Late Middle Age

Clerical shortcomings, especially when they were widespread, or, as in the case of the Great Schism, distinctly spectacular, were bound to affect the religious attitudes of the lay masses. Religion continued to be a powerful, possibly a dominant, influence in the life of the average European. At the same time, many persons, especially among the wealthy bourgeoisie, were affected by the prevailing spirit of worldliness. Perhaps for this very reason, there was evident a greater emphasis on religious externals. Popular veneration of relics bordered on the superstitious. Pilgrimages retained and increased their popularity.

In matters of popular devotion, the border line between superstition and orthodox practice is often hard to draw. The majority of Christians in the fifteenth century were illiterate and often came into contact with poorly trained priests. And perhaps because of a general loosening of ecclesiastical discipline, various weird beliefs became alarmingly popular. One was the peculiarly sinister belief in witchcraft.[2] Almost anyone who acted oddly, and especially lonely old women who perhaps had fallen into the habit of talking to themselves, became the object of popular suspicion and resentment as bewitched allies of the devil and sources of all manner of temporal and spiritual evil. So widespread was the delusion that many authorities shared and acted upon it; and in the course of the fifteenth century there developed a kind of epidemic of searching out "witches" and putting them to death.

The witchcraft delusion was but one example of a markedly pessimistic outlook on life which prevailed in the late middle age, especially in northern Europe. Perhaps men were abnormally absorbed in the contemplation of death because, in an age of much violence and recurring pestilence, death was ever present, and life for many was hard. At any rate, popular preachers could hold audiences by discourses, not so much on the hell fires of the hereafter, as on the spiritual struggles of the dying. Treatises on *The Art of Dying* had considerable vogue, as did contemporary woodcuts which abounded in skeletons and portrayed the "dance of death." [3]

---

[1] A famous example, often cited, is the case of Valencia, all of whose bishops for a period of a hundred years were Borgias, none of them resident.

[2] Witchcraft was a distortion of the church's teaching about the real existence of evil spirits—the devil and the fallen angels—into the popular notion that man could call such evil spirits to aid him against his enemies, and that some persons, "witches," were in communion with, and actually worshipped, the devil.

[3] For an example of the vogue in art, see above, p. 290.

If the historian must describe evil or unfortunate trends in the religious life of the late Middle Age, he cannot fail to remind his readers that the irregular is always more noticeable than the average. No doubt many, perhaps the great majority, of the clergy faithfully discharged their duties without attracting attention. There were fewer canonized saints than in earlier periods, particularly among the higher clergy, but there were some. It is also noteworthy that a considerable number of persons strove for a greater inner "experience of things divine." Such striving is known as mysticism. It was not novel to the fourteenth and fifteenth centuries. Far from it. But it stood out then against a background of worldliness and it represented, too, a spiritual reaction against scholastic rationalism and against mere externalism in religion. Mystical preachers seem to have appealed particularly to townsmen, who were now less under ecclesiastical influences than formerly.

Prominent among the noted mystics of the day was a German Dominican friar, usually known as Master Eckhart (*d.* 1327). A man of intellectual training who fully accepted the doctrines of the church, Eckhart preached to the common folk of the towns. Eschewing the customary scholastic methods, he sought rather to move the hearts of his hearers. Although he left no writings, his influence was great, especially in the Rhineland, and can perhaps best be judged by the lives and writings of some of his disciples. Of these, the best known were John Ruysbroeck, a Dutchman, and John Tauler and Henry Suso, both Germans.[1]

A similar spirit of longing for intimate personal communion with Christ can be seen in the life and work of Gerard Groote (1340–1384) of Deventer in Holland. Groote founded the organization known as the Brethren of the Common Life to which we have already referred.[2] In 1395 the Brethren adopted the Augustinian rule, and each separate house or monastery devoted itself to the copying of manuscripts and to teaching. Indeed, the pedagogical activities of the Brethren stimulated an educational reform throughout northwestern Europe. A number of famous scholars, including the great humanist Erasmus, were alumni of their schools. But above all, the Brethren inculcated a deep love of God and of one's fellow man. This movement came to be known as the "Devotio moderna," and from it, possibly from the pen of Thomas à Kempis (*d.* 1471), came one of the most popular devotional books of Christian literature, the *Imitation of Christ.*

Generally speaking, the *Devotio moderna* was unsympathetic to intellectualism or rational speculation in matters of religion. Instead, it was in line with an important trend of the late middle age in theological teaching—putting emphasis on the will rather than on the intellect. An earlier chapter called attention to the direction given philosophical studies by William of Ockham (*d.* 1349) and his followers. Ockhamism, with its questioning of the validity of rational speculation in matters of faith and its denial of any correspondence to reality of universals, or general ideas, was prevalent in the schools of the late middle age. Partly for this reason and partly because thirteenth-century scholasticism had given way in many places to pedantic and seemingly fruitless discussion of details, there was a marked lack of vigor and originality in contemporary theological teaching.

The church in the fifteenth century had successfully frustrated all attempts to alter its ancient constitution. This was an achievement of the first importance. In its espousal of the new learning and in the promotion of art, it had given brilliant leadership. But a comparable leadership in promoting much needed spiritual renewal was lacking. It seems evident that, as an organization, the church was not meeting or reducing the tensions of the early modern age.

---

[1] An exaggeration of Eckhart's teachings led to a type of mysticism which was condemned by the pope. Martin Luther, at a later date, seems to have been influenced by doctrines of this nature.

[2] See above, p. 317.

SELECT SUPPLEMENTARY READINGS FOR PART V

General. The interpretation of the period known as the late middle age or the renaissance has been and continues to be a subject of lively discussion, much of which revolves around the classic work of J. Burckhardt, *The Civilization of the Renaissance in Italy*, first published in German in 1860 and republished and translated many times since. See the recent edition, with introduction by B. Nelson and C. Trinkhaus, 2 vols. (1958). For further study of the concept of "renaissance," see K. H. Dannenfeldt, *The Renaissance, Medieval or Modern?* (1959); W. Ferguson, *The Renaissance in Historical Thought* (1948) and *Renaissance Studies* (1963); T. Helton, ed., A *Symposium on the Renaissance* (1961). Other general works are: *Cambridge Medieval History*, vols. VII and VIII; *New Cambridge Modern History*, vol. I (1957); E. P. Cheyney, *The Dawn of a New Era* (new ed. 1960); D. Hay, *The Italian Renaissance in Its Historical Background* (1962); J. H. Plumb, ed., *The Italian Renaissance* (1964); E. Lucki, *History of the Renaissance*, 5 vols. (1963–1965); M. P. Gilmore, *The World of Humanism* (1952); J. Huizinga, *The Waning of the Middle Ages* (1927); G. C. Sellery, *The Renaissance, Its Nature and Origins* (1950).

***Chapter* 22.** *Cambridge Economic History of Europe*, 3 vols. (1941, 1952, 1961); R. de Roover, *The Medici Bank* (1948), also *Money, Banking and Credit in Medieval Bruges* (1948) and *Rise and Decline of the Medici Bank* (1963).

***Chapter* 23.** A. Buchan, *Joan of Arc and the Recovery of France* (1958); H. Cam, *England before Elizabeth* (1950); O. Cartellieri, *The Court of Burgundy* (1929); P. Champion, *Louis XI* (tr. 1929); E. F. Jacob, *The Fifteenth Century* (England) (1961); M. M. McKisack, *The Fourteenth Century* (England) (1959); A. R. Myers, *England in the Later Middle Ages* (1952); E. Perroy, *The Hundred Years' War* (1951); G. M. Trevelyan, *England in the Age of Wycliffe* (1909); R. Pernoud, *Joan of Arc* (1961).

***Chapter* 24.** G. Barraclough, *The Origins of Modern Germany* (1947); J. D. Clarkson, A *History of Russia* (1961); O. Halecki, *Borderlands of Western Civilization* (1952); A. W. A. Leeper, A *History of Medieval Austria* (1941); G. Vernadsky and M. Karpovich, A *History of Russia*, vol. III (1953).

***Chapter* 25.** T. J. Oleson, *Early Voyages and Northern Approaches, 1000–1632* (1964). On Spain and Portugal, in addition to books cited above for chapter 17: J. H. Mariéjol, *The Spain of Ferdinand and Isabella* (tr. 1961). For the discoveries: B. W. Diffie, *Prelude to Empire: Portugal Overseas Before Henry the Navigator* (1960); J. E. Gillespie, A *History of Geographical Discovery* (1933); S. E. Morison, *Admiral of the Ocean Sea* (Columbus), 2 vols. (1942, and also a one-volume edition); S. E. Morison and M. Obregón, *The Caribbean as Columbus Saw It* (1964); A. P. Newton, *The Great Age of Discovery* (1932); E. Prestage, *The Portuguese Pioneers* (1933); E. Sanceau, *Henry the Navigator* (1947); C. McK. Parr, *Ferdinand Magellan, Circumnavigator* (1964); C. E. Nowell, ed., *Magellan's Voyage Around the World: Three Contemporary Accounts* (1962); P. Sykes, A *History of Exploration* (new ed., 1960). For Italy: W. M. Bowsky, *Henry VII in Italy* (1960); H. B. Cotterill, *Italy from Dante to Tasso* (1919); F. Chabod, *Machiavelli and the Renaissance* (1959); G. Mattingly,

Renaissance Diplomacy (1955); F. Schevill, *The Medici* (new ed., 1949), *History of Florence* (new ed., 1961), and *Siena* (new ed. with introduction by W. M. Bowsky, 1964).

***Chapter* 26.** In addition to the books cited under "General," above: R. Bolgar, *The Classical Heritage and Its Beneficiaries* (1954); R. W. Chambers, *Thomas More* (1935); J. Fletcher, *The Literature of the Italian Renaissance* (1934); J. Huizinga, *Erasmus* (tr. 1924); P. O. Kristeller, *The Classics and Renaissance Thought* (1955, new ed., 1961). On science, H. Butterfield, *The Origins of Modern Science* (1949); A. C. Crombie, *Medieval and Early Modern Science* (1959). For art, in addition to Gardner. Janson, and Pevsner cited above, p. 49; B. Lowry, *Renaissance Architecture* (1962); O. Benesch, *The Art of the Renaissance in Northern Europe* (1945). On music: P. H. Lang, *Music in Western Civilization* (1941). On printing: P. Butler, *The Origin of Printing in Europe* (1940); D. C. McMurtrie, *The Book, the Story of Printing and Bookmaking* (3rd ed., 1943).

***Chapter* 27.** L. E. Binns, *Decline and Fall of the Medieval Papacy* (1934); A. C. Flick, *The Decline of the Medieval Church* (1930); P. Hughes, *A History of the Church*, vol. III (1947); A. Hyma, *The Christian Renaissance, a History of the "Devotia Moderna"* (1924); J. Gill, *The Council of Florence* (1959); G. Mollat, *The Popes at Avignon, 1305–1378* (new tr. 1963).

From Charles V and Luther to Gustavus Adolphus and Philip IV

PART VI

EARLY MODERN RELIGIOUS UPHEAVAL

The interior of the Jesuit church of the *Gesù* in Rome (Vignola, *d.* 1573), redecorated seventeenth century.

Alinari photograph

TIMES AND IN THE WEST

Sixteenth century limestone medallions of the Emperor Charles V and his consort, Isabel of Portugal.

Courtesy Hispanic Society of America

WE DESCRIBE as "Early Modern Times" the sixteenth century and the first half of the seventeenth. In most respects they are but a continuation of the "Late Middle Age" of the fourteenth and fifteenth centuries. There is continuity in the strengthening of national monarchy, in the growth of commercial capitalism, in the development of printing, classical renaissance, and vernacular literature, in the menacing advance of the Moslem Turks in the "East," and in the expansion of the "West" across the Atlantic and into America.

The outstanding novelty of Early Modern Times is a religious upheaval throughout western and central Europe. It finds expression in a forceful revolt against the Catholic Church in the northern half of Germany and the Netherlands, in Scandinavia, Switzerland, England, and Scotland, and the establishment of a variety of separate Protestant churches and sects. It also finds expression in a reformation within the Catholic Church and a renewed zeal which enables it to maintain its hold on a majority of European countries and at the same time to secure compensation for its losses in Europe by missionary gains in America and the Far East.

The religious upheaval produces extraordinary bitterness and intolerance on the part of both Protestants and Catholics, and a series of religio-political wars. These wars begin with the unavailing efforts of the Emperor Charles V, in the first half of the sixteenth century, to keep the Holy Roman Empire strong and united and to use it, in conjunction with his Spanish inheritance, to dominate the Continent. They continue with the farflung but largely unsuccessful attempts of his son, Philip II, in the second half of the sixteenth century, to secure the supremacy of Spain and the defeat of Protestantism. They conclude with the Thirty Years' War, in the first half of the seventeenth century, when religious factors yield to dynastic and commercial, when political hegemony passes from Spain to France, and when the practical collapse of the Holy Roman Empire finally dispels any hope of providing a central power for a united Western Christendom.

CHAPTER 28

Emperor Charles V in Europe, Overseas and Against the Turks

A. Charles the First of Spain and Fifth of the Holy Roman Empire

When Charles was born in Ghent in 1500, it was clear that he would one day come into an extensive inheritance, but few could have realized that he would be lord of wider dominions than had been ruled by any previous European monarch. When he was six years old, the death of his father, Philip of Habsburg, gave him possession of the Netherlands and Imperial Burgundy (Franche Comté). When he was sixteen, the death of his grandfather Ferdinand made him King Charles I of Spain, with its dependencies in Italy and overseas in America. At nineteen, the death of his grandfather Maximilian brought him all the hereditary territories of the Habsburgs and the expectation of being chosen Holy Roman Emperor.

Though the title of emperor had come down in the Habsburg family continuously since 1438, the office was still elective, and in 1519 there were in addition to Charles two young and ambitious rulers who put forward their candidacies: Henry VIII of England, and Francis I of France. The latter was the more formidable rival in the election. By diplomacy and bribes Francis sought to win the backing of the church and the votes of the electors. Charles already ruled so many lands that it could easily be argued that he would have little time to devote to Germany or to his duties as Emperor.

But in the election Charles had certain advantages. The tradition of electing the Habsburgs was strong, and as a Habsburg Charles seemed more like a German than did Francis. In addition, Charles had special friends among the bankers of the time, and with their aid he was better able to play the game of bribery than his rival. He borrowed some money for the purpose from the Medici at Florence, and still more from the Fuggers, the German banking family of Augsburg which had long been loaning money to the Habsburgs. The Fuggers now surpassed the Medici and had more funds at their disposal than any other bankers in Europe. They had branch offices in Antwerp and a dozen other cities from which they financed merchants, towns, provinces, and kings. When the head of the house of Fugger, Jacob the Rich, opened his purse to Charles, it meant that the bribes of Francis could be easily matched and exceeded. In 1519 Charles gained the election, and in 1520 he was crowned as the Emperor Charles V at Aix-la-Chapelle (Aachen).

It was a sign of the times that capitalists could help make emperors. In the fifteenth century the center of capitalistic credit and banking had been in northern Italy, and particularly with the Medici family at Florence. But in the early sixteenth century it passed to Augsburg in southern Germany, where the family firms of the Welsers, the Hochstetters, the Meutings, and others

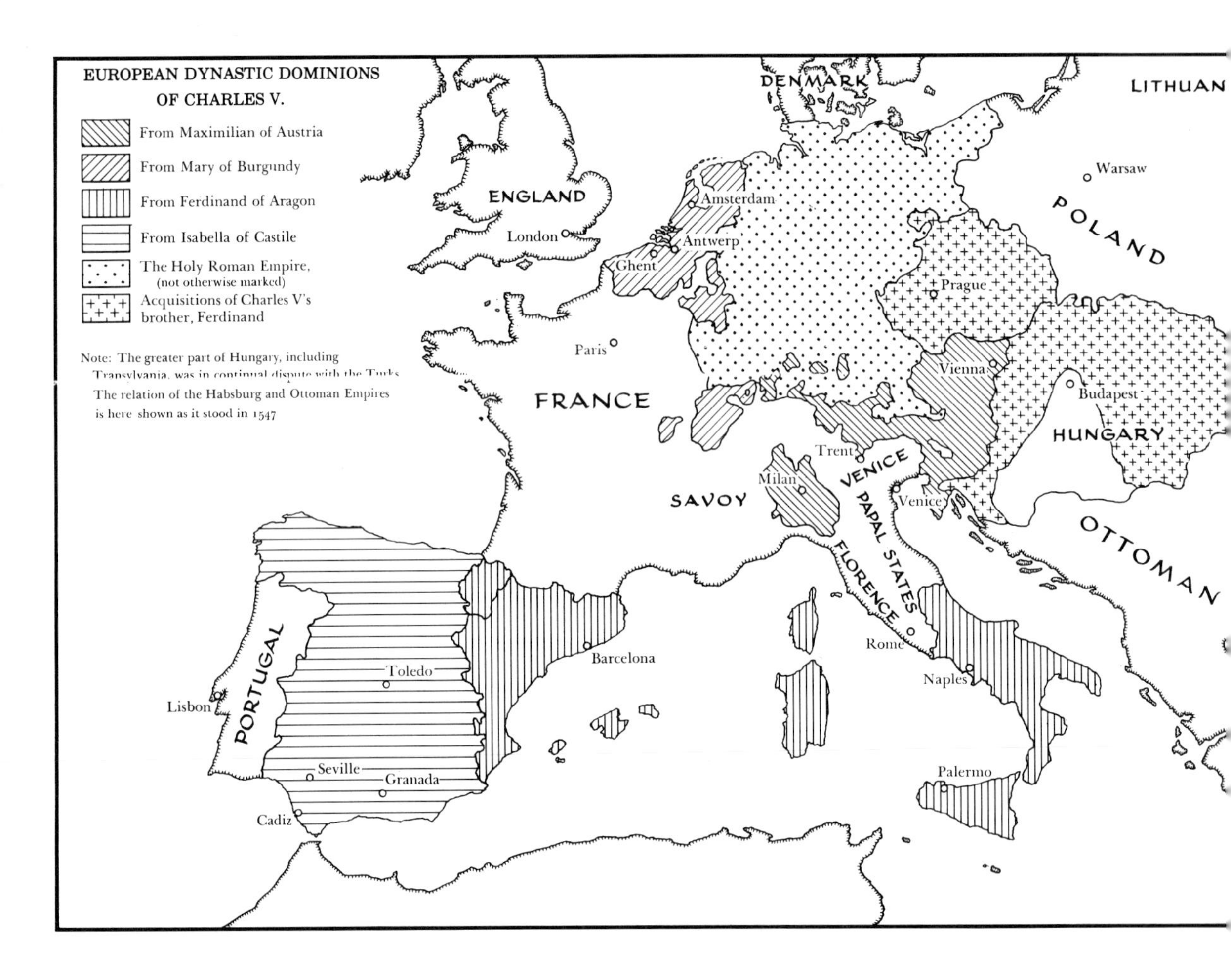

vied with the Fuggers. Many of the banker-merchants financed commercial and industrial ventures, but the Fuggers had two main interests—mining, and loans to the Habsburgs. They reaped rich profits from the copper, silver, and lead mines of the Tyrol and of Hungary. They loaned more and more money to the Habsburgs, until in 1560 Charles' son, Philip II of Spain, owed them some 4,000,000 gold gulden, a gigantic sum for those days.

Most of the great German and Italian bankers had offices in one of Charles' cities, Antwerp in the Netherlands. For by the sixteenth century Antwerp had displaced the older city of Bruges as the commercial center of northern and western Europe. There the products of the north, especially English cloth, were exchanged for those of the Mediterranean and for the new goods that began to come in from America and the Far East. Antwerp had a great Bourse, or Exchange (opened in 1460), for trade in goods, and another (opened in 1531) for financial transactions such as loans to merchants and kings. Its river harbor was thronged with shipping, its streets crowded with drays and carts. To Charles V, it was a great source of strength that he was ruler of the rich Netherlands and of the busy city of Antwerp.

Because he had been born in the Netherlands, had lived there during his boyhood, and spoke the local language (Flemish or Dutch), Charles V always thought of himself more as a Netherlander than as an Austrian or a Spaniard. He knew how to deal familiarly and in friendly fashion with the rich burghers of the towns. They, in turn, regarded him with pride and affection and even paid the taxes he levied without too much murmuring or discontent. In Spain, on the contrary, Charles was regarded, when he went there first in 1517, as a foreigner and he did not increase his popularity by making use there of advisers

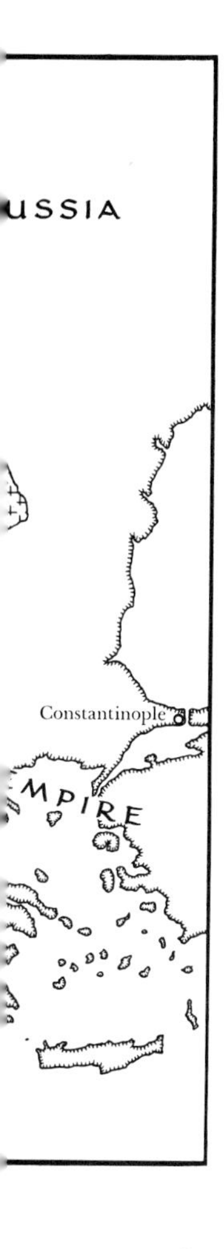

Francis I of France about 1525.
Jean Clouet.
Cuortesy Louvre Museum, Paris

and officials from the Netherlands. There was some hostility to him and even open revolt in various Spanish cities (1519–1520). But though Charles looked upon Spain merely as a source of wealth and military strength, he was able to crush all opposition and rule the country with a firm hand.

Charles was indeed an able ruler, who could adapt himself to the needs of the moment. If he was amiable in Ghent, he could be haughty in Madrid and stern in Vienna. Though he was afraid of mice and spiders, he was an able and courageous general on the field of battle. He could persuade as well as command, and he could employ guileful diplomacy as well as military force. All his life he showed a deep devotion to the Catholic faith. Thin of face and with the protruding lower jaw of the Habsburgs, Charles was anything but handsome. Yet his dignity and bearing were those of the great monarch that he truly was.

B. *Wars of Charles V in Europe*

During most of his reign, Charles V was at war with France. The French monarchy, which had done much to reëstablish itself following the Hundred Years' War, had, before the end of the fifteenth century, intervened actively in the affairs of Italy. The French King Charles VIII's expedition of 1494 has been discussed in a previous chapter. His successor, Louis XII (1498–1515) of the house of Orleans, continued the policy, adding the Orleanist claims to Milan to the older French-Angevin pretensions to Naples.[1] His efforts were unavailing, and they resulted, among other things, in the Spanish occupation of Naples (1504).

Louis' successor, Francis I (1515–1547), was therefore continuing an old Franco-Spanish rivalry both in pushing war into Italy and in attempting to win the Pyrenees

[1] Louis XII was the grandson of Valentina Visconti. See above, p. 280 *n*.

kingdom of Navarre which Ferdinand of Aragon had absorbed in 1512. But to Francis the entire complex of Habsburg territories offered a new problem. For it seemed as if these territories, more especially Spain, Franche Comté, and the Netherlands, were encircling France. On the other hand, Charles was determined to oppose all French pretensions beyond their frontiers and if possible to regain the French duchy of Burgundy which had been taken from his grandmother by Louis XI of France.

The war between Francis and Charles was, therefore, of wider scope than previous Franco-Spanish conflicts. Though it was fought at first mainly in Italy, it soon extended to other theatres. With various truces and treaties as interruptions, it was to be continued for more than a century. This series of conflicts was dynastic rather than national in character, in that disputes over inheritance and succession often outweighed more fundamental national interests.

By a brilliant victory at Marignano (1515), shortly after his accession, Francis regained Milan, which had been recently lost by Louis XII. But the forces of Charles V, aided by the pope, drove the French out again and went on to invade France. In turn, Francis pushed the Emperor's troops back. Finally, at Pavia in 1525, the army of Charles V completely crushed the French army and captured the French King. "Nothing is left to me," wrote Francis I to his mother, "save honor and life."

Francis won his release by agreeing to humiliating peace terms. But no sooner was he back in France, than he busied himself in winning the support of the pope and of other Italian rulers who were dismayed by the growing power of Charles. Hostilities were soon resumed, and the pope paid dearly for his change of sides, for in 1527 the unpaid and unruly soldiery of Charles V sacked and pillaged the city of Rome. Despite some aid from England, Francis made little headway, and the peace of Cambrai (1529) left all Italy under the rule or the influence of Charles V.

To make trouble for Charles, Francis sought help wherever he could find it. He made alliances with Scotland, Sweden, and Denmark, with rebellious princes in Germany, and even with the infidel Turks. Fighting occurred again from 1536 to 1538, and from 1542 to 1544. Neither the death of Francis I (1547) nor the abdication of Charles V (1556) ended the struggle, for war raged again from 1552 until the peace of Cateau-Cambrésis in 1559. By this treaty, France renounced once again its claims in Italy, leaving the entire peninsula under the control of Charles' Habsburg successors in Austria and Spain. But France gained something, for she was permitted to occupy the bishoprics of Metz, Toul, and Verdun, which were located in a position of high strategic importance on the northeast frontier of France, and gave to the French a foothold in Alsace and thus in the Holy Roman Empire.

From a larger point of view, the French gained by these many wars for they had checked somewhat the rising power of the

Habsburgs. In so doing they had adopted a policy of alliance with the Protestant princes of Germany which was to continue and to be intensified in the following century. Thus France had indirectly aided not only the Turks, but also the growth of Protestantism in Germany, by keeping Charles busy with foreign wars, when he might well have been putting down the ecclesiastical revolt in the Empire.

The difficulties in Germany were not merely the religious ones which will be examined in the next chapter. The German princes, great and small, were eagerly trying to increase their political power. They had made Charles, at his election as Emperor, grant them added rights over government and policy, and they could arouse a good deal of German national sentiment against him by painting him as a foreigner dominated by Spanish or other alien interests. Then, too, the rich burghers of the German towns opposed any taxes which would have increased the Emperor's power.

The lesser German nobility—the knights—under such fiery leaders as Ulrich von Hutten and Franz von Sickingen, were the most patriotic class, proud of being German and distrustful of foreign influence. At the beginning of his reign it looked as if Charles V could depend on the knights to help him against the princes and burghers. But at this very time, many of the knights welcomed the new Protestant movement as a way to end "foreign" control of the church in Germany. Thus when Charles took steps against the Protestants (1521) he alienated the knights. The next year under von Sickingen, the knights took arms and attacked the Catholic bishopric of Trier. Since the burghers and princes hated the unruly knights, they joined together and crushed them.

Nor were these the only troubles Charles

French sixteenth century castle architecture. Chambord, the favorite residence of King Francis I.

Courtesy French Government Tourist Office, New York

had to face in Germany, for the Lutheran princes banded together in a League at Schmalkald in 1531 and waged civil war off and on from 1546 to 1555, when the Peace of Augsburg temporarily settled the religious conflict.[1] Thus Charles V had on his hands not only almost continuous war with France, a foreign foe, but also almost equally continuous difficulties within Germany. To add to his problems, there was the ever-present threat to the east, the menace of the Moslem Turks.

C. Wars of Charles V against the Turks

Charles was concerned with the Turkish menace not only as Emperor and traditionally responsible for the Empire's eastern frontiers, but more particularly as Archduke of Austria and guardian of Vienna and the Danube valley. Moreover, his reign almost coincided with that of the greatest and ablest of the Turkish Sultans, Suleiman the "Magnificent" (1520–1566).

When Suleiman came to the throne at Constantinople, the Turks had already overrun most of the Balkan peninsula and the new Sultan soon renewed the victorious drive northward. In 1521 he captured Belgrade, and all of Serbia was soon under his sway. One of his greatest victories came five years later (1526) when he overwhelmed the Hungarian army on the field of Mohács. There perished a great portion of the Hungarian knights and nobles, and the king of Hungary (Louis II) fell on the field of battle. In 1529, Suleiman led his armies onward and laid siege to Vienna itself. All Christian Europe seemed threatened as the eastern marches crumbled. So strong was the defense of Vienna, however, that Suleiman raised the siege after three weeks, though his forces ravaged the surrounding countryside.

In the meanwhile, Ferdinand of Habsburg, brother of Charles V, laid claim to the throne of Hungary, secured his election to it, and tried to carry on the war against the Turks, more, perhaps, to acquire and defend new lands for himself than to free Hungary from the infidel. In 1547, Charles and Ferdinand were compelled to recognize the Turkish conquests in Hungary. By an agreement of that year, Suleiman left Ferdinand in possession of thirty-five counties of Hungary for which he agreed to pay the Turks a heavy annual tribute. The largest part of the country, including Budapest, became a Turkish province, while a third section centering in Transylvania was left under Turkish influence, though it was to be ruled by a Hungarian prince. Twice (1552 and 1566) did the Habsburgs try to conquer Transylvania, and twice Suleiman defeated them and consolidated the Turkish power. In many Hungarian towns, churches were turned into mosques.

The Hungarian King who fell at Mohács, Louis II, was also the elective King of Bohemia, still part of the Holy Roman Empire. After his death the Bohemians, in desperate fear of the advancing Turks, and wanting a ruler who could defend them, chose Ferdinand of Habsburg. Consequently, though it was not until the end of the following century that all of Hungary was recovered from the Turks, it and Bohemia were added to the Habsburg domains, to remain as such for nearly four hundred years.

Although at least nominal suzerainty over parts of central and western North Africa was claimed by the Turks, this was opposed by Charles who, as King of Spain and the Two Sicilies, was responsible for the Mediterranean interests of these countries. Since the fourteenth century the Spanish had held a small, fortified, rock island in front of the harbor of Algiers. In 1519 they sought to capture the city itself, whither had fled many of the Moors who had been expelled from Granada in 1492. The Spanish attack was repelled by a Turkish sea rover and admiral known as Khair-ed-Din, or Barbarossa (Redbeard), who had made himself master of the city and placed himself under the rule of the Turkish Sultan Suleiman the "Magnificent." Ten years later Barbarossa drove the Spanish even from their islet fortress.

To the east of Algiers, the same Barbarossa was also successful. Acting for Suleiman, he secured possession of Tunis. Then to check the expanding Turkish power in the Mediterranean, Charles V intervened. In 1535, with the Emperor in personal

[1] See below, p. 354.

command of the army and a Genoese admiral, Andrea Doria, in charge of the fleet, a Spanish expedition conquered Tunis and installed a native ruler as a Spanish vassal. Though the Spaniards long held strong fortresses on the Tunisian coast, they were never able to establish a firm rule over the country and in 1574 they were driven out and Tunisia became a Turkish province.

The Turkish rule at Algiers seemed to Charles V a special threat to the safety of Spanish commerce and even to Spain itself. Accordingly, in 1541, he led a large force against the city. But his luck was bad, for a storm destroyed many of his ships and his army of 30,000 men was defeated by the Algerians under a native prince, or pasha. In the ensuing years, the Moslem Barbarossa took a fleet to the south coast of France to support Francis I against Charles V, and on his way back to Constantinople the Turkish admiral ravaged and plundered the coast of Italy.

These forays and repulses in North Africa were really part of a great renewed struggle between Christian and Moslem for naval control of the Mediterranean. On the one side was Charles V, usually in alliance with Venice whose possessions among the islands and ports of the Near East were menaced. On the other side was Suleiman the Magnificent, aided by roving sea fighters like Barbarossa. On the whole, the Turks won in the first phases of the struggle, for they increased their control of North Africa, gained strong points on the Dalmatian coast across the Adriatic from Venice, conquered island after island, and repeatedly attacked the coasts of Sicily, South Italy, and even the Balearic Islands.

The crisis of the struggle was not reached till after both Suleiman and Charles V were dead. In 1570, a Turkish fleet captured Cyprus from the Venetians. Only Malta and Crete were left as Christian outposts in the eastern Mediterranean. Inspired by Pope Pius V, Genoa, Venice, and Spain joined with him to send a great fleet of 208 ships against the Moslems. It was led by Don John of Austria, a son of Charles V. On October 7, 1571, he inflicted a crushing defeat on a Turkish fleet of 273 vessels in

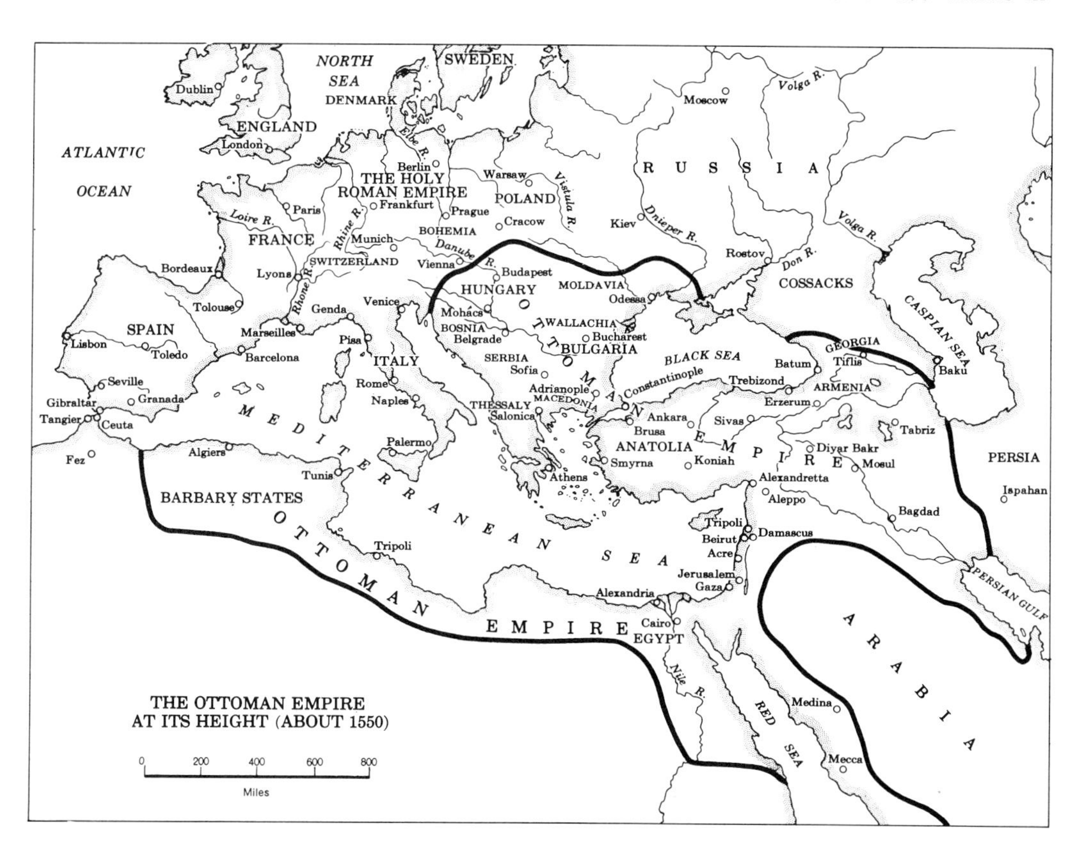

THE OTTOMAN EMPIRE AT ITS HEIGHT (ABOUT 1550)

the mouth of the Gulf of Lepanto. The cannon and tactics of the Christians proved superior. Most of the Turkish warships were sunk or driven ashore. Twenty thousand Turks, it is said, lost their lives.

The battle of Lepanto was the last great sea fight fought by large fleets of galleys. It was also in many ways the last of the Crusades. But it was more than that, for it marked a check to their sea power from which the Turks never recovered. Slowly their naval strength in the Mediterranean dwindled. In the seventeenth century, Moslem activity at sea was to be mainly in the form of piratical forays from cities like Algiers and Tunis on the north shore of Africa.

D. Charles and the Spanish and Portuguese Dominions Overseas

When Charles came to the throne of Spain in 1516, the foundations of the great Spanish overseas dominion had been laid. The work of Columbus and other explorers had made known the West Indies and much of the coasts of northern South America and of Central America. In 1513 Balboa had crossed the isthmus of Panama and seen the Pacific, while in the same year Ponce de Leon had discovered Florida. It was now, of course, universally realized that these lands were not Asia or the East Indies, but a "new world;" and it had been named "America."[1] The Portuguese meanwhile had been not only exploring and conquering important eastern areas from the Persian Gulf to the Spice Islands, but had also, through the work of Cabral, discovered and laid claim to the coast of Brazil. In order to arbitrate the rival claims of Spain and Portugal, Pope Alexander VI had drawn a "line of demarkation" (1493), as we have already said, from the north to the south pole, a hundred leagues west of the Azores, and then, by subsequent mutual agreement, the line had been moved some 270 leagues farther west. All lands to the east of the line (including Brazil, Africa, India and the East Indies) were to be a Portuguese monopoly for trade and colonization. All lands to the west of it (including the West Indies, North America, Central America, and South America, minus Brazil) were to be a Spanish monopoly.

[1] See above, p. 303.

In the years after 1516 the Spaniards pushed ahead rapidly with their tremendous work of exploring and conquering new lands. In 1519, an expedition under Alvarez de Piñeda sailed along the coast from Florida to Mexico. In the same year Ferdinand Magellan, a Portuguese in the service of Spain, set out with five ships and 243 men to open up a way to the East Indies by going south of South America. The expedition found a strait between the continent and Tierra del Fuego, crossed the Pacific, and discovered the Philippines where Magellan was killed in a fight with the natives. In 1522, one of his ships, the *Victoria*, got back to Spain with eighteen men. The world had been circumnavigated and no one could longer doubt that it was round or that the East could be reached by sailing west.

It was likewise in 1519 that the young

The Sultan Ahmet (Blue) Mosque in Istanbul (Constantinople), a sixteenth century building in which the Turks developed further the structural principles of Santa Sophia (in left background).

Courtesy Turkish Information Office, New York

Spaniard Hernando Cortez landed on the coast of Mexico with six or seven hundred men, eighteen horses, and a few cannon. Within a few years, he had accomplished the seemingly impossible, and conquered the rich and populous empire of the native Aztec Indians. A few years later, Francisco Pizarro conquered the extensive South American empire of the Incas.

The great work of the conquest forced Spain to develop a colonial system for the management of her new dominions. This task had been begun under Ferdinand and Isabella, but it really took definite form under Charles. Political control of the colonies was in the hands of a Council of the Indies. This Council sat as a court in important cases, made laws like a legislature, appointed viceroys, governors, and other officials, administered church affairs, and determined policies. Through it, the King was able to maintain firm control over all phases of colonial life.

In their treatment of the natives, the Spaniards were torn by two conflicting motives. On the one hand, bishops, priests, monks and friars, who had gone out from the homeland to win souls, wished to convert the natives and to treat them in a kindly manner as potential fellow Christians. On the other hand, many conquistadores and landowners, in their lust for wealth, were tempted to exploit the natives. In general, it may be said that the laws issued by the central government at Madrid were designed to protect the natives. But, such was the great distance between Spain and America, and so many were the involvements of the Spanish monarchy in Europe, that the laws were not effectively implemented. Thus it befell, for example, that after the native kingdoms had been despoiled of their gold and silver and the Spaniards had taken over the mines, the Indians were forced to provide the mine labor.

In 1545, Potosí in Peru, a veritable mountain of silver, was opened up, and other mines scarcely less rich were soon developed. For a century the New World was to pour a vast stream of silver into the Old. So great was this influx of precious metal that with it Spain could pay soldiers, build fleets, and bribe diplomats throughout the sixteenth century. It was this wealth, mined out of the earth by Indian laborers, that helped to make Spain the predominant country in Europe.

Not all Indians were treated badly. In the missions established by Franciscans, Dominicans, Jesuits, and other religious orders, many were protected with paternal kindness and taught the arts and crafts of civilized life. There were always some Spaniards who preached and worked against their greedy fellow countrymen and in behalf of the native Indians. For example, Bartolomé de Las Casas (1474–1566), Bishop of Chiapas in Mexico, is known as the Apostle of the Indies, because he devoted his every effort to champion the Indians and to secure laws which would improve their lot.

While the Spanish were creating a colonial empire in the new world, the Portuguese were building an empire of a different type in the east. Their far-flung possessions constituted a commercial rather than a colonial empire. The interest of the Portuguese centered in the spice trade over which they rapidly acquired a virtual monopoly. Two great leaders, Almeida, an admiral, and Albuquerque, a viceroy, followed up between 1505 and 1515 da Gama's voyage by ousting Arab traders and securing ports from the Persian Gulf to the Spice Islands. With their naval supremacy they held, fortified, and garrisoned the cities they captured and used them as centers of trade. Relatively little attempt was made to colonize or to extend Portuguese control beyond the coastal cities, for with a population of less than two million Portugal had little manpower to spare, and the Far Eastern countries were already densely inhabited.

Portuguese trade to the East was a royal monopoly, at least as regarded the all important spices. It was carried on by royal officials, with royal money, on royal ships. The profits were the king's and they were very great, for the Portuguese were able to buy pepper and other spices cheap in the East and sell them dear in Europe. Even so they undersold the Venetians, whose trade by the expensive overland routes rapidly dwindled after 1500. It was to Lisbon that ships came from all countries to secure the eastern spices. Until almost 1600, this little country of Portugal held all the storied eastern trade in its hands. When finally the Dutch and English broke into their preserve, then and only then did the Portuguese give much serious attention to their one great American colony of Brazil.

Thus it was that, for a hundred years after the original voyages of Columbus and da Gama, the countries which profited from the new discoveries were Spain and Portugal. Moreover, when the Spaniards—and later the Portuguese—settled in the New World, they were performing one of the major feats of modern history. They were transferring to that new and distant world their language, their religion, and Europe's Western civilization. By 1600 there were 150,000 Spaniards in America. Their political system was organized, and they were divided ecclesiastically into four archbishoprics and twenty-four bishoprics, including some 360 monasteries and convents. In some degree, European customs were merely superimposed on persisting native cultures. And it was some time before the schools and seminaries could rival their European counterparts. But if the universities of Mexico City and Lima had only small enrollment and limited facilities at the time of their establishment in 1551, they were the first institutions of higher learning in the New World. In many ways all the Americas south of the Rio Grande, with the exception of Brazil, were being made indelibly Spanish.

Such were the manifold concerns of the Emperor Charles V. They were, in fact, too much for one man. On his abdication in 1556, it had been decided that his eldest son, Philip, should inherit all his possessions with the exception of the Austrian lands and the presumption of election to the imperial title. These were to go to Charles' brother, Ferdinand. The formal act of abdication took place in the Netherlands where Charles had always been beloved. Worn out and broken in health by his many labors, he resigned his crowns, shed some tears, and went into retirement in a little house attached to a monastery in Spain.

Martin Luther and his friends. Lucas Cranach (*d.* 1553). Although John Frederick, Elector of Saxony and nephew of Frederick the Wise who had first protected Luther, dominates the picture, Luther can be seen at the extreme left, Melancthon at the extreme right, and Zwingli between Melancthon and the Elector.

Courtesy Toledo Museum of Art; gift of Edward Drummond Libbey, 1926

Gottes wort bleibt ewig.

Biblia/das ist/ die gantze Heilige Schrifft Deudsch.
Mart. Luth.
Wittemberg.
Begnadet mit Kürfürstlicher zu Sachsen freiheit.
Gedruckt durch Hans Lufft.

M. D. XXXIIII.

Title page of Luther's German translation of the Bible. Printed by Hans Lufft, Wittenberg, 1534.

Courtesy New York Public Library

CHAPTER 29

Protestant Revolt Against the Catholic Church

LUTHERANISM AND CALVINISM

A. Catholic Beliefs

Early in the sixteenth century the Catholic church which, except for occasional heresies, had universal acceptance throughout western and central Europe, was subjected to a major revolt which resulted in the formation of several new and separate, or as they came to be called, "Protestant," churches. The original Protestant movements from which others later diverged were three in number: (1) Lutheranism and (2) Calvinism, each so designated from the name of its founder, and (3) Anglicanism, named from the country of its origin. The weakness and corruption of the early sixteenth-century church, which a previous chapter has described,[1] contributed much to the spread of Protestantism. So also did certain political and economic factors. But Protestantism, at least in its origin, was essentially religious and involved serious questionings of basic doctrines of the Catholic faith. It may be well, therefore, to review briefly the principal articles of the Catholic faith in order better to understand where Protestants diverged.

Of central importance, it will be recalled, was belief in the Trinity, in the divinity of Jesus Christ, and in a divinely established church which, under the pope, was the ordained instrument to enable sinful human beings to attain salvation in the next world. The church was the custodian and dispenser of the sacraments. These, seven in number, were baptism, confirmation, confession and penance, the holy eucharist or Mass, extreme unction for the sick and dying, matrimony, and holy orders. Baptism was held to be essential for salvation since it cleansed the individual of all sin. Around the Eucharist or Lord's Supper, during which, at the words of the priest, the bread and wine were considered to be miraculously transformed into the very Body and Blood of Christ (transubstantiation), there had developed the elaborate and beautiful ritual of the Mass. The Mass, it should be added, was believed to be a sacrifice, a continuation of the sacrifice of Christ in his crucifixion.

In addition to these fundamental tenets, there had developed in the course of the centuries certain beliefs and practices which, although peripheral to the central articles of faith, had obtained widespread popularity. Indeed, it was the contention of some that certain of these, such as the invocation of saints and the issuance of indulgences, were often pursued at the expense of more important matters.

Since the distribution of indulgences was to precipitate the revolt of 1517, they require special explanation here. An indulgence, according to Catholic teaching, was the remission, in whole or in part, of the temporal punishment to be meted out to a person after his death for sins for which he had been sincerely sorry and had done penance. By means of an indulgence, the punishment of a soul in purgatory, the abode of those not yet ready for heaven, might be shortened (partial indulgence) or

[1] See above, pp. 325–333.

done away with altogether (plenary indulgence) by virtue of the authority conferred by Christ upon St. Peter to hold and use the "keys of the kingdom of heaven" and to "bind and loose" upon earth. In earlier times, indulgences were obtainable only after the performance of rather arduous tasks such as pilgrimages or crusades. Latterly, it had become customary only to require the penitent to say certain prayers or to perform some simple religious act. Among these might be a contribution of money for some religious purpose. The doctrine of indulgences was an extremely important matter in the early months of the Lutheran movement. After that, not being a tenet of major importance, it dropped into the background.

B. Luther and Lutheranism

Martin Luther (1483–1546) was born into a family of modest means. His father was a miner, able to give his son an education, and hopeful that he would follow the law. But Martin, a sensitive youth, entered the religious life as an Augustinian friar. He had studied at the university of Erfurt and he later taught at Wittenberg in Saxony. Intelligent and eloquent, though making no pretense at erudition, he was much influenced by the ideas of the *Devotio moderna* and by the contemporary philosophical and theological current of Ockhamism with its questioning of the role of the intellect in religious speculation.

Luther did not find in the religious life that inner peace which he sought. And as he studied the writings of St. Augustine and St. Paul, he gradually reached the conviction that, as a consequence of original sin, man's will was so corrupt as to be unable to do any works which could be "good" in the sight of God. Man could be saved, or in this life "justified," Luther came to think, not by anything he did but only by faith in God's infinite mercy. In other words, he was developing a doctrine of salvation, or justification, by faith alone, in opposition to the traditional Catholic doctrine of salvation through faith, sacraments, and good works.

Although Luther's ideas had grave theo-

Desiderius Erasmus. Hans Holbein the Younger (*d.* 1543).

Courtesy Louvre Museum, Paris

logical implication, it is possible that he might not have pursued them to further conclusions had it not been for the appearance in Wittenberg of an exceptionally glaring combination of ecclesiastical abuses. Pope Leo X, absorbingly interested in raising money to rebuild the great basilica of St. Peter's at Rome, had issued indulgences for which financial payments would be made and devoted to the cause. These indulgences were not popular and were not, in fact, preached in many places in Europe. But the young Albert of Hohenzollern was willing to permit their preaching in his German lands in return for one half of the proceeds. With this money he hoped to repay a debt to the banking house of Fugger which he had incurred in order to pay the pope for a dispensation to hold three episcopal sees at one time.

Now in 1517, the agent sent to Germany to dispose of the indulgences, a man named Tetzel, was employing methods that would today be termed those of high-pressure salesmanship. The commercial aspects of the transactions were heightened by the fact that agents of the banking house of the Fuggers accompanied Tetzel and took charge of the money that came in so as to ensure the repayment of certain loans they had made. To a considerable number of both clergy and laity, it appeared as if Tetzel was scandalously selling for cash something wholly spiritual.

It was this scandal which prompted Martin Luther to post on the church door at Wittenberg ninety-five *theses* or assertions which were designed to promote debate on the subject. But it must be emphasized that in his theses, Luther, who already had questioned the efficacy of "good works," was not only objecting to Tetzel and his methods, but was also questioning a commonly accepted doctrine and even the necessity of the church as an intermediary between man and God. "The Christian who has true repentance," wrote Luther, "has already received pardon from God altogether apart from an indulgence, and does not need one."

Probably Luther had, as yet, no intention of separating himself from the church. But as his theses were translated from Latin into German and circulated widely, he found himself in the midst of a growing protest to which he soon gave effective leadership. In 1519, in debates with prominent theologians, he began openly to question the status of both pope and church council and to proclaim that ultimate religious authority resided in Scripture. Even more significant were two pamphlets issued in 1520, the one calling on the German princes to take the initiative in purging the church of error, and the other, stating more explicitly his religious beliefs. Only two of the traditional seven sacraments, baptism and the eucharist, should be retained. In the latter, which was no longer considered a sacrifice, the doctrine of "consubstantiation" was substituted for transubstantiation. This meant that the bread and wine were not transformed into the Body and Blood of Christ, but that Christ was really present *with* and *in* the elements as fire is in a hot iron, to use Luther's own figure of speech.

In 1521, Pope Leo X excommunicated Luther, and the Diet of the Holy Roman Empire, meeting at Worms, placed him under the ban. Luther, however, was protected from both Pope and Emperor by the Elector of Saxony, Frederick the Wise; and he at once devoted himself to making a new German translation of the Bible which is still prized as a monument of German literature. Thus the break between Luther and the Catholic church was complete, and, despite many attempts of reasonable and moderate men to heal the breach, it widened and deepened.

Within the next few years, the Lutheran teachings spread like wildfire throughout northern and central Germany. They appealed to devout persons who were shocked by abuses in the church, to the worldly who saw a chance to appropriate church lands and riches for themselves, to patriots who wanted to nationalize the church, and to princes and nobles who were eager to increase their political power, as well as to those university professors and students who were impressed by Luther's theological arguments. To the movement, Luther gave effective leadership. Tirelessly he preached fiery sermons and wrote inflammatory pamphlets. German princes and peasants, burghers and clergymen rose against the church, seized its property, and abolished traditional forms of worship.

The peasants, in fact, went much too far to please princes and landlords. More victimized than any other class by the existing social and economic system, and now aroused by Luther's teachings and spurred on by fanatical leaders, the peasants thought the time had come to get rid of their economic burdens as well as their allegiance to the church. To us in the twentieth century, their demands seem quite modest. They wanted such things as the abolition of serfdom, the payment of wages for work done, the right freely to hunt and fish. They rose in open revolt in 1524 not only against the church but against their landlords and princes, many of whom had already repudiated Catholicism and become Lutheran.

Luther, appealed to by both sides, had a difficult decision to make. Shocked by the excesses of the rough peasantry, he chose the side of the nobles, and ended by urging them to put down the rising by any means available. The revolt was crushed in blood, and some fifty thousand peasants were slain. As a result not only did the lot of the peasants become worse in most of Germany, but Luther's influence among them declined, especially in south Germany.

Luther also failed to win wide support from among the humanists. Erasmus, for example, first saw in Luther simply one who might force the issue of much needed reform. Erasmus, however, was opposed not only to violence, but to any alteration in the fundamentals of the Catholic faith. It is significant, too, that Erasmus chose to break with Luther by publishing a pamphlet defending the freedom of the human will.

There was one humanist, however, who followed Luther. Melancthon became his right-hand man and a sort of unofficial theologian for him. When in 1530 the Emperor, who veered between attempts to suppress Lutheranism and efforts to achieve reconciliation, asked for a statement which could be used as a basis for a discussion held at Augsburg, Melancthon produced one which was moderate and careful. The "Augsburg Confession," as it was called, proved to be unacceptable to Catholic theologians, but it remained an integral part of the official teachings of the Lutheran church.

Thus it was that the princes of the Holy Roman Empire came to be divided into a Lutheran and a Catholic party. And in 1529 when Charles V, at that time confident of his authority, ordered the laws against heretics enforced, the Lutheran princes protested and were thereafter called "Protestants," a term which was to become general for all dissenters from the Catholic faith. In 1531, they banded together in the League of Schmalkald. And so it was that Charles, distracted by many problems outside Germany, was unable to put down Protestantism. At last in 1555 a sort of stalemate was reached and the two parties agreed to the so-called Peace of Augsburg, which provided: (1) each prince was to be free to dictate the religion of his subjects; (2) the Protestants were to retain all the church property they had seized up to 1552; (3) no form of Protestantism other than Lutheranism was to be tolerated; (4) Lutherans in states ruled by churchmen were not to be forced to become Catholics; (5) any churchman who became a Protestant was to give up his position and the lands that went with it. This last provision, called the "ecclesiastical reservation," was not strictly a part of the peace, but was added later by the Emperor and not fully accepted by the Protestants. It was to be a source of future trouble.

Thus between 1520 and 1555 Lutheranism won an established position and found general acceptance throughout the northern half of Germany. But its triumphs were not limited to Germany. To the north, Sweden broke away from Denmark in 1523 in a general uprising, and a new king, Frederick I (1523–1533), came to the throne of Denmark and Norway, while the Swedes chose Gustavus Vasa (1523–1560) as their ruler. Both the new rulers saw the possibility of increasing their political control and their power by adopting Lutheranism. Both met with considerable opposition, but by propaganda and legislation, and especially by force, they gradually converted their countries to the new faith. Catholicism died slowly in the Scandinavian lands, but before the end of the century they were firmly Lutheran.

Although the Lutheran churches established in north and central Germany and in Scandinavia were not organically united, and each was organized under the prince of the region, they retained a common faith and developed a modified liturgy in the vernacular. Moreover, much of the form of the old church organization was retained with bishops acting as administrative officials.[1] Considerable advances were made, too, in providing schools for the young. Judged in comparison with other sects, Lutheranism might be termed a moderate type of Protestantism.

C. *Emergence of Radical Sects*

Luther's conservatism is evident in his failure to come to any sort of agreement with certain of the more radical religious movements which emerged early in the sixteenth century. One contemporary leader, Thomas Münzer, who was denounced by Luther, and who took part in the Peasants' Revolt, went so far as to urge the overthrow of existing governments and the establish-

[1] At Upsala in Sweden, the title of archbishop was retained.

ment of a sort of communism. Even more shocking to conservative folk was John of Leiden (*d.* 1536), a Dutch tailor who taught that the Bible sanctioned polygamy and that he was the successor of King David. With a group of fanatical followers he seized the city of Münster and held it for a year until it was recaptured by the forces of its Catholic bishop.

A number of radical groups were what is known as "evangelical" in tendency, that is, they emphasized the emotional rather than the rational aspects of Christianity, and insisted on the literal inspiration of the Bible.[1] Most prominent among these were the Anabaptists, who believed that only adults should be baptized, since infants could not have had the necessary religious experiences. Although Thomas Münzer was an Anabaptist leader, most members of the sect were pious people who sought to lead pure and simple lives. Menno Simons (*d.* 1559), another reformer, preached a return to Biblical simplicity. He condemned as un-Christian the taking of oaths and the waging of war as well as the baptism of infants and is remembered as the founder of the Mennonite sect.

Another of Luther's contemporaries was Huldreich Zwingli (1484–1531), a well-born and well-educated Catholic priest who came to the Swiss canton of Schwyz. Though he first preached mainly against the practice of hiring out Swiss soldiers to foreign rulers, a business in which the church played a part, he soon came to attack ecclesiastical abuses and finally to denounce the supremacy of the pope and to insist that the Bible, not the church, was the true guide to faith and morals, and, as a consequence, that the ceremonies and traditions of the church were not truly Christian. Hence, he argued, the Eucharist was not a sacrament, but simply a memorial service.

Although Zwingli's teachings won considerable support in all but the original Forest Cantons, the vast majority of Swiss Protestants came to follow the doctrines of John Calvin, whose important movement we shall now consider.

[1] The word "evangelical" is derived from the Latin word for "gospel," *evangelium*.

D. Calvin and Calvinism

The second major branch of Protestantism—Calvinism—resembled the radical sects in departing farther from Catholic teaching. But unlike most of them, it built up a systematic body of theology and developed a strong church organization. Moreover, of all the Protestant religions it was the most international, the most widespread geographically.

The founder of Calvinism, John Calvin (1509–1564) was born of a middle-class family in Noyon in the French province of Picardy. He was educated first for the priesthood and then for a career as a lawyer. He was also, it seems, given somewhat to humanist studies then flourishing in Paris. France, like most other countries of Europe, was experiencing effects of the religious upheaval of the times, and Lutheran preachers had made themselves heard. But the French King Francis I, whose concordat with the pope (1516) conceded him wide power over the church in France, especially in the matter of the selection of bishops, adopted a stern policy toward religious dissent. He, and his successors, might find the Lutheran princes of Germany, or even the Turks, useful allies against the Catholic Habsburgs, but they were not minded, at least during the sixteenth century, to tolerate heresy within their own dominions.

At the age of twenty, Calvin became involved in the religious turmoil. He experienced a sudden "conversion" which he believed was a divine call to forsake Catholicism and to teach a purer Christianity. Despite his youth, followers soon gathered about him to learn from his lips how Christians might recapture the supposed simplicity of the early days of the church. In view of the attitude of the French government, Calvin prudently left his native country and settled at Basel in Switzerland. Here he came in contact with the teachings and the followers of Zwingli; and here he wrote his chief work, *The Institutes of the Christian Religion*. Published in 1536, the book was dedicated to Francis I, in the vain hope that it would win him over to the cause of the reformers.

Portrait of John Calvin by Lucas Cranach.
The Bettmann Archive

The *Institutes* proved of great historical importance. It is still regarded as a monument of French literature because of its cool, clear, dignified language. Orderly and concise, with an almost legal logic, it did for Protestant theology what the great medieval writers had done for that of the Catholic Church. In it are to be found the seeds, at least, of all the beliefs and practices of Calvinism.

The *Institutes* taught, and Calvin and his followers developed, certain special doctrines that have set the Calvinists apart from other sects. Like Zwingli, the Calvinists abandoned all the sacraments save baptism and the Lord's Supper, and the latter they regarded as merely a symbolic memorial. They stripped the church services of all rites and ceremonies for which they could not find express authority in the Bible. They did away with vestments, holy water fonts, stained glass windows, sacred images, incense, and organ music. The altar they set down in the body of the church and called it a communion table. They gave up the use of the crucifix and other symbols such as the ring in the marriage ceremony. In their public worship, they laid stress on the reading of scripture, the preaching of sermons, and the singing of psalms without instrumental accompaniment. Save for the Lord's prayer, which they found in the Bible, they used prayers devised extemporaneously for the occasion.

In church organization likewise, the Calvinists made many changes. They did away with bishops, archbishops, and regular clergy. They kept but one order of clergymen—the presbyters (priests or ministers)—who, aided by "elders" from the various congregations, governed the church through periodic local assemblies called synods.

Sixteenth-century Calvinism placed considerable emphasis on a special interpretation of the ancient doctrine of divine predestination. For it was held that the foreordination of all things by an omnipotent and eternal God precluded the freedom of the individual will. Thus, albeit with different reasoning, the Calvinists joined the Lutherans in questioning the Catholic teaching on free will. It must not be supposed, however, that the Calvinists' belief that those predestined to salvation, the "elect" or "saints," would go to heaven, the others to hell, resulted in a fatalism regarding human conduct. Few Protestants have been more systematic in promoting the good or "godly" life, few more energetic in advancing and expanding their religion. Calvinists frowned on light amusements such as dancing, games, and theatres; they insisted on a rigid observance of the Sabbath and on regular churchgoing; and they stressed the virtues of thrift, sobriety, and industry. Their way of life is known to us as "puritanical," a word coming down from the later English Calvinists.

In 1536 Calvin went to Geneva and helped to unite the followers of Zwingli and other reformers there and to throw off the rule of the Duke of Savoy who was upholding Catholicism. Soon, Calvin was made chief pastor and preacher of the city, and this position he held, save for a brief exile, till his death in 1564. Indeed, Geneva under Calvin became a theocracy, in which the civil administration was dominated by the religious governing body called the consistory. Thus offenses against religion were punished just as vigorously as crimes. When another reformer, the Spaniard Servetus, came to Geneva, Calvin had him tried for questioning the divinity of Christ, and burned at the stake. And the stern simplicity of life, the "puritanical godliness," in which Calvin believed, was rigidly enforced at Geneva.

While he was reforming Geneva, Calvin was also winning for himself the name of the "Protestant Pope." With unflagging energy he gave advice and guidance to a rapidly increasing number of followers all over Europe. Hundreds of earnest students and preachers came to Geneva to absorb Calvin's teaching. With others he carried on so extensive a correspondence his letters would fill thirty huge volumes.

E. The Expansion of Calvinism

Not only did most of Switzerland become Calvinist, but Geneva became a remarkably busy center for the propagation of Calvinism to various parts of Europe. And in those countries where it took root, often as a small but energetic minority, it was called the "Reformed Church." Thus German Calvinism came to be known as the German Reformed Church. In the northern Netherlands, where Calvinism achieved a notable success and won over a majority of the population, it was called the Dutch Reformed Church. Although Calvinist successes in Poland proved to be temporary, an important minority of the Hungarians, then under Turkish rule, adopted the Reformed faith.

In two instances, France and Scotland, the penetration of Calvinism was associated with important political developments. It was, in fact, in France, the native land of Calvin, that there occurred one of the most prolonged and dramatic struggles of the sixteenth century. We have noted that the French monarchy under Francis I (1515–1547) and Henry II (1547–1559) used its authority to repress all signs of Protestantism. In this it was not altogether successful, for Calvinism spread, especially among the middle class and in the south and west of France. By 1560 the French Calvinists, usually called Huguenots, had organized a nationwide church in Presbyterian fashion, had drawn up a confession of faith, and with their local meetings and larger synods had developed what almost amounted to a state within a state.

After the death of Henry II, his three sons, Francis II (1559–1560), Charles IX (1560–1574), and Henry III (1574–1589), ruled in succession. But most of the time, their mother, Catherine de' Medici, daughter of the Florentine banking family, was the real guide of royal policy. The whole period of these last three of the Valois kings was torn by a series of religious wars and by almost constant civil strife. Peaces and truces were made only to be broken in a few months. On the one side were the Huguenots, who had as leaders certain great nobles like Admiral Gaspard de Coligny (1519–1572), and Antoine de Bourbon (1518–1562), who was King of the principality of Navarre as well as a magnate of France. In the latter part of the wars, the leader of the Protestants was Antoine's son Henry, who took on an added importance as it became clear that Catherine de Medici's sons would leave no male heirs. Henry was only a distant cousin of the Kings, but he was next to them in line of succession to the throne.

On the opposing side, the leaders of the extreme Catholic party were a family by the name of Guise which had come to prominence in the first half of the century. Francis, duke of Guise (1519–1563), with his brother Charles who was called the Cardinal of Lorraine, played a leading role in the early stages of the religious strife. The Duke was an able general and had won renown by capturing Calais from the English in 1558. After his assassination by Protestants, his son Henry (1550–1588) became the prime leader of the Catholics. Popular with the people of Paris, Henry of Guise was able to form a powerful League to support the Catholic cause. There were moments when it looked as if he might be able to make himself king of France.

Between the extreme Protestant and Catholic parties stood Catherine de' Medici and her sons who ruled in succession. By and large, they sympathized with the Catholic cause, but they were more interested in maintaining and increasing the royal power. The devious policy of Catherine was usually aimed at playing off Protestant against Catholic so as to strengthen the crown. In this endeavor she often had the support of a group known as the "Politiques," who, though for the most part moderate Catholics, set peace and order and strong government ahead of religious considerations. France was to know no end to turmoil until those who thought like the Politiques grew strong enough to impose their views on embittered religious factions and a war-weary population.

Outside the country, the Spaniards were ever eager to fish in the troubled French waters. They supported the Catholic party with men and money. They several times invaded France with large armies. As long as France was rent by civil war, it was no threat to Spain. On the other hand, the Protestant party in France was aided from abroad, directly or indirectly, by the English who were at war with Spain, by the Dutch who were in revolt against their Spanish rulers, or by Protestant princes of Germany.

Many outrages were committed by both sides during the French wars of religion. There were assassinations and massacres of Catholics by Protestants, and of Protestants by Catholics. A particularly horrible example was the so-called massacre of St. Bartholomew's Day (1572). The Catholic party, under Henry of Guise, feared that the Protestant Coligny was winning too much influence over the mind of the weak King Charles IX. After an unsuccessful attempt to assassinate Coligny, Guise persuaded Catherine de' Medici and the King to consent to a general massacre of Protestants who had gathered in Paris to celebrate the marriage of Henry of Bourbon, King of Navarre, with the French King's sister, Margaret. When all was ready, the signal was given by the ringing of a church bell, and Guise's soldiers fell on the hapless Protestants. Coligny was murdered, and several thousand were slaughtered in Paris, and in the provinces, to which the butchery spread. Henry of Navarre escaped by rapidly feigning a conversion to Catholicism, which lasted only as long as he was in the King's power.

The later years of the French religious wars were filled with dramatic events. The last of the Valois kings, Henry III, who leaned to the Protestant side because he feared the growing power of Henry of Guise and his Catholic League, was driven from the capital city of Paris in 1588 by Guise's adherents in a rising known as the Day of Barricades. Soon afterwards, the Duke of Guise was lured to Blois by the King and assassinated by royal henchmen. The next year Henry III was assassinated by a fanatical monk. Then befell what the Catholics had dreaded. Henry of Navarre, the leader of the Protestants, became the rightful King of France as Henry IV.

For four years Henry IV waged war against his foes. But the Catholics would not willingly permit a Protestant to sit on the throne of St. Louis. At last, in 1593, the King removed most of the grounds for opposition by somewhat cynically abjuring Protestantism and becoming a Catholic. At this point, most followers of both parties were willing to come to terms, for the Catholics at least had a Catholic king and the Protestants a king whom they felt they could trust. But it was not until 1598 that the last of the rebellious nobles gave up and peace descended once more upon France. The French religious wars were over.

Henry IV marked the pacification of his kingdom by the Edict of Nantes (1598) which, for the time at least, settled the religious disputes in France. It granted to the Protestants liberty of conscience and of private worship throughout the country. Public worship was to be permitted them in two hundred towns listed by name and in the country houses or castles of something like three thousand nobles. Protestants, moreover, were accorded full civil and political rights, and, as a guarantee, they were privileged to hold and garrison some two hundred fortified towns. Thus the Huguenots, though never more than a minority of Frenchmen, won by their cohesion and by their persistence not only toleration but numerous political privileges.

In the British Isles, Calvinists were known as Presbyterians. Although never numerous in England, they did influence the development of Anglicanism. In Scotland, however, Calvinism took root and flourished. As elsewhere in Europe, there had been protests in Scotland against moral and financial abuses in the Catholic Church. But the primary causes of the religious over-turn seem to have been political. The kingdom had long been torn by the strife of great noble families, many of whom could rally small armies of clansmen from the Highlands.

In 1542, the premature death of King James V left the Scottish throne to his infant daughter Mary Stuart and opened the way for the nobles to seek more power at the expense of the Crown. In general, the Catholic clergy sided with the Crown and with the rule of the Queen's mother, a Frenchwoman, Mary of Guise. Many ambitious nobles, therefore, took up the Protestant cause as a means of reducing the royal power. Cardinal Beaton, archbishop of St. Andrews and primate of the Church in Scotland, strove to suppress Protestantism by the trial and execution of a number of its leaders. In retaliation, a group of Protestant nobles conspired together and in 1546 murdered the Cardinal and hung his body on the battlements of the castle of St. Andrews. Such was the tense situation in Scotland when John Knox appeared.

A Catholic priest born of peasant parents, John Knox (1515–1572) began openly in 1546 to attack the Catholic Church and to espouse the new religious ideas which were coming into Scotland from England and the continent. In fiery sermons, he preached the overriding authority of the Bible, and a stern puritanical morality. Mary of Guise and the Catholic court were still strong enough, however, to drive him into exile. After being imprisoned in France, Knox went to England, where he became a chaplain at the court of Edward VI and helped to swing the English church toward Protestantism. On the accession of the Catholic Mary Tudor to the English throne, Knox prudently departed for Geneva where he made the acquaintance of Calvin and discovered that in essential matters they were in agreement. From exile, Knox continued to exhort the Scottish Protestants with strongly worded letters and pamphlets.

In 1559, though still under sentence of death, Knox returned to Scotland and was soon the real leader of the Protestants. Meanwhile, Queen Mary Stuart had left Scotland, and by marriage to the short-lived Francis II had become Queen of France. Her absence weakened the Catholic cause, and local Calvinist, or Presbyterian, churches were being organized throughout Scotland. In 1560, a General Assembly of the Presbyterians met and adopted a rigidly Calvinist *Book of Discipline,* largely the work of Knox.

After the death of her husband, Mary Queen of Scots returned in 1561 to her native land. But she was too late to stem the tide of religious revolt and political opposition to the crown. The nobles prevented any increase in royal power, and Knox in public sermons fairly flayed the character and religion of the young Queen. Mary's marriage to her cousin Henry Stuart, Lord Darnley, who, like her, had a claim to the English throne, did little to strengthen her position. By him she gave birth to a son, James. Matters soon hastened to a climax. Darnley died under most mysterious circumstances. Mary married a nobleman named Bothwell who was suspected of Darnley's murder. The country was in a turmoil, and Mary was imprisoned by the nobles who opposed her. In 1568, she escaped and fled to England, to cast herself on the mercy of her cousin Elizabeth. But as a Catholic and the heir to the English throne, Mary was a dangerous person. Elizabeth kept her in confinement and eventually sent her to the scaffold.

Back in Scotland, the Presbyterians were triumphant. The Catholic adherents of Mary were put down by force of arms. Though her infant son was made King as James VI, the real power lay with groups of Protestant nobles who struggled among themselves but educated James in the new faith and imposed on the kingdom a rigid Calvinism in doctrine and church organization. By the end of the century Catholicism still lingered only in remote parts of the Highlands and among a few scattered families elsewhere.

Before the end of the sixteenth century, therefore, Calvinism had won adherents in many countries of Europe, and in some had exercised a major political as well as religious influence. Moreover, even where the official Calvinist reformed church was not established, Calvinist influences were often of great importance. Before many years, these influences, as well as official Calvinism, were to appear also in the expanding English possessions in the New World.

Queen Elizabeth I. Engraving by William Rogers (after Isaac Oliver).

Courtesy Museum of Fine Arts, Boston

CHAPTER 30

Revolt Against the Catholic Church: Anglicanism

A. Henry VIII and the Separation of the Church of England from the Papacy

In 1500 the Catholic Church seemed as firmly rooted in England as on the continent of Europe. A century later, the church in England had split off from Rome and become a separate national church, called Anglican, or the Church of England, with the king at its head. This change arose in large part from events which took place in the reign of Henry VIII (1509–1547). Henry VIII was the second king of the Tudor dynasty which, beginning with Henry VII, had pacified England following the Wars of the Roses and had obtained a firm control over the government and over Parliament.

The English, like Europeans elsewhere, had been influenced by criticisms of church abuses by the great humanists and scholars such as Colet, More, and Erasmus. It is possible that some traces of the teachings of John Wyclif lingered among the common people. And England was, of course, affected by the events on the continent. Lutheran teachings had come into England by 1521 and had aroused discussion in Oxford, Cambridge, and London. But despite the existence of strong national feeling and a desire among many for a thoroughgoing reform of the church, there was, at the accession of Henry VIII, no sign that religious revolt was imminent.

Moreover, Henry VIII for many years seemed to be a most devoted son of the Catholic Church. With his own royal hand he penned a bitter attack on the Lutheran teachings, and dedicated the work to the pope. The pope responded by conferring on the King the title "Defender of the Faith," which, ironically, the kings of England have borne ever since. In international politics, Henry VIII was on several occasions allied with Pope Leo X. In England, Henry's chief minister at first was the ambitious Thomas Wolsey, a cardinal of the Roman Church.

Indeed, it is difficult to see how England would have soon broken off from the Catholic Church, had it not been for the peculiar marital troubles of its ruler. Henry VIII had been married for many years to Catherine of Aragon,[1] and she had borne him six children of whom all save one daughter, Mary, had died. It seemed unlikely to Henry that she would give him the male heir he ardently desired. In addition, the King became smitten by the charms of Anne Boleyn, a maid-in-waiting at the court. Whatever his reasons, Henry VIII sought to have his marriage with Catherine annulled on the grounds that church law forbade a man to marry his brother's widow. To be sure, Pope Julius II had granted a dispensation authorizing the marriage. But Henry expressed doubt whether any pope could lawfully grant such a dispensation, and in any event, he argued, one pope might undo what another had

[1] She had previously been the widow of his older brother, Arthur. See above, p. 288.

Henry VIII. Hans Holbein the Younger (*d.* 1543).

Alinari photograph; National Gallery, Rome

done. Further, since the Wars of the Roses were of recent memory, the absence of a legitimate male heir seemed more than usually important.

The Pope, Clement VII, would have liked to oblige Henry VIII, though he was naturally reluctant to reverse a decision of one of his predecessors, and he knew that the Emperor Charles V, who was then dominant in Italy, would be incensed if his Aunt Catherine's marriage with Henry VIII was annulled. So the Pope procrastinated, and for several years delayed making any decision, hoping, no doubt, that in the meantime the matter might resolve itself. But the Pope did accede to Henry's wishes in the appointment, as the archbishop of Canterbury, of Thomas Cranmer, a cleric of marked Protestant leanings.

As the King grew more impatient, he began a campaign against what he now regarded as papal tyranny. In 1531, he was able to force an assembly of clergy to recognize him as the "supreme head" of the English church so far "as that is permitted by the law of Christ." But this proved to be but a preliminary step. For Henry then turned to Parliament, thereafter known as the "Reformation Parliament," and secured authorization to shut off payments to Rome and to appoint bishops without papal permission. Thereupon, convinced that no annulment was to be had from Rome, he secured from Cranmer declarations that his marriage with Catherine was null and void and his marriage to Anne Boleyn was legal and canonical. Meanwhile Cardinal Wolsey, who had failed to obtain the papal annulment, was forced out of office and died in disgrace. He was replaced as Lord Chancellor by Thomas More. But Henry's real right-hand man in these and subsequent negotiations was Thomas Cromwell, a layman and former secretary to Wolsey.

In 1534 the split with Rome was widened into formal separation when Parliament passed the Act of Supremacy which declared the King to be the "only supreme head on earth of the Church of England," and established penalties of treason for anyone who should deny the King's supremacy. An Act of Succession, validating Henry's heirs by both the new and the former marriage, followed and to this all were required to take an oath. Thomas More, the saintly John Fisher who was bishop of Rochester, and several lesser persons refused to do this, and were accordingly beheaded for clinging to their belief in the supremacy of the pope.[1] A popular pro-papal uprising in the north, called the "Pilgrimage of Grace," had to be put down by force of arms.

Lutherans and other Protestants were encouraged by these events to think that Henry VIII was moving in their direction. But in reality he adhered firmly to the old Catholic beliefs. He was a schismatic in that he had split off from Rome, but he insisted that he was no heretic. In 1539, Henry got Parliament to pass a law called the "six articles" which reaffirmed the chief points of the Catholic faith, including the miracle of transubstantiation, and provided severe penalties for any dissent from these doctrines. Thus, any Catholic who upheld

[1] More was imprisoned for refusing to take an oath to the Act of Succession. Throughout months of confinement in the Tower of London, he persistently refused to accept royal supremacy over the English church.

Thomas More. Hans Holbein the Younger (*d.* 1543).

Copyright, the Frick Collection, New York

the supremacy of the pope was beheaded, while any Protestant who denied transubstantiation was burned at the stake. The King's will was enforced in blood. Many died for political-religious offenses.

Meanwhile, Henry VIII had taken another significant step in an attack upon monasteries, though their alleged scandalous conduct was probably grossly exaggerated by the interested investigators whom Henry appointed and sent about the country. In general, the monks and nuns were supporters of the pope and opponents of the idea of royal supremacy, and hence were deemed disloyal. Still more important, the monasteries were possessed of broad lands and considerable wealth, and Henry was in need of funds. Accordingly, under the direction of Thomas Cromwell, the monasteries were suppressed by a series of acts and their property confiscated to the crown. Some of their wealth thus acquired, Henry used for ordinary expenses. A small portion went into new educational and charitable foundations, which were by no means an adequate replacement of those that were destroyed. A very large portion, Henry gave to his favorites and supporters, thus creating a new class of rich nobles and gentry, bound to the crown by gratitude and committed to the new religious situation by fear lest any change back toward the papacy might cost them the wealth they had newly obtained.

By his marriage to Anne Boleyn, Henry VIII had one daughter, Elizabeth. But Anne was found guilty of adultery and hence of treason, and was executed, thus leading to the King's third marriage, that with Jane Seymour, the mother of his only son, Edward, who succeeded him in 1547.[1]

B. Edward VI and Mary, and Religious Fluctuations in England

Under Henry VIII, the Church of England had split off from Rome, but remained Catholic in doctrine. Under his son Edward VI (1547–1553), the English church moved rapidly in the direction of Protestantism. Edward was but a child of nine when he came to the throne, and real power lay with various nobles who were eager to push the country toward Protestantism. Under their influence, Calvinists and Lutherans were allowed to preach freely. New articles of religion, drawn up to establish the position of the Anglican Church, were unmistakably Protestant in tone. Catholic service books were translated from Latin into English and edited, under the auspices of Archbishop Cranmer, as the *Book of Common Prayer* (1552), which made it clear that the eucharist was not to be regarded as a miracle. This denial of transubstantiation led to other changes. The "Mass" was henceforth to be called "Holy Communion," or the "Lord's Supper." The "altar" was called a "table." In the old churches, many changes were made. Altars and images were taken down, the former service books and stained glass windows destroyed.

On Edward's death in 1553, Mary, daughter of Catherine of Aragon, became Queen of England. Against continual

[1] Jane died in childbirth. Henry's subsequent wives were Catherine Howard, who was beheaded for adultery; Anne of Cleves, whom he promptly repudiated; and Catherine Parr, who managed to survive him.

pressure, she had clung stubbornly to the Catholic faith; and curiously, her rights to the succession had been protected by Parliament. Accordingly, despite a plot to bring a Protestant, Lady Jane Grey, to the throne, Mary was accepted. Now, too, according to the legislation of Henry VIII, she was head of the English church, and she immediately exercised her authority to restore it to Catholic usages and to communion with the papacy. She reinstated the bishops who had been put out of office in previous years. She obtained from Parliament the repeal of the church legislation of the two preceding reigns. England made its peace with the pope. A papal legate, Cardinal Reginald Pole, sailed up the Thames with a cross gleaming from the prow of his barge, and in full Parliament administered the absolution which freed the kingdom from the guilt incurred by its schism under Henry VIII and its heresy under Edward VI.

Nor did Mary stop here. The bishops who had supported the changes or who had married were dismissed from their offices. Similarly, something like a fifth of the clergy were deprived of their benefices, though some secured new ones if they put away their wives. Laws against heresy were revived, and some three hundred persons were put to death for violating them. Among these were four bishops and Archbishop Cranmer. Twice Cranmer recanted his Protestant beliefs and denounced the work he had done. But in the end he recanted his recantations and held in the flames the hand with which he had signed them. Thus Mary gave to Protestantism a number of martyrs, as her predecessors had martyred a number of Catholics, and her successor would put more to death. One result of Mary's persecutions was unexpected. Many English churchmen escaped punishment by taking refuge in Germany or Geneva. When in later years they came back to England, they returned more firmly Protestant than ever. With all her ardor for making England Catholic again, there was one step Mary did not dare to take. To reëstablish the monasteries and give them back their lands would have deprived many nobles and gentlemen of wealth they had gained and would have alienated them from the crown. Mary, therefore, left the church lands in private hands.

Jane Seymour, third wife of Henry VIII and mother of Edward VI. Hans Holbein the Younger (*d.* 1543).

Courtesy Foundation Johan van Maurits Mauritshuis, The Hague

To strengthen the Catholic pasition in England and to win foreign influence, Mary determined to marry her cousin, Philip II of Spain, although she was eleven years his senior. She took this step on the advice of the Emperor Charles V, who was not entirely disinterested in the matter, for he hoped by a union of England with the Netherlands and Spain to ring France about with hostile powers. The marriage was unpopular in England and its results were unhappy. Even those Englishmen who accepted the return to Catholicism tended to resent the influence of Philip and his Spanish courtiers. Spain was already embroiled in a war with France, and in the strife England lost to the French the port of Calais, the last remnant of the once extensive English holdings on the continent. Had an heir been born to Philip and Mary, the whole course of English and European political and religious history might have been different. But the couple were childless. When Mary died in 1558, her successor was her half-sister, Elizabeth, who by her birth was naturally inclined to uphold the Protestant position. Elizabeth was to undo all of Mary's work.

C. Elizabeth and the Final Establishment of Anglicanism

After all the shifts and changes of the preceding decades, the English church, under Elizabeth, definitely took on the form that in the future was to characterize it. And while it may seem surprising that many individual clergymen were able to accept all the revolutions of English religious policy which occurred in the mid-sixteenth century, it must be remembered that in England, as on the continent, there were many people who firmly believed in the right of the ruler to dictate the religious beliefs of his subjects. In addition, there were those who felt that to uphold royal authority in England was the only way to avoid disorder, civil war, and foreign aggression. Such sentiments were enormously intensified during the reign of Queen Elizabeth.

Elizabeth, herself, had a lingering affection for some of the older ways in religion. She liked the use of the crucifix in church services. She disliked married clergy. But her very birth made her uphold the swing back toward Protestantism, just as England's position in international affairs gradually forced her to align the country against Spain, the champion of Catholicism in Europe. And so it was that, in 1559, Parliament repealed the religious laws of Mary and passed once more the Act of Supremacy and the Act of Uniformity which enforced the use of Cranmer's *Book of Common Prayer*. Three years later Parliament enacted the *Thirty-Nine Articles,* a slightly modified version of the statement of doctrine that had been adopted under Edward. Since all but two of Mary's bishops refused to accept the new trend, Elizabeth put in a new set of bishops, including, as before, archbishops of Canterbury and York. Thus the official church of England, while embracing a modified Protestant theology, retained all the outward form of Catholic organization, save only the pope.

Elizabeth, no less than Mary, wanted all her subjects to conform to the new religious settlement. Liberty of public worship was denied to all dissenters from Anglicanism. A special court, the Court of High Commission, was set up to suppress heresy and enforce uniformity. Although royal commissioners tended at first to disregard private worship in the old faith, the persistence of plots to overthrow Elizabeth brought a change in governmental policy. For nearly twenty years (1568–1587), these plots revolved around the person of Mary, Queen of Scotland, who, it will be remembered, had been driven from her northern kingdom by a rebellious Calvinist nobility, and had sought refuge in England only to be imprisoned by Elizabeth. But Mary was not only a devoted Catholic; she was, should Elizabeth die childless, heiress to the throne of England.

Most of these plots originated outside of England and usually involved Spain. Moreover, as such activities continued, many Catholic clergy, including several Jesuits who had managed to enter England, and who were concerned simply to minister to English Catholics or to convert others, were held to be traitors. Thus, particularly from about 1583 onwards, the propagation of Catholicism in England was punishable by death as high treason, for it was held to involve political disloyalty to the Queen and support for a foreign ruler, the pope.[1] Some 250 Englishmen paid for their religious convictions with their lives. Eventually, as foreign affairs grew more tense, Elizabeth reluctantly consented to the execution of Mary (1587).

In the following year, Philip II of Spain, increasingly irritated by English attacks on Spanish shipping, made his last great effort to subdue England. The story of the Great Armada will occupy our attention in a subsequent chapter. Here two things must be noted. First, the failure of the Armada relieved England of the Spanish danger. Second, English Catholics rallied to the support of their country. The vast majority of them had nothing to do with the plots against the Queen, and wanted nothing more than to be left alone. Gradually it

[1] The papacy appears to have been ill-informed about religious conditions in England and overly optimistic about the strength of the Catholic cause. Pius V excommunicated Elizabeth in 1570 and declared her to be a usurper.

again became possible for them, now a small minority, by paying fines for themselves and their dependents, to worship in private.

It remains to mention another group of religious dissenters, those more extreme Protestants to whom the Anglican settlement seemed too reminiscent of the old Catholicism. Suppressed, as were Catholics, the non-Anglican Protestants were not, however, involved in accusations of treason. They did persist and gradually increased in numbers. Some were representatives of the Continental sects, Calvinists or Anabaptists. Many, much influenced by Calvinism, and known as Puritans because they wished to "purify" the Anglican church of all vestiges of Catholic practices, remained for a time nominal members of the official church. Others moved toward a democracy or congregationalism in church government. They tended to believe that each congregation should choose its own pastor, set up its own rules, and establish its own forms of worship. Such ideas were developed by Robert Browne (1550–1633). His followers, known as Brownists, Congregationalists, or Independents, were later to play an important role in both English and American history.

We have mentioned the course of religious events in Scotland. Very different was the story of the sixteenth century in Ireland. Henry VIII extended the royal authority over that eastern area of Ireland which the English managed to control. Monastery lands were seized and absorbed as greedily by Irish nobles and chiefs as were those in England by the English gentry. But, although there were abuses in the Catholic church in Ireland, there was no great popular feeling against it. As a consequence, the efforts of Edward VI and Elizabeth to introduce Anglicanism had only partial success in the Dublin area and in a few of the larger towns. During Elizabeth's reign, rebellions which were partly feudal revolts against the English conquerors, and partly religious protests against the imposition of Anglicanism, were all put down in blood. But Anglicanism made little headway and Catholicism became throughly intertwined with Irish patriotism.

D. The Elizabethan Age

Before concluding this chapter on the establishment of Anglicanism, it is important to observe that the sixteenth-century religious settlement in England occurred in an age of exceptionally brilliant national development. Various aspects of English life prospered. Parliament, though generally in support of royal policy, retained and strengthened its hold on the English government. Each change in English religious life had been promoted or ratified by an act of Parliament. Besides, England's power was being felt abroad as never before. For many years Elizabeth's complicated diplomacy, in which she played off the Netherlands, France, and Spain against each other, kept England out of open war. And at the same time English seamen, frequently with the encouragement and backing of the Queen, raided Spanish commerce and made piratical attacks on Spanish colonies. Raleigh and Hawkins, Cavendish and Gilbert, Grenville and a dozen others, won fame, fortune, and popular acclaim by "singeing the beard" of the Spanish King. When Drake returned in 1580 from a voyage around the world, his ships laden with twenty-six tons of silver not to mention coin, jewels, and gold, Elizabeth (who shared in the loot) knighted him on the quarter deck of the "Golden Hind."

The great national effort which involved the destruction of the Spanish Armada [1] and the defeat of Spain made Elizabeth, who had presided over the victory, a focus of patriotic fervor. In addition, during her long reign of nearly fifty years, England enjoyed a remarkable period of growth and prosperity, so that in later times Englishmen looked back with nostalgia to the gracious days of "good Queen Bess." The cloth industry flourished and found new markets on the continent. Companies were formed to trade with Russia, Africa, and the Near East. New industries were founded and won subsidies and support from the crown. If business was regulated by the long arm of the monarchy which reached into every sphere of life, still it also won popular support for the crown and favorable legislation. Fisheries grew and Parliament

[1] On the Armada, see below, pp. 388–389.

passed laws that people must, for national reasons, eat fish on Fridays and in Lent as they once had from religious motives.

Attempts were also made to found colonies. As early as 1497, a Genoese named John Cabot, in the service of Henry VII, had made a voyage from Bristol to Cape Breton Island in the Gulf of St. Lawrence. During Elizabeth's reign efforts were directed to the lands farther south, especially in "Virginia" (named after the Queen). But, though they showed the expansive energy of England, they met with no immediate success.

In agriculture, too, there was change and some prosperity. But here for the poorer classes there was suffering as well. Many of the manors changed over from grain-growing to sheep-raising, and considerable tracts of manorial land were "enclosed." Since it took fewer hands to tend a "sheep walk," many of the former cultivators were driven from their homes and into beggary. But if the peasant who lost his land, and, hounded from village to village, ended up in one of the new, prison-like national workhouses, had little cause to be enthusiastic about the trend of the times, still it was easy to forget him. The merchants with their new trade, the gentlemen with their new lands which had once belonged to the monasteries, the sailors spending their Spanish silver, all felt a sense of growth, expansion, and a most promising future.

Appropriately, there also occurred, in the time of Elizabeth, a most spectacular output of vernacular literature. The reasons for it cannot be disentangled, for they are compounded of the advent of an unusually large number of individual geniuses, the impact of the Italian renaissance, the development of a literary tradition, the freshness of a new age that was opening, the expanded horizons resulting from the geographical discoveries, business prosperity, the breaking away from the old lines of thought in religion and in philosophy, swelling pride in the nation and the monarch, and a dozen other factors. In any case, during the closing years of the sixteenth century and the opening decades of the seventeenth, there appeared in England a galaxy of writers whose work stands out for its beauty, its freshness, its power, and its charm. Though works of many types in poetry and prose were produced, the outstanding achievements were in the field of the drama, where plays had ceased to have a religious purpose and were being produced in London for the pleasure of persons of high and low degree.

Christopher Marlowe wrote half a dozen dramas in the tragic or historical vein which, despite an almost turgid eloquence, reached at times the very peak of poetic inspiration. Ben Jonson, in his plays, mixed scholarship and wit with insight into human nature and very real poetic power. Beaumont and Fletcher, who collaborated in dozens of dramas, turned out many routine products, but their best works had a gaiety and sparkle far above the ordinary.

Over all his competitors towered William Shakespeare. He would be remembered for the magic of his sonnets, had he never written for the stage. But it is his plays that won for him a unique position in the history of literature. It is remarkable that in every type of drama he produced incomparable masterpieces: in tragedy, such works as *Othello*, *Macbeth*, and *Hamlet*; in historical plays, such dramas as *Henry IV* and *Richard II*; in comedy, such varying types as *The Merry Wives of Windsor*, *Twelfth Night*, and *The Tempest*.

Despite the fact that his plays were for the ages, Shakespeare was a man of his own time, full of patriotism for England and respect for its Queen, having a sympathetic regard for England's Catholic past yet being curious about new ideas and new lands, heir to the thought of the renaissance yet able to address the generations to come.

Thus it was, that Anglicanism, the third great branch of Protestantism, took shape during an era of English resurgence. Of all the Protestant faiths it was the most national. Indeed, it was the only one which, until the independence of the United States, was exclusively associated with the development of a single country.[1]

[1] Following the establishment of independence, the Anglican Church in the United States, while maintaining the identical faith and many personal and other ties with the Church of England, became officially the Protestant Episcopal Church without attachment to the Crown.

The Council of Trent in Session. French sixteenth century engraving.

Courtesy Metropolitan Museum of Art, New York; Dick Fund, 1947

CHAPTER 31

Catholic Reformation, and the Cultural Life of the Sixteenth Century

A. *Reforming Popes and the Council of Trent*

The religious upheaval of the sixteenth century which gave rise to Lutheranism, Calvinism, Anglicanism, and the radical sects, had its counterpart in a great reform movement which swept through the Catholic Church to leave it both purified and strengthened. If Protestantism won most of northern and much of central Europe, still a rejuvenated Catholicism retained the loyalty of the rest of the continent, west of the area in which the Eastern Orthodox Church had long held sway.

It has already been noted that the prevailing weaknesses in the Catholic church in the fifteenth and early sixteenth centuries had prompted widespread demands for reform. And it will also be recalled that a vigorous reform had been promoted in the Spanish church by Cardinal Ximines.[1] This was destined to provide much of the impetus for a broader movement. Certainly, with the widening breach between Protestantism and the church, what had formerly been desirable now appeared imperative. But partly as a consequence of contemporary political conditions, and partly owing to the lack of vigorous leadership, it was only toward the middle of the sixteenth century that effective reform was promoted from Rome.

The change was first evident in the pontificate of Paul III (1534–1549). Pope Paul inaugurated a policy of appointing to high church offices men renowned for their virtue and learning rather than for their family position, their wealth, or their political influence. During the second half of the sixteenth century, this policy was well maintained by a series of upright and foresighted popes, such as Paul IV, Pius IV, St. Pius V, Gregory XIII, and Sixtus V. By the year 1600 a remarkable reformation had gradually been wrought in the personnel of the church, from the papacy, the cardinals, the *curia*, and the bishops, down to the parish priests and the monks. The worldly bishop and the ignorant priest became increasingly rare. To meet the challenge of Protestantism, the Catholic Church strove to recruit its officers from among its ablest sons.

The reforming zeal of the popes was supplemented and reënforced by the work of a general church council—the Council of Trent (1545–1563). It was no easy task in those troublesome times to hold a general council. But despite the many difficulties which long postponed its convocation and repeatedly interrupted its labors, the council which met at Trent on the boundary between the Italian- and German-speaking peoples consummated a great reform and contributed materially to the preservation of the Catholic faith. A few Protestant delegates attended certain of the sessions, but were able to obtain no acceptance of their views. The number and renown of the Catholic churchmen who did take part were such that the

[1] See above, p. 332.

Council of Trent easily ranked with the eighteen general councils which preceded it. Its final decrees were signed among others by six cardinals, three patriarchs, and 192 bishops and archbishops.

The work of the Council of Trent was twofold—dogmatic and reformatory. It was argued that the errors of the new religions might be refuted and the beliefs of the faithful better protected by a clear statement of Catholic doctrine, particularly on those matters which had been in dispute. Thus the main points of Catholic theology as it had long been accepted by all central and western Europe were confirmed. It was declared that historic tradition as well as the Bible was to be taken as the basis of the Christian religion and that the interpretation of the Holy Scriptures belonged exclusively to the church. The Protestant teachings about grace and justification by faith alone, and about the effects of original sin on the human will were condemned. The seven sacraments were pronounced indispensable. The miraculous and sacrificial character of the Lord's Supper (Mass) was reaffirmed. Belief in the invocation of saints, in the veneration of images and relics, in purgatory, and in indulgences was explicitly upheld, but precautions were taken to clear away some of the pernicious practices that had at times been connected with these doctrines. The spiritual authority of the Roman See over all Christians was confirmed, and the pope was recognized as the supreme interpreter in matters of faith and the incontestable chief of the bishops.

A volume of regulations on discipline constituted the second great achievement of the Council of Trent. The sale of church offices was forbidden. Bishops and other prelates were ordered to live in their respective dioceses, to abandon worldly pursuits, and to devote themselves entirely to spiritual labors. Seminaries were to be established for the proper education and training of priests. While Latin was retained as the official and liturgical language, frequent sermons were to be preached in the vernacular tongues. Indulgences were not to be issued for money, and no charge was to be made for conferring the sacraments.

The work of the Council did not produce changes overnight. More than fifty years after its close there was still controversy in France as to whether its decisions should be officially published there. But the seed sown by the Council had abundant fruit in the ensuing decades. The central government of the Catholic Church was completely reorganized. A uniform catechism was prepared at Rome and, by means of it, laymen were systematically instructed in the tenets and obligations of their religion. Revisions were made in the service books of the Church, and a new standard edition of the Latin Bible—the Vulgate—was issued.

Steps were taken, too, to check the spread of the Protestant teachings. The Council of Trent had begun work on a list of dangerous and heretical books, and this list, called the Index, was completed and published under Pope Pius IV (1559–1565). All Catholics were forbidden, without special permission, to read books listed in the Index. Under Pope Sixtus V (1585–1590) a "Congregation of the Index" was established to keep the prohibited list up-to-date.

To punish lapses in faith and conduct had been the function of the medieval ecclesiastical court of the Inquisition. In most Catholic lands, and especially in Italy and Spain, the personnel of the Inquisition was strengthened in the last half of the sixteenth century, and its work was pushed forward with redoubled zeal. Because it dealt with heresy and those who fell into heretical beliefs, it became for Protestants a symbol of Catholic persecution. As in other courts of the time, the proceedings of the Inquisition were secret and torture was used to extract confessions. Heretics judged guilty were sentenced to fasting and prayer and sometimes to fines and imprisonment. The church itself formally refused to put anyone, even a heretic, to death, but obstinate cases were sometimes "handed over to the secular arm," that is, to the lay government, for execution.

B. St. Ignatius Loyola and the Jesuits

To buttress and strengthen the Catholic Church in its trials during the sixteenth

Pope Paul III. Titian (*d.* 1576).

Courtesy National Museum, Naples

century, there arose several new religious orders. The largest and most famous of these new orders, and the one which did most to maintain Catholicism in southern Europe and to arrest the spread of Protestantism in the north, was the Society of Jesus, whose members are commonly known as Jesuits. The Society was founded by a Spaniard, St. Ignatius Loyola (1491–1556) in 1534 and its constitution was formally approved by Pope Paul III six years later.

In his younger days Loyola had been a soldier and, as a patriotic Spaniard, had fought bravely against the French in the armies of the Emperor Charles V. But while he lay wounded in a hospital, his leg shattered by a cannon ball, he chanced to read a life of Christ and biographies of several saints, which, he tells us, worked a great change within him. From a soldier of an earthly king, he would now become a knight of Christ and of the Church. Thus in the very year (1521) in which the German monk, Martin Luther, became the avowed and leading adversary of the Catholic Church, this Spanish warrior was starting on that remarkable career which was to make him a chief champion of Catholicism.

After a few years' trial of his new life, a pilgrimage to Jerusalem, and several rather footless efforts to serve the Church, Ignatius determined at the age of thirty-three to learn Latin and perfect his rather scanty education. It was while he was studying the classics, philosophy, and theology at the University of Paris that he made the acquaintance of a group of scholarly and pious men who became the first members of the Society of Jesus. Among this first group was Francis Xavier, the celebrated missionary, who, like Loyola, was eventually canonized as a saint. In 1537 Loyola was ordained a priest, and, despite the fact that for a time his intense zeal aroused the suspicion of the Spanish Inquisition, he amply proved his orthodoxy. His *Spiritual Exercises*, which he completed in 1548, became even more famous and influential in Catholic circles than Calvin's *Institutes* among Protestants.

Though the Society of Jesus was at first intended primarily for missionary work among the Moslems, it was speedily turned to other ends. In its organization, it showed the military instincts of its founder. To the usual three vows of poverty, chastity, and obedience, was added a fourth vow of special allegiance to the pope. Remembering his own educational difficulties, Loyola arranged that new members were to be carefully trained during a long novitiate. The whole order was placed under the personal direction of a general, resident in Rome. Loyola was the first general and served until his death. He understood that the church was now confronted by conditions of war rather than of peace. Accordingly, he directed that his brothers should not content themselves with prayers and works of peace, with charity and local benevolence, but should adapt themselves to the new circumstances of the time and should strive in a wide variety of ways to restore and strengthen the Catholic Church.

Thus it happened that the Jesuits, from the very start, rushed to the front in the religious upheaval and conflict of the sixteenth century. They distinguished themselves as teachers and as preachers, as advisers of kings and as diplomats, as missionaries and even as explorers. Realizing the importance of education, the Jesuits made it one of their primary duties to enlighten and train the young. As schoolmasters, they soon had no equals in Europe. No less a scholar and scientist than Francis Bacon said of Jesuit teaching, "Nothing better has been put into practice." In Catholic countries the Jesuits became the principal teachers in the universities, and their schools and colleges provided the best primary and secondary education.

By the unimpeachable purity of their lives, no less than by their learning and culture, the Jesuits won back popular respect for the Catholic clergy. In theological and philosophical controversies, they were opponents to be reckoned with. As preachers, too, they earned a high esteem by the clearness and simplicity of their sermons and instructions. Taking inspiration from their founder, many Jesuits displayed a soldierly courage and worked for Catholicism under conditions of the utmost peril. For example, the saintly Edmund Campion and the supple Robert Parsons entered England in disguise in 1580 to work and preach among the English Catholics. Though Parsons eluded the agents of Queen Elizabeth, Campion was caught and, after a partisan trial and repeated torture on the rack, was executed.

So successful were the Jesuits in their varied endeavors that they created for themselves many enemies. The Protestants came to regard them with dismay and loathing. Because of their political activities they were suspected of constant plotting. Their skill in logic led their opponents to charge that the Jesuits could make the worse appear the better reason. And in the religious recriminations of the time, their Protestant opponents accused them—quite erroneously—of believing that "the end justifies the means" and that any methods, however dubious or circuitous, were proper if they advanced the Catholic cause.

Even among Catholics there was a certain amount of opposition to the Jesuits. Older religious orders eyed their success with some envy and jealousy. But when the Society of Jesus celebrated its hundredth anniversary, it could look back on a proud record of achievements. Its eight hundred houses with fifteen thousand members represented a remarkable growth from the little band that had originally joined with St. Ignatius in Paris.

C. *Catholic Revival, Political and Religious*

In most of southern Europe, Protestantism in its various forms never represented more than a threat to the Catholic Church. Protestant preachers and teachers arose in Italy but they made slight headway, for Italy was bound more closely to the papal fortunes than any other country. Italians profited from the funds drawn in by the church from the rest of Europe. Italians held a large proportion of high church offices. Italian princes and nobles were often recipients of papal favors. Aided by the doctrinal clarity and the reform in discipline that followed the Council of Trent, the Catholic Church, through the Inquisition, through the Jesuits and the other new orders, and through a firm control of the schools and universities, was able to suppress all Protestant tendencies in Italy in the sixteenth century.

In Spain and Portugal, likewise, the kings supported the Catholic Church with consistency. Before the Protestant revolt broke out, Ferdinand and Isabella had persuaded the pope to transfer control of the Inquisition in Spain to the crown. Throughout the sixteenth century the Spanish Inquisition was employed for political as well as religious purposes and was supported by secular as well as ecclesiastical authority. As the champions of Catholicism in all Europe, Charles V and Philip II took good care that religious uniformity was maintained at home in Spain. In Germany, the influence of the Habsburgs and of the Catholic princes in the southern part of the country aided the forces of the Catholic revival, although in Bohemia, where the tradition of John Hus was still evident, the Habsburgs, up to the end of the sixteenth century, were not able to eliminate strong Protestant movements.

During the first half of the sixteenth century, conditions in the Catholic Church had been as bad in Poland as anywhere in Europe. It is not surprising, therefore, that Calvinists, Lutherans, and radical sects made considerable progress in Poland and that a fairly large number of Polish nobles went over to Protestantism. But here the forces of the Catholic revival soon gathered strength. King Sigismund II (1548–1572), despite his Calvinist wife, upheld the decisions of the Council of Trent and brought the Jesuits into Poland to stem the Protestant tide. As a consequence, the Catholic Church, reformed and strengthened, regained in Poland and Lithuania the ground it had briefly lost.

It was the Jesuits again, backed by the Habsburgs, who played a major role in Hungary in restricting Calvinists, Lutherans, and various heretical sects. On the other side of Europe in the Netherlands, the fate of the Catholic Church was closely tied with political developments. In the seven northern provinces, which eventually gained their independence from the Habsburgs, Calvinism became dominant, while in the ten southern provinces, where the Habsburgs continued to rule, almost all the people remained loyal to Catholicism.

In France, as has been related, Calvinism succeeded in establishing itself while still remaining the religion of a small but active minority. Toward the middle of the century the Catholic forces sought to do by propaganda and persuasion what political support was evidently failing to do. Aided by the reforms of the Council of Trent, by the activity of Jesuit preachers and teachers, and by a remarkable revival of national Catholic sentiment, the Catholic Church in France lost no more ground to the Protestants. In fact, during the first half of the seventeenth century a number of French Protestants returned to Catholicism

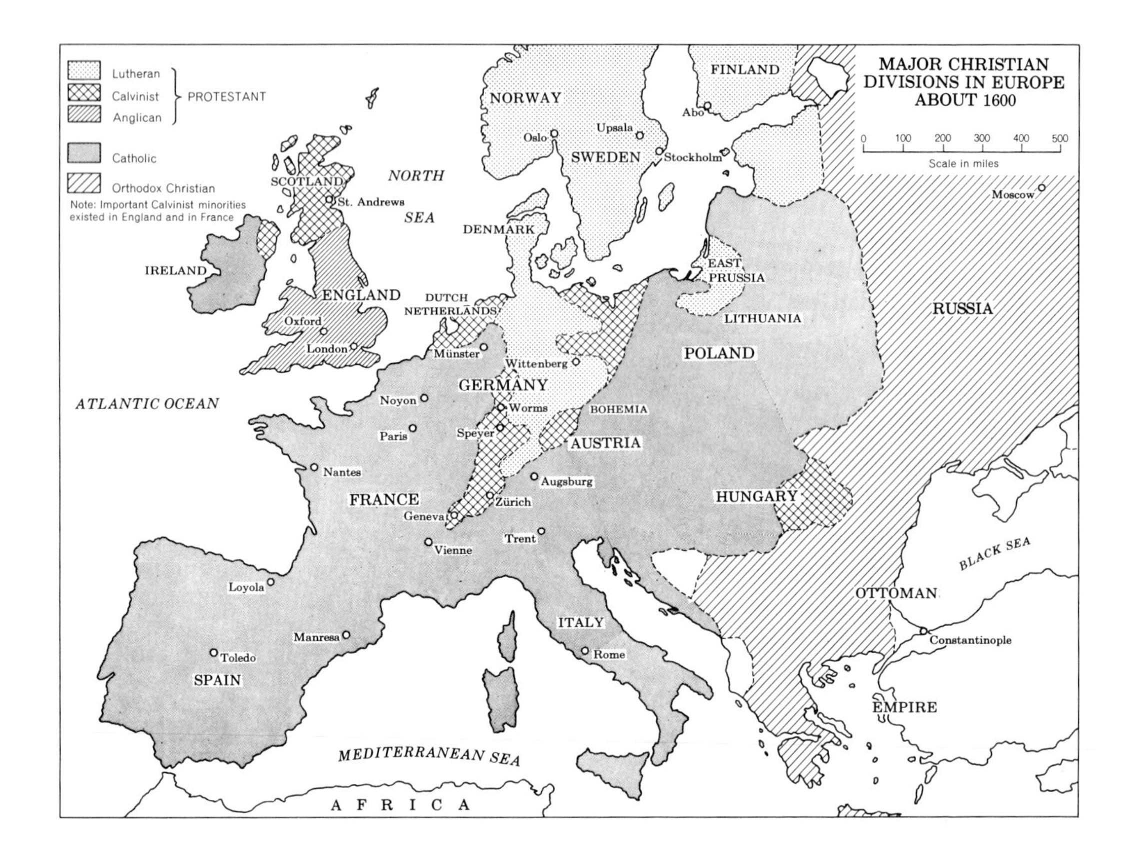

whether moved by religious conviction or by the hope of reward from the successors of Henry IV who seemed to be more sincerely devout than that monarch.

More important in the long run than ephemeral political support was a genuine religious revival. For before the end of the sixteenth century there was under way in Europe an extraordinary renewal of the Catholic faith. During the middle ages and especially in the late middle age, most Catholics had taken their religion as a habit and a mere matter of course. But the events of the sixteenth century brought about a change. Catholics had to defend their beliefs and examine their individual relations to their religious faith. Many became eager to prove by their lives and their acts that the fruits of Catholicism were both godly and goodly. They founded new orders to canalize their good works into fruitful lines. They organized new schools to educate the youth as able defenders of the faith. They wrote and read new books which proclaimed the mystical and divine mission of the Church. They were inspired by the martyrdom of priests and laymen who died in Protestant countries for their belief in Catholic Christianity.

Though the Jesuits were perhaps the most notable and most successful of the new Catholic orders that sprang up after the Protestant revolt, they were by no means unique. Some of the new orders were devoted to special kinds of service. Thus the Theatines, founded in 1524 by St. Cajetan and Giovanni Caraffa (later Pope Paul IV) had as their object the promotion of personal piety and the combating of heresy by preaching. The Capuchins, who arose at about the same time, were an offshoot of the older order of the Franciscans. Their chief mission was preaching to the poor and ministering to their spiritual needs. By 1619 when they were finally recognized as an independent order, they had fifteen hundred houses scattered throughout Catholic Europe.

A new kind of Catholic religious order,

called a "congregation," developed during the latter part of the sixteenth century. It consisted of secular priests, living and working together for a period under temporary vows. One such "congregation" was that of the Oratorians founded at Rome by St. Philip Neri. It grew up around evening meetings organized by St. Philip, at which there were readings, prayer, discussion, and musical selections with sacred settings which are still called "oratorios." The members undertook to preach in the evenings of weekdays at the various churches in Rome. The organization was formally recognized by the pope in 1575. Oratories, after the model of the original one, spread rapidly through Italy and France. With a loose, democratic organization, that made them in some respects almost like clubs for priests, they brought together many able men and some of the Oratories became famous for their scholars.

A somewhat similar order was that of the Oblates, founded by St. Charles Borromeo in 1578. Its members were pledged to aid the Church whenever and wherever they could, and in each diocese in which they were established, their services were at the immediate disposal of the local bishop.

While the new orders of varied types played a major role in the Catholic revival, the older organizations which had come down from the middle ages enjoyed a rebirth of activity and devotion. The Dominicans, for example, had long been famous as teachers in the universities and as the most active members of the Inquisition. In both roles, the troubled times of the sixteenth century called forth from them redoubled zeal. In most Catholic countries, the Chief Inquisitor was usually a learned Dominican. Among the Franciscans, too, there was a notable revival. Not only did this order give birth to the Capuchins, but it vied with them in promoting the Christian way of life exemplified by St. Francis of Assisi.

Amidst the revival of faith, the Catholic Church produced in the sixteenth century a number of famous saints. One of the most notable was St. Teresa (1515–1582), a Spanish Carmelite nun, whose spiritual experiences and beatific visions formed the substance of an extraordinary autobiography. St. Teresa wrote beautiful poetry as well as prose, and yet had time to found fourteen monasteries and sixteen convents. A somewhat different type was St. Francis de Sales (1567–1622). A wealthy noble of Savoy by birth, he founded the order of the Visitation for those strong in spirit but weak in body who could not endure the austerities of some of the other orders. But his greatest influence was through the gentleness, devoutness, and firmness of his personality. While still alive he was regarded by many as a saint and on a visit to Paris toward the end of his life he became the center of a veritable religious revival.

The renewal of mysticism, of devotion to the Church, and of faith in its divine mission led in the late sixteenth and early seventeenth centuries, not only to the formation of new religious orders, but also to the building of many churches, schools, and seminaries and to a remarkable growth of charitable organizations. The same impulses, combined with the fact of European expansion overseas, led to a tremendous outburst of Catholic missionary activity in far places.

D. *Catholic Overseas Missions*

During the sixteenth century the work of expansion overseas, of exploration and empire building, were almost exclusively in the hands of Spain and Portugal, lands which remained consistently loyal to Catholicism. From the start, one of the objectives of the Spanish and to a lesser degree of the Portuguese, in opening up new lands, was to win converts for the Catholic Church. Each expedition usually took with it priests and monks who ministered to the needs of emigrant Europeans and strove to bring Christianity to the natives.

Sometimes the conversion of native Americans or Asiatics was superficial and imposed by force. Sometimes it was strangely combined with economic oppression and exploitation. But if there was outcry against the ruthless methods of the conquerors, it came from priests like Bartolomé de las Casas who sought to protect the natives. And in America, at least in accessible areas,

Rome. St. Peter's. Facade and Piazza completed in the seventeenth century.

Courtesy Italian State Tourist Office, New York

Christianity largely replaced the cruel native religions.

One of the most remarkable missionary careers was that of St. Francis Xavier (1506–1552), friend and co-worker of St. Ignatius Loyola, and known for his labors in the Far East as the "Apostle of the Indies." Born of a noble family in Spanish Navarre, he received a thorough classical education at Paris. Then, won over to St. Ignatius' plans, he devoted himself to religious work. In 1541 he joined a mission which was being sent to the East Indies by the Portuguese king, and reached Goa the next year. There he began his missionary work. In the ensuing years he preached and taught and converted up and down the coast of India, then pushed on to Ceylon, Malacca, and the Spice Islands. Meeting a Japanese exile in Malacca, he was inspired to carry Christianity to Japan, and reached that little-known island empire in 1549. After a return trip to India, he died on his way to China where he had planned to continue his work.

Incredible stories are told of the hundreds of thousands of Asiatics who embraced Christianity as a result of Xavier's preaching. But it is clear that in the face of gigantic difficulties he began and organized missionary work in a dozen different areas. In Japan, indeed, so rapidly did Christianity grow in the last half of the sixteenth century that the native rulers felt called upon to suppress it by force as a threat to native institutions. The missionary activity in China of which Xavier had dreamed was actually accomplished by another Jesuit, Matteo Ricci (1552–1610), who spent twenty-seven years there. By his knowledge of science and mathematics, Ricci won the respect of the Chinese, and for a period he held an important place at the court of the emperor. It was Ricci and his fellow Jesuits who introduced western learning into China and gave Europe the first accurate knowledge of that country. Simultaneously, under Spanish auspices, the Philippine Islands were largely christianized.

On the other side of the world, Catholic missionaries—Franciscan, Jesuit, and Dominican—were laboring among the heathen in a somewhat different fashion. As Spanish rule expanded in America, the outposts of empire frequently consisted of missions organized by priests or monks to work among the natives. The mission normally consisted of a church surrounded by a small village. Here the Indians were gathered together, taught to till the soil, instructed in useful arts, protected from their Spanish rulers, and converted to Christianity. Over the mission ruled the priests or monks with a strict but kindly paternalism. As outposts, the missions had a political and military as well as a religious importance. They were indeed the knots with which the Spanish tied up the raveled edges of their empire.

In America, the Catholic missionaries accomplished a great deal that was a by-product of their religious work. Much of the exploration of Brazil and of the interior of South and Central America was accomplished by intrepid churchmen who boldly crossed mountains, sailed on rivers, and pierced jungles where no white man had ever preceded them. Into missions were introduced European plants and animals, and from them fruits and vegetables were sent back to Europe. The missionaries often compiled grammars and dictionaries of the native languages, translated the Bible into local tongues, and wrote works on the cultures and customs of the peoples among whom they labored. Thus they played an important role in Europeanizing the new lands and in introducing into Europe knowledge of overseas areas and peoples.

All the missionary activity overseas demanded organization and guidance from Rome. The demand was met in a preliminary way by Pope Gregory XIII, who originated, about 1582, a plan for the control of missionary activity. But this plan was not fully developed till 1622 when Pope Gregory XV organized the Congregation of the Propaganda and gave it charge of missionary work in non-Catholic countries. Five years later the College of the Propaganda was established to train missionaries.

After the close of the sixteenth century, other countries played a part in missionary endeavor. French priests explored the pathless wilderness of North America and gave their lives in efforts to convert the warlike Iroquois. England and, to a lesser degree, Holland made a beginning of Protestant missions overseas. Spain and Portugal continued their earlier endeavors. But the way had been opened, and the pattern for much of the later activity set, by the heroic efforts of the sixteenth-century pioneering missionaries who carried overseas the religious zeal and enthusiasm engendered by developments in Europe.

E. General Effects of the Religious Upheaval

It is difficult to determine clearly what were the effects of the religious events of the sixteenth century on other aspects of life, for in many cases they were entangled with older trends or with other new developments. But certain changes seem to have been closely associated with the religious revolution. One was, for example, an outburst of intolerance and fanaticism. In 1500 almost all the inhabitants of western and central Europe were Catholic Christians living in religious peace with one another. Seventy years later, in addition to Catholics, there were Lutherans, Calvinists, Anglicans, Anabaptists, Mennonites, and a dozen other sects, all quarreling with each other, persecuting and being persecuted.

Both Catholics and Protestants took arms to defend their creeds and there were battles and massacres and assassinations of the most ferocious sort. Prisoners of war and even women and children were often slaughtered without mercy. In countries remaining Catholic, the Inquisition, spies, police, and the army were employed to wipe out religious dissent. Protestants were often tortured and then burned at the stake. On the other hand, in lands which became Protestant, Catholics were banished or put to death and their property seized, while priests were hunted down like public enemies.

In the long run, but only in the long run, the Protestant revolt led to greater toleration, for in some lands two or more sects came to be so firmly established that people at length grew weary of strife between them, and governments less insistent on securing religious uniformity. Thus in Catholic France the Huguenots secured toleration by the Edict of Nantes in 1598. Poland showed signs of a tolerant policy in the sixteenth century, and Holland became quite tolerant in the seventeenth. In some American colonies of England, such as Rhode Island, Pennsylvania, and Maryland, toleration was the public policy at some time in the course of the seventeenth century. Modern religious tolerance is, however, more a result of the growth after 1700 of religious apathy and of rationalism, than a direct outcome of the religious upheaval of the sixteenth century.

One result of the fierce religious struggles that began with Luther was a growing strictness of morals and behavior. Each side accused the other of looseness and immorality. Protestants told with horror of the evil lives of Catholic priests and bishops. Catholics were equally horrified that the Protestants permitted divorce. To meet these charges both Catholic and Protestant strove to preach and to practice higher moral standards. Not only the Calvinists were puritantical. Everywhere efforts were made to put down swearing and blasphemy, to suppress lewd books, and to make sure that all ministers and priests led holy lives.

Similarly, both Catholics and Protestants were eventually driven to establish schools and improve their educational facilities. If they were to meet their opponents in debate, they must have the necessary intellectual tools at their disposal. Special efforts were made to see to it that priests, pastors, and ministers received proper instruction, and many new schools were founded especially to train them.

In a less direct way, the religious revolt may have led to an increase in individualism. The Catholic Church had always stressed unity in doctrine, and salvation through the church organization. Most of the reformers, on the other hand, tended to emphasize the relation of each individual to God. Each man was to read the Bible and interpret it for himself. The reformers were usually quite intolerant of anyone whose interpretation failed to coincide with their own. Yet in the long run, their teachings probably served to heighten the traditional Christian belief in the importance of the individual, and this not only in religious, but in economic and political life as well.

It can, for example, be argued that the religious revolt had some influence in aiding the rise of modern democracy. The emphasis on the worth of the individual is part of the democratic faith. Many of the radical sects organized their congregations in a democratic fashion. The Calvinists in France, England, Hungary, and elsewhere, because they were in a minority, stood against royal absolutism. But most of the new sects, even the Calvinists, were organized in an aristocratic fashion, and the principal Protestant leaders had little confidence in the ability of the masses to guide their own affairs.

In fact, the first effect of the religious upheaval was undoubtedly to strengthen the power of princes and kings, to increase the trend toward monarchical absolutism. In the Lutheran states of Germany and Scandinavia, in England, and even in Switzerland and Holland, the rulers added to their power by securing control of religious affairs at the same time that they increased their wealth by the seizure of church lands. In Catholic countries, too, the monarchs took advantage of the pope's difficulties to wring from him concessions that gave them greater power in church matters. In the three centuries immediately following Luther, rulers had much more absolute power than formerly.

Closely connected with this trend toward absolutism was a tendency toward "secularization," that is, the transfer to lay governments of the control of numerous activities which had formerly been handled by the church. In the middle ages, education, charity, and many legal matters had been in the hands of the church. When the power of the church was broken and its lands and endowments seized in Protestant countries, it became necessary for the government to step in to establish schools, to care for the poor and the sick, and to make laws on marriage

Statue of Moses. Michelangelo (*d.* 1564).

Alinari photograph

and the family. In the matter of charity, at least, the state was often a poor substitute for the church. The new work-houses were rarely an improvement on the old alms-houses.

In another sphere, the effects of the religious changes are less clear. Scholars are still arguing as to whether Protestantism hastened the rise of capitalism or not. It is clear that the church in the middle ages had disapproved not only the taking of interest on loans but also any undue eagerness to acquire wealth. It is equally clear that the Protestants and especially the Calvinists were more lenient about interest and stressed those virtues of thrift, sobriety, and hard work which are suitable to the growth of business and capitalism. But the first great capitalists arose in Catholic areas like north Italy, south Germany, and the southern Netherlands. Only later did the Protestant capitalists come to the fore. Perhaps the safest conclusion is that both the religious revolt and the rise of capitalism were caused by dozens of intertwined factors in the sixteenth century. It is, nonetheless, evident that by 1600 Calvinism was creating an environment very suitable for growing capitalism in Holland and in other areas.

F. Cultural Trends in the Sixteenth Century

The religious upheaval of the sixteenth century tended to bring to a close the great intellectual quickening of the renaissance. Italian humanism reached its climax with the pontificate of Leo X (1513–1521). Of the outstanding northern humanists, Johann Reuchlin (*d.* 1522), Philip Melancthon (*d.* 1560), John Colet (*d.* 1519). Thomas More (*d.* 1535), and the greatest of them, Desiderius Erasmus (*d.* 1536), all save Melancthon were mature men before Luther began his attacks on the church. Those who lived long enough were all diverted from their classical studies and literary work by religious controversy. It is true that the learning which they had brought to northern Europe, the knowledge of Greek and Hebrew and the critical scholarship, did not die out. But after 1520 or 1530 the new learning was put more and more to the service of theological and religious disputes. The arguments were not now concerned with the great Latin and Greek writers, but with the interpretation of the New Testament or the origins of papal supremacy.

In art, the impetus of the earlier "golden age" continued. Michelangelo (*d.* 1564) did much of his best work in painting, in sculpture and in architecture, after Luther posted his theses on the church door at Wittenberg. Titian (*d.* 1576), Veronese (*d.* 1588), Tintoretto (*d.* 1594), and the later Venetian painters were active through most of the sixteenth century. Spain boasted of El Greco (*d.* 1614); and Holbein (*d.* 1543), the German painter, who has preserved for us the likenesses of Henry VIII and many of his contemporaries, was followed by Lucas Cranach (*d.* 1553), to whom we owe portraits of Luther. And in the Netherlands, a great artistic genius, Peter Bruegel (*d.* 1569), was able not only to portray inimitably the people of his land in their rustic occupations and in moods of gaity, but also with bitter satire to expose their sufferings under the Spanish occupation.

In Palladio (*d.* 1580) Italian renaissance architecture reached a culmination which was to lead to the baroque early in the following century. Meanwhile, in England Elizabethan gentlemen were constructing gracious "Tudor" manor houses. And in France renaissance motifs influenced, but did not entirely replace, gothic features in the wonderful sixteenth-century *châteaux* of the Loire valley.

Appropriately too, in an age of monarchical consolidation, literature in the vernacular continued to flourish. We have mentioned the popularity of the German Bible of Luther and the great surge of Elizabethan literature. And we shall note later the literary achievements of Spain. In France, Calvin followed the original Latin edition of his *Institutes of the Christian Religion* with another version in French. In the first half of the sixteenth century, Rabelais (*d.* 1553), a humanist and admirer of Erasmus, produced his celebrated satires, *Pantagruel* and *Gargantua,* in a coarse but vigorous French. Somewhat later, Ronsard (*d.* 1585) and du Bellay (*d.* 1560), the founders of a group of French writers known as the *Pléiade,* were imparting to French literature a character at once more formal and more classical. And French literature was further enriched by the essays of Montaigne (*d.* 1592).

The sixteenth century also brought important achievements in music. Among the noted composers of the period, the name of Giovanni Pierluigi (*d.* 1594), more commonly known as Palestrina from the town of his birth, stands out. Palestrina composed a considerable quantity of ecclesiastical music, which is unsurpassed in its combination of technical skill, tonal appeal, and liturgical appropriateness. Setting himself against the over-elaborate style of some of his contemporaries, he produced masses and motets in which the music enhances and supports the words of the liturgy without dominating them. Although he exploited to the full the possibilities of polyphony, Palestrina made his music a natural accompaniment of religious worship and prayer.

In the sixteenth century there were other cultural developments which proved to be steps toward the creation of the modern spirit. These were notable advances in the field of science; and it is the influence of science, more perhaps than anything else, which distinguishes the modern mind and temper from that of earlier centuries. The scientific achievements of the sixteenth century owed much to the labors of the preceding generations, whose accomplishments at such places as Oxford, Paris, and Padua have been described. And while those men had contributed much to mathematics, chemistry, physics, and astronomy, they had, in general, not challenged the Ptolemaic concept of a geocentric universe.

In the year 1543, the year of his death, a Polish Catholic priest named Copernicus (1473–1543) put forward another theory in his work entitled *On the Revolutions of the Celestial Bodies*. He had found hints for his idea in the works of certain Greek and Roman authors. From these, by observations, calculations, and reflections, he developed the heliocentric theory, which held that the planets, including the earth, revolved around the sun.

The new theory was in every way superior to the old Ptolemaic system. It was far simpler and mathematically sounder. But it upset many old notions. Aristotle had taught that the sun moves around the earth. The common man thought he saw it so move. And churchmen had accepted this view, for it seemed to fit in with the notions which made the earth the great central stage on which the drama of man's salvation was being played. The Copernican theory which demoted the earth and its inhabitants to a secondary role, therefore, made its way but slowly. It was not accepted by most educated men before the middle of the seventeenth century.

In the meantime, however, further work was buttressing and demonstrating the validity of the new theory. Tycho Brahe (1546–1601), a Danish astronomer, made new and better observations of the movements of the heavenly bodies. Using Brahe's observations, a German named Kepler (1571–1630) worked out three mathematical statements or "laws" which described the way in which planets moved around the sun. The simplest of them declares that the path of a planet moving around the sun is an ellipse, with the sun at one of the two foci of the ellipse.

Most important of all, perhaps, was the work of the Italian Galileo (1564–1642). A great scientist in the fields of mechanics, mathematics, and optics as well as in astronomy, Galileo by his lectures at the University of Padua demonstrated and popularized the Copernican system. With a small telescope which he built (though the telescope does not seem to have been his invention), he showed that the sun was turning on its axis and that Jupiter was attended by moons revolving about it. These facts made it easier to believe that the earth turned daily on its axis and revolved around the sun. Unfortunately for Galileo, his enthusiastic desire to convert the church at once to the new astronomy got him into trouble. The church court of the Inquisition in 1616 condemned the Copernican system and in 1632 Galileo was found guilty of upholding it and punished for so doing.

It is noteworthy that it was a pope, Gregory XIII (1572–1585), who took advantage of the increasing astronomical knowledge to reform the calendar. The Julian calendar, in use since Roman times, had gotten ten days ahead of astronomical time. The new Gregorian calendar moved the date back by ten days and arranged to keep the calendar and the solar year in line by omitting the extra leap year day in all years ending in 00 (like 1700) unless the number of the year could be divided evenly by 400 (like 1600). The Gregorian calendar was quickly adopted by Catholic countries, more slowly by others. England accepted it only in 1751, and Russia not until 1922.

As in astronomy, great advances were made in mathematics. In Italy, Tartaglia (1506–1559) and Cardan (1501–1576) vied with each other in solving cubic equations. In Holland, Stevinus (1548–1620) wrote on decimal fractions, while in Scotland John Napier (1550–1617) invented logarithms and was the first to use the decimal point. In physics, great strides were made. The compound microscope was in use by about 1590 and the telescope a decade later. William Gilbert (1540–1603) experimented with magnetism. Galileo invented an air thermometer and an astronomical clock, while his work on falling bodies disposed of the old notion that heavy objects fall faster than light ones. Medicine and physiology were advanced by Paracelsus (1493–1541), half quack though he was, and by Vesalius (1514–1564) with his great treatise on anatomy. Not long after the end of the sixteenth century, William Harvey (1578–1657) discovered the circulation of blood from the heart through the arteries and back to the heart through the veins.

Similar progress was registered in half a dozen other fields. The expansion overseas, for example, greatly stimulated work in astronomy, geography, botany, and zoölogy. Men's minds were being expanded in many directions, most of which had but little connection with religious strife and controversy. Occasionally the two areas of thought collided. Giordano Bruno (1548–1600), an intemperate and stormy Italian, fell under the spell of the new science. He espoused the Copernican astronomy, jeered at the biblical miracles, and put the Hebrew scriptures on the level with pagan myths. He tried to work out a religious conception by which the whole of nature was conceived of as embodying and expressing the divine. He aroused the ire of Protestants and Catholics alike and was eventually burned at the stake in Rome. More important was the work of Francis Bacon (1561–1626), an English lawyer, courtier, official, and writer. In a series of writings, he developed a new philosophy adapted to the new science. He pleaded for induction, observation, and experiment, and insisted on the usefulness of scientific knowledge.

While some men pushed forward the frontiers of science and of thought, and others took part in fierce religious controversies, it must not be thought that most Europeans were engaged in intellectual pursuits. The vast majority of them still could not read or write. They toiled in the fields or worked at their crafts almost oblivious of many of the new developments. For them the world was still full of magic and superstitions. Even the upper classes still believed in witches, in astrology (the theory that stars influence men's lives), and in fabulous tales about distant lands. The great contributions in every field of thought were, in the sixteenth century as always, the work of a small elite of able thinkers. Yet in the long run these thinkers had more to do with the shaping of the world of today than even the kings and generals whose pomp and power dazzled the eyes of all.

It should also be remarked and emphasized that, overwhelming as was the impact on Western civilization of the religious upheaval, this did not entirely monopolize the energies of the early modern age.

CHAPTER 32

Successes and Failures of Philip II of Spain

A. Philip II, the Man and the Monarch

As Charles V had dominated the first half of the sixteenth century in Europe, so his son Philip II (1556–1598) dominated the second half. He came to the throne of Spain at a time when that country seemed at a peak of power and influence. At his death, a beginning of Spain's decline might have been detected. But during his reign he strove mightily to fulfill the manifold obligations which birth had placed upon him.

When Philip II in 1556, at the age of twenty-eight, became King of Spain, he did not fall heir to all the lands which his father had held. His uncle Ferdinand of Habsburg, who by election and marriage had become King of Bohemia and a part of Hungary, obtained the archduchy of Austria and was chosen to succeed Charles V as Holy Roman Emperor. Philip, however, received the impressive remainder of the family inheritance which included Spain, the Netherlands, Franche Comté, Milan, Naples, Sicily, and the Spanish holdings in North Africa, America, and the West Indies, together with the Philippines which had been claimed after Magellan's discovery of them in 1521 and further explored in 1542. Moreover, if Philip relinquished the German and Austrian holdings of his father, he nonetheless felt called upon to aid his relatives in those areas, and the family ties between the Habsburgs of Spain and Austria were drawn ever closer by new alliances. Ferdinand's son and successor married Philip's sister, and Philip's son and successor married Ferdinand's granddaughter.

Philip II has been represented as a deceitful and bigoted despot by English and Dutch writers, and by Spanish authors as the stalwart champion of Christian civilization. The judgment passed on Philip depends largely on the view taken of his policies, for the policies themselves are reasonably clear.

To begin with, Philip had a profound sense of dedication to the obligations of his office and a constant loyalty to the responsibilities placed upon him by his birth and heritage. Whatever he undertook he pursued to the end with extraordinary persistence, and no area of his scattered dominions—nor those of his Habsburg relatives in Germany—escaped his attention. Yet despite his widespread involvements, and in marked contrast to Charles V, Philip prized Spain as his native country and his most important possession. He spoke Spanish as fluently as his father had spoken Dutch. He surrounded himself with Spanish advisers, lived most of his life in Spain, and sought by every means to make Spain strong and powerful.

Finally, Philip was sincerely and piously attached to Catholicism. He abhorred Protestantism as a blasphemous rending of the seamless garment of the church and a grave menace to law and order. Confronted with a choice between the best interests of Spain and those of the church, he worked for the latter as he conceived them. His drastic use of the Inquisition, for example, undoubtedly promoted a kind of unity in Spain, but it was in the long run a unity dearly bought at the expense of the economic and political strength of the nation. No seeming failure of his policies could weaken Philip's belief in their fundamental excellence. What he did he did for the greater glory of God. Success or failure depended on the inscrutable will of the Almighty.

To carry out his policies, Philip was in some ways well-equipped. He had a boundless capacity for hard work. All day and much of the night he toiled over the reports and documents that came to him from his far-flung dominions. So conscientious was he that frequently the administration bogged down because the monarch was swamped in his paper work. He was more of a man of the desk and the pen than of the sword and the war horse. But if he preferred diplomacy to battle, he was ever ready to send his troops to fight for a cause that he conceived to be righteous. His conviction of his own righteousness made him intolerant of both political and religious dissent and led him to use wile, deceit, and even assassination to gain his ends.

Whatever his personal equipment, Philip faced tasks that in their multiplicity and difficulty were too much for any man, and he had to play a world role from a Spanish base that in itself presented many problems. Spain was a country of only nine or ten million people and it was composed of historically separate kingdoms, each with traditions and privileges. Philip II sought to further the work of national unification begun by his great-grandparents, Ferdinand and Isabella, and carried on by his father, because national unification implied uniformity and greater power for the crown. Absolutism and uniformity became the watchwords of his internal administration. Politically, Philip made little pretense of consulting the local legislatures or cortes about new laws, and although he convoked them to vote new taxes, he made it the rule that old taxes were to be considered as granted forever. Rejecting the older capitals of the Spanish peninsula, Philip embellished a formerly bleak area a few miles from Madrid near the geographical center of the country and there erected the magnificent but austere Escorial—combined palace and monastery. He made the nobles ornaments of the court rather than active statesmen, and put into the important offices lawyers and other subservient members of the middle class. Philip "the Prudent," as he came to be called, was the hard-working center of a complicated administration, which gradually became entangled in formal rules and much red tape.

Economically, the burdens Philip II placed on Spain were too heavy. More and more it had to finance his costly endeavors all over the world. If silver flowed in from America, it flowed out again with amazing rapidity to buy goods and support armies, for Philip did little to encourage industry or commerce within Spain. The ten per cent sales tax, called the *alcabala,* collected on each transaction, slowed down trade and hampered production. The great sheep-herding combine, the *Mesta,* won the support of the crown at the expense of other kinds of agriculture.

The expulsion of the Jews (1492) and the Moors (1502), led to the persecution of those (*Maranos* and *Moriscos*) who, as converts to Christianity, were allowed to remain. Thus Spain lost or lessened the contribution of some economically productive elements in the population. As the burdens of Philip's policy grew, Spain's ability to bear them decreased, and by the end of the century the country was staggering under the load.

One major addition to Spain's problems came in 1580, when Philip, eager to complete the political unity of the Iberian peninsula, laid claim to the throne of Portugal, whose king had just died. Philip bought off the duke of Braganza whose right to the Portuguese crown was better than his own, and sent in Spanish troops to take over the country. Despite Philip's efforts to placate the Portuguese by recognition of their constitutional rights and his endeavor to win over the nobility and country gentry by favors, Spanish rule was unpopular in Portugal. It was to be just sixty years until the Portuguese found an opportunity to reëstablish a native ruler. But in the meantime,

King Philip II of Spain. Sixteenth century marble bust.

Courtesy Metropolitan Museum of Art; bequest of Annie C. Kane, 1926

Spain had to defend Portugal and Portuguese trade and colonies, without receiving from that country much financial or military support.

A sign of the opposition to Philip's policies in Spain was the revolts he faced there. When he tried to stamp out heresy among the *Moriscos*, the descendants of the Moors in southern Spain, they rose in a bloody revolt in 1568, and were suppressed only after two years of bitter fighting. A revolt in Aragon in 1591 had to be put down by a Castilian army, and as a result the traditional rights and privileges of that kingdom were further reduced.

B. Spain's Many Problems Abroad

Of all the difficulties which Philip faced abroad, the most serious and most permanent was the revolt of the Netherlands which began about 1566, and was still in progress at his death in 1598. The prosperous Netherlanders objected to the burdensome taxes and the attempts to regulate their economy in the interests of Spain. Cities, provinces, and nobles alike resented the curtailment of long cherished rights and privileges. In addition, since Philip never understood Dutch ways, and appointed

El Escorial, the monastery-palace-mausoleum of Philip II of Spain.

Courtesy Spanish National Tourist Department, New York

Spaniards as governors and high officials in church and state, Spanish rule came to seem more and more like government by and for foreigners. Philip, who never visited the Netherlands after 1559, offered an unpleasant contrast to his father who had been at home in the Netherlands.

Finally, despite the rapid spread of Calvinism throughout the northern provinces of the Netherlands, Philip was resolved to force Catholicism upon all his subjects. He rearranged the bishoprics and increased their number. He issued decrees against religious dissent. He strengthened the Inquisition and employed it ruthlessly. Thus, for a combination of reasons, the Netherlanders found Spanish rule unbearable.

At first the opposition in the Netherlands was sporadic and ill-organized. But in 1566 a group of nobles and townsmen requested the Regent, Margaret of Parma, to urge Philip to abolish the Inquisition and to redress other grievances. The Regent, disquieted by the petitioners, was reassured by a courtier who exclaimed, "What, Madam, is your Highness afraid of these beggars?" The epithet was seized upon by the opponents of Philip. They called themselves

"Beggars" and used the old emblems of begging, the wallet and the bowl, as symbols.

Philip at first showed signs of wishing to pacify the Netherlands by concessions. But in the same year, 1566, the more radical Protestants, enraged at the religious decrees, took to arms and attacked Catholic churches, wrecking altars, breaking windows, and smashing images. The magnificent cathedral of Antwerp was irreparably ruined. To Philip there could be but one answer to such violence and sacrilege. In 1567 he sent his most famous general, the duke of Alba, with a large army and with instructions to reduce the people to submission.

In the next six years, Alba did his best to carry out his master's wishes. To try treason cases, he created an arbitrary court which won the name of the "Council of Blood." In the period of his rule, some eight thousand persons were executed, including two great nobles, Counts Egmont and Horn, who were patriots rather than religious fanatics. Taxes were increased, property confiscated, and thousands of Calvinists were forced into exile. So ruthless was Alba's rule that the Catholic townsmen of the southern Netherlands united with the Protestants of the north to oppose the Spanish tyranny. For a leader, the country found a nobleman, German by birth, French by title, who had large estates in the Netherlands and had held high offices there. He was William of Nassau, Prince of Orange (1533–1584), usually called William the Silent, though he was actually talkative to a normal degree.

At first the nondescript forces of William of Orange were easily routed by Alba. But soon a new factor developed. In 1569, William began to charter privateers to harass and prey upon Spanish shipping. These "Sea Beggars," as they were called, were mainly a wild and unruly lot, united by hatred of Spaniards and Catholics and by hope of loot. They were competent seamen and soon laid the foundations of Dutch naval power. They raided commerce, sailed up the numerous waterways, and before long had seized coastal towns and islands which served as secure bases for further operations.

When it was clear that Alba with his harsh tactics was making little headway, Philip replaced him, in 1573, with the more politic Requesens. But the new governor died three years later having accomplished little, and shortly after his death (1576) the unpaid Spanish soldiery mutinied and sacked the great commercial town of Antwerp with fire and sword, an event known as the "Spanish fury." Shocked by this happening, deputies from all seventeen provinces met and concluded an agreement known as the "Pacification of Ghent," by which they agreed to resist the Spaniards till Philip should abolish the Inquisition and reëstablish the old liberties. But before

Portrait of William the Silent. Willem Key (*d.* 1568).

Courtesy Foundation Johan Maurits van Nassau, Mauritshuis, The Hague

long, this union was broken up. Philip's governor from 1578 to 1592 in the Netherlands was Alexander Farnese, Duke of Parma. Adroitly mingling war with diplomacy, Parma sowed seeds of discord between the ten southern provinces, which were largely Catholic and industrial and in part French-speaking, and the seven northern provinces, which were largely Calvinist and commercial and wholly Dutch-speaking. In 1579 the southern provinces joined in the League of Arras to seek a reconciliation with Philip, while the northern provinces agreed, by the Union of Utrecht, to persevere in the fight for independence. Thereby the Netherlands were permanently split, and Spain kept possession of the southern portion (modern Belgium) throughout the next century.

Meanwhile, in the northern (Dutch) Netherlands, the struggle dragged on. In 1581, Philip proclaimed William of Orange a traitor and offered a reward for his person, dead or alive. William replied by a famous *Apology* in which he justified his acts. He was able to persuade the representatives of the northern provinces to proclaim their independence from Spain in an "Act of Abjuration." William was assassinated in 1584 by a Spanish agent, and Farnese captured Antwerp from the Protestants in the next year. But thereafter the Spanish made little headway against the stubborn Dutch.

Although the Dutch received some aid in men, munitions, and money from the German Protestants, from England, and from France, and, of course, profited from the defeat of the Armada in 1588, their ability to resist the might of Spain lay largely in their own resources. The rise of Dutch sea power enabled them to harass Spanish shipping and to cut sea communications between Spain and the Netherlands. At the same time their commerce built up their wealth and made possible the employment of mercenary soldiers. Moreover, the Spanish were operating at a distance from their base in difficult country peculiarly vulnerable to such Dutch tactics as opening the dykes.

Finally, in 1609, Philip's son and successor Philip III (1598–1621), made a twelve-year truce with the Dutch. During this interim, Dutch wealth and power grew apace and Holland was able to play a major role in the ensuing Thirty Years' War. At its conclusion in 1648, Spain reluctantly recognized that Holland was a free and independent nation.

The defeat of the Armada has been mentioned in connection with events in English history. As a major undertaking of Philip II it deserves further treatment here. In 1588, Philip had assembled to send forth against England what was called the "Invincible Armada," the most formidable fleet which Christendom had ever seen—130 ships, 8,000 seamen, 19,000 soldiers, and the flower of Spanish chivalry. It was placed under the command of the Duke of Medina-Sidonia, a man without important previous experience in maritime affairs. Out of a deeply felt sense of duty the Duke accepted and, remedying his lack of knowledge by careful study of all the problems he had to face, proved to be an extraordinarily able commander. But a combination of the failure of the Spanish authorities in the Netherlands to appear with invasion barges at the appointed rendezvous, the weather, and the clever tactics of the lighter and more maneuverable English craft, forced a break in what had for several days been a magnificently disciplined crescent formation. For Medina-Sidonia to bring his remaining, and now badly damaged, ships back to Spain by encircling the tip of Scotland was another rare feat of seamanship. As a military venture, the Armada was another failure of Philip II. As a saga of the seas, it is one of the most extraordinary in maritime annals.

It should be added that the defeat of the Armada brought feelings of relief not only to England. The Catholic French, no less than the Protestant Dutch, could breathe more easily. Indeed, Philip's French policy was also a failure. During the religious wars in France, Philip continually gave aid to the Catholic party and for a while his troops even held Paris. It took Henry IV nine years after he came to the French throne, in 1589, to expel the Spaniards from France. But at last Philip in the year of his death was forced to recognize the trend of events. France and Spain in 1598 signed the Peace of Vervins, which merely confirmed that of Cateau-Cambrésis.[1] Philip had poured out blood and money in France, and had little to show for his efforts.

Throughout his reign, Philip had constantly before him the menace of the Moslems. He had to continue the warfare against them in the western Mediterranean and north Africa, and Spain contributed the commander and the largest contingent to the fleet that won the great naval battle of Lepanto in 1571.[2] Far away, too, on the Hungarian plains, contingents of Spanish soldiery fought to help the Austrian Habsburgs stem the Turkish tide.

Finally, Philip was the almost undisputed master of Italy. The political complications which followed the long wars of his father continued to keep Italy divided. To many Italians this was a dark period of foreign occupation, a bleak contrast to the vitality of the middle ages and the brilliance of the renaissance.

Thus in every direction, Philip was faced with pressing difficulties, for Spain seemed so great and powerful that all eyed her with envy, and her very preëminence multiplied her enemies. Only in his overseas dominions did Philip see Spanish power wax and develop, for it was there that Spain not only maintained its position, but made notable advances.

C. *Spain Overseas*

In the work of developing the American conquests of Spain, the great features of the period of Philip II were the consolidation of Spanish rule, the development of mining, and the building up of the colonial system. Under the King the Council of the Indies continued, as far as the difficulty of communications permitted, to supervise the activities of the viceroys and governors in the New World. The King kept the church, too, subordinate to the crown and made it an instrument of political management as well as of religious instruction.

Interested though he might be in the growth of the church overseas, Philip was forced by his financial needs to pay even more attention to the mines of the new lands. The opening of the Potosí in Peru in 1545 and of Zacatecas in Mexico a year later had shown that the wealth to be secured by looting the old Indian civilizations was trifling compared to that which could be won by mining. Other mines were discovered and developed. The amalgam process, which employed mercury to separate the silver from the ore, came into use about 1576. It increased the yield of rich mines and made profitable the working of those of lower grade. By a happy chance Spain was the greatest producer of mercury in the world, so that the colonial demand quickly brought prosperity to the Spanish mercury mines.

In the early years of the Spanish conquest gold had outweighed silver in importance. But when Philip II came to the throne silver production was rising rapidly and in the decade 1561–1570 the imports of silver into Spain came greatly to surpass those of gold in value. Silver imports into Spain rose rapidly until they reached a peak in the last decade of the century, when they amounted to more than 1,230,000 pounds of fine silver. That figure is not very large in terms of

[1] See above, p. 342.
[2] See above, pp. 345–346.

modern production. But in the sixteenth century it was epoch making. These silver imports upset the economy of Spain and indeed of all Europe. They gave Spain a source of wealth and power that all the world envied. After 1600, the imports of silver into Spain slowly declined as some mines were exhausted, and more bullion was retained in America. In the decade of 1651–1660 they totaled only about 200,000 pounds.

As the wealth of the Americas became apparent, a colonial system for their economic exploitation was developed. As it grew, it came to be shaped by the importance of the silver imports. Under Philip II the chief purpose of the whole system was to secure more silver and to get it safely to Spain.

Charles V at first had let the German bankers, who were his subjects, play a part in developing America. But gradually restrictions of foreigners were increased, so that after 1556 trade and emigration were permitted only to Spaniards and, in theory at least, only to Castilians. Moreover, all merchandise was carried by royal ships, though on behalf of private merchants. All commerce with the colonies had to go in and out of the single port of Seville in Spain (from 1503 to 1717) and certain specified American ports (Havana, Puerto Bello, Nombre de Dios, Vera Cruz). For protection the ships were often sent in large fleets, and, after about 1560, two great fleets usually went each way every year. The *Flota* sailed in April for Havana and Vera Cruz, and the *Galleons* in August for Nombre de Dios. Both set out with sealed instructions and the routes were varied each time to thwart foreign pirates. From time to time stray ships were picked off, but so successful was the system that no fleet was captured till the Dutch took one in 1628, when Spanish power was already on the wane.

To control American trade and especially to keep track of the bullion, of which one-fifth went to the crown as a tax, the *Casa de Contratacion* (House of Trade) had been set up in 1503. It grew steadily in importance, and after 1543 it was aided by a sort of merchants' court called the *Consulado,* which settled disputes and tried commercial cases. The treasurer of the *Casa* had charge of receiving and registering all the bullion that came in, especially that part belonging to the crown. Stringent regulations were made and enforced by heavy penalties to prevent the smuggling of silver.

On paper Spain had a water-tight monopoly of all trade with her American colonies, and by keeping out foreigners she hoped to secure for herself all the silver produced. But from the early days, the Portuguese, the Dutch, the English, and the French cast envious eyes on the wealth of America. By the middle of the sixteenth century they were securing some share of the new riches, legally by selling goods needed for America, illegally by bribing Spanish merchants to ship goods for them and by sending vessels to the west to trade or plunder as opportunity offered. By the end of the century the Spaniards were having considerable difficulties and colonists could be tempted to trade illegally for the cheap goods brought in by foreigners, since under the restrictive Spanish system European wares sold at very high prices in America. Essentially, however, the Spanish colonial system was unshaken in 1600, and if foreigners were to nibble at its edges and even to win some of its outlying territories in the seventeenth century, it was to stand unshattered until after 1800.

One important addition to the Spanish overseas dominion under Philip II was the Philippine Islands, for it was during his reign that they were effectively occupied. In 1564, an expedition with five hundred men and four Augustinian friars was sent thither from Mexico, and the first permanent Spanish town was founded in the next year.

D. Successors of Philip II: Philip III and Philip IV, 1598–1665

Despite the many failures of Philip II, he has remained a symbol of the greatness of Spain, a greatness which endured for some decades after his death. He was followed by his son, Philip III (1598–1621), and his grandson, Philip IV (1621–1665). During the first part of this period most people thought of Spain as still the leading power

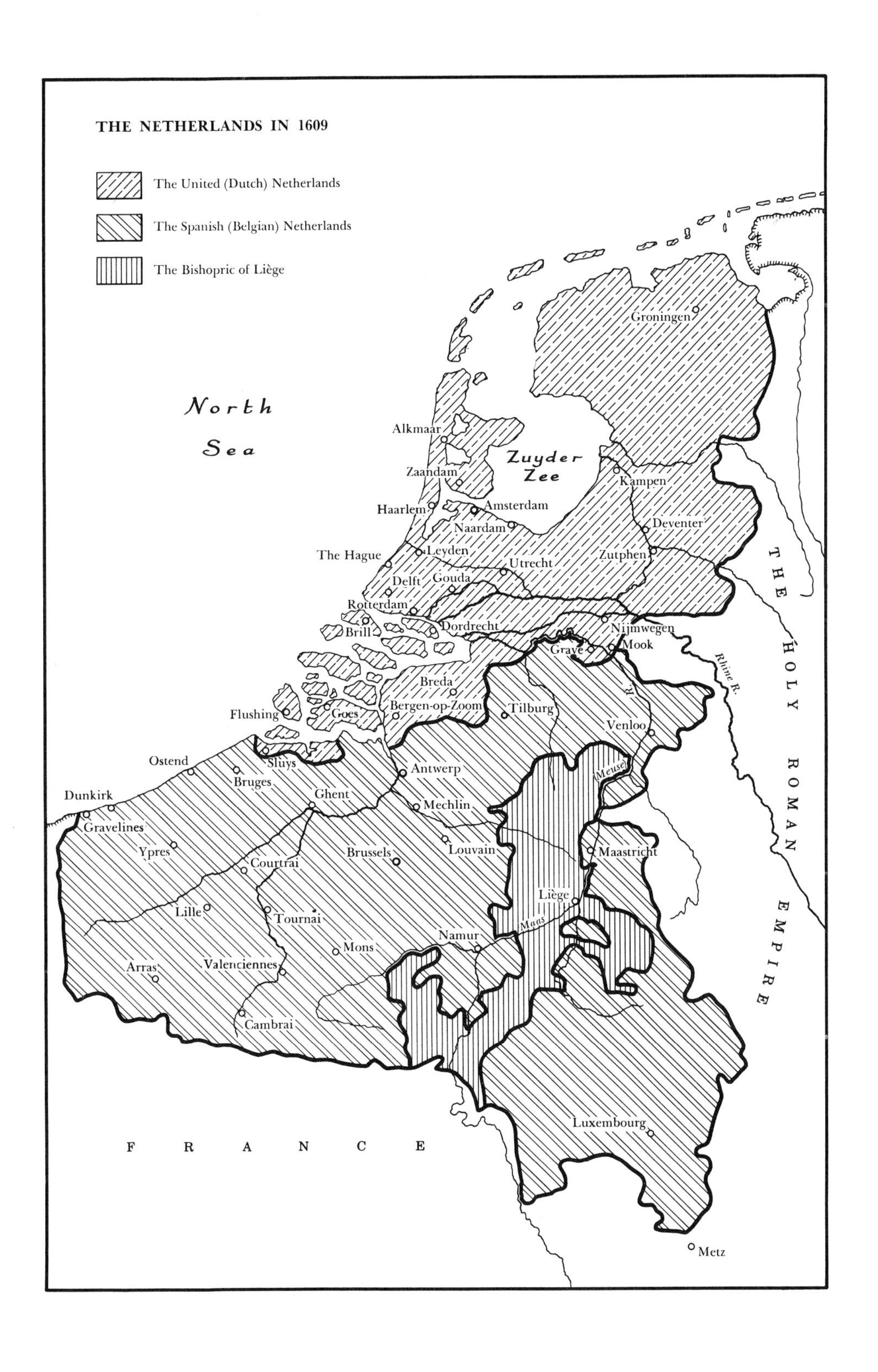
THE NETHERLANDS IN 1609
The United (Dutch) Netherlands
The Spanish (Belgian) Netherlands
The Bishopric of Liège
North Sea
Zuyder Zee
Groningen
Alkmaar
Zaandam
Kampen
Haarlem
Amsterdam
Naardam
Deventer
The Hague
Leyden
Utrecht
Zutphen
Delft
Gouda
Rotterdam
Dordrecht
Nijmwegen
Brill
Grave
Mook
Rhine R.
Breda
Bergen-op-Zoom
Tilburg
Flushing
Goes
Venloo
Ostend
Sluys
Antwerp
Bruges
Ghent
Meuse
Dunkirk
Mechlin
Gravelines
Ypres
Courtrai
Brussels
Louvain
Maastricht
Liège
Lille
Tournai
Maas
Namur
Mons
Arras
Valenciennes
Cambrai
Luxembourg
FRANCE
THE HOLY ROMAN EMPIRE
Metz

Cardinal Don Fernando Nino de Guevara. El Greco (d. 1614).

Courtesy Metropolitan Museum of Art; bequest of Mrs. H. O. Havemeyer, 1929, The H. O. Havemeyer Collection

of Europe. By its end, Spain, impoverished and weakened through long wars, had clearly yielded the foremost place to France.

The opening decades of the seventeenth century seemed auspicious for Spain. Henry IV of France, who had disliked and distrusted the Habsburgs but after 1598 had kept peace with them, was assassinated in 1610 as he was about to attack the Spanish Netherlands. He was succeeded by his wife, Marie de Medici, as Regent, a weak ruler who sought to curry Spanish favor and who married her young son, Louis XIII, to a Spanish princess in order to promote the friendship of the two countries. Similarly in England, Queen Elizabeth, who had rallied the forces of the country against Spain, was succeeded in 1603 by James I, who admired Spain, sought a Spanish alliance, and tried unsuccessfully to marry Charles, his son and heir, to a Spanish princess. Besides, the struggle between Spain and Holland reached something of a stalemate in 1609 with the twelve-year truce negotiated between the two countries. Philip III hoped to muster Spanish forces and resources to crush the stubborn Dutch at the end of the truce in 1621. The flow of silver from America to Spain began to show signs of slackening after 1600, but since it did not drop precipitately till after 1630, Spain could continue to count on a constant influx of bullion.

Within Spain there were some signs of trouble and decay. Philip III was upright and pious, but weak, incompetent, and pleasure-loving. Unlike his father, he took little part in the affairs of government; and power was exercised by courtiers and favorites, especially the duke of Lerma and his son, the duke of Uceda. Philip II had kept the nobles at a distance or used them in his military forces. Under Philip III, they swarmed about the court seeking favors and pensions. Luxury grew apace. The expenses of the royal household increased fourfold, and money was spent lavishly and frivolously. The stiff Spanish etiquette grew yet more rigid, till court life was crowded with forms and ceremonies. Public administration became increasingly inefficient and corrupt, and foreigners began to say that any Spanish official could be bought for a price.

Meanwhile public finances and currency were falling into disorder, so that the Spanish monarchy throughout the seventeenth century was either bankrupt or tottering on the brink of bankruptcy most of the time. Religious and political intolerance led to the expulsion in 1610 of the *Moriscos* who, it was feared, might aid the Moors of North Africa in an invasion. The *Moriscos* were able artisans and farmers, and their expulsion was something of a blow to Spanish prosperity.

A sign of Spanish weakness was the inability to defend the Portuguese overseas empire which had been annexed to Spain in 1580. The English formed a competitive East India Company in 1600 and two years later the Dutch consolidated one out of several smaller companies. By the end of Philip III's reign in 1621, the Dutch were firmly established in the Spice Islands and in India and, together with the English, they had taken over a large part of the eastern trade. In 1622 the English captured Ormuz, the key to the Persian Gulf and its commerce. Eleven years later the Portuguese were driven out of Bengal.

But if Spain gave signs of decay, it also was able to make an impressive show of cultural achievement. For this was the era of the immortal *Don Quixote* of Cervantes (*d.* 1616) and the dramas of Lope de Vega (*d.* 1635) and Calderón (*d.* 1681). In painting, El Greco (*d.* 1614) was finishing at Toledo the long career which had produced so many strangely moving masterpieces, while Ribera (*d.* 1652), Velasquez (*d.* 1660), Zurbarán (*d.* 1664), and Murillo (*d.* 1682) brought Spanish artistic achievement of the era to a brilliant climax.

When Philip III died in 1621, the Thirty Years' War had been under way for some three years. For Spain this struggle was to endure not for thirty but for 41 years. In its course the hollowness of Spain's seeming strength was to be made apparent, and the proud monarchy of Charles V and Philip II was to be humbled by the Bourbons of France.

King Philip IV of Spain. Velasquez (*d.* 1660).

CHAPTER 33

The Age of the Thirty Years' War, 1618–1648

A. Issues at Stake in the War

In 1618 there broke out in Bohemia (modern Czechoslovakia) a struggle which was to rack Europe for a generation and more. The Bohemian revolt which began the conflict was not in any real sense its cause, but rather the spark that ignited a conflagration which had been long in the making. Though the Habsburgs of Austria had been kings of Bohemia for almost a hundred years, the monarchy there had been traditionally elective. The Habsburgs had come to look upon it as one of their hereditary dominions, but the Bohemians felt differently.

Now in 1618, the Holy Roman Emperor was Matthias, and since he was childless his heir was Ferdinand of Styria, a man of blameless life and resolute character, devoted to the cause of absolutism and intensely loyal to the Catholic Church. In Austria and Hungary, few opposed the prospective accession of Ferdinand. But in Bohemia, where three types of Protestants (Lutherans, Calvinists, and so-called Utraquists who were followers of the old Hussite doctrines) were numerous, the advent of so staunch a Catholic as ruler was regarded with dismay. Having conspired together to preserve their political and religious independence, a group of Bohemian noblemen invaded the room in the palace at Prague where some of the Emperor's envoys were stopping and threw them out the window into the moat sixty feet below. Though the envoys were but slightly injured, it was clear that the Bohemians were bent on flouting imperial authority.

The next spring, the throne of Bohemia became vacant through the death of Matthias, and the Bohemian estates formally deposed the Habsburgs and elected Frederick, Count Palatine of the Rhine, to be their King. They chose Frederick partly because he was the leading Calvinist prince of Germany and partly because they thought he would receive support from his father-in-law, James I of England. In this hope they were disappointed, for they never received from England much more than benevolent good wishes. Frederick accepted the throne and was crowned in Prague with due formality in 1619.

Despite minor sympathetic risings in Hungary and Austria, it took the Habsburgs little over a year to crush what they regarded as a revolt in Bohemia against their just rule. Ferdinand had succeeded Matthias and had been elected Holy Roman Emperor. He arranged with his cousin, Philip III of Spain, to have the Palatinate, Frederick's home territory, invaded by a Spanish army. Then securing the aid of Maximilian of Bavaria and a famous Bavarian general, Tilly by name, he invaded Bohemia and, at White Hill outside Prague, Ferdinand's forces in November 1620 inflicted an overwhelming defeat on the Bohemian army. Frederick fled and thus earned the title of the "Winter King," for he had ruled so short a period in his new kingdom. Ferdinand was reinstated as ruler of Bohemia. Many Czech nobles lost their lives and their estates. The

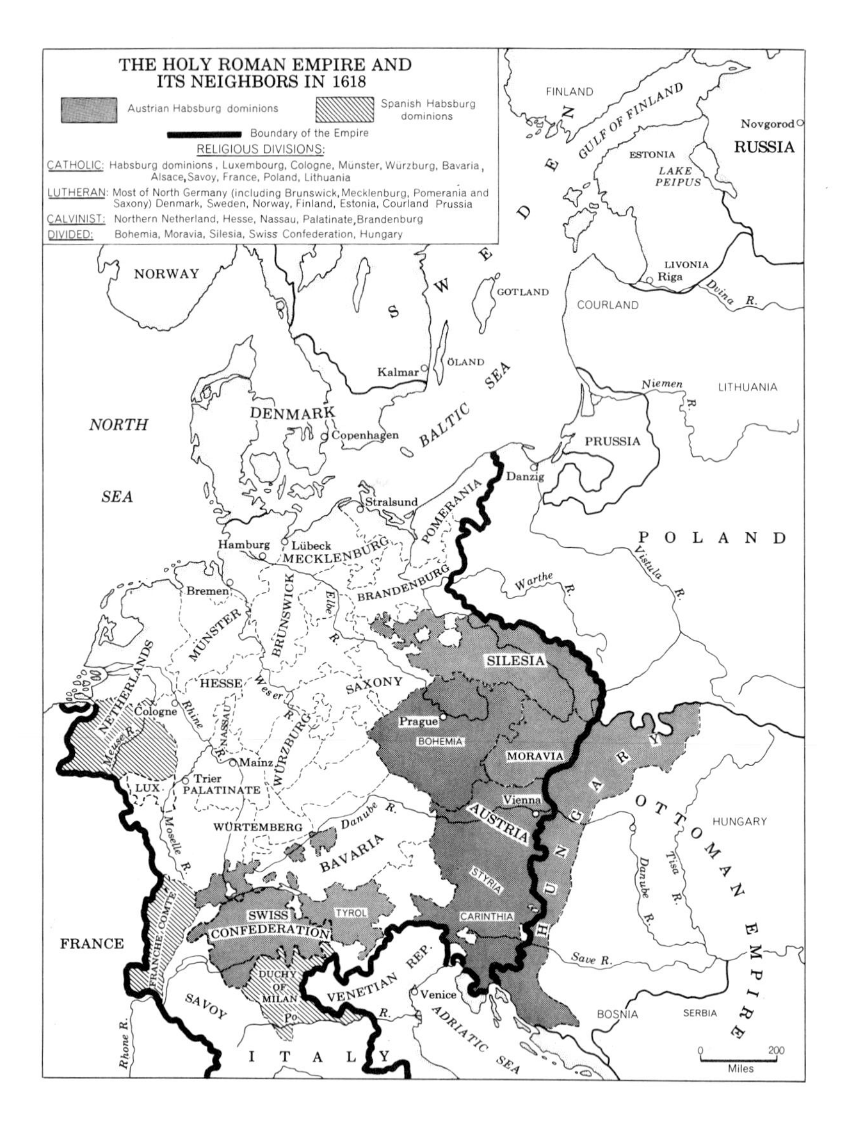

practice of all forms of Protestantism was forbidden. Frederick's Palatinate was turned over to Bavaria, and Bavaria's ruler Maximilian was recognized as an elector of the Holy Roman Empire.

Most of the Lutheran princes in Germany, led by the tactful John George of Saxony, had remained aloof from the struggle, hoping to win favors and concessions from the Emperor. The war might have ended with the crushing of Bohemian independence, had there not been a whole series of issues in Germany and Europe which demanded settlement and which were sufficient to keep half the continent embroiled for three decades. Of these issues the religious was the most prominent in the early stages of the war, and the dynastic in the later stages. But it will be simplest to discuss them all at this point.

The provisions of the religious peace of Augsburg of 1555 [1] were no longer adequate to meet new situations which had since arisen. First, it had been made before Calvinism became strong in Germany. While it gave satisfactory status to Lutherans and Catholics, it did not recognize Calvinism, and in the ensuing years the Calvinists became strong not only in Bohemia but in central and southern Germany as well. Second, the Emperor had added to the peace of Augsburg a provision called the "ecclesiastical reservation" which forbade the further alienation of Catholic lands. The Protestants refused to recognize this provision,

[1] See above, p. 354.

and Protestant rulers continued to seize church lands when opportunity offered, and there were also a number of cases where Catholic ecclesiastics, bishops or abbots, became Protestant and turned their church holdings into personal estates. The Catholic revival had now gained great strength, spearheaded in many areas by the activities of the Jesuits. Yet Protestantism was still active and seeking to gain new converts. The forces of a rejuvenated Catholicism met the advancing Protestants head on.

The Holy Roman Empire, where the Bohemian revolt had occurred, had failed completely, as previous chapters have indicated, to achieve the kind of consolidation characteristic of France and Spain. Indeed, long before the Peace of Augsburg (1555), the history of the Empire had become the history of its separate states. Certainly in the seventeenth century these states, Protestant and Catholic alike, were determined to thwart any attempt on the part of ambitious emperors to revive a long dormant imperial authority.

Furthermore, the German states which opposed the Habsburg Emperors, particularly in the final stages of the Thirty Years' War, were to be aided by the Bourbon rulers of France who in the seventeenth century, no less than their Valois predecessors of the sixteenth, felt that their country was encircled in a threatening fashion by Habsburg power and that France could gain in strength and prestige only by defeating the Habsburgs. Between Habsburg and Bourbon, therefore, the dynastic stakes were clear; they were nothing less than predominance in Europe.

In addition to the religious and dynastic issues, both of which were continuations of sixteenth-century problems, there had arisen other matters which concerned the Baltic and its trade. Denmark, through its traditional authority in the straits which gave access to the Baltic, was able to collect dues on ships passing by and was also in a good strategic position to extend its commerce and its territory. But so also was Sweden, which, having won its independence from Denmark nearly a hundred years earlier, was growing in military power and in commercial and territorial ambitions. Nor were these the only powers interested in the Baltic. The old Hanseatic cities of Lübeck and Bremen were eager to maintain their commerce and prosperity. Brandenburg, the northern electorate of the Holy Roman Empire, was ambitious to become a Baltic power as a consequence of the war. Even Spain, France, and England were desirous of increasing their commerce with the Baltic countries. And the Netherlands, having already won a major share in the North Sea trade, was anxious to improve its position in the Baltic.

In all these matters, one factor is increasingly evident. The divided condition of Germany, accentuated by religious conflict, dynastic struggles, and economic rivalry, was inviting foreign intervention. By the early seventeenth century, the German problem was an international concern.

B. Phases and Course of the War

The Bohemian phase of the Thirty Years' War had been brief (1618–1620), and in it the religious issues had been outstanding, though Czech patriotism was likewise involved. It had ended in the triumph of the Habsburgs and of Catholicism and a ruthless crushing of Bohemian Protestantism. In 1621, Philip IV succeeded Philip III as King of Spain. Since that year marked the end of the Spanish-Dutch truce and since things seemed to be going well for the Habsburgs in Europe, the new King renewed the war with Holland in the hope of reconquering it. Both France and England espoused the cause of Holland. But the French campaign against the Spanish was badly managed, an English attack on Cadiz was repulsed, and a Dutch expedition against Brazil was driven off. In 1625, Spain's success reached a climax, for after a long and painful siege a Spanish army captured the important Dutch town of Breda.

In the meantime, the Protestant princes of Germany had grown increasingly alarmed as they witnessed the triumphs of the Habsburgs of both Austria and Spain and the expansion of Catholic Bavaria. It seemed as if the balance of power in Europe was being upset in favor of the Catholics. At this juncture, Christian IV (1588–1648) of Denmark opened the second, or Danish,

The Club-foot. Painting by José Ribera (*d.* 1652).

Courtesy Louvre Museum, Paris

phase of the war in Germany. An ambitious and impulsive ruler, Christian, as duke of Holstein, was a member of the Holy Roman Empire and like most of the other princes was eager to check any increase in Habsburg power. As King of Denmark and Norway, he was desirous of extending his influence over the northern coasts of Germany and his control over the trade of the Baltic. As a Lutheran, he wished to support his fellow Protestants in their privileges and in their possession of lands seized from the Catholic Church. For these reasons, Christian IV, supported by grants of money from England and aided by many of the German Protestant princes, invaded Germany in 1625.

Against the Danish invasion, Tilly, general of the imperial forces, might have had difficulty in making headway. But fate seemed to have raised up in the nick of time another defender of the Habsburg cause in the person of a remarkable adventurer, Wallenstein. This man had made himself enormously rich out of the confiscated estates of Czech Protestants. He had secured permission from the Emperor Ferdinand II to raise an independent army of his own to restore order in the Empire and expel the Danes. By liberal promises of pay and plunder he had recruited a force of some 50,000 men, soldiers of fortune like himself. Italian, Swiss, Spaniard, German, Pole, Irishman, and Scot, Protestant and Catholic, were welcomed into his army by Wallenstein. Bound together by loyalty to its leader and hope of gain, it was made into an effective military machine by Wallenstein's genius. Supplied from his Czech lands, it became a sort of moving military state. It plundered and ravaged as it went, dragging in its train a motley throng of camp followers, men, women, and children. Where Wallenstein's army had been, it was said that a crow could scarce find sustenance.

The fighting in the Danish phase of the war was in northern Germany. At Lutter (1626), Tilly's forces, combined with those of Wallenstein, crushed the army of Christian IV. The Lutheran states were left at the mercy of the Catholics, and Brandenburg, hastily joining the Habsburg cause, aided Ferdinand's generals in expelling the Danes from German soil. Only lack of naval control in the Baltic and North Seas prevented the victors from seizing Denmark and winning complete mastery of the German Baltic coast. Thus, for example, the city of Stralsund, aided by Danish and Swedish ships which brought in supplies and evacuated non-combatants, successfully withstood an eleven-week siege in 1628 by Wallenstein, who dreamed of carving out a Baltic state for himself and who swore to take the city, "though it were chained to heaven." The desperate straits of Christian IV and the growth of suspicious activity on the part of Sweden resulted in the peace of Lübeck (1629), by which the Danish King was left in possession of Jutland, Schleswig, and Holstein, but deprived of the German bishoprics which various members of his family had taken from the Catholic Church.

As a result of these successes, the Emperor Ferdinand II in the same year (1629) felt strong enough to sign an edict of "Restitution," which restored to the Catholic Church all the lands taken from it in violation of the principle of "ecclesiastical reservation" of the peace of Augsburg of 1555. The edict was executed by imperial commissioners, all Catholics, who worked so effectively that within three years Catholicism in Germany recovered three bishoprics, thirty Hanse towns, and nearly a hundred monasteries, to say nothing of numerous parish churches. Up till then, the weight of the Habsburg power had fallen mainly on Calvinists, but at this point the Lutheran princes became thoroughly alarmed. The enforcement of the edict of Restitution seemed likely to deprive them of many fair lands and to strengthen greatly the position of the Emperor and of the Catholic league which supported him. This dismay of the Lutherans seemed to promise a favorable opportunity for intervention by the foremost Lutheran power—Sweden. In addition, the Emperor weakened his position in 1630, by dismissing, at the behest of the Catholic league, the rapacious but able Wallenstein.

The King of Sweden was Gustavus Adolphus (1611–1632), the grandson of Gustavus Vasa who had established both the independence and the Lutheranism of his country. Gustavus Adolphus was one of the most attractive figures of his age—in the prime of life, tall, fair, blue-eyed, well-educated, and versed in seven languages, fond of music and poetry, skilled and daring in war, impetuous and versatile. A rare combination of idealist, general, and practical man of affairs, Gustavus Adolphus dreamed of making of Protestant Sweden the leading power of northern Europe, and of the Baltic sea a Swedish lake. Setting to work vigorously to achieve his ends, he had occupied Finland and Estonia and had forced Russia in 1617 to recognize these territories as Swedish possessions. Then by a stubborn conflict with Poland (1621–1629) he had secured for Sweden the province of Livonia and the mouth of the Vistula river. In these wars in the eastern Baltic, he had matured his military genius and become a master in handling both artillery and cavalry.

No sooner was his war with Poland ended than Gustavus Adolphus turned his attention to northern Germany. He feared lest the Emperor, gaining control of the coastal cities there, might build up a Baltic sea power threatening Sweden. He viewed with alarm the decline of the Protestant cause, and the edict of Restitution promised him aggrieved allies among the Lutheran princes. It was likewise at this very time that Cardinal Richelieu, chief minister of King Louis XIII of France, was seeking some effective means of prolonging the war in Germany so that France might profit from the defeat and humiliation of the Habsburgs. In Richelieu's mind, cardinal of the Roman church though he was, national and dynastic reasons had more weight than religious ones. He agreed to support Gustavus with money and arms, and asked only that the Protestant leader accord liberty of Catholic worship in conquered districts.

Gustavus Adolphus, landing in Pomerania in 1630, inaugurated the third, or Swedish, phase of the war in Germany. He proceeded to occupy the chief northern fortresses and to seek alliances with the influential but reluctant Protestant electors of Brandenburg and Saxony. While Gustavus tarried at Potsdam in these negotiations, Tilly and the imperialists succeeded after a long siege in capturing the Lutheran stronghold of Magdeburg (May 1631). The fall of the city was attended by a mad massacre of the garrison and of armed and unarmed citizens in the streets, houses, and churches. At least 20,000 perished; wholesale plundering and a general conflagration completed the havoc. Gustavus Adolphus, now joined by the electors of Brandenburg and Saxony and by many other Protestant princes of northern Germany, advanced into Saxony, where, in September 1631, he avenged the destruction of Magdeburg by decisively defeating the smaller army of Tilly on the Breitenfeld, near Leipzig. Tilly was himself thrice wounded and escaped from the field with some difficulty.

Gustavus then turned southwestward, making for the Rhine valley, with the idea of forming a union with the Calvinist princes. Only the prompt protest of his powerful ally, Cardinal Richelieu, prevented the Catholic archbishoprics of Cologne, Trier, and Mainz from passing immediately under Swedish control. Next, Gustavus Adolphus moved east and invaded Bavaria. Tilly, who had reassembled his forces, failed to check the invasion and lost his life in a fierce battle on the Lech (April 1632). The victorious Swedish King, now acclaimed by German Protestants as their liberator, at once made ready to carry the war into the hereditary dominions of the Austrian Habsburgs. As a last resort, Ferdinand II recalled Wallenstein and gave him full control of his free-lance army. About the same time, the Emperor concluded an especially close alliance with Philip IV of Spain.

The memorable contest between the two generals—Gustavus Adolphus and Wallenstein—was brought to a tragic close in November of the same year, 1632, on the fateful field of Lützen. Wallenstein was defeated, but Gustávus was killed. Although the Swedes continued the struggle, their army was not large, and they possessed no general of the calibre of their fallen King. On the other hand, Wallenstein's loyalty to the Emperor was suspect. He had earlier offered to coöperate with Gustavus, and rumors reached Ferdinand II that he was engaged in self-seeking negotiations with the Protestants. In February 1634, Wallenstein was assassinated in his camp by a group of imperialists whose very names (Piccolomini, Gordon, Devereux, Leslie, Butler) indicate the motley nature of the armies of soldier-adventurers warring in Germany at the time.

The removal of both Wallenstein and Gustavus Adolphus, the economic exhaustion of the whole Empire, and the eagerness of the Protestant princes, and the Emperor as well, to rid Germany of foreign soldiers and foreign intervention—all these developments seemed to point to the possibility of concluding the third, or Swedish, period of the war, not as advantageously for the imperial cause as would have been possible earlier, but at any rate by some sort of compromise. In fact, in May 1635, a treaty was signed at Prague between the Emperor and a number of the German princes, whereby the former would gain control of the military forces of the Empire, the leagues of the princes would be dissolved, captured territory would be restored, and church lands would remain in the hands of those who actually held them in 1627, two years before the edict of Restitution was issued. On this basis a fairly satisfactory peace seemed possible. But from such a peace, the Emperor would doubtless have emerged in a considerably strengthened position, and this was contrary to the desires of Richelieu and what he conceived to be the interests of France.

C. *French Intervention and the Peace of Westphalia*

After the death of Gustavus Adolphus it became increasingly evident to Richelieu that France might have to abandon its policy of merely aiding the enemies of the Habsburgs with money. It was the peace of Prague which made it clear that if Richelieu wished to keep the war going to weaken and defeat the Habsburgs he would have to use more direct methods. Richelieu accordingly declared open war on Spain in 1635, and began the final, or French, phase of the war, which was to last thirteen years, almost as long as the other three periods put together. In the earlier phases, religious considerations had been prominent, though German and Baltic questions were also important. In the last period, with Catholic France warring on Catholic Spain and the Emperor, the issues were clearly dynastic, and religious matters played only a secondary role. Furthermore, while Richelieu was eager to humble the Austrian Habsburgs and to add to the French holdings in Alsace, his major designs were against Austria's close ally, Philip IV of Spain. The wily French Cardinal could count upon the Swedes and a number of the German princes to keep up the fight against the Emperor, while French armies attacked the encircling dominions of the Habsburg King of Spain.

From 1635 onward Philip IV had to wage a very different war from that he had previously carried on. Before 1635 he had aided his Austrian kinsmen and sought vainly to crush Holland. After 1635, he was confronted by such violent attacks from the French in the Belgian Netherlands, in Franche Comté, in northern Italy and in Spain itself, that he had frequently to abandon the offensive against Holland and also against the German Protestants. From the start Richelieu's keen strategic eye had discerned the importance of the Valtelline, an Alpine valley which offered the only practicable route by which the Spaniards could bring supplies and men from Italy to the Rhineland and Germany. In that valley, therefore, repeated campaigns were fought and much of the time the French were able to prevent its use by the Spanish.

At first, the Spanish armies, composed mainly of veterans of a dozen campaigns and led by able and tested generals, seemed superior to the French forces, which totaled some 200,000 men but lacked adequate training and competent commanders. In 1636 a large Spanish army invaded northern France and almost captured Paris. The next year, another Spanish force invaded southern France. Gradually, however, the balance shifted. Spanish armies made less and less headway against the French. As the latter gained in experience and acquired more capable generals, they began to press the Spaniards back in the Netherlands, in the Rhineland, in northern Italy, and in southern France.

By 1640, Philip IV was threatened with the disintegration of his dynastic empire. In that year, while the Dutch, with French aid, were successfully maintaining their independence and making inroads into Brazil, an assembly of nobles at Lisbon proclaimed the deposition of Philip IV as King of Portugal. In his place, they put John IV, the head of the native noble family of Braganza and a relative of the king whom Philip II had succeeded in 1580 when he made himself ruler of Portugal. Shortly after 1640, other revolts against Philip IV broke out in Naples and Catalonia (Aragon). Valiantly but hopelessly the Spanish struggled on. The Neapolitans were repressed and so were the Catalans eventually, despite military, naval, and financial aid they received from France. Milan was successfully defended and the Belgian Netherlands were grimly held. But these defensive endeavors quite exhausted the resources of Philip IV. He was unable to recover Portugal or to make headway against the Dutch or the French. In 1643, the long-standing prestige of Spanish arms was shattered when in a fair fight at Rocroi the brilliant young French general, later known as the Grand Condé, crushingly defeated a large body of the far-famed Spanish infantry.

Meanwhile, the fortunes of war had been fluctuating in Germany. For a time the Habsburg Emperor, with the aid of Maximilian of Bavaria and other Catholic princes, more than held his own against the Swedes and the Protestant German princes. But the waning strength of Spain enabled the French to send larger and larger forces into Germany against the Emperor, with increasingly decisive results. Though negotiations for a general peace were undertaken in 1641 by Ferdinand III (who had become Emperor on the death of his father in 1637), they bore no fruit until after the death of Cardinal Richelieu in 1642 and the occupation of Bavaria by the French in 1646. So complicated were the questions involved that after the diplomats had been conferring for many months as to the peace terms, it was decided to hold a general debate to determine what had been the issues over which the war had been fought. At last in 1648, by a series of treaties concluded at Münster and Osnabrück in Westphalia, the Thirty Years' War was ended and peace restored within the Holy Roman Empire. But in signing the peace treaties the Emperor, under pressure from the French, abandoned his Spanish kinsman and ally, Philip IV, and the war between Spain and France dragged on for eleven more years—years that were long and costly for the Spaniards

The peace of Westphalia left the Austrian Hapsburgs in undisputed possession of their dominions in Austria, Hungary, and Bohemia. But its political provisions deprived them of any effective control over the Holy Roman Empire and at the same time wrought numerous changes within the Empire. (1) Practically, each prince was invested with sovereign authority in his own territory; each prince was in effect free to make war, peace, or alliances, without let or hindrance by the Emperor. (2) France obtained Alsace, except the free city of Strasbourg, and was confirmed in the possession of the bishoprics of Metz, Toul, and Verdun. (3) Sweden received the part of Pomerania controlling the mouth of the Oder, and the bishopric of Bremen surrounding the city of that name and dominating the mouths of the Elbe and Weser. (4) France and Sweden, thus securing lands in the Empire and acting as guarantors of the peace, got the right to interfere in German affairs, and Sweden got a voice in the imperial diet. (5) Brandenburg annexed eastern Pomerania and several bishoprics, while Saxony and a number of other smaller states gained or lost certain territories. (6) The Palatinate was divided between Maximilian of Bavaria and the son of Frederick, the "Winter King," and both Bavaria and the Palatinate were henceforth to be electorates. (7) Switzerland and Holland were formally recognized as states free and independent—Holland of the Spanish Habsburgs, and Switzerland of the Austrian Habsburgs.

In addition to the political provisions, the peace of Westphalia included certain stipulations about religion. (1) Calvinists were to share all the privileges of their Lutheran fellow-Protestants. (2) Any piece of church property was guaranteed to such Catholic or Protestant as held it on January 1, 1624 (1618 for Württemberg, Baden, and the Palatinate). (3) An equal number of Catholics and Protestants were to sit in certain imperial courts. (4) The ruler could determine the official religion of each German state, but (except for the hereditary lands of the Habsburgs) he must permit liberty of private worship, freedom of conscience, and the right to emigrate.

D. Results of the Thirty Years' War, and the Continuing Franco-Spanish War to 1659

The Thirty Years' War, concluded in 1648, gave a more or less definite solution to the vexing issues which had given rise to it. In the religious sphere the Calvinists won recognition and equality, and the further alienation of Catholic lands was halted. More important, the conflict between an advancing Protestantism and a rejuvenated Catholicism was ended. After 1648 there was little further change in the

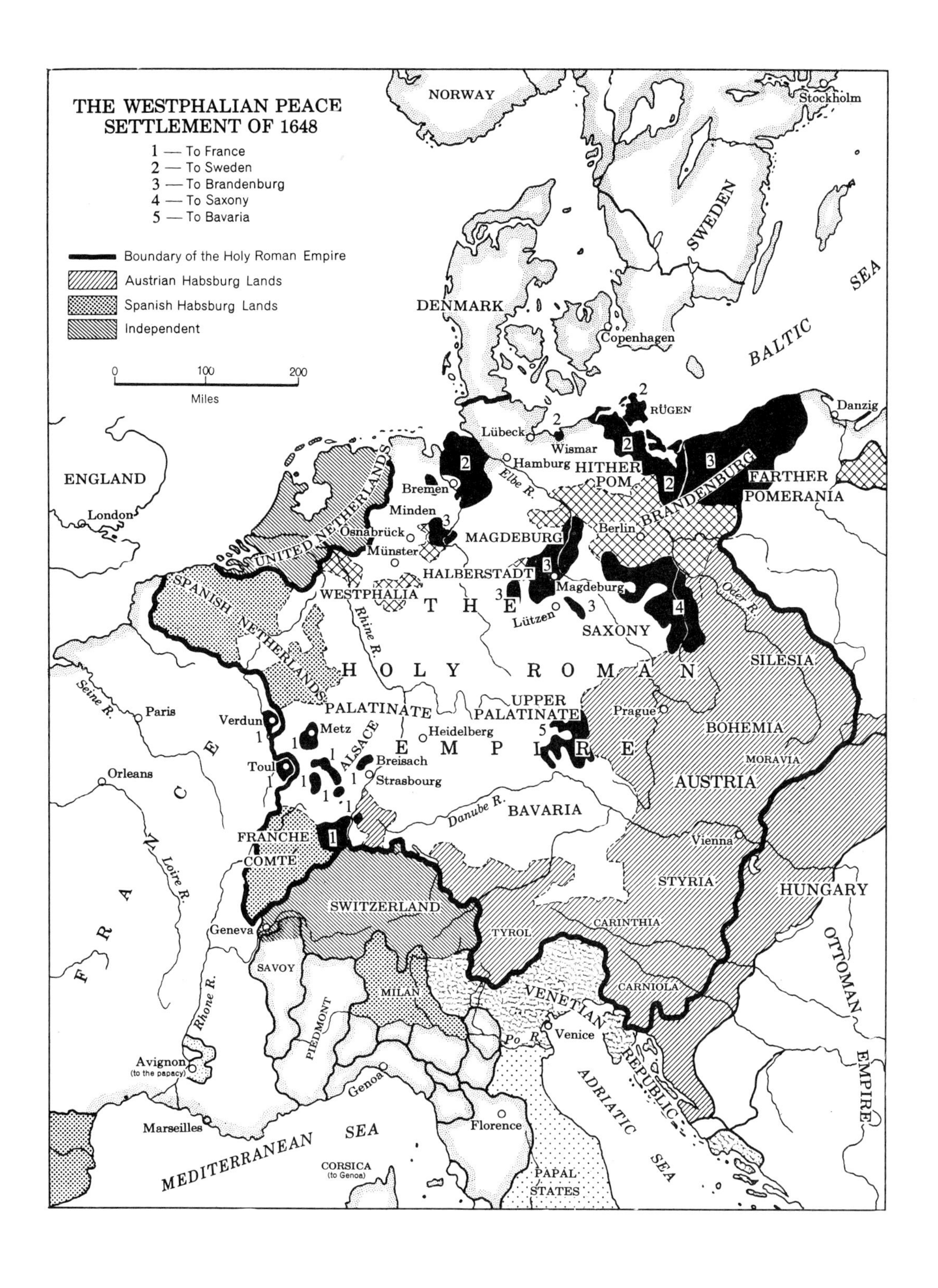
THE WESTPHALIAN PEACE SETTLEMENT OF 1648
1 — To France
2 — To Sweden
3 — To Brandenburg
4 — To Saxony
5 — To Bavaria
Boundary of the Holy Roman Empire
Austrian Habsburg Lands
Spanish Habsburg Lands
Independent
0
100
200
Miles
NORWAY
Stockholm
SWEDEN
BALTIC SEA
DENMARK
Copenhagen
RÜGEN
Danzig
Lübeck
Wismar
Hamburg
HITHER POM.
BRANDENBURG
FARTHER POMERANIA
ENGLAND
London
UNITED NETHERLANDS
Bremen
Minden
Osnabrück
Münster
MAGDEBURG
Berlin
HALBERSTADT
Magdeburg
Lützen
SAXONY
Elbe R.
Oder R.
SPANISH NETHERLANDS
WESTPHALIA
Rhine R.
THE HOLY ROMAN EMPIRE
SILESIA
PALATINATE
UPPER PALATINATE
Prague
BOHEMIA
MORAVIA
AUSTRIA
Seine R.
Paris
Verdun
Metz
ALSACE
Heidelberg
Toul
Breisach
Strasbourg
Orleans
FRANCE
Danube R.
BAVARIA
FRANCHE COMTÉ
Vienna
Loire R.
SWITZERLAND
STYRIA
HUNGARY
Geneva
TYROL
CARINTHIA
OTTOMAN EMPIRE
SAVOY
CARNIOLA
MILAN
VENETIAN REPUBLIC
PIEDMONT
Rhone R.
Po R.
Venice
Avignon
(to the papacy)
Genoa
ADRIATIC SEA
Marseilles
Florence
MEDITERRANEAN SEA
CORSICA
(to Genoa)
PAPAL STATES

religious affiliation of the peoples of the various sections of Germany. In part, the cessation of religious strife in Germany after the peace of Westphalia was due to the exhaustion of the country. In part, it arose from a definite decrease in religious zeal.

Ten years before the end of the war, it had become fairly clear that the religious questions were side issues as compared with political and dynastic matters. Even the pope had been on several occasions accused of favoring the "Protestant" side in the war. Furthermore, as the seventeenth century progressed, it became clear that all over Europe religious bitterness was waning and that, through force of circumstances, tolerance was gradually increasing. In the last half of the century some of the wars had religious aspects, but more and more clearly the main issues were national and dynastic, territorial and economic.

On the whole it can be argued that in Germany the Thirty Years' War represented a victory, partial and qualified, but still a victory, for the forces of Catholicism. Not only had the further advance of Protestantism been checked, but also considerable areas had been won back for the Catholic Church. The triumphs of the Habsburgs in the early years of the war had enabled them to crush Protestantism in Bohemia. At the same time, with the aid of the Jesuits and other religious orders, they had almost wiped out Protestantism in Austria and greatly reduced it in Hungary. The Calvinists in the Palatinate and the upper Rhineland were sharply decreased in number by the course of the war and by Austrian and Bavarian influence. By 1648 the Catholic revival had won back almost all the areas that were to be recovered from Protestantism. Henceforth, its forces were to be expended in strengthening the religious life of Catholic countries in Europe and in winning converts overseas.

The Thirty Years' War helped to prepare the way for the emergence of the modern state-system of Europe, with its formulated principles of international law and diplomacy. Modern diplomatic usages had originated among the Italian states in the fifteenth century [1] and had been adopted by the monarchs of Spain, Portugal, France England, and other countries for the con duct of inter-state business. Yet the modern state-system could not fully emerge as long as one European power—the Holy Roman Empire—claimed even a nominal jurisdiction over states which aspired to, and were capable of, independent existence. The Treaty of Westphalia, by conceding full sovereignty to the member states of the Empire, even in matters of foreign policy, climaxed a development which had been going on since the Golden Bull of 1356 [1] and had made of the Empire merely a nominal federation of self-governing principalities.

Accordingly from the negotiations and treaties of Westphalia emerged the novel principle that all independent sovereign states, regardless of size, were essentially equal. Henceforth, the public law of Europe was to be made by diplomats and by congresses of ambassadors representing theoretically equal sovereign states. The Peace of Westphalia pointed the new path—a path that was made clearer by the fact that with the definite success of the Protestant revolt the pope could no longer speak with spiritual authority to all the rulers. To the Protestant states he was now only a petty Italian prince with somewhat sinister religious connections. Even the Catholic kings, if they still listened to the pope with respect on spiritual matters, were often inclined to ignore his behests when they interfered with political or national ambitions.

Another aspect of international relations was emphasized in the first half of the seventeenth century. It was the Thirty Years' War with its revolting cruelty which turned the attention of a considerable number of scholars to the need of formulating rules for the protection of non-combatants in time of war, the treatment of the sick, wounded, and prisoners, the prohibition of wanton pillage and other horrors which shocked the awakening humanitarianism of the time. The foremost of such scholars was Hugo Grotius (1583–1645), whose famous treatise *On the Laws of War and Peace* (1625) was published in the midst of the struggle.

[1] See above, p. 306 *n*.

[1] See above. pp. 274, 291.

In the Baltic, the results of the Thirty Years' War were somewhat inconclusive. From a political and military point of view, Sweden emerged as the strongest power. Encircled by Swedish-held lands, the Baltic was almost the Swedish lake of which Gustavus Adolphus had dreamed. But the population and resources of Sweden were not sufficient to enable it to maintain such an extensive dominion for long. Sweden was to play the role of a great power for only about seventy years after the Peace of Westphalia. Then the rise of Russia and of Prussia would thrust Sweden back into a secondary position. Commercially, the Thirty Years' War did not effect much real change. The Dutch had had the lion's share of the Baltic trade in 1617. They still had it in 1649.

In the dynastic sphere, the results of the Thirty Years' War were more definite. It marked the decline of the Habsburgs of Austria and Spain and the rise of the Bourbons of France. By French intervention, the Habsburg Emperor had been humbled, deprived of any real control of Germany as a whole, and thrust back upon his own hereditary dominions as his sole remaining source of strength. The Spanish Habsburgs had likewise been checked and weakened by 1648, but for them the war was not ended in 1648. Cardinal Mazarin, who in 1642 had succeeded Richelieu as chief minister of France, forced upon the Austrian Habsburgs the peace of Westphalia in 1648, and, despite internal troubles in France, maintained with mounting success the struggle with the Spanish Habsburgs until 1659.

The war was continued under disastrous conditions for Spain. To be sure, Philip IV had terminated the long struggle with Holland by the Peace of Westphalia. But though he had emptied the Spanish treasury and bled white the Spanish manpower to serve the Habsburg cause, though Spanish armies had borne the brunt of the fighting all over Europe and Spanish colonies and commerce had suffered repeatedly from attacks by the French, English, and Dutch, still in 1648 the Emperor Ferdinand III felt obliged to reject his cousin Philip's pleas for aid from Austria and to leave Spain to continue alone the war with the French Bourbons. Valiantly the Spanish soldiers fought on; doggedly the Spanish King declined to make concessions. But in time, French pressure became unbearable. French generals, like the brilliant Turenne, won victories in the Belgian (Spanish) Netherlands and in northern Spain. France gained an ally in Portugal and toward the end secured another ally in England. At long last, in 1659, Philip IV bowed to the inevitable and signed with France the treaty of the Pyrenees.

At the beginning of the century Spain had appeared to be the wealthiest and strongest state in Europe. The treaty of the Pyrenees formally registered the end of Spanish predominance and the beginning of that of France. Spain quickly sank to the status of a second-rate power. The provisions of the treaty were not of themselves of prime importance. But they were as favorable to France as they were unfavorable to Spain. (1) Spain ceded to France the province of Roussillon at the eastern end of the Pyrenees. (2) Spain ceded to France a southern strip of the Belgian Netherlands, including the province of Artois and several fortified towns. (3) Philip IV agreed to the marriage of his daughter Maria Theresa to the young King Louis XIV of France. In return for a large dowry, Louis XIV agreed to renounce for himself and his heirs any right to inherit the Spanish dominions. But since Spain was now poor, the dowry was never paid, and Louis XIV was left with a claim to the Spanish inheritance.

One result of the Thirty Years' War which arose from its length and extent, rather than from any issue involved, was the widespread havoc and destruction in Germany. There were few areas in the country which had not at one time or another been ravaged or plundered, and there is no doubt that the prosperity and civilization of Germany received a terrific set-back from which it took decades to recover. But the disastrous effects of the war upon Germany must not be exaggerated.[1] No section of Germany was fought

[1] Certain modern German historians, searching for an explanation of the backwardness of their country before 1870, exaggerated the disasters of the Thirty Years' War and assumed general conditions from purely local happenings.

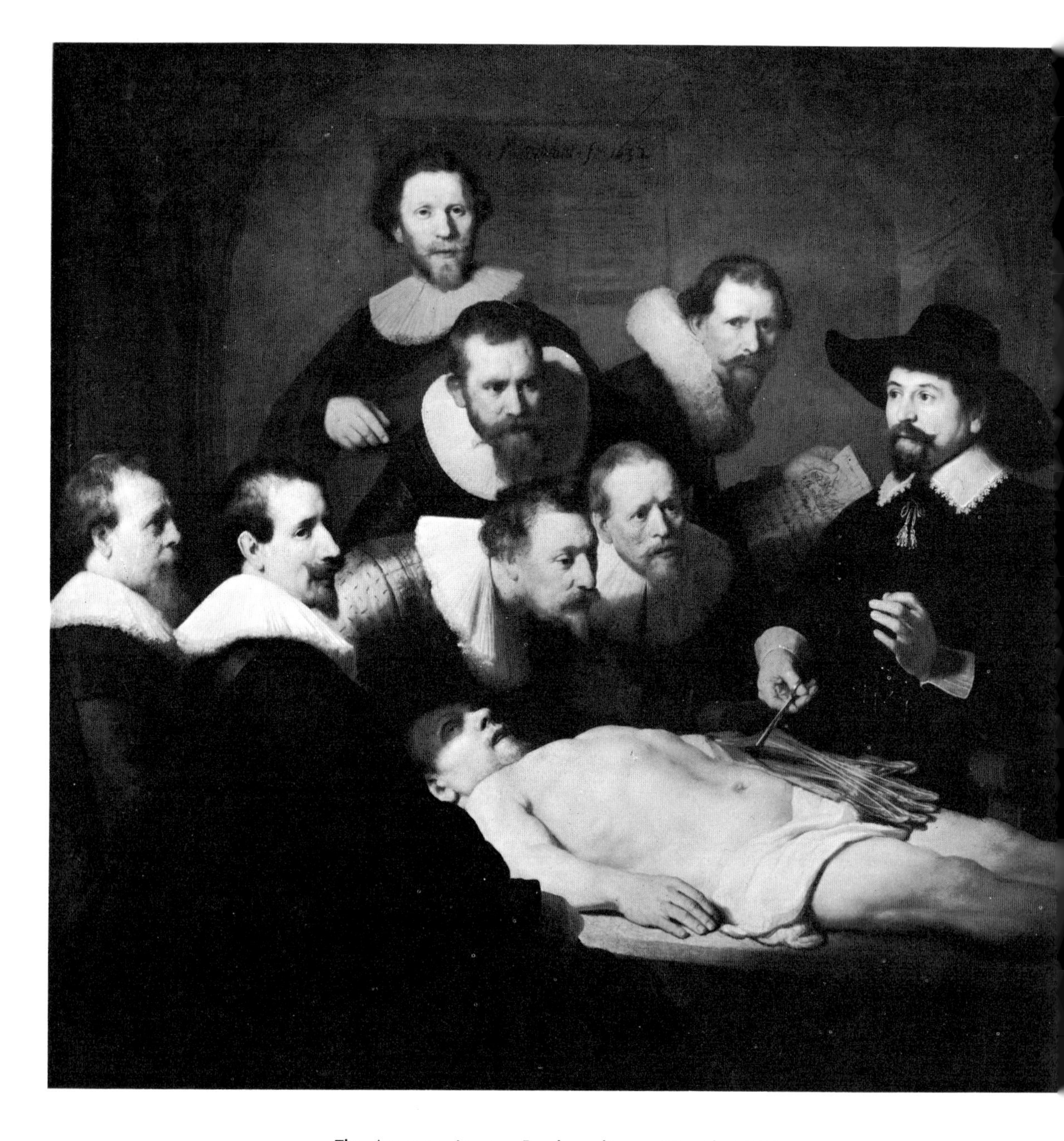

The Anatomy Lesson. Rembrandt van Rijn (*d.* 1669).

Courtesy Foundation Johan Maurits van Nassau, Mauritshuis, The Hague

over continuously for thirty years or even for a major portion of that time. It is also a misunderstanding of history to impute to seventeenth-century Germany a political failure. The Germans no more failed in the seventeenth century than had the Italians in the fifteenth. Indeed, the Germans of those days would have undoubtedly regarded the arrangements of Westphalia as a landmark in an important progress toward the emancipation of their respective states. Moreover, some of these states, in the course of time, participated not only in the political but also in the cultural development of Europe. The latter subject it will be well to consider briefly before passing on to a later age. But meanwhile let us say something of an

important economic occurrence—the so-called "price revolution."

E. Economics and the Price Revolution of Early Modern Times

During the sixteenth century, when the Spanish empire was at its height, the influence of European overseas expansion was increasingly felt throughout western Europe. One of the most remarkable developments was the rise in prices which resulted largely from the imports of precious metals and which served to intensify the growth of capitalism. The quantity of gold and silver in Europe in 1500 is not known. But when all allowances are made for bullion buried, lost, used in the arts, or sent to the East, and for bullion produced in Europe, secured from Africa, or smuggled into Spain unregistered from America, it seems clear that the amount of precious metals in Europe was about tripled between 1500 and the middle of the seventeenth century.

In that same period, prices of goods and wages roughly tripled in Europe. The price rise started in Spain and moved out from that center, affecting first the nearer and then the further lands, as these secured some portion of the Spanish treasure. Wages usually tended to rise more slowly than prices, a fact which had important results, for manufacturers tended to get more for their products while paying relatively less wages. Thus, for more than a century the cards were stacked in favor of the industrialist; and the man who could make the most goods (the capitalist producer with many people working for him in a shop or under the putting-out system) made the most money. In addition, rising prices favored the merchant, for the goods he had in storage or on ships tended to rise in price while he held them. In short, the remarkable price rise favored the big business man—the new capitalist—and helped to make capitalism a success and to fix it on Europe. In a similar way, the increased supply of the precious metals speeded the transition to a money economy, made it easier to accumulate large stocks of money, and encouraged the use of credit devices, bills of exchange, and the like, based on money in both trading and banking.

We have already noted that even before 1500, landowners (including ecclesiastical establishments) whose incomes were derived from money rents, fees, and dues long fixed by custom or by contract, were at a disadvantage in an economy of rising prices. This situation was accentuated in the sixteenth century, as fixed incomes could obviously purchase fewer of the luxury goods which were in demand. Although English landlords, many of whom had appropriated former monastic lands, or who were busy enclosing vast tracts for sheep raising, succeeded better than their French confrères in adjusting to the expanding money economy, no area in western Europe was unaffected. By the end of the sixteenth century, many big estates in France had been mortgaged and many nobles had lost their land. The buyers were officials or merchants who in one way or another had profited from the price rise. In most countries of Europe, while some nobles lost their old status, new persons appeared in the ranks of the upper classes.

The price rise, with its attendant contribution to capitalistic economy, was but one of the highly important results of overseas expansion. The new overseas trade brought to Europe a steadily increasing flow of foreign commodities and took from it a rapidly growing stream of goods needed in the Far East or in the American colonies, such as textiles, tools, munitions, hardware, glass, and trinkets. Thus, commerce grew and stimulated industry. The new fisheries off Newfoundland gave employment to thousands of Europeans, and dried or salted fish became an increasingly valuable item of consumption. It was the Atlantic that was now the highway of trade and the road to riches. The ports of the Mediterranean and the Baltic, while still busy with ships, were overshadowed by the new commercial centers on the Atlantic coast. Throughout most of the sixteenth century, the chief northern port city was Antwerp with its exceptionally fine harbor and its renowned *bourse* or "stock exchange." But Antwerp suffered during the Spanish-Dutch wars and by the early seventeenth century was being rivaled by Amsterdam. For it was the northern Netherlands which, as it won its independence from Spain, attained to the commercial supremacy of northwestern Europe.

Since Spain seemed for long to be profiting most directly and to the greatest extent from the new lands overseas, other countries strove to get some share of Spanish silver, or tried to find new lands rich in mines for themselves. Moreover, the example of Spain fastened on Europe a pattern of economic thought and policy known as mercantilism. Almost every country adopted laws designed to bring in bullion and to retain the precious metals. Sometimes this was done directly by paying extra for bullion, forbidding its export, and limiting its use in plate, jewelry, or clothes. Increasingly, it was done indirectly by encouraging, usually by customs duties and tariff laws, a favorable balance of trade, that is, an excess of exports over imports.

The products from overseas, whether long known and now secured in increasing quantities, or brought to Europe for the first time, made possible new luxuries. Dyes like indigo, cochineal, and brazilwood, replaced older products. Silk, furs, ostrich plumes, and ivory; perfumes like musk, civet, sandalwood, and ambergris; rich rugs, carpets, and shawls, all aided the display or comfort of the upper classes. Old spices from the east such as pepper, nutmegs, cinnamon, and cloves were more plentiful; while new flavors were introduced from America, like allspice, chocolate, and vanilla. Guinea fowl were brought in by the Portuguese from Africa, and turkeys from America by the Spanish. Though they were not in common use till much later, the tomato and the potato and Indian corn (or maize) were likewise introduced into Europe from America.

It was truly an age of expanding horizons. Any year might bring word of a new land, rich and populous, or wild and strange. Any year might see some new exotic product brought in for the use of Europeans. Any hazardous voyage might win for its backers a fortune. The world was larger and stranger than anyone had thought.

F. Culture in the Early Seventeenth Century: Emergence of the Baroque

It was inevitable in the circumstances of the sixteenth and early seventeenth centuries that intellectual horizons should be broadened. The great French essayist, Montaigne (*d.* 1592), writing about Brazilian cannibals, gained a new perspective on

France. Astronomy was stimulated by the new half of the heavens seen below the equator. Geography grew by leaps and bounds as men like Gerard Mercator (1512–1594) put on to maps the new discoveries that were reported. Botany was enriched by the description of exotic plants which found their way into books like the *Herball* (1597) of John Gerard. New animals and birds were brought home as curiosities. New medicines, like quinine from South America, aided the doctors. New products like tobacco brought with them a train of social changes and opportunities for importers, manufacturers, and tradesmen.

Perhaps because the late sixteenth and early seventeenth centuries constituted an age of expanding horizons and growing fortunes, there was in art a tendency toward the grandiose and the ornate. The art of the seventeenth century is generally classified as "baroque," a term of uncertain origin, but probably first used with deprecatory connotation. But if baroque art was lavish, it was also complex, dynamic, and emotional. In southern Europe, it was closely associated with the Catholic reformation, with the Jesuits, and above all with Rome, which was fast acquiring the baroque aspect which it still possesses.

It was in the early decades of the seventeenth century that the great St. Peter's basilica was finally completed. Maderna extended the nave and added the façade. Bernini (*d.* 1680), a sculptor as well as an architect, did most of the interior decorations, including the baldachino (canopy) over the high altar, and he designed the magnificent *piazza* with its colonnades. Early Italian baroque painters, Caravaggio (*d.* 1610) and Carracci (*d.* 1609), were followed by others who produced in churches and private palaces enormous and magnificent ceiling paintings.

It was in this same age that the Spanish painting, which was described in the preceding chapter, reached its apogée. Meanwhile, Rubens (*d.* 1640), a Flemish artist who had lived in Italy, epitomized the baroque painting of the north. Another Fleming, Van Dyck (*d.* 1641), is especially noted for his portraits.

As the northern Netherlands was winning its independence from Spain and developing a commercial empire, it was also becoming one of the cultural centers of Europe. The university of Leiden won an enviable reputation and attracted many students from abroad. And while some Dutch artists, notably Hals (*d.* 1666), painting for a bourgeois public, portrayed people and scenes from everyday life, and others, such as Vermeer (*d.* 1675), produced small pictures to hang in private homes, the great Rembrandt (*d.* 1669) was creating something much more profound.

All the aspects of the life of the early seventeenth century, political, economic, and cultural, were to find foremost expression ultimately in France and there to be modified by characteristics peculiarly French. For with the ending of Spanish military and political predominance, Spanish (and Italian) cultural preëminence notably declined. The future lay with France, and to this nation, on the eve of a period of exceptional brilliance, in which French culture matched French political achievement, we shall next turn.

SELECT SUPPLEMENTARY READINGS FOR PART VI

General. *The New Cambridge Modern History*, vol. II (1958); S. B. Clough and C. W. Cole, *Economic History of Europe* (1952); A. J. Grant, *History of Europe, 1494–1610*, 2 vols. (1948); V. H. H. Green, *Renaissance and Reformation* (1952); H. J. Grimm, *The Reformation Era, 1500–1650* (1958); E. H. Harbison, *The Age of the Reformation* (1955): C. J. H. Hayes, *Political and Cultural History of Modern Europe*, vol. I (1936); P. Smith, *The Age of the Reformation* (1920).

Chapter 28. K. Brandi, *Charles V* (tr. 1939); R. T. Davies, *The Golden Century of Spain* (1937); J. Lynch, *Spain Under the Habsburgs*, vol. I, *Empire and Absolutism, 1516–1598* (1964); J. H. Elliott, *Imperial Spain, 1496–1716* (1964); R. Ehrenberg, *Capital and Finance in the Age of the Renaissance* (1928); C. H. Haring, *The Spanish Empire in America, 1492–1815* (1946); H. Holborn, *History of Modern Germany*, vol. I (1959); R. B. Merriman, *Suleiman the Magnificent* (1944) and *The Rise of the Spanish Empire in the Old World and the New*, vol. III (1925); F. L. de Gomara, *Cortes: the Life of the Conqueror by His Secretary* (1964); C. Gibson, *The Aztecs Under Spanish Rule—1519–1810* (1964); J. H. Parry, *Europe and a Wider World, 1415–1715* (1949, new ed., *The Establishment of the European Hegemony*, 1961); J. Streider, *Jacob Fugger the Rich* (1931).

Chapter 29. Books dealing with the Reformation in general, in addition to those cited above under "General": R. H. Bainton, *The Reformation of the Sixteenth Century* (1952); L. Cristiani, "The Reformation on the Continent," *The Reformation* (1936), vol. IV of *European Civilization*, ed. E. Eyre; P. Hughes, *A Popular History of the Reformation* (1960); A. Hyma, *Renaissance to Reformation* (1951); G. L. Mosse, *The Reformation* (1953); F. Mourret, *A History of the Catholic Church*, vol. V (tr. 1930); L. Pastor, *History of the Popes*, vols. VI ff. For Lutheranism: R. H. Bainton, *Here I Stand: a Life of Martin Luther* (1950); H. Holborn, *History of Modern Germany*, vol. I; C. Manschreck, *Melancthon: the Quiet Reformer* (1958); E. G. Schweibert, *Luther and His Times* (1950); J. Clayton, *Luther and His Work* (1937). On Calvinism: A. Dakin, *Calvinism* (1946); A. J. Grant, *The Huguenots* (1934); G. Harkness, *John Calvin: the Man and His Ethics* (1931); R. N. C. Hunt, *Calvin* (1933); A. Hyma, *Life of John Calvin* (1943). On France and the religious wars: F. C. Palm, *Calvinism and the Religious Wars* (1932); J. E. Neale, *The Age of Catherine de Medici* (1943). On the much debated question of the reformation and capitalism, including bibliography: R. H. Green, *Protestantism and Capitalism: the Weber Thesis and Its Critics* (1959).

Chapter 30. General histories of England: S. T. Bindoff, *Tudor England* (1950); J. B. Black, *The Reign of Elizabeth, 1558–1603* (1959); J. D. Mackie, *The Earlier Tudors, 1485–1558* (1952); J. McCollum, *The Age of Elizabeth* (1961); C. Read, *The Tudors* (1936); A. L. Rowse, *The Elizabethan Age*, 2 vols. (1951, 1955); G. W. O. Woodward, *A Short History of Sixteenth-Century England* (1963); L. Stone, *The Crisis of the Aristocracy, 1558–1641* (1965). For selected biographies and for the English reformation: R. W. Chambers, *Thomas More* (1938); C. W. Ferguson, *Naked to Mine Enemies: the Life of Cardinal Wolsey* (1958); F. Hackett, *Henry VIII* (1929); P. Hughes, *The Reformation in England*, 3 vols. (1951–1954); F. E. Hutchinson, *Cranmer* (1951); A. F. Pollard, *Thomas Cranmer* (1904), *Henry VIII* (1913), and *Wolsey* (1929); F. M. Powicke, *The Reformation in England* (1941); J. E. Neale, *Queen Elizabeth I* (1934); N. B. Morrison, *Mary, Queen of Scots* (1961).

Chapter 31. In addition to the general histories of the church, cited above for Chapter 29: J. Brodrick, S. J., *The Origin of the Jesuits* (1940) and *The Progress of the Jesuits, 1556–1579* (1947); P. Dudon, *St. Ignatius Loyola* (1950); M. P. Harney, S. J., *The Jesuits in History* (1941); G. H. Dunne, S. J., *A Generation of Giants: the Story of the Jesuits in China in the Last Decades of the Ming Dynasty* (1962); G. Sansom, *A History of Japan, 1334–1615* (1961); H. Jedin, *A History of the Council of Trent* (1957); B. J. Kidd, *The Counter-Reformation* (1933); H. Daniel-Rops, *The Catholic Reformation* (1962). For the culture of the sixteenth century: H. Butterfield, *The Origins of Modern Science* (1949); A. C. Crombie, *Science in the Later Middle Ages and Early Modern Times* (1959); M. Boas, *The Scientific Renaissance, 1450–1630* (1962); H. Gardner, *Art Through the Ages* (1959); K. Holl, *The Cultural Significance of the Reformation* (1948, 1959); P. Lang, *Music in Western Civilization* (1941); R. Murray, *Political Consequences of the Reformation* (1926); N. Pevsner, *An Outline of European Architecture* (1957).

Chapter 32. A. Castro, *The Structure of Spanish History* (1954); C. E. Chapman, *Colonial Hispanic America* (1933); B. Chudoba, *Spain and the Empire, 1519–1634* (1952); R. T. Davies, *The Golden Century of Spain* (1937); P. Geyl, *Revolt of the Netherlands, 1555–1609* (1937); C. H. Haring, *The Spanish Empire in America* (1947); J. H. Mariejol, *Philip II, the First Modern King* (tr. 1934); C. Petrie, *Philip II of Spain* (1963); G. Mattingly, *The Armada* (1959); G. J. Marcus, *A Naval History of England*, vol. I, *The Formative Centuries* (1961); R. B. Merriman, *The Rise of the Spanish Empire*, vol. IV, *Philip the Prudent* (1934); W. T. Walsh, *Philip II* (1937); C. V. Wedgwood, *William the Silent* (1944).

Chapter 33. P. Geyl, *The Netherlands Divided, 1609–1648* (1936); C. R. Boxer, *The Dutch Seaborne Empire, 1600–1800* (1965); H. Holborn, *History of Modern Germany*, vol. I (1959); M. Roberts, *Gustavus Adolphus: a History of Sweden, 1611–1632*, vol. I (1953); C. V. Wedgwood, *The Thirty Years' War* (1939). For Richelieu and French intervention in the Thirty Years' War, see p. 496 under Chapter 34. For economic and cultural developments, in addition to the books cited above for Chapter 32: E. F. Hecksher, *Mercantilism*, 2 vols. (1935); L. B. Packard, *The Commercial Revolution* (1927); J. H. Parry, *Europe and a Wider World*; P. Smith, *History of Modern Culture*, vol. I (1930); D. M. Frame, *Montaigne* (1965). On art: the works of Gardner and Pevsner, cited above for Chapter 31.

APPENDIX

Partial List of European Sovereigns

I. EMPERORS

Roman

Augustus, 27 B.C.–14 A.D.
Tiberius, 14–37 A.D.
Gaius, 37–41
Claudius, 41–54
Nero, 54–68
Vespasian, 69–79
Titus, 79–81
Domitian, 81–96
Nerva, 96–98
Trajan, 98–117
Hadrian, 117–138
Antoninus Pius, 138–161
Marcus Aurelius, 161–180
Commodus, 180–193
Septimius Severus, 193–211
Caracalla, 211–217
Macrinus, 217–218
Elagabalus, 218–222
Alexander Severus, 222–235
Maximinus, 235–238
Philip, 244–248
Decius, 249–251
Aurelian, 270–275
Diocletian, 284–305
Constantius, 305–311
Constantine, 311–337
Constantius II, 337–361
Julian, 361–363
Valens, 364–378
Theodosius, 379–395

East Roman (Byzantine)

Arcadius, 395–408
Theodosius II, 408–450
Marcian, 450–457
Leo I, 457–474
Zeno, 474–491
Anastasius I, 491–518
Justin I, 518–527
Justinian, 527–565
Justin II, 565–578
Maurice, 582–602
Heraclius, 610–641
Justinian II, 685–711
Leo III, 717–741
Constantine VI, 780–797
Irene, 797–802
Nicephoras I, 802–811
Leo V, 813–820
Michael III, 842
Basil I, 867–886

West Roman

Honorius, 395–423
Valentinian III, 423–455

Julius Nepos, 474–475
Romulus "Augustulus," 475–476

Frankish Roman

Charlemagne, 800–814
Louis, the Pious, 814–840
Lothair, 840–855
Louis II, 855–875
Charles II, the Bald, 877–881
Charles III, the Fat, 881–887

East Roman (Byzantine)—Cont.	***Holy Roman (German)***	
Constantine VII, 912–959	Henry I, the Fowler, 919–936	SAXON
Nicephoras II, Phocas, 963–969	Otto I, the Great, 936–973	"
	Otto II, 973–983	"
Basil II, 976–1025	Otto III, 983–1002	"
	Henry II, 1002–1024	"
	Conrad II, 1024–1039	FRANCONIAN
Constantine IX, 1042–1054	Henry III, 1039–1056	"
Isaac I, 1057–1059	Henry IV, 1056–1106	"
Romanus IV, 1067–1071		
Alexius I, Comnenus, 1081–1118	Henry V, 1106–1125	"
John II, 1118–1143	Lothair II, 1125–1137	"
Manuel I, 1143–1180	Conrad III, 1138–1152	HOHENSTAUFEN
Andronicus I, 1183–1185	Frederick I, Barbarossa, 1152–1190	"
Isaac II, 1185–1195		
Alexius III, 1195–1203	Henry VI, 1190–1197	"
	Philip of Swabia, 1198–1208	
	Otto IV, 1208–1215	GUELF
	Frederick II, 1220–1250	HOHENSTAUFEN
Michael VIII, Palaeologus, 1259–1282	Conrad IV, 1250–1254	"
Andronicus II, 1282–1328	Rudolf I, 1273–1291	HABSBURG
	Adolf, 1292–1298	NASSAU
	Albert I, 1298–1308	HABSBURG
Andronicus III, 1328–1341	Henry VII, 1308–1313	LUXEMBOURG
	Louis IV, 1314–1347	BAVARIAN
John V, 1341–1391	Charles IV, 1347–1378	LUX-BOHEMIAN
Manuel II, 1391–1425	Wenceslas, 1378–1400	"
John VI, 1425–1448	Sigismund, 1410–1437	"
Constantine XI, 1448–1453	Albert II, 1438–1439	HABSBURG
	Frederick III, 1440–1493	"

Holy Roman (German)	***Ottoman (Turkish Sultans)***	***Russian (Tsars)***
	Mohammed II, 1451–1481	
Maximilian I, 1493–1519	Bayezid I, 1481–1512	Ivan III, the Great, 1462–1505
Charles V, 1519–1556	Selim I, 1512–1520	Basil IV, 1505–1533
Ferdinand I, 1556–1564	Suleiman II, the Magnificent, 1520–1566	Ivan IV, the Terrible, 1533–1584
Maximilian II, 1564–1576	Selim II, 1566–1574	
Rudolf II, 1576–1612	Murad III, 1574–1595	Theodore I, 1584–1598
Matthias, 1612–1619	Mohammed III, 1595–1603	Boris Godunov, 1598–1605
Ferdinand II, 1619–1637	Murad IV, 1623–1640	Michael Romanov, 1613–1645
Ferdinand III, 1637–1657	Ibrahim, 1640–1648	Alexius, 1645–1676

II. POPES (Partial List)

Peter, d. about 67 A.D.
Clement I, 88–97
Alexander I, 105–115
Sixtus I, 115–125
Pius I, 140–154
Soter, 166–175
Victor I, 189–199
Calixtus I, 217–222
Urban I, 222–230
Stephen I, 254–257
Felix I, 269–275
Marcellus I, 308–309
Sylvester I, 314–336
Julius I, 337–352
Liberius, 352–366
Damasus I, 366–384
Innocent I, 401–417
Leo I, 440–461
Symmachus, 498–514
Vigilius, 537–556
Gregory I, 590–604
Boniface IV, 608–615
Honorius I, 625–640
Martin I, 649–654
Eugene I, 654–657
Agatho, 678–682
Leo II, 682–683
Sergius I, 687–701
Gregory II, 715–731
Gregory III, 731–741
Zacharius, 741–752
Stephen III, 752–757
Paul I, 757–768
Hadrian I, 772–795
Leo III, 795–816
Gregory IV, 827–844
Leo IV, 847–855
Nicholas I, 858–867
John VIII, 872–882
Formosus, 891–896
John X, 914–928
John XII, 955–963
Sylvester II, 999–1003
John XIX, 1024–1032
Benedict IX, 1032–1045
Leo IX, 1049–1054
Gregory VII, 1073–1085
Urban II, 1088–1099
Paschal II, 1099–1118
Honorius II, 1124–1130
Innocent II, 1130–1143
Eugene III, 1145–1153
Hadrian IV, 1154–1159
Alexander III, 1159–1181
Lucius III, 1181–1185
Celestine III, 1191–1198
Innocent III, 1198–1216
Honorius III, 1216–1227
Gregory IX, 1227–1241
Celestine IV, 1241
Innocent IV, 1243–1254
Alexander IV, 1254–1261
Urban IV, 1261–1265
Clement IV, 1265–1271
Gregory X, 1271–1276
John XXI, 1276–1277
Nicholas III, 1277–1281
Martin IV, 1281–1285
Honorius IV, 1285–1288
Nicholas IV, 1288–1292
Celestine V, 1294
Boniface VIII, 1294–1303
Benedict XI, 1303–1304
Clement V, 1305–1314
John XXII, 1316–1334
Benedict XII, 1334–1342
Clement VI, 1342–1352
Innocent VI, 1352–1362
Urban V, 1362–1370
Gregory XI, 1370–1378
Urban VI, 1378–1389
Boniface IX, 1389–1404
Innocent VII, 1404–1406
Gregory XII, 1406–1417
Martin V, 1417–1431
Eugene IV, 1431–1447
Nicholas V, 1447–1455
Calixtus III, 1455–1458
Pius II, 1458–1464
Paul II, 1464–1471
Sixtus IV, 1471–1484
Innocent VIII, 1484–1492
Alexander VI, 1492–1503
Pius III, 1503
Julius II, 1503–1513
Leo X, 1513–1521
Hadrian VI, 1522–1523
Clement VII, 1523–1534
Paul III, 1534–1549
Julius III, 1550–1555
Marcellus II, 1555
Paul IV, 1555–1559
Pius IV, 1559–1565
Pius V, 1566–1572
Gregory XIII, 1572–1585
Sixtus V, 1585–1590
Urban VII, 1590
Gregory XIV, 1590–1591
Innocent IX, 1591–1592
Clement VIII, 1592–1605
Paul V, 1605–1621
Gregory XV, 1621–1623
Urban VIII, 1623–1644
Innocent X, 1644–1655

III. OTHER SOVEREIGNS

Kings of England

King	House
William I, 1066–1087,	Norman
William II, 1087–1100,	"
Henry I, 1100–1135,	"
Stephen, 1135–1154,	"
Henry II, 1154–1189,	Angevin (Plantagenet)
Richard I, 1189–1199,	"
John, 1199–1216,	"
Henry III, 1216–1272,	"
Edward I, 1272–1307,	"
Edward II, 1307–1327,	"
Edward III, 1327–1377,	"
Richard II, 1377–1399,	"
Henry IV, 1399–1413,	Lancaster
Henry V, 1413–1422,	"
Henry VI, 1422–1461	"
Edward IV, 1461–1483,	York
Edward V, 1483,	"
Richard III, 1483–1485,	"
Henry VII, 1485–1509,	Tudor
Henry VIII, 1509–1547,	"
Edward VI, 1547–1553,	"
Mary I, 1553–1558,	"
Elizabeth I, 1558–1603,	"
James I, 1603–1625,	Stuart
Charles I, 1625–1649, (*Cromwell*)	"

Kings of France

King	House
Hugh Capet, 987–996,	Capetian
Robert, 996–1031,	"
Henry I, 1031–1060,	"
Philip I, 1060–1108,	"
Louis VI, 1108–1137	"
Louis VII, 1137–1180	"
Philip II, Augustus, 1180–1223,	"
Louis VIII, 1223–1226,	"
Louis IX, 1226–1270,	"
Philip III, 1270–1285	"
Philip IV, the Fair, 1285–1314,	"
Louis X, 1314–1316,	"
Philip V, 1316–1322,	"
Charles IV, 1322–1328,	"
Philip VI, 1328–1350,	Valois
John, 1350–1364,	"
Charles V, 1364–1380,	"
Charles VI, 1380–1422,	"
Charles VII, 1422–1461,	"
Louis XI, 1461–1483,	"
Charles VIII, 1483–1498,	"
Louis XII, 1498–1515,	"
Francis I, 1515–1547,	"
Henry II, 1547–1559,	"
Francis II, 1559–1560,	"
Charles IX, 1560–1574,	"
Henry III, 1574–1589,	"
Henry IV, 1589–1610,	Bourbon
Louis XIII, 1610–1643,	"
Louis XIV, 1643–1715,	"

Kings in the Iberian Peninsula

Castile	*Aragon*	*Portugal*
Alphonso V, 999–1027		
Ferdinand I, 1028–1065		
Alphonso VI, 1065–1109	Alphonso I, 1104–1134	Alphonso I, 1112–1185
Alphonso VII, 1137–1157		
Alphonso VIII, 1158–1214	Alphonso II, 1162–1196	
	Peter II, 1196–1213	Sancho I, 1185–1211
Henry I, 1214–1217	James I, 1213–1276	Alphonso II, 1211–1223
Ferdinand III, 1217–1252		Sancho II, 1223–1248
Alphonso X, 1252–1284	Peter III, 1276–1285	Alphonso III, 1248–1279
Sancho IV, 1284–1296	Alphonso III, 1285–1291	Diniz, 1279–1325
Ferdinand IV, 1296–1312	James II, 1291–1327	
Alphonso XI, 1312–1350	Alphonso IV, 1327–1336	Alphonso IV, 1325–1357
Peter I, 1350–1368	Peter IV, 1336–1387	Peter I, 1357–1367
Henry II, 1368–1379		Ferdinand I, 1367–1383
John I, 1379–1390	John I, 1387–1395	John I, 1385–1443
Henry III, 1390–1406	Martin I, 1395–1410	
John II, 1406–1454	Ferdinand I, 1414–1416	
	Alphonso V, 1416–1458	Alphonso V, 1443–1481
Henry IV, 1454–1474	John II, 1458–1479	
Isabella I, 1474–1504	Ferdinand II, 1479–1516	John II, 1481–1495
Philip I, 1504–1506		Manuel I, 1495–1521

Spain		
Ferdinand V, 1506–1516		
Charles I, 1516–1556		John III, 1521–1557
Philip II, 1556–1598,	HABSBURG	Sebastian, 1557–1578
		Henry, 1578–1580
Philip III, 1598–1621,	"	(*To Spain, 1580–1640*)
Philip IV, 1621–1665,	"	John IV, 1640–1656

Kings in Scandinavia

Denmark	***Norway***	***Sweden***
Harold, 935–985		
Svend, 985–1014	Olaf I, 996–1000	Olaf, 993–1024
Knut, 1014–1035	Olaf II, 1016–1029	
Hardiknut, 1035–1042	Magnus, 1035–1047	
Svend II, 1047–1076	Harold III, 1047–1066	
	Magnus III, 1095–1103	
Waldemar I, 1157–1182	Magnus V, 1161–1184	Eric IX, 1150–1162
Knut VI, 1182–1202		
Waldemar II, 1202–1241	Haakon IV, 1217–1262	Earl Birger, 1248–1266
	Haakon V, 1299–1319	Magnus, 1279–1290
Waldemar IV, 1340–1375	Haakon VI, 1350–1380	
	Olaf III, 1380–1387	Albert, 1365–1388
Margaret, 1387–1412		
Christian I, 1448–1483		
Hans, 1483–1513		
Christian II, 1513–1523		
Frederick I, 1523–1533		Gustavus I, Vasa, 1523–1560
Christian III, 1533–1559		
Frederick II, 1559–1588		Eric XIV, 1560–1568
		John III, 1568–1592
Christian IV, 1588–1648		Gustavus II, Adolphus, 1611–1632
Frederick III, 1648–1670		Christina, 1632–1654

Kings of Poland, Bohemia, and Hungary

Poland	***Bohemia***	***Hungary***
Boleslav I, 992–1025		Stephen I, 997–1038
Casimir I, 1025–1058	Bretislav I, 1037–1055	Andrew I, 1046–1066
Boleslav II, 1058–1091		Ladislas I, 1077–1095
	Vratislav II, 1061–1092	Koloman, 1095–1116
	Bretislav II, 1092–1110	
	Vladislav I, 1111–1125	
Boleslav III, 1102–1139	Sobeslav, 1125–1140	
	Vladislav II, 1140–1173	
		Bela III, 1173–1196
	Ottakar I, 1197–1230	Andrew II, 1205–1235
	Wenceslas I, 1230–1253	Bela IV, 1235–1270
	Ottakar II, 1253–1278	Ladislas IV, 1272–1290
	Wenceslas II, 1278–1305	Andrew III, 1290–1301
	Wenceslas III, 1305–1306	
Ladislas I, 1306–1333	John of Luxembourg, 1310–1346	Charles I, 1308–1342
Casimir III, 1333–1370	Charles, 1346–1378	
Louis of Hungary, 1370–1382		Louis I, 1342–1382
Ladislas II, 1386–1434	Wenceslas IV, 1378–1419	Sigismund, 1387–1437
Ladislas III, 1434–1444	Sigismund, 1419–1437	
	Albert, 1437–1439	John Hunyadi, 1446–1456
Casimir IV, 1447–1492	Ladislas, 1440–1457	Matthias I, 1458–1490
	George Podiebrad, 1458–1471	Vladislav of Bohemia, 1490–1516
John Albert, 1492–1501	Vladislav III, 1471–1516	Louis of Bohemia, 1516–1526
		Ferdinand of Austria, 1527–1564
Sigismund I, 1506–1548	Louis, 1516–1526	
Sigismund II, 1548–1572	Ferdinand of Austria, 1526–1564	(*Same Rulers as Austria, after 1527*
	(*Same Rulers as Austria, after 1526*	

Kings of Poland, Bohemia, and Hungary

Poland

Boleslav I, 992–1025
Casimir I, 1025–1058
Boleslav II, 1058–1091
Boleslav III, 1102–1139
Ladislas I, 1306–1333
Casimir III, 1333–1370
Louis of Hungary, 1370–1382
Ladislas II, 1386–1434
Ladislas III, 1434–1444
Casimir IV, 1447–1492
John Albert, 1492–1501
Sigismund I, 1506–1548
Sigismund II, 1548–1572
Henry of Valois, 1573–1574
Stephen Bathory, 1575–1586
Sigismund III, 1587–1632
Ladislas IV, 1632–1648
John II Casimir, 1648–1668
John III Sobieski, 1674–1696
Augustus II of Saxony, 1697 1733
Augustus III, 1733–1763
Stanislaus II, Poniatowski, 1763–1795

Bohemia

Bretislav I, 1037–1055
Vratislav II, 1061–1092
Bretislav II, 1092–1110
Vladislav I, 1111–1125
Sobeslav, 1125–1140
Vladislav II, 1140–1173
Ottakar I, 1197–1230
Wenceslas I, 1230–1253
Ottakar II, 1253–1278
Wenceslas II, 1278–1305
Wenceslas III, 1305–1306
John of Luxembourg, 1310–1346
Charles, 1346–1378
Wenceslas IV, 1378–1419
Sigismund, 1419–1437
Albert, 1437–1439
Ladislas, 1440–1457
George Podiebrad, 1458–1471
Vladislav III, 1471–1516
Louis, 1516–1526
Ferdinand of Austria, 1526–1564
(*Same Rulers as Austria, 1526–1918*)

Hungary

Stephen I, 997–1038
Andrew I, 1046–1066
Ladislas I, 1077–1095
Koloman, 1095–1116
Bela III, 1173–1196
Andrew II, 1205–1235
Bela IV, 1235–1270
Ladislas IV, 1272–1290
Andrew III, 1290–1301
Charles I, 1308–1342
Louis I, 1342–1382
Sigismund, 1387–1437
John Hunyadi, 1446–1456
Matthias I, 1458–1490
Vladislav of Bohemia, 1490–1516
Louis of Bohemia, 1516–1526
Ferdinand of Austria, 1527–1564
(*Same Rulers as Austria, 1527–1918*)

INDEX

Index

Aachen, 123, 124
Abbasid dynasty, 104, 107
Abelard, Peter, 233, 241-242
Abu Bakr, Caliph, 104
Abu'l-Abbas, Caliph, 104
Acre, 177
Actium, battle of, 35
Act of Abjuration, 388; of Succession, 362; of Supremacy, 362, 365; of Uniformity, 365
Adalbert of Prague, 147
Adelaide, Empress, 143
Adhemar of Puy, Bishop, 169
Adolf of Holstein, 176
Adrianople, battle of (378), 66
Aeschylus, 22
Aetius, 68
Africa, 71
Agathias, 95
Agincourt, battle of, 281
Agricola, Rudolph, 316
Agriculture, 154-159, 198-199, 266-268, 367
Aids, feudal, 133-134
Aistulf, King, 118
Akkad, 7-8
Alamans, 63-64, 68
Alans, 66, 67
Alaric, 66, 67
Alba, Duke of, 386-387
Albert II, Emperor, 292
Albert, "the Bear," of Brandenburg, 176
Albert, Bishop, 176
Albert of Hohenzollern, 352
Alberti, Leon Battista, 315, 319, 322-323
Albertus Magnus, 242
Albigensians, 206, 234, 235-236. *See* Catharism
Al-Biruni, 108
Albornoz, Cardinal, 309, 327
Albuquerque, 348
Alchemy, 108
Alcuin, 123-124, 125
Aldhelm, 97
Aldine Press, 316
Aleppo, 180
Alexander, "the Great," 24-25, 33
Alexander III, Pope, 176, 216-217, 227, 237
Alexander VI, Pope, 303, 310, 346
Alexander Nevski, 223
Alexandria, 25, 26, 90, 103
Alexius Commenus I, Emperor, 154, 168, 169, 224
Al-Farabi, 108
Alfred, "the Great," of England, 126, 127, 146
Algebra, 107
Alhambra, 108, 109
Ali, Caliph, 104
Al-Khwarizmi, 107
Almeida, 348
Alphabet, Cyrillic, 88, 151
Alphonso V, of Aragon, 302
Alphonso X, of Castile, 211
Alphonso, the Magnanimous, 309, 315
Al-Razi, 108
Alsace, 342, 402
Altenberg, 217
Alvarez de Piñeda, 346
Amalfi, 189
Ambrose, Saint, 44, 59, 60
Amenophis IV, Pharaoh, 10
America, 303, 346, 377, 389-390
Amiens, 226
Ammianus, Marcellinus, 58
Amorites, 7
Amsterdam, 273, 408
Anabaptists, 355, 366
Andrew II, of Hungary, 222
Angelico, Fra, 320, 324
Angevins, 201-202
Angles, 68
Anglican Church. *See* Church, Anglican
Anglo-Saxons. *See* Saxons
Anjou, 285
Ankara, Battle of (1402), 304
Anne Boleyn, 361-362, 363
Anne of Brittany, 286
Anselm, Saint, 145, 240
Anthony, Saint, 93
Antioch, 54, 150, 169, 170, 177, 178, 179, 181
Antoine de Bourbon, 357
Antoninus Pius, Emperor, 38
Antony, Mark, 34
Antwerp, 273-274, 340, 387, 408
Apostolic See. *See* Papacy
Apprentices, Guild, 195-197
Aquinas. *See* Thomas Aquinas, Saint
Aquitaine, 205, 277, 279
Arabia (Arabs), 63 *n.*, 86, 99-104, 305
Arabian Nights, 108
Aragon, 145, 176, 189, 190, 209, 220, 300-302, 385. *See* Spain
Aramaeans (Aramaic), 8-9, 14
Arcadius, Emperor, 66
Archimedes, 26-27, 107
Architecture, ancient, 11, 22-23, 39; medieval, 256-257, 258-259, 322-323; modern, 380
Arianism (Arius), 47-48, 69, 70, 73, 81
Ariosto, 319
Aristarchus, 27
Aristophanes, 22
Aristotle, 20, 22, 24, 27, 46, 97, 107, 108-109, 240, 241-242, 381
Arius. *See* Arianism
Arles, 143
Armada, "Invincible," 365-366, 388-389
"Armagnacs," 280, 282
Armenia (Armenians), 38, 296
Arnold of Brescia, 216
Arras, congress of, 283; league of, 388
Art, ancient, 11-12, 18, 22-23, 39, 60-61; medieval, 125, 150-151, 256-259, 319-323; modern, 380
Artevelde, Jaques van, 278
Arthur, King, 252
Artois, 405
Aryan, 14
Ascalon, 178
Assur, 12. *See* Assyria

Assyria, 8, 12–13, 38
Astrolabe, 190
Astrology, 108
Astronomy, 11, 381–382
Asturias, 103
Aswan, 6
Athanasius, Saint, 47
Athens, 19, 20–21, 24, 48, 82
Attila, 68–69
Aue, Hartmann von, 252
Augsburg, confession of, 354; peace of (1555), 344, 354, 396, 399
Augustine, Saint, of Canterbury, 87, 88, 94
Augustine, Saint, of Hippo, 44, 59–60, 66, 162, 240, 314, 352
Augustinians, 233 *n.*
Augustus Caesar, 35, 38, 39
Ausonius, 58
Austrasia, 117
Austria, 290
Avars, 86, 119
Averroes, 243, 318
Avicenna, 108
Avignon, 325–327
Avitus, Bishop, 92
Azores, 300

Babylon, 7–8, 10, 14
"Babylonian Captivity," Jewish, 12; papal, 325–327
Bacon, Francis, 382
Bacon, Roger, 234, 243, 318
Bagdad, 104, 106, 107
Bajazet, Sultan, 304
Balboa, 346
Baldwin, of Jerusalem, 177
Balearic Islands, 176
Bamberg cathedral, 138
Banalités, 158
Bandinelli, Cardinal, 216
Banking, 270–271
Bannockburn, battle of, 205
"Barbarian," 63 *n.*
Bardi family, 270
Baroque, 408–409
Barricades, day of, 358
Basel, council of, 331; treaty of (1499), 294
Basil, Saint, 93–94
Basil II, Emperor, 150
Bavaria, 143, 396
Baybars, 182, 186
Bayeux tapestry, 140–141
Beaton, Cardinal, 359
Beatrice of Burgundy, 214
Beaumont, 367
Becket, Thomas à, 202–203, 237, 239
Bede, Venerable, 97–98
Bedford, Duke of, Regent, 281
"Beggars," Dutch, 387
Beirut, 177
Belisarius, 71, 81, 95
Bellini, Gentile, 320
Benedict Biscop, 98
Benedict, Saint, of Aniane, 94
Benedict, Saint, of Nursia, 93–95
Benedictines, 94–95, 161, 233
Benevento, 143; treaty of, 216
Beowulf, 126
Berbers, 63 *n.*, 81, 103
Bernard, Saint, of Clairvaux, 233, 242
Bernini, 409
Bessarion, Cardinal, 314, 331 *n.*
Bethlehem, 168, 177
Bibars, 182, 186
Bible, 43, 59. *See* New Testament; Old Testament
Bishops, 92–93, 232
Bisticci, Vespasiano da, 315
"Black Death," 186 *n.*, 265, 266, 271, 279, 286, 287, 318, 327
"Black Prince," 279, 280
Blanche of Castile, 207
Boccaccio, Giovanni, 314, 318–319
Boethius, 69, 96–97, 240
Bohemia, 143, 147, 221–222, 294, 395–397. *See* Czechoslovakia
Boiardo, 319
Bokhara, 78
Boleslav I, "the Brave," of Poland, 147
Boleslav III, of Poland, 222
Bologna, 312; university of, 145, 243, 247–248
Bonaventura, Saint, 234
Boniface VIII, Pope, 205, 237, 325
Boniface, Saint, 87, 89, 117, 209
Book of Kells, 97, 98
Borgia, Caesar, 310
Boris I, of Bulgaria, 127, 151
Bothwell, Earl of, 359
Botticelli, 320, 329
Bourgeoisie (middle class), 194
Bourges, Pragmatic sanction of, 286
Bouvines, battle of, 206, 218
Bracton, Henry de, 205
Braganza family, 384, 401
Brahe, Tycho, 381
Brandenburg, 177, 293, 397, 400, 402
Brant, Sebastian, 319
Brazil, 349
Breitenfeld, battle of, 400
Bremen, 402
Brethren of the Common Life, 316, 333
Brétigny, treaty of, 279
Bridget, Saint, of Sweden, 327
Britain, 35, 38, 68, 81. *See* England
Brittany, 87, 286
Bronze Age, 6
Browne, Robert, 366
Bruce, Robert, 205
Bruegel, Peter, 380
Bruges, 188, 190, 272; Matins of, 270 *n.*
Brunelleschi, 322, 323
Bruno, Archbishop, 144
Bruno, Giordano, 382
Budé, Guillaume, 315, 317
Bulgaria (Bulgars), 126–127, 150, 224, 297
"Bull," 230 *n.*
Burgos, 173
Burgundians, 64, 68
Burgundy, 143, 268, 284–285
Byblos, 9, 11
Byelorussia, 222, 298. *See* White Russians
Byzantine Church. *See* Church, Eastern Orthodox
Byzantine Empire, 77–86, 102–103, 150–151, 153–154, 181–182, 222, 224–225, 297–298, 303–305
Byzantium, 18, 61 *n.* *See* Constantinople

Caboche, Simon, 280
Cabot, John, 367
Cabral, 346
Caesar, Augustus. *See* Augustus Caesar
Caesar, Julius. *See* Julius Caesar
Caesarius, Bishop, 92
Cairo, 103, 105
Cajetan, Saint, 374
Calais, 279, 357, 364
Calderon, 393
Calendar, Gregorian, 381–382; Julian, 381
Calicut, 300
Caligula, Emperor, 38
Caliphate, 103–106
Calvin, John, 355–357, 359, 380
Calvinism (Calvinists), 356–359, 363, 366, 378, 380, 402
Cambrai, peace of, 342
Cambridge, university of, 248
Cambyses, of Persia, 14
Campion, Edmund, 372
Canary Islands, 274
Canossa, 165
Canterbury, 97
Cape Breton Island, 367
Cape of Good Hope, 300
Capet, Hugh, 123, 139, 141
Capetian family, 123
Capitalism, 270, 407–408

Capitularies, 120
Capuchins, 374
Caracalla, Emperor, 39, 54–55
Caraffa, Giovanni, 374. *See* Paul IV, Pope
Caravaggio, 409
Cardan, 382
Cardinals, College of, 227–230
Carinthia, 290
Carmelites, 233 *n.*, 375
Carniola, 290
Carolingian Empire, 120–123
Carolingian family, 117–123, 143
Carracci, 409
Carthage, 9, 19, 30, 32–33, 67
Casa de Contratacion, 390
Casimir "the Great," 296
Cassian, Saint John, 94
Cassel, battle of, 277
Cassiodorus, 69, 97
Castelnau, Peter de, 235
Castile, 145, 176, 209–211, 300–302. *See* Spain
Catalans (Catalonia), 300
Cateau-Cambrésis, treaty of, 342, 389
Catharism, 235–236
Catherine of Aragon, 288, 361–362, 363
Catherine de' Medici, 357, 358
Catherine, Saint, of Siena, 327
Catholicism. *See* Church, Catholic
Cauchon, Bishop, 282
Cavendish, 366
Caxton, 316
Celtes, Conrad, 316
Cervantes, 393
Ceuta, 299
Ceylon, 78
Chaeronea, 24
Chalcedon, 18; council of, 48, 82, 88
Chaldeans, 12
Châlons, battle of, 68
Champagne, 192
Chansons de Geste, 164
Charlemagne, 114, 117, 118–126, 164
Charles I, Emperor. *See* Charlemagne
Charles II, "the Bald," Emperor, 122, 123
Charles III, "the Fat," Emperor, 123, 129
Charles IV, Emperor, 291, 294, 314
Charles V, Emperor, 288, 339–349, 354, 362, 364, 371, 373, 390
Charles of Anjou and Naples, 211, 220
Charles, "the Bold," of Burgundy, 284–285
Charles I, of France. *See* Charlemagne
Charles III, "the Simple," of France, 129
Charles V, of France, 279–280, 317
Charles VI, of France, 280, 281
Charles VII, of France, 282–283, 286
Charles VIII, of France, 285–286, 310, 317 *n.*
Charles IX, of France, 357, 358
Charles, "the Bad," of Navarre, 279
Charles I, of Spain, 339. *See* Charles V, Emperor
Charles Borromeo, Saint, 375
Charles, of Lorraine, Cardinal, 357
Charles Martel, 103, 117
Charles, the Dauphin. *See* Charles V, of France
Chaucer, 319
Chauliac, Guy de, 318
China, 7 *n.*, 79, 186, 326, 376–377
Chivalry, 133–135, 268
Chosroes, of Persia, 86, 102
Christendom. *See* Christianity; Church
Christian I, of Denmark, 294
Christian IV, of Denmark, 397–399
Christianity, 40–48, 59–60, 106. *See* Church
Chrysoloras, Manuel, 314
Church, Anglican, 361–367; Byzantine, 167; Catholic, in ancient Roman Empire, 44; in middle ages, 70, 73, 80, 82, 87–98, 135–137, 161–170, 174, 192–193, 227, 230–238, 325–333, 351–352, 368–380; Eastern Orthodox, 174, 298, 331. *See* Calvinists; Huguenots; Lutherans; Methodists; Presbyterians; Protestants; Reformed; etc.
Cicero, 39, 46
Cid, El, 145, 252
Ciompi, revolt of the, 307
Cistercians, 176, 198–199, 233
Cities, 192–198
Civitas, Roman, 38–39, 92
Clarendon, Assize of, 202; Constitution of, 202
Clement, Saint, Pope, 44
Clement III, anti-pope, 165
Clement V, Pope, 325–326
Clement VII, Pope, 362
Clement, VII, anti-pope, 327
Cleopatra, 34
Clergy, Regular, 233–234; Secular, 231–233
Clericis laicos, 205, 209
Clermont, council of, 168
Clermont-Ferrand, 160
Clovet, Jean, 341
Clovis, King, 69–70, 117
Cluny, abbey of, 161–162, 168, 233
Cnossus, 12
Coeur, Jacques, 270–271, 283
Coimbra, 248
Coinage, 192
Colet, John, 317, 361, 380
Coligny, Gaspard de, 357, 358
College, 247
Collège de France, 315, 317
Coloni, 55, 58, 64, 73, 92
Colonies, Greek, 18–19; Phoenician, 9, 19, 30; Portuguese, 299–300, 346, 348–349; Spanish, 300–303, 346–348, 349
Colosseum, 39
Colossus of Rhodes, 26
Columba, Saint, 87
Columbanus, Saint, 87, 93, 94
Columbus, Christopher, 302–303, 346
Commerce, medieval, 153–154, 189–192, 271–274; modern, 407–408
Commines, Philippe de, 319
Common Law. *See* Law, English Common
Commons, House of, 287
Conciliar movement, 329–331
Concordat (1516), 331
Condé, 402
Condottieri, 306, 326
Confederation, Swiss, 293. *See* Switzerland
Congregationalists, 366. *See* Independents
Conrad II, Emperor, 143, 144
Conrad IV, Emperor, 220
Conrad, of Arles, 143
Conradin, 220
Consistory, 230
Constance, council of, 329–330; treaty of, 216, 217, 219
Constance, of Sicily, 211, 217
Constantine I, Emperor, 45–46, 47, 56, 57, 60, 61, 66, 91, 118
Constantine Porphyrogenotus, 151
Constantinople, 61, 77, 79, 86, 103, 169, 181–182, 298, 304–305; council of, 90; patriarch of, 90, 91, 305; university of, 150
Copenhagen, university of, 294
Copernicus, 381
Copyholder, 266
Cordova, 107
Corinth, 18, 20, 33, 44
Corinthian style, 23, 26

Corpus Juris Civilis, 80
Corsica, 103, 126, 154
Cortenuova, battle of, 219
Cortes, Spanish, 211
Cortez, Hernando, 347
Cosmas Indicopleustes, 95
"Council of Blood," 387
Cracow, university of, 296
Cranach, Lucas, 350, 356, 380
Cranmer, Thomas, 363, 364
Crécy, battle of, 278–279
Credit, 192–193
Crete, 9, 12, 17
Croatia (Croats), 150, 222
Cromwell, Thomas, 362, 363
Croton, 18
Crusades, First, 167–170; Second, 176; Later, 179–183, 303–304; Albigensian, 206
Cuba, 302
Cumae, 18
Curia, papal, 227, 230, 326
Curiales, 57, 58
Curia Regis, 132, 201, 207, 208
Cyprus, 181, 345
Cyrene (Cyrenaica), 18
Cyril, Saint, 87–88, 151
Cyrus, of Persia, 14, 15
Czechoslovakia (Czechs), 143. *See* Bohemia; Moravia

Dacia, 38, 54
Dalmatia, 150
Damascus, 104
Danelaw, 127
Danes, 127. *See* Denmark
Dante, 253–254, 314, 326
Danzig, 296
Darius I, of Persia, 19
Darius III, of Persia, 24
Darnley, Lord, 359
Dauphiné, 279 *n.*, 292
David, of Judah, 9
David I, of Scotland, 175
Delian League, 24
Della Robbia, Andrea, 322
Della Robbia, Luca, 322
Demarcation, Papal Line of, 303, 346
Denmark, 146–147, 221, 294, 354, 397, 399
Desalquier, Anselm, 274–275
Desiderius, King, 118
Deventer, 316
Devotia moderna, 333, 352
Diaz, Bartolomeo, 300
Diaz, Rodrigo, 145, 252
Diet, of Holy Roman Empire, 291
Diocletian, Emperor, 53, 55, 56–57, 60–61, 66, 78
Diplomatic relations, 404
Domesday Book, 201
Dominic, Saint, 234
Dominicans, 183, 233–236, 375
Donatello, 321, 322
Donation of Constantine, 118 *n.*, 315
Donatus, 58–59
Doria, Andrea, 345
Doric style, 23
Drake, Sir Francis, 366
Du Bellay, 380
Dunstable, 323
Dürer, Albrecht, 295, 321
Dutch. *See* Netherlands, Dutch
Dyarchy, Roman, 35, 56

"Early Middle Age," 114–171
"Early Modern Times," 338
East India Company, Dutch, 393; English, 393
East Prussia, 296
"Ecclesiastical Reservation," 396–397
Eckhart, Master, 333
Edessa, 170, 177, 180
Education, medieval, 123–124
Edward I, of England, 175, 203, 204–205
Edward II, of England, 205
Edward III, of England, 277, 278, 279, 280, 286–287, 328
Edward IV, of England, 288
Edward VI, of England, 359, 363, 366
Egmont, Count, 387
Egypt, 6–7, 9–10, 11, 14, 24–25, 34–35, 102, 103, 181
Einhard, 118, 124
Elamites, 8
Eleanor, of Aquitaine, 202, 205, 253
Electors of Holy Roman Empire, 291
El Greco, 380, 391, 393
Elizabeth I, of England, 359, 360, 363, 364–367, 393
Empire, Byzantine. *See* Byzantine Empire
Empire, Carolingian, 120–123
Empire, Holy Roman, 141–144, 289–294, 395–404
Empire, Roman. *See* Roman Empire
Empire, Russian. *See* Russia
England, early medieval, 87, 97, 127, 146; later medieval, 201–206, 277–284, 286–288; in early modern times, 361–367
Ephesus, 20, 26; council of, 48, 238
Epicurus, 27
Erasmus, Desiderius, 316–317, 323, 333, 352, 354, 361, 380
Eratosthenes, 27
Eric V, of Denmark, 221
Eric IX, of Sweden, 221
Ericson, Leif, 128
Eschenbach, Wolfram von, 252
Escorial, 384, 386–387
Estates General, French, 208, 279, 286
Estonia, 176, 399
Ethiopia, 78–79, 300. *See* Abyssinia
Etruscans, 29–30
Euclid, 26, 107
Eugenius III, Pope, 233
Eugenius IV, Pope, 331
Euripides, 22
"Evangelical," 355
Exarchs, Byzantine, 78

Fairs, medieval, 191–192
Far East, 78
Farnese, Alexander, 388
Fatimites, 105
Faubourg, 193. *See* Towns, medieval
Feltre, Vittorino da, 315
Ferdinand I, Emperor, 383
Ferdinand II, Emperor, 399, 400
Ferdinand III, Emperor, 402
Ferdinand, of Aragon, 300, 309, 339
Ferdinand of Habsburg, 344
Ferdinand of Styria, 395. *See* Ferdinand II, Emperor
Ferrara, council of, 331
"Fertile crescent," 5
Feudalism, 131–137
Fiefs, 132
Finland, 221, 295, 399
Fisher, Saint John, 362
Flanders (Flemish), 154, 199, 277–278. *See* Netherlands
Fletcher, 367
Florence, 198, 307–308; council of, 298, 314
Florida, 346, 474
Foederati, 65, 67, 68, 69
Fondachi, 271
Fortunatus, 97
Fouquet, Jean, 268 *n.*, 285, 321
France, ancient (*see* Gaul, Franks); medieval, 139–141, 201–202, 205–209, 245–246, 251–252, 277–286; in 16th century, 341–343, 357–358, 373–374; in 17th century, 401–405
Franche Comté, 280, 285, 290 *n.*

Francis I, of France, 317, 331, 339, 341–342, 355, 357
Francis II, of France, 357, 359
Francis, duke of Guise, 357
Francis of Assisi, Saint, 234, 328, 375
Francis de Sales, Saint, 375
Francis Xavier, Saint, 372, 376
Franciscans, 183, 233–234, 375; Spiritual, 328
Franconia, 143
Franconian dynasty, 144
Franks, 63, 68, 69–70
Frankish State, 117–129. *See* France
Frederick I, Barbarossa, Emperor, 181, 213–217
Frederick II, Emperor, 177, 206, 211, 218–220, 253, 289
Frederick III, Emperor, 292
Frederick I, of Denmark, 354
Frederick of Hohenzollern, 293
Frederick of the Palatinate, 395–396, 402, 403
Frederick, "the Wise," of Saxony, 350, 353
Froissart, Jean, 319
Fueros, 301
Fugger family, 270, 274, 339, 340, 352
Fulbert of Chartres, 145
Fulda, 116
Funcken, Johannes, 274

Gaiseric, 67
Galen, 107, 108, 243, 317
Galileo, 318, 381
Gallicanism, 331 *n.*
Gama, Vasco da, 348
Gaul, 34, 70, 81, 103. *See* France
Geneva, under Calvin, 356–357
Genoa, 154, 169, 189, 198, 274, 308
Gentile, Fabriano da, 320
Geoffrey of Monmouth, 252
Geoffrey Plantagenet, 201–202
Gerard, John, 409
Gerbert, 144. *See* Sylvester II, Pope
Germanic languages, 122
Germanus, Bishop, 92
Germany (Germans), ancient, 63–75; medieval, *see* Holy Roman Empire
Gerson, Jean, 329 *n.*
Ghent, pacification of, 387–388
Ghibelline, 216
Ghiberti, 311, 322
Ghirlandaio, 320
Gilbert, Sir Humphrey, 366
Gilbert, William, 382
Giotto, 253, 320, 322
Glanville, Ranulf de, 205
Glebe, 158
Godfrey of Bouillon, 177
Golden Bull (1212), 221; (1222), 222; (1356), 274, 291, 404
Golden Fleece, Order of, 268
Goliardic verse, 249
Goths, 64. *See* Ostrogoths; Visigoths
Gozzoli, Benozzo, 320
Graeco-Persian Wars, 19, 24
Granada, 108, 109, 176, 300
Gratian, 243
Greece (Greeks), ancient, 16–27, 29, 30, 33 *n.*, 39; medieval, *see* Byzantine Empire
Greek fire, 78
Greenland, 128, 147, 221, 273 *n.*
Gregorian Chant, 92, 254
Gregory I, "the Great," Pope, 87, 91–92, 96, 126
Gregory VII, Pope, 115, 162, 237
Gregory IX, Pope, 219, 227, 236 *n.*, 246
Gregory XI, Pope, 327
Gregory XII, Pope, 330
Gregory XIII, Pope, 369, 377, 381–382
Gregory XV, Pope, 377
Gregory of Tours, 92, 97
Grenville, Sir Richard, 366
Grey, Lady Jane, 364
Groote, Gerard, 333
Grosseteste, Robert, 243, 318
Grotius, Hugo, 404
Guarino, Verona da, 315
Guebara, Cardinal de, 391
Guelf, 213, 216, 218
Guesclin, Bertrand du, 279–280
Gui, Bernard, 236 *n.*
Guicciardini, 319
Guido of Arezzo, 145, 256
Guilds, craft, 195, 269; journeyman, 195, 269–270; merchant, 195
Guinea, 275
Guiscard, Robert, 165
Guise family, 357
Gundebaud, 73
Guntrum the Dane, 127
Gustavus I, Vasa, of Sweden, 354, 399
Gustavus II, Adolphus, of Sweden, 399–400
Gutenberg, Johann, 316, 319

Habsburg family, 290, 292, 293, 297, 373, 383
Hadrian, Emperor, 38
Hadrian IV, Pope, 125, 216
Hals, Frans, 409
Hamitic languages, 5
Hammurabi, 8, 10
Hannibal, 33
Hanseatic League, 272–273, 294, 295–296
Harold, "Bluetooth," of Denmark, 146
Harold, of England, 146
Harold, "Fairhair," of Norway, 147
Harold Hardrada, 146
Harun al-Raschid, Caliph, 107
Harvey, William, 382
Hastings, battle of, 146
Hatshepsut, of Egypt, 4
Hattin, battle of, 181
Havana, 390
Hawkins, John, 366
Hebrews, 9. *See* Jews; Judaism
Hegius, Alexander, 316
Hejira, 101
Hellas (Hellenes), 18
"Hellenistic," 25–27
Heloise, 242 *n.*
Henry I, "the Fowler," 123, 143
Henry II, Emperor, 138, 164 *n.*
Henry III, Emperor, 144, 164
Henry IV, Emperor, 144, 165–166, 169
Henry V, Emperor, 166, 222
Henry VI, Emperor, 211, 217
Henry VII, Emperor, 290
Henry I, of England, 201
Henry II, of England, 175, 201–203, 205, 237, 277
Henry III, of England, 204, 237, 277
Henry IV, of England, 280, 287
Henry V, of England, 280–281, 288
Henry VI, of England, 281, 288
Henry VII, of England, 271, 288, 339, 361, 366, 367
Henry VIII, of England, 288, 361–363, 364
Henry II, of France, 357
Henry III, of France, 357, 358
Henry IV, of France, 358, 389, 393
Henry, duke of Guise, 357, 358
Henry, of Navarre, 357, 358. *See* Henry IV, of France
Henry, "the Lion," of Saxony, 176, 213–214, 216
Henry, "the Navigator," Prince, 299–300, 318
Heraclius, Emperor, 86, 102
Heresy, 47–48, 234–238
Heriot, 158
Herjolfson, Bjarni, 128
Herman of Metz, Bishop, 165
Herman of Salza, 177

Herodotus, 22
Hildebrand, 115, 162. *See* Gregory VII, Pope
Hipparchus, 27
Hippocrates, 22, 107, 243, 317
Hippodrome, 79, 80
Hittites, 7, 8
Hochstetter family, 339
Hohenstaufen family, 213, 218, 220–221
Hohenzollern family, 293
Holbein, Hans, 321, 352, 362, 363, 364, 380
Holland, 388, 402. *See* Netherlands, Dutch
Holstein, 177
Holy Land, 183, 219. *See* Palestine
Holy Roman Empire, 141–144, 289–294, 395–404
Holy See. *See* Papacy
"Holy War," 164, 167
Homer, 17–18, 22
Honorius, Emperor, 66
Honorius III, Pope, 218–219, 234
Horace, 39, 48
Horn, Count, 387
Hosius, 88
Hroswita, 144
Hugh, of Lusignan, 206
Hugenots, 357
Humanism, Renaissance, 313–317
Humbert, Cardinal, 167
Hundred Years' War, 266, 268, 277–284, 326
Hungary (Hungarians), 127, 147, 150, 222, 296–297, 344
Huns, 65, 68–69, 126, 127
Hus, John, 291, 328–329, 330, 373
Hutten, Ulrich von, 343

Iceland, 128, 147, 221, 294
Iconoclasm, 90–91, 117, 120 *n.*, 150
Ictinus, 22
Idrisi, 108
Ignatius Loyola, Saint, 370–372, 376
Ikhnaton, Pharaoh, 10, 11
Île de France, 139, 141, 207
"Independents," 366. *See* Congregationalists
Index, Congregation of, 370
India, 7 *n.*, 103, 107, 300, 376, 393
Indies, Council of, 389
Indo-European, 5. *See* Aryan
Indonesia, 106
Indulgence, 169, 351–352, 370
Industry, medieval, 153–154, 192–193, 268–271
Innocent III, Pope, 176, 181, 204, 206, 217–218, 227, 230, 234, 235, 237, 246
Innocent IV, Pope, 220, 227, 236
Inquisition, papal, 236, 282–283, 370; Spanish, 301, 331, 372, 373
Investiture controversy, 164–166
Ionic style, 23
Iran, 14. *See* Persia
Ireland, 87, 94, 97, 127–128, 175, 366
Irnerius, 243
Iron Age, 6
Isabella, of Castile, 288, 300–302
Isidore of Kiev, 289, 331 *n.*
Isidore of Seville, 97
Islam, 99–109, 305. *See* Moslems
Istanbul. *See* Constantinople
Italy, ancient, 32; in middle ages, 81, 82, 118 *n.*, 145–146, 189–190, 214–220, 305–311
Ivan III, of Russia, 298

Jadwiga, of Poland, 296
Jaffa, 177
Jagiello, of Lithuania, 296
James I, of England, 393
James IV, of Scotland, 288
James V, of Scotland, 359
James VI, of Scotland, 359. *See* James I, of England
Janissaries, 305
Japan, 186, 376
Jaqueries, 279
Jenghis Khan, 186
Jerome, Saint, 44, 59, 66
Jerome of Prague, 330
Jerusalem, 12, 15, 48, 168, 170, 177, 178, 179, 180, 181, 182
Jesuits, 371–373, 409
Jesus Christ, 40–43, 47
Jews, 15, 192–193, 210, 296, 301, 384
Joan of Arc, 282–283
John II, Commenus, Emperor, 224
John XII, Pope, 143–144
John XXII, Pope, 290, 326, 328
John XXIII, Pisan Pope, 330
John, "the Fearless," of Burgundy, 280, 281, 284
John, of England, 203, 204, 206, 218
John II, "the Good," of France, 279
John I, of Portugal, 299
John IV, of Portugal, 401
John Asen II, of Bulgaria, 224
John, Don, of Austria, 345
John Frederick, of Saxony, 350
John George, of Saxony, 396
John Hunyadi, 297
John of Ephesus, 95
John of Gaunt, 328
John of Leiden, 355
John of Montecorvino, 183, 326
John of Plano, Carpini, 186
John of Salisbury, 239
John, Saint, 43
John Scotus Erigena, 124
Jonson, Ben, 367
Judea, 41
Judaism, 41–43
Julian, Emperor, 46
Julius Caesar, 34, 48, 63
Julius II, Pope, 361
Jury trial, 202
Justinian, Emperor, 71, 78, 79–82, 90, 95
Jutes, 68

Ka'aba, 100, 101
Kadesiya, battle of, 103
Kadijah, 100
Kairwan, 103
Kalmar, Union of, 294
Karnak, 11
Kempis, Thomas a, 333
Kepler, 381
Khair-ed-Din (Barbarossa), 344
Kiev, 128, 147, 150, 222
Knighthood, 163–164
Knights Hospitallers of St. John, 179, 325 *n.*
Knights of the Sword, 176
Knights Templar, 179, 325
Knox, John, 359
Knut, of Denmark, 146
Koran, 100, 105
Kublai Khan, 186
Kurland, 176

Laborers, statute of, 287–288
Ladislas I, of Hungary and Poland, 297
Ladislas II, of Bohemia and Hungary, 297
Ladislas III, of Poland and Hungary, 304; of Naples, 309
Lancastrian family, 288
Lanfranc, 145
Langland, William, 288, 319
Langton, Stephen, 204
Languages, 2, 5–6, 30, 39, 75, 78, 98, 105, 122, 240, 251
Langue d'oc, 176, 252, 253

Langue d'oil, 164, 252
Las Casas, Bartolomé de, 348, 375–376
Las Navas de Tolosa, battle of, 176
"Late Middle Age," 264
Lateran Council, Third, 230; Fourth, 230, 234, 238
Latin, 30, 39, 240
Laurentian Library, 315
Law, Canon, 243; English common, 202; Germanic, 72–73; maritime, 274 *n.*; Roman, 38, 39, 80, 243
Lay investiture. *See* Investiture controversy
League, Catholic, 358
League of the Common Weal, 285
Lech, battle of the, 400
Lechfeld, battle of, 143
Legnano, battle of, 217
Leif Ericson, 128
Leo III, Emperor, 90, 103, 117, 150
Leo I, "the Great," Pope, 48, 69, 88, 91
Leo III, Pope, 121
Leo IV, Pope, 126
Leo IX, Pope, 144, 146, 162
Leo X, Pope, 308, 315, 323, 331, 352, 353, 361, 380
Leon, 145, 176
Leonidas, 19
Lepanto, battle of, 345–346, 389
Lerma, Duke of, 393
Liberal Arts, 59, 239
Liege-lord, 133
Line of Demarcation, 303, 346
Lippi, Fra Filippo, 320
Lisbon, 176
Literature, ancient, 22, 30, 39, 58–60; medieval, 251–254, 319, 367; early modern, 380–381
Lithuania, 177, 296
Little Russians. *See* Ukraine
Livonia, 177, 399
Livy, 39
Logic, 240
Lollards, 287
Lombard League, 216–217, 219
Lombard, Peter, 241
Lombards, 64, 71, 81, 82, 117. 118
Lope de Vega, 393
Lords, House of, 286–287
Lorenzo, "the Magnificent." *See* Medici
Lorraine, 123, 143 *n.*
Lorris, Guillaume de, 252
Lothair, Emperor, 122, 123
Lothair II, 123
Lotharingia, 123
Louis, the Pious, Emperor, 122
Louis II, "the German," Emperor, 122, 123
Louis, of Bavaria, Emperor, 290, 328
Louis II, of Bohemia and Hungary, 344
Louis VI, of France, 205, 207
Louis VII, of France, 205, 207, 208
Louis IX, of France, 181, 207, 237, 277
Louis XI, of France, 268, 271, 284–286, 321
Louis XII, of France, 310, 341
Louis XIII, of France, 393, 400
Louis XIV, of France, 405
Louis, Duke of Orléans, 280
Low Countries. *See* Flanders; Holland; Netherlands
Loyola, Ignatius. *See* Ignatius Loyola
Lübeck, treaty of, 399
Luke, Saint, 41–43
Lull, Raymond, 183 *n.*
Lupus, Abbot, 124
Luther, Martin, 316 *n.*, 333 *n.*, 350–355, 372
Lutherans, 352–354, 363
Lutter, battle of, 399
Luxor, 11
Lydia, 14
Lyons, 292

Macedonia, 24–25
Machiavelli, 310, 319
Madeira, 300
Maderna, 409
Magdeburg, 400
Magellan, Ferdinand, 346
Magna Carta, 203, 204
Magna Graecia, 18
Magyars, 126–127, 143. *See* Hungary
Malocello, 274
Malory, Thomas, 319
Malta, 302
Mamun, "the Great," Caliph, 107
Manfred, 220
Manichaeism, 43, 59, 235
Manor, medieval, 156 *n.* *See* Seigneurial regime
Manuel I, Comnenus, Byzantine Emperor, 224
Manzikert, battle of, 167
Maranos, 301, 384
Marathon, 19
Marcel, Étienne, 279
Marches, 119
Marchfeld, battle of, 290
Marcus Aurelius, Emperor, 38, 45, 53
Margaret, of Denmark and Norway, 294
Margaret, of Parma, 386
Maria Theresa, of Spain and France, 405
Marie de' Medici, 393
Marignano, battle of, 331 *n.*, 342
Marius, 34
Mark, Saint, 43
Markets, 190–191
Marlowe, Christopher, 367
Marionites, 178
Marseilles, 18, 154
Marsiglio of Padua, 328
Martianus Capella, 59
Martin V, Pope, 330
Martin, Saint, of Tours, 94
Martini, Simone, 320
Mary, Blessed Virgin, 41, 42, 48, 238
Mary, of Burgundy, 285, 290 *n.*
Mary (Tudor), of England, 363–365
Mary, of Guise, 359
Mary (Stuart), of Scotland, 359, 365
Massaccio, 320
Mathematics, 243, 245, 282
Matilda, of England, 201
Matilda, Countess, 165
Matthew, Saint, 43, 44
Matthias, Emperor, 395
Matthias Corvinus, of Hungary, 297
Maximilian I, Emperor, 285, 290 *n.*, 292
Maximilian, of Bavaria, 395, 402
"Mayor of the Palace," 117
Mazarin, Cardinal, 405
Mecca, 100, 101, 105
Mecklenburg, 177
Medes, 12–14
Medici family, 307–308, 339; Catharine de', 357, 358; Cosimo de', 270, 307, 314, 315; Lorenzo de', "the Magnificent," 270, 307–308, 314, 315, 319; Marie de', 393
Medicine, 243, 282
Medina, 101
Medina Sidonia, Duke of, 388–389
Megara, 18
Meissen, 293
Melancthon, Philip, 350, 354, 380
Melfi, constitution of, 211
Memling, Hans, 321
Menno Simons (Mennonites), 355

Mercantilism, 408
Mercator, Gerard, 409
Merchant Adventurers, 271
Merovingian dynasty, 69–70, 117
Mersen, treaty of, 123
Mesopotamia, 6, 7, 38, 103. *See* Assyria; Babylonia; Persia
Methodius, Saint, 87–88, 151
Metz, 342, 402
Meung, Jean de, 319
Meuting family, 339
Mexico, 347, 389
Michael Cerularius, Patriarch, 167
Michael, Paleologus, Emperor, 224
Michelangelo, 322, 379, 380
Michelozzo, 323
"Middle Ages," 114
Middle Class. *See* Bourgeoisie
Miesko I, of Poland, 147
Milan, 198, 307; Edict of (313), 45–46. *See* Lombardy
Miletus, 18, 20
Miltiades, 19
Ming, dynasty, 186 *n.*
Mining, medieval, 192, 274
Minnesingers, 253
Mirandola, Pico della, 314, 317
Missi dominici, 119
Missionaries, Christian, 375–377
Mithradates, of Pontus, 34
Mithras (Mithraism), 15, 47
Model Parliament, 203, 205
Mogul Empire, 186
Mohacs, battle of, 344
Mohammed, 99, 100–101, 104
Mohammed II, Sultan, 304
Mohammedanism. *See* Islam; Moslems
Monasticism, 79, 93–95
Mongol Empire (Mongols), 183–186, 222, 223
Monica, Saint, 59
Monophysites, 48, 82, 90, 95
Montaigne, 381, 408–409
Montecassino, 94
Monte-Gargano, 145
Montfort, Simon de, 204
Montpellier, university of, 248
Moors, 63 *n.*, 81, 103, 384
Moravia, 143, 147. *See* Czechoslovakia
More, Saint Thomas, 317, 361, 362, 363, 380
Moriscos, 301, 384, 385, 393
Moscow, Grand-duchy of, 298; patriarch of, 298
Moslems, 100–109, 126, 167–170, 176, 181–183, 243, 245, 301
Mozarabas, 209–210
Mudejares, 210
Müller, Johannes, 318
Mundius, 318
Münster, 355; treaty of, 402
Münzer, Thomas, 354–355
Murad I, Sultan, 303
Murad II, Sultan, 304
Murillo, 393
Music, Gregorian, 92, 254; medieval, 254, 256, 323; modern, 381
Mycenae, 9, 17
Mysticism, 333

Nantes, edict of, 358
Napier, John, 382
Naples, 145–146, 211, 309. *See* Two Sicilies
Narses, 71, 81
Naucratis, 18
Navarre, 123 *n.*, 145, 209, 342
Navigation, medieval, 274–275
Nazareth, 168, 177
"Near East," 1, 4–15
Nebuchadnezzar, of Babylon, 12
Neolithic Age, 6
Neo-Platonism, 47, 60
Nero, Emperor, 38, 45
Nestorians (Nestorius), 48, 186 *n.*
Netherlands, 280, 284, 290 *n.*, 373, 392; Belgian, 405; Dutch, 385–389, 393. *See* Burgundy; Flanders; Holland
Neustria, 117
Newfoundland. 128
New Testament, 43
Nicaea, council of, 47, 88; second council, 120, 121 *n.*, 150
Niccoli, Niccolò, 315
Nicene Creed, alteration of the, 121 *n.*
Nicholas II, Pope, 146
Nicholas V, Pope, 315
Nicholas of Cusa, 316
Nicomedia, 61
Nicopolis, battle of, 304
Niebelungenlied, 252
Nika riots, 79, 80
Nile river, 6
Nineveh, 12
Nobility, 266, 268
Nogaret, 209
Nombre de Dios, 390
Normandy, 129, 175, 201–202, 281
Normans, 145–147
Norsemen, 126, 127–129, 175
Norway, 127, 128, 147, 221, 294, 354
Novgorod, 128, 224

Oblates, 375
Ockham, 352
Octavian. *See* Augustus Caesar
Odo, Count, 123, 129
Odovakar, 69
Olaf, Saint, of Norway, 147
Old Testament, 42, 43
Oleg, 128
Omar, Caliph, 104
Omar Khayyam, 108
Oratorians, 375
Orléans, 282
Ormuz, 393
Orthodox Church, 174, 298, 331
Osman, Sultan, 303
Osnabrück, treaty of, 402
Ostrogoths, 64, 65, 69, 71, 81
Otto I, Emperor, 127, 141 *n.*, 143
Otto II, Emperor, 144
Otto III, Emperor, 144
Otto IV, Emperor, 206
Otto, of Brunswick, 218
Ottokar I, of Bohemia, 221
Ottokar II, of Bohemia, 222, 290
Oxford, university of, 248

Padua, 248
Paganism, Graeco-Roman, 46, 58, 82
Painting, 319–321
Palatinate, 402
Paleolithic Age, 6
Palestine, 8, 41, 86, 102, 179
Palestrina, 381
Palladio, 380
Palmyra, 99
Papacy, 88–92
Papal State, 309–310
Paracelsus, 382
Paris, 198, 244; university of, 145, 245–247
Parlements, French, 208
Parliaments, English, 286–287, 366
Parsons, Robert, 372
Parthenon, 1
Patrick, Saint, 87, 94
Patrimony of St. Peter, 91, 118. *See* Papal State
Paul, Saint, 43, 44, 47
Paul III, Pope, 369, 371
Paul IV, Pope, 369, 374
Paul the Deacon, 124, 125
Pausanius, 19
Pavia, 71; battle of, 342; council of, 330–331
Peace of God, 134, 137, 153, 163
Peasants, medieval, 157–159, 199, 266
Peloponnesian war, 23, 24

Pepin I, King, 118. *See* Pepin III, Mayor of Palace
Pepin II, Mayor of Palace, 117
Pepin III, "the Short," Mayor of Palace, 118. *See* Pepin I, King
Pericles, 21, 22
Perpetual Pact, Swiss, 293
Persia, 12–15, 19, 24, 54, 79, 86, 102, 103, 104. *See* Iran
Peru, 389
Perugino, 320
Peruzzi family, 270
Peter, Saint, 44; basilica of, 352, 376, 409
Peter III, of Aragon, 176
Peter Lombard, 241
Peter "the Hermit," 169
Peterborough cathedral, 112–113
Petrarch, 294, 314, 318, 326
Pharisees, 43
Phidias, 23
Philip, "the Bold," of Burgundy, 280
Philip, "the Good," of Burgundy, 284
Philip I, of France, 166
Philip II, Augustus, of France, 181, 198, 206–207, 218, 246
Philip IV, "the Fair," of France, 205, 207–209, 237, 278, 325
Philip VI, of France, 277, 278
Philip II, of Macedonia, 24
Philip I, of Spain (Habsburg), 339
Philip II, of Spain, 340, 364, 365, 373, 383–390, 393
Philip III, of Spain, 388, 390, 393, 395, 397
Philip IV, of Spain, 390, 393, 394, 397, 400, 401–402, 405–406
Philip, of Swabia, 218
Philip Neri, Saint, 375
Philip of Valois. *See* Philip VI of France
Philippines, 106, 346, 377, 383, 390
Philistines, 9
Philosophy, 21–22, 240
Phoenicia (Phoenicians), 9. *See* Carthage; Sidon, Tyre
Physics, 282
Piast dynasty, 147
Picardy, 285
Piccolomini, Aeneas Silvius, 315. *See* Pius II, Pope
Picts, 67, 68
Piedmont. *See* Sardinia
Pierluigi, Giovanni, 381
Pie-powder, 191
"Pilgrimage of Grace," 362
Pilgrimages, 167–168
Pindar, 22
Pinzon brothers, 302
Pirates, 190, 191
Pisa, 154, 169, 189, 194; council of, 329
Pisan, Christine de, 319
Pisano, Niccolo, 321–322
Pius II, Pope, 315
Pius IV, Pope, 369, 370
Pius V, Pope, 345, 365 *n.*, 369
Pizarro, Francisco, 347
Plantagenet. *See* Angevin
Platea, battle of, 19
Plato, 20, 22, 46, 240, 314
Plautus, 39
Plethon, 314
Pliny, the Younger, 38, 45
Plotinus, 47, 97
Podestà, 216
Poitiers, battle of, 279
Poland, 147, 177, 221–222, 296–297, 373, 399–400
Pole, Reginald, Cardinal, 364
Politiques, French, 358
Poliziano, Angelo, 314, 319
Pollentia, battle of, 66
Polo, Marco, 186, 302; Maffeo, 186; Nicolo, 186
Polygnotus, 23
Pomerania, 177, 222, 402
Pomerelia, 296. *See* West Prussia
Pompey, Gnaeus, 34
Ponce de Leon, 346
Portugal, 145, 176, 209, 299–300, 346, 348–349, 384–385, 393, 401–402
Praemunire, statute of, 287, 326 *n.*
Pragmatic Sanction of Bourges, 331 *n.*
Prague, treaty of, 400–401; university of, 294
Praxiteles, 23
Premonstratensians, 162 *n.*, 176
Presbyterians, 358–359
Prester, John, 186 *n.*, 300
Price Revolution, 406–407
Principate, Roman, 35, 55
Printing, 316
Procop, 330
Procopius, 95
Propaganda, Congregation of the, 377
Protestants, 354
Provence, 292
Provisors, statute of, 287, 326 *n.*
Prudentius, 60
Prussia, 177. *See* Brandenburg; East Prussia
Psellus, Michael, 150–151
Ptolemy, 27, 95, 107, 108, 302, 317, 381
Punic Wars, 32–33
Punt, 7
Puritans, 356, 366
Pyrenees, treaty of the, 405
Pythagoras, 21

Rabelais, François, 380
Raleigh, Walter, 366
Rameses II, Pharaoh, 11
Rammelsberg, 154
Raphael, 320, 321
Ravenna, 62, 69, 71, 74, 82, 83
Raymond VI, of Toulouse, 207, 235
Raymond VII, of Toulouse, 207, 235–236
Raymond Lull, 183 *n.*
"Realism," Medieval, 240
Reformation. *See* Revolt, Protestant
Reformation, Catholic, 369–377
Reformed Church, Dutch, 359
Reims, 282
Reliefs, 132–133
Religion, ancient Pagan, 10, 35, 46, 58; ancient Persian, 14–15. *See* Christianity; Church; Hebrews; Islam; Jews; Judaism; Moslem
Rembrandt, 406, 409
Remigius, Bishop, 92
Renaissance, Byzantine, 151; Carolingian, 123–126; classical, 264, 313–323
Requesens, 387
Restitution, edict of, 399, 400
Reuchlin, Johann, 316, 317, 380
Revolt, Protestant, on the Continent, 351–360; in Britain, 361–366
Ribera, 393, 398
Ricci, Matteo, 376–377
Richard I, of England, 181, 183, 198, 200
Richard II, of England, 280, 287, 288, 328
Richard III, of England, 288
Richelieu, Cardinal, 400–401, 402
Rienzo, Cola di, 309
Rigaud, Eudes, 232
Robert Grossteste. *See* Grossteste, Robert
Robert Guiscard, 146
Robert of Geneva, 329
Rocroi, battle of, 402
Roger I, Guiscard, of Sicily, 146, 211
Roger II, of Sicily, 108, 211
Roland, Song of, 164
Rollo, 129
Roman Catholic Church. *See* Church, Catholic

Roman Empire, 34–39, 52–61, 65–71, 74–75. *See* Byzantine Empire; Holy Roman Empire
Roman law. *See* Law, Roman
Roman Republic, 29–34
"Romania," 75
Rome, 48, 103, 118 *n.*, sack of (1527), 342
Romulus "Augustulus," 69
Roncaglia, diet at, 216
Ronsard, 380
Roses, Wars of the, 288
Rouen, 281, 282
Roussillon, 405
Rudolf I, Emperor, 290, 293
Rurik, 128
Russia, 128–129, 147, 150, 186, 222–223, 298
Ruthenians. *See* Ukraine
Ruysbroeck, John, 333

Sacraments, 43, 351, 353, 356, 370
Saint Bartholomew's Day, massacre of, 358
St. Mark's at Venice, 151
St. Peter, 44; basilica of, 352, 376, 409
Saladin, Sultan, 181
Salamanca, university of, 248
Salamis, 19
Salerno, university of, 145, 248–249
Salic law, 278 *n.*
Samarkand, 78
Samogitia, 296
Santa Sophia, 76, 79, 80, 95–96, 305, 346–347
Santiago de Compostela, 145, 164, 168
Sappho, 22
Saracens, 126, 145, 164. *See* Moslems
Sardinia, 103, 126, 154, 176 *n.*, 302
Sargon II, of Assyria, 12
Sarmatians, 64
Savonarola, 308, 315
Saxon dynasty, 123, 143
Saxons, 64, 118–119
Saxony, 143, 213–214, 293, 400, 402
Scandinavia, 127–129, 221, 354. *See* Denmark; Norsemen, Norway, Sweden
Schism, Great, 327–330
Schleswig, 143
Scholasticism, 240
Schools, cathedral, 124, 145; monastic, 124. *See* Education
Science, medieval, 243, 245, 318; modern, 381–382
Scipio "Africanus," 33
Scotland (Scots), 67, 68, 87, 128, 175, 205, 277, 294, 359–360
Sculpture, 321–322
"Sea Beggars," 387
"Secularization," 378, 380
Seigneurial regime, 156–159
Selim I, Sultan, 305
Seljuk Turks. *See* Turks, Seljuk
Semitic, 5
Senate, Roman, 31, 32
Seneca, 46
Sennacherib, of Assyria, 12
Separatists. *See* Congregationalists
Serbia (Serbs), 150, 297, 344.
Serfdom (Serfs), 157
Servetus, 356
Servites, 233 *n.*
Seymour, Jane, 363, 364
Sforza, Galeazzo, 310 *n.*; Ludovico, 307
Shakespeare, William, 367
Shiites, 104
Shipping, 190
Sicilian Vespers, 176, 270 *n.*, 309
Sicily, 103, 109, 145–146, 175, 190, 211, 218–220, 302. *See* Two Sicilies
Sickingen, Franz von, 343
Sidon, 9, 177
Sidonius Apollinaris, 59
Sigismund, Emperor, 291–292, 293, 303–304, 330
Sigismund, II, of Poland, 373
Silesia, 177
Silver, Spanish, 348
Simony, 135, 161, 164, 165
"Six Articles," 362
Sixtus IV, Pope, 310, 318
Sixtus V, Pope, 369, 370
Slavery, 10, 21, 33, 157, 300
Slavs, 82, 86, 126–127. *See* Bohemia; Croatia; Moravia; Poland; Russia; Serbia
Sluter, Claus, 322
Sluys, battle of, 278
Socrates, 20, 22
Solomon, of Israel, 9
Sophia Palaeologus, 298
Sophists, 20
Sophocles, 22
Sorbon, Robert de, 247
South America. *See* America
Spain, 67, 71, 81, 103, 104–105, 109, 145, 176, 209–211, 300–303, 383–393, 402–405. *See* Aragon; Castile; Granada; Leon; Navarre
Spanish America, 346–348, 349
Sparta, 19, 20, 24
Spice Islands, 393
Spoleto, 143
Star Chamber, Court of, 288
Stephen II, Pope, 118
Stephen I, Saint, of Hungary, 127, 147
Stephen Dushan, of Serbia, 297
Stevinus, 382
Stilicho, 66
Stoicism, 27, 46
Stralsund, 399; treaty of (1370), 273
Strasbourg Oaths, 122
Strassburg, Gottfried von, 252
Styria, 290
Suevi, 34, 64, 66, 67
Suger, Abbot, 207
Suleiman II, "the Magnificent," Sultan, 344
Sulla, 34
Sumer, 7–8
Sunnites, 104
Surgery, 243
Suso, Henry, 330
Swabia, 143
Sweden (Swedes), 128–129, 147, 221, 294–296, 354, 399–400, 402, 405
Switzerland, 293–294, 402
Sylvester I, Pope, 118 *n.*
Sylvester II, Pope, 144, 147. *See* Gerbert
Symmachus, 58
Syracuse, 16, 18, 19
Syria, 8, 86, 102, 104, 177

Taborites, 330
Tacitus, 39, 58, 63
Tamerlane, 304
Tancred of Hauteville, 146
Tannenberg, battle of (1410), 296
Tartaglia, 382
Tatars (Tartars), 183–186, 298. *See* Mongols
Tauler, John, 333
Technology, 274–275
Terence, 39
Teresa, Saint, 375
Tetzel, 352–353
Teutonic Knights, 176–177, 220, 222, 295–296
Thales, 21
Theatines, 374
Themistocles, 19
Theodora, Empress, 80, 81, 82, 95
Theodore, of Tarsus, 97
Theodoric, 62, 69, 96
Theodosius, Emperor, 46, 66, 72
Theodulf, of Orleans, 125
Theology, 240
Theophano, 144
Thermopylae, 19

Thirty Years' War, 395–405
Thomas à Kempis, 333
Thomas Aquinas, Saint, 234, 242–243, 254, 318
Thrace, 24
Thucydides, 22
Thuringia, 143, 293
Thutmose III, of Egypt, 7
Tigranes, of Armenia, 34
Tigris-Euphrates, 6
Tilly, 395, 398–399, 400
Timbuktu, 275
Tintoretto, 380
Titian, 320, 371, 380
Toledo, 145, 210
Toleration, religious, 378
Tolls, 190–191
Tomislav, of Croatia, 150
Toul, 342, 402
Toulouse, university of, 248
Tours, battle of, 103
Towns, medieval, 192–198
Trade. *See* Commerce
Trajan, Emperor, 38, 45
Transylvania, 344
Trebizond, 225
Trent, council of, 368–370, 373
Tripoli, in Africa, 190; in Syria, 177, 179, 181
Troubadours, 253
Troy, 9, 17
Troyes, Chretien de, 252
Troyes, treaty of, 281, 282
Truce of God, 134, 137, 163
Tudor family, 288, 361–365
Tunis (Tunisia), 105, 181, 190, 345
Turkestan, 103
Turks, Ottoman, 303–305, 344–346; Seljuk, 167–169
Tut-ankh-amen, Pharaoh, 11
Two Sicilies, 302. *See* Naples; Sicily
Tyre, 9, 177

Uceda, Duke of, 393
Ukraine (Ukrainians), 222, 288
Umayyad Dynasty, 104–105, 106
Universities, 245–249
Upsala, university of, 294
Urban II, Pope, 168–169, 170
Urban VI, Pope, 327, 330
Uri, 293
Usury, 192–193, 268–269
Utraquists, 330 *n.*, 395
Utrecht, Union of, 388

Valencia, 176, 300
Valens, Emperor, 65–66
Valla, Lorenzo, 315
Vandals, 64, 66, 67–68, 71, 81
Van der Weyden, Roger, 321
Van Dyck, 409
Van Eyck, Jan, 321
Varangians, 128–129, 150
Varna, battle of, 297
Vasco da Gama, 300
Vassalage (Vassals), 132–133
Vatican Library, 315
Velasquez, 393, 394
Venetia (Venice), 82, 151, 153–154, 178, 181, 189–190, 198, 217, 224, 271–272, 297, 308–309; peace of, 224; siege of (1529), 344
Verdun, 342, 402; treaty of (843), 122
Vergil, 35, 38
Vermeer, 409
Vernaculars, 318–319
Veronese, 380
Verrocchio, 322
Vervins, treaty of, 389
Vesalius, 382
Vespucci, Amerigo, 303
Viborg, 295
Vienna, siege of (1529), 346
Vigilius, Pope, 90
Vikings, 127–129. *See* Norsemen
Villani, Giovanni, 319
Villehardouin, 183
Villon, François, 319
Vinci, Leonardo da, 275, 320
Vinland, 128
Virginia, 367
Visconti family, 307
Visigoths, 64, 65–67, 81
Visitation, Order of, 375
Vitalian, Pope, 97
Vives, Juan Luis, 317
Vladimir, of Kiev, 147, 150
Vulgate, 59, 370

Waldensians, 235
Wales, 68, 175, 205
Wallenstein, 399, 400
Walter the Penniless, 169
Wars, religious, 357–358
Watling Island, 302
Welser family, 339
Wenceslas, of Bohemia, 294
Werner, der Gartenaere, 252
Western civilization defined, 1–2
West Indies, 303
Westphalia, peace of (1648), 402, 403
West Prussia, 296
Wettin family, 293
Whitby, Synod of, 88–89, 97
White Hill, battle of, 395
White Russians, 222. *See* Byelorussia
William I, "the Conqueror," of England and Normandy, 146, 166, 201
William, "the Silent," of the Netherlands, 387–388
William IX, of Aquitaine, 253
William of Champeaux, 241
William of Ockham, 318, 333
William of Rubruquis, 186
William of Tyre, 178, 183
Willibrord, 87, 89
Winfrid, 87
Witchcraft, 332
Wittelsbach family, 290
Wittenberg, university of, 352
Wolsey, Cardinal, 361, 362
Worms, concordat of, 166, 214; diet of (1521), 383
Writing, 10–11
Wycliffe, John, 287, 328–329

Xenophon, 22
Xerxes, of Persia, 19
Ximines de Cisneros, Cardinal, 317–318, 332, 369

Yarmuk, battle of, 102
Yaroslav, of Kiev, 147, 150
Yorkist family, 288
Yugoslavia (Yugoslavs), 86, 127. *See* Serbia

Zaccaria, 182
Zacharias, Pope, 118
Zacuto, Abraham, 318
Zeno, 27
Zeno, Emperor, 69
Zipangu, 186. *See* Japan
Ziska, 330
Zoroaster (Zoroastrians), 15, 43, 59
Zurburan, 393
Zwingli, Huldreich, 350, 355, 356